MW00577575

A SYNTAX GUIDE
FOR READERS OF THE
GREEK NEW TESTAMENT

A SYNTAX GUIDE
FOR READERS OF THE
GREEK NEW TESTAMENT

CHARLES LEE IRONS

ISBN 978-0-8254-4382-4

Printed in the United States of America

16 17 18 19 20 / 5 4 3 2 1

Contents

Introduction / 7
Works Cited / 13
Abbreviations / 17

Chapter One: The Gospel of Matthew / 21
Chapter Two: The Gospel of Mark/ 81
Chapter Three:The Gospel of Luke / 123
Chapter Four: The Gospel of John / 199
Chapter Five: The Acts of the Apostles / 249
Chapter Six: The Epistle to the Romans / 333
Chapter Seven: The First Epistle to the Corinthians / 369
Chapter Eight: The Second Epistle to the Corinthians / 397
Chapter Nine: The Epistle to the Galatians / 423
Chapter Ten: The Epistle to the Ephesians / 437
Chapter Eleven: The Epistle to the Philippians / 449
Chapter Twelve: The Epistle to the Colossians / 459
Chapter Thirteen: The First Epistle to the Thessalonians / 467
Chapter Fourteen: The Second Epistle to the Thessalonians / 475
Chapter Fifteen: The First Epistle to Timothy / 481
Chapter Sixteen: The Second Epistle to Timothy / 489
Chapter Seventeen: The Epistle to Titus / 495
Chapter Eighteen: The Epistle to Philemon / 499
Chapter Nineteen: The Epistle to the Hebrews / 501
Chapter Twenty: The Epistle of James / 533
Chapter Twenty-One: The First Epistle of Peter / 543
Chapter Twenty-Two: The Second Epistle of Peter / 557
Chapter Twenty-Three: The First Epistle of John / 567
Chapter Twenty-Four: The Second Epistle of John / 575
Chapter Twenty-Five: The Third Epistle of John / 577
Chapter Twenty-Six: The Epistle of Jude / 579
Chapter Twenty-Seven: The Revelation of John / 585

Index of Subjects / 607

Introduction

This *Syntax Guide* is intended to assist readers of the Greek New Testament by providing brief explanations of intermediate and advanced syntactical features of the Greek text. It also provides suggested translations to help the reader make sense of unusual phrases and difficult sentences. Many tools are readily available for students wanting to read continuous portions of the Greek New Testament. For example, there are numerous parsing tools, both print editions and widely used electronic Bible software packages. There are also reader's lexica and reader's editions of the Greek New Testament that provide contextual glosses for vocabulary occurring under a certain number of times and in some cases parsing of select verbs and verbal forms.[1] This *Syntax Guide* does not duplicate the help provided by such tools. Rather, it picks up where these other tools leave off, presupposes their use, and moves on to more complex issues of syntax, translation, some textual criticism, and limited exegesis. The intent is to provide concise notes enabling the reader to make sense of the Greek text at a level of linguistic communication one step higher than the word to the syntactical level of the phrase, clause, or sentence.

---

1. The best reader's lexicon is Michael H. Burer and Jeffrey E. Miller, *A New Reader's Lexicon of the Greek New Testament* (Grand Rapids: Kregel, 2008). The two main reader's editions are Richard J. Goodrich and Albert L. Lukaszewski, *A Reader's Greek New Testament* (3rd ed; Grand Rapids: Zondervan, 2015), and Barclay M. Newman and Florian Voss, *The Greek New Testament: A Reader's Edition* (Peabody: Hendrickson, 2015). This *Syntax Guide* can be used in conjunction with any of these tools.

One of my aims in creating this *Syntax Guide* is to encourage students, pastors, and others to devote themselves to reading large portions of the Greek New Testament and, ideally, all of it. This can be a challenge given the disconnect between the necessarily simplified grammar learned in elementary Greek and the actual, real-life Greek of the New Testament. This disconnect can be overcome only by immersing oneself in the actual text. The best way to improve one's facility in biblical Greek is to read the text continuously and synthetically with minimal interruption.[2] By eliminating the need to stop and look up intermediate, advanced, or unusual grammatical features of the Greek text, I have sought to streamline the reader's experience so that true learning of New Testament Greek can occur organically through familiarity with the actual text *in extenso*. When used together with a reader's edition and/or a parsing guide (whether print or electronic), this *Syntax Guide* will enable students of the Greek New Testament to read large portions of text at a time, thereby strengthening their ability to read the New Testament in the original.

Although this *Syntax Guide* provides some lexical information and very limited parsing in select cases, glosses and parsing are not the focus. The primary aim is to provide concise explanations of syntactical, clause-level features that may not be immediately obvious to the beginner. Such features may be something as simple as the genitive absolute, which occurs frequently in the Greek New Testament, or the fact that in Greek neuter plural subjects take singular verbs. In a great number of cases, there is no specific grammatical rule to be noted, but rather suggested translations of difficult phrases, clauses and verses are given to assist the reader. These translations are usually taken from English versions familiar to evangelicals. The New American Standard Bible, the English Standard Version, and the New International Version are employed most frequently, but other English versions are also quoted on occasion when they prove helpful.

In addition, it is surprising how the various particles, prepositions, and common utility words like καί are used in a variety of ways,

---

2. Philip H. Towner, "Preface," *The* UBS *Greek New Testament: A Reader's Edition*.

including some that are unusual and quite unexpected. The preposition ἐπί has 18 different uses according to the standard lexicon of the Greek New Testament.[3] Rather than spending precious time hunting down explanations for less common or non-standard usages in a lexicon or grammar, the work has been done for the reader. In most cases, citations have been given pointing the student to the standard Greek grammars and lexica for further study. In some cases, lengthier notes are provided in which a number of exegetical or interpretive options are listed. The goal has been to be as objective as possible in setting out the range of scholarly views. However, a certain degree of subjectivity is unavoidable. The options are listed from least likely to more or most likely, so that the last option listed is the one I regard as most likely.

Analysis of syntax often entails making judgments about the various uses of a certain grammatical form, giving rise to a particular meaning in that context. This *Syntax Guide* uses the traditional categories of usage as given in the standard grammars of New Testament Greek.[4] However, I recognize that more recent linguistic approaches to Greek grammar have challenged the traditional categories. Many contemporary scholars prefer not to use labels such as "the objective genitive" or "the ingressive aorist," for they seem to imply that the genitive or the aorist actually contains within itself an entire range of discrete meanings. It is argued, rather, that "the objective genitive" and "the ingressive aorist" are really only different ways in which the genitive or the aorist form can be used, and that the various meanings are not inherent to the form itself but arise from its use in particular contexts. Another way of putting the matter is that these categories should not be taken as semantic values but as pragmatic

---

3. Walter Bauer, Frederick W. Danker, W. F. Arndt, and F. W. Gingrich, *A Greek-English Lexicon of the New Testament and Other Early Christian Literature* (3rd ed.; Chicago: University of Chicago Press, 2000).
4. For categories of usage, I rely mainly on Friedrich Blass, Albert Debrunner, and Robert W. Funk, *A Greek Grammar of the New Testament and Other Early Christian Literature* (Chicago: University of Chicago Press, 1961), and Daniel B. Wallace, *Greek Grammar Beyond the Basics: An Exegetical Syntax of the New Testament* (Grand Rapids: Zondervan, 1996).

functions.[5] I defend my use of the traditional terminology, not because I reject this important insight, but because new reference grammars incorporating the insights of modern linguistics have yet to be written. Inventing new terminology would be inappropriate in a work of this nature. Linguistically sophisticated users may mentally gloss the traditional labels as descriptors of context-conditioned pragmatic functions.

I have chosen to continue using the term "deponent," even though I am agnostic about whether it is a genuine syntactical category in Greek. I use the term merely because I believe it is helpful for the beginning student to note when verbs that are middle or passive in form are best translated with an active verb in English.[6]

With regard to the contentious debate over tense and aspect in the Greek verb system, it is not necessary to defend a particular position for the purposes of this *Syntax Guide*. My own view is that the Greek verb, in the indicative mood, generally communicates temporal distinctions in addition to aspectual ones. With regard to the aorist, my working assumption is that it is generally used to indicate that the action is being viewed as a simple event in the past, with the notion of pastness being communicated as a semantic value by the augment. Occasionally, the aorist indicative does not denote a past event but an action viewed as a fact without regard to time; such instances are noted in the *Syntax Guide* using traditional categories such as "constantive/global aorist" or "gnomic aorist." Of course, the aorist when used in the imperative or subjunctive mood, or as a participle, lacks the augment and therefore does not communicate past time as part of its semantic value, although aorist participles often have a past meaning due to the pragmatics of their use in historical narratives.[7]

---

5. For the distinction between semantics and pragmatics, see Constantine R. Campbell, *Basics of Verbal Aspect in Biblical Greek* (Grand Rapids: Zondervan, 2008), 22–24.
6. For the case against deponency as a genuine syntactical category in Greek, see Jonathan T. Pennington, "Deponency in Koine Greek: The Grammatical Question and the Lexicographical Dilemma," *Trinity Journal* 24 (2003): 55–76.
7. Some scholars argue that tense is not a semantic value of the Greek verb, even in the indicative mood, although they do recognize that temporal

A notable feature of this work is the extent to which I have attempted to recognize Hebraic constructions, Semitic interference, and Septuagintisms in the syntax of the Greek New Testament, noting, where applicable, representative passages in the Septuagint where the syntactical feature can be seen in the Bible of Greek-speaking Judaism.

This *Syntax Guide* closely follows the critical edition of the Greek New Testament presented in the 27th and 28th Editions of the Nestle-Aland *Novum Testamentum Graece* published by the Deutsche Bibelgesellschaft (Stuttgart). However, significant textual variants, especially those which appear to have arisen in connection with perceived syntactical difficulties, are also discussed.

---

reference can, and often does, appear at the pragmatic level. For a helpful overview of the history of the debate, see Campbell, *Basics*, 26–33.

Works Cited

The following is a list of abbreviations of the reference works and commentaries cited. Those indicated in bold below are the "constant witnesses" cited with great frequency throughout. Users of this *Syntax Guide* need not consult any of these reference tools in order to understand the notes. However, those engaging in more detailed exegetical study will benefit from consulting the works cited.

Aune   Aune, David E. *Revelation 1–5*. WBC 52A. Dallas: Word
            Books, 1997.

Barrett   Barrett, C. K. *A Commentary on the First Epistle to the
            Corinthians*. HNTC. New York: Harper & Row, 1968.

BDAG   Bauer, Walter, Frederick W. Danker, W. F. Arndt, and F. W.
            Gingrich. *A Greek-English Lexicon of the New Testament
            and Other Early Christian Literature*. 3rd ed. Chicago:
            University of Chicago Press, 2000.

BDF   Blass, Friedrich, Albert Debrunner, and Robert W. Funk.
            *A Greek Grammar of the New Testament and Other Early
            Christian Literature*. Chicago: University of Chicago
            Press, 1961.

Works Cited

Beale   Beale, G. K. *The Book of Revelation*. NIGTC. Grand Rapids: Eerdmans, 1999.

Black   Black, Matthew. *An Aramaic Approach to the Gospels and Acts*. 3rd ed. Peabody: Hendrickson, 1998.

Burton   Burton, Ernest de Witt. *The Epistle to the Galatians*. ICC. New York: Scribner's, 1920.

Carson   Carson, D. A. *The Gospel According to John*. Grand Rapids: Eerdmans, 1991.

Charles   Charles, R. H. *The Revelation of St. John*. 2 Vols. ICC. Edinburgh: T. & T. Clark, 1920.

Cranfield   Cranfield, C. E. B. *A Critical and Exegetical Commentary on the Epistle to the Romans*. ICC. 2 Vols. Edinburgh: T&T Clark, 1975, 1979.

Cremer   Cremer, Hermann. *Biblico-Theological Lexicon of New Testament Greek*. Fourth English Edition. Translated by William Urwick. Edinburgh: T&T Clark, 1895.

Fee   Fee, Gordon D. *The First Epistle to the Corinthians*. NICNT. Grand Rapids: Eerdmans, 1987.

Fitzmyer   Fitzmyer, Joseph A. *The Acts of the Apostles*. AB 31. New York: Doubleday, 1998.

Geldenhuys Geldenhuys, Norval. *The Gospel of Luke*. NICNT. Grand Rapids: Eerdmans, 1983.

Green   Green, Joel B. *The Gospel of Luke*. NICNT. Grand Rapids: Eerdmans, 1997.

Harris   Harris, Murray J. *The Second Epistle to the Corinthians*. NIGTC. Grand Rapids: Eerdmans, 2005.

Hawthorne   Hawthorne, Gerald F. *Philippians*. WBC 43. Waco: Word Books, 1983.

Hodge   Hodge, Charles. *Commentary on the Epistle to the Romans*. Rev. ed. Philadelphia: William S. & Alfred Martien, 1864.

HR   Hatch and Redpath. *Concordance to the Septuagint*. 3 vols. Clarendon: Oxford, 1897, 1906.

Lane   Lane, William L. *Hebrews*. WBC 47AB. Waco: Word Books, 1991.

Lincoln   Lincoln, Andrew T. *Ephesians*. WBC 42. Dallas: Word Books, 1990.

LSJ   Liddell, Scott, Jones, and MacKenzie. *A Greek-English Lexicon*. 9th ed. Oxford, 1996.

M   Moule, C. F. D. *An Idiom Book of New Testament Greek*. 2nd ed. Cambridge: Cambridge University Press, 1959.

Marshall   Marshall, I. Howard. *The Gospel of Luke*. NIGTC. Grand Rapids: Eerdmans, 1978.

Metzger   Metzger, Bruce M. *A Textual Commentary on the Greek New Testament*. Second Edition. Stuttgart: Deutsche Bibelgesellschaft, 1994.

Moo   Moo, Douglas J. *The Epistle to the Romans*. NICNT. Grand Rapids: Eerdmans, 1996.

Thayer   Thayer, Joseph H. *A Greek-English Lexicon of the New Testament.* 4th ed. Edinburgh: T. & T. Clark, 1896.

W   Wallace, Daniel B. *Greek Grammar Beyond the Basics: An Exegetical Syntax of the New Testament.* Grand Rapids: Zondervan, 1996.

Z   Zerwick, Maximilian. *Biblical Greek Illustrated By Examples.* Trans. by Joseph Smith. Rome: Pontifical Biblical Institute, 1963.

ZG   Zerwick, Max and Mary Grosvenor. *A Grammatical Analysis of the Greek New Testament.* 3rd ed. Rome: Pontifical Biblical Insitute, 1988.

Abbreviations

1s	First person singular
2s	Second person singular
3s	Third person singular
1p	First person plural
2p	Second person plural
3p	Third person plural
abs.	Absolute
acc.	Accusative
adj.	Adjective
adv.	Adverb(ial)
alt.	Alternative translation given in margin or footnote
bec.	Because
ch.	Chapter
cp.	Compare
dat.	Dative
ESV	English Standard Version
fem.	Feminine
fig.	Figurative(ly)
gen.	Genitive
hapax	*Hapax legomenon* (occurring only once)
Heb.	Hebrew
Hebr.	Hebraic
impf.	Imperfect
impv.	Imperative

indef.	Indefinite
indic.	Indicative
inf.	Infinitive
intrans.	Intransitive
KJV	King James Version
lit.	Literal(ly)
LXX	Septuagint
masc.	Masculine
mid.	Middle
mng.	Meaning
mod.	Modified
MS(S)	Manuscript(s)
NA	Nestle-Aland, *Novum Testamentum Graece*
NASB	New American Standard Bible
neg.	Negative
neut.	Neuter
NIV	New International Version
nom.	Nominative
NRSV	New Revised Standard Version
NT	New Testament
OT	Old Testament
pass.	Passive
perf.	Perfect
pl.	Plural
plupf.	Pluperfect
prep.	Preposition(al)
ptc.	Participle
ref.	Reference
sc.	Scilicet – it is permitted to understand
see	See notes or commentary
sg.	Singular
subj.	Subjunctive
s.v.	Sub verbo/voce – under the word
trans.	Transitive
v./vv.	Verse/verses

voc.	Vocative
vs.	Versus
Vulg.	Vulgate
w/o	Without
w.r.t.	With respect to

Chapter One

The Gospel of Matthew

Matthew 1

1:1 | βίβλος γενέσεως Ἰ. Χρ. – nom. abs. (W 49–50); allusion to "the book of the generations" (LXX Gen 2:4; 5:1)

1:2 | Ἀβραὰμ ἐγέννησεν τὸν Ἰσαάκ = LXX 1 Chron 1:34 – note the unexpected definite article τόν before the name of the person begotten, and so throughout vv. 2–16. Formula used in the LXX genealogies: x ἐγέννησεν τὸν y (see LXX Gen 5:6ff; 10:8ff; 1 Chron 2:10ff)

1:6 | ἐκ τῆς τοῦ Οὐρίου = "by the [wife] of Uriah" (highlighting David's adultery) (cp. ἡ τοῦ Κλωπᾶ, John 19:25)

1:11 | ἐπί + gen. = "at the time of" (BDAG ἐπί 18a) | μετοικεσία ("deportation") is from μετοικέω < μετά + οἰκέω = "change one's abode"

1:16 | ἐγεννήθη – in contrast with the active form ἐγέννησεν used repeatedly in vv. 2–16a, the sudden pass. in ref. to Jesus stands out – Jesus is begotten by God.

1:18 | δέ = "now" (W 674) | οὕτως ἦν = "took place in this way" (ESV), "was as follows" (NASB), adv. functioning as adj. (BDF §434(1); BDAG οὕτως 2) | μνηστευθείσης ... gen. abs. ("after his mother

Mary had been betrothed to Joseph") | Subject of εὑρέθη is same as the noun of the gen. abs. (Mary), which is unusual (BDF §423(4)) | πρὶν ἤ = "before," the Ionic/Koiné equivalent of πρίν in Attic (see BDAG); on πρίν + inf., see BDF §395; W 596 (cp. Matt 26:43, 75); "before they came together [in marriage]" (BDAG συνέρχομαι 3) | εὑρέθη ἐν γαστρὶ ἔχουσα = "she was found to be with child," εὑρίσκω + supplementary ptc. (BDF §416(2))

1:18, 23 | ἐν γαστρὶ ἔχω (2x) = "be pregnant" (BDAG γαστήρ 2; LXX Gen 16:4)

1:19 | ἐβουλήθη aorist of βούλομαι; takes complementary inf., "decide to" | λάθρᾳ = "secretly," adverbial dat. (W 161 n59)

1:20 | ἐνθυμηθέντος – pass. in form but active in mng. (deponent); gen. abs., "after he had reflected on these things" | ἄγγελος κυρίου = "an (or the) angel of the Lord" (cp. 1:24; 2:13, 19; 28:2) (see discussion at W 252) | κατ᾽ ὄναρ = "in a dream" (cp. 2:12, 13, 19, 22; 27:19) | φοβηθῇς – deponent | τὸ γεννηθέν = lit. "the thing [child] that has been begotten," divine pass. (see v. 16)

1:21 | Ἰησοῦς – in LXX "Joshua" (Yahweh is salvation) is spelled Ἰησοῦς, probably an intentional allusion to the OT Joshua

1:22 | τοῦτο ὅλον = "all this"

1:23 | ἕξει – future of ἔχω | ὅ ἐστιν μεθερμηνευόμενον = "which when translated means" (BDAG εἰμί 2cα; μεθερμηνεύω [< μετά + ἑρμηνεύω]) | μεθ᾽ ἡμῶν = μετὰ ἡμῶν

1:25 | αὐτήν = "her" (= Mary) | ἕως οὗ = "until" (BDAG ἕως 1bβℵ) (cp. 13:33)

Matthew 2

2:1 | τοῦ δὲ Ἰησοῦ γεννηθέντος = "now after Jesus was born," gen.

abs. | παραγίνομαι εἰς = "become present in" a place (BDAG παρ. 1a; εἰς 1aδ)

2:2 | αὐτοῦ τὸν ἀστέρα = τὸν ἀστέρα αὐτοῦ ("his star") – on position of gen. pronoun, see BDF §284

2:4 | ἐπυνθάνετο – verbs of asking tend to prefer impf. tense (BDF §328) | ποῦ ὁ Χριστὸς γεννᾶται = "where the Messiah is [to be] born," present retained in indirect discourse (W 537–9)

2:6 | ἡγούμενος = "ruler," anarthrous substantivized adjectival ptc. (BDF §264(6))

2:7 | τὸν χρόνον ... ἀστέρος = "the time of the star's appearing"

2:8 | ἐπάν (< ἐπεὶ ἄν) + aorist subj. = "when," "as soon as" (BDF §455(1)) | κἀγώ = καὶ ἐγώ = "I too"

2: 9 | οἱ = "they" (= the magi); οἱ δὲ ἀκούσαντες = "now when they heard" | ἐπάνω οὗ = "over [the place] where" (BDAG ἐπάνω 1b); οὗ = "where," gen. of ὅς that has become an adv. of place

2:12 | χρηματίζω – since verb has connotation of a divine message or oracle, could be translated "being warned by God" (NASB) (see v. 22) | κατ' ὄναρ = "in a dream" (cp. vv. 13, 19, 22; 1:20; 27:19) | μὴ ἀνακάμψαι – complementary inf. with verb of commanding (BDF §392(1)(d)) | δι' ἄλλης ὁδοῦ = "by another [ἄλλος, η, ον] way" (ὁδός is fem.)

2:13 | ἀναχωρησάντων αὐτῶν – gen. abs. | μέλλω + inf. = "be about to" | τοῦ ἀπολέσαι – gen. articular inf. expressing purpose ("in order to kill")

2:14 | ὁ = "he" (= Joseph); ὁ δὲ ἐγερθεὶς παρέλαβεν = "then he got up and took" (see v. 21) | νυκτός – gen. of time ("at night")

2:16 | ἐμπαίζω – lit. "mock," here "trick" – "Then Herod, when he realized that he had been tricked by the magi, became very angry" | ἀποστείλας ἀνεῖλεν = "sent [soldiers who] killed," Semitic graphic ptc. (Z §363) (cp. Mk 6:17; Acts 7:14; Rev 1:1) | παρὰ τῶν μάγων = "from the wise men" (BDAG παρά A3aγ).

2:19 | τελευτήσαντος = "when Herod died," gen. abs.

2:20 | οἱ ζητοῦντες – categorical pl. referring to Herod (W 404)

2:22 | βασιλεύω + gen. of region ruled | ἐκεῖ ἀπελθεῖν = "to go there" (BDAG ἀπέρχομαι 1b)

2:23 | εἰς = ἐν (cp. 2:1; 4:13) | Ναζωραῖος – see BDAG for possibilities

Matthew 3
3:2 | ἤγγικεν = "has drawn near, is on the verge of arriving" (cp. 4:17)

3:3 | βοῶντος = "of (some)one crying out," anarthrous substantival ptc. (cp. Mk 1:3; Lk 3:4)

3:4 | ἀπὸ τριχῶν καμήλου = "[made] from the hairs of a camel"

3:5 | περίχωρος, ον = "neighboring," here as subst., "the neighboring region"

3:5–6 | ἐξεπορεύετο, ἐβαπτίζοντο – distributive iterative impfs. (W 547); note switch from sg. to pl.

3:7 | ἐπὶ τὸ βάπτισμα = "for baptism, to get baptized," ἐπί + acc. as marker of purpose (BDAG ἐπί 11) | ἡ μέλλουσα ὀργή = "the wrath to come" (cp. Luke 3:7) (BDAG μέλλω 3)

3:9 | μὴ δόξητε λέγειν = "do not presume to say" (NRSV)

3:10 | κεῖμαι πρός = "is lying at," ready to fell the tree | ποιοῦν (neut. present ptc.) καρπόν = "producing fruit" (BDAG ποιέω 2g)

3:11 | μέν ... δέ = "on the one hand ... on the other hand" (BDAG μέν 1a) | ὁ ὀπίσω μου ἐρχόμενος = "the one coming after me" | ἐν (2x) = "with," Hebr./instrumental ἐν (BDF §219; BDAG ἐν 5b)

3:13 | τοῦ βαπτισθῆναι = "in order to be baptized," gen. articular inf.

3:14 | διεκώλυεν = "was trying to prevent," conative impf. (W 550)

3:15 | ἄφες ἄρτι = "let it be so now" (ESV, NIV) | πρέπον ἐστὶν ἡμῖν + inf. = "it is fitting for us to" | πληρῶσαι πᾶσαν δικαιοσύνην = "to bring about the fulfillment of all righteousness," i.e., all the good fruit (vv. 8, 10) and obedience (4:1–11) that God demanded through his law but failed to find in Israel (cp. 7:19; 15:13; 21:19, 34, 41).

3:17 | ἐν ᾧ εὐδόκησα (cp. Mark 1:11; Luke 3:22) – possible interpretations of the aorist: (1) "on whom my pleasure has just now fallen," immediate past aorist (W 564–5; M 11) (unlikely, bec. same statement is made both earlier and later; cp. 12:18; 17:5; 2 Pet 1:17); (2) "on whom my electing pleasure has fallen," referring to the eternal decree of God by which he foreordained his Son to be the Messiah (Benjamin W. Bacon, "Supplementary Note on the Aorist εὐδόκησα, Mark i.11," *JBL* 20 [1901]: 28–30); or (3) "with whom I am well pleased," constative/global aorist, stressing the fact of God's pleasure w/o regard to time (W 557)

Matthew 4

4:2 | ἡμέρας ... τεσσαράκοντα – acc. for extent of time (W 202) | ὕστερον = "afterwards," adv. acc.

4:3 | λέγω ἵνα = "order that," with ἵνα used in attenuated sense (BDAG ἵνα 2aδ; λέγω 2c)

4:4 | ζάω ἐπί + dat. (2x) = "live on" (BDAG ἐπί 6a)

4:6 | ἐντέλλομαι – deponent; implied subject is God (v. 7): "To his angels he will give orders concerning you" (LXX Ps 91:11–12)

4:10 | ἐὰν πεσὼν προσκυνήσῃς μοι = "if you fall down and worship me," attendant circumstances ptc.

4:13 | εἰς Καφ. τὴν παραθαλασσίαν = "in Capernaum which is by the sea." τήν identifies adj. παραθαλασσίαν as modifying Καφ. attributively (W 306–7). τήν agrees with Καφ. in case, gender, and number. Note fulfillment of Scripture: παραθαλασσίαν (v. 13) → ὁδὸν θαλάσσης (v. 15) → παρὰ τὴν θάλασσαν (v. 18)

4:15 | ὁδὸν θαλάσσης = "toward the sea" (LXX Isa 9:1), lit. translation of Heb.; ὁδός effectively functions here as preposition (BDF §§161, 166; BDAG ὁδός 1)

4:16 | τοῖς καθημένοις … αὐτοῖς – pleonastic pronoun; anacoluthon (BDF §§297; 466(4)) (cp. 5:40)

4:17 | ἀπὸ τότε = "from then on" | ἤγγικεν (see 3:2)

4:18, 20, 21 | ἀμφίβληστρον (< ἀμφί + βάλλω = "cast on either side") = "casting-net," whereas δίκτυον = generic "fishing net"

4:20, 22 | οἱ = "they"

4:21 | ἄλλους δύο ἀδελφούς = "two other brothers" | Ἰάκωβον τὸν τοῦ Ζεβεδαίου = "Jacob/James, the [son] of Zebedee"

4:24 | ἡ ἀκοὴ αὐτοῦ = "his fame" (ESV), "news about him" (NASB) (cp. 14:1; BDAG ἀκοή 4a) | τοὺς κακῶς ἔχοντας ποικίλαις νόσοις = "those sick with all kinds of diseases," κακῶς ἔχειν = "to be sick," οἱ κακῶς ἔχοντες = "those who are sick" (BDAG ἔχω 10b) | [τοὺς] βασάνοις συνεχομένους = "those suffering with pains/torments" | σεληνιάζομαι (< σελήνη = "moon") = lit. "be moonstruck," presumably bec. epileptic seizures were thought to be caused by the moon (cp. 17:15)

Matthew 5

5:1 | καθίσαντος αὐτοῦ = "after he sat down," gen. abs.

5:3 | οἱ πτωχοί – cp. 11:5; LXX Isa 61:1

5:3–10 | Note emphatic position of αὐτοί/αὐτῶν (8x): "for it is they who ..." (ὅτι αὐτοί, vv. 4–9), or "for to them belongs ..." (ὅτι αὐτῶν, vv. 3, 10)

5:11 | κατά + gen. = "against" (BDAG κατά A2bβ)

5:13 | μωραίνω normally means "make foolish" but here context requires "make tasteless" (cp. Lk 14:34); John Lightfoot: "Μωρανθῆ suits very well with the Hebrew word תפל, which signifies both *unsavoury* and a *fool*" (quoted by Black 166) | ἐν τίνι = "with what?" | εἰ μὴ βληθὲν ἔξω καταπατεῖσθαι – difficult, possibly corrupt; other MSS have εἰ μὴ βληθῆναι ἔξω καὶ καταπατεῖσθαι ("except to be cast out and trampled")

5:15 | Subject of καίουσιν and τιθέασιν is indef. "they" or "people"

5:16 | οὕτως = "in the same way," pointing to moral of figure (BDAG οὕτως 1b) | ὑμῶν τὰ καλὰ ἔργα – on word order, see comment at 2:2

5:19 | ὃς ἐάν (or ἄν) = "whoever" (and throughout ch. 5); ἐάν sometimes used in place of ἄν after relatives (BDF §107; BDAG ἐάν 3) | ὃς ἐὰν λύσῃ = "whoever annuls" (BDAG λύω 4), subj. in indef. relative clause; the potential element belongs to the subject rather than the verb (W 478–9) (and throughout ch. 5)

5:20 | πλεῖον (adv. acc.) + gen. of comparison = "more greatly than" (BDAG πολύς 2bβ)

5:21 | τοῖς ἀρχαίοις (cp. v. 33) could be translated "by the ancients," but probably "to the ancients" | οὐ φονεύσεις – imperatival future, usually employed in LXX quotations of OT categorical injunctions (BDF §362; W 569; M 178–9) (cp. vv. 27, 33, 43)

5:22 | ἐγὼ δὲ λέγω ὑμῖν (also vv. 28, 32, 34, 39, 44) = "but *I* say to you," emphatic ἐγώ of messianic authority – as the crowds perceived (7:28–29) | ἔνοχος εἰς τὴν γέενναν = "guilty [enough to go] into the fiery hell" (NASB), pregnant construction (BDAG εἰς 10d)

5:23 | κἀκεῖ = καὶ ἐκεῖ = "and there"

5:24 | ὕπαγε πρῶτον διαλλάγηθι = "first go and be reconciled" (NIV), asyndeton: the impv. ὕπαγε is almost always followed by another impv. w/o a connective (BDAG ὑπάγω 2a; BDF §461(1))

5:25 | ἕως ὅτου + indic. = "while" (BDAG ἕως 2c) | μήποτε + aorist subj. = "lest"

5:28 | πρὸς τό + inf., indicating intent (BDF §402(5)) (cp. 6:1; 13:30; 23:5)

5:29–30 | ἵνα – final sense attenuated; functions as inf. (BDAG ἵνα 2)

5:32 | παρεκτὸς λόγου πορνείας = "except on the ground of sexual immorality" (ESV) (BDAG λόγος 2d) | ποιέω + inf. = "cause someone to do something" (BDAG ποιέω 2hα) | ἀπολελυμένην = "a divorced woman"

5:33 | ἀποδίδωμι = "perform" (ESV), "fulfill" (NASB), "keep" (NIV 1984) (BDAG ἀποδίδωμι 2c)

5:34–36 | ὀμνύω ἐν = "swear by," ἐν replacing acc. under Hebr. influence (BDAG ὀμνύω; BDF §149; W 204–5) (cp. 23:16–22)

5:34 | μή ... ὅλως = "not ... at all"

5:35 | ὀμνύω εἰς = "swear by" (BDAG εἰς 6)

5:37 | τὸ περισσὸν τούτων = "anything more than these," with τούτων as gen. of comparison (BDF §185(1)) | ἐκ τοῦ πονηροῦ – if masc. (ὁ πονηρός), "from the evil one" (NIV), i.e., the devil (BDAG πονηρός 1bβ); if neut. (τὸ πονηρόν), "of/from evil" (NASB, ESV), i.e., from evil motives (BDAG πονηρός 1bγ)

5:39 | τῷ πονηρῷ – masc. (ὁ πονηρός) (BDAG πονηρός 1bα), "the evil person" as a class (generic article; W 227) | τὴν ἄλλην [sc. σιαγόνα]

5:40 | αὐτῷ – pleonastic pronoun; anacoluthon (BDF §§297; 466(4)); lit. "to the person wishing [τῷ θέλοντι] to sue you and take your shirt, give to him [αὐτῷ] your coat also" (cp. 4:16)

5:43 | ὁ πλησίον = "the one who is near," "neighbor," extremely common in LXX; substantivized adverb/preposition (W 232; BDF §266)

5:46–47 | οὐχί = "Do not ... ?" (expects affirmative answer) | τὸ αὐτό = "the same" (BDAG αὐτός 3b)

5:47 | τί περισσὸν ποιεῖτε; = "what are you doing that is remarkable?" (BDAG περισσός 1), "what more are you doing than others?" (ESV, NASB)

Matthew 6
6:1 | προσέχω + μή + inf. (ποιεῖν) = "take care not to" | δικαιοσύνη = "righteous deed, charity" (BDAG δικαιοσύνη 3b) | πρὸς τό + inf. – see 5:28 | αὐτοῖς = "by them"

6:2 | δοξάζω (pass.) = "be praised, honored"

6:3 | σοῦ δὲ ποιοῦντος = "but when *you* give alms," gen. abs. | ἡ ἀριστερὰ/δεξιὰ [χείρ] – ellipsis of substantive with adj. attributives (BDF §261(6))

6:5 | ἔσεσθε – imperatival future *not* in OT quotation – quite rare (W 569; BDF §362)

6:6 | τῷ πατρί σου τῷ ἐν τῷ κρυπτῷ = "to your father who is in secret" (cp. v. 18)

6:7 | βατταλογέω = "meaningless repetition" (NASB), onomatopoetic | ἐν = "because of" (BDAG ἐν 9a)

6:8 | ὧν χρείαν ἔχετε = "the things of which you have need" | πρὸ τοῦ + inf. = "before" | ὑμᾶς – acc. subject with inf. (αἰτῆσαι)

6:9 | πάτερ – voc.

6:10 | ὡς ... καί = "as ... so" (BDAG καί 2c; ὡς 2a) (cp. Acts 7:51; Gal 1:9; Phil 1:20)

6:11 | ἐπιούσιος, ον – mng. uncertain; unattested in extra-biblical Greek; could be translated (1) "necessary for existence," (2) "for today," (3) "for the following day," (4) "for the future," (5) "coming," i.e., eschatological (see BDAG ἐπιούσιος and commentaries for discussion) | σήμερον (adv.) = "today"

6:13 | τοῦ πονηροῦ – as in 5:37, could be masc., "the evil one," or neut., "evil" (cp. 2 Thess 3:3)

6:19 | σής, ἡ = "moth" (here as larvae) | βρῶσις, ἡ = "eating, consuming" "The interp *corrosion, rust* finds no support outside this passage" (BDAG βρῶσις); "moth and eating" = hendiadys for "larvae that eat clothing" | διορύσσω – Since houses were typically made of earthen bricks, thieves would "dig" a whole in the wall in order to break in.

6:22 | ὁ λύχνος ... ὁ ὀφθαλμός = "the eye is the lamp of the body" | ἁπλοῦς = "single, without guile, sincere, straightforward" (BDAG ἁπλοῦς), *simplex* (Vulgate); opposite of διπλοῦς = "twofold" (LSJ)

6:23 | τὸ σκότος πόσον = "how great is that darkness!"

6:24 | δυσί = dat. of δύο | ἤ ... ἤ = "either ... or" | μισήσει and ἀγαπήσει – gnomic futures (W 571) | ἀντέχομαι and καταφρονέω take gen.

6:25 | τῇ ψυχῇ ὑμῶν = "for your life," dat. of advantage (BDF §188(1)) | τῆς τροφῆς and τοῦ ἐνδύματος – gens. of comparison

6:26 | ὅτι can be left untranslated: "Look at the birds of the air: they ..." (ESV); prolepsis (cp. v. 28), i.e., anticipation of the subject of the subordinate clause by making it the object of the main clause (BDF §476(2)) | καί = "and yet" (BDAG καί 1bη) | οὐχ ὑμεῖς μᾶλλον διαφέρετε αὐτῶν = "are you not much more valuable than they?" (NIV); μᾶλλον is pleonastic (BDAG μᾶλλον 1) and heightens the comparative (BDF §246); αὐτῶν, gen. of comparison (BDAG διαφέρω 4)

6:27 | μεριμνῶν = "by means of worrying" (W 628–30)

6:28 | καταμάθετε τὰ κρίνα τοῦ ἀγροῦ πῶς αὐξάνουσιν = "consider the lilies of the field, how they grow" (ESV), prolepsis (cp. v. 26)

6:29 | οὐδέ = "not even"

6:30 | Subject is ὁ θεός, and direct object is τὸν χόρτον ... βαλλόμενον ("the grass of the field which exists today and tomorrow is cast into the furnace")

6:34 | μεριμνάω + εἰς = "be anxious for" (BDAG εἰς 2aβ); + gen. (BDF §176(2))

Matthew 7

7:2 | ἐν ᾧ (2x) = "with whatever"

7:3 | τί δὲ βλέπεις; = "why do you look at?" | τήν goes with δοκόν (fem.)

7:4 | πῶς ἐρεῖς; = "how can you say?" | ἄφες ἐκβάλω = "let me take out," impv. of ἀφίημι reinforces hortatory subj. to form single idiomatic phrase; leave ἄφες untranslated (BDAG ἀφίημι 5b; BDF §364(1–2); W 464–5) (cp. 27:49)

7:6 | μήποτε + future indic. and aorist subj. = "lest" | ἐν = "with," Hebr./instrumental ἐν (BDF §219; BDAG ἐν 5b) | ῥήγνυμι = "tear in pieces" (with their teeth)

7:9–10 | Anacolutha (BDF §469) | μή = "he will not ..., will he?"

7:11 | οἶδα + inf. = "know how to" (BDAG οἶδα 3)

7:12 | πάντα ὅσα ἐάν = "all things whatsoever" (KJV); on ἐάν for ἄν, see 5:19, 32 | ἵνα – final sense attenuated; functions as inf. (BDAG ἵνα 2)

7:14 | τί = "how!" (BDAG τίς 3)

7:15 | ἅρπαξ (adj.) = "ravenous, rapacious, greedy for prey" (< ἁρπάζω = "seize, steal, make off with")

7:16, 20 | ἀπό = "by" with verbs of perceiving (ἐπιγινώσκω) (BDAG ἀπό 3d)

7:16 | μήτι ... "Surely they do not gather ... do they?" (BDAG μήτι)

7:17 | οὕτως – cp. 5:16

7:17–19 | ποιέω (5x) = "produce, yield" (BDAG ποιέω 2g)

7:20 | ἄρα γε = "so then" (NASB)

7:21–22 | κύριε (4x) – voc.

7:23 | ὅτι recitative – marker of direct discourse, rendered with quotation marks (BDAG ὅτι 3; BDF §397(5)) | οἱ ἐργαζόμενοι = "you workers," articular ptc. with implied 2p from impv. ἀποχωρεῖτε (BDF §412(5)) | τὴν ἀνομίαν = "lawlessness," article with abstract noun (W 226)

7:24, 26 | μου τοὺς λόγους τούτους (2x) = "these words of mine"

7:25, 27 | προσ-πίπτω/-κόπτω – prefix takes dat. object (BDF §202 s.v. προσ-)

7:28 | καὶ ἐγένετο ὅτε = "and it came to pass, when" (KJV), Septuagintism (BDF §§4; 442(5); BDAG γίνομαι 4f) | ἐπί after verbs which express feelings = "at" (BDAG ἐπί 6c)

7:29 | ἦν διδάσκων = "he was teaching," impf. periphrastic (W 648)

Matthew 8
8:1, 5 | καταβάντος/εἰσελθόντος αὐτοῦ = "when he came down/ entered," gen. abs.

8:3 | ἥψατο αὐτοῦ – verbs of touching take gen. object (W 132)

8:4 | ὅρα + μή + aorist subj. = "see to it that you do not" (BDAG ὁράω B2; BDF §364(3)), though here with μηδενί (dat. of μηδείς) | ὕπαγε σεαυτὸν δεῖξον = "go and show yourself," asyndeton (see 5:24) | BDAG εἰς 4f

8:6, 14 | βάλλω = "lie on a sickbed" (BDAG βάλλω 1b) (cp. 9:2)

8:7 | ἐγὼ ἐλθὼν θεραπεύσω αὐτόν = "I will come and heal him." The aorist ptc. ἐλθών takes on a future mng. bec. of the tense of the controlling verb, but still refers to action antecedent to that of the main verb.

8:8 | ἵνα for epexegetical inf. (BDAG ἵνα 2cβ; W 476) | μου ὑπὸ τὴν στέγην = ὑπὸ τὴν στέγην μου (BDF §473(1)) (cp. Lk 7:6) | εἰπὲ λόγῳ = "say the word," cognate dat. (W 168)

8:9 | καὶ γὰρ ἐγώ = "for I too"

8:10 | παρά + dat. = "with" (BDAG παρά B4)

8:13 | BDAG ὡς 1bβ

8:15 | ἥψατο + gen. (see v. 3)

8:16 | οἱ κακῶς ἔχοντες = "those who are sick" (see 4:24; 9:12)

8:18 | εἰς τὸ πέραν = "to the other side" (v. 28)

8:19 | εἷς functions here as an indef. article (BDAG εἷς 3) | ὅπου ἐάν = ὅπου ἄν = "wherever" (see 5:19)

8:20 | οὐκ ἔχει ποῦ + subj. = "has nowhere to" (BDAG ποῦ 1b)

8:23 | ἐμβάντι αὐτῷ – unusual; it looks like gen. abs. changed to dat. case by attraction with the second αὐτῷ ("when he got into the boat, his disciples followed him") (cp. 9:27–28)

8:27 | ποταπός ἐστιν οὗτος = "what kind of [a man] is this?"

8:28 | εἰς τὸ πέραν (see v. 18) | δύο δαιμονιζόμενοι = "two demon-possessed men" | μὴ τινά = "no one"

8:29 | τί ἡμῖν καὶ σοί; – variety of translations: "what have you to do with us?" (ESV), "what business do we have with each other?" (NASB), "what do you want with us?" (NIV), "leave us in peace! do not bother us!" (BDF §127(3)), "what do we have in common?" (W 150–1)

8:32 | κατά + gen. = "down" (BDAG κατά A1a)

8:33 | οἱ βόσκοντες = "the herdsmen" | τὰ τῶν δαιμονιζομένων = "what had happened to the demoniacs"

Matthew 9

9:2 | προσέφερον = "some people were bringing," indef. 3p subject (BDF §130(2)) (cp. vv. 17, 32) | βάλλω – see 8:6, 14

9:4 | πονηρά = "evil thoughts" (NIV)

9:10 | καὶ ἐγένετο ... καί = "and it came to pass ... that," common construction in Hebrew narrative, mediated by LXX (BDAG καί 1bβ) | συν-ανάκειμαι + dat. = "recline at table with"

9:12 | ἔχω χρείαν + gen. (ἰατροῦ) = "have need of something" | οἱ κακῶς ἔχοντες (see 4:24; 8:16)

9:13 | τί ἐστιν = "what [this] means" (BDAG εἰμί 2cα) (cp. 12:7)

9:14 | πολλά = "often," adv. acc.

9:15 | οἱ υἱοὶ τοῦ νυμφῶνος = lit. "the sons of the bridal chamber," i.e., "the bridegroom's attendants" (BDAG νυμφών 2) (cp. Mk 2:19; Lk 5:34) | ἐφ᾽ ὅσον = "as long as" (BDAG ἐπί 18cβ) | μετ᾽ = μετά

9:16 | ἐπίβλημα ῥάκους = "a patch of unshrunk cloth," gen. of material (W 91) | αἴρω = "take [something] away" | αὐτοῦ = "its," i.e., the garment's ("its patch takes something away from the garment")

9:17 | βάλλουσιν (2x) indef. 3p subject (see v. 2) | εἰ δὲ μή γε = "otherwise"

9:18 | εἷς as indef. article (BDAG εἷς 3) – see 8:19 | ὅτι recitative – see 7:23

9:20 | δώδεκα ἔτη – acc. for extent of time (W 202)

9:20, 21, 29 | Verbs of touching take gen. (3x) (cp. 8:3)

9:22 | θύγατερ – voc.

9:24 | κατα-γελάω takes gen. object bec. of κατα- prefix (BDF §181)

9:25 | κρατέω + gen. has a note of tenderness, in contrast with κρατέω + acc. (cp. 12:11; 28:9) which indicates grasping the whole of (W 132)

9:27–28 | παράγοντι ... ἐλθόντι – see 8:23

9:30 | ἐμβριμάομαι – deponent

9:31 | διεφήμισαν αὐτόν = they "spread the news about him" (NASB)

9:32 | προσήνεγκαν – indef. 3p subject (see v. 2)

9:33 | Substantival οὕτως = "something like this" (BDAG οὕτως 2) (cp. Mk 2:12)

9:34 | Hebr./instrumental ἐν – see 7:6

9:35 | περιάγω + acc. of place traversed = "travel throughout," intransitive (BDAG περιάγω 2; BDF §308)

9:36 | σπλαγχνίζομαι περί + gen. = "have pity on," with verbs of emotion (BDAG περί 1c; BDF §229(2)) (cp. 20:24) | ἐσκυλμένοι καὶ ἐρριμμένοι = "harassed and helpless" (ESV), "distressed and dejected" (BDAG σκύλλω 1; ῥίπτω 2)

9:37 | μέν ... δέ (see 3:11)

9:38 | δέομαι + gen. of person to whom request is addressed

Matthew 10
10:1 | ἐξουσία + gen. = "authority over"

10:2 | τὰ ὀνόματά ἐστιν – neut. pl. subjects take sg. verbs

10:4 | ὁ Καναναῖος (Aramaism) = ὁ ζηλωτής (Lk 6:15; Acts 1:13) = "the Zealot" (BDAG Καναναῖος)

10:5 | εἰς ὁδὸν ἐθνῶν = "toward the Gentiles" (cp. 4:15)

10:9 | μὴ κτήσησθε ... εἰς τὰς ζώνας = "do not acquire ... [to put it] into your belts," pregnant construction (BDAG κτάομαι 1; εἰς 10d)

10:10 | εἰς ὁδόν = "for the journey" (BDAG ὁδός 2) | ἄξιος + gen. = "worthy of, entitled to"

10:11 | εἰς ἥν ἄν = "into whatever" | ἐξετάσατε τίς = "find out who" (ESV) | κἀκεῖ = καὶ ἐκεῖ

10:13 | μέν ... δέ = "on the one hand ... on the other hand" | ἡ εἰρήνη ὑμῶν (2x) = "your [blessing of] peace" (NASB) (cp. Lk 10:13)

10:15 | ἀνεκτός (< ἀνέχομαι) = "bearable, tolerable" | ἤ = "than" (BDAG ἤ 2a)

10:18 | ἐπί + acc. = "before," marker of legal proceeding (BDAG ἐπί 10)

10:22 | ἔσεσθε μισούμενοι = "you will be hated," future periphrastic (W 567, 648–9) | ὁ ὑπομείνας = "the one who endures," substantival gnomic aorist ptc. with generic ref. (W 615 n8)

10:23 | ὅταν ... ἑτέραν = "when they persecute you in one city, flee to the next"

10:25 | ἀρκετὸν [ἐστιν] + dat. + ἵνα = "[it is] enough for ... to" (BDF §§187(8), 393(2))

10:27 | ὃ εἰς τὸ οὖς ἀκούετε = "what you hear [whispered] in [your] ear" (NASB) (cp. εἰς τὰ ὦτα, Lk 1:44; Acts 11:22; Jas 5:4)

10:28 | BDAG ἀπό 1c/5c (cp. 14:26) | καὶ ψυχὴν καὶ σῶμα = "both soul and body"

10:29 | ἀσσαρίου = "for an assarion," gen. of price (W 122) | ἄνευ τοῦ πατρὸς ὑμῶν – options: "without the cognizance (or permission) of your Father" (M 82), "apart from the will of your Father" (NIV 1984), "outside your Father's care" (NIV 2011)

10:30 | ὑμῶν δὲ καὶ αἱ τρίχες = "*even* the hairs of your head"

10:32 | ἐν + dat. (2x) – equivalent to simple dat. (BDF §220) | κἀγώ = καὶ ἐγώ = "I too"

10:33 | ὅστις ἂν ἀρνήσηται = "whoever denies," subj. in indef. relative clause; the potential element belongs to the subject rather than the verb (W 478-9)

10:36 | "A man's enemies [will be] the members of his household"

10:37-38 | μου ἄξιος (3x) = "worthy of me"

10:39 | ὁ εὑρών ... ὁ ἀπολέσας = "whoever finds ... whoever loses," substantival gnomic aorist ptcs. with generic ref. (W 615 n8)

10:41-42 | εἰς ὄνομα (3x) = "because he is a" (NIV, ESV) (BDAG ὄνομα 3)

10:42 | ψυχρόν, τό = "cold water," substantivized adj. | μόνον goes with ποτήριον = "even a cup of cold water"

Matthew 11

11:1 | τοῦ διδάσκειν καὶ κηρύσσειν – gen. articular infs., expressing purpose

11:3 | προσδοκῶμεν – could be indic. ("are we waiting for another?") or deliberative subj. ("are we to wait for another?")

11:6 | ὃς ἐάν = "whoever" (see 5:19) | σκανδαλίζομαι ἐν = "take offense at" (cp. 13:57)

11:9, 11 | προφήτου, Ἰωάννου, αὐτοῦ – gens. of comparison

11:10 | ἄγγελος = "a human messenger serving as an envoy" (BDAG ἄγγελος 1)

11:12 | ἕως ἄρτι = "until now"

11:16 | ὅμοιος + dat. of person or thing compared (cp. 13:31ff) | τοῖς ἑτέροις = "to the other [children]," ellipsis (BDF §241)

11:19 | ἀπό = ὑπό = "by" (BDAG ἀπό 5eβ) | ἄνθρωπος φάγος = "a glutton," pleonastic ἄνθρωπος (BDAG ἄνθρωπος 4aε)

11:20 | αἱ πλεῖσται δυνάμεις αὐτοῦ = "most of his miracles"

11:21 | πάλαι ἂν μετενόησαν = "they *would have* repented long ago" (also v. 23)

11:23 | μὴ ἕως οὐρανοῦ ὑψωθήσῃ; = "you will not be exalted to heaven, will you?" | τῆς σήμερον [sc. ἡμέρας] – ellipsis (BDF §241(2))

11:26 | ἔμπροσθεν σου = "before you," reverential form of "to you" (BDAG ἔμπροσθεν 1bδ)

11:27 | ᾧ ἐάν + subj. = lit. "to whomever," i.e., "anyone to whom" (cp. Lk 10:22), relative clause functioning as subject; on ἐάν for ἄν, see 5:19

Matthew 12
12:1 | τοῖς σάββασιν = "on the sabbath," pl. for sg. (BDAG σάββατον 1bβ)

12:2 | ἔξεστιν = "be lawful/permitted" – see vv. 4, 10, 12

12:7 | τί ἐστιν = "what [this] means" (cp. 9:13) | οὐκ ἂν κατεδικάσατε = "you would not have condemned" (cp. 11:21, 23)

12:10 | χεῖρα ἔχων ξηράν = ἔχων χεῖρα ξηράν | κατηγορέω – κατα- prefix takes gen. object (BDF §181)

12:12 | προβάτου – gen. of comparison | ὥστε = "therefore" (BDAG ὥστε 1a)

12:13 | ἀπεκατεστάθη – note the double augment (BDF §69(3)) (cp. Mk 3:5; 8:25; Lk 6:10) | ἡ ἄλλη [sc. χεῖρ] – ellipsis

12:14 | συμβούλιον λαμβάνειν = "to form a plan/plot," Latinism: *consilium capere* (BDF §5(3)(b); BDAG συμβούλιον 3) (cp. 22:15; 27:1, 7; 28:12) | κατ᾿ αὐτοῦ = "against him"

12:18 | εἰς ὃν εὐδόκησεν – see note on 3:17

12:20 | ἕως ἂν ἐκβάλῃ εἰς νῖκος τὴν κρίσιν = "until he brings justice to victory" (ESV); unusual usage of ἐκβάλλω = "bring something about, bring" (BDAG ἐκβάλλω 5)

12:22 | δαιμονιζόμενος τυφλὸς καὶ κωφός = "a demon-possessed man who was blind and mute" (NASB) | τὸν κωφόν – acc. subject of infs. λαλεῖν and βλέπειν (W 192)

12:23 | μήτι typically expects negative answer: "This man cannot be the Son of David, can he?" (NASB), but can also be used when questioner is in doubt concerning the answer (BDAG μήτι): "Could this be the Son of David?" (NIV) (cp. John 4:29)

12:24 | Οὗτος οὐκ ἐκβάλλει ... "this man does not cast out demons except by Beelzebul"

12:24, 27, 28 | Hebr./instrumental ἐν (4x) (see 7:6)

12:25 | καθ' ἑαυτῆς (2x) = κατὰ ἑαυτῆς = "against itself" (BDAG κατά A2bγ)

12:26 | ἐφ' ἑαυτόν = ἐπὶ ἑαυτόν = "against himself" (BDAG ἐπί 12b)

12:27 | κριταὶ ὑμῶν – objective gen. with verbal noun

12:31 | ἡ τοῦ πνεύματος βλασφημία = "speaking against/denigrating the Spirit" – objective gen. with verbal noun (W 118)

12:32 | ἐν τῷ μέλλοντι [sc. αἰῶνι] – ellipsis

12:33 | ἤ ... ἤ = "either ... or"

12:34 | πῶς + present indic., rare (BDF §366(4)); normally πῶς takes deliberative subj. (e.g., 23:33; 26:54)

12:35 | ἐκβάλλω (2x) = "bring out" (NASB) (BDAG ἐκβάλλω 3)

12:36 | πᾶν ῥῆμα ... περὶ αὐτοῦ ("for it") – anacoluthon after πᾶς (BDF §466(3)) | ἀποδίδωμι λόγον = "give an account"

12:40 | τρεῖς ἡμέρας καὶ τρεῖς νύκτας (2x) – acc. for extent of time

12:41 | μετανοέω εἰς = "repent at, in the face of" (BDAG εἰς 10a) (cp. Lk 11:32)

12:45 | πονηρότερα ἑαυτοῦ = "more evil than itself," gen. of comparison | τὰ ἔσχατα … τῶν πρώτων = "the last state … the first state" | τῇ γενεᾷ ταύτῃ – dat. of ref./respect (W 144)

12:49 | ἐκτείνας τὴν χεῖρα αὐτοῦ ἐπὶ τοὺς μαθητάς = "stretching out his hand toward his disciples" (BDAG ἐπί 4bα)

12:50 | ὅστις ἂν ποιήσῃ = "whoever does," subj. in indef. relative clause (cp. 5:19, 21; 10:33)

Matthew 13

13:1 | ἐξελθὼν τῆς οἰκίας = "went out of the house," ἐκ- prefix of ἐξ-έρχομαι takes gen. (BDF §181)

13:2 | ὥστε … καθῆσθαι = "so that he got into a boat and sat down" (ESV) | αὐτόν as acc. subject of inf.

13:3 | τοῦ σπείρειν – gen. of the articular inf., final sense (BDF §400(5))

13:4 | ἐν τῷ σπείρειν αὐτόν = "as he sowed," Septuagintism (BDF §404) (v. 25)

13:4ff | ἅ … ἄλλα = "some [seeds] … other [seeds]" – neut. pl. σπέρματα implied bec. cognate with verb σπείρω (cp. vv. 24, 27, 37, σπείρω σπέρμα; also v. 18, τὸ ἐσπαρμένον for τὸ σπέρμα) | Neut. pl. subjects take sg. verbs (BDF §133)

13:5–6 | Subject of εἶχεν is the implied "seeds" – "where they did not have much soil" | διὰ τὸ μὴ ἔχειν (2x) = "on account of not having" (BDF §402(1)), articular inf.

13:7 | ἐπὶ τὰς ἀκάνθας = "among the thorns" (BDAG ἐπί 4bδ) (cp. v. 22, εἰς)

13:8 | δίδωμι καρπόν = "produce/yield fruit" (BDAG δίδωμι 9)

13:11 | ὅτι recitative

13:12 | καὶ ὃ ἔχει = "even what he has" (cp. 25:29)

13:13 | βλέποντες (also v. 14), ἀκούοντες – concessive ptcs., "though seeing ... though hearing" (NIV); also cognate ptcs. (BDF §422)

13:14 | αὐτοῖς = "in their case" (ESV, NASB), dat. of ref./respect (see 12:45) | ἀκοῇ ἀκούσετε = lit. "with hearing you will hear," cognate dat. (W 168–9); "a Hebr. turn of speech lending emphasis to the vb" (ZG) | ἀκοῇ ... ἴδετε = "you will be ever hearing but never understanding; you will be ever seeing but never perceiving" (NIV)

13:15 | μήποτε + subj. = "lest" | ἰάσομαι – future continuing subj. to designate some further consequence (BDF §369(3))

13:16 | ὑμῶν – placed up front for emphasis ("but blessed are *your* eyes")

13:18 | τὸ ἐσπαρμένον = "what has been sown," i.e., τὸ σπέρμα

13:19 | παντός ... συνιέντος = "when anyone hears ... and yet does not understand," gen. abs. | Anacoluthon after πᾶς – παντός ἀκούοντος is resumed by ἐν τῇ καρδίᾳ αὐτοῦ (BDG §466(3))

13:19, 20, 22, 23 | ὁ σπαρείς (4x) = "the one sown" (aorist pass. ptc.)

13:22 | εἰς τὰς ἀκάνθας = "among the thorns" (BDAG εἰς 1aε) (cp. v. 7, ἐπί)

13:22–23 | Ptcs. continued by finite verbs (BDF §468(3))

13:23 | ὃς δή = "he is just the one who" (BDF §451(4)), "who indeed" (BDAG) | ποιέω (also v. 26) – see 7:17–19 | ὃ μέν ... ὃ δέ ... ὃ δέ ... = "in one case ... in another ... in another" (ESV) (BDF §250)

13:24 | ὡμοιώθη = lit. "has become like" (aorist pass.) – could be (1) Semitic stative perfect with present meaning (W 565), or (2) genuine past tense indicating that the kingdom "has made its appearance [in the person of Christ] like ..." (ZG)

13:25 | ἐν τῷ καθεύδειν τοὺς ἀνθρώπους = "while his men [i.e. his servants] were sleeping" (v. 4) | αὐτοῦ ὁ ἐχθρός = "his enemy" | ἐπισπείρω = "sow *on top of* a crop," agricultural technical term (BDAG) | ἀνὰ μέσον = "among"

13:26 | ἐφάνη καὶ τὰ ζιζάνια = "the tares *also* appeared"

13:27 | οὐχὶ ἔσπειρας; = "did you not sow?" | πόθεν; = "from what source?" (BDAG πόθεν 2); "Where then did the weeds come from?" (NIV)

13:28 | ἐχθρὸς ἄνθρωπος = "an enemy," pleonastic ἄνθρωπος (BDAG ἄνθρωπος 4aε) | θέλεις ἀπελθόντες συλλέξωμεν αὐτά; = "Do you want us to go and pull them up?" (NIV)

13:30 | ἄφετε + inf. + acc. = "let both grow together" (BDAG ἀφίημι 5a) | πρὸς τό + inf., indicating intent, "to burn them up" (NASB) (cp. 5:28)

13:31 | ὅμοιος + dat. of person or thing compared (cp. vv. 33, 44, 45, 47, 52)

13:32 | μέν ... δέ = "though ... yet" | μικρότερον/μεῖζον + gen. of comparison

13:33 | εἰς takes acc., so εἰς ἀλεύρου σάτα τρία = εἰς σάτα τρία ἀλεύρου = "in three measures of flour" | ἕως οὗ = "until" (BDAG ἕως 1bβℵ) (cp. 1:25) | ὅλον [sc. τὸ ἄλευρον] = "[the] whole [batch of flour]," ellipsis (BDAG ὅλος 1bγ) | "until the whole batch of flour became leavened" (cp. 1 Cor 5:6 || Gal 5:9)

13:35 | κεκρυμμένα ἀπὸ καταβολῆς κόσμου = "things hidden from/since the foundation of the world" (BDAG ἀπό 2b) (cp. 25:34)

13:41 | πάντα τὰ σκάνδαλα = "all stumbling blocks" (NASB), "all causes of sin" (ESV) (cp. 16:23; 18:7)

13:44 | ἀπὸ τῆς χαρᾶς = "because of the joy," ἀπό indicates motive (BDAG ἀπό 5c) | αὐτοῦ = "over it," i.e., the treasure

13:45 | Pleonastic ἄνθρωπος – see v. 28

13:46 | πέπρακεν – aoristic perfect (BDF §343(1); W 578)

13:47 | ἐκ παντὸς γένους συναγαγούσῃ = "gathering [fish] of every sort"

13:48 | Antecedent of ἥν is σαγήνη | ἀναβιβάσαντες … ἔβαλον – subject is "they" | τὰ καλά and τὰ σαπρά – substantivized adjs. (BDF §263(4))

13:49 | ἀφορίζω ἐκ μέσου = "take out from among"

13:52 | Pleonastic ἄνθρωπος – see vv. 28, 45 | τῇ βασιλείᾳ – dat. of respect | ἐκβάλλω = "bring out" (see 12:35)

13:54, 56 | πόθεν τούτῳ; (2x) = lit. "from whence to him?" (dat. of possession); more idiomatically, "where did this man get?"

13:56 | πρὸς ἡμᾶς = "with/among us" (BDAG πρός 3g)

13:57 | σκανδαλίζομαι ἐν = "take offense at" (cp. 11:6; 26:31, 33)

13:58 | διά + acc. = "because of"

Matthew 14
14:1 | ἡ ἀκοὴ Ἰησοῦ – see 4:24

14:2 | BDAG ἀπό 3aβ | αἱ δυνάμεις = "these miraculous powers" (ESV)

14:4 | ἔλεγεν γάρ = "for John had been saying," pluperfective impf. (W 549) (cp. Mk 6:18) | ἔξεστιν – see 12:2

14:5 | θέλων = "although wishing," concessive ptc. (cp. 21:46) | ἔχω τινα ὡς = "consider someone to be [something]" (BDAG ἔχω 6; BDF §157(3))

14:6 | γενεσίοις γενομένοις = "when H's birthday celebrations had come" – dat. abs., modeled after the Latin ablative abs. (M 44–45)

14:7 | ὅθεν = "so [much] that" (NASB), "therefore" (BDAG) | μεθ' ὅρκου = "with an oath" | ὃ ἐάν = "whatever"

14:8 | ἡ = "she"

14:9 | λυπηθείς – concessive ptc. | διά + acc. = "because of," could modify λυπηθείς but probably modifies ἐκέλευσεν: "although he was saddened, yet because of his oaths and his dinner guests the king commanded [it] to be given" | Subject of δοθῆναι is ἡ κεφαλή of John – same syntagmatic verb/noun combination in vv. 8, 11 (cp. 27:58)

14:13 | κατ' ἰδίαν = "by himself" (cp. v. 23) | πεζῇ (adv.) = "on foot," "by land," opposite of ἐν πλοίῳ ("by boat")

14:14 | ἐπί after verbs which express feelings (BDAG ἐπί 6c) (cp. 7:28)

14:15 | ἡ ὥρα ἤδη παρῆλθεν = "the hour is already late" (NASB), "the day is now over" (ESV), "the time is already past" (BDAG παρέρχομαι 2) | ἀπολύω = "send away" (BDAG ἀπολύω 3) (cp. vv. 22–23; 15:23, 32, 39)

14:16 | οὐ χρείαν ἔχουσιν ἀπελθεῖν = "they don't need to go away" | δότε αὐτοῖς ὑμεῖς φαγεῖν = "*you* give them [something] to eat"

14:17 | οὐκ ἔχομεν ὧδε εἰ μή = "we don't have [anything] here except"

14:19 | Brachylogy: "and the disciples [gave them] to the crowds"

14:20 | τὸ περισσεῦον = "what was left over"

14:22 | Subject of ἠνάγκασεν is "he" (= Jesus) | εἰς τὸ πέραν = "to the other side" | ἕως οὗ ἀπολύσῃ τοὺς ὄχλους = "while he sent the crowds away" (BDAG ἕως 2c), ἕως οὗ + subj. w/o ἄν (BDF §383(2))

14:24 | ἀπέχω + acc. for extent of space (W 202) = "be a certain distance from" (BDAG ἀπέχω 4) – "the boat was already many stadia from the land"

14:25 | τετάρτῃ φυλακῇ = "in the fourth watch," dat. of time (W 155)

14:26 | BDAG ἀπό 1c/5c (cp. 10:28)

14:28 | εἰ σὺ εἶ = "if [it] is you"

14:31 | Verbs of grasping and touching (v. 36) take gen. | εἰς τί; = "why?"

14:33 | θεοῦ υἱός – anarthrous but definite per Colwell's rule: "Definite predicate nouns which precede the verb usually lack the article" (W 257, 263–4)

14:35 | ἀπέστειλαν = "they sent [word]" (NASB) | οἱ κακῶς ἔχοντες (see 4:24)

14:36 | παρεκάλουν αὐτὸν ἵνα μόνον = "they implored him that they might just" (NASB), attenuated ἵνα (BDAG ἵνα 2aγ); μόνον – adv. acc. (BDAG μόνον 2a) | παρεκάλουν – distributive iterative impf. (W 546) | ὅσοι = "as many as" (NASB, ESV), "all who" (NIV)

Matthew 15
15:2–3 | διὰ τί; (2x) = "why?"

15:2 | ὅταν + present subj. = "whenever"

15:4 | θανάτῳ τελευτάτω = "let him die the death," similar to cognate dat. for emphasis, i.e., "let him surely die" (cp. 13:14)

15:5 | Δῶρον ὃ ἐὰν ἐξ ἐμοῦ ὠφεληθῇς = lit. "it is a gift [for God], whatever you would be benefitted by me," mng.: "whatever I might have given you has already been set aside for God"

15:8 | πόρρω (adv.) ἀπέχει ἀπ᾽ ἐμοῦ = "is far away from me" (BDAG ἀπέχω 4)

15:14 | τυφλὸς τυφλὸν ἐὰν ὁδηγῇ = ἐὰν τυφλὸς τυφλὸν ὁδηγῇ

15:16 | ἀκμήν = *adhuc* (Vulgate), "still," "as yet," "even now," adv. acc., from ἀκμή = "highest point," "critical moment" (LSJ ἀκμή)

15:18 | κἀκεῖνα = καὶ ἐκεῖνα

15:20 | τὸ φαγεῖν = "eating," articular inf. with anaphoric ref. to the eating previously mentioned in v. 2 (BDF §399)

15:22 | κακῶς δαιμονίζεται = "is suffering terribly from demon-possession" (NIV 1984) (cp. κακῶς πάσχει in ref. to demon-possession, 17:15,18)

15:23 | ἀπολύω (vv. 32, 39) = "send away" (see 14:15)

15:24 | οὐκ ... εἰ μή = lit. "not ... except," mng. "only" (cp. 5:13; 11:27; 12:24; 16:4)

15:27 | καὶ γάρ = "for even," where γάρ supports an unexpressed thought that must be supplied (BDAG γάρ 1e): "Yes, Lord, [nevertheless, I may still partake of the children's bread], for even the dogs ..." | τὰ κυνάρια = "little house dogs," not street dogs | ἀπό – substitute for partitive gen. (BDAG ἀπό 1f) | τῶν κυρίων αὐτῶν – "of their masters," i.e., the children (τέκνα) in v. 26

15:31 | "So the crowd marveled as they saw ..." (NASB) | Ἰσραήλ is gen.

15:32 | ἤδη ἡμέραι τρεῖς = "for three days now," rare use of nom. for extent of time (BDF §144; W 64; cp. Mark 8:2) | οὐκ ἔχουσιν τί φάγωσιν = "they do not have anything to eat," lit. "they do not have what they might eat," subj. in indirect question (W 478) | ἀπολύω (vv. 23, 39) | νήστεις (acc. pl. of νῆστις) (adj.) = "not eating, fasting, hungry" | οὐ θέλω + inf. (ἀπολῦσαι) = "I am not willing to send them away hungry | μήποτε + subj. = "lest"

15:33 | πόθεν ἡμῖν; = lit. "from whence to us?" dat. of possession | "Where in this deserted area would we get enough loaves to satisfy such a large crowd?"

Matthew 16

16:1 | πειράζοντες ἐπηρώτησαν αὐτόν = "to test him they asked him" (ESV); πειράζοντες – telic adverbial ptc. (W 635–6 and n60)

16:3 | "[There will be] a storm today, for the sky is red and threatening"

(NASB), στυγνάζω (< στυγνός = "gloomy, sad") = "be gloomy, dark, lowering"

16:5 | εἰς τὸ πέραν = "to the other side"

16:6, 11, 12 | προσέχω ἀπό (3x) = "beware of"

16:8 | ὅτι = "that" (not "because")

16:11 | πῶς οὐ νοεῖτε = "how is it that you do not understand?"

16:12, 13, 15 | προσέχειν and εἶναι (2x) – indirect discourse

16:18 | κἀγώ = καὶ ἐγώ | μου τὴν ἐκκλησίαν = τὴν ἐκκλησίαν μου | κατισχύω – κατα- prefix takes gen. (BDF §181)

16:19 | ὃ ἐάν (2x) = ὃ ἄν = "whatever" | ἔσται + perfect pass. ptc. (2x) = "shall have been bound/loosed," future perf. periphrastic (W 647–9; BDF §352) (cp. 18:18; Lk 12:52; Heb 2:13)

16:20 | Attenuated ἵνα (BDAG ἵνα 2aδ)

16:21 | ἀπὸ τότε = "from that time on" | δεῖ + acc. (αὐτόν) + four infs. = "it is necessary for him to ..." | πολλά = adv. acc. – πολλὰ παθεῖν = "to suffer greatly" | ἀπό = "at the hands of" (BDAG ἀπό 5eβ)

16:22 | ἵλεώς σοι – Septuagintism (BDF §128(5)), see LXX 2 Kgdms 20:20; 23:17; its meaning is interpreted by next clause, οὐ μὴ ἔσται σοι τοῦτο (for οὐ μή + future indic., see BDF §365; M 157)

16:23 | σκάνδαλον εἶ ἐμοῦ – either (1) "you are an offense to me," or (2) "you are tempting me to sin" (BDAG σκάνδαλον 2–3); taking ἐμοῦ as objective gen.

16:24 | εἴ τις for ὅστις (BDAG εἰ 7) (cp. 18:28)

16:26 | τὴν ψυχὴν αὐτοῦ ζημιωθῇ – acc. with pass. (BDF §159(2)) | ἀντάλλαγμα (< ἀντί + ἀλλάσσω ["exchange"]) + gen. = "in exchange for," ἀντι- prefix takes gen. (cp. 20:28)

16:28 | τῶν ὧδε ἑστώτων = "of those standing here," partitive gen. (W 84) | Verb of tasting takes gen. (θανάτου) | ἕως ἄν + subj. = "until"

Matthew 17
17:1 | μετά + acc. = "after" (BDAG μετά B2a) | κατ' ἰδίαν = "by themselves"

17:4 | One is tempted to translate, "it is good for us to be here" (NIV, NASB), but ἡμᾶς is acc. and subject of inf., hence: "it is good *that* we are here" (ESV) (BDF §409(3))

17:5 | ἔτι αὐτοῦ λαλοῦντος = "while he was still speaking," gen. abs. | ἐν ᾧ εὐδόκησα (cp. 2 Pet 1:17) – see note on 3:17 | ἀκούω + gen. = "give careful attention to, listen to, heed" (BDAG ἀκούω 4)

17:7 | Verbs of touching take gen.

17:8 | μόνον (adj.) = "alone" (NASB); it is not that they saw "only" Jesus but that when they saw Jesus, he was "alone"

17:10 | δεῖ + acc. (Ἠλίαν) + inf. (ἐλθεῖν) = "Elijah must come"

17:12 | ἐν αὐτῷ – equivalent to simple dat. | οὕτως καί = "so also" | μέλλω + inf. = "is destined to" (BDAG μέλλω 2a), "will certainly" (ESV) | ὑπ' αὐτῶν = "at their hands"

17:14 | ἐλθόντων πρὸς τὸν ὄχλον = "when [they] came to the crowd," gen. abs. with noun or pronoun (e.g., αὐτῶν, v. 9) omitted

(BDF §423(3)) (cp. v. 26) | γονυπετέω τινά = "kneel down before someone in petition" (BDAG γονυπετέω)

17:15 | μου τὸν υἱόν = τὸν υἱὸν μου | σεληνιάζομαι = lit. "be moonstruck" (see 4:24) | Subject of πίπτει is the man's son: "he often falls"

17:17 | ἕως πότε ἀνέξομαι ὑμῶν; = "how long am I to put up with you?" deliberative future (W 570); verbs of emotion (ἀνέχομαι) take gen. (BDF §176(1))

17:20 | "Because of the littleness of your faith" | ὡς = "as small as" (NIV)

17:24 | οἱ τὰ δίδραχμα λαμβάνοντες = "the collectors of the two-drachma tax" (the temple tax) | οὐ τελεῖ; = "does he not pay?" (cp. Rom 13:6)

17:25 | ἐλθόντα εἰς τὴν οἰκίαν = "when [Peter] came into the house" – looks like a gen. abs. changed to acc. by attraction with αὐτόν | προφθάνω + acc. (αὐτόν) + supplementary ptc. (λέγων) = "be ahead of someone in some activity" (BDAG προφθάνω; BDF §414(4)); here: "Jesus spoke to him first" (ESV, NASB), "Jesus was the first to speak" (NIV) | τί σοι δοκεῖ; = "what do you think?" (BDAG δοκέω 2bα) (cp. 18:12) | οἱ βασιλεῖς – pendent nom., a type of anacoluthon (W 51; BDF §466(2))

17:26 | εἰπόντος – gen. abs., with Peter as implied subject (BDF §423(3)) (cp. v. 14)

17:27 | τὸν ἀναβάντα πρῶτον ἰχθὺν ἆρον = "take the first fish that comes up"

Matthew 18
18:1, 4 | μείζων – comparative for superlative (BDAG μέγας 4a)

18:6 | ἵνα almost seems to mean "if" here | μύλος ὀνικός = lit. "a donkey millstone," worked by donkey-power (BDAG ὀνικός; μύλος 2)

18:7 | ἀπό = "because of" (BDAG ἀπό 5a)

18:8–9 | καλόν σοί ἐστιν + inf. (2x) = "it is better for you to" (BDAG καλός 2dγ), positive for comparative (BDF §245(3)) | κυλλὸν ἢ χωλόν, ἢ δύο χεῖρας ἢ δύο πόδας ἔχοντα = "or ... than ... or" (see also ἤ = "than" in v. 9)

18:10 | διὰ παντός = "continually"

18:12 | τί ὑμῖν δοκεῖ; = "what do you think?" (BDAG δοκέω 2bα) (cp. 17:25) | ἐὰν γένηταί τινι ἀνθρώπῳ ἑκατὸν πρόβατα = "if a man owns a hundred sheep" (NIV), dat. of possession (W 150); neut. pl. subjects (πρόβατα) take sg. verbs (γένηται) (BDF §133)

18:13 | καὶ ἐὰν γένηται εὑρεῖν αὐτό = "if it turns out that he finds it" | χαίρω ἐπί + dat. = "rejoice over," with verbs of emotion (BDAG ἐπί 6c)

18:14 | Reverential ἔμπροσθεν (BDAG ἔμπροσθεν 1bδ; BDF §214(6)), "of your father" (cp. 11:26)

18:16 | ἔτι ἕνα ἢ δύο = "one or two *others*" (BDAG ἔτι 2b)

18:17 | καὶ τῆς ἐκκλησίας = "*even* to the church"

18:18 | ὅσα ἐάν (2x) = "whatever" | ἔσται + perfect pass. ptc. (2x) = "shall have been bound/loosed" (see 16:19)

18:19 | δύο ...ἐξ ὑμῶν = "two of you" | περὶ παντὸς πράγματος οὗ ἐὰν αἰτήσωνται = "about anything that they may ask" | γενήσεται αὐτοῖς παρὰ τοῦ πατρός μου = lit. "it shall be done for them *from* my Father" (BDAG παρά A3aβ), not "by my Father"

18:20 | εἰς τὸ ἐμὸν ὄνομα = "in my name" (BDAG ὄνομα 1dγ)

18:22 | ἑβδομηκοντάκις (adv.) ἑπτά = could be (1) "seventy times seven times," or (2) "seventy-seven times" (BDAG ἑβδομηκοντάκις; BDF §248(2)) (cp. LXX Gen 4:24)

18:23 | Pleonastic ἄνθρωπος (BDAG ἄνθρωπος 4aϵ) | ἠθέλησεν – aorist of θέλω | συναίρω λόγον = "settle an account" (v. 24 without λόγον) (cp. 25:19)

18:24 | ἀρξαμένου αὐτοῦ συναίρειν = "as he began the settlement" (NIV), gen. abs. | εἷς as indef. article (BDAG εἷς 3); λόγον is supplied from v. 23 | μυρίων ταλάντων – objective gen. with verbal noun (ὀφειλέτης)

18:25 | μὴ ἔχοντος αὐτοῦ ἀποδοῦναι = "since he did not have [the means] to repay" (NASB), gen. abs. | πραθῆναι = "to be sold into debt bondage" | ἀποδοθῆναι = "repayment to be made"

18:27 | Verbs of emotion (σπλαγχνίζομαι) take gen. (BDF §176(1)) | ἀπέλυσεν αὐτόν = "he released him" from the threat of being sold into slavery

18:28 | ἔπνιγεν = "he began to choke him," inceptive impf. | εἴ τι ὀφείλεις ("if you owe anything") for ὅ τι ἂν ὀφείλῃς ("whatever you owe") (BDF §376; BDAG εἰ 7) (cp. 16:24)

18:29 | ὁ σύνδουλος αὐτοῦ = "his fellow-servant" gen. of association (W 128–30) (cp. vv. 31, 33)

18:30 | τὸ ὀφειλόμενον = "what was owed" (v. 34)

18:31 | τὰ γενόμενα (2x) = "what had happened"

18:33 | Acc. σε as subject of inf. (ἐλεῆσαι)

18:34 | ἕως οὗ + subj. = "until"

Matthew 19
19:1 | καὶ ἐγένετο … = "and it came to pass, when Jesus had finished these words, [that] he departed from Galilee" (see 26:1)

19:3 | πειράζοντες – telic adverbial ptc. (see 16:1) | κατὰ πᾶσαν αἰτίαν = "for any reason" (BDAG κατά B5aδ)

19:5 | ἔσονται εἰς – predicate nom. replaced by εἰς + acc. in LXX quotation (BDAG εἰς 8aβ)

19:8 | ὅτι recitative | πρός + acc. = "because of" (BDAG πρός 3eα; BDF §239(8))

19:9 | μὴ ἐπὶ πορνείᾳ = "not on the basis of immorality" (BDAG ἐπί 6a; μή 1a); cp. wording of exception clause at 5:32 | ἄλλην = "another [woman]"

19:10 | οὕτως – adv. used as adj. (BDF §434(1))

19:11 | ἀλλ' οἷς δέδοται = "but [those] to whom it has been granted"

19:12 | ἐγεννήθησαν οὕτως = "were born that way"

19:13, 15 | τὰς χεῖρας = "his hands"

19:14 | ἐλθεῖν – complementary inf. to both impvs.: "Let the children come to me and do not hinder them from coming to me"

19:16 | εἷς = "someone," equivalent to τις (BDAG εἷς 3a; BDF §247(2))

19:17 | εἷς ἐστιν ὁ ἀγαθός = "there is [only] one who is good" (BDAG εἷς 2b) (cp. 23:8–10)

19:18 | ποίας; = "which [commandments]?" (BDAG ποῖος 2bα) (cp. 22:36) | τό introduces the scriptural quotation; untranslatable (BDAG ὁ 2hα)

19:19 | ὁ πλησίον σου = "your neighbor" (see 5:43)

19:22 | ἀπῆλθεν λυπούμενος = "he went away grieving," adverbial ptc. of emotion or attitude (W 627–8) | ἦν ἔχων = "he owned," periphrastic (W 647–8)

19:24 | ἤ = "than"

19:27 | τί ἄρα ἔσται ἡμῖν; = "what then will there be for us?" i.e., what will be our reward?

19:28 | θρόνος δόξης αὐτοῦ = "his glorious throne," attributive gen. (W 86–7) (cp. 25:31) | καθήσεσθε καὶ ὑμεῖς = "you also will sit," repeating and resuming ὑμεῖς at beginning of sentence | κρίνειν here does not mean "pass an unfavorable verdict," but has Hebr. neutral sense, "act/function as a judge" (cp. LXX Exod 18:13, 22; Lev 19:15), even "rule" (LXX 4 Kgdms 15:5; Ps 2:10) (cp. Lk 22:30)

19:30 | πολλοί … πρῶτοι = "many first ones will be last," etc.

Matthew 20

20:1 | Pleonastic ἄνθρωπος (BDAG ἄνθρωπος 4ae) | ἅμα πρωΐ = "early in the morning" | εἰς τὸν ἀμπελῶνα αὐτοῦ – either (1) "for his vineyard" (ESV, NASB), taking εἰς as equivalent to dat. of advantage (BDAG εἰς 4g), or (2) "[to go] into his vineyard," pregnant construction (BDAG εἰς 10d) (rightly NIV; confirmed by vv. 4, 7).

20:2 | ἐκ δηναρίου = "for a denarius," equivalent to δηναρίου (BDAG ἐκ 4b); gen. of price (W 122) (cp. v. 13) | τὴν ἡμέραν = "for the day," acc. for extent of time (see v. 6)

20:3, 5, 6, 9 | περί + acc., of time (4x) = "at about" (BDAG περί 2b; M 62)

20:6 | ὅλην τὴν ἡμέραν = "all day long" (NIV), acc. for extent of time (W 202) | ἀργός = "unemployed, idle" (BDAG), "doing nothing" (NIV) (not to be confused with ἀγρός)

20:9–10 | ἀνά (2x) = "each, apiece" (BDAG ἀνά 3)

20:11 | ἐγόγγυζον = "they began to grumble" (NIV), ingressive impf.

20:12 | ἴσους ἡμῖν αὐτοὺς ἐποίησας = "you have made them equal to us"

20:13 | ἑνὶ αὐτῶν = "to one of them," ἑνί is dat. of εἷς | δηναρίου – gen. of price (cp. v. 2)

20:15 | "Am I not permitted to do what I wish with what is my own?"

20:17 | παραλαμβάνω τινὰ κατ᾽ ἰδίαν = "take someone aside" for a private talk

20:18 | κατακρίνω τινὰ θανάτῳ = "condemn someone to death" (BDF §195(2); BDAG θάνατος 1bα)

20:19 | εἰς τό + inf. = "in order to" (BDAG εἰς 4f; BDF §402(2))

20:20 | προσκυνοῦσα καὶ αἰτοῦσα – usually attendant circumstance ptcs. with aorist main verbs are also aorist (W 640–2), so these present ptcs. are unusual; perhaps they are modeled on the historical/dramatic present (W 526–9)

20:21 | εἰπὲ ἵνα = "command that" (BDAG λέγω 2c; ἵνα 2aδ) | ἐκ (2x) = "at, on" (BDAG ἐκ 2)

20:24 | ἀγανακτέω περί + gen. = "be indignant with/at," with verbs of emotion (BDAG περί 1c; BDF §229(2)) (cp. 9:36)

20:25 | Verbs of ruling take gen. (BDF §§177, 181)

20:28 | λύτρον ἀντὶ πολλῶν = "a ransom in the place of many" (see extended discussion of ἀντί at W 365–7)

20:31 | ἐπιτιμάω τινι ἵνα = "scoldingly warn/tell someone to," where ἵνα introduces that which the censure or warning is intended to bring about (BDAG ἐπιτιμάω 1; ἵνα 2aδ) | οἱ = "they" | μεῖζον = "all the more," adv. acc.

20:34 | Verbs of touching take gen.

Matthew 21

21:2 | ὄνος = "donkey," can be male or female; here female (δεδεμένην, αὐτῆς, and τὴν ὄνον (v. 7))

21:3 | ἐάν τις ὑμῖν εἴπῃ τι = "if anyone says anything to you" | ὅτι recitative | αὐτῶν goes with χρείαν – "the Lord has need of them" | Subject of ἀποστελεῖ is the undefined "s/he" implied by "anyone" (τις) | αὐτούς refers to the donkey and her colt

21:5 | σοι = "to you," dat. of destination (W 147), in Hebrew with verbs of motion (BDF §192) | ἐπιβεβηκώς = "mounted" (NASB, ESV)

21:8 | ὁ πλεῖστος ὄχλος = either (1) "most of the crowd" (NASB, ESV), genuine superlative, or (2) "a very large crowd" (NIV), elative force (BDF §60(2); BDAG πολύς 2cα) | Sg. subject with pl. verb (ἔστρωσαν), bec. ὄχλος is collective; *constructio ad sensum* (BDF §134(1c)) | ἑαυτῶν τὰ ἱμάτια = "their own cloaks," as distinct from the disciples' (v. 7)

21:9, 15 | ὡσαννά (3x) = Aramaic shout of praise, equivalent to δόξα (Luke 19:38)

21:11 | ὁ ἀπό – repetition of article with prepositional attributive (BDF §272) | ἀπό for ἐκ (BDF §209(3))

21:13 | ποιέω + double acc. = "make x into y" (BDAG ποιέω 2hβ)

21:16 | θηλαζόντων = "of nursing babies," ptc. used as substantive w/o article (BDF §§264(6); 413(1)); θηλάζω here = "*take* nourishment from the breast" (contrast 24:19)

21:19 | μία (< εἷς) functions as indef. article (BDF §247(2)) | ἐπὶ τῆς ὁδοῦ = "by the road," ἐπί + gen. (BDAG ἐπί 2a) | ἐπ᾽ αὐτήν = "up to it," ἐπί + acc. with verb of motion (BDAG ἐπί 4b)

21:21 | τὸ τῆς συκῆς = "what was done to the fig tree" (cp. 8:33), either objective gen. or gen. of ref. (W 128) | κᾂν = καὶ ἄν

21:22 | πάντα ὅσα ἄν = "all things whatsoever" (KJV) (cp. 7:12) | πιστεύοντες = "if you believe" (NIV), conditional ptc. (W 632)

21:23 | αὐτῷ διδάσκοντι = "to him as he was teaching" (ESV)

21:24 | ἐρωτήσω ὑμᾶς κἀγὼ λόγον ἕνα – double acc. of person and thing (W 181–2) | κἀγώ (2x) = καὶ ἐγώ = "I too" | λόγος = "question" (BDAG λόγος 1aβ) | ὃν ἐὰν εἴπητέ μοι = "which if you tell me" (NASB)

21:26 | ἔχω τινα ὡς = "consider someone to be [something]" (see 14:5)

21:29 | ὕστερον – adv. acc. (v. 37)

21:32 | οὐδέ = "not even" (BDAG οὐδέ 3); "and you, when you saw [the tax collectors and prostitutes believing John], did *not even* later change your mind so as to believe him" | τοῦ πιστεῦσαι – gen. articular inf., expressing purpose

21:34 | ὁ καιρὸς τῶν καρπῶν = "the season for fruit" (ESV), "harvest time" (NASB)

21:35 | ὃν μέν ... ὃν δέ ... ὃν δέ = "the one ... the other ... the other"

21:36 | πλείονας τῶν πρώτων = "more than the first," gen. of comparison

21:41 | κακοὺς κακῶς ἀπολέσει αὐτούς – play on words, "he will bring those *wretches* to a *wretched* end" (NASB) (BDF §488(1a))

21:42 | λίθον ὅν – inverse attraction, i.e., the case of the antecedent is assimilated to the case of the relative pronoun (BDF §295) | γίνεσθαι εἰς + acc. – functions as predicate nom., due to Semitic interference (BDAG εἰς 8aα) | παρὰ κυρίου ἐγένετο αὕτη = "this came about from the Lord" (NASB), "this was the Lord's doing" (ESV, BDAG παρά A2) | Fem. αὕτη instead of neut. τοῦτο, lit. translation of Hebrew (BDF §138(2); M 182)

21:44 | ἐφ᾽ ὃν δ᾽ ἂν πέσῃ = "on whomever it falls" | ὁ λίθος is subject of both πέσῃ and λικμήσει

21:45 | ὅτι λέγει = "that he was speaking," present to express relative time in indirect discourse (BDF §324; W 537–9)

21:46 | ζητοῦντες = "although they were seeking," concessive ptc. (cp. 14:5) | ἔχω τινα εἰς – see v. 26 but with εἰς as marker of predicate acc. (BDAG εἰς 8b; BDF §157(5))

Matthew 22

22:2 | ποιέω = "give" when used of meals or banquets (BDAG ποιέω 2f) | γάμους – pl. with sg. mng. (vv. 3, 4, 9), "wedding celebration"

22:5 | οἱ = "they" | ὃς μέν ... ὃς δέ = "the one ... the other"

22:9 | αἱ διέξοδοι τῶν ὁδῶν = "the main highways" (NASB); διέξοδος = "the place where a main street cuts (through) the city boundary and goes (out) into the open country" (BDAG διέξοδος)

22:10 | τε καί = "both ... and" | γάμος here = "wedding hall" (BDAG γάμος 3) | ἀνακειμένων – verbs of "filling" take gen., "filled with dinner guests"

22:11–12 | ἔνδυμα γάμου (2x) = "wedding garment," descriptive gen. (W 79)

22:15 | συμβούλιον λαμβάνειν = "to form a plan/plot" (Latinism: *consilium capere*) (BDF §5(3)(b); BDAG συμβούλιον 3) (cp. 12:14; 27:1, 7; 28:12)

22:16 | οὐ μέλει σοι περὶ οὐδενός = "you care for no one" | οὐ βλέπεις εἰς πρόσωπον ἀνθρώπων = "you do not regard people's face" | "You aren't swayed by men, because you pay no attention to who they are" (NIV 1984)

22:17 | εἰπὲ οὖν ἡμῖν τί σοι δοκεῖ = "tell us then; what do you think?" (BDAG δοκέω 2bα) (cp. v. 42; 17:25)

22:19 | τὸ νόμισμα τοῦ κήνσου = "the coin used for paying the tax," gen. of purpose (W 100)

22:23 | λέγοντες μὴ εἶναι ἀνάστασιν = "who say there is no resurrection"

22:25 | παρ᾽ ἡμῖν = "with/among us" (BDAG παρά B1bβ)

22:26 | ἕως τῶν ἑπτά = lit. "until the seven," i.e., "down to the seventh" (NASB)

22:27 | ὕστερον δὲ πάντων = "last of all," adv. acc.

22:31 | τὸ ῥηθὲν ὑμῖν ὑπὸ τοῦ θεοῦ = "what was spoken to you by God"

22:34 | ἐπὶ τὸ αὐτό = "at the same place, together"

22:35 | πειράζων αὐτόν = "to test him," telic ptc. (cp. 16:1; 19:3)

22:36 | μεγάλη (also v. 38) = "greatest," positive for superlative (BDF §245(2))

22:37 | Hebr./instrumental ἐν (3x)

22:39 | ὁ πλησίον σου = "your neighbor" (see 5:43; 19:19)

22:44 | ἐκ = "at" (cp. 20:21) (BDAG ἐκ 2)

22:46 | "nor did anyone dare from that day on to question him further"

Matthew 23

23:2 | ἐκάθισαν = either (1) "sit" (ESV), gnomic aorist (W 562), or (2) "have seated themselves" (NASB), perfective aorist denoting continuing effect (BDF §342(1))

23:5 | πρὸς τό + inf., indicating intent (see 5:28)

23:8–10 | εἷς ἐστιν (3x) = "there is [only] one" (BDAG εἷς 2b) (cp. 19:17)

23:9 | The first ὑμῶν is oddly positioned, but is probably to be taken with πατέρα, and then an object such as τινα must be supplied: "Do not call [anyone] on earth your father" (NASB). However, several Western MSS have ὑμῖν instead (cp. Vulgate *vobis*), so no extra word need be supplied: "Do not call for yourselves a father on earth." | εἷς γάρ ἐστιν ὑμῶν ὁ πατὴρ ὁ οὐράνιος = "for you have one Father – the one in heaven" (NRSV)

23:11 | ὁ μείζων ὑμῶν = "the greatest among you," comparative for superlative (BDF §60(1)), and ὑμῶν as partitive gen. (W 84) | ὑμῶν διάκονος = "your servant," taking ὑμῶν as objective gen. with verbal noun (διάκονος < διακονέω)

23:13 | ἔμπροσθεν τῶν ἀνθρώπων = "in peoples' faces" (ESV) | τοὺς εἰσερχομένους = "those who would enter" (ESV), present ptc. for conative impf. (BDF §339(3))

23:15 | περιάγω + acc. of place traversed = "travel about on," intransitive (BDAG περιάγω 2; BDF §308) | ἡ ξηρὰ [γῆ] = "the dry [land]," ellipsis of substantive with adjectival attributive (BDF §241(1)) | ὅταν γένηται = "when he becomes [one]," i.e., a proselyte

23:16–22 | ὀμνύω ἐν (13x) = "swear by" (see 5:34–36)

23:16, 18 | ὀφείλει = "he is obligated, bound by his oath," Rabbinic usage (BDAG ὀφείλω 2bα)

23:20–22 | ὁ ὀμόσας (3x) = "whoever swears," substantival gnomic aorist ptc. with generic ref. (W 615 n8)

23:23 | πίστις probably means "faithfulness" here (BDAG πίστις 1a) | ταῦτα ἔδει ποιῆσαι – the subject of ποιῆσαι must be supplied: "These are the things that [you/ὑμᾶς] ought to have done without neglecting the others" | κἀκεῖνα = καὶ ἐκεῖνα

23:24 | διϋλίζω – see BDAG for discussion of KJV's misleading "strain at"

23:25 | γέμω usually takes simple gen., but here ἐκ + gen. (BDAG ἐκ 4aζ; BDF §164) | ἁρπαγή = possibilities: (1) "robbery," (2) "what has been stolen, plunder," or (3) "greediness, rapacity" (BDAG ἁρπαγή 1–3) | ἀκρασία = "lack of self-control, self-indulgence"

23:26 | Φαρισαῖε τυφλέ = "you blind Pharisee," voc. sg.

23:30 | εἰ ἤμεθα = "if we had lived," second class conditional indic. (W 450–1, 694–6) | αὐτῶν κοινωνοὶ ἐν τῷ αἵματι = "partners with them in [shedding] the blood," gen. of association (W 129)

23:32 | πληρώσατε – aorist impv., "fill up the measure [of the guilt] of your fathers!"

23:33 | πῶς φύγητε = "how will you escape?" – deliberative rhetorical subj. (W 467; BDF §366(1))

23:34 | ἐξ αὐτῶν (2x) = "some of them," partitive ἐκ functioning as object (BDAG ἐκ 4aγ; BDF §164(2))

23:35 | ἔλθῃ ἐφ᾽ ὑμᾶς = "might be laid to your account" – cf. ἥξει ἐπί (v. 36)

23:37 | ὃν τρόπον = "in the manner in which," "just as," adv. acc. (BDF §160)

23:39 | "you will not see me *from now on* [ἀπ᾽ ἄρτι] until you say ..."

Matthew 24
24:1 | "Jesus came out from the temple and was going away"

24:5, 11, 24 | πλανάω (3x) = "mislead, deceive" in active sense

24:6 | μελλήσετε ἀκούειν = "you will hear"

24:7 | κατὰ τόπους = "in place after place" (BDAG κατά B1a)

24:12 | διὰ τό + inf. + acc. = "because of the increase of wickedness" (NIV) (W 597)

24:13 | ὁ ὑπομείνας = "the one who endures," substantival gnomic aorist ptc. with generic ref. (W 615 n8)

24:15 | τὸ βδέλυγμα τῆς ἐρημώσεως = "the abomination that causes desolation" (NIV), gen. of product? (W 106)

24:17 | ἆραι τὰ ἐκ τῆς οἰκίας αὐτοῦ = lit. "to remove the things that are *out of* his house" (!) – two possible solutions: (1) pregnant construction for ἆραι τὰ ἐν τῆς οἰκίας αὐτοῦ ἐξ αὐτῆς (M 74; Thayer ἐκ III; BDAG ἐκ 6a; BDF §437); (2) many MSS (cp. Mk 13:15), have τι ("anything") instead of τά

24:19 | αἱ ἐν γαστρὶ ἔχουσαι = "pregnant women" (see 1:18, 23) | θηλάζω here = "*give* nourishment at the breast" (contrast 21:16)

24:20 | χειμῶνος – gen. of time (W 122) | σαββάτῳ – dat. of time (W 155)

24:21 | οὐδ' οὐ μὴ γένηται = "nor ever will occur" (W 468)

24:24 | δίδωμι of signs and wonders = "produce, cause to appear" (BDAG δίδωμι 4)

24:29 | δίδωμι of heavenly bodies = "give light, shine" (BDAG δίδωμι 4)

24:31 | ἀπ' ἄκρων ... αὐτῶν = "from one end of heaven to the other"

24:32 | ὅταν ἤδη ... ἀπαλός = "when its branch has already become tender"

24:33 | ἐπὶ θύραις = "at the doors" (BDAG ἐπί 2b)

24:35 | οὐ μή + aorist subj. for emphatic negation (W 468)

24:41 | δύο ἀλήθουσαι = "two women [will be] grinding," fem. ptc.; ἔσονται implied from v. 40 | ἐν = "at" (BDAG ἐν 1c)

24:43 | ἐκεῖνο precedes its referent, the ὅτι clause (BDF §291(5))

| εἰ ἤδει = "if he had known," plupf. in protasis of second class condition (W 695 n25) | φυλακή = "watch of the night," dat. of time (also vv. 42, 44) | ἔρχεται – futuristic present (BDF §323(2))

24:44 | ᾗ οὐ δοκεῖτε ὥρᾳ = "at an hour when you do not think [he will come]"

24:46 | ἐλθών – "whom his master, *when he comes*, finds so doing"

24:47 | τὰ ὑπάρχοντα (< ὑπάρχω) = "possessions" – see 25:14

24:50 | ᾗ (2x) – attraction to case of antecedent (W 339)

Matthew 25

25:1 | εἰς ὑπάντησιν τοῦ νυμφίου = "to meet the bridegroom" (see v. 6); taking τοῦ νυμφίου as objective gen. with verbal noun (ὑπάντησις < ὑπαντάω)

25:5 | χρονίζοντος τοῦ νυμφίου – gen. abs.

25:6 | μέσης νυκτός – gen. of time

25:8 | ἐκ τοῦ ἐλαίου ὑμῶν = "some of your oil" (BDF §164; BDAG ἐκ 4aε) | σβέννυνται = "are going out," progressive present (W 518)

25:9 | μήποτε οὐ μὴ ἀρκέσῃ ἡμῖν καὶ ὑμῖν = "certainly there would never be enough for us and you too!" emphatic (W 468; BDAG μήποτε 4)

25:10 | ἀπερχομένων αὐτῶν ἀγοράσαι = "while they were on their way to buy the oil" (NIV); gen. abs. with complementary inf. | αἱ ἕτοιμοι = "the [virgins] who were ready," two endings in pl. (BDAG ἕτοιμος; BDF §59(2))

25:11 | ὕστερον – adv. acc. | καὶ αἱ λοιπαὶ παρθένοι = "the other virgins also"

25:14 | ὥσπερ γάρ = "for [the kingdom of heaven – v. 1] is like," introducing a parable (BDF §§453(4), 482) | ἀποδημῶν = "about to leave on a journey," he has not left yet, see v. 15 (W 626)

25:15 | ἑκάστῳ κατὰ τὴν ἰδίαν δύναμιν = "to each according to his ability"

25:16 | ἠργάσατο ἐν αὐτοῖς = "traded/invested with them," i.e., the talents (ἐν for simple dat.)

25:19 | συναίρω λόγον = "settle an account" (cp. 18:23–24)

25:21, 23 | πιστὸς ἐπί + acc. (2x) = "faithful over" (BDAG ἐπί 9c; BDF §233(2))

25:24 | ὁ εἰληφώς = "the possessor," perfect with continuing effect (BDF §342(1))

25:24, 26 | ὅθεν (2x) = ἐκεῖθεν οὗ/ὅπου = "from where" (BDF §437)

25:25 | ἴδε ἔχεις τὸ σόν = lit. "See, you have what is yours" (NASB); more idiomatically, "See, here is what belongs to you" (NIV)

25:26 | ὀκνηρός = "possessing ὄκνος (a state involving shrinking from something, 'holding back, hesitation, reluctance'), idle, lazy, indolent" (BDAG ὀκνηρός)

25:27 | ἔδει – impf. of δεῖ | ἔδει σε οὖν βαλεῖν = "then you ought to have put" (NASB), acc. σε as subject of inf. (cp. 26:35)

25:29 | τῷ ἔχοντι παντί (= "to everyone who has") seems to be equivalent to παντὶ τῷ ἔχοντι (cp. Lk 19:26), but it is an unusual word order, which may explain why some MSS drop παντί | τοῦ μὴ ἔχοντος – pendent gen. anticipating the pleonastic resumptive pronoun αὐτοῦ (ZG; BDF §297; W 329–30) (contrast Lk 19:26) | καὶ ὃ ἔχει = "even what he has" (cp. 13:12)

25:31 | θρόνος δόξης αὐτοῦ = "his glorious throne" – see 19:28

25:33 | ἐρίφιον = "goat" (synonym of ἔριφος) | ἐκ (2x) – see 20:21

25:35 | ἐδώκατέ μοι φαγεῖν = "you gave me [something] to eat," taking φαγεῖν as equivalent to a substantive (BDF §§390(2); 409(2)); cp. Mark 5:43

25:40, 45 | ἐφ' ὅσον (2x) = "to the degree that," "in so far as" (BDAG ἐπί 13)

25:40 | ἑνὶ τούτων τῶν ἀδελφῶν μου τῶν ἐλαχίστων = "to one of the least of these brothers of mine"

Matthew 26
26:1 | καὶ ἐγένετο ... = "and it came to pass, when Jesus had finished all these words, [that] he said to his disciples" (see 19:1)

26:2 | γίνεται and παραδίδοται – futuristic presents (BDF §323(1,2)) | εἰς τό + inf. = "in order to" (BDAG εἰς 4f; BDF §402(2))

26:5 | Ellipsis (BDF §481) | ἵνα μή = "lest"

26:7 | ἀλάβαστρον μύρου βαρυτίμου = "an alabaster jar of very expensive perfume" (NIV), gen. of content (W 92) | ἀνακειμένου = "as he was reclining at the table" (NIV)

26:8 | εἰς τί; = "why?"

26:9 | πολλοῦ = "for a large sum of money," gen. of price (W 122)

26:10 | ἠργάσατο – aorist ind. of ἐργάζομαι, "she had done a good deed to me"

26:12 | "when she put this perfume on my body, she did it to prepare me for burial," πρὸς τό + inf. indicating intent | Cp. LXX Gen 50:2: "And Joseph ordered his servants, the undertakers/embalmers, to prepare his father for burial" (καὶ προσέταξεν Ιωσηφ τοῖς παισὶν αὐτοῦ τοῖς ἐνταφιασταῖς ἐνταφιάσαι τὸν πατέρα αὐτοῦ) (see LSJ ἐνταφιαστής)

26:13 | ὅπου ἐάν = "wherever" | λαληθήσεται καὶ ὃ ἐποίησεν αὕτη = "even what she did will be spoken of" | εἰς μνημόσυνον αὐτῆς = "in memory of her," purpose clause (BDAG εἰς 4f)

26:15 | τί θέλετέ μοι δοῦναι κἀγὼ ὑμῖν παραδώσω αὐτόν; – two possibilities for this unusual usage of καί: (1) conditional: "what are you willing to give me *if* I hand him over to you?" (BDAG κἀγώ 5; W 689); or (2) purpose: "what are you willing to give me *so* I will hand him over to you?" (BDF §442(2))

26:16 | ἀπὸ τότε = "from then on" (NIV, NASB), "from that moment" (ESV) | ἐζήτει εὐκαιρίαν = "he [began] looking for a good opportunity" (NASB), ingressive/inceptive impf. (W 544)

26:17 | τῇ πρώτῃ τῶν ἀζύμων = "on the first [day] of the Feast of Unleavened Bread," pl. used for festivals (BDF §141(3); BDAG ἄζυμος 2) | ποῦ θέλεις ἑτοιμάσωμεν = "where do you want us to prepare?" deliberative subj. (W 465–7)

26:18 | πρὸς τὸν δεῖνα = "to a certain man" | πρὸς σέ = "at your house" | ποιῶ τὸ πάσχα = "I will celebrate the Passover" (BDAG ποιέω 2f); futuristic present (BDF §323; M 7)

26:22 | εἷς ἕκαστος = "each one" (NASB), "one after another" (ESV)

26:22, 25 | μήτι (2x) expects negative answer: "Surely it is not I, is it?" (BDF §427(2))

26:23 | ὁ ἐμβάψας = "the one who dips," substantival aorist ptc. lacks temporal ref. (BDF §339); cp. present ptc. (ὁ ἐμβαπτόμενος) in Mk 14:20

26:24 | καλόν = "better," positive for comparative (BDAG καλός 2dγ; BDF §245)

26:25 | ὁ παραδιδοὺς αὐτόν = "the one who is betraying him," substantival present ptc. with ingressive-futuristic force (W 537) (cp. vv. 46, 48)

26:28 | περί = ὑπέρ – cp. Mk 14:24; Lk 22:20 (M 63)

26:29 | ἀπ᾽ ἄρτι = "from now on"

26:31, 33 | σκανδαλίζομαι ἐν (2x) = "take offense at" (cp. 11:6; 13:57)

26:32 | μετὰ τό + inf. + acc. (subject of inf.) = "after I have been raised" (BDF §402(3))

26:34 | πρίν + acc. (subject) + aorist inf. (BDAG πρίν αβ; BDF §395) | τρίς modifies ἀπαρνήσῃ (repeated in v. 75)

26:35 | δέῃ = present subj. of δεῖ | κἂν δέῃ με σὺν σοὶ ἀποθανεῖν = "even if it is necessary for me to die with you," acc. με as subject of inf. (cp. 25:27) | ὁμοίως καί = "likewise also"

26:36 | αὐτοῦ = "here," neut. gen. of αὐτός used as deictic adv. (BDAG αὐτοῦ) | ἕως οὗ + subj. = "while" (BDAG ἕως 2c)

26:38 | ἕως + gen. = "to the point of" (BDAG ἕως 5)

26:39, 42 | Πάτερ (2x) – voc.

26:40 | ἔρχεται ... εὑρίσκει ... λέγει – historical presents (W 529) | οὕτως = "so, ...?" introducing a question (BDAG οὕτως 1b) | μίαν ὥραν = "for one hour," acc. for extent of time

26:42, 44 | ἐκ δευτέρου/τρίτου = "a second/third time," ἐκ + gen. equivalent to simple gen. of time (BDAG ἐκ 5bβ)

26:42 | τοῦτο and αὐτό – neuts. referring back to τὸ ποτήριον τοῦτο (v. 39)

26:43 | αὐτῶν οἱ ὀφθαλμοί = οἱ ὀφθαλμοὶ αὐτῶν

26:45 | τὸ λοιπόν = "for the remainder of the time," acc. for extent of time | παραδίδοται – ingressive-futuristic present (W 537)

26:46 | ὁ παραδιδούς με = "my betrayer," substantival aorist ptc., lacking temporal ref. (cp. vv. 25, 48)

26:47 | ἔτι αὐτοῦ λαλοῦντος = "while he was still speaking," gen. abs. (BDAG ἔτι 1aβ)

26:48 | ὃν ἂν φιλήσω αὐτός ἐστιν = "whomever I kiss, he is the one"

26:50 | ἐφ᾽ ὃ πάρει – difficult; most translations supply missing impv.: "[do] what you have come for" (cp. BDAG ὅς 1bβכ), taking its omission as aposiopesis due to strong emotion (BDF §§482, 300(2)). If impv. is not supplied, then it becomes a question: "what are you here for?" (ZG; Z §223); but interrogative ὅς is doubtful (BDAG ὅς 1bα, 1iβ). In any case, ἐπί is marker of purpose (BDAG ἐπί 11), and πάρει is a perfective present (BDAG πάρειμι 1a; BDF §322; W 532)

26:51 | αὐτοῦ τὸ ὠτίον = τὸ ὠτίον αὐτοῦ

26:52 | πάντες οἱ λαβόντες μάχαιραν = "all who take up the sword," substantival gnomic aorist ptc. with generic ref. (W 615 n8)

26:53 | ἤ as interrogative particle (BDAG ἤ 1dα; BDF §440(1)) | παρίστημι + dat. = "put at one's disposal" | ἄρτι = "at once" (BDAG ἄρτι 2) | πλείω δώδεκα λεγιῶνας ἀγγέλων = "more than 12 legions of angels"

26:54 | πῶς + dubitative subj. = "how will?" (BDF §366)

26:55 | ὡς ἐπὶ λῃστήν = "as [one goes out] against an insurrectionist" (see BDAG ὡς 2b; ἐπί 12b; λῃστής 2) | καθ' ἡμέραν = "day after day" (ESV), "daily" (BDAG κατά B2c) | ἐκαθεζόμην = "I used to sit," customary impf. (W 548)

26:57 | οἱ = "they," article as pronoun (W 211)

26:58 | ἀπὸ μακρόθεν = "at a distance" | ἕως + gen. = "as far as," functioning as a preposition | ἰδεῖν τὸ τέλος = "to see the end" (ESV), "outcome" (NIV, NASB)

26:59 | ἐζήτουν = they "kept trying to obtain" (NASB), conative impf. (W 550) | κατά + gen. = "against" (BDAG κατά A2bβ)

26:60 | "and they did not find [any], even though many false witnesses came forward" (concessive ptc., gen. abs.) | ὕστερον – adv. acc.

26:61 | διὰ τριῶν ἡμερῶν = "after three days" (BDAG διά A2c; BDF §223(1))

26:62 | οὐδέν ... καταμαρτυροῦσιν; – possible punctuations: (1) "Have you nothing to answer? What is it that these men are accusing you of?" or (2) "Have you nothing to answer what these men are accusing you of?" (BDF §298(4); §299(1)) | κατα-μαρτυροῦσιν takes gen. object (σου) bec. of κατα- prefix (BDF §181)

26:64 | ἀπ' ἄρτι = "from now on," is puzzling; three possibilities: (1) ἀπ' ἄρτι could be taken with καθήμενον rather than ὄψεσθε (cp.

Luke 22:69), but word order makes this difficult; (2) possibly it is a different word, ἀπαρτί = "certainly, definitely" (BDF §12; BDAG ἀπαρτί); (3) most likely, Jesus is refering to his imminent resurrection/ ascension as proleptic of his parousia.

26:65 | τί ἔτι χρείαν ἔχομεν μαρτύρων; = "what further need have we of witnesses?" (BDAG ἔτι 1bβ)

26:67 | οἱ δὲ ἐράπισαν = "others slapped him" (cp. 28:17) (BDF §250)

26:71 | ἄλλη [παιδίσκη] = "another [servant girl]" | τοῖς ἐκεῖ = "to those [who were] there"

26:72, 74, 75 | ὅτι recitative (3x)

26:73 | μετὰ μικρόν = "after a little while" | καὶ γάρ = "for indeed" | ἡ λαλιά σου δῆλόν σε ποιεῖ = "your accent gives you away" (NIV)

26:75 | πρίν ... ἀπαρνήσῃ με (see v. 34)

Matthew 27

27:1 | συμβούλιον λαμβάνειν = "to form a plan/plot" (Latinism: *consilium capere*) (BDF §5(3)(b); BDAG συμβούλιον 3) (cp. v. 7; 12:14; 22:15; 28:12)

27:3 | Subject of κατεκρίθη is Jesus: "Then when Judas, his betrayer, saw that Jesus was condemned ..." (ESV)

27:4 | ἥμαρτον παραδούς = "I have sinned in that I betrayed," ptc. defining more exactly the action of the main verb (BDF §339(1); W 628–9) | τί πρὸς ἡμᾶς; = "what is that to us?" (BDAG πρός 3eγ; BDF §299(3)) | σὺ ὄψῃ = "see to it yourself" (ESV), "that's your responsibility" (NIV) (see BDAG ὁράω B3)

27:6 | εἰς τὸν κορβανᾶν = "into the treasury" | τιμὴ αἵματος = lit.

"the price of blood," money paid for a bloody deed (BDAG τιμή 1) |
ἐστιν – neut. pl. subjects (τὰ ἀργύρια) take sg. verbs

27:7 | συμβούλιον λαμβάνειν = "to form a plan/plot" (v. 1) | ἐξ αὐτῶν
= "with them," i.e., τὰ ἀργύρια | εἰς ταφὴν τοῖς ξένοις = "as a burial
place for strangers," εἰς as marker of predicate acc. (BDAG εἰς 8b)

27:9 | τιμάω = "price; set a price" (BDAG τιμάω 1) | τὴν τιμὴν
τοῦ τετιμημένου ὃν ἐτιμήσαντο = lit. "the price of the one
having been priced, on whom a price was set by the sons of Israel" |
ἀπό = ὑπό – see 11:19

27:10 | ἔδωκαν αὐτὰ εἰς τὸν ἀγρὸν τοῦ κεραμέως = "they paid
them [= the 30 pieces of silver] for the Potter's Field" (BDAG δίδωμι
6a; εἰς 4d)

27:12 | ἐν τῷ κατηγορεῖσθαι αὐτόν = "while he was being accused"
(BDF §404(1))

27:13 | πόσα σου καταμαρτυροῦσιν = "how many things they tes-
tify against you" – on gen. σου, see 26:62

27:14 | πρὸς οὐδὲ ἓν ῥῆμα = "not even to a single charge" (ESV),
taking ῥῆμα in Hebr. sense, "thing, matter" (BDAG ῥῆμα 2)

27:15 | κατά + acc., as marker of time, "at" (BDAG κατά B2a) |
εἰώθει = "was accustomed," plupf. with past (or impf.) force (W
586) | ἕνα δέσμιον = "one prisoner" | ὃν ἤθελον = "whom they
wanted" (impf.)

27:16 | εἶχον = "they were holding [in prison]" (impf.) | τότε = "at
that time"

27:17 | τίνα θέλετε ἀπολύσω (aor. subj.) ὑμῖν = lit. "whom do you
want that I should release for you?" deliberative subj. (W 465–7)

27:19 | μηδὲν σοὶ καὶ τῷ δικαίῳ ἐκείνῳ = "have nothing to do with that righteous man" | πολλά = "greatly," adv. acc. | κατ᾽ ὄναρ = "in a dream" (cp. 1:20; 2:12, 13, 19, 22)

27:20 | Note that ἀπόλλυμι ("destroy, kill," v. 20) and ἀπολύω ("release," vv. 15, 17, 21, 26) are different words | ἵνα functions as inf. (BDAG ἵνα 2)

27:21 | τίνα ἀπὸ τῶν δύο; = "which of the two?" taking ἀπό as substitute for partitive gen. (BDAG ἀπό 1f) (cp. 15:27)

27:21, 22 | ἀπολύσω and ποιήσω – deliberative subjs. (W 465–7)

27:22 | ποιέω τί τινα = "do something with someone," ποιέω + double acc. (BDAG ποιέω 4a)

27:24 | οὐδὲν ὠφελεῖ = "he was accomplishing nothing" | ἀθῷός ἀπό = "innocent of," Septuagintism, e.g., LXX Gen 24:41

27:25 | Supply a 3s impv. such as ἔστω or ἐλθάτω (cp. 23:35) (BDF §480(5))

27:27 | συνήγαγον ἐπ᾽ αὐτὸν ὅλην τὴν σπεῖραν = "they were gathering the whole cohort around him" (lit., "to him")

27:29 | βασιλεῦ – voc.

27:30 | ἐμπτύω/τύπτω εἰς = "spit/beat on" (BDAG εἰς 1aγ)

27:31 | ἐκ(ἐν)δύω (trans.) + double acc. of person and thing (W 181–2) | τὴν χλαμύδα = "the [scarlet] robe" (NASB), anaphoric article referring back to the previously mentioned χλαμὺς κοκκίνη (v. 28) (W 217) | εἰς τό + inf. = "in order to" (BDAG εἰς 4f; BDF §402(2)) | αὐτόν (= Jesus) does double duty as direct object of both ἀπήγαγον and σταυρῶσαι

27:32 | ἄνθρωπος Κυρηναῖος = "a man of Cyrene" in Libya (thus, a diaspora Jew)

27:35 | βάλλοντες κλῆρον = "by casting lots," ptc. of means (W 628)

27:36 | "and [the soldiers] sat down and were keeping watch over him there"

27:37 | τὴν αἰτίαν αὐτοῦ γεγραμμένην = "the written charge against him," objective gen. (αὐτοῦ); predicate adjectival ptc. (W 619)

27:38 | BDAG ἐκ 2 (cp. 20:21)

27:40 | ὁ καταλύων ... οἰκοδομῶν = "he who would destroy/build," present ptcs. functioning as conative impfs. (BDF §339(3))

27:42 | βασιλεὺς Ἰσραήλ = "the King of Israel," Colwell's rule: "Definite predicate nouns which precede the verb usually lack the article" (W 257, 263)

27:43 | ῥυσάσθω = "let him rescue [him]" | εἰ θέλει αὐτόν = "if he takes pleasure in him" (BDAG θέλω 3b)

27:44 | τὸ αὐτό = "in the same way," adv. acc. (BDF §§154; 160; BDAG αὐτός 3b)

27:45 | ἀπό ... ἕως = "from ... until"

27:46 | περί + acc., when used of time = "at about" (BDAG περί 2b; M 62) (cp. 20:3) | θεέ – voc. | ἐγκατέλιπες = (1) "Why did you forsake me?" aorist for past event, present results not prominently contemplated (M 11 n1); or (2) "Why have you forsaken me?" consummative aorist (W 559)

27:47 | τινές ... ἀκούσαντες = "when some of those standing there

heard this" (NIV) | ὅτι recitative | φωνέω = "summon, call for"
(BDAG φωνέω 3)

27:48 | πλήσας ὄξους = "filled it with sour wine," verbs of filling take gen.

27:49 | ἄφες ἴδωμεν = "let us see" (NASB), impv. of ἀφίημι rein-
forces hortatory subj. to form single idiomatic phrase; leave ἄφες un-
translated (BDAG ἀφίημι 5b; BDF §364(1–2); W 464–5) (cp. 7:4) |
σώσων = "to save," future ptc. expressing purpose (BDF §§351; 418(4))

27:51 | σχίζω εἰς δύο = "tear in two" (BDAG εἰς 4e)

27:54 | θεοῦ υἱός = "the Son of God," Colwell's rule (cp. v. 42)

27:56 | ἐν αἷς = "among whom" | ἦν – see BDF §135(1)(a) for ex-
planation of sg. rather than pl. verb with more than one subject (cp.
v. 61; 28:1) | ἡ τοῦ Ἰακώβου καὶ Ἰωσὴφ μήτηρ = "the mother
of James and Joseph"

27:57 | τοὔνομα = τὸ ὄνομα = "by name," acc. of respect (BDF §160)
| ὃς καὶ αὐτὸς ἐμαθητεύθη τῷ Ἰησοῦ = "who himself had also
become a disciple of Jesus" (NASB)

27:60 | τῇ θύρᾳ – dat. bec. of prefix of προσ-κυλίω (BDF §202)

27:63 | ἐκεῖνος ὁ πλάνος = "that deceiver" (NIV, NASB), "that im-
poster" (ESV) | ἔτι ζῶν = "when he was still alive" (BDAG ἔτι 1aβ)
| ἐγείρομαι – futuristic present (BDF §323(1); M 7)

27:64 | μήποτε + aor. subj. = "lest" | ἀπὸ τῶν νεκρῶν (cp. 28:7) = ἐκ
νεκρῶν (cp. 17:9) (W 363 n17) | τῆς πρώτης – gen. of comparison

27:65 | ἔχετε κουστωδίαν – ambiguous; ἔχετε could be (1) indic.
("you have a guard"), or (2) impv. ("take a guard") | ἀσφαλίσασθε ὡς
οἴδατε = "make it as secure as you know how" (BDAG ὡς 1a)

27:66 | μετὰ τῆς κουστωδίας = "along with the guard" (NASB), μετά as marker of attendant circumstances (BDAG μετά A3b); the literal sealing of the tomb and the posting of the guard are distinct actions; instrumental μετά ("by means of a guard") is possible but unattested in NT.

Matthew 28

28:1 | ὀψέ + gen. = "after" (BDF §164(4); BDAG ὀψέ 3) | τῇ ἐπιφωσκούσῃ – dat. of time | μίαν σαββάτων = "the first [day] of the week" (BDAG σάββατον 2b) | "Now after the Sabbath, as it began to dawn toward the first [day] of the week" (NASB) | ἦλθεν – for explanation of sg., see 27:56

28:2 | ἄγγελος κυρίου = "an (or the) angel of the Lord" (cp. 1:20, 24; 2:13, 19) (see W 252)

28:4 | οἱ τηροῦντες = "the guards"

28:7 | ἀπὸ τῶν νεκρῶν – see 27:64

28:9 | 'Ιησοῦς usually has the article in Matt; there may be theological significance in its absence here in first narrative mention after resurrection (BDF §260(1)) | αἱ = "the women," article used as pronoun | κρατέω + acc. = "take hold" or "grasp" the whole of, in contrast with tenderness of κρατέω + gen. (9:25) (W 132; BDAG κρατέω 3b) | αὐτοῦ τοὺς πόδας = τοὺς πόδας αὐτοῦ = "his feet"

28:10 | ἀπαγγείλατε ... ἵνα ἀπέλθωσιν = "tell them to go," ἵνα equivalent to inf. (BDAG ἵνα 2) | κἀκεῖ = καὶ ἐκεῖ = "and there"

28:11 | τὰ γενόμενα = "what had happened," see 18:31

28:12 | συμβούλιον λαμβάνειν = "to form a plan/plot" (Latinism: consilium capere) (BDF §5(3)(b); BDAG συμβούλιον 3) (cp. 12:14; 22:15; 27:1, 7) | ἀργύρια ἱκανά = "a large sum of money" (BDAG ἱκανός 3b)

28:13 | ὅτι recitative | νυκτός – gen. of time | ἡμῶν κοιμωμένων – gen. abs., "while we were asleep"

28:14 | ἐὰν ἀκουσθῇ τοῦτο ἐπὶ τοῦ ἡγεμόνος = "if this should come to the governor's ears" (NASB) | πείθω could also be translated "conciliate, satisfy" (BDAG) | ἀμέριμνον ποιεῖν τινα = "to keep someone out of trouble" (BDAG ἀμέριμνος) (on ποιέω + acc. object + acc. predicate adj., see BDAG ποιέω 2hβ)

28:15 | ἐποίησαν ὡς ἐδιδάχθησαν = "they did as they were instructed" | παρὰ Ἰουδαίοις = "among Jews" (BDAG παρά B1bγ), absence of article may indicate that this story circulated among some or many Jews

28:15, 17 | οἱ = "they," article used as pronoun

28:16 | οὗ (adv.) = "where" | εἰς τὸ ὄρος οὗ ἐτάξατο αὐτοῖς ὁ Ἰησούς = "to the mountain where Jesus had told them [to go]" (NIV), must supply a complementary inf. such as πορεύεσθαι (BDAG τάσσω 2b)

28:17 | οἱ δὲ ἐδίστασαν = "but some doubted" (cp. 26:67) (BDF §250)

28:19 | πορευθέντες μαθητεύσατε = "go and make disciples of," aorist attendant circumstances ptc. + aorist impv. (see W 645) | πάντα τὰ ἔθνη = "all the Gentiles" | εἰς τὸ ὄνομα = "in the name" (see BDAG ὄνομα 1dγ)

28:19–20 | βαπτίζοντες ... διδάσκοντες = "by baptizing ... by teaching," ptcs. of means (W 628–30); these are the means of making disciples (see W 645)

28:20 | πάντα ὅσα = "everything that" | πάσας τὰς ἡμέρας = lit. "for all the days," usually translated "always," acc. for extent of time (W 202)

Chapter Two

The Gospel of Mark

Mark 1

1:1 | Ἀρχή – nom. abs. (W 49–50) | Ἰησοῦ Χριστοῦ – could be subjective gen. ("the gospel preached by Jesus Christ," cp. v. 14) or objective gen. ("the gospel about Jesus Christ"), or both (W 121) | υἱοῦ θεοῦ is probably original; see commentaries

1:2 | ἄγγελος = "a human messenger serving as an envoy" (BDAG ἄγγελος 1)

1:3 | βοῶντος = "of (some)one crying out," anarthrous substantival ptc. (cp. Matt 3:3; Lk 3:4)

1:4 | Ignore [ὁ] ("John appeared, baptizing in the wilderness and preaching"); or, following other MSS, take ὁ βαπτίζων as a title (as in 6:14) and omit καί ("John the Baptizer appeared in the wilderness, preaching")

1:5 | ἐξεπορεύετο, ἐβαπτίζοντο – distributive iterative impfs. (W 547); note switch from sg. to pl., *constructio ad sensum*

1:6 | ἐνδεδυμένος τρίχας καμήλου = lit. "clothed with camel's hairs," mng. he "wore clothing made of camel's hair" (NIV) (cp. Matt 3:4)

1:7 | ἰσχυρότερός μου = "mightier than I," gen. of comparison |
Relative clause introduced by οὗ followed by pleonastic pronoun
αὐτοῦ (BDF §297), "the strap *of whose* sandals" | κύψας λῦσαι =
"to stoop down and untie," attendant circumstances ptc. (W 640;
pace BDF §418(5))

1:9 | καὶ ἐγένετο ἐν ἐκείναις ταῖς ἡμέραις = "and it came to pass
in those days [that]" (BDAG γίνομαι 4f) | εἰς = ἐν (cp. v. 5) (BDAG
εἰς 1bγ; BDF §205)

1:10 | ἀναβαίνων = "as he came up" (M 102) | εἶδεν σχιζομένους
τοὺς οὐρανούς = "he [= Jesus] saw the heavens being torn open"
(ESV) | καταβαῖνον – neut. ptc. in agreement with τὸ πνεῦμα

1:11 | ἐν σοὶ εὐδόκησα (= Luke 3:22) = "with you I am well pleased,"
constative/global aorist, stressing the fact of God's pleasure w/o regard
to time (W 557), as evidenced by use of aor. both before (Matt 12:18
quoting Isa 42:1) and after his baptism (Matt 17:5; 2 Pet 1:17); for
other options see note at Matt 3:17

1:13 | τεσσεράκοντα ἡμέρας – acc. for extent of time (W 202)

1:14 | μετὰ τό + inf. – "after John was arrested" (W 594–5)

1:15 | πιστεύω ἐν – occurs only 2x in NT (cp. John 3:15) (M 80)

1:15, 37, 40 | ὅτι recitative (3x), represented by quotation marks
(BDAG ὅτι 3)

1:17 | ποιήσω ὑμᾶς γενέσθαι = "I will cause you to become" (BDAG
ποιέω 2hα)

1:19 | ὀλίγον = "a little farther," acc. for extent of space (W 202) | καὶ
αὐτούς = "and them in the boat mending the nets" (BDF §442(9));
similar to "and him crucified" (1 Cor 2:2)

1:21 | εἰσπορεύονται – historical/dramatic present; commonly used in the Gospels to make the narrative more vivid (W 526) | τοῖς σάββασιν = "on the Sabbath," dat. of time when (W 155; BDF §200(3)); Semitic pl. with sg. meaning (BDAG σάββατον 1bβ; BDF §141(3))

1:22 | ἐπί after verbs which express feelings = "at" (BDAG ἐπί 6c) | ἦν διδάσκων = "he was teaching," impf. periphrastic (W 648)

1:23 | ἐν πνεύματι ἀκαθάρτῳ = "having/with an unclean spirit," sociative use of ἐν (BDF §§198(2); 219(4); Z §116) (Luke 4:33 has ἔχων instead)

1:24 | τί ἡμῖν καὶ σοί; – see variety of translations at Matt 8:29 | Ἰησοῦ Ναζαρηνέ – vocative | οἶδά σε τίς εἶ = "I know you, who you are," prolepsis, i.e., anticipation of the subject of the subordinate clause by making it the object of the main clause (BDF §476(2))

1:27 | ὥστε συζητεῖν ... τοῦτο; = "so that they queried among themselves, saying, 'What is this?'" (W 346) (ὥστε + inf. of result) | κατ᾽ ἐξουσίαν = "with authority" (BDAG κατά B5bβ) | καὶ τοῖς πνεύμασι ... ἐπιτάσσει = "he commands *even* the unclean spirits"

1:29 | ἐξελθόντες ἦλθον (pl.) = "they went out ... and came into the house" makes sense until you come to "with James and John." For this reason, other MSS have sg. ("he went out ... and came into the house"), which is supported by sg. pronouns referring to Jesus in immediate context: αὐτῷ (vv. 27, 30); αὐτοῦ (v. 28) (Metzger)

1:31 | ἤγειρεν αὐτὴν κρατήσας τῆς χειρός – attendant circumstances ptcs. usually precede main verb (W 642); transpose in translation: he "took her by the hand and lifted her up" (ESV) (BDF §339) | Verbs of touching/grasping take gen., though κρατέω can take either gen. or acc.

1:32, 34 | κακῶς ἔχειν (2x) = "to be sick"

1:34 | πολλοὺς κακῶς ἔχοντας ποικίλαις νόσοις = "all who were sick with various kinds of diseases" | ᾔδεισαν – plupf. with simple past force (W 586)

1:35 | ἔννυχα (< νύξ) λίαν = "while it was still quite dark," "long before daylight" | κἀκεῖ = καὶ ἐκεῖ = "and there," conjunctive καί (contrast v. 38) | προσηύχετο – progressive or ingressive impf. (W 543–5), setting scene for the disciples coming and interrupting him while in prayer

1:37 | πάντες ζητοῦσίν σε = "all are [right now] searching for you," progressive present (W 518)

1:38 | ἄγωμεν – hortatory subj. (W 464) | τὰς ἐχομένας κωμοπόλεις = "the neighboring towns" (BDAG ἔχω 11b), attributive adjectival ptc. (W 618) | καὶ ἐκεῖ = "there also," adverbial καί (contrast v. 35) | εἰς τοῦτο γὰρ ἐξῆλθον – could be (1) prosaic: "for that is why I went out [to a desolate place to pray]" (cp. ἐξῆλθεν, v. 35); or, more likely, (2) theological: "for it was for this purpose that I came forth [from God]" (see parallel, Luke 4:43; cp. ἐξῆλθον/-εν in John 8:42; 13:3; 16:27–30; 17:8)

1:39 | εἰς (2x) = ἐν

1:40–41 | ἔρχεται, λέγει – historical presents

1:41 | αὐτοῦ – possessive pronoun with τὴν χεῖρα ("his hand"), not gen. object of ἥψατο (W 239) | καθαρίσθητι = "be cleansed!" pronouncement imperative, i.e., speech act fulfilled at moment of speaking (W 492, 440 n109)

1:44 | ὅρα μηδενὶ μηδὲν εἴπῃς = "see that you say nothing to anyone" | ἅ = "what" or "the sacrifices that" (NIV); Matt 8:4 (parallel) has τὸ δῶρον ὅ

1:45 | ὁ = "he," article as pronoun | πολλά = "freely," adv. acc., intensifies the verb (BDAG πολύς 3aβ) | ὥστε + infinitive of result: "so that he [Jesus] was no longer able to enter a city openly"

Mark 2

2:1 | δι' ἡμερῶν = "several days afterward" (BDAG διά A2c), "after some days" (BDF §223(1)) | ἀκούσθη ὅτι ἐν οἴκῳ ἐστίν = "it became known that he was in the house" (BDAG ἀκούω 3e); anarthrous, definite noun after preposition (ἐν οἴκῳ) (W 247); present (ἐστίν) retained in indirect discourse (W 537–9)

2:2 | ὥστε μηκέτι χωρεῖν μηδὲ τὰ πρὸς τὴν θύραν = "so that there was no longer any room, not even at the area around the door"

2:3 | αἰρόμενον ὑπὸ τεσσάρων = "carried by four men"

2:4 | ἐξορύξαντες χαλῶσι = "after digging [a hole in the roof] they lowered the mat," attendant circumstances ptc. + historical present

2:5, 9 | σου αἱ ἁμαρτίαι = αἱ ἁμαρτίαι σου = "your sins"

2:7 | τί οὗτος οὕτως λαλεῖ; = "why does this man speak this way?" | εἰ μὴ εἷς ὁ θεός (see 10:18) = "except God alone" (BDAG εἷς 2c); Luke 5:21 (parallel) has μόνος instead of εἷς

2:10 | ἐξουσία + inf. = "authority to"

2:12 | ἄρας – attendant circumstances ptc. (W 640) | οὕτως οὐδέποτε εἴδομεν = "we have never seen anything like this"

2:15 | καὶ γίνεται κατακεῖσθαι αὐτόν ... καί = "and it comes to pass as he is reclining ... that" (BDAG γίνομαι 4e/f; καί 1bβ) | ἦσαν γὰρ πολλοὶ καὶ ἠκολούθουν αὐτῷ = "for there were many *who* followed him" (NIV, ESV) (BDAG καί 1aε; BDF §471(4))

2:16 | Second ὅτι = "why?" (cp. 9:11, 28) – rare (M 159)

2:17 | χρεία + gen. = "need of" | κακῶς ἔχειν = "to be sick"

2:18 | διὰ τί; = "why?" | σοί = "your" (nom. pl. of σός)

2:19 | οἱ υἱοὶ τοῦ νυμφῶνος = lit. "the sons of the bridal chamber," i.e., "the bridegroom's attendants" (BDAG νυμφών 2) (cp. Matt 9:15; Lk 5:34) | ἐν ᾧ = "while" – "while the bridegroom is with them the wedding guests cannot fast, can they?" | ὅσον χρόνον = "as long as" (BDAG ὅσος 1b)

2:21 | ἐπίβλημα ῥάκους ἀγνάφου = "a patch [made out] of un-shrunk cloth," gen. of material (W 91) | αἴρει τὸ πλήρωμα ἀπ᾽ αὐτοῦ τὸ καινὸν τοῦ παλαιοῦ = "the patch pulls away from it, the new from the old" (NASB)

2:21, 22 | εἰ δὲ μή (2x) = lit. "otherwise" (NASB), or "if he does" (ESV)

2:22 | οἶνον νέον εἰς ἀσκοὺς καινούς – ellipsis; must supply some form of the verb βάλλω ("one puts" or "they put")

2:23 | καὶ ἐγένετο = "and it came to pass that" (BDAG γίνομαι 4e/f) | ὁδὸν ποιεῖν = "to make a path"

2:24, 25 | τί; (v. 24) = "why?" but τί (v. 25) = "what"

2:24, 26 | ἔξεστιν (2x) = "be lawful/permitted"

2:25 | ὅτε χρείαν ἔσχεν = "when he was in need"

2:26 | ἐπὶ Ἀβ. ἀρχιερέως = (1) "in the time of Ab. the high priest" (BDAG ἐπί 18a) (but see 1 Sam 21:1ff), or (2) "in the passage about Ab. the high priest" (1 Sam 22:20–22; 23:6, 9; 30:7) (cp. ἐπὶ τοῦ βάτου, Mk 12:26; BDAG ἐπί 2a); John W. Wenham, "Mark 2:26," *JTS* 1.2 (Oct 1950): 156

2:27 | διά + acc. (2x) = "because of, for the sake of" (BDAG διά B2a)

2:28 | κύριος ... καὶ τοῦ σαββάτου = "lord even of the Sabbath"

Mark 3

3:1 | ἐξηραμμένην ἔχων τὴν χεῖρα = ἔχων τὴν χεῖρα ἐξηραμμένην ="having the hand withered/paralyzed"

3:2 | παρετήρουν αὐτὸν εἰ ... θεραπεύσει αὐτόν = "they were watching him [to see] *whether* he would heal him," εἰ as marker of indirect question (BDAG εἰ 5bα)

3:3 | ἔγειρε εἰς τὸ μέσον = "get up [and stand] in the middle," pregnant construction (BDAG εἰς 10d)

3:5 | συλλυπούμενος = "deeply grieved," συν- prefix strengthens mng. | ἐπί + dat. = "at" after verbs of emotion (BDAG ἐπί 6c) | ἀπεκατεστάθη ("was restored") has eschatological connotation; cp. ἀποκατάστασις (Acts 3:21); note the double augment (BDF §69(3)) (cp. 8:25; Matt 12:13; Lk 6:10)

3:6 | συμβούλιον ἐδίδουν = they "began to plot" (NIV), "to conspire" (BDAG δίδωμι 17a), ingressive impf. (W 544) | κατ᾽ αὐτοῦ = "against him"

3:7–8 | πολὺ πλῆθος (2x) = "a large crowd" (NIV); collective sg. subject with pl. verbs (W 400)

3:8 | ἀκούοντες ὅσα ἐποίει = "when they heard [about] everything that he was doing"

3:9 | εἶπεν ... ἵνα πλοιάριον προσκαρτερῇ αὐτῷ = "he told his disciples that a boat should stand ready for him" (NASB), attenuated ἵνα (BDAG ἵνα 2aδ)

3:10 | αὐτοῦ refers to Jesus (verbs of touching take gen.) | ὅσοι εἶχον μάστιγας = "all those who had illnesses," subject of ἅψωνται | μάστιξ = "scourge," illness sent by God as punishment for sin (LXX Ps 89:32) (Thayer) (cp. 5:29, 34)

3:11–12 | Distributive iterative imperfects (W 546)

3:11 | ὅταν αὐτὸν ἐθεώρουν = "whenever they saw him," ὅταν + indic. (BDAG ὅταν 1bγ; BDF §382(4))

3:12 | πολλά = "sternly" (see 1:45)

3:13 | οὓς ἤθελεν αὐτός = "those whom he himself wanted"

3:20 | ὥστε μὴ δύνασθαι αὐτοὺς μηδὲ ἄρτον φαγεῖν = "to such an extent that they could not even eat a meal" (NASB), μηδέ continues the negation (BDF §445(2))

3:21 | οἱ παρ' αὐτοῦ = "his relatives" (BDAG παρά A3b; BDF §237(2))

3:22 | Hebr./instrumental ἐν (BDF §219(1))

3:26 | τέλος ἔχει = "is at an end"

3:27 | ἀλλά indicates that the preceding is a settled matter, forming transition to something new (BDAG ἀλλά 3) | οὐ δύναται οὐδείς ... εἰσελθών ... διαρπάσαι = "no one can go in and plunder" | ἐὰν μή = "unless"

3:28 | πάντα ... βλασφημήσωσιν = "everything shall be forgiven to the sons of men – their sins and whatever blasphemies they may utter"

3:34 | τοὺς περὶ αὐτὸν κύκλῳ καθημένους = "those who were sitting around him in a circle"

Mark 4

4:1 | πλεῖστος = "huge," elative, i.e., not a true superlative but used to intensify mng. (M 98; W 303)

4:2 | ἐδίδασκεν αὐτοὺς ἐν παραβολαῖς πολλά = "he was teaching them many things in parables" (note that πολλά is acc. not dat.)

4:4 | καὶ ἐγένετο – see 2:15, 23 | ἐν τῷ σπείρειν = "as he sowed" (BDF §404(1)) | ἦλθεν τὰ πετεινά – neut. pl. subjects take sg. verbs

4:4–8 | ὃ μέν ... ἄλλο = "one [seed] ... another [seed]"

4:5–6 | διὰ τὸ μὴ ἔχειν (2x) = "on account of its not having"

4:7 | εἰς = "among" (BDAG εἰς 1aε) (also v. 18)

4:7–8 | δίδωμι καρπόν (2x) = "produce/yield fruit" (BDAG δίδωμι 9)

4:8 | It is tempting to take ἀναβαίνοντα as acc. sg. masc. modifying καρπόν but as the following αὐξανόμενα shows, both are nom. neut. pl. ptcs. agreeing with ἄλλα (Metzger): "Other seeds fell into the good soil, *and as they grew up and increased*, they yielded a crop and produced thirty, sixty, and a hundredfold" (NASB) | Textual variant: Aramaic ἔν (3x) or distributive εἰς (3x) (BDF §§207(2); 248(3); BDAG εἰς 4b; εἰς 7) (cp. v. 20)

4:10 | ὅτε ἐγένετο κατὰ μόνας = "when he was alone" (BDAG μόνος 3) | ἐρωτάω = "ask someone [acc.] about something [acc.]" ("they were asking him about the parables") | οἱ περὶ αὐτὸν σὺν τοῖς δώδεκα = "those around him with the twelve" (ESV), "his followers, along with the twelve" (NASB) (BDF §228; cp. Lk 22:49)

4:11 | ἐκείνοις ... γίνεται = "those outside receive everything in parables" (BDAG γίνομαι 4bγ)

4:12 | ἀφεθῇ αὐτοῖς = "it may be forgiven them"

4:13 | οἶδα = "understand" (BDAG οἶδα 4) | καί introduces apodosis which is also a question (BDAG καί 1bθ; BDF §442(8)): "[If] you do not understand this parable, how *then* will you understand any (lit. all) of the parables?" | πᾶς can come close to mng. "any" (BDF §275(3))

4:15 | NA punctuation is confusing: it is clearer to take the ὅπου clause as modifying τὴν ὁδόν and καὶ ὅταν as the start of a new clause: "These are the ones who are beside the road where the word is sown; and when they hear ..." (NASB)

4:17 | γενομένης θλίψεως ἢ διωγμοῦ = "when tribulation or persecution arises," gen. abs.

4:19 | αἱ περὶ τὰ λοιπὰ ἐπιθυμίαι = "desires for other things" (BDAG περί 2d)

4:21 | μήτι ἔρχεται ὁ λύχνος = "a lamp is not brought, is it?" (BDAG ἔρχομαι 3) | οὐχ = "is it not [brought]?"

4:22 | οὐ γάρ ἐστίν [τι] κρυπτόν = "for nothing is hidden" | ἐὰν μή = ἀλλά = "except" (BDF §448(8)) | ἐλθεῖν εἰς φανερόν = "to come to light"

4:24 | βλέπετε τί ἀκούετε = "consider carefully what you hear" (NIV) (BDAG βλέπω 6c) | ἐν ᾧ = "with whatever"

4:25 | καὶ ὃ ἔχει = "even what he has"

4:26 | Lit. "Thus [οὕτως] is the kingdom of God, as if [ὡς] a man should cast seed on the ground" (BDAG οὕτως 2); on ὡς ἄνθρωπος βάλῃ see BDAG ὡς 2dγ; BDF §380(4); M 23

4:27 | νύκτα καὶ ἡμέραν – acc. for extent of time, iterative (W 202)

A Syntax Guide for Readers of the Greek New Testament

| ὡς οὐκ οἶδεν αὐτός = "in such a way as he himself does not know" (BDAG ὡς 1a)

4:28 | πλήρη[ς] σῖτον = "fully ripened grain" (BDAG πλήρης 2); πλήρη is proper; if πλήρης is read, then it is indeclinable adj. (Metzger)

4:29 | ὅταν δὲ παραδοῖ ὁ καρπός = lit. "when the crop permits," i.e., when it is ripe (BDAG παραδίδωμι 4) | ὅτι = "because" (W 460–1)

4:30 | ἐν τίνι αὐτὴν παραβολῇ θῶμεν = "in what figure of speech can we present it?" (BDAG τίθημι 1bα)

4:31 | ὡς κόκκῳ is unusual; appears to be modeled after ὅμοιος + dat. (cp. vv. 30–31 with Matt 11:16) | Supply copula: "[it is] like" | ὄν = "though being," concessive ptc.

4:31–32 | πάντων τῶν σπερμάτων/λαχάνων – gen. of comparison

4:32 | καὶ ὅταν σπαρῇ = "yet when it is sown," resumptive clause after concessive participial phrase; καί = "yet" (BDAG καί 1bη)

4:33 | τοιαύταις παραβολαῖς πολλαῖς = "with many such parables," dat. of means (W 162) | ἐλάλει – customary impf. (W 548) | καθὼς ἠδύναντο ἀκούειν = "as much as they could understand" (NIV)

4:34 | κατ᾽ ἰδίαν = "privately"

4:35 | διέλθωμεν = "let us cross over," hortatory subj. (W 464)

4:36 | παραλαμβάνουσιν αὐτόν = "[the disciples] took him along with them" | ὡς ἦν = "just as he was" (he was in the boat since v. 1) (BDAG ὡς 2dβ)

4:38 | οὐ μέλει σοι ὅτι = "is it not a concern to you that?" impersonal

4:39 | πεφίμωσο – rare perf. impv. (W 485 n96; 718 n16); solemn and emphatic (BDF §346)

Mark 5

5:2 | ἐξελθόντος αὐτοῦ ἐκ τοῦ πλοίου = "when he [= Jesus] got out of the boat," gen. abs. | ἐν πνεύματι ἀκαθάρτῳ = "having an unclean spirit," sociative use of ἐν (BDF §§198(2); 219(4); Z §116) (cp. v. 25; 1:23)

5:3 | οὐδὲ ἁλύσει οὐκέτι οὐδεὶς ἐδύνατο αὐτὸν δῆσαι = "even with a chain, no one was able to bind him anymore"

5:4 | "because he had often been bound with shackles and chains, and the chains had been torn apart by him and the shackles broken in pieces" (NASB)

5:5 | διὰ παντός = "continually" | νυκτὸς καὶ ἡμέρας – gens. of time

5:7 | τί ἐμοὶ καὶ σοί – cp. 1:24; see note at Matt 8:29 | υἱέ – voc. | τὸν θεόν = "by God," acc. of oath (BDF §149; W 204–5)

5:8 | ἔλεγεν γάρ = "for [Jesus] had said," pluperfective impf. (W 549) (cp. 6:18)

5:9 | σοί, μοί – dats. of possession

5:10 | πολλά = "earnestly" (cp. v. 23; 1:45)

5:11 | πρός + dat. = "near" (BDAG πρός 2a)

5:13 | κατά + gen. = "down" | ὡς with numerals means "about" (BDAG ὡς 6) | Subject of ἐπνίγοντο is the pigs not the demons

5:14 | οἱ βόσκοντες αὐτούς = "the ones herding them [the pigs]," the herdsmen | τὸ γεγονός = "the thing that had happened"

5:15 | τὸν ἐσχηκότα τὸν λεγιῶνα = "the one who had had the legion"

5:16 | πῶς goes with διηγήσαντο: "And those who had seen it described to them *what* [BDAG πῶς 1bα] had happened to the demon-possessed man" (ESV)

5:18 | ὁ δαιμονισθείς = "the man who had been demon possessed" | ἵνα μετ' αὐτοῦ ᾖ = "that he might be with [accompany] him"

5:19 | τοὺς σούς < οἱ σοί = "your own people/family" (BDAG σός bα) | καὶ ἠλέησέν σε = "and [how] he had mercy on you" (NASB); hendiadys: "all that the Lord in his mercy has done" (ZG)

5:23 | πολλά = "earnestly" (cp. v. 10) | ὅτι recitative | ἐσχάτως ἔχει = "is at the point of death" | ἵνα ἐλθὼν ἐπιθῇς ... = "come and lay your hands on her," imperatival ἵνα (W 476–7; M 144; BDAG ἵνα 2g), or mixed construction joined in thought with παρακαλεῖ (BDF §387(3))

5:23, 28, 34 | Most English versions render σῴζω "heal, be healed," but "save, be saved" better captures theological significance of miracles of healing.

5:25 | οὖσα ἐν ῥύσει αἵματος = "having a flow of blood," sociative ἐν (see v. 2)

5:26 | πολλά = "greatly," "terribly," adv. acc. (see 1:45) | τὰ παρ' αὐτῆς πάντα = "all that she had"

5:27, 28, 30, 31, 41 | Verbs of touching/grasping take gen.

5:28 | ἔλεγεν – possibly iterative impf., as she musters up courage (W 547, 697) | κἄν = "just" (BDAG κἄν 3); Matt has μόνον (Matt 9:21)

5:29 | ἔγνω τῷ σώματι = "she felt in her body" (NASB; BDAG γινώσκω 4c)

5:29, 34 | On μάστιξ, see note at 3:10

5:30 | τὴν ἐξ αὐτοῦ δύναμιν ἐξελθοῦσαν = lit. "the power from him going from him" (pleonastic)

5:32 | τὴν τοῦτο ποιήσασαν = "the woman who had done this"

5:33 | εἰδυῖα ὃ γέγονεν αὐτῇ = "knowing what had happened to her"

5:34 | εἰς εἰρήνην = "in peace" (BDAG εἰς 9; BDF §206(1)) (cp. Lk 7:50; 8:48)

5:35 | ἔτι αὐτοῦ λαλοῦντος = "while he was still speaking," gen. abs. | ἔρχονται – supply anonymous subject "they" | ἀπὸ τοῦ ἀρχισυναγώγου = "from the synagogue leader," i.e., sent by him

5:38 | κλαίοντας καὶ ἀλαλάζοντας = "people weeping and wailing" | πολλά = "loudly" (cp. vv. 10, 23, 26, 43; see 1:45)

5:40 | κατα-γελάω takes gen. object bec. of κατα- prefix (BDF §181)

5:41 | κρατέω + gen. has a note of tenderness, in contrast with κρατέω + acc. (cp. Matt 12:11; 28:9) which indicates grasping the whole of (W 132) | τὸ κοράσιον – nom. instead of voc. (BDF §147(3))

5:43 | πολλά = "sternly, strictly" (cp. v. 38) | ἵνα μηδεὶς γνοῖ τοῦτο = "that no one should know about this" | εἶπεν δοθῆναι αὐτῇ φαγεῖν = "he ordered that [something] should be given to her to eat," taking φαγεῖν as equivalent to a substantive (BDF §§390(2); 409(2), cp. 6:37; Matt 25:35); pass. inf. as complement of verb of commanding (BDF §392(4); BDAG λέγω 2c)

Mark 6

6:2 | πόθεν τούτῳ ταῦτα = "where did this man get these things?" (dat. of possession) | καὶ αἱ δυνάμεις ... = lit. "and such are the miracles being done through his hands" (BDAG τοιοῦτος baℵ), a statement when one would expect a third question; scribes wrestled with this (Metzger)

6:5 | οὐδεμία = "any," double negatives reinforce each other | ἐπιτίθημι τὰς χεῖρας + dat. of person(s) on whom hands are placed (cp. 5:23)

6:6 | θαυμάζω διά + acc. = "marvel at"

6:7 | δύο δύο = "two by two," Semitic idiom (BDF §248(1); M 182) | ἐξουσία + gen. = "authority over"

6:8, 12 | ἵνα (2x) – final sense attenuated (BDAG ἵνα 2aδ)

6:8–9 | Mixture of direct and indirect discourse (BDF §470(2)) – παρήγγειλεν αὐτοῖς ἵνα (indirect) ... μὴ ἐνδύσησθε (direct)

6:8 | εἰς ὁδόν = "for the journey" (BDAG ὁδός 2) | μὴ εἰς τὴν ζώνην χαλκόν = "no money [to put it] into your belt," pregnant construction (BDAG εἰς 10d)

6:10 | ὅπου ἐάν = lit. "wherever" (NASB), but could be translated more idiomatically "whenever" (NIV, ESV) (see BDAG ὅπου 1aβ/δ)

6:11 | ὃς ἂν τόπος = "whatever place"

6:12 | ἐκήρυξαν ἵνα μετανοῶσιν = "they preached that people should repent"

6:13 | ἤλειφον, ἐθεράπευον – distributive iterative impfs. (W 546) | ἐλαίῳ – dat. of material (W 169–70)

6:14 | φανερός = "well known" | τὸ ὄνομα αὐτοῦ = "his [= Jesus'] name"

6:15 | προφήτης ὡς εἷς τῶν προφητῶν = "[He is] a prophet, like one of the prophets [of old]" (NASB)

6:16 | ὃν ἐγὼ ἀπεκεφάλισα Ἰωάννην, οὗτος ἠγέρθη = "the very one whom I beheaded, John, has been raised" (BDAG οὗτος 1aε)

6:17–29 | Digression narrating events that had occurred earlier

6:17 | ἀποστείλας ἐκράτησεν = "sent [soldiers who] arrested," Semitic graphic ptc. (Z §363) (cp. Matt 2:16; Acts 7:14; Rev 1:1)

6:18 | ἔλεγεν γάρ = "for John had been telling Herod," pluperfective impf. (W 549) (cp. 5:8) | ἔξεστιν = "be lawful/permitted" (see 2:24, 26)

6:20 | ἀκούω + gen. of person being listened to (αὐτοῦ) (2x) | πολλά = "greatly, very" (see 1:45), "he was very confused/perplexed"

6:21 | τοῖς γενεσίοις αὐτοῦ = "on his birthday," dat. of time | ποιέω = "give" when direct object is a banquet (BDAG ποιέω 2f) | οἱ πρῶτοι = "the leading men"

6:22 | τῆς θυγατρὸς αὐτοῦ Ἡρῳδιάδος = "his daughter Herodias," but see vv. 17–19; alternative reading is to be preferred: τῆς θυγατρὸς αὐτῆς τῆς Ἡρῳδιάδος = "the daughter of Herodias herself" (Metzger) | Subject of ἤρεσεν is the daughter of Herodias

6:22–23 | ὃ ἐάν = ὅ τι ἐάν = "whatever"

6:26 | περίλυπος γενόμενος = "although he was very sorry," concessive ptc. | ἀθετῆσαι αὐτήν = "to refuse her" (NASB), "to break his word to her" (ESV) (see BDAG ἀθετέω 2); αὐτήν refers to the daughter of Herodias

6:27 | σπεκουλάτορα is direct object of ἀποστείλας, and a dat. pronoun referring to the same must be supplied as object of ἐπέταξεν (cp. v. 39): "the king sent an executioner and ordered [sc. αὐτῷ/him] to bring John's head"

6:28 | αὐτήν (2x) refers to the head (κεφαλή – fem.) of John the Baptist

6:31 | Δεῦτε ὑμεῖς αὐτοὶ κατ᾽ ἰδίαν = "come away by yourselves" | ὀλίγον = "a while," acc. for extent of time

6:33 | εἶδον – subject is to be inferred from context, "the people" | ἐπέγνωσαν – must supply direct object αὐτούς from preceding clause, i.e., Jesus and the disciples | "The people saw them going, and many recognized them and ran there together on foot from all the cities, and got there ahead of them" (NASB), where "together" represents συν- prefix in συν-τρέχω

6:34 | εἶδεν – subject is Jesus | ἐπί + dat. = "on" after verbs of emotion (BDAG ἐπί 6c)

6:35 | ἤδη ὥρας πολλῆς γενομένης = "when it was already quite late," gen. abs. | πολλή when modifying ὥρα (2x) = "late" (BDAG πολύς 3aα) | ἤδη ὥρα πολλή = "the hour is now late," supply ἐστίν

6:37 | φαγεῖν (2x) = "[something] to eat," cp. 5:43 | ἀπελθόντες ἀγοράσωμεν = "should we go and buy?" deliberative subj. (W 465–6) | δηναρίων διακοσίων = "for 200 denarii," gen. of price (W 122)

6:38 | γνόντες = "when they found out [how many loaves there were]," aorist ptc. is indicator of mng. (BDAG γινώσκω 2) (cp. 15:45)

6:39–40 | συμπόσια συμπόσια = πρασιαὶ πρασιαί = "in groups," distributive doubling, Semitic idiom (BDF §493(2); M 182)

6:40 | "They sat down in groups of hundreds and of fifties" (NASB), or "in a great rectangle, a hundred by fifty" (M 59); note: 100 x 50 = 5,000 (v. 44)

6:43 | ἦραν κλάσματα δώδεκα κοφίνων πληρώματα = "they gathered (enough) pieces to fill twelve baskets" (BDAG πλήρωμα 1a) | καὶ ἀπὸ τῶν ἰχθύων = "and remnants of the fish," ἀπό as partitive gen. (BDAG ἀπό 1f)

6:45 | Subject of ἠνάγκασεν is Jesus | ἕως αὐτὸς ἀπολύει τὸν ὄχλον = "while he himself is dismissing the crowd" (BDAG ἕως 2a)

6:48 | βασανιζομένους ἐν τῷ ἐλαύνειν = lit. "being tormented as they progressed," i.e., "making headway painfully" (ESV), "straining at the oars" (NASB) | ἤθελεν παρελθεῖν αὐτούς = "was ready to pass by them" (BDAG θέλω 2)

6:49 | ἔδοξαν ὅτι φάντασμά ἐστιν = "they thought it was a ghost," present retained in indirect discourse (W 537–9)

6:50 | λάλω μετά = "speak to" (NIV, ESV) (M 61; BDAG μετά A2cα)

6:52 | οὐ συνῆκαν ἐπὶ τοῖς ἄρτοις = "they had not gained any insight from the incident of the loaves" (NASB) (see BDAG συνίημι; ἐπί 6a)

6:55 | κακῶς ἔχειν = "to be sick" | ὅπου ἤκουον ὅτι ἐστίν = "where they heard that he was," present retained in indirect discourse (W 537)

6:56 | ὅπου ἄν = "whenever" | κἄν = "just" (BDAG κἄν 3) | ὅσοι ἄν = "all who" | αὐτοῦ = "it," the fringe; verbs of touching take gen. | σῴζω (pass.) = "to be saved," i.e., restored to health (BDAG σῴζω 1c)

Mark 7
7:2 | Prolepsis (BDF §476(2)) – see 1:24

7:3 | πυγμῇ = lit. "with the fist," probably means with one clenched fist turned about in the hollow of the other hand; "thoroughly" (NRSV) (see BDAG πυγμή 1 for other suggestions)

7:3, 4, 8 | κρατέω (3x) = "adhere strongly to, hold" (BDAG κρατέω 6a)

7:4 | ἀπ' ἀγορᾶς = "[when they return] from market places," pregnant construction (BDF §209(4)) | βαπτίζω = "wash ceremonially for purpose of purification" (BDAG βαπτίζω 1) | ἄλλα πολλά ἐστιν = "there are many other things" – neut. pl. subjects take sg. verbs (BDF §133) | κρατεῖν = "in order to hold," inf. of purpose (W 590)

7:6 | ὁ = "he," article as pronoun | καλῶς = "rightly" (BDAG καλῶς 4b)

7:7 | μάτην = "in vain," adv. acc. | διδάσκοντες ... ἀνθρώπων = "teaching as doctrines the commandments of men" (ESV)

7:9 | καλῶς ἀθετεῖτε = "you are experts at setting aside" (NASB), "you have a fine way of rejecting" (ESV); ironic (BDAG καλῶς 6; BDF §495(2))

7:11 | Δῶρον, ὃ ἐὰν ἐξ ἐμοῦ ὠφεληθῇς = lit. "[It is] a gift [devoted to God], whatever you would be benefitted by me," mng.: "whatever I might give you has already been set aside for God"

7:13 | ἀκυροῦντες = "thus nullifying," circumstantial ptc. expressing result (W 637–9)

7:15, 23 | Neut. pl. subjects take sg. verbs (cp. v. 4)

7:17 | ἀπό = "away from" (BDAG ἀπό 4) | ἐπερωτάω + double acc. (see 4:10)

7:19 | αὐτοῦ εἰς τὴν καρδίαν = εἰς τὴν καρδίαν αὐτοῦ | καθαρίζων πάντα τὰ βρώματα – circumstantial ptc. expressing result (W 637), or pendent nom. ptc. (W 51, 654; BDF §137(3)); parenthetical clause modifies λέγει (v. 18): "In saying this, Jesus declared all foods clean" (NIV) (see πειράζοντες – 10:2)

7:24 | οὐδένα ἤθελεν γνῶναι = "he wanted no one to know [that he was there]" | καὶ οὐκ ἠδυνήθη λαθεῖν = "yet he could not be hidden" (BDAG καί 1bη)

7:25 | ἧς εἶχεν τὸ θυγάτριον αὐτῆς ... = "whose little daughter had an unclean spirit," with pleonastic personal pronoun αὐτῆς (BDF §297)

7:26 | τῷ γένει = "by birth"

7:27 | οὐκ ἔστιν καλόν + inf. = "it is not right/good to"

7:28 | ἀπὸ τῶν ψιχίων = "some of the crumbs," substitute for partitive gen. (BDAG ἀπό 1f)

7:31 | ἀνὰ μέσον = "in the midst of" (see commentaries re. geographical problem)

7:32 | κωφὸν καὶ μογιλάλον = "a man who was deaf and had a speech impediment" (ESV)

7:33 | ἀπολαβόμενος αὐτὸν ἀπὸ τοῦ ὄχλου κατ᾽ ἰδίαν = "taking him aside from the crowd privately" (ESV) | Verbs of touching take gen.

7:36 | ὅσον ... μᾶλλον περισσότερον = "the more he was ordering them, all the more were they proclaiming"

Mark 8
8:1 | "In those days, when there was again a large crowd and they had nothing to eat" (NASB), gen. abs.; ὄχλος is sg. in form but pl. in mng.; hence shift to pl. ἐχόντων (*constructio ad sensum*)

8:1–2 | τί φάγωσιν (2x) = "anything to eat," subjunctive in indirect deliberative question (W 478)

8:2 | ἤδη ἡμέραι τρεῖς = "for three days now," rare use of nom. for extent of time (BDF §144; W 64; cp. Matt 15:32)

8:4 | Πόθεν τούτους δυνήσεταί τις ὧδε χορτάσαι ἄρτων ἐπ' ἐρημίας; = "From what source (i.e., how) will anyone be able to satisfy these people with bread here in this desolate place?" | χορτάζω = "feed/satisfy someone [acc.] with something [gen.]" (M 33)

8:7 | It is interesting that Jesus blesses the fishes (but see Metzger) | εἶπεν καὶ ταῦτα παρατιθέναι = "he ordered [them] to distribute these *also*" (BDAG λέγω 2c); usually pass. infinitive is used with verbs of commanding (BDF §392(4)), so it is not surprising that some MSS have παραθῆναι: "he ordered that these also be distributed"

8:8 | περισσεύματα κλασμάτων ἑπτὰ σπυρίδας = "the leftovers of the broken pieces, seven basketfuls"

8:9 | ὡς with numerals means "about" (BDAG ὡς 6)

8:12 | τί; = "why?" | εἰ δοθήσεται σημεῖον = "no sign will be given," Hebr. oath formula; emphatic denial expressed by aposiopesis (BDF §454(5); BDAG εἰ 4; M 179)

8:13 | πάλιν ἐμβάς = "he again got into the boat" (supply εἰς τὸ πλοῖον from v. 10)

8:14 | εἰ μὴ ἕνα ἄρτον οὐκ εἶχον = "except for one loaf, they did not have [any bread] with them in the boat"

8:15 | βλέπετε ἀπό + gen. = "beware of" (BDAG βλέπω 5) (cp. 12:38)

8:16–17 ὅτι (2x) = "about the fact that" (BDAG ὅτι 2b)

8:16 | ἔχουσιν – present retained in indirect discourse (W 537–9)

8:19–20 | εἰς (2x) = "for," equivalent to dat. of advantage (BDAG εἰς 4g)

8:22–23 | Verbs of touching and grasping take gen.

8:23 | εἴ τι βλέπεις; = lit. "whether do you see anything?" mixing direct and indirect discourse; some MSS fix this by dropping the final ς, changing the verb from 2s to 3s: "whether he sees anything"

8:24 | ὅτι = "for"

8:25 | ἀπεκατέστη – note the double augment (BDF §69(3)) (cp. 3:5)

8:26 | μηδὲ = "don't even"

8:27 | ἐν τῷ ὁδῷ = "on the way"

8:27, 29 | Acc. με as subject of inf. (εἶναι) in indirect discourse

8:29 | Ὑμεῖς δὲ τίνα με λέγετε εἶναι; = "But you, who do *you* say that I am?" – note emphatic position of ὑμεῖς

8:30 | ἵνα μηδενὶ λέγωσιν περὶ αὐτοῦ = "to tell no one about him"

8:31 | πολλὰ παθεῖν = "to suffer greatly" (see 1:45)

8:34 | καὶ ἀκολουθείτω μοι = "*and then* let him follow me" (BDAG καί 1bζ)

8:35, 38 | ὃς ἐάν (2x) = ὃς ἄν = "whoever"

8:37 | "For what could [subjunctive] a man give in exchange for his soul?"

8:38 | καὶ ὁ υἱός ... ἐπαισχυνθήσεται = "the Son of Man will *also* be ashamed"

Mark 9

9:1 | οὐ μὴ γεύσωνται – emphatic negation subj. (W 468) | γεύομαι ("taste, experience") takes gen.

9:2 | κατ᾽ ἰδίαν μόνους = "by themselves alone"

9:3 | τὰ ἱμάτια αὐτοῦ ἐγένετο – neut. pl. subjects take sg. verbs | στίλβοντα λευκὰ λίαν = "radiant, intensely white" (ESV), "dazzling white" (NIV) | οἷα γναφεὺς ἐπὶ τῆς γῆς οὐ δύναται οὕτως λευκᾶναι = "as no launderer on earth can whiten them" (NASB)

9:4 | ἦσαν συλλαλοῦντες – impf. periphrastic (W 648)

9:5 | ποιήσωμεν – hortatory subj. (W 464)

9:8 | οὐκέτι οὐδένα εἶδον = "they no longer saw anyone" (the double negative does not cancel itself out but reinforces negative mng.) | μόνον (adj.) = "alone" (NASB) (see Matt 17:8)

9:9 | ἃ εἶδον = "what they had seen" | εἰ μὴ ὅταν = "until"

9:10 | τὸν λόγον ἐκράτησαν πρὸς ἑαυτούς – could be (1) "they kept the matter to themselves" (ESV) (BDAG κρατέω 6c; λόγος 1αε), or (2) "they seized upon that statement" (NASB), taking πρὸς ἑαυτούς with συζητοῦντες ("discussing among themselves") | τί ἐστιν τὸ ἐκ νεκρῶν ἀναστῆναι = "what rising from the dead means" (BDAG εἰμί 2c); note also articular inf., τὸ ἀναστῆναι

9:11 | First ὅτι; = "why?" (cp. v. 28; 2:16) – rare (M 159)

9:12–13 | μέν ... ἀλλά = "to be sure ... but" (BDAG μέν 1αβ) | γράφω ἐπί + acc. (2x) = "write about" (BDAG ἐπί 14bα)

9:12 | καὶ πῶς; = "how then?" (BDAG καί 1bθ; BDF §442(8)) | πολλὰ πάθη – see 8:31

9:13 | καί ... καί = "*not only* has Elijah come, *but* they *also* did to him whatever they wanted" (BDAG καί 1f)

9:14 | Καὶ ἐλθόντες πρὸς τοὺς μαθητὰς εἶδον = "And when they came [back] to the [other] disciples, they saw ..."

9:17 | εἷς ἐκ τοῦ ὄχλου = "someone from the crowd" (BDAG εἷς 3a; ἐκ 4aα)

9:18 | ὅπου ἐάν = "whenever" (see 6:10, 56) | εἶπα = "I asked" (BDAG λέγω 2a/c)

9:19 | ἕως πότε; (2x) = "how long?" | ἀνέχομαι + gen. = "put up with someone"

9:20 | αὐτόν (4x): 1st & 4th = the boy; 2nd & 3rd = Jesus | ἰδών ... τὸ πνεῦμα – masc. ptc. with neut. noun, *constructio ad sensum* (BDF §134(3)) | καὶ πεσών ... ἐκυλίετο ἀφρίζων = "and [the boy] fell to the ground and was rolling around, foaming at the mouth," the subject has shifted from τὸ πνεῦμα to the boy, who has been foregrounded by the 4th αὐτόν

9:21 | Πόσος χρόνος ἐστὶν ὡς τοῦτο γέγονεν αὐτῷ; = "How long has it been since this [state] befell him?" – unusual use of ὡς (M 133; BDAG ὡς 8b); present retained in indirect discourse (W 537–9)

9:22 | καί ... καί = "*both* into the fire *and* into the water" (BDAG καί 1f) | εἴ τι δύνῃ = "if you can [do] anything"

9:23 | Τὸ Εἰ δύνῃ – τό functions as quote marks: "'If you can?'" (BDAG ὁ 2hα; M 110)

9:26 | κράξας ... σπαράξας (see v. 20) | πολλὰ σπαράξας = "violently convulsing him" (see 1:45), or could denote frequency, "fit after fit" (M 35) | ὥστε τοὺς πολλοὺς λέγειν = "so that the crowd said" (BDAG πολύς 2αβ‎‏‎א‎)

9:28 | ὅτι = "why?" (v. 11)

9:29 | Hebr./instrumental ἐν (2x)

9:30 | οὐκ ἤθελεν ἵνα τις γνοῖ = "he did not want anyone to know" (where he was)

9:31 | παραδίδοται – futuristic present (BDF §323(1); M 7; W 535–6)

9:34 | μείζων – comparative with superlative mng. (BDAG μέγας 4a)

9:37 | ὃς ἄν (2x) = "whoever" (also v. 42) | ἓν τῶν τοιούτων παιδίων = lit. "one of such children," i.e., "one child such as this"

9:37 | ἐπὶ τῷ ὀνόματί μου = "in my name" (BDAG ἐπί 17); "when my name is confessed" (BDAG ὀνόμα 1dγ‏‎ⅎ‎) (cp. v. 42: "one of these little ones who believes in me")

9:38 | ἐκωλύομεν αὐτόν = "we tried to stop him," conative impf. (BDF §326; M 9; W 550)

9:41 | ἐν ὀνόματι ὅτι Χριστοῦ ἐστε = "under the category that you belong to Christ" (BDAG ὀνόμα 3), or "on the claim, on the basis that" (BDF §397(3)) (cp. Matt 10:41–42)

9:42, 43, 45, 47 | καλόν (4x) = "better," positive with comparative mng. (BDAG καλός 2dγ; BDF §245(3)) | καλόν ἐστίν σε – would expect σοι ("for you") – mixing of constructions (subjects of infs. are acc.) | ἤ = "than"

9:50 | ἐν τίνι = "with what?"

Mark 10

10:2 | εἰ = "whether" | πειράζοντες αὐτόν = "in order to test him," telic ptc. (W 635–6 n60)

10:3 | οἱ = "they," article as pronoun | ἐπέτρεψεν ... ἀπολῦσαι = "Moses permitted [a man] to write a certificate of divorce and send [her] away" (NASB)

10:5 | πρὸς τὴν σκληροκαρδίαν ὑμῶν = "with reference to (i.e., because of) the hardness of our heart" (BDAG πρός 3eα), "in view of" (M 53)

10:8 | ἔσονται εἰς = "shall become," εἰς as predicate marker (BDAG εἰς 8αβ)

10:10 | εἰς = ἐν | "in the house *again*" (see 9:28, 33)

10:11 | ἐπ᾽ αὐτήν could be (1) "against" the first wife, or (2) "with" the second one (BDAG μοιχάω 1b)

10:12 | ἐὰν αὐτὴ ἀπολύσασα ... = "if the woman herself divorces her husband and marries another man, she commits adultery"

10:13 | προσέφερον = "they were bringing," indef. 3p subject (BDF §130(2)) | ἵνα αὐτῶν ἅψηται = ἵνα ἅψηται αὐτῶν = "that he might touch them," verbs of touching take gen.

10:15 | ὃς ἂν μή ... οὐ μή + aorist subjunctive = "whoever does not ... will never," emphatic negation subj. (W 468)

10:17 | εἰς ὁδόν = "on the way" (BDAG ὁδός 2) | εἷς = τις = "someone" (BDAG εἷς 3a; BDF §247(2)) | γονυπετέω τινά = "kneel down before someone in petition" (BDAG)

10:18 | Τί με λέγεις ἀγαθόν; = "Why do you call me good?" (BDAG λέγω 4) | εἰ μὴ εἷς ὁ θεός = "except God alone" (see 2:7)

10:20, 22 | ὁ (2x) = "he," article as pronoun

10:22 | ἦν ἔχων = "he had," periphrastic (W 647)

10:23–24 | πῶς δυκσόλως = πῶς δύσκολόν ἐστιν = "how difficult it is!"

10:25 | ἤ = "than"

10:26 | καὶ τίς; = "who then?" (BDAG καί 1bθ)

10:27 | παρά + dat. (3x) = "with, for" (BDAG παρά 3)

10:29–30 | Lit.: "There is no one who has left ... but (ἐὰν μή) he will receive" (see smoother parallels: Matt 19:29–30; Luke 18:29–30)

10:32 | Periphrastic (2x) (see v. 22) | τὰ μέλλοντα αὐτῷ συμβαίνειν = "what was going to happen to him"

10:33 | ὅτι recitative | ἀναβαίνομεν – ingressive-futuristic present (W 537)

10:35 | θέλομεν ... ἡμῖν = "we want you to do for us whatever we ask you"

10:35, 37 | ἵνα (2x) – final sense attenuated; equivalent to inf. (BDAG ἵνα 2)

10:37 | σου ἐκ δεξιῶν = ἐκ δεξιῶν σου | ἐκ (2x) = "at, on" (BDAG ἐκ 2)

10:40 | ἀλλ' οἷς ἡτοίμασται = "but [it belongs to those] for whom it has been prepared"

10:42 | οἱ δοκοῦντες ἄρχειν = "those who are reputed to be rulers" (BDAG δοκέω 2aβ) | ἄρχω + gen. = "rule over"

10:45 | καὶ γάρ = "for even"

10:46 | "As he was leaving Jericho with his disciples and a large crowd" (NASB), gen. abs. | ὄχλος ἱκανός = "a large crowd" (BDAG ἱκανός 3a)

10:47 | ἀκούσας ὅτι Ἰησοῦς ὁ N. ἐστιν = "when he heard that it was Jesus the Nazarene" (NASB); present retained in indirect discourse (W 537–9)

Mark 11
11:1, 4 | πρός + acc. (2x) = "at, near" (BDAG πρός 3g)

11:2 | οὐδεὶς ἀνθρώπων = lit. "no one of humans" | ἐφ᾽ ὃν οὐδεὶς οὔπω ἀνθρώπων ἐκάθισεν = "on which no one has ever sat," double negatives reinforce | λύσατε αὐτὸν καὶ φέρετε = "untie it and bring [it]," ellipsis of the pronoun, with αὐτόν understood a second time

11:3 | τί; = "why?" | ὁ κύριος αὐτοῦ χρείαν ἔχει = "the Lord has need of it," taking αὐτοῦ with χρείαν not κύριος | εὐθύς here must mean "as soon as he is done with it" | "he [= the Lord] will send it back here," taking ἀποστέλλει as futuristic present (M 7); "The Lord needs it and will send it back here shortly" (NIV) | ἀποστέλλω πάλιν = "send back" (BDAG πάλιν 1a)

11:4 | ἔξω = "outside," adv. modifying δεδεμένον | ἐπὶ τοῦ ἀμφόδου = "by the street" (BDAG ἐπί 2a)

11:5 | τί; = "what?"

11:8 | πολλοί – subject; τὰ ἱμάτια – direct object | ἄλλοι δὲ στιβάδας κόψαντες = "others [spread] leafy branches which they had cut from the fields" (NASB)

11:11 | ὀψίας ἤδη οὔσης τῆς ὥρας = "since the hour was already late" (BDAG ὄψιος 1), gen. abs.

11:13 | εἰ ἄρα τι εὑρήσει ἐν αὐτῇ = lit. "if perhaps he might find any [fruit] in it," taking ἄρα = "perhaps" (BDAG ἄρα 3)

11:14 | Μηκέτι … μηδείς φάγοι = "may no one ever eat," voluntative optative (W 481), "vehemently prohibitive" (M 136)

11:16 | ἵνα – final sense attenuated | σκεῦος = "merchandise" (NIV, NASB), "anything" (ESV)

11:18 | Object of ἤκουσαν must be supplied: they "heard [this]," i.e., what Jesus was saying about them in v. 17 | πῶς + deliberative subj. = "how" (BDAG πῶς 1bβ), "a way to" (ESV)

11:22 | πίστις θεοῦ = "faith in God," objective gen. (W 116)

11:23 | ὃς ἂν εἴπῃ … ἔσται αὐτῷ = "whoever says … and does not doubt … but believes … it will be for him" | ὃ λαλεῖ γίνεται = "what he says is going to happen" (futuristic present)

11:25 | Rare use of ὅταν + present indic. (M 133; BDF §382(4)) | εἴ τι ἔχετε κατά τινος = "if you have anything against anyone"

11:29 | λόγος = "question" (BDAG λόγος 1aβ)

11:32 | ἅπαντες εἶχον τὸν Ἰ. ὄντως ὅτι προφήτης ἦν = lit. "they all held John really, that he was a prophet," i.e., "they all held that John really was a prophet." Anacoluthon: the ἔχω τινα construction (BDAG ἔχω 6) should have been completed with predicate acc., but was continued instead by ὅτι, resulting in prolepsis (BDF §§408; 476(1)). Imperfect retained in indirect discourse (ἦν for "had been," since John was dead) (W 552–3; BDF §330).

Mark 12

12:2 | τῷ καιρῷ = "at [harvest] time," dat. of time | ἀπὸ τῶν καρπῶν = "of the fruit," ἀπό + gen. as substitute for partitive gen. (BDAG ἀπό 1f)

12:4–5 | κἀκεῖνον (2x) = καὶ ἐκεῖνον

12:5 | οὓς μέν ... οὓς δέ = "some ... others"

12:6 | ἔτι ἕνα εἶχεν, υἱὸν ἀγαπητόν = "he had one more [to send], a beloved son" | ἔσχατον = "last of all, finally," adv. acc.

12:6–7 | ὅτι recitative (2x)

12:7 | πρὸς ἑαυτούς = "to one another" | ἀποκτείνωμεν = "let us kill," hortatory subj.

12:10 | οὐδέ + aorist indic. = "Have you not even ...?" (BDAG οὐδέ 3; BDF §445(2)) | εἰς – marker of predicate nom. with γίνεσθαι | See additional notes on syntax of LXX Ps 118:22–23 at Matt 21:42

12:12 | Second καί = "and yet" (BDAG καί 1bη) (NASB) | πρὸς αὐτούς = "with reference to them" (BDAG πρός 3eα), almost "against them" (M 53)

12:14 | οὐ μέλει σοι περὶ οὐδενός = "you care for no one," i.e., for their opinion | οὐ βλέπεις εἰς πρόσωπον ἀνθρώπων = "you do not regard people's face" | "You aren't swayed by men, because you pay no attention to who they are" (NIV 1984) | ἐπ' ἀληθείας = "in accordance with the truth" (BDAG ἐπί 8) (cp. v. 32) | δῶμεν (2x) = "shall we pay?" deliberative subj.

12:15 | αὐτῶν τὴν ὑπόκρισιν = τὴν ὑπόκρισιν αὐτῶν

12:16 | οἱ = "they," article as pronoun

12:19 | ἐάν τινος ἀδελφὸς ἀποθάνῃ = "if a man's brother dies" | Imperatival ἵνα (BDAG ἵνα 2g; BDF §§387(3); 470(1))

12:22 | ἔσχατον πάντων = "last of all," adv. acc. (cp. 1 Cor 15:8) | καὶ ἡ γυνή = "the woman also"

12:23 | γυναῖκα = "as wife," double acc. of object-complement (W 182–7)

12:26 | περὶ τῶν νεκρῶν ὅτι ἐγείρονται = lit. "concerning the dead, that they are raised," prolepsis (BDF §476) | ἐπὶ τοῦ βάτου = lit. "at the bush," i.e., in the passage about the burning bush (BDAG ἐπί 2a)

12:27 | πολύ = "greatly," adv. acc. (BDAG πολύς 3aγ)

12:28 | ἀκούσας αὐτῶν συζητούντων = "heard them debating" (NIV) | καλῶς as an adv. = "well" (BDAG καλῶς 4b) | πάντων (masc./neut.) – frozen form (BDF §164(1)); should be πασῶν (fem.) in agreement with ἐντολή

12:30–31 | ἀγαπήσεις (2x) – imperatival future, only in OT quotations (W 569)

12:32 | καλῶς as an exclamation = "Quite right! Well said!" (BDAG καλῶς 4c)

12:33 | τό (2x) – two possibilities: either (1) functions as quote marks (see 9:23), or (2) articular infinitive ("to love") | πάντων ... θυσιῶν – gen. of comparison

12:34 | ἰδὼν αὐτόν ὅτι – prolepsis (BDF §476) | οὐδεὶς οὐκέτι = "no one any more," double negatives reinforce

12:36 | ἐκ δεξιῶν μου = "on my right" (BDAG ἐκ 2); pl. used in directions (BDF §141(2))

12:37 | λέγει = "calls" (BDAG λέγω 4) | καὶ πόθεν αὐτοῦ ἐστιν υἱός; = "how then is he his son?" (BDF §442(8); BDAG καί 1bθ; πόθεν 3)

12:38 | βλέπετε ἀπό + gen. = "beware of" (BDAG βλέπω 5) (cp. 8:15) | θέλω followed by inf. or acc. (here both) = "like" (BDAG θέλω 3)

12:40 | οἱ κατεσθίοντες – pendent nominative ptc. (W 51, 654) | προφάσει = "for appearance's sake" (NASB; BDAG), adverbial dat. (W 161–2) | μακρά – adv. acc.

12:41 | ἔβαλλον – distributive iterative impf. (W 502, 546–7)

12:43 | πάντων τῶν βαλλόντων = "than all the [other] contributors," gen. of comp.

12:44 | ἔβαλον – constative/global aor., separate contributions of individuals treated as a whole (BDF §332(2); W 502–3, 557) | ἐκ τοῦ περισσεύοντος αὐτοῖς = "out of their abundance" (BDAG περισσεύω 1aβ), dat. of possession

Mark 13
13:2 | οὐ μή + aor. subj. (2x) – emphatic negation (W 468)

13:3 | κάθημαι εἰς = "sit on" (BDAG κάθημαι 1a; εἰς 1aδ) | κατ᾽ ἰδίαν = "privately"

13:4 | μέλλω + present inf. = future | συντελέω can mean "fulfill, accomplish" (BDAG συντελέω 2); "What [will be] the sign when all these things will be accomplished?"

13:6 | ἐπὶ τῷ ὀνόματί μου = "in my name" (BDAG ἐπί 17) (cp. 9:37)

13:8 | κατὰ τόπους = "in place after place" (BDAG κατά B1a)

13:9 | εἰς συναγωγάς = "in synagogues" | εἰς μαρτύριον = "as/for a testimony"

13:11 | ἄγω = "arrest" (BDAG ἄγω 2) | ὃ ἐάν = "whatever"

13:13 | ἔσεσθε μισούμενοι = "you will be hated," future periphrastic

(W 567, 648–9) | ὁ ὑπομείνας = "the one who endures," substantival gnomic aorist ptc. with generic reference (W 615 n8)

13:14 | τὸ βδέλυγμα τῆς ἐρημώσεως = "the abomination that causes desolation" (NIV), gen. of product? (W 106) | τὸ βδέλυγμα (neut.) ... ἑστηκότα (masc.), *constructio ad sensum* (BDF §134(3)); masc. gender of ptc. may support future-individual interpretation of antichrist (see ZG); though cp. ἑστός (neut.) in Matt 24:15 | ὅπου οὐ δεῖ = "where he ought not [to stand/be]," ellipsis of inf.

13:16 | εἰς τὰ ὀπίσω = "back [home]"

13:17 | ἐν γαστρὶ ἔχω = "be pregnant"

13:18 | "Pray that it may not happen in the winter" | χειμῶνος – gen. of time (W 122)

13:19 | τοιαύτη – pleonastic (BDF §297): "Those days will be a tribulation such as has not occurred since the beginning of creation"

13:22 | πρὸς τό + inf. – indicates intent | δίδωμι of signs and wonders = "produce, cause to appear" (BDAG δίδωμι 4)

13:24 | δίδωμι of heavenly bodies = "give light, shine" (BDAG δίδωμι 4)

13:25 | ἔσονται πίπτοντες = "will be falling," future periphrastic (M 18; W 648–9)

13:28 | ὅταν ἤδη ὁ κλάδος αὐτῆς ἁπαλὸς γένηται = "when its branch has already become tender"

13:29 | ἐπὶ θύραις = "at the doors"

13:30 | οὐ μή + aorist subj. – emphatic negation | μέχρις οὗ = "until"

13:31 | οὐ μή + future indic. instead of expected aorist subj. (παρέλθωσιν, Matt 24:35), possibly due to attraction with preceding παρελεύσονται (BDF §365(1)); signifies emphatic negation (W 468)

13:34 | "[It is] like a man away on a journey [who] left his house and gave his slaves authority, to each his task, and ordered the doorkeeper to keep alert"

13:35a, 36 | γρηγορεῖτε ... μὴ ἐλθών = "Keep alert, therefore (...) lest, when he comes suddenly, he finds you sleeping"

13:35b | ἤ ... ἤ ... ἤ ... ἤ = "whether ... or ... or ... or" | Note that v. 35b ("for you do not know when the master of the house is coming, whether ... or ... or ... or") is a parenthesis – see above

Mark 14

14:1 | "Now Passover-and-Unleavened-Bread was two days away," sg. verb (ἦν) because subject viewed as single entity | τὰ ἄζυμα – pl. used for names of festivals (BDF §141(3)) (cp. v. 12) | μετά δύο ἡμέρας = "after two days [from now]," i.e., two days away

14:2 | μήποτε + fut. indic. for aor. subj. (BDF §§369(2); 370(2)) (cp. Heb 3:12)

14:3 | ἀλάβαστρον μύρου νάρδου πιστικῆς πολυτελοῦς = "an alabaster jar [full] of perfume of nard – pure and expensive" | μύρου – gen. of content (W 92) | "[and] she broke the alabaster jar [and] poured it over his head" | κατα-χέω + gen. of thing liquid is poured over (BDF §181)

14:4 | ἀγανακτSοῦντες πρὸς ἑαυτούς – either (1) "indignantly remarking to one another" (NASB) (cp. 12:7), or (2) "said to themselves indignantly" (ESV), i.e., "within themselves, inwardly" (ZG) | εἰς τί; = "why?" | τοῦ μύρου – objective gen.

14:5 | ἠδύνατο = "could have," impf. (BDF §358) | ἐπάνω + numbers

= "more than" (BDAG ἐπάνω 2) (cp. 1 Cor 15:6) | δηναρίων τριακοσίων – gen. of price (W 122)

14:6 | κόπους παρέχω τινι = "trouble someone" | ἐν ἐμοί = "to me" (BDAG ἐν 8)

14:7 | ὅταν θέλητε δύνασθε αὐτοῖς εὖ ποιῆσαι = "whenever you wish you can do good to them" (NASB)

14:8 | ὃ ἔσχεν ἐποίησεν = "she has done what she could" (BDAG ἔχω 5) | προλαμβάνω + inf. = "do something ahead of time"

14:9 | ὅπου ἐάν = "wherever" | καὶ ὃ ἐποίησεν αὕτη λαληθήσεται = "what this woman has done will *also* be spoken of" (NASB)

14:12 | ὅτε τὸ πάσχα ἔθυον = "when they [i.e., the Jews] were sacrificing the Passover lamb," or "when it was customary to sacrifice" (NIV), customary impf. (W 548)

14:13 | ὕδατος – gen. of content (W 92)

14:14 | ὅπου ἐὰν εἰσέλθῃ = "wherever he enters" | ὅτι recitative

14:18 | εἷς ἐξ ὑμῶν παραδώσει με ὁ ἐσθίων μετ' ἐμοῦ = "one of you will betray me – one who is eating with me" (NASB)

14:19 | εἷς κατὰ εἷς = "one by one" – κατά + nom. looks like bad grammar (M 60) but probably colloquial (cp. John 8:9) | μήτι ἐγώ = "Surely not I?" (NASB), μήτι expects negative response

14:21 | μέν ... δέ = "one the one hand ... on the other" | καλόν = "better" (BDAG καλός 2dγ) | Supply ἦν (BDF §360(1)): "[It would have been] better for him if that man had never been born" | εἰ οὐκ ἐγεννήθη – οὐ for μή (BDF §428(2); M 149)

14:28 | μετὰ τὸ ἐγερθῆναί με = "after I have been raised" (W 594–5)

14:29 | εἰ καί ... ἀλλά = "even if ... yet certainly" (BDAG ἀλλά 4a)

14:32 | ἕως + subj. = "while" (BDAG ἕως 2b)

14:35 | Attenuated ἵνα (BDAG ἵνα 2aγ)

14:37 | μίαν ὥραν – acc. for extent of time

14:40 | ἦσαν καταβαρυνόμενοι – impf. periphrastic (W 648) | αὐτῶν οἱ ὀφθαλμοί = οἱ ὀφθαλμοὶ αὐτῶν

14:41 | τὸ τρίτον = "for the third time," adv. acc. | Καθεύδετε τὸ λοιπόν – various possibilities, but most translate: "Are you still sleeping and resting?" (NASB; ESV; NIV); τὸ λοιπόν = "for the remainder of the time" (BDAG λοιπός 3aα; BDF §160) | ἀπέχει – uncertain, probably = "it is enough" (but see BDAG ἀπέχω 1–3 for other options) | παραδίδοται – ingressive-futuristic present (W 537)

14:42 | ὁ παραδιδούς με = "my betrayer," present substantival ptc. with ingressive-futuristic force (cp. vv. 41, 44)

14:44 | "Now the one betraying him had given them a signal, saying ..." | ὃν ἂν φιλήσω αὐτός ἐστιν = "whomever I kiss, he is the one"

14:47 | εἷς [τις] = "a certain one," εἷς often replaces τις as an indef. article, but here both are used pleonastically (Z §155; BDAG εἷς 3c) | αὐτοῦ τὸ ὠτάριον = τὸ ὠτάριον αὐτοῦ

14:48 | BDAG ὡς 2b

14:49 | καθ᾽ ἡμέραν = "every day" | ἀλλ᾽ ἵνα πληρωθῶσιν αἱ γραφαί – possibilities: (1) "but [this has taken place] so that the Scriptures may be fulfilled" (BDF §448(7)) (cp. Matt 26:56); (2) "but let the Scriptures be fulfilled" (ESV), imperatival ἵνα (BDAG ἵνα 2g; M 144; W 476–7); (3) "but so that the Scriptures may be fulfilled [do what you came to do]"

14:51 | ἐπὶ γυμνοῦ = "over his naked body" | κρατοῦσιν – historical present for ingressive aorist (BDF §337(1))

14:54 | ἕως ἔσω εἰς τὴν αὐλήν = "right into the courtyard" | ἦν ... θερμαινόμενος = "he was ... warming himself," impf. periphrastic (W 648); reflexive (W 417) | πρὸς τὸ φῶς = "at the fire" (BDAG φῶς 2)

14:55 | κατὰ τοῦ Ἰησοῦς μαρτυρίαν = "testimony against Jesus" (BDAG κατά A2bβ) (cp. vv. 56–57) | εἰς τό + inf. = "in order to," purpose (BDF §402(2)) | οὐχ ηὕρισκον – negated impf. rather than aorist = "they could find none" in spite of repeated attempts (BDF §327)

14:58 | διὰ τριῶν ἡμερῶν = "within three days" (BDAG διά 2b)

14:59 | "Yet even then their testimony did not agree" (NIV)

14:60 | οὐκ ἀποκρίνῃ ... καταμαρτυροῦσιν; – possible punctuations: (1) "Have you nothing to answer? What is it that these men are accusing you of?" or (2) "Have you nothing to answer what these men are accusing you of?" (BDF §§298(4); 299(1)) | κατα-μαρτυροῦσιν takes gen. object (σου) bec. of κατα- prefix (BDF §181)

14:62 | ἐκ = "at, on" (BDAG ἐκ 2) | ἐκ δεξιῶν καθήμενον τῆς δυνάμεως = καθήμενον ἐκ δεξιῶν τῆς δυνάμεως = "seated at the right hand of Power" (i.e., of Yahweh), echoing LXX Ps 110:1 (Εἶπεν ὁ κύριος τῷ κυρίῳ μου Κάθου ἐκ δεξιῶν μου)

14:64 | τί ὑμῖν φαίνεται; = "how does it seem to you?" (NASB), "what is your decision?" (ESV) (BDAG φαίνω 5)

14:65 | ῥαπίσμασιν αὐτὸν ἔλαβον = lit. "they received him with blows," colloquialism mng. "they beat him up," "they worked him over"

(BDAG λαμβάνω 5); on other hand, "blows" could be slaps to face (see BDAG ῥαπίζω, ῥάπισμα)

14:68 | Οὔτε οἶδα οὔτε ἐπίσταμαι σὺ τί λέγεις = "I neither know nor understand what you mean" (BDAG λέγω 1bβ)

14:70 | μετὰ μικρόν = "after a little while"

14:71 | τὸν ἄνθρωπον τοῦτον ὃν λέγετε = "this man you are talking about" (NASB) (BDAG λέγω 1bβ)

14:72 | ἐκ δευτέρου = "a second time" | ὡς – practically equivalent to ὅ (BDAG ὡς 1bβ) | ἐπιβαλὼν ἔκλαιεν is difficult: (1) "he began to weep" (NASB; BDF §308), or (2) "he broke down and wept" (ESV; NIV); see BDAG ἐπιβάλλω 2b

Mark 15

15:1 | συμβούλιον ποιέω = "reach a group decision after deliberation," Latinism (BDF §5(3)(b))

15:3–4 | κατηγορέω takes gen. object (αὐτοῦ/σοῦ) bec. of the κατα-prefix (BDF §181) | πολλά = "of many things" (cp. πόσα = "how many things," v. 4)

15:6 | κατὰ ἑορτήν = "at the feast" | ἀπέλυεν = "he would customarily release," customary impf. (see v. 8)

15:8 | "And the crowd came up and began to ask Pilate to do as he usually did for them" (ESV), ἐποίει as customary impf. (W 548)

15:14 | Τί γὰρ ἐποίησεν κακόν; = "Why, what crime has he committed?" – when γάρ is used in questions, leave untranslated (BDAG γάρ 1f)

15:15 | τὸ ἱκανὸν ποιέω + dat. = "satisfy someone," Latinism (BDF

§5(3)(b)) | παρέδωκεν τὸν Ἰησοῦν φραγελλώσας ἵνα σταυρωθῇ = lit. "he handed Jesus over, after having him flogged, to be crucified" (φραγελλώσας is in an odd position; Matt 27:26 has a more natural word order)

15:16 | ἔσω τῆς αὐλῆς = "further into the palace," gen. with adverb (BDF §184) | ὅ – should be fem. ἥ in agreement with αὐλή, but changed to neut. in agreement with predicate πραιτώριον – gender attraction (W 338; BDF §134)

15:19 | αὐτοῦ τὴν κεφαλήν = τὴν κεφαλὴν αὐτοῦ | τίθημι τὰ γόνατα = "bend the knees," Latinism (BDAG τίθημι 1bγ; BDF §5(3)(b))

15:21 | παράγοντά τινα Σ. Κ. = "a passer-by, a certain Simon of Cyrene"

15:23 | "And they were attempting to give [ἐδίδουν] him wine mixed with myrrh, but he did not accept it," conative impf. (W 551)

15:24 | βάλλω κλῆρον ἐπί + acc.= "cast lots for something" (BDAG ἐπί 14bα; κλῆρος 1) | τίς τί ἄρῃ = "[to decide] what each should take," double interrogative used distributively (BDF §298(5))

15:25 | καὶ ἐσταύρωσαν αὐτόν = "*when* they crucified him" (BDAG καί 1bγ; BDF §442(4); Z §455δ)

15:27 | ἐκ (2x) = "at, on" (BDAG ἐκ 2)

15:29 | ὁ καταλύων τὸν ναὸν καὶ οἰκοδομῶν = "he who would destroy the temple and (re)build it," voluntative present ptcs. (W 534); one article governing two ptcs. (W 274–5)

15:30 | καταβάς – attendant circumstances ptcs. usually precede main verb (W 642), but in this case the order is logical: "Save yourself, and come down from the cross!"

15:31 | ἐμπαίζοντες πρὸς ἀλλήλους = "ridiculing [him] among themselves"

15:34 | εἰς τί; = "why?" | ἐγκατέλιπες = (1) "Why did you forsake me?" aorist for past event, present results not prominently contemplated (M 11 n1); or (2) "Why have you forsaken me?" consummative aorist (W 559)

15:35 | φωνέω τινα = "call for someone" (BDAG φωνέω 4)

15:36 | γεμίζω ὄξους = "fill with sour wine," verbs of filling take gen. (BDF §172) | περι-τίθημι τί τινι = "put something on/around something," compound verbs with περι- take dat. (BDF §202) | ἄφετε ἴδωμεν = "let us see" (NASB), impv. of ἀφίημι reinforces hortatory subj. to form single idiomatic phrase; leave ἄφετε untranslated (BDAG ἀφίημι 5b; BDF §364(1–2); W 464–5) (cp. Matt 27:49)

15:38 | σχίζω εἰς δύο = "tear in two" (BDAG εἰς 4e)

15:39 | ἐξ ἐναντίας + gen. = "right in front of" (NASB), "facing" (ESV) | οὕτως = "in this manner," referring to the φωνὴ μεγάλη that Jesus uttered just prior to his death (note repetition of ἐξέπνευσεν – vv. 37, 39)

15:40 | ἦσαν θεωροῦσαι – impf. periphrastic | ἡ ... μήτηρ = "the mother of James the younger and of Joses" (Ἰωσῆτος is gen. of Ἰωσῆς)

15:41 | "who [αἵ], when he was in Galilee, used to follow him and minister to him," customary imperfects

15:44 | ἐθαύμασεν εἰ ἤδη τέθνηκεν – not "wondered if he was dead" (NASB), but "expressed surprise that he was already dead" (M 154; BDAG εἰ 2) (cp. 1 John 3:13) | γνοὺς ... = "when he found out from the centurion [that it was true that Jesus was dead]," aorist ptc. is indicator of semantic usage (BDAG γινώσκω 2) (cp. 6:38)

15:47 | ἡ Ἰωσῆτος = "the [mother] of Joses" | ἐθεώρουν ποῦ τέθειται = they "saw where he was laid" (ESV)

Mark 16
16:1 | ἵνα ἐλθοῦσαι ἀλείψωσιν αὐτόν = "so that they might come and anoint him," ἐλθοῦσαι as attendant circumstances ptc. (fem. pl. in agreement with the three women named)

16:2 | τῇ μιᾷ τῶν σαββάτων = "on the first [day] of the week" | ἀνατείλαντος τοῦ ἡλίου = "the sun having risen," gen. abs.

16:8 | εἶχεν αὐτὰς τρόμος καὶ ἔκστασις = "trembling and astonishment had seized them" (ESV) (BDAG ἔχω 3d)

Shorter ending of Mark
"And they promptly reported all these instructions to Peter and his companions. And after that, Jesus Himself sent out through them from east to west the sacred and imperishable proclamation of eternal salvation" (NASB).

τὰ παρηγγελμένα = "instructions"
συντόμως = "promptly," adv. modifying ἐξήγγειλαν
ἐξήγγειλαν = "they reported," subject is the women of vv. 1–8
τοῖς περὶ τὸν Π. = "to Peter and those with him" (BDAG περί 2aδ)
καὶ αὐτὸς ὁ Ἰησοῦς = "even Jesus himself"
ἀπό ... δύσεως = "from east to west," from western perspective?
ἐξαπέστειλεν – subject is Jesus; direct object is τὸ κήρυγμα
δι' αὐτῶν = "through them," i.e., the apostles

Longer ending of Mark
16:9 | ἀναστάς ... ἐφάνη = Jesus "arose and appeared" | πρώτῃ σαββάτου = "on the first [day] of the week"

16:10 | ἐκείνη πορευθεῖσα ἀπήγγειλεν = "she went and reported [it]" | τοῖς ... κλαίουσιν = "to those who had been with him, as they were mourning and weeping"

16:10, 11, 13, 20 | ἐκεῖνος (4x) weakened to a pronoun (BDF §291(6))

16:11 | κἀκεῖνοι = καὶ ἐκεῖνοι | ὅτι ζῇ καὶ ἐθεάθη ὑπ' αὐτῆς = "that he was alive and had been seen by her," i.e., by Mary Magdalene; present and aorist expressing relative time in indirect discourse (BDF §324; W 537)

16:12 | δυσὶν ἐξ αὐτῶν περιπατοῦσιν = "to two of them as they were walking"

16:14 | ὕστερον = "later," adv. acc. | "because they had not believed those who had seen him risen"

16:15 | πάσῃ τῇ κτίσει = "to all creation," i.e., to every person

16:16 | ὁ πιστεύσας καὶ βαπτισθείς = "the one who believes and is baptized," substantival gnomic aorist ptcs. with generic reference (W 615 n8; 621 n22; 688); also Granville Sharp rule (W 274)

16:17 | σημεῖα ... ταῦτα = "these signs"

16:17–18 | Categorical plurals? (see interesting discussion in W 405–6)

16:18 | κἂν ... βλάψῃ = "and if they drink any deadly poison, it will not hurt them" (ESV) (BDAG κἄν 1; but see W 405) | καλῶς ἕξω = "be well," future: "will recover"

16:19 | μὲν οὖν = "so then," continues the narrative (M 162; BDAG μέν 2e; BDF §451(1)) | μετὰ τό + inf. = "after he had spoken to them" (BDF §402(3)) | ἐκ = "at, on" (BDAG ἐκ 2)

16:20 | τοῦ κυρίου συνεργοῦντος ... βεβαιοῦντος = "while the Lord was working with them ... and confirming," gen. abs.

Chapter Three

The Gospel of Luke

Luke 1

1:1–4 | The prologue is "a beautiful period" (BDF §464) with the following tripartite structure:

Protasis	Apodosis
Πολλοί	κἀμοί
ἐπεχείρησαν ἀνατάξασθαι διήγησιν	ἔδοξε καθεξῆς γράψαι
καθώς ...	ἵνα ἐπιγνῷς ...

1:1 | τὰ πεπληροφορημένα ἐν ἡμῖν πράγματα = "the events that have occurred among us in fulfillment [of God's βουλή – 7:30; Acts 2:23; 4:28; 13:36; 20:27]" (BDAG πληροφορέω 1a; πρᾶγμα 1)

1:2 | οἱ ... γενόμενοι = "those who were eyewitnesses and servants of the word"

1:3 | ἔδοξε μοι + inf. (γράψαι) = "it seemed good to me to," "I resolved to" (BDAG δοκέω 2bβ) | κἀμοί = καὶ ἐμοί = "to me as well" | Adverb ἀκριβῶς modifies either (1) παρηκολουκηθότι – "having investigated everything *carefully* from the beginning" (NASB); or (2) γράψαι – "to write to you *precisely* [and] in an orderly sequence" | κράτιστος = "excellent, noble," superlative in form but elative ("very") in force (BDF §60; W 303) (cp. Acts 24:3)

1:4 | ἵνα ἐπιγνῷς ... τὴν ἀσφάλειαν = "that you might know the certainty" | περὶ ὧν κατηχήθης λόγων τὴν ἀσφάλειαν = τὴν ἀσφάλειαν [τῶν] λόγων περὶ ὧν κατηχήθης (BDAG κατηχέω 1; BDF §294(5)) = "the certainty of the things concerning which you have been taught"

1:5 | ἐγένετο ... ἱερεύς τις = "it came to pass in the days of Herod King of Judea [that there was] a certain priest" (BDAG γίνομαι 4f)

1:7 | αὐτοῖς – dat. of possession | προβεβηκότες ἦσαν – perf. periphrastic (W 649)

1:8 | ἐν τῷ ἱερατεύειν αὐτόν = "as he was serving as priest" (W 595); ἐν τῷ + inf. is "characteristically Lucan usage" (M 76); Septuagintism (BDF §404)

1:9 | ἔλαχε τοῦ θυμιᾶσαι εἰσελθών = "he was chosen by lot to enter and offer incense," gen. of articular inf., expressing purpose (BDF §400(3))

1:11 | ἄγγελος κυρίου = "an (or the) angel of the Lord" (cp. 2:9; Matt 1:20, etc.) (see discussion at W 252)

1:14 | ἔσται σοι = "you will have," dat. of possession | χαίρω ἐπί + dat. = "rejoice at," with verbs of emotion (BDAG ἐπί 6c) (cp. v. 47; 2:20, 47; 13:17)

1:15 | Verbs of filling (πίμπλημι) take gen. of content (πνεύματος ἁγίου) (cp. v. 41) (W 92–4) | ἔτι ἐκ κοιλίας μητρὸς αὐτοῦ = "while he is still in his mother's womb" (BDAG ἔτι 1aγ)

1:17 | ἐν φρονήσει δικαίων = "to the wisdom of the just" (BDF §218; BDAG ἐν 3), use of ἐν for εἰς here is "quite astonishing" (M 76, 205)

1:18 | κατὰ τί; = "how shall I know this?" (cp. LXX Gen 15:8)

1:20 | ἔση σιωπῶν = "you shall be dumb," future periphrastic (M 18; W 648–9) | ἄχρι ἧς ἡμέρας γένηται ταῦτα = "until the day when these things take place," incorporation of the antecedent in the relative clause (BDF §294(5)); should be ἄχρι τῆς ἡμέρας ἧς [or ἐν ᾗ] γένηται ταῦτα (cp. Acts 1:2, 22) | ἀνθ' ὧν = "because" (M 71) | εἰς τὸν καιρὸν αὐτῶν = "at their proper time," εἰς = ἐν (BDF §206(1); M 68–9)

1:21 | ἐν τῷ χρονίζειν αὐτόν = "that he was taking so long" (see v. 8) (BDAG ἐν 7)

1:23 | καὶ ἐγένετο ὡς ... ἀπῆλθεν = "and after ..., he went," Hebr. pleonastic ἐγένετο, common in Luke (BDF §§442(5); 472(3)) (BDAG ὡς 8a)

1:24 | μῆνας πέντε – acc. for extent of time

1:25 | ὅτι recitative | ἐν ἡμέραις αἷς = "in the days when"

1:29 | ποταπὸς εἴη ὁ ἀσπασμὸς οὗτος = "what sort of greeting this might be," either potential optative without ἄν (Z §§339(2); 346), or oblique optative (BDF §386(1); W 483)

1:31 | συλλαμβάνω ἐν γαστρί = "become pregnant"

1:34 | ἄνδρα οὐ γινώσκω = "I have not known a man," perfective present (W 533)

1:35 | τὸ γεννώμενον ἅγιον κληθήσεται υἱὸς θεοῦ – two options (see M 107): (1) to take τὸ γεννώμενον (substantival ptc.) as the subject and ἅγιον as predicate adjective, with υἱὸς θεοῦ in apposition thereto: "the child to be born will be called holy—the Son of God" (ESV) (for ἅγιον κληθήσεται, cp. 2:23), or (2) to take τὸ ἅγιον (substantival adjective) as the subject, with γεννώμενον as attributive thereto, and υἱὸς θεοῦ as the predicate: "the holy one to be born will be called the Son of God" (NIV); in either case, present ptc. γεννώμενον denotes future event (BDF §339(2); Z §283).

1:36 | καὶ αὐτή = "she too" | οὗτος μὴν ἕκτος ἐστὶν αὐτῇ = "this is now her sixth month," dat. of possession

1:37 | οὐκ ... πᾶν ῥῆμα = "nothing" (BDF §302(1)) (cp. LXX Gen 18:14)

1:39 | ἡ ὀρεινὴ [χώρα] = "the hill country," adjective with mentally supplied noun (M 96) (cp. v. 65)

1:41 | ἀσπασμὸς τῆς Μαρίας – subjective gen.

1:41, 44 | ὡς + aorist = "when" (BDAG ὡς 8a; BDF §455(2)) (cp. 2:15, 39)

1:41, 67 | πνεύματος ἁγίου = "with the Holy Spirit," gen. of content; verbs of filling take gen. (cp. v. 53)

1:43 | καὶ πόθεν μοι τοῦτο; = "why is this granted to me?" (ESV), "how have I deserved this?" (BDAG καί 1bθ; πόθεν 3) | ἵνα equivalent to explanatory inf. after τοῦτο (BDAG ἵνα 2e; BDF §394)

1:44 | ὡς ἐγένετο ἡ φωνὴ τοῦ ἀσπασμοῦ σου εἰς τὰ ὦτά μου = "when the sound of your greeting reached my ears" (ESV) (cp. εἰς τὰ ὦτα in Matt 10:27; Acts 11:22; Jas 5:4) | ἐσκίρτησεν ἐν ἀγαλλιάσει = "leaped for joy"

1:45 | ἡ πιστεύσασα ὅτι ἔσται – ὅτι is ambiguous: either (1) "she

who believed *that* there would be," or (2) "she who believed, *for* there
will be" | τελείωσις τοῖς λελαλημένοις = "a fulfillment of (lit. to)
the things that were spoken" | παρὰ κυρίου = "from the Lord," the
things were not spoken by the Lord directly but through the angel (BDF
§237(1); M 51)

1:47 | ἀγαλλιάω ἐπί + dat. = "rejoice in" (BDAG ἐπί 6c) (v. 14)

1:48 | ἀπὸ τοῦ νῦν = "from now on"

1:49 | ὁ δυνατός = "the Mighty One"

1:50 | εἰς γενεὰς καὶ γενεάς = lit. "to generations and generations"
(BDF §493(2)) (cp. LXX Ps 49:11)

1:51 | κράτος = "a specific product of resident strength, mighty deed"
(BDAG κράτος 2), neut. sg. acc., direct object of ἐποίησεν – "he
has performed mighty deeds" | Hebr./instrumental ἐν | διανοίᾳ
καρδίας αὐτῶν = "in the thoughts of their hearts," dat. of respect
(ZG) | κράτος and διανοίᾳ are sg. where English idiom uses pl.

1:53 | ἀγαθῶν = "with good things," gen. of content (W 92–4)

1:54 | ἀντιλαμβάνομαι takes gen.; Ἰσραήλ is gen., object not subject
| μνησθῆναι – inf. of result (BDF §391(4)); μιμνήσκομαι takes gen.
(cp. v. 72)

1:56 | ὡς with numerals = "about"

1:57 | τῇ δὲ Ἐ. = "now for Elizabeth," moved forward for emphasis,
shift of focus from Mary (BDF §472(2)) | ὁ χρόνος τοῦ τεκεῖν
αὐτήν = "the time for her to give birth," gen. of articular inf. after certain substantives (BDF §400(1)) (cp. 2:6)

1:58 | μεγαλύνω ἔλεος μετά + gen. = "show great mercy to someone" (BDAG μεγαλύνω 1; μετά A2αγ:) (the usual construction uses ποιέω – cp. v. 72; 10:37; LXX Gen 24:12, etc.)

1:59 | ἐκάλουν αὐτό Z. = "they were going to call him Zachariah," voluntative imperfect (W 551) | ἐπὶ τῷ ὀνόματι τοῦ πατρὸς αὐτοῦ = "after his father," as we would say in English (under BDAG ἐπί 17) (cp. LXX 2 Esdras 17:63)

1:61 | ὅτι recitative

1:62 | τὸ τί ἂν θέλοι καλεῖσθαι αὐτό = "what he wanted him to be called," either oblique optative (BDF §386(1)), or potential optative (W 483–4; ZG) | τό changes direct question into indirect (BDAG ὁ 2hα; BDF §267(2)); common in Luke-Acts and twice in Paul: τὸ τί (1:62; 19:48; Acts 22:30; Rom 8:26); τὸ τίς (9:46; 22:23, 24); τὸ πῶς (22:2, 4; Acts 4:21; 1 Thess 4:1)

1:65 | ἐγένετο ἐπὶ πάντας φόβος τοὺς περιοικοῦντας αὐτούς = ἐγένετο φόβος ἐπὶ πάντας τοὺς περιοικοῦντας αὐτούς = "fear came on all those living around them" (NASB), "fear came on all their neighbors" (ESV); ἐπὶ πάντας moved forward for emphasis (BDF §472(2)); acc. pl. αὐτούς is direct object of περι-οικέω (περί + acc. = "around") | ἡ ὀρεινή – cp. v. 39

1:66 | τί ἄρα τὸ παιδίον τοῦτο ἔσται; = "what then will this child be?" (ESV) (BDAG ἄρα 1b; BDF §299(2))

1:68, 78 | ἐπισκέπτομαι (2x) = "visit; exercise oversight on behalf of; make an appearance to help" (BDAG)

1:70 | οἱ ἅγιοι ἀπ᾽ αἰῶνος προφῆται = "the holy prophets of long ago"

1:72 | μιμνήσκομαι takes gen. (cp. v. 54)

1:73, 77, 79 | τοῦ + inf. expressing purpose (W 610; BDF §400(5)(6))

2:20 | ἐπί + dat. after verbs of emotion = "for" (BDAG ἐπί 6c)

2:21 | Second καί introduces apodosis (Hebr. influence, BDF §442(7); BDAG καί 1bδ): "And when the eight days to circumcise him were fulfilled, his name was called Jesus, the name that was called by the angel before he was conceived in the womb" | ἡμέραι + τοῦ + inf. = "days to," tending toward consecutive sense (BDF §400(2)) | πρὸ τοῦ + aorist inf. = "before" (BDF §403; M 74; W 596)

2:22–24 | ἀνήγαγον αὐτὸν εἰς Ἰ. παραστῆσαι τῷ κυρίῳ ... καὶ τοῦ δοῦναι θυσίαν = "they brought him to Jerusalem to present [him] to the Lord ... and to offer sacrifice," second inf. with τοῦ for clarity (BDF §400(6)); both infs. used in final sense (M 128)

2:23 | Parenthesis

2:24 | νοσσός = "the young of a bird," thus νοσσοί περιστερῶν = "the young of pigeons or doves"

2:26 | ἦν αὐτῷ κεχρηματισμένον = "it had been revealed to him," plupf. periphrastic (M 19; W 649) | μὴ ἰδεῖν θάνατον = "that he would not see death," inf. in indirect discourse (W 603–5); aorist inf. for future inf. (ZG); acc. αὐτόν as subject of inf. is to be supplied from previous clause (αὐτῷ) (BDF §§406–7) | πρὶν ἤ + subj. = "before" (BDF §383(3))

2:27–28 | "And when the parents brought the child Jesus in so that they [αὐτούς] might do according to the custom of the law concerning him, he himself took it into his arms and blessed God and said," ἐν τῷ + inf. = "when" (see 1:8); first καί of v. 28 introduces apodosis

2:32 | εἰς = "for" in the sense of "serving as" (BDAG εἰς 4d), also understood before δόξαν | ἐθνῶν ... λαοῦ σου = "to the Gentiles ... to your people," objective gens. with verbal nouns

2:33 | ἦν … θαυμάζοντες – impf. periphrastic; sg. finite verb with pl. ptc., not ungrammatical (BDF §135(1)(d))

2:35 | καὶ σοῦ αὐτῆς τὴν ψυχήν = "even your own soul" (NASB); τὴν ψυχήν is direct object of διέρχομαι, "the climax of contradiction (the Cross) being obliquely implied in the suffering of Mary" (ZG) | ἐκ πολλῶν καρδιῶν διαλογισμοί = "thoughts of (or from) many hearts," either gen. of source made explicit with addition of ἐκ, or ἐκ for simple gen.

2:36 | ζήσασα μετὰ ἀνδρός = "she had lived with her husband," aorist ptc. referring to a concluded period of time many decades earlier | ἔτη ἑπτά – acc. for extent of time | ἀπὸ τῆς παρθενίας = lit. "from when she was a virgin" (ESV), i.e., "after her marriage" (NASB)

2:37 | αὐτὴ χήρα ἕως ἐτῶν ὀγδοήκοντα τεσσάρων = either (1) "she remained a widow for 84 years" after her husband's death, or (2) more likely, "she remained a widow until the age of 84" (BDAG ἕως 1bα) | τοῦ ἱεροῦ – gen. of separation after verb with ἀπο- prefix (ἀφίστημι) (W 107–9) | νύκτα καὶ ἡμέραν – acc. for extent of time

2:38 | αὐτῇ τῇ ὥρᾳ = "at that very moment," dat. of time

2:39 | ὡς + aorist = "when"

2:40 | πληρόω (pass.) + dat. = "filled with" (BDF §195(2))

2:41 | ἐπορεύοντο = "his parents used to go," customary impf. (W 548) | κατ᾽ ἔτος = "every year"

2:42–43 | Four subordinate clauses (a–d) before the two main clauses (e–f): "(a) And when he became twelve years of age, (b) *on one of their trips up [to Jerusalem] according to the custom of the Feast and* (c) *after they had completed the days [of the Feast]*, (d) as his parents were returning home, (e) the boy Jesus stayed behind in Jerusalem, and (f) his parents were unaware of it," the two clauses in italics are gen. abs.

2:44 | ἡμέρας ὁδόν = "a day's journey"

2:47 | BDAG ἐπί 6c | Possible hendiadys (BDF §442(16))

2:48 | κἀγώ = καὶ ἐγώ | ὀδυνώμενοι ἐζητοῦμέν σε = we "have been anxiously searching for you" (NIV), ptc. of manner (W 627–8)

2:49 | Τί ὅτι; = "how [is it] that?" (W 460), i.e., "why?" | ἐν τοῖς τοῦ πατρός = either (1) "about my Father's business" (KJV; M 75), or (2) "in my Father's house" (ESV; BDAG ἐν 1a)

Luke 3
3:2 | ἡγεμονεύοντος … τετρααρχοῦντος (3x) = "when Pontius Pilate was governor of … when so-and-so was tetrarch of," etc., gen. abs. (cp. 2:2) | ἐπί + gen. = "in the time of, under" (BDAG ἐπί 18a) (cp. 4:27) | ἐγένετο ἐπί + acc. = "came to" (BDAG ἐπί 14bβ)

3:4 | βοῶντος = "of (some)one crying out," anarthrous substantival ptc. (cp. Matt 3:3; Mk 1:3)

3:5 | ταπεινωθήσεται – sg. possibly bec. the subject is viewed as a single entity, and to rhyme with πληρωθήσεται | ἔσται – neut. pl. subjects take sg. verbs; interestingly, εὐθείαν is sg. as well (contrast λείας) | εἰς (2x) – marker of predicate nom. (BDAG εἰς 8)

3:7 | ἡ μέλλουσα ὀργή = "the wrath to come" (cp. Matt 3:7) (BDAG μέλλω 3)

3:9 | ἐκκόπτεται & βάλλεται – futuristic (W 536) or gnomic presents (W 524)

3:10, 11, 14 | ἐπηρώτων (2x), ἔλεγεν – iterative imperfects (W 547)

3:10, 12, 14 | ποιήσωμεν (3x) – deliberative subjunctives (W 466)

3:13 | πλέον παρά + acc. = "more than" (BDAG παρά C3; M 51) | πράσσω = "collect or exact" taxes (BDAG πράσσω 1b) (cp. 19:23)

3:14 | καὶ στρατευόμενοι = "soldiers also"

3:15 | "Now while the people were in a state of expectation and all were wondering in their hearts about John, as to whether he was the Christ, John answered ..." (NASB) | μήποτε αὐτὸς εἴη ὁ Χριστός – optative εἴη in indirect discourse after μήποτε means "whether perhaps" (BDF §§370(3); 386(2))

3:16 | μέν ... δέ = "on the one hand ... on the other hand" | βαπτίζω – distributive present – John performs the action repeatedly, though presumably baptizing each person only once (W 521) | ἔρχεται – futuristic present (W 536) | ἰσχυρότερός μου = "mightier than I," gen. of comparison | οὗ ... αὐτοῦ = "the strap *of whose* sandals," relative clause introduced by οὗ followed by pleonastic pronoun αὐτοῦ under Semitic influence (BDF §297; Z §201) (cp. v. 17)

3:17 | διακαθᾶραι & συναγαγεῖν – purpose infs. (W 590)

3:18 | μὲν οὖν – summarizes what has been narrated in order to transition to new subject (BDF §451(1); M 162) | πολλὰ καὶ ἕτερα – acc. object of παρακαλέω (BDAG παρακαλέω 2); "So with many other exhortations he preached the gospel to the people" (NASB)

3:19 | περὶ πάντων ὧν ἐποίησεν πονηρῶν = περὶ πάντων [τῶν] πονηρῶν ὧν ἐποίησεν = "concerning all the wicked things that he had done," incorporation of the antecedent in the relative clause (BDF §294(5))

3:20 | προσέθηκεν καὶ τοῦτο ἐπὶ πᾶσιν = "he added *this also* to them all," τοῦτο points to what follows: "he locked John up in prison"

3:21–22 | ἐγένετο + three infs. (BDAG γίνομαι 4e): "It came to pass (...) that heaven was opened and the Holy Spirit came down ... and a voice from heaven occurred," where (...) = "(a) *after* all the people had been baptized and (b) *after* Jesus had been baptized and *as* he was praying," clause (a) is ἐν τῷ + aorist inf. construction (BDF §404(2); Z §390); clause (b) is gen. abs. composed of an antecedent aorist ptc. (βαπτισθέντος) and a contemporaneous present ptc. (προσευχομένου)

3:22 | ἐν σοὶ εὐδόκησα (= Mark 1:11) = "with you I am well pleased," see Matt 3:17 for discussion of other options

3:23 | αὐτὸς ἦν Ἰησοῦς ... ὡσεὶ ἐτῶν τριάκοντα = "Jesus himself was about thirty years of age" | ἀρχόμενος – present circumstantial ptc. of ἄρχω ("begin"), takes inf. complement, implied from context: "when he began [to do his work]" | "being [ὤν], as was supposed, the son of Joseph"

Luke 4

4:1 | ἐν τῷ πνεύματι = "by the Spirit," ἐν + dat. of agency with pass. (BDAG ἐν 6) (cp. ὑπὸ τοῦ πνεύματος, Matt 4:1) (*pace* W 373, who questions this category) | ἐν τῇ ἐρήμῳ = εἰς τὴν ἔρημον (textual variant; Matt 4:1; Mk 1:12), ἐν used for εἰς (BDF §218; BDAG ἐν 3; M 205 note for p. 76)

4:2 | ἡμέρας τεσσεράκοντα – acc. for extent of time | πειραζόμενος = "to be tempted," telic ptc. (W 636 n60) (cp. πειρασθῆναι, Matt 4:1) | οὐκ ἔφαγεν οὐδέν = "he ate nothing," double negatives reinforce (BDF §431(2)) | συντελεσθεισῶν αὐτῶν = "when those [days] were completed," gen. abs.; antecedent of αὐτῶν is ταῖς ἡμέραις ἐκείναις | ἐπείνασεν = "he became hungry," inceptive aorist (W 558)

4:3 | λέγω + dat. + ἵνα = "command x to," with ἵνα used in attenuated sense as substitute for inf. (BDAG ἵνα 2aδ; λέγω 2c)

4:4 | ζάω ἐπί + dat. = "live on" (BDAG ἐπί 6a)

4:6 | τὴν ἐξουσίαν ταύτην ἅπασαν καὶ τὴν δόξαν αὐτῶν = lit. "all this authority and their glory," awkward bec. antecedent of αὐτῶν is unstated, but can be inferred (cp. πάσας τὰς βασιλείας τοῦ κόσμου, Matt 4:8) | ᾧ ἐὰν θέλω = "to whomever I want"

4:7 | σύ moved forward for emphasis

4:8, 12 | προσκυνήσεις, λατρεύσεις, ἐκπειράσεις – imperatival futures, usually employed in LXX quotations of OT categorical injunctions (BDF §362; W 569; M 178–9) (cp. 18:20)

4:10 | τοῦ pleonastically prefixed to inf.; LXX's literal rendering of Hebrew לְ + inf. construct (BDF §400(7); Z §386)

4:13 | ἄχρι καιροῦ = "until an opportune time"

4:14 | καθ' ὅλης τῆς περιχώρου = "throughout the whole surrounding region" (BDAG κατά A1c; BDF §225) (cp. 23:5)

4:15 | αὐτός used in weakened sense as pronoun, picking up on αὐτοῦ and signaling shift of subject (BDF §277(3))

4:16 | κατὰ τὸ εἰωθὸς αὐτῷ = "according to his custom," dat. of possession (BDF §189(1)) | ἡ ἡμέρα τῶν σαββάτων = "the Sabbath day" (cp. LXX Exod 20:8) (BDAG σάββατον 1bβ; BDF §141(3))

4:18 | οὗ εἵνεκεν = "because" | ἀποστέλλω ἐν ἀφέσει = "set free" (NASB; BDAG ἀποστέλλω 2b) (LXX Isa 58:6), ἐν + dat. denoting manner, functioning as auxiliary in periphrasis for adv. (BDAG ἐν 11)

4:20 | ἦσαν ἀτενίζοντες – impf. periphrastic

4:21 | ὅτι recitative

4:22 | μαρτυρέω + dat. = "speak well of someone" (BDAG μαρτυρέω 2) | BDAG ἐπί 6c | τῆς χάριτος = "gracious, winsome," gen. of quality (W 86; BDF §165; Z §40) | Οὐχὶ υἱός ἐστιν Ἰωσὴφ οὗτος; = "Is this not Joseph's son?"

4:23 | παραβολή here = "proverb" | ἰατρέ – vocative | εἰς = ἐν | καὶ ὧδε = "here as well"

4:25 | ἐπ' ἀληθείας = "truly" (BDAG ἐπί 8) | ἐπί + acc. = "for three years and six months" (BDAG ἐπί 18cβ) | ὡς + aorist = "when"

4:27 | ἐπί + gen. = "in the time of, under" (BDAG ἐπί 18a) (cp. 3:2)

4:28 | Verbs of filling take gen. (θυμοῦ) | πάντες ... ἐν τῇ συναγωγῇ = "all [the people] in the synagogue"

4:29 | ὥστε + inf. is usually consecutive, but here final/purposive (M 140; BDAG ὥστε 2b; BDF §391(3); W 591 n5; Z §352) | ἡ πόλις ... αὐτῶν = "their city"

4:31, 38, 44 | ἦν + present ptc. (3x) = impf. periphrastic

4:31 | ἐν τοῖς σάββασιν = "on the Sabbath," Hebr. pl. (see v. 16)

4:32 | BDAG ἐπί 6c

4:32, 36 | ἐν ἐξουσίᾳ (2x) = "with authority" (BDAG ἐν 11)

4:34 | τί ἡμῖν καὶ σοί – see translation possibilities at Matt 8:29 | οἶδά σε τίς εἶ = "I know you, who you are," prolepsis, i.e., anticipation of the subject of the subordinate clause by making it the object of the main clause (BDF §476(2))

4:35 | μηδὲν βλάψαν αὐτόν = "without doing him any harm" (BDAG βλάπτω)

4:40 | δύνοντος τοῦ ἡλίου = "while the sun was setting," gen. abs. | ἅπαντες ὅσοι εἶχον ἀσθενοῦντας = "all those who had any who were sick" (NASB, ESV) | ὁ δέ – shift of subject (prepared for by preceding αὐτόν); article used as pronoun | ἑνὶ ἑκάστῳ αὐτῶν = "on each one of them" | τὰς χεῖρας = "his hands" | "he laid his hands on each one of them and healed them," ἐπιτιθείς as attendant circumstances ptc. (W 644) | ἐθεράπευεν – iterative impf.

4:41 | καὶ δαιμόνια = "demons also," neut. pl. subjects take sg. verbs | ἐπιτιμῶν οὐκ εἴα αὐτὰ λαλεῖν = "rebuking them, he was not letting them speak" | ὅτι ᾔδεισαν τὸν χριστὸν αὐτὸν εἶναι = "because they knew that he was the Christ"

4:42 | ἦλθον ἕως αὐτοῦ = "they came to where he was," ἕως + gen. of person who is in a certain place (BDAG ἕως 3a) | κατεῖχον (conative impf.) ... = "they were trying to keep him from going away from them," τοῦ μή + inf. = "so that not" (BDF §400(4))

4:43 | καὶ ταῖς ἑτέραις πόλεσιν = "to the other towns *also*" | δεῖ + acc. + inf. = "it is necessary for someone to do something" (here: "it is necessary for me to preach the good news of the kingdom")

4:44 | εἰς = ἐν

Luke 5
5:1 | ἐγένετο ... καί αὐτός = "it came to pass ... *that* he himself was standing" (BDAG καί 1bβ; BDF §442(5); Z §389) (cp. v. 12) | ἐν τῷ + present infs. (ἐπικεῖσθαι & ἀκούειν) = "as the crowd was surrounding him and listening to the word of God" (BDF §404(1); Z §390) (cp. v. 12) | ἐπίκειμαι + dat. = "crowd around someone"

5:2 | οἱ δὲ ἁλιεῖς ἀπ' αὐτῶν ἀποβάντες ἔπλυνον τὰ δίκτυα = "Now the fishermen got out of them [i.e., the two boats] and were washing their nets," ἀποβαίνω ἀπό + gen. = "get out of" (BDAG ἀποβαίνω 1; ἀπό 1a)

5:3 | ὃ ἦν Σίμωνος = "which was Simon's," gen. of possession | ὀλίγον = "a short distance," acc. for extent of space | ἐκ τοῦ πλοίου ἐδίδασκεν = "he was teaching from the boat" (BDAG ἐκ 2)

5:4 | ὡς + aorist = "when" | παύομαι (mid.) + supplementary ptc. = "cease doing something" (BDF §414(2); BDAG παύω 2) | ἐπανάγαγε εἰς τὸ βάθος = "put out into the deep" | εἰς ἄγραν = "in order to catch something" (BDAG εἰς 4f)

5:7 | κατανεύω τινί + inf. = "signal to someone," with message indicated by complementary inf. (BDF §§396–7) | τοῦ ἐλθόντας συλλαβέσθαι = "to come and help them," pleonastic τοῦ prefixed to inf. (BDF §400(7); Z §386) | ὥστε βυθίζεσθαι αὐτά = "so that they were in danger of sinking" (BDF §338(1)) or "so that they began to sink" (W 593), present indicating an "unaccomplished tendency" (Z §274)

5:9 | θάμβος ἐπί + dat. = "amazement because of" (BDAG ἐπί 6c) (cp. θαμβέω ἐπί + dat., Mark 10:24)

5:10 | ὁμοίως δὲ καί = "likewise also James and John [fell down at Jesus' feet]" | ἀπὸ τοῦ νῦν = "from now on" | ἔσῃ ζωγρῶν = "you will be catching," future periphrastic (W 648–9)

5:11 | Antecedent temporal ptc. (καταγαγόντες) followed by attendant circumstances ptc. (ἀφέντες): "And after they brought their boats to the land, they left everything and followed him." "The focus … is not on what the disciples left … but on their following Jesus" (W 643).

5:12 | "While he was in one of the cities, behold, [there was] a man covered with leprosy" (NASB, supplying ἦν); see v. 1 for both the ἐγένετο … καί and the ἐν τῷ + present inf. constructions | πλήρης + gen. = "covered with" (BDAG πλήρης 1b) | δέομαι – deponent (pass. in form but active in mng.), with gen. of person petitioned (αὐτοῦ)

5:13 | Verbs of touching take gen.

5:14 | Mixture of indirect and direct discourse (BDF §470(2)) | Direct object of προσένεγκε must be supplied (cp. τὸ δῶρον, Matt 8:4) | BDAG εἰς 4f

5:15 | ὁ λόγος περὶ αὐτοῦ = "the news about him" (NIV) (cp. 7:17)

5:16 | ἦν + two present ptcs. = impf. periphrastic

5:17 | ἐγένετο ... καί αὐτός (see v. 1) | οἳ ἦσαν ἐληλυθότες = "who had come," plupf. periphrastic (W 649) | δύναμις κυρίου ἦν εἰς τὸ ἰᾶσθαι αὐτόν = "the power of the Lord was present for him to perform healing" (NASB); εἰς τό + inf. (W 611); acc. αὐτόν as subject of inf.

5:18 | φέροντες ... ἐζήτουν – either (1) ptc. continued with a finite verb (ZG; Z §375), or more likely, (2) supply ἦσαν after ἰδού ("behold, [there were] men") (cp. v. 12) | ἦν παραλελυμένος (cp. v. 24) is probably not plupf. periphrastic, but perf. ptc. as predicate adjective ptc. (W 583 n33) | ζητέω + inf. = "try to do something" (BDAG ζητέω 3d)

5:19 | μὴ εὑρόντες ποίας εἰσενέγκωσιν αὐτόν = "not finding any [way] to bring him in" (ποίας [ὁδοῦ] – BDAG ποῖος 2bβ; BDF §186(1)) | διά + acc. = "because of"

5:20 | ἄνθρωπε – voc. | ἀφέωνται = "are forgiven," intensive or resultative perf. (W 576) (cp. 13:12)

5:24 | Direct discourse broken by insertion of εἶπεν to prepare for apostrophe directed to the paralytic (BDF §470(3))

5:25 | ἐφ᾽ ὃ κατέκειτο = "what he had been lying on" (i.e., τὸ κλινίδιον, vv. 19, 24) (BDAG ἐπί 1cα)

5:26 | Verbs of filling take gen. | παράδοξα = "incredible things," neut. pl.

5:27 | BDAG ἐπί 1cγ

5:29 | ποιέω of meals and banquets, "give" (BDAG ποιέω 2f) | αὐτῷ = "for him," i.e., for Jesus | οἳ ἦσαν κατακείμενοι = "who were re-clining," impf. periphrastic

5:30 | οἱ γραμματεῖς αὐτῶν = "their [= the Pharisees'] scribes"

5:31 | ἔχω χρείαν + gen. (ἰατροῦ) = "have need of" (BDAG χρεία 1) | κακῶς ἔχειν = "to be sick"

5:33 | First οἱ = "they," article as pronoun | πυκνά = "often," neut. pl. as adv. acc. | ὁμοίως καὶ οἱ τῶν Φαρ. = "likewise also the [disciples] of the Pharisees" | οἱ δὲ σοί = "but your [disciples]"

5:34 | Μὴ δύνασθε ... ποιῆσαι νηστεῦσαι; = "You cannot force ... to fast, can you?" (BDAG ποιέω 2hα) | οἱ υἱοὶ τοῦ νυμφῶνος = lit. "the sons of the bridal chamber," i.e., "the bridegroom's attendants" (BDAG νυμφών 2) (cp. Matt 9:15; Mk 2:19) | ἐν ᾧ ... ἐστιν = "while the bridegroom is with them"

5:35 | ἐλεύσονται ἡμέραι, καὶ ὅταν ... τότε = either (1) "the time will come when ... and then" (ESV) (BDAG ἡμέρα 3b; BDF §442(4)), or (2) "[the] days will come; and when ... then" (NASB) (BDF §382(3)). Overall mng. is captured by (1), but presence of καί before ὅταν (rather than before τότε as in Matt 9:15; Mk 2:20) favors (2).

5:36 | ἔλεγεν δὲ καὶ παραβολὴν πρὸς αὐτούς = "he *also* told them a parable" (ESV), aoristic impf. (W 542) (cp. 6:39) | ὅτι recitative | οὐδείς ... παλαιόν = "No one tears a piece of cloth from a new garment and puts it on an old garment" (NASB), σχίσας as attendant circum-stances ptc.

5:36–37 | εἰ δὲ μή γε (2x) = "otherwise"

5:38 | βλητέον = "must be put," verbal adjective (BDF §65(3))

Luke 6

6:1 | ἐγένετο διαπορεύεσθαι αὐτόν = "It happened that he was going through" (BDAG γίνομαι 4e) (see 3:21–22), acc. αὐτόν as subject of inf.

6:26: | τοῖς σάββασιν = "on the Sabbath," Hebr. pl. (cp. 4:16, 31)

6:2, 4, 9 | ἔξεστιν (3x) = "is permitted/lawful"

6:4 | ὡς = "how," marker of discourse content (BDAG ὡς 5) | οὓς – relative pronoun referring back to τοὺς ἄρτους τῆς προθέσεως ("which no one but the priests alone is permitted to eat") | τοὺς ἱερεῖς – acc. as subject of inf.

6:6 | ἐγένετο + two infs. – see v. 1

6:7 | εἰ = "to see whether" (BDAG εἰ 5b) | ἵνα εὕρωσιν κατηγορεῖν αὐτοῦ = "so that they might find [cause] to accuse him" – the full expression is εὑρίσκω αἰτίαν, "find a basis for a charge" (John 18:38; 19:4, 6; Acts 13:28); note that κατηγορέω (usually) takes gen. object

6:8 | τῷ ξηρὰν ἔχοντι τὴν χεῖρα = τῷ ἔχοντι τὴν ξηρὰν χεῖρα

6:10 | ὁ = "he," article as pronoun | ἀπεκατεστάθη – note the double augment (BDF §69(3)) (cp. Matt 12:13; Mk 3:5; 8:25)

6:11 | Verbs of filling take gen. | τί ἂν ποιήσαιεν = "what they might do," either oblique optative (BDF §386(1)), or potential optative (ZG; Z §339(2))

6:12 | ἐγένετο + inf. – see vv. 1, 6 | Acc. αὐτόν as subject of inf. |
ἦν διανυκτερεύων – impf. periphrastic | προσευχὴ τοῦ θεοῦ =
"prayer to God," objective gen. (W 117 n126)

6:16 | ὃς ἐγένετο προδότης = "who became a traitor"

6:17 | καὶ ὄχλος πολύς = "and [there was] a great crowd," supplying ἦν

6:18 | οἱ ἐνοχλούμενοι ἀπὸ πνευμάτων ἀκαθάρτων = "those
troubled *by* unclean spirits," either ἀπό = ὑπό (BDAG ἀπό 5eβ), or
causal ἀπό (M 73)

6:19 | ζητέω – see 5:18 | Verbs of touching take gen. | ἰᾶτο – iter-
ative impf.

6:22 | ἐκβάλλω = "force/drive out; expel someone from a group" (BDAG;
cp. John 9:34–35; Gal 4:30; 3 John 10) | ἕνεκα + gen. = "because of"

6:23, 26 | κατὰ τὰ αὐτά = "in the same way"

6:26 | λέγω καλῶς + acc. = "speak well of someone" (BDAG καλῶς 3)

6:29 | ἀπὸ τοῦ αἴροντός σου τὸ ἱμάτιον καὶ τὸν χιτῶνα μὴ
κωλύσῃς = "whoever takes away your coat, do not withhold your
shirt from him *either* (καὶ)" (NASB), κωλύω τι ἀπό τινος = "withhold something from someone" (cp. LXX Gen 23:6) (BDAG κωλύω
2; BDF §180(1))

6:30 | τὰ σά = "what is yours"

6:31 | ἵνα instead of supplementary inf. (BDAG ἵνα 2aα)

6:32–34 | χάρις (3x) = "credit, favorable response" (BDAG χάρις 2b)
(cp. 1 Pet 2:19–20) | καὶ [οἱ] ἁμαρτωλοί (3x) = "*even* sinners"

6:34 | ἐὰν δανίσητε παρ' ὧν ἐλπίζετε λαβεῖν = "if you lend [to those] from whom you expect to receive," omission of the antecedent is common (M 130)

6:37 | ἀπολύω here = "pardon" (BDAG ἀπολύω 1)

6:38 | δώσουσιν = "they will give," indef. pl. subject to avoid the divine name (BDF §130(1–2); Z §2) (cp. 12:20, 48; 16:9)

6:39 | εἶπεν δὲ καὶ παραβολὴν αὐτοῖς = "he *also* told them a parable" (cp. 5:36) | μήτι expects negative answer ("a blind man cannot ... can he?")

6:40b | Take κατηρτισμένος as temporal adverbial ptc. (W 623–6) and supply μαθητής from v. 40a: "But once fully trained, every [disciple] will be like his teacher"

6:41, 46 | τί; (2x) = "why?"

6:42 | ἄφες ἐκβάλω = "let me take out," impv. of ἀφίημι reinforces hortatory subj. to form single idiomatic phrase; leave ἄφες untranslated (BDAG ἀφίημι 5b; BDF §364(1–2); W 464–5) | αὐτός ... οὐ βλέπων = "when/while you yourself do not see," second person continued implicitly from δύνασαι ... σου | διαβλέψεις ... ἐκβαλεῖν = "you will clearly see [so as] to take out," inf. of purpose | τὸ κάρφος could be direct object of ἐκβαλεῖν only (as in Matt 7:5), or first of διαβλέψεις and then doing double duty as direct object of ἐκβαλεῖν ("then you will clearly see the speck that is in your brother's eye so as to take it out")

6:43 | πάλιν = "on the other hand" (BDAG πάλιν 4)

6:44 | συλλέγουσιν & τρυγῶσιν – indef. pl., "they/people" (BDF §130)

6:47 | μου τῶν λόγων = τῶν λόγων μου | τίνι ἐστὶν ὅμοιος = "whom he is like"

6:48 | ἔσκαψεν καὶ ἐβάθυνεν = "dug deep," hendiadys (BDF §471(4); Z §460) | διὰ τὸ καλῶς οἰκοδομῆσθαι αὐτήν = "because it had been well built," διὰ τό + inf. (BDF §402(1))

Luke 7
7:1 | εἰς τὰς ἀκοὰς τοῦ λαοῦ = "in the ears/hearing of the people" (BDAG ἀκοή 3), εἰς = ἐν (BDF §205; Z §99)

7:2 | ἑκατοντάρχου τινος δοῦλος = "the servant of a certain centurion" | κακῶς ἔχων = "being sick" | μέλλω + inf. = "be about to" | ἔντιμος + dat. = "valuable to someone," here, to the centurion (αὐτῷ)

7:3 | ὅπως ἐλθὼν διασώσῃ = "asking him to come and save his slave," with verbs of asking ὅπως equivalent to inf. (BDAG ὅπως 2b); ἐλθών, attendant circumstances ptc.

7:4 | ἄξιός ἐστιν ᾧ παρέξῃ τοῦτο = "he is worthy to whom you will grant this" or "he deserves that you grant him this" (BDAG παρέχω 3b); qualitative-consecutive relative clause, "such that" (BDF §379); ἄξιος ᾧ = *dignus qui* (Latinism; M 192); παρέξῃ – future for subj. (Z §343)

7:6 | ἐπορεύετο – impf. describing action in progress when some other action takes place (Z §275); "Jesus was going with them, and as he [was going and] was now [ἤδη] not far off from the house" | αὐτοῦ ἀπέχοντος – gen. abs. | μὴ σκύλλου = "don't trouble yourself," reflexive (W 417) | ἵνα for epexegetical inf. (BDAG ἵνα 2cβ; W 476)

7:7 | διὸ οὐδὲ ἐμαυτὸν ἠξίωσα πρὸς σὲ ἐλθεῖν = "therefore I did not even consider myself worthy to come to you" | εἰπὲ λόγῳ = "say the word," cognate dat. (W 168)

7:8 | καὶ γὰρ ἐγώ = "for I also"

7:10 | οἱ πεμφθέντες = "those who had been sent"

7:11 | ἐν τῷ/τῇ ἑξῆς – textual issue; either (1) "soon afterward," supplying χρόνῳ to go with τῷ (cp. 8:1), or (2) "the next day," supplying ἡμέρᾳ to go with τῇ (cp. 9:37; Acts 21:1; 25:17; 27:18) (see Metzger)

7:12 | ὡς + aorist = "when" | "When he approached the gate of the city, behold a dead man was being carried out," καί as Hebr. marker of apodosis (cp. 2:21) (BDAG καί 1bδ; BDF §442(7); Z §457) | τῇ πύλη – dat. of destination (W 147–8) | τεθνηκώς = "a dead man" | μονογενὴς υἱὸς τῇ μητρὶ αὐτοῦ = "the only begotten son of his mother," dat. of possession (cp. 8:42; 9:38) | ὄχλος τῆς πόλεως ἱκανός = "a large crowd from the city," gen. of source

7:13 | BDAG ἐπί 6c

7:14 | Verbs of touching take gen.

7:15 | Subject of ἔδωκεν is Jesus

7:16 | ὅτι recitative (2x)

7:17 | ὁ λόγος οὗτος περὶ αὐτοῦ = "this report about him" (ESV) (cp. 5:15)

7:19 | προσδοκῶμεν – could be indic. ("are we waiting for another?") or deliberative subj. ("are we to wait for another?")

7:23 | ὃς ἐάν = "whoever" | σκανδαλίζω ἐν τινι = "take offense at someone"

7:24 | ἀπελθόντων τῶν ἀγγέλων Ἰωάννου = "after John's messengers left" (NIV), aorist gen. abs.

7:24, 27 | ἄγγελος (2x) = "a human messenger serving as an envoy" (BDAG ἄγγελος 1)

7:25 | οἱ ... ὑπάρχοντες = "those who are"

7:25, 26 | ἀλλά (2x) = "but if not that, then" (ZG; BDF §448(4))

7:28 | μείζων + gen. of comparison (Ἰωάννου & αὐτοῦ) = "greater than" | ἐν γεννητοῖς γυναικῶν = "among those born of women" (cp. clearer word order at Matt 11:11)

7:29–30 | Parenthetical comment by Luke

7:29 | πᾶς ὁ λαὸς ἀκούσας καὶ οἱ τελῶναι = "when all the people heard this, and the tax collectors too" (ESV) | βαπτισθέντες τὸ βάπτισμα Ἰωάννου = "having been baptized with the baptism of John," ptc. of means and acc. of the retained object with pass. (BDF §159; W 197)

7:29, 35 | δικαιόω = "acknowledge/prove someone to be right" (BDAG δικαιόω 2a), common usage in extra-biblical Gk | ἐδικαιώθη – gnomic aorist (M 13)

7:32 | ἃ λέγει = "who say," antecedent of ἅ (neut. pl.) is παιδίοις (dat. neut. pl.)

7:35 | ἀπό = ὑπό (BDAG ἀπό 5eβ)

7:36 | τις τῶν Φαρισαίων = "one of the Pharisees"

7:38 | παρὰ τοὺς πόδας τινός = "at someone's feet" (BDAG παρά C1c) (cp. 8:35, 41; 17:16) | κλαίουσα – ptc. of manner (W 627–8)

7:39 | καλέω = "invite" | ἐγίνωσκεν ἄν ... ἅπτεται αὐτοῦ = "he would know who and what sort of woman [it is] that is touching him"

7:40 | ἔχω σοί τι εἰπεῖν = ἔχω τι εἰπεῖν σοί | ὁ δέ ... φησίν = "he says" | εἰπέ = "say it"

7:41 | δύο χρεοφειλέται ἦσαν δανιστῇ τινι = "a certain money lender had two debtors," dat. of possession

7:42 | ἔχω + inf. = "be able to" (BDAG ἔχω 5) – "when they could not pay," gen. abs. | τίς αὐτῶν; = "which of them," partitive gen. (BDF §164(1)

7:43 | ᾧ τὸ πλεῖον ἐχαρίσατο = "[the one] whom he forgave more"

7:44 | σου εἰς τὴν οἰκίαν = εἰς τὴν οἰκίαν σου

7:45 | ἀφ' ἧς εἰσῆλθον (with ὥρας understood) = "from [the time] that I came in" (BDF §241(2))

7:47 | οὗ χάριν ... ὅτι = "for this reason ... [i.e.,] because" | The ὅτι clause is not connected with ἀφέωνται but with λέγω, and is not causal but inferential (BDAG ὅτι 4b). It is not that she is forgiven because of her acts of love for Jesus, but that her acts of love are the fruit of her being forgiven by him (cp. vv. 42–43, 47b). "I can say with confidence that her sins are forgiven, because her love is evidence of it" (M 147; cp. Z §422).

7:49 | ὃς καὶ ἁμαρτίας ἀφίησιν = "who *even* forgives sins"

7:50 | πορεύου εἰς εἰρήνην = "go in peace" (BDAG εἰς 9; BDF §206(1)) (cp. 8:48; Mk 5:34) (לְשָׁלוֹם → εἰς εἰρήνην, LXX Judges 18:6 [A text]; 1 Kgdms 1:17; 20:42)

Luke 8

8:1 | ἐν τῷ καθεξῆς = "soon afterward" (cp. 7:11) | κατὰ πόλιν καὶ κώμην = "from one town and village to another" (BDAG κατά B1d) (cp. v. 4; 13:22)

8:2 | αἳ ἦσαν τεθεραπευμέναι = "who had been healed," plupf. periphrastic (W 649) | τεθ. ἀπὸ πνευμάτων πονηρῶν καὶ ἀσθενειῶν

= "healed *of* evil spirits and of sicknesses" (cp. 13:11) | Substitution of another active verb (ἐξεληλύθει) for the usual pass. (ἐξεβέβλητο) (BDF §315) (cp. 4:41)

8:3 | τὰ ὑπάρχοντά τινι = "someone's property, possessions, means" (BDAG)

8:4 | κατὰ πόλιν = "from town after town" (cp. v. 1)

8:5 | τοῦ σπεῖραι = "to sow," final sense (BDF §400(5)) | ἐν τῷ σπείρειν αὐτόν = "as he was sowing" (BDF §404(1))

8:5–8 | ὃ μέν ... καὶ ἕτερον ... καὶ ἕτερον = "one [seed] ... and another [seed]," etc.

8:6 | διὰ τὸ μὴ ἔχειν = "on account of not having" (BDF §402(1))

8:9 | τίς αὕτη εἴη ἡ παραβολή = "what this parable might mean" (BDAG εἰμί 2cα – cp. v. 11) (on optative, see note at 1:29)

8:10 | ὑμῖν δέδοται γνῶναι = "to you it has been granted [by God] to know" | τοῖς λοιποῖς ἐν παραβολαῖς = "but to the rest [it is given] in parables"

8:11 | ἔστιν αὕτη ἡ παραβολή = "this is the meaning of the parable" (NIV) (BDAG εἰμί 2cα) (cp. v. 9)

8:12, 14 | οἱ ἀκούσαντες (2x) = "those who hear," substantival gnomic aorist ptc. used generically (W 615 n8)

8:12 | ἵνα μὴ πιστεύσαντες σωθῶσιν = "so that they may not believe and be saved"

8:13 | "Those [seeds which fell] on the rock [are] those who, when they hear, receive the word with joy; and [since] these have no root, they believe for a time and fall away in time of testing." | πρὸς καιρόν = "for a time" (BDAG καιρός 1a) (cp. 1 Cor 7:5)

8:14 | πορευόμενοι = "as they go on their way" (ESV) (see M 209) | ὑπό goes with συμπνίγονται = "are choked by"

8:14–15 | τὸ πεσόν = "that which fell" – note ellipsis in v. 15, τὸ [πεσόν] | τὸ πεσόν ... οὗτοί εἰσιν – shift from sg. to pl., *constructio ad sensum*

8:18 | καὶ ὃ δοκεῖ ἔχειν = "*even* what he thinks he has"

8:20 | ἰδεῖν θέλοντές σε = θέλοντες ἰδεῖν σε = "wanting to see you"

8:22 | ἐγένετο ... καὶ αὐτός – see 5:1 | ἐν μιᾷ τῶν ἡμερῶν = "on one of [those] days" | διέλθωμεν = "let us cross over," hortatory subj.

8:23 | πλεόντων αὐτῶν – gen. abs. | λαῖλαψ ἀνέμου = "a wind-storm," attributive gen. | συνεπληροῦντο = "they were being swamped"

8:25 | Epexegetical use of ὅτι (W 459–60) | καὶ τοῖς ἀνέμοις καὶ τῷ ὕδατι = "*even* the winds and the water" (BDF §444(3))

8:27 | ἐξελθόντι δὲ αὐτῷ ἐπὶ τὴν γῆν = "when Jesus stepped ashore" (NIV), ὑπαντάω takes dat. | χρόνῳ ἱκανῷ = "for a long time," dat. of time

8:28 | τί ἐμοὶ καὶ σοί – see possibilities at Matt 8:29 | δέομαι + gen. of person asked (cp. v. 38)

8:29 | πολλοῖς χρόνοις = "many a time" (ESV), "on many occasions" (M 43), dat. of time | ἐδεσμεύετο ... ἠλαύνετο = "he had been bound ... he would be driven," iterative pluperfective impfs. (W 549) | φυλασσόμενος = "being kept under guard" | Third καί = "and yet"

(BDAG καί 1bη) | ἠλαύνετο ... ἐρήμοις = "he [= the demoniac] would be driven by the demon into desolate places"

8:31 | παρεκάλουν αὐτόν = "they [= the demons] were imploring him [= Jesus]"

8:31–32 | Attenuated ἵνα (2x) for inf. after παρακαλέω (BDAG ἵνα 2aγ)

8:33 | κατά + gen. = "down" (BDAG A1a)

8:34–35 | τὸ γεγονός (2x) = "what had happened" (cp. v. 56; 24:12)

8:34 | εἰς (2x) = ἐν (Z §99)

8:35 | ἐξῆλθον ... ἦλθον ... εὗρον ... ἐφοβήθησαν – subject of these plurals is implied "people" from the town and surrounding countryside (vv. 34, 37) | καθήμενον ... παρὰ τοὺς πόδας τοῦ Ἰησοῦ = "sitting at Jesus' feet" (BDAG παρά C1c) (cp. v. 41; 7:38; 17:16) (cp. πρός, 10:39)

8:38 | ἐδεῖτο αὐτοῦ ... εἶναι σὺν αὐτῷ = "the man begged him [= Jesus] [to be allowed] to be with him [= Jesus]," δέομαι + gen. of person asked (cp. v. 28) + complementary inf. (BDF §392(1c)) | ἀπολύω = "send away"

8:39 | καθ' ὅλην τὴν πόλιν κηρύσσων = "proclaiming throughout the whole city" (ESV, NASB), "all over town" (NIV) (BDAG κατά B1a)

8:40 | ἐν τῷ ὑποστρέφειν τὸν Ἰησοῦν = "while Jesus was [lit. is] returning" (BDF §404(1); Z §390); acc. τὸν Ἰ. as subject of inf. (cp. v. 42) | ἦσαν προσδοκῶντες – impf. periphrastic; collective sg. subject (ὁ ὄχλος) with pl. verb (W 400–1)

8:41 | παρὰ τοὺς πόδας τινός – cp. v. 35

8:42 | θυγάτηρ μονογενὴς ἦν αὐτῷ = "he had an only begotten daughter," dat. of possession (cp. 7:12; 9:38) | ὡς with numerals = "about" | αὐτὴ ἀπέθνησκεν = "she was dying," progressive impf. (Z §273)

8:43 | οὖσα ἐν ῥύσει αἵματος = "having a flow of blood," sociative use of ἐν (BDF §§198(2); 219(4); Z §116) | ἀπὸ ἐτῶν δώδεκα = "for 12 years" (BDAG ἀπό 2bα) | ἀπ᾽ οὐδενός = "by no one," ἀπό = ὑπό (BDAG ἀπό 4eβ)

8:44–47 | Verbs of touching take gen. (4x)

8:44 | ἔστη = "stopped" (BDAG ἵστημι B1)

8:45 | ἀρνουμένων πάντων = "while they were all denying it" (NASB), gen. abs.

8:47 | τρέμουσα ἦλθεν = "she came trembling," ptc. of manner (W 627–8) | δι᾽ ἣν αἰτίαν ἥψατο αὐτοῦ ἀπήγγειλεν … ὡς ἰάθη = "she announced why she had touched him … and how she had been healed"

8:48 | εἰς εἰρήνην = "in peace" (BDAG εἰς 9) (cp. 7:50)

8:49 | ἔρχεται – historical present (M 7) | τις παρὰ τοῦ ἀρχισυναγώγου = "someone from [the house of] the synagogue leader" (Jairus himself is with Jesus) | ὅτι recitative

8:51 | τινα … εἰ μή = "anyone except"

8:53 | κατα-γελάω takes gen. object bec. of κατα- prefix (BDF §181)

8:54 | κρατέω + gen. has a note of tenderness, in contrast with κρατέω + acc. (cp. Matt 12:11; 28:9) which indicates grasping the whole of (W 132) | ἡ παῖς – nom. instead of voc. (BDF §147(3))

8:55 | αὐτῇ δοθῆναι φαγεῖν = "that [something] be given her to eat," taking φαγεῖν as equivalent to a substantive (BDF §§390(2); 409(2))

8:56 | ὁ = "he" (= Jesus), article as pronoun | τὸ γεγονός = "what had happened" (cp. vv. 34–35)

Luke 9

9:3 | εἰς τὴν ὁδόν = "for the journey" (BDAG ὁδός 2) | ἔχειν – imperatival inf. (M 126; BDF §389); "do not have two tunics"

9:4 | εἰς ἣν ἂν οἰκίαν εἰσέλθητε = "whatever house you enter" (cp. 10:5)

9:6 | κατὰ τὰς κώμας – see 8:1

9:7 | διὰ τὸ λέγεσθαι = "because it was said"

9:7–8 | ὑπό τινων ... ὑπό τινων ... ἄλλων = "by some ... by some ... [by] others"

9:10 | κατ᾽ ἰδίαν = "by himself"

9:11 | τοὺς χρείαν ἔχοντας θεραπείας = "those needing to be healed" (see 5:31)

9:12 | καὶ ἀγρούς goes with εἰς ("that they might go into the surrounding villages and farms")

9:13 | φαγεῖν = "[something] to eat," inf. equivalent to substantive (BDF §§390(2); 409(2)) (cp. Matt 25:35; Mk 5:43; 6:37) | πλεῖον ἤ = "more than" | εἰ μήτι = "unless perhaps" | εἰς πάντα τὸν λαόν = "for all these people," εἰς for dat. of advantage (BDAG εἰς 4g)

9:18 | ἐν τῷ εἶναι αὐτὸν προσευχόμενον = "while he was praying" | κατὰ μόνας = "alone" | τίνα με λέγουσιν οἱ ὄχλοι εἶναι; = "who do the crowds say that I am?" – interrogative pronoun τίνα is predicate; acc. με as subject of inf. (W 195 n71)

9:22 | ὅτι recitative | πολλὰ παθεῖν = "to suffer greatly," adv. acc. | ἀπό = ὑπό (BDAG ἀπό 4eβ; cp. 8:43)

9:23 | καθ᾽ ἡμέραν = "daily" (BDAG κατά B2c)

9:24, 26 | ὃς ἄν (3x) = "whoever"

9:25 | κερδήσας ... ἀπολέσας = "if he should gain ... but if he loses," adverbial ptc. equivalent to a condition (W 632)

9:27 | αὐτοῦ = "here," neut. gen. of αὐτός functioning as deictic adverb | Verbs of tasting take gen.

9:28 | μετὰ τοὺς λόγους τούτους ὡσεὶ ἡμέραι ὀκτώ = "about eight days after these sayings," rare use of nom. (ἡμέραι) for extent of time (BDF §144; W 64)

9:29 | ἐγένετο – not "and it came to pass" but "became": "The appearance of his face *became* different and his clothes [*became*] white."

9:31 | μέλλω + inf. = "be about to" (here impf.)

9:32 | ἦσαν βεβαρημένοι ὕπνῳ = "they had become heavy with sleep," plupf. periphrastic (W 649) (cp. v. 45)

9:33 | ποιήσωμεν = "let us make," hortatory subj.

9:36 | "And they kept silent and reported to no one in those days any of the things which they had seen" (NASB) ("in those days," in contrast with the time after Jesus' ascension, when the apostles did proclaim these events) | οὐδὲν ὧν = οὐδὲν τούτων ἅ = "none of the things which," relative pronoun assimilated to the case of the omitted demonstrative (BDF §294(4))

9:37 | ἐν τῇ ἑξῆς ἡμέρᾳ = "on the next day"

9:38, 40 | δέομαι (deponent) takes gen.

9:38 | μονογενής μοί = "my only begotten [son]," dat. of possession (cp. 7:12; 8:42), connotation, "precious to me"

9:39 | μετὰ ἀφροῦ = lit. "with foaming," i.e., "so that he foams at the mouth" (ESV)

9:41 | ἕως πότε; = "how long?" | πρός + acc. = "with" | ἀνέχομαι takes gen.

9:42 | ἔτι προσερχομένου αὐτοῦ = "even while the boy was coming" (NIV), gen. abs.

9:43 | BDAG ἐπί 6c (2x)

9:44 | μέλλω + present pass. inf. = "is about to be" (ESV), "is going to be" (NASB)

9:45 | ἦν παρακεκαλυμμένον = "it had been concealed," plupf. periphrastic (cp. v. 32)

9:46 | τό changes direct question into indirect (BDAG ὁ 2hα) (see 1:62) | εἴη – for options re. optative, see 1:29

9:49 | ἐκωλύομεν = "we tried to stop," conative impf. (W 550–1)

9:51 | ἐγένετο ... καὶ αὐτός = "it came to pass ... *that* he" (see 5:1)

9:52 | ἄγγελος = "a human messenger serving as an envoy" (BDAG ἄγγελος 1) | ὡς ἑτοιμάσαι αὐτῷ = "to make preparations for him," rare construction in NT (M 138 n1; BDF §391(1); BDAG ὡς 9b) (cp. Acts 20:24); but see textual variant ὥστε

9:53 | Lit. "for his face was proceeding to Jerusalem" (cp. LXX 2 Kgdms 17:11)

9:54 | θέλεις εἴπωμεν = "do you want us to command?" deliberative subj. introduced by θέλεις (ZG; BDF §366(3)) (cp. 18:41)

9:57 | ὅπου ἐάν = "wherever"

9:58, 62 | "his head," "his hand," article as possessive pronoun

9:61 | τοῖς εἰς τὸν οἶκόν μου = "to those in my household," εἰς = ἐν (Z §100)

Luke 10
10:1 | ἀνὰ δύο = "two by two" | μέλλω + inf. – see 9:31

10:2 | μέν ... δέ = "on the one hand ... on the other hand"

10:4 | κατὰ τὴν ὁδόν = "on the way"

10:5 | εἰς ἣν ἂν εἰσέλθητε οἰκίαν = εἰς ἣν οἰκίαν ἂν εἰσέλθητε = "whatever house you enter" (cp. vv. 8, 10; 9:4)

10:6 | ἡ εἰρήνη ὑμῶν = "your [blessing of] peace" (cp. Matt 10:13 NASB)

10:7 | τὰ παρ' αὐτῶν = "what they give you" (NASB) – see BDAG παρά A3bβ

10:11 | ὑμῖν = "against you," dat. of disadvantage

10:12, 14 | τινι ἀνεκτότερον ἢ τινι = "more bearable for x than for y"

10:17 | καὶ τὰ δαιμόνια = "even the demons"

10:17, 20 | Neut. pl. subjects (τὰ δαιμόνια, τὰ πνεύματα & τὰ ὀνόματα) take sg. verbs (ὑποτάσσεται [2x] & ἐγγέγραπται)

10:18 | ἐθεώρουν τὸν Σατανᾶν ... πεσόντα = "I saw [constantly or repeatedly] Satan's fall," taking as aorist ptc. πεσόντα as global, "embracing the whole process of the defeat of Satan from the fall of Lucifer throughout the whole history of salvation to the full and final victory in the Last Judgment" (Z §269).

10:19 | ἐξουσίαν τοῦ πατεῖν = "authority to trample," pleonastic τοῦ prefixed to inf. (BDF §400(7); Z §386) | οὐδέν – subject of ἀδικήσῃ = "nothing will ever harm you," double negatives reinforce (BDF §431(3))

10:21 | πάτερ, κύριε – vocs. | ὁ πατήρ – nom. for voc. | ἔμπροσθέν σου = "to you," reverential (BDAG ἔμπροσθεν 1bδ) (cp. Matt 11:26)

10:22 | ᾧ ἐάν + subj. = lit. "to whomever," i.e., "anyone to whom" (cp. Matt 11:27), relative clause functioning as subject; ἐάν for ἄν (BDF §107; BDAG ἐάν 3)

10:23 | κατ᾽ ἰδίαν = "privately"

10:25 | νομικός τις = "a lawyer," adjectival use of indef. pronoun (W 347) (cp. vv. 30, 31, 33) | ἐκπειράζων = "to test," telic ptc. (W 637) | ποιήσας – adverbial ptc. expressing a condition: "what, if I do it, will I inherit eternal life" (cp. ὁ ποιήσας, Rom 10:5; Gal 3:12)

10:27 | ἀγαπήσεις – imperatival future (see 4:8, 12)

10:29 | θέλων = "because he wished," causal ptc. (M 102) | καὶ τίς; = "who then?" (BDAG καί 1bθ) (cp. 18:26)

10:30 | λῃσταῖς περιέπεσεν = "fell into the hands of robbers," dat. of destination (cp. ἐμπίπτω εἰς + acc., v. 36) | οἳ καί = "who also"

10:31 | κατὰ συγκυρίαν = "by chance"

10:32–33 | ἐλθεῖν κατά (2x) = "to come up to/upon" (BDAG κατά B1b)

10:34–35 | ἐπιμελέομαι (2x) takes gen. object

10:35 | ἐκβαλὼν ἔδωκεν = "he took out two denarii and gave them" (δύο δηνάρια does double duty as object of both verbs) | ὅ τι ἂν προσδαπανήσῃς … σοι = "whatever more you spend, when I return I will repay you"

10:36 | "Which of these three do you think *proved to be* [BDAG γίνομαι 7] a neighbor to the man who fell into the robbers' [hands]?" (NASB) | ὁ πλησίον (= "neighbor") is indeclinable; gen. pl. = τῶν πλησίον

10:37 | ποιέω ἔλεος μετά τινος = "show mercy to one" (Septuagintism)

10:39 | τῇδε ἦν = "she had," dat. of possession | πρὸς τοὺς πόδας τοῦ κυρίου = "at the Lord's feet" (cp. παρά 8:35)

10:40 | οὐ μέλει σοι; = lit. "isn't it a care to you?" (impersonal), i.e., "don't you care?" | μόνην με κατέλιπεν = "has left me alone," μόνην is fem. in agreement with the referent of με (= Martha) | εἰπὲ αὐτῇ ἵνα = "tell her to" (BDAG λέγω 2c)

Luke 11
11:1 | ὡς + aorist = "when, after" (BDAG ὡς 8a)

11:2 | πάτερ – voc.

11:3 | ἐπιούσιος – see options at Matt 6:11 | τὸ καθ' ἡμέραν = "each day," adv. acc., with meaningless article (BDF §160)

11:4 | καὶ γὰρ αὐτοί = "for we ourselves also"

11:5 | τίς ἐξ ὑμῶν; = "which of you?" ἐξ for partitive gen. after interrogative pronoun (BDAG ἐκ 4aβ; BDF §164) (cp. v. 11) | μεσονυκτίου (< μέσος + νύξ) = "at midnight," gen. of time (W 122)

11:5, 7 | εἴπῃ (2x) – hypothetical or parabolic subj. (M 23)

11:6 | ἐξ ὁδοῦ = "on a journey"

11:7 | κἀκεῖνος = καὶ ἐκεῖνος | κόπους παρέχω τινί = "cause someone trouble," "bother someone" | εἰς = ἐν (BDF §205; Z §100) | τὰ παιδία ... εἰσίν – rule that neut. pl. nouns take sg. verbs is often not followed where the noun designates persons (BDF §133(1))

11:8 | εἰ καί = "even though" (BDAG εἰ 6e; W 663; M 167) (cp. 18:4) | ἀναστάς is attendant circumstance ptc. denoting action logically prior to δώσει, "even though he will not get up and give him," cp. more proper order in v. 7 (ἀναστὰς δοῦναι) and in next clause (ἐγερθεὶς δώσει) | διὰ τὸ εἶναι φίλον αὐτοῦ = "because he is his friend" | διά γε τὴν ἀναίδειαν αὐτοῦ = either (1) "to avoid the shame-lessness that will be attributed to him if he does not help," taking the referent of αὐτοῦ as the already-in-bed neighbor (Green 448 n46); or (2) more naturally, "yet because of his impudence," taking the clause as referring to the shamelessness of the at-the-door neighbor (see BDAG ἀναίδεια) | ὅσων [gen. pl. of ὅσος] χρήζει = "as much as he needs"

11:11 | Lit. "Which father among you will his son ask for a fish, and will he give him a snake instead of a fish?" (mixing of constructions)

11:13 | πονηροὶ ὑπάρχοντες = "though being evil," concessive ptc.

11:14 | ἦν ἐκβάλλων – impf. periphrastic | ἐγένετο + aorist gen. abs. + indic. = "it came to pass, when the demon had gone out, that the mute man spoke"

11:15, 18, 19, 20 | Hebr./instrumental ἐν (5x) (cp. Matt 12:24; Mk 3:22)

11:15–16 | τινὲς δὲ ἐξ αὐτῶν ... ἕτεροι δέ = "some of them ... while others"

11:16 | πειράζοντες – telic ptc.; direct object is an implied αὐτόν ("him"), not σημεῖον (which goes with ἐζήτουν)

11:17 | αὐτῶν τὰ διανοήματα = τὰ διανοήματα αὐτῶν

11:18 | εἰ δὲ καὶ Σατανᾶς = "if Satan *also*" | Indirect discourse: λέγω + inf. + acc. με as subject of inf. – "For you say that I cast out demons by Beelzebul"

11:19 | ὑμῶν κριταί = "your judges," objective gen. (W 116)

11:21 | ἐν εἰρήνῃ ἐστὶν τὰ ὑπάρχοντα αὐτοῦ = "his possessions are safe" (NIV), "undisturbed" (NASB), neut. pl. subjects take sg. verbs

11:22 | ἐπάν (< ἐπεὶ ἄν) + subj. = "when" (cp. v. 34) (BDF §455(1)) | ἰσχυρότερος αὐτοῦ = "someone stronger than he," anarthrous substantival (W 294) comparative adj. + gen. of comparison (cp. 14:8)

11:24 | ὅταν + subj. = "when" (cp. v. 34)

11:26 | ἑαυτοῦ (= "than itself") & τῶν πρώτων (= "than the first"), gens. of comparison | γίνεται τὰ ἔσχατα – neut. pl. subjects take sg. verbs | τὰ ἔσχατα ... τῶν πρώτων = "the last state ... the first state"

11:27 | ἐγένετο ... = "it came to pass, as he was saying these things, that ..." | Acc. αὐτόν as subject of inf. | ἐπαίρω φωνήν = "raise one's voice" | τις γυνὴ ἐκ τοῦ ὄχλου = "a certain woman from the crowd," ἐκ for partitive gen. | μαστοὶ οὓς ἐθήλασας = "the breasts you have sucked" (BDAG θηλάζω 2)

11:28 | μενοῦν μακάριοι = "blessed rather [are]," adjective μακάριοι in first predicate position followed by articular noun (W 307)

11:29 | τῶν ὄχλων ἐπαθροιζομένων = "as the crowds were increasing" (NASB), gen. abs.

11:31–32 | ἐν τῇ κρίσει (2x) = "at the judgment" | πλεῖον + gen. of comparison (2x) = "something greater than"

11:32 | μετανοέω εἰς = "repent at, in the face of" (BDAG εἰς 10a) (cp. Matt 12:41)

11:34 | ὁ λύχνος ... ὁ ὀφθαλμός σου = "your eye is the lamp of the body" (ESV) | ἁπλοῦς = "single, without guile, sincere, straightforward" (BDAG), *simplex* (Vulgate); opposite of διπλοῦς = "twofold" (LSJ) | ὅταν (see v. 24) & ἐπάν (see v. 22) + apodotic καί (2x; BDAG καί 1bδ; Z §457)

11:36 | μὴ ἔχον μέρος τι σκοτεινόν = "with no dark part" | ὡς ὅταν = "as when" | τῇ ἀστραπῇ = "with its flash/ray of light," dat. of means (W 162)

11:38 | βαπτίζω = "wash ceremonially for purpose of purification" (BDAG βαπτίζω 1)

11:39 | Verbs of filling take gen.

11:40 | "Did not he who made the outside make the inside also?" (NASB)

11:41 | "But give that which is within as charity" (NASB)

11:42 | ἡ ἀγάπη τοῦ θεοῦ = "love for God," objective gen. (W 118) | κἀκεῖνα = καὶ ἐκεῖνα

11:44 | ἐστὲ ὡς = "you are like" | οἱ ἄνθρωποι [οἱ] περιπατοῦντες ἐπάνω οὐκ οἴδασιν = "the people who walk over [them] are unaware [of it]" (NASB)

11:45 | ταῦτα λέγων καὶ ἡμᾶς ὑβρίζεις = "in saying these things you insult us *as well*" (cp. καὶ ὑμῖν, v. 46), ptc. of means

11:46 | καὶ αὐτοί = "while you yourselves" (NASB) | ἑνί + gen. = "with one of," dat. of means | προσψαύω + dat. = "touch something"

11:49 | ἐξ αὐτῶν = "[some] of them," partitive ἐκ functioning as object (BDAG ἐκ 4aγ; BDF §164(2))

11:50–51 | ἐκζητέω ἀπό τινος (cp. LXX Gen 9:5; 42:22; 2 Kgdms 4:11; Ps 9:12; Ezek 3:18, 20); "this generation will be held responsible for the blood of all the prophets" (NIV)

11:52 | τοὺς εἰσερχομένους = "those who would enter," present ptc. for conative impf. (BDF §339(3)) (cp. Matt 23:13)

11:53 | κἀκεῖθεν = καὶ ἐκεῖθεν = "and from there" | δεινῶς ἐνέχειν = "to be very hostile" (BDAG), "to oppose him fiercely" (NIV) | ἀποστοματίζειν αὐτὸν περὶ πλειόνων = either (1) "to interrogate him concerning many subjects," "to besiege him with questions" (NIV), or (2) "to provoke him to speak about many things" (ESV; cp. BDAG ἀποστοματίζω)

11:54 | θηρεῦσαί τι ἐκ τοῦ στόματος αὐτοῦ = lit. "to catch something out of his mouth," i.e., "to catch him in something he might say" (BDAG θηρεύω)

Luke 12
12:1 | ἐν οἷς = "under these circumstances" (NASB; BDAG ὅς 1kγ), "at which juncture" (M 76, 197) | ἐπισυναχθεισῶν ... ὥστε ... = "when many thousands of the crowd had gathered together (gen. abs.)

with the result that they were stepping on one another" (BDAG ὥστε 2aβ) | πρῶτον (adv.) – Jesus spoke "first" to his disciples, then to all the people (vv. 15, 41, 54) | προσέχειν ἑαυτῷ ἀπό + gen. = "to be on one's guard against" (cp. 20:46; 21:34); ἀπὸ τῆς ζύμης ... τῶν Φαρισαίων = "against the leaven of the Pharisees"

12:3 | ἀνθ' ὧν = "therefore" (ESV; BDAG ἀντί 5)

12:4 | μὴ ἐχόντων περισσότερόν τι ποιῆσαι = "are unable to do anything further," ἔχω + inf. = "be able to" (BDAG ἔχω 5)

12:5 | μετὰ τὸ ἀποκτεῖναι = "after killing" (BDF §402(3)) | τόν ... ἔχοντα ἐξουσίαν + inf. = "the one having authority to" (BDF §393(5))

12:6 | ἀσσαρίων δύο – gen. of price

12:7 | ἀλλὰ καί = "but also" (BDAG ἀλλά 3) | πολλῶν στρουθίων – gen. of comparison

12:8 | πᾶς ὃς ἄν = "everyone who" | ὁμολογέω ἐν τινι (2x) = "confess or acknowledge someone" (Semitism; BDF §220; M 183)

12:9 | ὁ ἀρνησάμενος = "the one who denies," substantival gnomic aorist ptc. used generically (W 615 n8)

12:10 | Hostile εἰς (2x) = "against" (BDAG εἰς 4cα)

12:11 | ἐπί + acc. = "before," marker of legal proceeding (BDAG ἐπί 10)

12:12 | ἐν αὐτῇ τῇ ὥρᾳ = "in that same (very) hour" (M 93, 122) | ἃ δεῖ εἰπεῖν = "what you ought to say"

12:15 | οὐκ ἐν τῷ περισσεύειν ... αὐτῷ = "one's life does not consist in the abundance of his possessions" (ESV), αὐτῷ as dat. of possession

12:19 | ψυχή (2x) = "self" (M 185; BDAG ψυχή 2g): "I'll say to my-self" (NIV)

12:20 | ἀπαιτοῦσιν = "they will demand," indef. pl. subject as periph-rasis for God and/or his angels (BDF §130(1–2); Z §2) (cp. v. 48; 6:38) | τίνι ἔσται; = "who will get?" (NIV), dat. of possession | Neut. pl. subjects (ἅ) take sg. verbs (ἔσται)

12:21 | οὕτως = "this is how it is for"

12:22 | τῇ ψυχῇ ... τῷ σώματι = "for your life ... for your body," dats. of advantage (BDF §188)

12:23 | πλεῖον + gen. of comparison = "more than"

12:24 | οἷς οὐκ ἔστιν = "they do not have," dat. of possession

12:24, 27 | "Consider the x, that/how they ...," prolepsis (BDF §476)

12:26 | "So if you are not capable of even the smallest thing, why do you worry about the rest?" (BDAG δύναμαι c)

12:27 | οὐδέ = "not even"

12:28 | ἐν ἀγρῷ τὸν χόρτον ... βαλλόμενον – whole phrase is object of ἀμφιάζει

12:30 | ὑμῶν ὁ πατήρ = ὁ πατὴρ ὑμῶν (cp. v. 32) = "your Father" | χρῄζω takes gen. object (τούτων)

12:32 | εὐδόκησεν = "has determined/resolved/willed" (BDAG εὐδοκέω 1)

12:33 | σής, ἡ = "moth" (here as larvae) (cp. Matt 6:19–20)

12:35 | "Let your loins be girded and [your] lamps burning"

12:36 | Repeat main verb from v. 35 (ἔστωσαν): "Be like men" | γάμοι (pl.) = "wedding feast" (BDF §141(3); BDAG γάμος 1a) (cp. 14:8) | ἐλθόντος καὶ κρούσαντος – gen. abs.

12:37 | Translate ἐλθών last: "whom the master finds awake *when he comes*" (cp. v. 43) | ἀνακλίνω is transitive – "cause someone to recline for a meal"

12:38 | κἄν (2x) = καὶ ἐάν = "whether" | εὕρῃ οὕτως = "finds them so," i.e., awake (cp. v. 37: εὑρήσει γρηγοροῦντας)

12:40 | ᾗ ὥρᾳ ... ἔρχεται = "is coming at an hour that you do not suppose," incorporation of the antecedent in the relative clause (BDF §294(5))

12:41 | ἢ καὶ πρὸς πάντας = "or to everyone as well"

12:42 | τοῦ διδόναι = "to give," gen. of articular inf. in final sense (BDF §400)

12:43 | ἐλθών = "when he comes" (cp. v. 37)

12:44 | BDAG ἐπί 9b

12:47–48 | δαρήσεται πολλάς/ὀλίγας [sc. πληγάς – BDF §154] = "he will be beaten with many/few [blows]," retention of acc. with pass. (M 32–33)

12:47 | πρὸς τὸ θέλημα = "in accordance with the will" (BDAG πρός 3εδ)

12:48a | ὁ δὲ μὴ γνούς – ellipsis; supply τὸ θέλημα τοῦ κυρίου αὐτοῦ from v. 47 | ποιήσας ἄξια πληγῶν = "committed deeds worthy of a flogging" (NASB)

12:48b | αὐτοῦ & αὐτόν – Semitic pleonastic personal pronouns (M 176; BDF §297) and anacolutha after πᾶς (BDF §466(3)) | αἰτήσουσιν = "they will demand," indef. pl. subject as periphrasis for God and/or his angels (cp. v. 20)

12:49 | τί θέλω εἰ ἤδη ἀνήφθη = "how I wish it were already kindled!" (NASB; NIV; BDF §§299(4), 360(4)); BDAG τίς, τί 3. See discussion of this difficult clause in Z §405; M 137, 187; Black 123.

12:50 | ἕως ὅτου + subj. = "until" (cp. 13:8)

12:51 | ἀλλ᾽ ἤ = "but rather"

12:52 | ἔσονται διαμεμερισμένοι = "will be divided," future perf. periphrastic (W 647–9; BDF §352) (cp. Matt 16:19; 18:18; Heb 2:13) | ἀπὸ τοῦ νῦν = "from now on"

12:52–53 | BDAG ἐπί 12a (8x)

12:53 | "They will be divided, father against son," etc.

12:54 | ἐπὶ δυσμῶν = "in the west" (BDAG δυσμή), pl. for the four directions (BDF §141(2); cp. 13:29)

12:56 | πῶς; = "how is it that?" (NIV) (BDAG πῶς 1aβ)

12:57 | "Why don't you judge for yourselves what is right?" (NIV)

12:58 | ὡς = "while, as" | ἐπ᾽ ἄρχοντα = "before the magistrate" (BDAG ἐπί 10) | δὸς ἐργασίαν + inf. = "make an effort to" (Latinism: *da operam*) (M 192; BDF §5(3)(b)) | ἀπολλάσσω ἀπό τινος = "settle the matter with someone" | μήποτε + subj. = "lest"

Luke 13

13:1 | ἐν αὐτῷ τῷ καιρῷ = "at that very time" | ὧν τὸ αἷμα = "whose blood"

13:2 | First ὅτι = "that," second ὅτι = "because"

13:2, 4 | παρά + acc. (2x) = "worse/more than"

13:2, 5 | ἐὰν μή = "unless"

13:6 | συκῆν εἶχέν τις πεφυτευμένην = "a man had a fig tree which had been planted" (not periphrastic, *pace* Dana-Mantey as quoted W 647)

13:7 | ἰδοὺ τρία ἔτη = "behold, [it has been] three years," supply copula | ἀφ' οὗ = "since" (BDAG ἀπό 2bγ) | ἔρχομαι & εὑρίσκω = "I have been coming ... and I have not found [any]," extending-from-past presents (W 519–20; M 8; BDF §322) (cp. 15:29) | ζητῶν = "seeking," telic ptc. (W 637) | ἱνατί καί; = "why at all?" καί after interrogative (Z §459; BDF §442(14))

13:8 | καὶ τοῦτο τὸ ἔτος = "for this year too" (NASB), "for one more year" (NIV), acc. for extent of time | ἕως ὅτου + subj. = "until" (cp. 12:50)

13:9 | κἄν = καὶ ἐάν = "and if" | εἰς τὸ μέλλον = "in the coming [year]" or "in the future" (M 68) | Suppression of the first apodosis (BDF §454(4)): "and if it bears fruit next year, [fine]; but if not, cut it down" (NASB)

13:10–11 | ἦν διδάσκων & ἦν συγκύπτουσα – impf. periphrastics

13:10 | ἐν τοῖς σάββασιν = "on the Sabbath," Hebr. pl.

13:11 | Supply ἦν after ἰδού | πνεῦμα ἀσθενείας = "a disabling spirit" (ESV), a spirit which produces ἀσθενεία (cp. 8:2), gen. of product (W 106) | ἔτη δεκαοκτώ – acc. for extent of time | εἰς τὸ παντελές – either (1) goes with ἀνακῦψαι, "could not *fully* straighten herself" (ESV), or (2) goes with μὴ δυναμένη, "could not straighten up *at all*" (NASB) (see BDAG παντελής 1a/b)

13:12 | γύναι – voc. | ἀπολέλυσαι = "you are set free of," intensive or resultative perfect (W 574–6) (cp. 5:20); takes gen. bec. of ἀπο- prefix (M 90)

13:13 | τὰς χεῖρας = "his hands," article for possessive pronoun (W 215)

13:14–15 | τῷ σαββάτῳ (2x) = "on the Sabbath," dat. of time (W 155–7)

13:16 | ταύτην ... οὐκ ἔδει λυθῆναι = "should not this woman ... be set free?" (NIV) | ἰδοὺ δέκα καὶ ὀκτὼ ἔτη – could be acc. for extent of time, but with Semitic interjection (M 183), probably parenthetical nom. (BDF §144): "... whom Satan hath bound, lo, these eighteen years" (KJV)

13:17 | "and the entire crowd was rejoicing over all the glorious things being done by him" (NASB) (BDAG γίνομαι 2a)

13:19 | γίνομαι εἰς – Semitic εἰς for predicate nom., common LXX construction (BDAG εἰς 8aα)

13:21 | εἰς = ἐν | ἕως οὗ = "until"

13:22 | κατὰ πόλεις καὶ κώμας = "from one city and village to another" (NASB) (see 8:1) | πορείαν ποιεῖσθαι = "to journey," periphrasis for πορεύεσθαι (BDAG ποιέω 7a)

13:23 | εἰ – marker of question: "Are there few who are being saved?" (BDAG εἰ 5)

13:25 | ἀφ᾽ οὗ = "when once" (cp. v. 7) | Fourth καί = Semitic marker of apodosis ("*then* he will answer you ...") (Z §457; BDF §442(7); BDAG καί 1bδ)

13:25, 27 | οὐκ οἶδα ὑμᾶς πόθεν ἐστέ – prolepsis (BDF §476(2))

13:30 | εἰσὶν ἔσχατοι/πρῶτοι = "there are last/first ones"

13:32 | πορευθέντες εἴπατε = "go and tell," attendant circumstances ptc. (W 640) | ἐκβάλλω ... ἀποτελῶ ... τελειοῦμαι – futuristic presents (M 7; W 537)

13:32, 33 | τῇ τρίτῃ & τῇ ἐχομένῃ = "the third [day]" & "the next [day]"

13:34 | ὃν τρόπον = "in the manner in which," "just as," adv. acc. (BDF §160)

13:35 | ἥξει ὅτε = "[the time] comes when"

Luke 14

14:1 | καὶ ἐγένετο ... καί = "and it came to pass ... *that*" (Z §389) | ἐν τῷ ἐλθεῖν ... = "when he went into the house of one of the leaders of the Pharisees ... to eat bread" (NASB) (Z §390) | σαββάτῳ = "on the Sabbath" (cp. v. 3; see 13:14–15)

14:5 | "Which one of you has a son or an ox that falls into a well ...?" | υἱὸς ἢ βοῦς – "because the collocation of the two words appeared to be somewhat incongruous, copyists altered υἱός either to ὄνος or to πρόβατον" (Metzger)

14:8 | γάμοι (pl.) = "wedding feast" (see 12:36) | ἐντιμότερός σου = "someone more distinguished than you," anarthrous substantival comparative adj. + gen. of comparison (cp. 11:22) | μήποτε + subj. = "lest" (cp. v. 12) | ᾖ κεκλημένος – subj. perfect periphrastic (W 649) | "lest someone more distinguished than you has been invited by him"

14:9 | ὁ σὲ καὶ αὐτὸν καλέσας = "he who invited [both] you and him"

14:10 | ὁ κεκληκώς = "the one who has invited you" (NASB), "your host" (ESV) | ἵνα + future indicative (ἐρεῖ) (M 23; Z §340; BDF §369(2))

14:11 | πᾶς ὁ = "everyone who"

14:12, 13, 16 | ποιέω + dinner/banquet (3x) = "give" (BDAG ποιέω 2f)

14:12 | μήποτε καὶ αὐτοὶ ἀντικαλέσωσίν σε = "lest they *also* invite you in return" (ESV) | γένηται σοι = "you may receive" (BDAG γίνομαι 4bγ), dat. of advantage

14:14 | οὐκ ἔχουσιν + inf. = "they cannot" (BDAG ἔχω 5)

14:15 | ὅστις = "everyone who" (cp. v. 27)

14:17 | ἤδη ἕτοιμά ἐστιν = "[all things] are now ready," supplying πάντα (as many MSS do; cp. Matt 22:4); neut. pl. subjects take sg. verbs

14:18 | ἀπὸ μιᾶς (adv.) = "unanimously, alike" (BDAG ἀπό 6); the noun to be supplied is unclear (BDF §241(6)), probably "with one voice" | ἔχω ἀνάγκην + inf. = "I must"

14:18–19 | ἔχε με παρῃτημένον (2x) = "consider me excused" (NASB; BDAG ἔχω 6)

14:20 | διὰ τοῦτο = "for this reason," retrospective *conceptual* antecedent (W 333), referring to the man's newlywed status

14:22 | γέγονεν ὃ ἐπέταξας = "what you ordered has been done"

14:24 | γεύομαι + partitive gen. of thing tasted (BDF §169(3))

14:26 | εἴ τις ἔρχεται πρός με = "if anyone comes to me," general first class condition (W 706) | ἔτι τε καί = "furthermore" (BDAG), "yes, and even" (NASB)

14:28 | τίς ἐξ ὑμῶν; = "which of you?" (cp. v. 33; 15:4) | εἰ ἔχει εἰς ἀπαρτισμόν = "if he has [enough] to complete it"

14:29 | ἵνα μήποτε = "lest," a strengthened form of ἵνα μή (Marshall) | θέντος ... ἰσχύοντος – gen. abs. (cp. v. 32)

14:31 | ἐν = "along with" (BDAG ἐν 5aα; M 78)

14:32 | ἐρωτάω τὰ πρὸς εἰρήνην = "ask for terms of peace" (BDAG εἰρήνη 1a); on τὰ πρός, see M 106; BDAG πρός 3eβ (cp. 19:42)

14:33 | πᾶς ἐξ ὑμῶν = "any one of you" (cp. v. 28) | ἀποτάσσω usually takes dat. of personal object, "say farewell to, take leave of" someone; here figuratively with dat. of impersonal object: "Any one of you who does not say farewell to all his possessions cannot be my disciple."

14:34 | ἐὰν δὲ καὶ τὸ ἅλας = "but if *even* the salt" | μωραίνω normally means "make foolish" but here context requires "make tasteless" (see note at Matt 5:13) | Of course, salt itself cannot become tasteless, but the impure salt-rock that contains the salt can | ἐν τίνι; = "with what?"

14:35 | εὔθετος εἰς – either (1) "fit for" (BDAG εἰς 4g), or (2) "fit [to be thrown] into," pregnant construction (BDAG εἰς 10d) (see BDAG εὔθετος)

Luke 15
15:1 | ἦσαν ἐγγίζοντες – impf. periphrastic | ἀκούω + gen. of person heard

15:2 | ὅτι recitative

15:4 | τίς ἄνθρωπος ἐξ ὑμῶν; = "which man of you?" (cp. 14:28) | ἐξ αὐτῶν ἕν = "one of them" | πορεύομαι ἐπί + acc. = "go after" (BDAG ἐπί 4bα)

15:7 | χαρὰ ἔσται ... ἤ = "there will be [more] joy over one sinner who repents *than* over 99 righteous" (BDAG ἤ 2bα) | οἵτινες οὐ χρείαν ἔχουσιν μετανοίας = "who do not need to repent" (NIV) (see 5:31)

15:8 | τίς γυνή ... οὐχί; = "what woman does not?" | δραχμὰς ἔχουσα δέκα = "having ten drachmas" | ἕως οὗ + subj. = "until"

15:10 | χαρὰ ἐνώπιον + gen. = either (1) "joy among" (ZG; BDAG ἐνώπιον 2b), or (2) "cause for joy in the eyes of" (BDAG χαρά 2; BDF §214(6))

15:12 | ὁ νεώτερος αὐτῶν = "the younger of them," comparative of νέος + partitive gen. | τὸ ἐπιβάλλον μέρος τῆς οὐσίας = "the share of the estate that falls to me" (NASB)

15:12, 18, 21 | πάτερ (3x) – voc.

15:13 | μετ᾽ οὐ πολλὰς ἡμέρας = "not many days later" (BDAG μετά B2a; πολύς 1aα) (cp. Acts 1:5) | ζῶν ἀσώτως = "in reckless living" (ESV), ptc. of means; as the older son says in v. 30, the younger son is guilty of both *moral* recklessness, living with "reckless abandon, debauchery" (BDAG ἀσωτία), and *financial* recklessness, "the verb σῴζω refers to preservation, hence ἀσωτία generally denotes 'wastefulness'" (BDAG ἀσωτία), hence "wastefully, prodigally" (BDAG ἀσώτως)

15:14 | δαπανήσαντος αὐτοῦ πάντα = "after he had spent everything," gen. abs. | κατὰ τὴν χώραν ἐκείνην = "throughout that region" (BDAG κατά B1a)

15:16 | χορτασθῆναι ἐκ = "to be satisfied with" (BDAG ἐκ 4aζ)

15:17 | ἔρχομαι εἰς ἐαυτόν = "come to one's senses" | περισσεύομαι + gen. = "have an abundance of something" | λιμῷ = "because of a famine," dat. of cause (W 168)

15:22 | πρῶτος = "special" (BDAG πρῶτος 2aα), "best" (NASB)

15:23 | φαγόντες εὐφρανθῶμεν = "let's eat and celebrate," attendant circumstances ptc. + hortatory subj.

15:24 | ἦν ἀπολωλώς = "had been lost," plupf. periphrastic (W 649)

15:25 | ὡς ἐρχόμενος ἤγγισεν τῇ οἰκίᾳ = "as he approached the house," graphic ptc., implicit in the main verb (ZG; Z §363); dat. of destination (W 147)

15:26 | τί ἂν εἴη ταῦτα = "what these things could mean," potential optative (ZG; Z §356; BDAG εἰμί 2cα)

15:27 | First ὅτι is recitative; second ὅτι is causal (BDAG ὅτι 4a) | ὅτι ὑγιαίνοντα αὐτὸν ἀπέλαβεν = "because he has gotten him back safe and sound" (BDAG ἀπολαμβάνω 2)

15:29 | τοσαῦτα ἔτη = "all these years" (NIV), acc. for extent of time | δουλεύω = "I have been serving," extending-from-past present (W 519–20; M 8; BDF §322) (cp. 13:7)

15:32 | ἔζησεν = "came to life," ingressive aorist (M 10; W 558–9)

Luke 16

16:1 | οὗτος διεβλήθη αὐτῷ = "this man [= the manager] was the subject of a complaint made to him [= the rich man, the manager's boss]" (on deictic pronoun, see BDF §290(1)) | ὡς + present ptc. = "as one who" (BDAG ὡς 3aγ; BDF §425(3)) (cp. 23:14)

16:2 | οὐ δύνῃ ἔτι + inf. = "you can no longer" (BDAG ἔτι 1bβ)

16:3 | ποιήσω – deliberative subj. | ὅτι = "seeing that, now that" (ZG)

16:4 | ἔγνων τί ποιήσω = "I know what I'll do," immediate past aorist (W 565; M 7, 11) | ἵνα ... δέξωνταί με = "so that ... [people] may receive me"

16:5 | ἕνα ἕκαστον + gen. = "each one of" (NIV, NASB)

16:6–7 | σου τὰ γράμματα = τὰ γράμματα σου = "your promissory note, bill"

16:8 | εἰς τὴν γενεάν = "in relation to their own kind" (BDAG εἰς 5; γενεά 1); this usage of γενεά may help explain Matt 24:34 ‖ Mk 13:30 ‖ Lk 21:32

16:8–9 | τῆς ἀδικίας (2x) (cp. 18:6) = "dishonest" (v. 8), "unrighteous" (v. 9), Hebr. attributive gen. (W 86–88)

16:9 | ἐκ + gen. = "by means of" (BDAG ἐκ 3f) | δέξωνται = "they may receive," possibly indef. pl. subject to avoid the divine name (BDF §130(1–2); Z §§2, 236) (cp. 6:38; 12:20, 48)

16:11–12 | τίς; (2x) = "who?"

16:11 | πιστεύω τινί τι = "entrust someone with something" (BDAG πιστεύω 3)

16:13 | ἤ ... ἤ = "either ... or" (BDAG ἤ 1b) | ἀντέχω & καταφρονέω take gen.

16:14 | ἐκμυκτηρίζω (< μυκτήρ, "nostril") = "sneer at someone" (BDAG, NIV), "deride by turning up the nose" (Thayer)

16:17 | εὐκοπώτερόν ἐστιν + acc. + inf. + ἤ + acc. + inf. = "it is easier for x to ... than for y to ..." (BDAG ἤ 2a; εὔκοπος) (cp. 18:25)

16:18 | ὁ ἀπολελυμένην ἀπὸ ἀνδρὸς γαμῶν = "he who marries (ὁ γαμῶν) a woman who is divorced from her husband"

16:19 | καθ᾽ ἡμέραν = "every day"

16:20 | πρός + acc. = "at"

16:21 | χορτάζεσθαι ἀπό τινος = "to eat one's fill of something," equivalent to partitive gen. (BDAG ἀπό 1f) (cp. ἐκ at 15:16) | ἀλλὰ καί = "but also" (BDAG ἀλλά 3), "moreover, even" (ESV)

16:22 | ἐγένετο + acc. (subject) + inf. = "it came to pass that the poor man died"

16:23 | ὑπάρχων ἐν βασάνοις = "being in torment" (BDAG ἐν 2b)

16:24 | ὕδατος = "in water," gen. of place within which (W 124) (*pace* M 43; ZG)

16:26 | καὶ ἐν πᾶσι τούτοις = "and besides all this" (ESV)

16:28 | ἔχω γὰρ πέντε ἀδελφούς – parenthetical | ὅπως διαμαρτύρηται αὐτοῖς = "that he [αὐτόν (v. 27), i.e., Lazarus (v. 24)] may warn them"

16:31 | οὐδέ ... πεισθήσονται – note placement of ἐάν clause inside main clause; if placed outside, after πεισθήσονται, the syntax becomes clearer: οὐδὲ πεισθήσονται, ἐάν τις ἐκ νεκρῶν ἀναστῇ = "neither will they be persuaded, though one rose from the dead" (KJV)

Luke 17

17:1 | ἀνένδεκτόν ἐστιν + acc. + μή + inf. = "it is impossible for ... not to come," i.e., they are sure to come | Pleonastic τοῦ + inf. (Z §386) | πλὴν οὐαὶ δι᾽ οὗ ἔρχεται = "but woe [sc. αὐτῷ, to the one] through whom they come," neut. pl. subjects (τὰ σκάνδαλα) take sg. verbs

17:2 | λυσιτελεῖ αὐτῷ εἰ ... ἢ ἵνα = "it would be better for him if ... than that," attenuated ἵνα after impersonal expression (BDAG ἵνα 2b; ἤ 2a)

17:4 | ἑπτάκις τῆς ἡμέρας = "seven times a day," gen. of time during which (W 122–4) (cp. 18:12)

17:6 | ἄν + ind. (2x) = "could say," "would have obeyed," apodosis of unreal condition (ZG; Z §310)

17:7 | εἰσελθόντι – dat. in agreement with αὐτῷ as indirect object of ἐρεῖ

17:8 | ἀλλ᾽ οὐχὶ ἐρεῖ = "will he not rather say?" expects affirmative answer (BDAG οὐχί 3) | ἑτοίμασον τί δειπνήσω = "prepare something for me to eat," aorist impv. bec. specific action in view (M 20, 135)

17:9 | ἔχω χάριν τινι = "thank someone"

17:10 | ὃ ὠφείλομεν ποιῆσαι πεποιήκαμεν = "we have done [only] that which we ought to have done" (NASB)

17:11 | ἐγένετο ... καὶ αὐτός = "it came to pass ... *that* he himself" (see 5:1; 9:51) | διὰ μέσον Σ. καὶ Γ. = "along the border between S. and G." (NIV)

17:11, 14 | ἐν τῷ + inf. = "as ..." (see 1:8)

17:12 | εἰσερχομένου αὐτοῦ = "as he was entering," gen. abs.

17:15 | BDAG μετά A3b – marker of attendant circumstances

17:16 | παρὰ τοὺς πόδας τινός = "at someone's feet" (see 7:38)

17:18 | οὐχ εὑρέθησαν ὑποστρέψαντες δοῦναι δόξαν τῷ θεῷ; = "were none found returning to give glory to God?" (ZG); predicate ptc. (W 618) + purpose inf. (W 590) | εἰ μὴ ὁ ἀλλογενὴς οὗτος = "except this foreigner"

17:20 | BDAG μετά A3b (cp. v. 15)

17:21 | ἐντὸς ὑμῶν = either (1) "in your midst" (NASB), or (2) "within you" (NIV 1984), i.e., in your hearts (see BDAG ἐντός)

17:23 | διώκω = "run after" (BDAG διώκω 4a)

17:24 | ἐκ τῆς ὑπὸ τὸν οὐρανὸν εἰς τὴν ὑπ᾽ οὐρανόν = "from one place on earth to another," since "under heaven" = "on earth" (BDAG οὐρανός 1b)

17:25 | πολλὰ παθεῖν = "to suffer greatly," adv. acc.

17:28 | ὁμοίως καθώς ... = "Likewise, as it was in the days of Lot" – some commentators think the comparison is left unfinished (Marshall); on other hand, if vv. 28b–29 are set off as parenthetical, the comparison is completed in v. 30 (καθώς ... κατὰ τὰ αὐτά = "as it was ... so will it be," ESV)

17:30 | κατὰ τὰ αὐτά = "in the same way" (BDAG κατά 5bα) | ᾗ ἡμέρᾳ = "on the day when"

17:31 | ὃς ἔσται = "the one who will be"

17:35 | ἐπὶ τὸ αὐτό = "at the same place"

Luke 18
18:1 | πρὸς τὸ δεῖν + inf. + acc. = "to the effect that they ought to" (BDF §402(5)), "about the need of praying" (BDAG πρός 3eα)

18:3 | ἤρχετο – iterative impf. | ἐκδίκησόν με ἀπό + gen. = "see to it that I get justice against" (BDAG); cp. *T. Levi* 2:2: "I performed justice for our sister Dinah against Hamor" (ἐποίησα τὴν ἐκδίκησιν τῆς ἀδελφῆς ἡμῶν Δίνας ἀπὸ τοῦ Ἐμμώρ)

18:4 | ἐπὶ χρόνον = "for a while" | εἰ καί = "even if" (BDAG εἰ 6e) (cp. 11:8)

18:5 | διὰ τό + inf. = "because" (BDF §402(1)) | γε = "yet" (BDAG γε aα) | ὑπωπιάζω (see BDAG) = either (1) lit. "give a black eye, strike in the face" or (2) fig. "wear down" | εἰς τέλος – adv. prep. phrase, could (1) modify ἐρχομένη and be rendered "continually" (ZG; NASB), or (2) modify ὑπωπιάζῃ (in fig. sense, "wear down") and be rendered "in the end, finally" (BDAG τέλος 2bγ), "eventually" (NIV), "completely" (BDF §207(3))

18:6 | ὁ κριτὴς τῆς ἀδικίας = "the unrighteous judge," Hebr./attributive gen. (W 86–88; cp. 16:8–9)

18:7 | οὐ μή + aorist subj. normally expresses emphatic negation (cp. v. 17), but here as question expresses emphatic affirmation (BDF §365(4)): "Will not God ... ?" (cp. John 18:11; Rev 15:4) | ἡμέρας καὶ νυκτός – gen. of time | καὶ μακροθυμεῖ ἐπ' αὐτοῖς – see commentaries; main options: (1) "despite his patience with them," adversative/concessive καί (M 178; ZG); (2) "and will he delay long over them?" (NASB), answered in the negative, v. 8a (see BDAG μακροθυμέω 2–3; ἐπί 6c)

18:8 | ἐν τάχει = "speedily," periphrasis for adv. (BDAG ἐν 11)

18:10 | ὁ εἷς ... ὁ ἕτερος = "the one ... the other"

18:11 | πρὸς ἑαυτόν – could modify (1) προσηύχετο, "was praying to himself" (NASB; BDAG πρός 3g), or (2) σταθείς, "standing by himself" (ESV); difficult to decide: option (2) is supported by word order, but then contrast with tax collector "standing far off" (v. 13) is weakened | ἢ καί = "or even"

18:12 | δὶς τοῦ σαββάτου = "twice a week," gen. of time during which (see 17:4) (BDAG σάββατον 2a)

18:14 | δεδικαιωμένος παρ' ἐκεῖνον = "justified rather than the other" (ESV), Hebr. comparative expressing exclusion (BDF §245a; παρά C3) (cp. Rom 1:25; Heb 1:9)

18:15 | Verbs of touching take gen.

18:17 | ὃς ἂν μή + aorist subj. = "whoever does not" | οὐ μή + aorist subj. for emphatic negation (W 468) (cp. v. 7)

18:18 | τί ποιήσας = lit. "having done what," i.e., "what must I do to," adv. aorist ptc. expressing a condition on which the fulfillment of the idea indicated by the main verb (κληρονομήσω) depends (W 632)

18:19 | λέγω + double acc. = "call someone something" (BDAG λέγω 4) | εἰ μὴ εἷς ὁ θεός = "except God alone" (BDAG εἷς 2c)

18:20 | Imperatival futures, usually employed in LXX quotations of OT categorical injunctions (BDF §362; W 569; M 178–9) (cp. 4:8, 12)

18:22 | ἔτι ἕν σοι λείπει = lit. "one thing is still lacking to you," i.e., "one thing you still lack," dat. of possession (BDF §189(3))

18:25 | εὐκοπώτερόν ἐστιν + acc. + inf. + ἤ + acc. + inf. = "it is easier for x to ... than for y to ..." (see 16:17)

18:26 | καὶ τίς; = "who then?" (BDAG καί 1bθ) (cp. 10:29)

18:27 | Neut. pl. subjects take sg. verbs

18:28 | τὰ ἴδια = "home, possessions" (BDAG ἴδιος 4b)

18:29–30 | "There is no one who has left ... who will not receive"

18:31 | τῷ υἱῷ τοῦ ἀνθρώπου – either (1) dependent on γεγραμμένα: "written ... concerning the Son of Man," dat. of reference/respect (W 146) (some MSS have περὶ τοῦ υἱοῦ τοῦ ἀνθ.), or (2) dependent on τελεσθήσεται: "fulfilled ... upon the Son of Man," dat. of disadvantage (W 143) (ZG)

18:33 | τῇ ἡμέρᾳ τῇ τρίτῃ = "on the third day," dat. of time (W 155–6)

18:35 | τυφλός τις = "a blind man"

18:36 | τί εἴη τοῦτο = "what this might mean," either potential optative w/o ἄν (Z §356) or oblique optative (W 483) (see 1:29)

18:37 | παρέρχεται – present retained in indirect discourse (W 537)

18:39 | Attenuated ἵνα equivalent to inf. (BDAG ἵνα 2aδ)

18:40 | ἐγγίσαντος αὐτοῦ = "when he [= the blind man] came near," gen. abs.

18:41 | τί σοι θέλεις ποιήσω; = "what do you want me to do for you?" deliberative subj. introduced by θέλεις (see 9:54)

Luke 19
19:1 | τὴν Ἰεριχώ is object of both εἰσελθών & διήρχετο – "he entered Jericho and was passing through it" | διήρχετο – conative impf., in progress but not complete (W 550)

19:2 | καὶ αὐτός (2x) – possible Semitism (M 121, 176; BDF §277(3))

19:3 | ἐστίν – present retained in indirect discourse (W 537) (cp. v. 22) | ἀπὸ τοῦ ὄχλου = "because of the crowd" (BDAG ἀπό 5a) | τῇ ἡλικίᾳ = "in stature," dat. of respect with adj. (W 144; Z §53)

19:4 | εἰς τὸ ἔμπροσθεν = "ahead," pleonasm (BDF §484), the προ-prefix in προτρέχω already means "ahead" (BDAG ἔμπροσθεν 1a; cp. v. 28) | ἐκείνης = "that way" – adv. gen. of ἐκεῖνος, fem. in agreement with an understood ὁδοῦ, gen. of place (BDF §186(1)) | μέλλω + inf. = "be about to"

19:5 | ὡς + aorist = "when"

19:5–6 | σπεύσας (2x) = "hurry/hurried and," attendant circumstances ptc. (W 644)

19:8 | δίδωμι & ἀποδίδωμι – either instantaneous performative presents (W 517; also called "aoristic," BDF §320), or futuristic presents (ZG; W 535)

19:11 | προσθείς + verb = "do something again" (Septuagintism; BDF §392(2); BDAG προστίθημι 1c; M 177) (cp. 20:11–12) | διὰ τό + inf. + acc. (subject) = "because he was near Jerusalem and [because] they supposed that ..."

19:12, 15 | λαβεῖν βασιλείαν (2x) = "to acquire kingship" (BDAG βασιλεία 1a), with ἑαυτῷ (v. 12): "to have himself appointed king" (NIV)

19:13 | ἐν ᾧ [sc. χρόνῳ] ἔρχομαι = "during the [sc. time] that I am coming," i.e., "until I come" (ZG; M 76, 133; BDF §383(1))

19:15 | καὶ ἐγένετο ... καί = "and it came to pass ... that" (see 14:1) | ἐν τῷ ἐπανελθεῖν αὐτόν = "when he returned" | εἶπεν φωνηθῆναι αὐτῷ = "he ordered that they be summoned to him" (BDAG λέγω 2c)

19:17 | ἴσθι ἐξουσίαν ἔχων = "be holding authority," periphrastic, emphasizing the adjectival idea inherent in the ptc. (BDAG εἰμί 11f)

19:20 | ἣν εἶχον = "which I kept" (BDAG ἔχω 3b)

19:22 | εἰμί – present retained in indirect discourse (cp. v. 3)

19:23 | καὶ διὰ τί; = "why then?" (BDAG καί 1bθ) | κἀγὼ [= καὶ ἐγὼ] ἐλθὼν σὺν τόκῳ ἂν αὐτὸ ἔπραξα = "and at my coming I might have collected it with interest" (ESV), unreal condition, with ἂν + aorist indic. in apodosis (ZG; Z §313; BDF §360(2)) | πράσσω = "collect or exact" interest (BDAG πράσσω 1b) (cp. 3:13)

19:26 | καὶ ὃ ἔχει = "even what he has"

19:28 | ἐπορεύετο ἔμπροσθεν = "he was going on ahead," adverbial use (cp. v. 4)

19:30 | τὴν κατέναντι κώμην = "the village opposite (us)," adverbial use (BDAG κατέναντι 2a)

19:31, 33 | διὰ τί; = τί; = "why?"

19:31, 34 | αὐτοῦ χρείαν ἔχει (2x) = χρείαν ἔχει αὐτοῦ = "has need of it" (see 5:31)

19:37 | ἐγγίζοντος αὐτοῦ = "as he was drawing near" (to Jerusalem), gen. abs. | ἤδη πρὸς τῇ καταβάσει τοῦ Ὄ. τῶν Ἐ. = lit. "already at the descent of [= the road that goes down the slope of] the M. of O.," i.e., "already on the way down the M. of O." (ESV) | ἤρξαντο χαίροντες αἰνεῖν τὸν θεόν = they "began joyfully to praise God" (NIV), ptc. of manner/emotion (W 627–8) | περὶ πασῶν ὧν εἶδον δυνάμεων (normally: περὶ πασῶν [τῶν] δυνάμεων ἃς εἶδον) = "for all the miracles which they had seen" (BDAG ὅς 1εγ), note that ἅς changes into ὧν by attraction with πασῶν (ZG)

19:42 | "If you only knew this day, even you, what makes for peace!" aposiopesis (BDAG εἰ 4; BDF §482)

19:43 | First καί = "when" (BDAG καί 1bγ; BDF §442(4); Z §455δ) (cp. 23:44)

19:44 | ἀνθ᾽ ὧν = "because" | τὸν καιρὸν τῆς ἐπισκοπῆς σου = "the time of God's coming to you" (NIV), σου as objective gen.

19:47 | ἦν διδάσκων – impf. periphrastic | τὸ καθ᾽ ἡμέραν = "daily," adv. acc.

19:48 | οὐχ εὕρισκον τὸ τί ποιήσωσιν = lit. "they were not finding what they might do," or "they could not find any way to do it" (NIV), τό changes direct question into indirect (BDAG ὁ 2hα) (see 1:62) | ἐξεκρέματο αὐτοῦ ἀκούων = "were hanging upon him as they were listening [to him]," αὐτοῦ doing double duty as object; both ἐκκρεμάννυμι & ἀκούω can take gen.

Luke 20
20:1 | ἐν μιᾷ τῶν ἡμερῶν + gen. abs. = "on one of the days while he was" (NASB)

20:3 | ἐρωτήσω ὑμᾶς κἀγὼ [= καὶ ἐγὼ] λόγον = "I will *also* ask you a question" (BDAG λόγος 1aβ)

20:6 | πεπεισμένος ἐστιν = the people "are convinced," πεπεισμένος is virtually an adj., with little reference to time (M 18)

20:9 | χρόνους ἱκανούς = "for a long time," acc. for extent of time

20:10 | καιρῷ = "when the time came" (ESV), "at harvest time" (NIV), dat. of time | ἐξαπέστειλαν αὐτὸν δείραντες κενόν = they "beat him and sent him away empty-handed," action of aorist ptc. previous to main verb (M 99)

20:11, 12 | προστίθημι + inf. (2x) = "do something again" (cp. 19:11)

20:14 | ἀποκτείνωμεν – hortatory subj.

20:17 | γίνομαι εἰς – see 13:19

20:18 | ἐφ᾽ ὃν ἄν = "upon whomever"

20:19 | Third καί is adversative, "but" (BDAG καί 1bη; Z §455β) | πρὸς αὐτούς = "with reference to them" (BDAG πρός 3εα)

20:20 | ὑποκρινομένους ἑαυτοὺς δικαίους εἶναι = "who pretended to be sincere" (NIV), reflexive pronoun with reflexive mid. = redundant mid. (W 418–9) | ὥστε + inf. expressing purpose (see 4:29) (M 143)

20:20, 26 | ἐπιλαμβάνομαι + double gen. (2x) = "catch someone in something" | αὐτοῦ – verbs of grasping/catching take gen. | λόγου/ῥήματος = "in something he said" (BDAG λόγος 1αβ; ῥῆμα 1)

20:21 | λαμβάνω πρόσωπον = "show favoritism or partiality" (Septuagintism) | ἐπ᾽ ἀληθείας = "in accordance with the truth, truly" (BDAG ἐπί 8)

20:22 | πανουργία = "craftiness, trickery, lit. 'readiness to do anything'" (BDAG)

20:26 | BDAG ἐπί 6c

20:28 | ἵνα with imperatival force – "he is to take" (BDAG ἵνα 2g)

20:35 | οἱ καταξιωθέντες τυχεῖν + gen. = "those who are considered worthy of taking part in" (NIV)

20:36 | Negative + ἔτι = "no longer" (BDAG ἔτι 1bβ)

20:37 | ὅτι = "that" | καὶ Μωϋσῆς = "even Moses" | ἐπί + gen. = "in the passage about" (BDAG ἐπί 2a) (cp. Mk 2:26; 12:26)

20:42 | ἐκ = "at, on" (BDAG ἐκ 2)

20:43 | ἕως ἄν + subj. = "until"

20:44 | καὶ πῶς; = "how then?" (BDAG καί 1bθ; BDF §442(8))

20:45 | ἀκούοντος παντὸς τοῦ λαοῦ = "in the hearing of all the people" (ESV), gen. abs.

Luke 21

21:1 | τούς ... πλουσίους = "the rich," with βάλλοντας as attributive (W 618)

21:3 | πλεῖον + gen. of comparison = "more than all [the others]"

21:4 | ἔβαλον εἰς τὰ δῶρα = "threw in among the (other) gifts" (ZG), "put into the offering" (NASB) (see BDAG δῶρον)

21:5 | καί τινων λεγόντων = "and while some [of the disciples] were remarking," gen. abs. | ὅτι λίθοις καλοῖς καὶ ἀναθήμασιν κεκόσμηται = "that it was adorned with beautiful stones and votive gifts" (NASB), for κοσμέω (pass.) + dat., see BDAG κοσμέω 2aβ (cp. Rev 21:19)

21:6 | ταῦτα ἃ θεωρεῖτε = "as for these things which you are looking at" (NASB), possibly acc. of respect (ZG); more likely, pendent nom. (W 51–2)

21:7, 11 | Neut. pl. subjects take sg. verbs

21:7 | μέλλω + inf. = "be about to"

21:9 | οὐκ εὐθέως τὸ τέλος = "the end will not come right away" (NIV)

21:11 | κατὰ τόπους = "in various places"

21:13 | "It will lead to an opportunity for your testimony" (NASB); "This will result in your being witnesses to them" (NIV 1984); εἰς + acc. expressing result (M 70; BDAG εἰς 4e)

21:14 | θέτε ἐν ταῖς καρδίαις ὑμῶν = "make up your minds"

21:15 | στόμα = "utterance, eloquence" (BDAG στόμα 2)

21:16 | ἐξ ὑμῶν = "some of you," partitive ἐκ functioning as object (BDAG ἐκ 4aγ; BDF §164(2))

21:17 | ἔσεσθε μισούμενοι – future periphrastic

21:21 | αὐτῆς & αὐτήν – both refer to Jerusalem (v. 20), translated "the city"

21:22 | ἡμέραι ἐκδικήσεως – Semitic adjectival gen. (M 175) | τοῦ + inf. could be telic or consecutive

21:23 | ἐν γαστρὶ ἔχω = "be pregnant" (BDAG γαστήρ 2; LXX Gen 16:4; etc.)

21:24 | πεσοῦνται – pl. referring to collective sg. (ὁ λαός), *constructio ad sensum* (BDF §134(1a)) | ἄχρι οὗ + subj. = "until"

21:25 | ἐν ἡλίῳ καὶ σελήνη = "in the sun and moon," anarthrous but definite monadic nouns (W 248–9) | ἐθνῶν – subjective gen. | ἐν ἀπορίᾳ ἤχους θαλάσσης καὶ σάλου = "in perplexity at the roaring of the sea and the waves" (NASB), taking ἤχους as gen. of cause (ZG) | Note that ἦχος can be masc., or neut. as here (see two entries in BDAG)

21:26 | ἀποψυχόντων ἀνθρώπων = "people fainting," gen. abs. | ἀπό = "from," in the sense "because of" (BDAG ἀπό 5c) + two gens. (φόβου & προσδοκίας) (cp. 22:45; 24:41) | τὰ ἐπερχόμενα τῇ οἰκουμένῃ = "the things which are coming upon the world" (NASB)

21:28 | ἀρχομένων τούτων γίνεσθαι = "as these things are beginning to take place," gen. abs.

21:30 | ἀφ' ἑαυτῶν = "for yourselves"

21:32 | ἕως ἄν + subj. = "until" | Neut. pl. subjects take sg. verbs

21:33 | οὐ μή + future indic. instead of expected aorist subj. (παρέλθωσιν, Matt 24:35), possibly due to attraction with preceding παρελεύσονται (BDF §365(1)); signifies emphatic negation (W 468)

21:37 | ἦν διδάσκων – impf. periphrastic | τὰς ἡμέρας ... τὰς δὲ νύκτας = "during the day ... but at night" | εἰς = ἐν

21:37, 38 | ηὐλίζετο & ὤρθριζεν – iterative impfs.

Luke 22

22:2, 4 | τό changes direct question into indirect (BDAG ὁ 2ha; πῶς 1ba) (see 1:62) – "how they might get rid of him" (v. 2), "how he might betray him" (v. 4)

22:6 | τοῦ + inf. – telic | ἄτερ ὄχλου = "in the absence of a crowd" (ESV)

22:7 | ἔδει + inf. (θυέσθαι) = "had to be sacrificially slaughtered"

22:11 | φάγω – subj. in final relative clause (Z §343; BDF §378)

22:12 | κἀκεῖνος = καὶ ἐκεῖνος

22:15 | ἐπιθυμίᾳ ἐπεθύμησα = "I have earnestly desired," Greek rendering of Hebrew inf. abs. construction (LXX Gen 31:30) (M 177–8; Z §60) | πρὸ τοῦ με παθεῖν = "before I suffer" (BDF §§395; 403), with acc. με as subject of inf. (BDF §406(3))

22:16 | ἕως ὅτου + subj. = "until"

22:18 | ἀπὸ τοῦ νῦν = "from now on" (cp. v. 69) | ἕως οὗ + subj. = "until"

22:19 | εἰς τὴν ἐμὴν ἀνάμνησιν = "in order to remember me" (BDAG εἰς 4f)

22:20 | μετὰ τό + inf. = "after" (W 594–5) | τὸ ὑπὲρ ὑμῶν ἐκχυννόμενον = "which is poured out for you," article functioning as relative pronoun (W 213–15) referring all the way back to τὸ ποτήριον (M 31 n1)

22:21, 22 | παραδιδόντος & πορεύεται – ingressive futuristic presents (W 537)

22:22 | μέν ... πλήν = "indeed ... but" (BDAG μέν 1aγ) | κατὰ τὸ ὡρισμένον = "in accordance with the (divine) decree" (BDAG ὁρίζω 2a)

22:23, 24 | τό – see vv. 2, 4

22:23 | τίς ἐξ αὐτῶν = "which one of them" | ἄρα simply enlivens the question (BDAG ἄρα 1b) | εἴη – either potential optative without ἄν (Z §356) or oblique optative (W 483) (see 1:29) | ὁ μέλλων + inf. = "the one who is going to," substantival ptc. (W 619) | τοῦτο (acc.) is direct object of πράσσειν, referring to act of betraying Jesus (vv. 21–22) | "And they began to discuss among themselves which one of them it might be who was going to do this thing" (NASB)

22:26 | ὑμεῖς δὲ οὐχ οὕτως = "but you [are] not [to act] in this way" (BDAG οὕτως 1b), ellipsis (BDF §480(5))

22:29 | κἀγώ = καὶ ἐγώ | βασιλείαν does double duty as object of both διατίθεμαι & διέθετο | διατίθημι βασιλείαν τινι = "covenantally bestow kingship on someone" (throughout LXX, διατίθημι διαθήκην = "make a covenant," e.g., for covenanting with regard to kingship, see LXX 2 Kgdms 5:3)

22:30 | τὰς δώδεκα φυλὰς κρίνοντες τοῦ Ἰσραήλ = κρίνοντες τὰς δώδεκα φυλὰς τοῦ Ἰσραήλ (cp. Matt 19:28) = "judging the 12 tribes of Israel" | κρίνειν here does not mean "to pass an unfavorable verdict," but has Hebr. neutral sense, "to act/function as a judge" (cp. LXX Exod 18:13, 22; Lev 19:15; 3 Kgdms 3:9; 8:32; 4 Kgdms 15:5; etc.)

22:31 | ἐξητήσατο ὑμᾶς τοῦ σινιάσαι = "asked for you, to sift [you]," ὑμᾶς doing double duty as object of both verbs (BDAG ἐξαιτέω) | τοῦ + inf. – telic (BDF §400(5))

22:33 | ἕτοιμος + inf. = "ready to do something" | καί ... καί = "both ... and"

22:34 | ἕως τρίς με ἀπαρνήσῃ εἰδέναι = "until you have denied three times that you know me," indirect discourse; but note that με is the direct object (not the subject) of the inf.

22:35 | ὑστερέω + gen. = "lack something" (BDAG ὑστερέω 3a) | οὐθενός = older Attic spelling of οὐδενός (BDF §33) (cp. 23:14)

22:36 | ὁ μὴ ἔχων is elliptical; supply μάχαιραν

22:37 | τό introduces Scripture quotation | καὶ γάρ = "for indeed" | τὸ [sc. γεγραμμένον] περὶ ἐμοῦ = "what is written about me" (NIV, ESV, ZG) | τέλος ἔχει = "is nearing accomplishment" (ZG), "is reaching its fulfillment" (NIV) (of fulfillment of Scriptural prophecy; see BDAG τέλος 1), ingressive-futuristic present (W 537)

22:39 | κατὰ τὸ ἔθος = "as was his custom" (ESV, NASB), article as possessive pronoun

22:40 | γενόμενος ἐπί = "when he arrived at" (BDAG γίνομαι 6c) (cp. John 6:21)

22:41 | ὡσεὶ λίθου βολήν = "about a stone's throw," acc. for extent of space (W 202) | τίθημι τὰ γόνατα = "kneel"

22:43 | ἐνισχύω – here, transitive = "strengthen someone"

22:45 | ἀναστὰς ἀπὸ τῆς προσευχῆς = "when he rose from prayer" | ἀπὸ τῆς λύπης = "because of, from sorrow" (BDF §210(1); BDAG ἀπό 5c) (cp. 21:26; 24:41)

22:47 | φιλῆσαι – inf. of purpose (BDF §390)

22:48 | φιλήματι – dat. of means (W 162)

22:49 | οἱ περὶ αὐτόν = "those around him," i.e., his disciples (BDF §228) (cp. Mk 4:10) | τὸ ἐσόμενον = "what was going to happen," fut. ptc. (BDF §351(2)) | εἰ πατάξομεν = "shall we strike?" Septuagintal use of εἰ to introduce direct question (Z §401; BDF §440(3)); deliberative fut. indic. (BDF §366(2)) | ἐν μαχαίρῃ = "with the sword," Hebr./instrumental ἐν

22:50 | εἷς τις ἐξ αὐτῶν (cp. John 11:49) = "a certain one of them," εἷς often replaces τις as an indef. article, but here both are used pleonastically (Z §155; BDAG εἷς 3c)

22:51 | ἐᾶτε ἕως τούτου = either (1) "No more of this!" (ESV); or (2) supply αὐτούς as implied object: "Let them go thus far," i.e., as far as arresting me (Marshall) | Verbs of touching take gen.

22:52 | Article τούς governs ἀρχιερεῖς, στρατηγούς, and πρεσβυτέρους, and causes them to be viewed as a single entity | παραγενομένους ἐπ᾽ αὐτόν = "who had come out against him," attributive ptc.

22:53 | καθ᾽ ἡμέραν = "every day" | ὄντος μου – gen. abs.

22:55 | περιαψάντων ... συγκαθισάντων – gen. abs.; the subject is "they" and must be supplied from the αὐτῶν at end of sentence

22:56 | πρὸς τὸ φῶς = "in the firelight" (NIV)

22:57, 58, 60 | γύναι, ἄνθρωπε (2x) – vocatives

22:58 | μετὰ βραχύ = "a little later" (BDAG βραχύς 2)

22:59 | διαστάσης ὡσεὶ ὥρας μιᾶς = "after about an hour had passed" (NASB), gen. abs. | ἄλλος τις = "another man" (NASB)

22:60 | ἔτι λαλοῦντος αὐτοῦ = "while he [= Peter] was still speaking," gen. abs.

22:61 | ὡς = "that," marker of discourse content (BDAG ὡς 5) | ὅτι recitative

22:66 | ὡς + aorist = "when"

22:68 | "and if I asked you, you would not answer" (NIV)

22:69 | ἀπὸ τοῦ νῦν – see v. 18 | ἔσται καθήμενος – future periphrastic | ἐκ δεξιῶν = "at the right hand," ἐκ answers question "where?" (BDAG ἐκ 2)

22:71 | τί ἔτι ἔχομεν μαρτυρίας χρείαν; = "what further need have we of testimony?" (see 5:31) (BDAG ἔτι 1bβ) | αὐτοὶ γὰρ ἠκούσαμεν = "for we ourselves have heard" (M 121)

Luke 23
23:1 | ἐπί = "before," marker of legal proceeding (BDAG ἐπί 10)

23:2 | κατηγορέω takes gen. (cp. v. 10) | εὕραμεν = εὕρομεν (Z §489; BDF §81(3)) | λέγοντα ἑαυτὸν Χριστὸν βασιλέα εἶναι =

"declaring himself to be king Messiah," inf. + acc. as subject of inf. (BDF §406(1); BDAG λέγω 2e)

23:5 | καθ᾽ ὅλης τῆς Ἰουδαίας = "throughout all Judea" (BDAG κατά A1c; BDF §225) (cp. 4:14)

23:6 | εἰ = "whether" (BDAG εἰ 5bα) |

23:6–7 | ἐστίν (2x) – present retained in indirect discourse (W 537)

23:7 | ἐκ τῆς ἐξουσίας Ἡρῴδου ἐστίν = "he comes from Herod's jurisdiction" (BDAG ἐξουσία 6) | ὄντα καὶ αὐτόν ... ἡμέραις = "who was also in Jer. at that time" (NIV)

23:8 | ἐξ ἱκανῶν χρόνων = "for a long time" (BDAG ἐκ 5a) | διὰ τὸ ἀκούειν περὶ αὐτοῦ = "because he had been hearing about him" (BDF §402(1)) | ἦν γὰρ θέλων ... ἤλπιζεν = "for he had been wanting ... and had been hoping," pluperfective imperfects (W 549)

23:9 | Hebr./instrumental ἐν

23:10 | κατηγορέω takes gen. (cp. v. 2)

23:12 | προϋπῆρχον γὰρ ἐν ἔχθρᾳ ὄντες πρὸς αὐτούς = "for before this they had been at enmity with each other" (ESV) | ἐν ἔχθρᾳ = "in a state of enmity" (BDAG ἐν 2b) | Textual problem: (1) πρὸς αὐτούς (NA), (2) πρὸς ἑαυτούς (Majority Text), or (3) contracted form πρὸς αὐτούς (Z §210) – "the simple pronoun does not appear to be admissible here" (BDF §287); "a reflexive is clearly required" (M 119)

23:14 | ὡς + present ptc. = "as one who" (BDAG ὡς 3aγ; BDF §425(3)) (cp. 16:1) | οὐθέν = οὐδέν (cp. 22:35) | "And behold, having examined him before you, I have found in this man no cause for the things of which you accuse him"

23:15 | "nothing worthy of death has been done *by him*," taking αὐτῷ as Classical dat. of agent – quite rare in NT (BDF §191; Z §59; W 165)

23:18 | παμπληθεί (< πᾶν + πλῆθος) (adverbial dat.) = "all together," of a crowd shouting in unison

23:19 | Parenthetical editorial comment by Luke | διὰ στάσιν ... καὶ φόνον = "for insurrection and for murder" (cp. v. 25) | στάσιν τινὰ γενομένην = "a certain insurrection that had taken place"

23:21–23 | οἱ ... ὁ ... οἱ = "they ... he ... they," articles functioning as pronouns

23:22 | τρίτον = "the third time," adv. acc. | τί γὰρ κακὸν ἐποίησεν οὗτος; = "why, what crime has this man committed?" (BDAG γάρ 1f)

23:23 | κατίσχυον = "began to prevail" (NASB), ingressive impf.

23:24 | "Pilate decided that their demand should be granted" (BDAG αἴτημα), γενέσθαι = lit. "be done," but in collocation with αἴτημα, "be granted" | τόν ... βεβλημένον = "him who had been thrown" into prison

23:26 | Σίμωνά τινα Κυρηναῖον ἐρχόμενον ἀπ᾽ ἀγροῦ = "one Simon of Cyrene who was coming in from the countryside" | ἐπιλαμβάνομαι (as a verb of grasping) takes gen., but here acc. (although see widely supported textual variant; BDF §170(2))

23:28 | θυγατέρες – voc. pl. | κλαίω + ἐπί + acc. (3x) = "weep over" | πλήν = ἀλλά = "but rather" (BDAG πλήν 1b)

23:31 | ἐν (2x) for simple dat., "to" | ποιοῦσιν – impersonal "they" | τί γένηται; = "what will happen?" subj. in doubtful/deliberative question (BDF §366(1))

23:33 | ὃν μέν ... ὃν δέ = "the one ... the other" | ἐκ (2x) answers question "where?" (see 22:69)

23:36 | προσερχόμενοι = "coming up [to him]" | προσφέρω = "offer"

23:39 | οὐχὶ σύ ...; = "are you not ...?"

23:40 | οὐδὲ σύ ...; = "do you not ...?" | ἐν τῷ αὐτῷ κρίματι = "under the same sentence of condemnation"

23:41 | ἡμεῖς μέν ... οὗτος δέ = "we indeed ... but *this* man," emphatic (M 122) | ἄξια ὧν ἐπράξαμεν ἀπολαμβάνομεν = "we are getting just deserts [ἄξια] for the things we did"

23:42 | ἄτοπος = lit. "not in its proper place," here: "behaviorally out of place, wrong, improper" (BDAG ἄτοπος 2) | μιμνήσκομαι takes gen. (cp. 24:8)

23:44 | Second καί = "when" (see 19:43)

23:45 | τοῦ ἡλίου ἐκλιπόντος = "because the sun stopped shining" or "was eclipsed," causal ptc. (W 631) | μέσον = "down the middle," adv. acc.

23:49 | οἱ γνωστοὶ αὐτῷ = "his acquaintances, friends" (see 2:44)

23:51, 55 | ἦν συγκατατεθειμένος & ἦσαν συνεληλυθυῖαι – plupf. periphrastics (W 583, 649)

23:53 | οὐκ οὐδεὶς οὔπω = "no one ever," combinations of negatives have strengthening effect (BDF §431(2))

23:54 | ἐπέφωσκεν = lit. "was dawning," but since the Sabbath begins on Friday evening, "was about to begin" (ingressive impf.)

23:55 | "Now the women who had come with him out of Galilee followed, and saw the tomb and how his body was laid" (NASB)

23:56b–24:1 | μέν ... δέ = "And although they rested on the Sabbath" (taking a break from preparing the spices, v. 56a), "on the first day of the week they came to the tomb bringing the spices which they had prepared" on Friday evening.

Luke 24

24:1 | ἡ μία τῶν σαββάτων = "the first [sc. ἡμέρα/day] of the week" (BDAG σάββατον 2b) | ὄρθρου βαθέως = lit. "at deep (i.e., very early) dawn," gen. of time (BDF §186(2))

24:2 | ἐγένετο ... καί = "it came to pass ... that" (cp. v. 15; 5:12; 14:1)

24:6 | ἔτι ὤν = "while he was still" (cp. v. 44)

24:7 | "saying concerning the Son of Man that it is necessary for him to be handed over," prolepsis: anticipation of the subject/object of subordinate clause by making it the object of main clause (BDF §476(3))

24:8 | μιμνήσκομαι takes gen. (cp. 23:42)

24:11 | "These words seemed to them to be nonsense" (BDAG ἐνώπιον 3; λῆρος)

24:12 | τὸ γεγονός = "what had happened" (cp. 8:34–35, 56)

24:13 | καὶ ἰδοὺ δύο ... ἦσαν πορευόμενοι – Hebr. "and behold" + ptc., but improved by addition of ἦσαν (impf. periphrastic) (BDF §353(1)) | ἀπέχουσαν σταδίους ἑξήκοντα ἀπὸ Ἰερ. = "which was 60 stadia from Jer." (about 7 miles) | σταδίους – acc. for extent of space (M 34; W 201)

24:15 | ἐγένετο ... καί = "it came to pass ... *that*" (cp. v. 2)

24:16 | ἐκρατοῦντο = "were held back, restrained" (BDAG κρατέω 5) | τοῦ μὴ ἐπιγνῶναι αὐτόν = "from recognizing him"

24:19 | ἀνὴρ προφήτης = "a prophet," adjectival use of substantive (BDF §242)

24:20 | ὅπως – unusual: either (1) it means "how," unique in NT (BDAG ὅπως 1; BDF §300(1)); or (2) adopt textual variant ὡς (BDF §443(1)) | τε ... καί = "*both* handed him over ... *and* crucified him" (W 672)

24:21 | ἐστίν – present retained in indirect discourse (W 537) | ὁ μέλλων + inf. = "he who was going to" | ἀλλά γε καί = "indeed" (BDAG ἀλλά 3) | σὺν πᾶσιν τούτοις = "besides (or in addition to) all this" (BDAG σύν 3b; cp. NASB) | τρίτην ταύτην ἡμέραν ἄγει – unusual; probably based on idiom "spend, observe" a period of time (BDAG ἄγω 4), but used here impersonally: "it is spending the third day," i.e., "this is now the third day" (see M 27) | ἀφ' οὗ = "since" (BDAG ἀπό 2bγ) (cp. 13:7, 25)

24:22 | ἀλλὰ καί = "but also" (BDAG ἀλλά 3) | ὀρθριναί – predicate adj., rendered as adv. in English (BDF §243) (cp. δευτεραῖοι, Acts 28:13)

24:23 | λέγουσαι καὶ ὀπτασίαν ἀγγέλων ἑωρακέναι = "saying that they had even [καί] seen a vision of angels," indirect discourse (M 153) | οἳ λέγουσιν αὐτὸν ζῆν = "who [the angels] said that he was alive," indirect discourse

24:25 | βραδεῖς τῇ καρδίᾳ = "slow of heart," dat. of respect (W 144; Z §53)

24:28 | οὗ (adv.) = "where" | προσποιέω + inf. = "act as though were"

24:29 | πρὸς ἑσπέραν ἐστίν = "it is getting toward evening" (NASB; BDAG πρός 3bα; ἑσπέρα; M 53)

24:31 | αὐτῶν ... οἱ ὀφθαλμοί = "their eyes" | ἄφαντος ἐγένετο = "he disappeared"

24:35 | τὰ ἐν τῇ ὁδῷ = "what had happened on the way/journey" (BDAG ὁδός 2)

24:37 | ἐδόκουν πνεῦμα θεωρεῖν = "they thought they were seeing a ghost" (BDAG πνεῦμα 4b; cp. v. 39)

24:41 | ἀπὸ τῆς χαρᾶς = "for joy" (BDAG ἀπό 5c) (cp. 21:26; 22:45)

24:46 | γέγραπται παθεῖν τὸν Χριστὸν καὶ ἀναστῆναι = "it is written that the Christ would suffer and rise," indirect discourse

24:49 | ἕως οὗ + subj. = "until"

24:53 | διὰ παντός = "continually"

Chapter Four

The Gospel of John

John 1

1:1 | θεὸς ἦν ὁ λόγος = "the Word was God." Why is θεός anarthrous? Because it is a qualitative predicate nom. By this construction, John affirms that the Word belongs to the category θεός (deity), and yet is not to be equated with ὁ θεός (the Father, who is distinguished from the Word by the phrase πρὸς τὸν θεόν). "It would be pure Sabellianism to say 'the Word was ὁ θεός'" (Westcott, quoted M 116). See Wallace's helpful discussion (W 266–9).

1:3 | οὐδὲ ἕν = "not even one thing" | ὃ γέγονεν – two options: (1) if taken with v. 4, "that which came into existence," or (2) if taken with v. 3, "that has come into being" (NASB)

1:5 | καταλαμβάνω means "lay hold of," "grasp" either (1) in the neutral intellective sense: "understand," "comprehend," or (2) with hostile intent: "overtake," "overcome," "overpower" (see BDAG καταλαμβάνω 1, 2b, 4). Could be deliberate double mng. (M 197).

1:6, 14 | παρά + gen. (2x) = "from"

1:7 | εἰς μαρτυρίαν = either (1) "as a testimony/witness," predicate nom. (BDAG εἰς 8a), or (2) "for the purpose of testimony/witness" (BDAG εἰς 4f; ZG)

1:9 | ἐρχόμενον could be neut. nom. (modifying τὸ φῶς) or masc. acc. (modifying ἄνθρωπον) – hard to decide

1:10, 11 | καί (2x) = "and yet" (BDAG καί 1bη)

1:11 | τὰ ἴδια (neut.) = "home, possessions," whereas οἱ ἴδιοι (masc.) = "associates, relations, compatriots" (see BDAG ἴδιος 4a/b): "He came to his own world, and yet this own people did not receive him."

1:14 | μονογενής = either (1) "only one of his kind, only," or (2) more likely, "only begotten," *unigenitus* (Vulgate) (cp. v. 18; 3:16; 18; 1 John 4:9, also 5:18)

1:15 | ὃν εἶπον = "of whom I said" (rough – would expect a preposition like περί or ὑπέρ – see v. 30) | πρῶτος + gen. = "before" (cp. v. 30), as though it were πρότερος + gen. of comparison (M 42)

1:16 | Epexegetical καί = "that is" (BDAG καί 1c) | ἀντί + gen. = "upon" (BDAG ἀντί 2; NASB; ESV), "one blessing after another" (NIV 1984), "a succession of favours" (M 71)

1:17 | ἐγένετο – pl. subject with sg. verb bec. ἡ χάρις καὶ ἡ ἀλήθεια viewed as one concept ("grace-and-truth")

1:18 | εἰς = ἐν (BDF §205). "One must beware of insisting overmuch on the use of εἰς in contexts where a connotation of motion would be welcome to the theologian" (Z §102). "One cannot press the idea of motion here, as though the meaning is 'who was *into* the bosom of the Father'" (W 360).

1:19 | σὺ τίς εἶ; = "you, who are you?" prolepsis (BDF §476)

1:20 | ὅτι recitative (cp. v. 32)

1:21 | τί οὖν; = "what then?"

1:22 | οὖν = "so," used as transition to continue narrative, not strictly inferential (BDF §451(1); BDAG οὖν 2b); occurs ~200x in John | ἵνα ἀπόκρισιν δῶμεν = "[tell us] so that we may give an answer," brachylogy; final clause after a question (BDF §483) (cp. 9:36)

1:24 | ἀπεσταλμένοι ἦσαν = "they had been sent," plupf. periphrastic (W 649); extensive plupf. (W 585–6) in parenthetical remark (see ESV)

1:26, 31, 33 | ἐν (4x) = "with," Hebr./instrumental ἐν (BDF §219; BDAG ἐν 5b)

1:27, 33 | οὗ ... αὐτοῦ & ἐφ' ὅν ... ἐπ' αὐτόν – Hebr. pleonastic personal pronouns (BDF §297)

1:30 | ὑπέρ = περί (BDAG ὑπέρ A3; BDF §231(1))

1:31 | κἀγώ = καὶ ἐγώ (cp. vv. 33–34)

1:32 | καταβαῖνον ... καὶ ἔμεινεν – ptc. continued by finite verb (BDF §468(3))

1:35, 40 | ἐκ (2x) equivalent to partitive gen.

1:38, 41 | ὃ λέγεται μεθ. ... ὃ ἐστιν μεθ. – editorial parentheses inserted in direct discourse (BDF §465(2)) (cp. 4:25)

1:39 | ὡς with numbers = "about"

1:45 | ὃν ἔγραψεν Μωϋσῆς = "the one of whom Moses wrote" (cp. v. 15)

1:48 | πόθεν; = "how?" (BDAG πόθεν 3) | πρὸ τοῦ σε Φίλιππον φωνῆσαι = "before Philip called you," πρό + gen. articular inf. (BDF §403) | ὑπό + acc. = "under" (BDAG ὑπό B1b; BDF §232(1)), but ὑποκάτω + gen. (v. 50)

1:50 | First ὅτι = "because," second ὅτι = "that"

John 2

2:2 | ἐκλήθη ὁ Ἰησοῦς καὶ οἱ μαθηταὶ αὐτοῦ = "Jesus was invited and [so were] his disciples," compound subject with sg. verb (W 401)

2:3 | ὑστερήσαντος οἴνου = "when the wine gave out," gen. abs.

2:4 | τί ἐμοὶ καὶ σοί = "of what concern is that to you or me?" (BDF §299(3)), "what does that have to do with us?" (NASB); for other possibilities see Matt 8:29 | γύναι – voc.

2:5 | ὅ τι ἂν λέγῃ ὑμῖν = "whatever he tells you"

2:6 | κατά + acc. = "for the purpose of, for" (BDAG κατά B4)

2:7 | γεμίζω ὕδατος = "fill with water," verbs of filling take gen. of content (BDF §172) (cp. 6:13) | ἕως ἄνω = "to the brim"

2:8 | οἱ = "they," article as pronoun

2:9 | ὡς + aorist = "when" (cp. v. 23) | γεύομαι normally takes gen., but occasionally acc., as here (BDF §169(3)) (cp. Heb 6:5) | τὸ ὕδωρ οἶνον γεγενημένον = "the water which had become wine" | οἱ δὲ διάκονοι ... τὸ ὕδωρ = "(but the servants who had drawn the water knew)" (NASB), parenthetical editorial comment

2:10 | ὅταν + aorist subj. = "when" | τὸν ἐλάσσω = "[then he serves] the inferior [wine]," ellipsis

2:12 | οὐ πολλοί = "not many," "a few" (BDAG πολύς 1aα)

2:15 | τῶν κολλυβιστῶν ... τὸ κέρμα = "the coins [collective sg.] of the money changers"

2:16 | οἱ τὰς περιστερὰς πωλοῦντες = "sellers of doves," substantivized ptc. | ποιέω + double acc. = "turn x into y" (BDAG ποιέω 2hβ) (cp. 4:46)

2:18 | ὅτι ταῦτα ποιεῖς – where ὅτι (in collocation with δεικνύω in the previous clause) takes on the mng. "proving that" (NIV: "to prove your authority to do all this")

2:19–20 | ἐν τρίσιν ἡμέραις (2x) = "within three days" (BDAG ἐν 10a)

2:20 | οἰκοδομήθη – note absence of temporal augment (BDF §67(1)); could be constative/global aorist (M 11; W 557) or consummative aorist (W 560–1): "It took 46 years to build this temple" (NASB), or "It has taken ..." (ESV) | τεσσεράκοντα καὶ ἓξ ἔτεσιν – dat. instead of acc. for extent of time (ZG; Z §54; BDF §200(2)); numerals above three are indeclinable

2:21 | ὁ ναὸς τοῦ σώματος αὐτοῦ = "the temple which is his body," gen. of apposition; "the Shekinah glory, which had long ago departed from the temple, now resides in Jesus bodily" (W 98)

2:23 | ὡς + impf. = "while" (BDAG ὡς 8b) | αὐτοῦ τὰ σημεῖα = τὰ σημεῖα αὐτοῦ

2:24 | πιστεύω τινι τι = "entrust something to someone" (BDAG πιστεύω 3) | First αὐτόν = "himself" (other MSS have ἑαυτόν), intensive-reflexive (W 349) | διὰ τὸ αὐτὸν γινώσκειν πάντας = "because he knows all people" (not "all things," which would be neut. pl. πάντα)

John 3

3:2 | νυκτός = "at night," gen. of time within which (W 123)

3:3, 7 | ἄνωθεν (2x) can mean "again" or "from above" (v. 31)

3:4 | γέρων ὤν = "when he is old," temporal present ptc.

3:6 | τὸ γεγεννημένον (2x) = "that which is born"

3:7, 14 | δεῖ (2x) = "must" (+ inf. + acc. as subject of inf.)

3:8 | ὅπου θέλει πνεῖ = "blows where it wishes"

3:11 | μαρτυρέω + acc. = "bear witness to, declare, confirm" (BDAG μαρτυρέω 1b) (cp. v. 32); usually, μαρτυρέω + dat. or περί + gen.

3:14 | καθώς ... οὕτως = "as ... so"

3:15, 16 | πᾶς ὁ πιστεύων (2x) = "everyone who believes," "whoever believes," ongoing/continual present (W 521–22, 620–1)

3:15 | πιστεύω ἐν – occurs only 2x in NT (cp. Mk 1:15) (M 80)

3:16 | οὕτως ... ὥστε = either (1) "so much ... that" (BDAG οὕτως 3), taking ὥστε = ἵνα (BDAG ὥστε 2b; BDF §391(3)), or (2) more likely, "in this way ... namely" (BDAG οὕτως 2)

3:18 | κέκριται – gnomic perf. (W 580)

3:19 | μᾶλλον τὸ σκότος ἤ = "darkness rather than" | αὐτῶν τὰ ἔργα = τὰ ἔργα αὐτῶν (cp. αὐτοῦ τὰ ἔργα, v. 21)

3:20, 21 | Neut. pl. subjects (τὰ ἔργα) take sg. verbs (ἐλεγχθῇ & ἐστίν)

3:22 | ἐβάπτιζεν – iterative impf. (W 547)

3:23 | ἦν βαπτίζων – impf. periphrastic | ὕδατα πολλὰ ἦν – neut. pl. subjects take sg. verbs | παρεγίνοντο καὶ ἐβαπτίζοντο = "[people] were coming and being baptized," distributive iterative impfs. (W 546–7)

3:24 | οὔπω ἦν βεβλημένος = "had not yet been thrown," plupf. periphrastic

3:25 | ἐκ τῶν μαθητῶν Ἰωάννου = either (1) "on the part of John's disciples," or (2) possibly equivalent to dat., τισὶν ἐκ τῶν μ. (BDF §164(2)) | μετὰ Ἰουδαίου = "with a Jew," but many MSS have pl. Ἰουδαίων

3:26 | ὅς ... ἴδε οὗτος = "[he] who ... behold, that one"

3:27 | οὐ δύναται ... οὐδὲ ἕν = "a man can receive nothing," double negatives reinforce

3:28 | αὐτοὶ ὑμεῖς μοι μαρτυρεῖτε = "you yourselves can bear me witness" | First ὅτι = "that," while second and third are ὅτι recitative; however, second ὅτι is probably a scribal addition. John may have have then rectified the omission by adding the ὅτι recitative after ἀλλά (see BDF §470(1))

3:29 | χαρᾷ χαίρει = "rejoices with joy," Hebr. cognate dat. (W 168–9; Z §60; M 178)

3:32 | ὅ ... τοῦτο = "*what* he has seen and heard, *of that* he testifies" (NASB) (for μαρτυρέω + acc., cp. v. 11)

3:33 | ὁ λαβών = "whoever receives," substantival gnomic aorist ptc. with generic ref. (W 615 n8) | αὐτοῦ τὴν μαρτυρίαν = τὴν μαρτυρίαν αὐτοῦ

3:34 | ὅν = "[he] whom" | οὐκ ἐκ μέτρου = "without measure"

3:35 | ἐν = εἰς (M 75–6; BDF §§217(2); 218)

John 4

4:1 | ὡς ἔγνω ὁ Ἰησοῦς = "when Jesus learned" (ESV; BDAG γινώσκω 2) | πλείονας ἤ = "more than"

4:2 | καίτοιγε = "although," in parenthesis (BDAG καί 2iδ; BDF §450(3))

4:6 | ἐκ = "because of" (BDAG ἐκ 3dβ) | οὕτως = "thus," i.e., wearied (κεκοπιακώς) | ὡς with numerals = "about" (BDAG ὡς 6)

4:7, 9, 10 | πεῖν (3x) = "[something] to drink," inf. equivalent to substantive when used with δίδωμι (BDF §§390(2); 409(2–3)), like φαγεῖν (v. 33; Matt 25:35; Mk 5:43; 6:37)

4:9 | πῶς σύ ... οὔσης; = "How is it that you, being a Jew, ask [for something] to drink of me, being a Samaritan woman?"

4:10 | Second class conditional (contrary to fact) (W 694–5) | Second καί could be epexegetical: "If you knew the gift of God, *that is* (καί), who it is who says to you" (Z §455ζ) | Aorist + ἄν (2x) = "would have"

4:11 | οὔτε ... καί – rare (BDF §445(3); BDAG οὔτε)

4:12 | μείζων + gen. of comparison | ἐξ αὐτοῦ = "of it," i.e., the well

4:12–14 | πίνω + ἐκ for partitive gen. (3x) (BDF §169(2))

4:14 | ὅς δ' ἄν + aorist subj. = "but whoever drinks"

4:18 | νῦν ὅν ἔχεις = "the man you now have" (NIV) | τοῦτο ἀληθὲς εἴρηκας – either (1) take ἀληθές as predicate with understood ἐστίν, "what you have said is true," or (2) take ἀληθές as adverbial neut. acc., "you have said that with some truth" (ZG)

4:21 | γύναι – voc.

4:21–24 | προσκυνέω can take dat. (vv. 21, 23a) or acc. (vv. 22 [2x], 23b, 24) direct object; difficult to discern any difference in mng. (W 173 n90)

4:23 | ἔρχεται ὥρα καὶ νῦν ἐστιν = "an hour is coming and is now here," ἔρχεται is ingressive-futuristic present (W 537) | καὶ γάρ = "for indeed" | ὁ πατὴρ τοιούτους ζητεῖ τοὺς προσκυνοῦντας αὐτόν = "the Father is seeking such people to worship him" (ESV), "the Father wants people of this kind as his worshippers" (ZG)

4:24 | πνεῦμα – anarthrous qualitative predicate nom. (like θεός in 1:1c)

4:25 | ἔρχεται – futuristic present (W 536) | ὁ λεγόμενος Χρ. – could be the words of the Samaritan woman, or editorial parenthesis inserted in direct discourse (BDF §465(2)) (cp. 1:38, 41)

4:27 | ἐπὶ τούτῳ = "at this point" (NASB; cp. M 50), "just then" (NIV, ESV) | λάλω μετά + gen. (2x) = "converse with" in a friendly or at least non-hostile manner (M 61; BDAG μετά A2cα) | First τί; = "what?" but second τί; = "why?"

4:28 | "So the woman left her water jar," οὖν used as transition to continue narrative (see 1:22)

4:29 | πάντα ὅσα = "everything that" | μήτι typically expects negative answer: "This is not the Christ, is it?" (NASB), but can also be used when questioner is in doubt concerning the answer (BDAG μήτι): "Could this be the Messiah?" (NIV) (cp. Matt 12:23)

4:30 | ἤρχοντο = "they began coming," ingressive impf. (W 545). Wallace points out that the crowd of Samaritans is coming to Jesus but has not yet arrived; they appear on the scene in v. 35 when Jesus says, "Lift up your eyes, and see that the fields are white for harvest."

4:31 | ἐν τῷ μεταξύ = "meanwhile" (BDAG ἐν 10a; μεταξύ 1bα)

4:33 | φαγεῖν = "[something] to eat" (see πεῖν in vv. 7, 9, 10)

4:34 | Attenuated ἵνα equivalent to inf. (BDAG ἵνα 2cα) | αὐτοῦ τὸ ἔργον = τὸ ἔργον αὐτοῦ

4:35 | ἔτι = "yet," of time not yet come (BDAG ἔτι 1c) | καί = "and then" (BDAG καί 1bζ) | ἔρχεται – futuristic present (BDF §323(2); Z §278) | ἔτι τετράμηνός ἐστιν καὶ ὁ θερισμὸς ἔρχεται = lit. "there are yet four months, and then comes the harvest" (NASB); more idiomatically, "there are still four months before the harvest comes" (BDAG ἔτι 1c; ZG)

4:36 | ἵνα ὁ σπείρων ὁμοῦ χαίρῃ καὶ ὁ θερίζων = "so that sowers and reaper may rejoice together" (ESV)

4:37 | ἄλλος ... ἄλλος = "one ... another"

4:38 | ὅ = "that for which"

4:39 | πολλοί ... τῶν Σαμαριτῶν = "many of the Samaritans"

4:40 | δύο ἡμέρας – acc. for extent of time (W 201)

4:41 | πολλῷ πλείους = "many more"

4:45 | πάντα ἑωρακότες ὅσα ἐποίησεν = ἑωρακότες πάντα ὅσα ἐποίησεν = "having seen all that he had done" (ESV) | ἐν τῇ ἑορτῇ = "at/during the [Passover] Feast" (cp. 2:13ff, 23) (BDAG ἐν 10b/c)

4:46 | ποιέω + double acc. = "turn x into y" (BDAG ποιέω 2hβ)

4:47 | μέλλω + inf. = "be about to"

4:49 | πρίν + inf. = "before"

4:51 | ἤδη αὐτοῦ καταβαίνοντος = "as he was still on his way down," gen. abs. | ζῇ – present retained in indirect discourse (W 537)

4:52 | κομψότερον ἔχω = "feel better" (BDAG ἔχω 10b), with ingressive aorist ἔσχεν = "he got better" (W 559; M 10) | ὥραν ἑβδόμην = "at the seventh hour" (= 1:00 p.m.); unusual use of acc. for time at which (M 34); would expect dat. (see W 203, Chart 16, "The Cases for Time")

4:54 | ἐλθών ἐκ = "when he had come from"

John 5
5:2 | ἔστιν = "there is" | ἐπὶ τῇ προβατικῇ [sc. πύλη] = "by the Sheep [Gate]" (BDF §241(6))

5:5 | "A man was there who had been ill for 38 years" (NASB) (BDAG ἔχω 7b; M 101), acc. for extent of time

5:6 | γνούς = "when he learned" (NIV) (BDAG γινώσκω 2), aorist ptc. | ὅτι πολὺν ἤδη χρόνον ἔχει = "that he had been [ill] for a long time now," for this usage of ἔχω with indications of time/age, cp. v. 5; ἔχει as extending-from-past present (W 519–20)

5:7 | ἵνα ... βάλῃ με = "to put me," attenuated ἵνα equivalent to inf. | ὅταν ταραχθῇ τὸ ὕδωρ = "when the water is stirred up" | ἐν ᾧ = "while"

5:10 | ἔξεστιν = "it is lawful/permitted"

5:13 | ὄχλου ὄντος = "while (or since) there was a crowd," gen. abs. | ὁ ἰαθείς = "the man who had been healed"

5:13, 15 | ἐστίν (2x) – present retained in indirect discourse

5:14 | ἵνα μή = "lest" | χεῖρόν τι = "something worse"

5:17 | ἕως ἄρτι = "until now" | κἀγώ = καὶ ἐγώ = "and I too"

5:18 | μᾶλλον = "even more" | λύω = either (1) "repeal, annul, abolish" ("In John, Jesus is not accused of breaking the Sabbath, but of doing away with it as an ordinance" [BDAG λύω 4]), or (2) "break" in the sense of "violate" (most English versions) | λέγω + double acc. (2x) = "call someone something" (BDAG λέγω 4) (cp. 15:15) | ἴσος + dat. = "equal with"

5:19 | ἀφ᾽ ἑαυτοῦ = "of his own accord" (ESV) (cp. v. 30) | ἃ ἂν ἐκεῖνος ποιῇ = "whatever he [= the Father] does" | ταῦτα καὶ ὁ υἱὸς ὁμοίως ποιεῖ = "these things the Son also does in like manner" (NASB)

5:20 | πάντα ἃ = "all that" | μείζονα τούτων ἔργα = "greater works than these," gen. of comparison (cp. v. 36)

5:21, 26 | ὥσπερ ... οὕτως καί (2x) = "just as ... so also"

5:22 | οὐδέ ... οὐδένα = "judges no one," negatives reinforce

5:24 | ὁ ... ἀκούων καὶ πιστεύων = "the one who hears and believes" | μεταβέβηκεν – gnomic perf. (W 580)

5:26–27 | δίδωμι = "grant [authority] to do something" (BDAG δίδωμι 13)

5:28 | οἱ ἐν τοῖς μνημείοις = "those who are in the tombs"

5:33 | ὑμεῖς ἀπεστάλκατε = "you sent [a delegation] to John" (cp. 1:19)

5:35 | πρὸς ὥραν = "for a time" (BDAG πρός 3bβ; ὥρα 2b)

5:36 | μείζω + gen. of comparison

5:37 | ὁ πέμψας με πατήρ = "the Father who sent me"

5:38 | μένοντα = "remaining, abiding," present ptc. | ὅτι = "for" (BDAG ὅτι 4b) | ὃν ἀπέστειλεν ἐκεῖνος = "[the one] whom he has sent"

5:40 | καί = "and yet" (BDAG καί 1bη)

5:42 | ἔγνωκα ὑμᾶς ὅτι … οὐκ ἔχετε = lit. "I know you, *that* you do not have," i.e., "I know that you do not have," prolepsis (Z §207) | ἡ ἀγάπη τοῦ θεοῦ = could be (1) "love for God," objective gen., or (2) "God's love," subjective gen.

5:44 | δόξαν παρὰ ἀλλήλων λαμβάνοντες = "when you receive glory from one another," conditional adverbial ptc.

5:45 | κατηγορέω takes gen. object (ὑμῶν) (2x)

John 6
6:2 | Shift from sg. (ἠκολούθει) to pl. (ἐθεώρουν) due to collective singular ὄχλος (*constructio ad sensum*) | BDAG ἐπί 8

6:6 | πειράζων αὐτόν = "to test him (= Philip)," telic ptc. (W 635–7) | αὐτὸς γὰρ ᾔδει τί ἔμελλεν ποιεῖν = "for he himself knew what he would do" (ESV)

6:7 | διακοσίων δηναρίων ἄρτοι = "200 denarii worth of bread," gen. of price (W 122) | ἀρκοῦσιν αὐτοῖς ἵνα ἕκαστος βραχύ τι λάβῃ = "enough for each of them to get a little," attenuated ἵνα

6:9 | ἀλλὰ ταῦτα τί ἐστιν εἰς τοσούτους; = "but what are they for so many?" (ESV); "but how far will they go among so many?" (NIV) | BDAG εἰς 4g

6:10 | ποιέω + acc. + inf. = "make someone do something" (BDAG ποιέω 2ha) | τὸν ἀριθμόν = "with reference to number," acc. of respect (W 203–4; M 33) | ὡς with numerals = "about"

6:11 | ὁμοίως καὶ ἐκ τῶν ὀψαρίων ὅσον ἤθελον = "likewise also of the fish as much as they wanted" (NASB)

6:12 | ἵνα μή τι ἀπόληται = "so that nothing may be lost/wasted"

6:13 | ἐγέμισαν δώδεκα κοφίνους κλασμάτων = "they filled twelve baskets with fragments," verbs of filling take gen. of content (W 94) (cp. 2:7)

6:14 | ὃ ἐποίησεν σημεῖον = [τὸ] σημεῖον ὃ ἐποίησεν – incorporation of the antecedent into the relative clause, with omission of article (BDF §294(5)) | ὁ ἐρχόμενος = "who is to come," futuristic present ptc.

6:15 | γνούς – see 5:6

6:17 | σκοτία ἤδη ἐγεγόνει = "by now darkness had fallen," intensive plupf., emphasis on resultant state (W 585)

6:18 | ἀνέμου μεγάλου πνέοντος = "because a strong wind was blowing" (ESV), causal gen. abs.

6:19 | σταδίους – acc. for extent of space (W 202)

6:21 | ἐγένετο ἐπί = "arrived at" (BDAG γίνομαι 6c) (cp. Lk 22:40) | εἰς ἣν ὑπῆγον = "to which they were going," conative impf. (W 550)

6:23 | ἄλλα – neut. pl. of ἄλλος, not to be confused with ἀλλά

6:25 | πότε ὧδε γέγονας; = "when did you get here?"

6:26 | ὅτι (2x) = "because"

6:27 | ἐργάζομαι τὴν βρῶσιν = "work for food" (BDAG ἐργάζομαι 2e; M 33)

6:28, 30, 34 | εἶπον (3x) – can be either 1s or 3p aorist of λέγω (here 3p)

6:29 | τὸ ἔργον τοῦ θεοῦ = "the work God requires," descriptive gen.? (W 79) | ἵνα equivalent to explanatory inf. after demonstrative (BDAG ἵνα 2e; BDF §394) (cp. v. 50; 15:8; 17:3) | ὃν ἀπέστειλεν = "[him] whom he has sent" | ἐκεῖνος (i.e., God the Father) is the subject of ἀπέστειλεν

6:30 | τί ἐργάζῃ; = "what work are you doing?" (BDAG ἐργάζομαι 2a)

6:31, 45 | ἔστιν γεγραμμένον (2x) – perf. periphrastic (W 649)

6:33 | ὁ καταβαίνων καὶ διδούς = "the one who comes down and who gives life," two present ptcs. governed by one article; Granville Sharp Rule (W 274)

6:36 | καί ... καί ... = "*although* you have seen me, *yet* you do not believe" (BDAG καί 2f)

6:39 | ἵνα πᾶν ὃ δέδωκέν μοι μὴ ἀπολέσω ἐξ αὐτοῦ – anacoluthon (BDF §466(3)). John begins with a positive construction (which might have read: "that all he has given me I might raise up in the last day") but switches midstream to a negative construction, then catches himself and inserts a belated ἐξ αὐτοῦ (lit. "[any] of them"). To correct the anacoluthon in translation, we have to retroject ἐκ earlier in the sentence: "that *of* all he has given me I might not lose any *of* them." | αὐτοῦ and αὐτό – collective neut. sg. pronouns in agreement with πᾶν, best translated "of them" and "them" respectively.

6:42 | οὗ ἡμεῖς οἴδαμεν τὸν πατέρα καὶ μητέρα = "whose father and mother we know"

6:44 | κἀγώ = καὶ ἐγώ (cp. vv. 54, 56, 57)

6:45 | διδακτοὶ θεοῦ = "taught by God," i.e., hearing from the Father and learning (v. 45b); θεοῦ = gen. of agency (W 126) | πᾶς ὁ ἀκούσας καὶ μαθών = "whoever hears and learns," substantival gnomic aorist ptcs. with generic ref. (W 615 n8)

6:46 | οὐχ ὅτι τὸν πατέρα ἑώρακέν τις = "not that *anyone* has seen the Father"

6:53, 54, 56 | αὐτοῦ τὸ αἷμα = τὸ αἷμα αὐτοῦ – ditto for μου τὴν σάρκα/τὸ αἷμα

6:57 | καθώς ... καί = "just as ... so also" (BDAG καί 2c) | ὁ ζῶν πατήρ = "the living Father" | διά + acc. (2x) = "because of" | κἀκεῖνος = καὶ ἐκεῖνος

6:60 | πολλοὶ ἐκ τῶν μαθητῶν αὐτοῦ = "many of his disciples"

6:62 | ἐὰν οὖν = "then what if ..." i.e., would you still take offense? – aposiopesis (BDF §482) | τὸ πρότερον – adv. acc. (BDAG πρότερος 1bβ)

6:64 | εἰσὶν ἐξ ὑμῶν τινες οἵ = "there are some of you who," ἐκ for partitive gen. (cp. vv. 70–71) | ὁ παραδώσων αὐτόν = "the one who would betray him," future ptc.

6:65 | διὰ τοῦτο εἴρηκα ὑμῖν ὅτι = "this is why I told you that"

6:66 | ἐκ τούτου = either (1) temporal "from this time" (NIV) or (2) logical "as a result of this" (NASB) (ZG; M 72–3; BDAG ἐκ 3e) (cp. 19:12) | ἀπέρχομαι εἰς τὰ ὀπίσω = "turn back," "go away," "leave"

6:67 | μὴ καὶ ὑμεῖς θέλετε ὑπάγειν; = "you do not want to go away also, do you?" (NASB), μή expects negative response

6:70–71 | εἷς ἐκ (2x) = "one of" (cp. v. 64)

6:70 | καί = "and yet" (BDAG καί 1bη) | διάβολος = "a devil," possibly "the devil" (W 249)

John 7
7:2 | ἡ σκηνοπηγία = "the Feast of Booths" (cp. LXX Deut 16:16; 2 Macc 1:9)

7:3 | ἵνα + future indic.; infrequent (BDF §369(2); M 139; W 699 n35) | σοῦ τὰ ἔργα = τὰ ἔργα σοῦ

7:4 | οὐδείς τι ποιεῖ = "no one does anything" | Coordination for subordination – "For no one does anything in secret *while/when* [καί] he himself seeks to be [known] publicly" (NASB) (BDF §442(4)) | αὐτός ... εἶναι – nom. with inf.; rare (BDF §405(1))

7:7 | Neut. pl. nouns (τὰ ἔργα) take sg. verbs (ἐστίν)

7:10 | ὡς ... τότε = "when ... then" | καὶ αὐτός = "he himself also"

7:12 | οἱ μέν ... ἄλλοι δέ = "some ... others" | ἀγαθός ἐστιν = "he is a good man"

7:13 | διὰ τὸν φόβον τῶν Ἰουδαίων = "for fear of the Jews," objective gen.

7:14 | ἤδη τῆς ἑορτῆς μεσούσης = "when the feast was now half over," gen. abs.

7:15 | πῶς ... μὴ μεμαθηκώς; = "how has this man become learned, having never been educated?" (NASB); "... without having been taught?" (NIV)

7:17–18, 28 | ἀπό + reflexive (3x) = "on one's own [authority/initiative]"

7:19 | καί = "and yet" (BDAG καί 1bη) | τί; = "why?"

7:23 | ἄνθρωπος = "a male person" (BDAG ἄνθρωπος 3), "a boy" (NIV) | ἐμοὶ χολᾶτε ὅτι = "are you angry with me because …?"

7:24 | κατ' ὄψιν = "by outward appearances" | κρίνειν τὴν δικαίαν κρίσιν – cognate acc. (M 33)

7:25 | ὅν = "[the man] whom"

7:26 | παρρησίᾳ = "boldly," dat. of manner (W 162) | ἔγνωσαν = "concluded" (NIV), effective aorist (ZG; Z §252) | "Can it be that the [Jewish] rulers have indeed concluded that this man is the Messiah?" (BDAG μήποτε 3a)

7:27 | τοῦτον οἴδαμεν πόθεν ἐστίν – prolepsis (BDF §476(2)) (cp. 9:29)

7:28 | κἀμε = καὶ ἐμέ | καί … καί = "not only … but also" ("you not only know me, but you also know where I am from") (BDAG καί 1f) | Third καί = "and yet" (BDAG καί 1bη)

7:29 | ὅτι παρ' αὐτοῦ εἰμί = "for I am from him" | κἀκεῖνος = καὶ ἐκεῖνος

7:31 | πλείονα σημεῖα ὧν = πλείονα σημεῖα τούτων ἅ – the relative pronoun, which includes the demonstrative, has been assimilated to the case of the omitted demonstrative (BDF §294(4)) (cp. 17:9) | "When the Messiah comes, he will not perform more signs than those which this man has performed, will he?"

7:33 | ἔτι χρόνον μικρὸν μεθ' ὑμῶν εἰμί = "I will be with you a little longer," futuristic present

7:35, 39 | μέλλω + inf. (3x) = "be about to"

7:38 | ποταμοί … ὕδατος ζῶντος = "rivers of living water"

7:39 | Subject of ἔμελλον is οἱ πιστεύσαντες

7:40 | ἐκ τοῦ ὄχλου = "some in the crowd," partitive ἐκ functioning as subject (BDAG ἐκ 4aγ; BDF §164(2))

7:41 | ἄλλοι … οἱ δέ = "others … still others" | μή expects negative answer (cp. vv. 47, 48, 51, 52)

7:41–42 | ἔρχεται (2x) = "is to come," futuristic present

7:43 | δι' αὐτόν = "because of him" (NASB), "over him" (ESV)

7:44 | τινὲς ἐξ αὐτῶν = "some of them"

7:45 | διὰ τί; = "why?"

7:47 | μὴ καὶ ὑμεῖς πεπλάνησθε; = "you *also* have not been deceived, have you?" (BDAG πλανάω 2cδ) (cp. v. 12)

7:48 | "No one of the rulers or Pharisees has believed in Him, has he?" (NASB)

7:50 | τὸ πρότερον – adv. acc. (BDAG πρότερος 1bβ) | εἷς ὢν ἐξ αὐτῶν = "who was one of them"

7:51 | "Does our law condemn anyone without first hearing him to find out what he is doing?" (NIV 1984)

John 8
8:2 | ὄρθρου = "early in the morning," gen. of time (W 122)

8:3–4 | ἐπί + dat. (2x) = "at the time of, in" (ZG; BDAG ἐπί 18b)

8:5 | σὺ οὖν τί λέγεις; = "you, then, what do you say?" prolepsis (BDF §476)

8:6 | πειράζοντες = "to test him," telic adverbial ptc. | ἵνα ἔχωσιν κατηγορεῖν αὐτοῦ = "that they might have [grounds] for accusing him" (NASB), inf. used as substantive (cp. 4:7, 9, 10)

89 | εἷς καθ' εἷς = "one by one," preposition + nom. is "bad" grammar; but in this case it is a colloquial expression (cp. Mark 14:19) | Subject of κατελείφθη (= "left") is Jesus

8:11 | ἀπὸ τοῦ νῦν = "from now on"

8:14 | κἄν = καὶ ἐάν = "even if" (BDAG κἄν 2)

8:17 | δύο ἀνθρώπων ἡ μαρτυρία = "the testimony of two people"

8:19 | εἰ ἐμὲ ᾔδειτε, καὶ τὸν πατέρα μου ἂν ᾔδειτε = "if you knew me, you would know my Father *also*," second class condition (past contrary-to-fact) (W 694–5) (cp. 4:10; 5:46)

8:22 | μήτι ἀποκτενεῖ ἑαυτόν; = "Surely he is not going to kill himself, is he?" μήτι expects negative answer; more emphatic than μή (hence "surely")

8:25 | Τὴν ἀρχὴν ὅ τι καὶ λαλῶ ὑμῖν – obscure. Τὴν ἀρχήν is probably adv. acc.: "[I am] what I have been saying to you *from the beginning*." Others take it as a question; see commentaries for other possibilities.

8:26 | BDAG εἰς 4c

8:27 | "They did not realize that he had been speaking to them about the Father" (NASB), λέγειν τινα = "to speak about someone" (BDF §151(1))

8:30 | ταῦτα αὐτοῦ λαλοῦντος = "as he was saying these things," gen. abs.

8:33 | οὐδενὶ δεδουλεύκαμεν πώποτε = "we have never been enslaved to anyone"

8:38 | ἃ ἑώρακα παρά = lit. "what I have seen from," possibly "heard from" (BDAG ὁράω A1b) | παρὰ τῷ πατρί ... παρὰ τοῦ πατρός = "from *my* Father ... from *your* father," article as possessive pronoun (BDF §278; W 215)

8:39 | ἐποιεῖτε – impf. (many MSS add ἄν) = "you would be doing"

8:42 | καὶ ἥκω – could (1) be taken with ἐκ τοῦ θεοῦ, "I proceeded forth and have come from God" (NASB), or (2) be independent, "I came from God and now am here" (NIV 1984)

8:43 | ὅτι = "because"

8:44 | ἐκ τοῦ πατρὸς τοῦ διαβόλου = "of your father the devil," gen. of apposition (W 98; BDF §268(2)) | ἐκ τῶν ἰδίων = "from his own nature" (NASB), "out of his own character" (ESV), "from his own well-stocked supply" (BDAG ἴδιος 4b) | ψεύστης ἐστὶν καὶ ὁ πατὴρ αὐτοῦ = "he is a liar and the father *of it* [= lies, falsehood]," *constructio ad sensum*, collective sg. (Z §45; BDF §282(3))

8:45 | ἐγὼ δὲ ὅτι τὴν ἀλήθειαν λέγω = "but I, because I speak the truth," prolepsis

8:48 | οὐ καλῶς λέγομεν ἡμεῖς = "do we not rightly say ...?"

8:50 | ἔστιν ὁ ζητῶν καὶ κρίνων = "there is One who seeks it, and he is the judge" (ESV)

8:52 | Verb of tasting takes gen. (θανάτου)

8:53 | μείζων + gen. of comparison = "greater than" | τίνα σεαυτὸν ποιεῖς; = "who do you make yourself out (claim/pretend) to be?" (BDAG ποιέω 2hβ)

8:55 | κἂν εἴπω = "if I were to say" | ἔσομαι ὅμοιος ὑμῖν ψεύστης = "I would be a liar like you"

8:56 | Attenuated ἵνα equivalent to inf. (BDAG ἵνα 2aα)

8:57 | πεντήκοντα ἔτη οὔπω ἔχεις = "you are not yet 50 years old" (cp. 5:5–6) (BDAG ἔχω 7b)

8:58 | ἐγὼ εἰμί = "I AM" (cp. LXX Exod 3:14; Isa 41:4; 43:10; 46:4) (W 530–1)

8:59 | ἐκρύβη καὶ ἐξῆλθεν – second verb should be ptc., i.e., ἐκρύβη ἐξελθών = "he hid himself among the people and so escaped" (BDAG καί 1aε; BDF §471(4))

John 9

9:1 | παράγων = "as he passed by" (BDAG παράγω 3) | ἐκ γενετῆς = "from birth," of the time when something begins (BDAG ἐκ 5a; M 72–3)

9:2 | Ecbatic ἵνα (BDAG ἵνα 3; W 473)

9:3 | οὔτε ... οὔτε = "neither ... nor" | ἀλλ' ἵνα – (1) possibly imperatival ἵνα (Z §415; BDAG ἵνα 2g): "but let the works of God be revealed" (ZG; M 145); (2) more likely ellipsis: "on the contrary [this happened] in order that ..." (BDF §448(7)) | Neut. pl. noun viewed as collective sg. (τὰ ἔργα τοῦ θεοῦ) with sg. verb (φανερωθῇ) (W 399)

9:4 | "We (ἡμᾶς) must do the works of him who sent me (μέ)" – to correct the incongruity some scribes changed ἡμᾶς to ἐμέ ("I must do the works of him who sent me"), while others changed μέ to ἡμᾶς ("We must do the works of him who sent us") | ἕως + indic. = "as long as, while" (BDAG ἕως 2a)

9:5 | ὅταν + subj. (ὦ) = "while"

9:6 | ἐπέχρισεν αὐτοῦ τὸν πηλόν ἐπὶ τοὺς ὀφθαλμούς = "he smeared the mud on his eyes." Though αὐτοῦ is oddly placed, it probably goes with τοὺς ὀφθαλμούς (cp. vv. 11, 15) (BDF §473(1)). Some scribes found it difficult and omitted it.

9:7 | νίπτεσθαι εἰς = "to wash oneself in" (BDAG εἰς 1bγ) (cp. βαπτίζεσθαι εἰς, Mark 1:9)

9:8 | οἱ θεωροῦντες αὐτὸν τὸ πρότερον ὅτι προσαίτης ἦν = "those who previously saw that he had been a beggar" | τὸ πρότερον – adv. acc. (cp. 6:62; 7:50)

9:9, 11, 17 | ὅτι recitative (4x)

9:9 | ἐκεῖνος ἔλεγεν = "he kept saying" (ESV, NASB), "he himself insisted" (NIV), iterative impf. (W 546)

9:10, 11, 14, 17, 21, 26, 30 | σου/μου/αὐτοῦ οἱ ὀφθαλμοί = οἱ ὀφθ. σου/μου/αὐτοῦ

9:13 | τόν ποτε τυφλόν = "the man who once was blind"

9:14 | ἐν ᾗ ἡμέρᾳ = ἐν [τῇ] ἡμέρᾳ ἐν ᾗ – incorporation of the antecedent into the relative clause, with omission of article (BDF §294(5))

9:15 | μου ἐπὶ τοὺς ὀφθαλμούς = ἐπὶ τοὺς ὀφθαλμούς μου

9:16 | ἐν αὐτοῖς = "among them" (cp. 10:19)

9:18 | ἕως ὅτου = "until" | "They did not believe concerning him that he had been (ἦν) blind and had regained his sight, until they called the parents of him who had regained his sight," impf. (ἦν) to express relative time (BDF §330)

9:19 | ἄρτι = νῦν (cp. vv. 21, 25)

9:21, 23 | ἡλικίαν ἔχει (2x) = "he is of age" (cp. ἔχω in 5:5–6; 8:57)

9:22–23 | Parenthesis – note the intricate chiastic logic: (a) His parents said "¹Ask him; ²he is of age," because (ὅτι) they feared the Jews (v. 22a); (b) why did they fear the Jews? Because (γάρ) the Jews had agreed to excommunicate anyone who confessed Jesus as the Christ (v. 22b); (a´) that is why (διὰ τοῦτο) they said, "²He is of age; ¹ask him" (v. 23)

9:22 | ἤδη ... γένηται = "for the Jews had already agreed that [BDAG ἵνα 2aα] if anyone confessed Him to be Christ, he was to be put out of the synagogue" (NASB)

9:23 | The ESV strangely leaves v. 23 out of the parenthesis

9:24 | ἐκ δευτέρου = "a second time" (BDAG ἐκ 5bβ) | δὸς δόξαν τῷ θεῷ = "give God the praise" by telling the truth; an adjuration (BDAG δόξα 3)

9:25 | τυφλὸς ὤν = "though I was blind," present ptc. used in reference to the past (BDF §339(3))

9:27 | τί; = "why?"

9:29 | Μωϋσεῖ (dat.) = "to Moses" | τοῦτον δὲ οὐκ οἴδαμεν πόθεν ἐστίν = "*but as for this man*, we do not know where he is from," prolepsis (BDF §476(2)) (cp. 7:27)

9:30 | ἐν τούτῳ γὰρ τὸ θαυμαστόν ἐστιν = "well, here is an amazing thing" (NASB) | καὶ ἤνοιξέν μου τοὺς ὀφθαλμούς = "*and yet* he opened my eyes" (BDAG καί 1bη) (cp. 10:39)

9:32 | ἐκ τοῦ αἰῶνος οὐκ ἠκούσθη = "since the beginning of time it has never been heard" (NASB), "from time immemorial" (M 73) (BDAG ἐκ 5a) | τυφλοῦ γεγεννημένου = "of someone born blind"

9:33 | Second class (contrary to fact) condition (W 694)

9:34 | ἐν ἁμαρτίαις σὺ ἐγεννήθης ὅλος = "you were born entirely in sins" (NASB), "altogether, wholly" (BDAG ὅλος 2), "through and through" (ZG); "you were steeped in sin at birth" (NIV)

9:34–35 | ἐκβάλλω (2x) = "expel someone from a group," e.g., synagogue (BDAG ἐκβάλλω 1; cp. Lk 6:22; Gal 4:30; 3 John 10) | Pleonastic ἔξω (2x) (cp. 12:31)

9:36 | καί introducing a question (BDAG καί 1bθ) | ἵνα πιστεύσω εἰς αὐτόν = "[tell me] that I may believe in him," brachylogy; final clause after a question (BDF §483) (cp. 1:22)

9:37 | καί ... καί = "not only ... but also" ("Not only have you seen him, but also he is the one who is speaking with you!") (BDAG καί 1f)

9:39 | First εἰς = "for," denoting purpose (BDAG εἰς 4f); second εἰς = "into" | εἰς κρίμα ἐγὼ εἰς τὸν κόσμον τοῦτον ἦλθον = "for judgment I came into this world," κρίμα has connotation of "separation" (BDAG κρίμα 6); "Jesus' presence constitutes a judgment between men according as they believe in or reject him" (ZG) (cp. 3:17–21; 8:47; 10:26–27; Lk 2:34)

9:40 | ἐκ τῶν Φαρισαίων οἱ μετ' αὐτοῦ ὄντες = "some of the Pharisees who were with him," partitive ἐκ functioning as object (BDAG ἐκ 4aγ; BDF §164(2))

John 10

10:1 | ἡ αὐλὴ τῶν προβάτων = "the sheepfold"

10:3 | τὰ ἴδια πρόβατα = "his own sheep" (cp. v. 12) | κατ᾽ ὄνομα = "by name"

10:4 | ὅταν τὰ ἴδια πάντα ἐκβάλῃ = "when he has brought out (or led out) all his own [sheep]" (BDAG ἐκβάλλω 2)

10:6 | ἐκεῖνοι δὲ οὐκ ἔγνωσαν τίνα ἦν ἃ ἐλάλει αὐτοῖς = "but they did not understand what it was that he had been saying to them" | τίνα ἦν ἃ = "what were the things that," neut. pl. subjects take sg. verbs

10:7 | ἡ θύρα τῶν προβάτων = "the door for the sheep," gen. of purpose (BDF §166; but W 100 n76)

10:10 | καὶ περισσὸν ἔχωσιν = "and have it abundantly" (NASB, ESV), "and have it to the full" (NIV), "beyond what is necessary" (BDAG περισσός 2a)

10:12 | ὁ μισθωτὸς καὶ οὐκ ὢν ποιμήν = "he who is a hired hand and not a shepherd" (NASB) | οὗ οὐκ ἔστιν τὰ πρόβατα ἴδια = "for whom they are not 'his own sheep,'" neut. pl. subjects take sg. verbs (also vv. 6, 16, 21)

10:13 | οὐ μέλει αὐτῷ περὶ τῶν προβάτων = lit. "it is not of concern to him about the sheep," i.e., "he doesn't care about the sheep" (cp. 12:6)

10:15 | κἀγώ = καὶ ἐγώ

10:16 | κἀκεῖνα = καὶ ἐκεῖνα

10:18 | ἀπ᾽ ἐμαυτοῦ = "of my own accord" (ESV)

10:19 | ἐν τοῖς Ἰουδαίοις = "among the Jews" (cp. 9:16)

10:20 | τί αὐτοῦ ἀκούετε; = "why do you listen to him?"

10:21 | ταῦτα τὰ ῥήματα οὐκ ἔστιν δαιμονιζομένου = "these words are not [those] of a demon possessed man"

10:24 | ἕως πότε; = "how long?" | αἴρω τὴν ψυχήν τινος = lit. "lift up someone's soul," i.e. keep someone in suspense (BDAG αἴρω 5)

10:26 | οὐκ ἐστὲ ἐκ τῶν προβάτων τῶν ἐμῶν = lit. "you are not of my sheep," "you are not part of my flock" (ESV), ἐκ for partitive gen.

10:28 | οὐ μή + aor. subj. + εἰς τὸν αἰῶνα = lit. "not to eternity," Hebr. way of saying "never" | οὐ + future + τις = "no one will"

10:29 | πάντων μεῖζον = "greater than all," gen. of comparison

10:32 | διὰ ποῖον αὐτῶν ἔργον = either (1) lit. "for which category of works of these?" (W 356 n85), or (2) more likely, "for which work of these?" taking ποῖος as equivalent to τίς (BDAG ποῖος 2aα) | λιθάζετε = "are you trying (or about) to stone," conative (M 8; ZG) or tendential (W 535) present

10:34 | οὐκ ἔστιν; = "is it not?" | ὅτι recitative

10:35 | εἰ ἐκείνους εἶπεν θεούς = "if he called them gods" (BDAG λέγω 4)

10:36 | ὃν ὁ πατὴρ ἡγίασεν = "[him] whom the Father sanctified/consecrated" | First ὅτι is recitative (cp. v. 34); second ὅτι = "because"

10:38 | κἄν = καὶ ἄν = "even if" | ἵνα γνῶτε καὶ γινώσκητε = "that you might *come* to know [aorist subj.] and *continue* to know [present subj.]"

10:39 | καί = "and yet" (BDAG καί 1bη)

10:40 | τὸ πρῶτον = "earlier," adv. acc. (BDAG πρῶτος 1aβ; cp. 12:16; 19:39)

10:41 | μέν ... δέ = "although ... yet"

John 11
11:1 | ἦν τις ἀσθενῶν = "there was a certain sick man," substantival anarthrous present ptc. (W 619; BDF §§264(6); 413)

11:2 | Parenthesis: "(Now it was the Mary who anointed the Lord ... whose brother was sick)," from author's time-frame (BDF §339(1)) | ταῖς θριξὶν αὐτῆς = "with her hair," instrumental dat. (W 162–3)

11:3 | ὅν = "[he] whom"

11:4 | οὐκ ἔστιν πρὸς θάνατον = "does not lead to death" (ESV) (BDAG πρός 3cγ) | ὑπὲρ τῆς δόξης τοῦ θεοῦ = "for the sake of [i.e., to reveal] the glory of God" (BDAG ὑπέρ A1b) (cp. Rom 1:5)

11:6 | ἐν ᾧ ἦν τόπῳ = ἐν [τῷ] τόπῳ ᾧ ἦν = "in the place where he was," incorporation of the antecedent into the relative clause, with omission of article (cp. 6:14; 9:14)

11:7, 15, 16 | ἄγωμεν = "let us go," hortatory subj.

11:9 | δώδεκα ὧραι τῆς ἡμέρας = "12 hours in the day," gen. of time (W 124); ἡμέρα = the period between sunrise and sunset (BDAG ἡμέρα 1)

11:11 | πορεύομαι – futuristic present (W 536)

11:12 | σωθήσεται = "he will get better" (NIV) (cp. Mark 5:28) (BDAG σῴζω 1c)

11:13 | ἐκεῖνοι ἔδοξαν = "they thought" | ἡ κοιμήσεως τοῦ ὕπνου = lit. "the sleep of sleep," i.e., "literal sleep" (NASB), gen. of apposition (W 98–9)

11:15 | χαίρω ὅτι = "glad that," with ὅτι clause giving the reason (BDAG χαίρω 1; ὅτι 1e) | The ἵνα clause immediately follows and completes διά + acc. (cp. v. 42), but in translation clarity is enhanced if moved to end: "I am glad *for your sakes* that I was not there, *so that you may believe*" (NASB)

11:16 | ἄγωμεν καὶ ἡμεῖς = "let us *also* go"

11:17 | τέσσαρας ἤδη ἡμέρας ἔχοντα ἐν τῷ μνημείῳ = "had already been in the tomb for four days" (NIV) (cp. 5:5–6; 8:57; 9:21, 23 for this use of ἔχω)

11:18 | ὡς ἀπό σταδίων δεκαπέντε = "about 15 stadia away" (BDAG ἀπό 4)

11:20 | ἔρχεται = "was coming," present retained in indirect discourse

11:21, 32 | εἰ ἦς ὧδε (2x) = "if you had been here"

11:25 | κἂν = "even if"

11:31 | δόξαντες = "supposing" (cp. v. 13)

11:33 | τοὺς συνελθόντας αὐτῇ Ἰουδαίους = "the Jews who had come with her," συν- prefix requires dat. pronoun (αὐτῇ) | ἐνεβριμήσατο τῷ πνεύματι = "he was deeply moved in his [human] spirit," dat. of respect (ZG; Z §53); a strong term with possible hints of anger (see commentaries) (cp. v. 38; Matt 9:30; Mk 1:43; 14:5) | ἐτάραξεν ἑαυτόν = "he threw himself into inner turmoil," "he became greatly agitated"

11:37 | ποιέω = "cause, bring it about that" (BDAG ποιέω 2hα) – "Could not this man ... have kept this man also from dying?" (NASB)

11:39 | ὁ τετελευτηκώς = "the dead man" (cp. ὁ τεθνηκώς, v. 44)

11:42 | διὰ τὸν ὄχλον ... ἵνα πιστεύσωσιν (cp. v. 15) = "for the sake of the crowd ... that they may believe," from collective sg. to pl. (*constructio ad sensum*)

11:44 | δεδεμένος τοὺς πόδας καὶ τὰς χεῖρας = "bound hand and foot," acc. of respect (BDF §160; W 203) | ἄφετε αὐτὸν ὑπάγειν = "let him go [home]"

11:45 | οἱ ἐλθόντες πρὸς τὴν Μαριάμ = "who had come to visit Mary" (NIV)

11:47 | συνάγω συνέδριον = "convene a meeting of the Sanhedrin" | τί ποιοῦμεν; = "What are we going to do?" rare use of present indicative in deliberative sense (BDF §366(4)) | ὅτι = "for"

11:48 | ἐὰν ἀφῶμεν αὐτὸν οὕτως = "if we let him [go on] like this" | ἡμῶν καὶ τὸν τόπον καὶ τὸ ἔθνος = "both our place [= the temple] and our nation" (on καί ... καί, see BDF §444(3))

11:49 | εἷς τις ἐξ αὐτῶν (cp. Lk 22:50) = "a certain one of them," εἷς often replaces τις as an indef. article, but here both are used – pleonastic (Z §155; BDAG εἷς 3c) | ὑμεῖς οὐκ οἴδατε οὐδέν = "you know nothing at all," double negatives reinforce

11:49, 51 | τοῦ ἐνιαυτοῦ ἐκείνου (2x) = "that year," gen. of time (W 124)

11:51 | ἀφ' ἑαυτοῦ = "on his own initiative" | μέλλω + inf. = "be about to"

11:54 | εἰς Ἐφραὶμ λεγομένην πόλιν = "to a city called Ephraim" | κἀκεῖ = καὶ ἐκεῖ

11:57 | δεδώκεισαν ἐντολάς = "they had given orders" | ἵνα ἐάν τις γνῷ ποῦ ἐστιν μηνύσῃ = "that if anyone found out where he was, they should report [it]," present (ἐστιν) retained in indirect discourse

John 12

12:1 | πρὸ ἓξ ἡμερῶν τοῦ πάσχα = "six days before the Passover," Hellenistic construction (BDF §213; BDAG ἡμέρα 2c)

12:3 | λίτραν μύρου[1] νάρδου[2] πιστικῆς[2] πολυτίμου[1] = "a pound of extremely expensive perfume made of pure nard," [1]partitive gen. (W 84), [2]gen. of material (W 91) | ἐπληρώθη ἐκ = "filled with" (BDAG ἐκ 4aζ)

12:5 | τριακοσίων δηναρίων = "for 300 denarii," gen. of price (W 122)

12:6 | οὐχ ὅτι περὶ τῶν πτωχῶν ἔμελεν αὐτῷ = lit. "not because it was of concern to him about the poor," i.e., "not because he cared about the poor" (cp. 10:13) | τὰ βαλλόμενα ἐβάσταζεν = "he used to pilfer the contributions" (BDAG βάλλω 3b; βαστάζω 3b), customary impf.

12:7 | ἄφες αὐτὴν ἵνα ... τηρήσῃ αὐτό – Option (1) BDAG τηρέω 2: "let her alone, so that she may *save it* [= the perfume] for the day of my burial." But since vv. 3–5 imply that she has used up all the perfume, others adopt option (2) BDAG τηρέω 3 (cp. 9:16; 14:15): "let her alone, so that she may *observe it* [= the Jewish burial custom (cp. 19:40); see NASB note] in anticipation of the day of my burial," or "let alone, [she did this] in order to observe it," etc. Some also suggest imperatival ἵνα (ZG; BDAG ἵνα 2g), which could go with either mng. of τηρέω: "let her alone, let her save it (or observe it)," etc.

12:11 | πολλοί ... τῶν Ἰουδαίων = "many of the Jews" | δι᾽ αὐτόν = "on account of him [= Lazarus]" | ὑπῆγον ... καὶ ἐπίστευον = "were going away and believing," distributive iterative imperfects (W 546)

12:13 | εἰς ὑπάντησιν αὐτῷ = "to meet him"

12:16 | αὐτοῦ οἱ μαθηταί = οἱ μαθηταὶ αὐτοῦ | τὸ πρῶτον = "at first," adv. acc. (BDAG πρῶτος 1aβ; cp. 10:40; 19:39) | ἦν γεγραμμένα = "had been written," plupf. periphrastic; neut. pl. subjects take sg. verbs | ἐπ᾽ αὐτῷ = "about him" (BDAG ἐπί 14a) | ταῦτα ἐποίησαν αὐτῷ = "they did these things to him [= Jesus]" | Coordination instead of subordination or hendiadys: "that what they had done to him had been recorded in scripture" (ZG; BDF §442(4, 16))

12:17 | ἐμαρτύρει (absolute) = "continued to testify [about him]" (NASB) | ὁ ὄχλος ὁ ὢν μετ᾽ αὐτοῦ ὅτε = "the crowd that was with him when"

12:18 | τοῦτο αὐτὸν πεποιηκέναι τὸ σημεῖον = "that he had performed this sign," indirect discourse; acc. αὐτόν as subject of inf.; τοῦτο goes with τὸ σημεῖον

12:19 | οὐκ ὠφελεῖτε οὐδέν = "you are accomplishing nothing" (BDAG ὠφελέω 2) (cp. Matt 27:24); more idiomatically: "this is getting us nowhere" (NIV)

12:21 | κύριε = "sir," voc.

12:23 | "The hour has come for the Son of Man to be glorified," attenuated ἵνα equivalent to inf. after nouns of time (BDAG ἵνα 2d) (cp. 13:1; 16:2, 32)

12:24 | ἐὰν μή + subj. = "unless"

12:26 | ἐὰν ἐμοί τις διακονῇ (2x) = "if anyone serves me" | Second καί = "also"

12:27 | καὶ τί εἴπω; = "what *then* shall I say?" deliberative subj., with καί introducing a question (BDAG καί 1bθ) (cp. v. 34) | ἀλλὰ διὰ τοῦτο ἦλθον εἰς τὴν ὥραν ταύτην = "No, it was for this very reason I came to this hour" (NIV)

12:28 | καί ... καί = "not only ... but also" ("not only have I glorified it, but I will also glorify it again") (BDAG καί 1f)

12:31 | Pleonastic ἔξω (cp. 9:34)

12:32 | κἀγώ = καὶ ἐγώ | μέλλω + inf. = "be about to"

12:34 | καὶ πῶς σὺ λέγεις = "how is it *then* that you say" (cp. v. 27)

12:35 | ἐν ὑμῖν = "among you"

12:35–36 ὡς + present indicative (2x) = "while"

12:37 | τοσαῦτα αὐτοῦ σημεῖα πεποιηκότος = "even though he had performed so many signs," concessive gen. abs.

12:40 | ἰάσομαι – future continuing a series of subjunctives to designate some further consequence (BDF §369(3))

12:42 | ὅμως μέντοι = "nevertheless" | καὶ ἐκ τῶν ἀρχόντων πολλοί = "many *even* of the authorities"

12:43 | ἡ δόξα τῶν ἀνθρώπων ... τοῦ θεοῦ = "the honor/approval/ praise (BDAG δόξα 3) that comes from humans ... from God," gens. of source (cp. 5:41, 44 where παρά + gen. is used) | μᾶλλον ἤπερ (= ἤ) = "rather than" (BDAG μᾶλλον 3c; ἤ 2eβ)

12:46 | φῶς = "as the Light"

12:47 | μου ... τῶν ῥημάτων = "my words" (cp. v. 48) | καὶ μὴ φυλάξῃ = "and does not keep [them]"

12:49 | ἐξ ἐμαυτοῦ = "on my own authority/initiative" | λαλήσω could be either aor. subj. or fut. indic. | "what to say and what to speak" (NASB), "what to say and how to say it" (NIV 1984)

John 13

13:1 | ἡ ὥρα ἵνα μεταβῇ = "his hour to depart," attenuated ἵνα equivalent to inf. after nouns of time (BDAG ἵνα 2d) (cp. 12:23; 16:2, 32)

13:2 | Two genitive absolutes | βάλλω εἰς τὴν καρδίαν ἵνα = "put [the idea] into the heart to," attenuated ἵνα equivalent to inf. | τὴν καρδίαν ... Ἰούδας Σίμωνος Ἰσκαριώτου = "the heart of Judas Iscariot, son of Simon"

13:3 | εἰδώς = "[Jesus] knowing"

13:4 | Finally, the main verbs – subject is Jesus

13:5 | βάλλω of liquids = "pour" (BDAG βάλλω 3b)

13:6, 8 | μου ... τοὺς πόδας (2x) = τοὺς πόδας μου (cp. v. 9)

13:8 | μέρος μετ᾽ ἐμοῦ = "share/part with me" (cp. Rev 20:6; 22:19)

13:9 | μὴ μόνον ἀλλὰ καί = "not only but also"

13:10 | ὅλος = "all over" (BDAG ὅλος 1bγ)

13:11 | τὸν παραδιδόντα αὐτόν = "who was going to betray him," futuristic present (W 536) | ὅτι recitative

13:13 | ὁ διδάσκαλος καὶ ὁ κύριος – nom. of appellation (W 61; BDF §143)

13:14 | καὶ ὑμεῖς = "you also"

13:15 | καθώς ... καί = "just as ... so also" (BDAG καί 2c) (cp. v. 33) | ἵνα ... καὶ ὑμεῖς ποιῆτε = "that you also should/must do," ἵνα with imperatival nuance

13:16 | μείζων + gen. of comparison (2x) = "greater than" | ἀπόστολος (< ἀποστέλλω) = "one who is sent," "messenger"

13:18 | ἐγὼ οἶδα τίνας ἐξελεξάμην = "I know whom I have chosen," interrogative in place of relative pronoun (BDF §298(4); Z §221) | ἀλλ' ἵνα = "but [this sovereign election is] in order that" (BDF §448(7)) (cp. Mk 14:49) | ἐπ' ἐμέ = "against me" (BDAG ἐπί 12b)

13:19 | ἀπ' ἄρτι (= "from now on") or ἀπάρτι (= "even now") | πρὸ τοῦ γενέσθαι = "before it comes to pass" (BDF §403; W 596) | ἵνα πιστεύσητε ὅταν γένηται = ἵνα ὅταν γένηται πιστεύσητε (cp. 14:29) = "so that, when it does come to pass, you may believe"

13:20 | ἄν τινα πέμψω = "whomever I send"

13:22 | ἀπορούμενοι περὶ τίνος λέγει = "at a loss [to know] about whom he was speaking"

13:24 | "So Simon Peter motioned to him to inquire who it might be [τίς ἂν εἴη] about whom he was speaking," potential optative (Z §356); present (λέγει) retained in indirect discourse

13:26 | ᾧ ἐγὼ βάψω ... καὶ δώσω = "to whom I will dip ... and give," coordination for subordination (ZG) | αὐτῷ = Semitic pleonastic pronoun (BDF §297)

13:27 | ὃ ποιεῖς = "what you are about to do," ingressive-futuristic present (W 537) | τάχιον = "quickly," comparative in form but not in mng. (BDAG ταχύς 1bβ)

13:28 | πρὸς τί = "with respect to what," i.e., "why" (BDAG πρός 3eα) | "None of those reclining [οὐδεὶς τῶν ἀνακειμένων] knew why [πρὸς τί] he had said this [τοῦτο] to him [αὐτῷ]"

13:29 | ὧν χρείαν ἔχομεν = "[the things] of which we have need" | τοῖς πτωχοῖς ἵνα τι δῷ = "that he should give something to the poor," imperatival ἵνα

13:32 | Textual problem: (a) phrase in brackets accidentally deleted by some scribes due to homoeoteleuton; (b) logical step-parallelism (vv. 31–32) is characteristically Johannine (Metzger) and necessary to make sense of the argument. First ἐν αὐτῷ = "in Jesus," second ἐν αὐτῷ = "in God the Father himself"

13:33 | καθὼς εἶπον τοῖς Ἰουδαίοις ... καὶ ὑμῖν λέγω = "as I said to the Jews ... so also I say to you" (cp. v. 15) | ὅτι recitative

13:34 | ἵνα ἀγαπᾶτε (2x) has imperatival force (BDAG ἵνα 2g; BDF §387(3))

13:35 | ἐν ἀλλήλοις = "among one another" (BDAG ἐν 1d) (cp. Rom 15:5)

13:38 | ἕως οὗ + aor. subj. = "until"

John 14
14:1 | πιστεύετε (2x) – could be present indicative or imperative

14:2 | Two possible punctuations, depending on whether ὅτι is taken as marker of discourse content ("that") or as logical ground ("for"): (1) "If it were not so, would I have told you *that* I go to prepare a place for you?" (ESV); (2) "If it were not so, I would have told you; *for* I go to prepare a place for you" (NASB)

14:3 | ἔρχομαι – futuristic present (W 536) (also vv. 18, 28) | καὶ ὑμεῖς ἦτε = "you also may be"

14:7 | Textual issue – either (1) negative: "if you had known (ἐγνώκειτε) me [which you do not], you would have known (ἐγνώκειτε ἄν) my Father also" (NASB, ESV) (cp. 8:19), or (2) positive: "if you have come to know me (ἐγνώκατε) [as in fact you do], you shall know (γνώσεσθε) my Father also" (see Metzger) | ἀπ᾽ ἄρτι (= "from now on") or ἀπάρτι (= "even now") (cp. 13:19)

14:9 | τοσούτῳ χρόνῳ = "so long," dat. for acc. of time (W 156; Z §54), note textual variant in acc. | εἰμί = "I have been" | μεθ᾽ ὑμῶν = μετὰ ὑμῶν (cp. vv. 16, 30)

14:12 | κἀκεῖνος = καὶ ἐκεῖνος | μείζονα [ἔργα] τούτων – gen. of comparison

14:13 | ὅ τι ἄν = "whatever"

14:16 | κἀγώ = καὶ ἐγώ (also vv. 20–21) | μεθ᾽ ὑμῶν = μετὰ ὑμῶν

14:17 | οὐδὲ γινώσκει = "nor knows [him]," αὐτό as object of θεωρεῖ is understood as object of γινώσκει as well | παρ᾽ ὑμῶν = παρὰ ὑμῶν (cp. vv. 24–25)

14:18 | ἔρχομαι – (see vv. 3, 28)

14:19 | ἔτι μικρὸν καί = "yet a little while and," i.e., "soon" (BDAG μικρός 1dβ) (cp. 16:16–19) | ὅτι ἐγὼ ζῶ καὶ ὑμεῖς ζήσετε = "because I live, you *too* will live"

14:22 | καὶ τί γέγονεν ὅτι; = "what *then* has happened that?" καί introducing a question (BDAG καί 1bθ) | μέλλω + inf. = "be about to"

14:28 | ἐχάρητε ἄν ὅτι = "you would be glad that" (NIV) | Third ὅτι = "for" | ὁ πατὴρ μείζων μού ἐστιν = "the Father is greater than I," gen. of comparison; it is a personal, not an ontological, superiority

14:30 | οὐκέτι πολλὰ λαλήσω μεθ᾽ ὑμῶν = "I will no longer talk much with you" (ESV), "I will not speak with you much longer" (NIV 1984) | ἐν ἐμοὶ οὐκ ἔχει οὐδέν = "he has no claim on me" (ESV)

14:31 | ἀλλ' ἵνα = "but [this is happening] in order that" (BDF §448(7)) (cp. 13:18)

John 15
15:2 | Subject of αἴρει & καθαίρει is ὁ πατήρ μου (v. 1) | καθαίρω ("clean, cleanse," when applied to horticulture, "clear, prune") is to be distinguished from καθαιρέω ("destroy"); καθαίρω is related to the word καθαρός, which explains the play on words in v. 3 ("You are already clean," i.e., pruned)

15:4 | μείνατε – constative aorist impv. (W 720–1) | ἀφ' ἑαυτοῦ = "by itself" | οὕτως οὐδὲ ὑμεῖς = "so neither [can] you [bear fruit] unless you abide in me," brachylogy (δύναται καρπὸν φέρειν is to be understood from the preceding καθώς clause)

15:5 | οὐ δύνασθε ποιεῖν οὐδέν = "you can do nothing," reinforcing double neg.

15:6 | ὡς τὸ κλῆμα = "like a branch"

15:7 | ὃ ἐὰν θέλητε αἰτήσασθε = "ask whatever you wish"

15:8 | ἐν τούτῳ [prospective] ... ἵνα (cp. v. 12) | ἐμοὶ μαθηταί = "my disciples," dat. of possession

15:9 | καθώς ... κἀγώ = "just as ... so also I" (BDAG καί 2c) (cp. 13:15)

15:12, 17 | ἵνα ἀγαπᾶτε (2x) – cp. 13:34

15:15 | λέγω + double acc. (2x) = "call someone something" (BDAG λέγω 4) (cp. 5:18) | ὅτι = "for"

15:16 | ὅ τι ἄν αἰτήσητε = "whatever you ask" (cp. 16:23) | ἵνα ... δῷ ὑμῖν = "so that he [= the Father] may give [it] to you"

15:18 | πρῶτον + gen. = "before"

15:19 | τὸ ἴδιον = "its own" | ὅτι δέ ... διὰ τοῦτο = "but because ... for this reason [retrospective]"

15:20 | μνημονεύω takes gen. (cp. 16:21) | καὶ τὸν ὑμέτερον τηρήσουσιν = "they will keep yours [= your word] also," ellipsis of λόγον, implied by τόν

15:22 | ἀφ᾽ ὑμῶν = ἀπὸ ὑμῶν

15:23 | οὐκ ἐρωτήσετε οὐδέν = "you will not ask me anything," reinforcing double neg. | ὁ ἐμὲ μισῶν καὶ τὸν πατέρα μου μισεῖ = "the one who hates me hates my Father *also*" | οὐδεὶς ἄλλος = "no one else"

15:24 | καί ... καί (2x) = "both ... and"

15:25 | ἀλλ᾽ ἵνα – imperatival (cp. 9:3; 13:18; 14:31) | δωρεάν – adv. acc.

15:27 | "You also will testify, because you have been with me from the beginning" (NASB), taking μαρτυρεῖτε as futuristic present, and ἐστέ as perfective present indicating "duration ... of an act up to and including the present" (BDF §322; W 532)

John 16

16:2 | ἀλλά = "indeed" (ESV), "in fact" (NIV) (BDAG ἀλλά 3; BDF §448(6)) | "An hour is coming for everyone who kills you to think ...," attenuated ἵνα equivalent to inf. after nouns of time (BDAG ἵνα 2d) (cp. v. 32; 12:23; 13:1) | πᾶς ὁ ἀποκτείνας ὑμᾶς = "whoever kills you," substantival gnomic aorist ptc. with generic ref. (W 615 n8) | δόξῃ λατρείαν προσφέρειν = "think he is offering," present indic. converted to inf. in indirect discourse (W 604)

16:4 | First αὐτῶν goes with ὥρα ("their hour"); second αὐτῶν is object of μνημονεύω and picks up ταῦτα ("that you may be remember them [= the things I told you]")

16:5 | οὐδεὶς ἐξ ὑμῶν = "none of you," ἐκ for partitive gen.

16:12 | ἔτι = "still" | ἄρτι = "now"

16:13 | ἀφ᾽ ἑαυτοῦ = "on his own authority" | τὰ ἐρχόμενα = "the things that are to come"

16:15 | πάντα ὅσα ἔχει ὁ πατὴρ ἐμά ἐστιν = "all that the Father has is mine," neut. pl. subjects take sg. verbs

16:16, 17, 19 | μικρὸν καί (6x) = "a little while and," i.e., "soon" (cp. 14:19)

16:17 | ἐκ τῶν μαθητῶν αὐτοῦ = "some of his disciples," partitive ἐκ functioning as subject (BDAG ἐκ 4aγ; BDF §164(2))

16:17–18 τί ἐστιν τοῦτο; (2x) = "what does this mean?" (BDAG εἰμί 2cα)

16:18 | τό functions as quote marks (BDAG ὁ 2hβ)

16:19 | ζητέω = "deliberate" (BDAG ζητέω 2) | ὅτι ("that") resumes περὶ τούτου ("about this") – "Are you deliberating with each other *about this, that* [or the fact that] I said ...?"

16:20 | γίνομαι εἰς = "change/turn into" (BDAG γίνομαι 5a)

16:21 | ἡ γυνὴ ὅταν τίκτῃ – prolepsis (BDF §476) | διὰ τὴν χαρὰν ὅτι ἐγεννήθη ἄνθρωπος εἰς τὸν κόσμον = "because of her joy that a child is born into the world" (NIV)

16:23 | ἄν τι αἰτήσητε = "whatever you ask" (cp. 15:16)

16:24 | ἕως ἄρτι = "until now"

16:27 | παρά + gen. = "from" (BDAG παρά A1)

16:28 | ἀφίημι = "I am leaving"

16:30 | ἐν τούτῳ – retrospective

16:32 | ὥρα ... ἵνα (see v. 2) | εἰς τὰ ἴδια = "to his own home" (BDAG ἴδιος 4b) | καὶ οὐκ εἰμὶ μόνος = *"and yet* I am not alone" (BDAG καί 1bη)

16:33 | ἐν τῷ κόσμῳ θλῖψιν ἔχετε = "in the world you have tribulation" (NASB); ESV & NIV follow textual variant ἕξετε (future)

John 17
17:1 | πάτερ – voc. (cp. vv. 5, 11, 21, 24, 25) | σου τὸν υἱόν = τὸν υἱὸν σου

17:2 | ἐξουσία + gen. = "authority over" | πᾶν ὃ δέδωκας αὐτῷ = "all that you have given him" (cp. 6:39); prolepsis (BDF §476) of the object as if it were the subject; then after the verb, it is changed to indirect object using dat. pl. pronoun (αὐτοῖς)

17:3 | ὅν = "[him] whom"

17:4 | ἵνα ποιήσω = "to do," attenuated ἵνα equivalent to inf.

17:5 | παρά + dat. = "with/beside," spatial proximity (BDAG παρά B1bγ) | πρὸ τοῦ + inf. = "before the world was" | παρὰ σοί goes with εἶχον

17:6 | σου τὸ ὄνομα = τὸ ὄνομά σου (cp. v. 26) | σοὶ ἦσαν = "they were yours," dat. of possession (cp. v. 9) | κἀμοί = καὶ ἐμοί

17:7–8 | παρά + gen. (2x) = "from"

17:9 | περὶ ὧν = "for [those] whom," attraction of the relative (see 7:31)

17:10 | Neut. pl. subjects take sg. verbs

17:12 | ὁ υἱὸς τῆς ἀπωλείας = "the son of perdition," Hebr. attributive gen. (W 86)

17:15 | Attenuated ἵνα (2x) after verb of requesting = "that" (BDAG ἵνα 2aγ)

17:17 | ἐν τῇ ἀληθείᾳ = "by the truth," Hebr./instrumental ἐν | σός = "your"

17:19, 21 | καὶ αὐτοί (2x) = "they too"

17:24 | Attenuated ἵνα after verb of desiring = "that" (BDAG ἵνα 2aα)

17:26 | ἥν = "[with] which"

John 18

18:2, 5 | ὁ παραδιδοὺς αὐτόν (2x) – ingressive-futuristic present ptc.

18:3 | ἐκ τῶν ἀρχιερέων καὶ ἐκ τῶν Φαρισαίων ὑπηρέτας = "temple police from the chief priests and from the Pharisees"

18:4 | πάντα τὰ ἐρχόμενα ἐπ᾽ αὐτόν = "all that was going to befall him"

18:6 | χαμαί (adv.) = "to the ground"

18:10 | αὐτήν = μάχαιραν | τῷ δούλῳ – dat. of possession

18:11 | οὐ μή + aorist subj. normally expresses emphatic negation (W 468), but here as question expresses emphatic affirmation (BDF §365(4)): "Shall I not ... ?" (cp. Lk 18:7; Rev 15:4)

18:13 | ἀρχιερεὺς τοῦ ἐνιαυτοῦ ἐκείνου = "that year's high priest," not gen. of time bec. not used adverbially

18:14 | ἦν δὲ Καϊάφας ... = "it was Caiaphas who had advised the Jews that"

18:15–16 | γνωστὸς τῷ ἀρχιερεῖ = "known to the high priest," while γνωστὸς τοῦ ἀρχιερέως = "known by the high priest," gen. of agency (W 126)

18:16 | πρός + dat. = "at" (BDAG πρός 2a)

18:21 | τοὺς ἀκηκοότας = "those who have heard [me]"

18:22 | ταῦτα αὐτοῦ εἰπόντος = "when he said these things," gen. abs.

18:26 | συγγενὴς ὢν οὗ ἀπέκοψεν Πέτρος τὸ ὠτίον = "being a relative of [the man] whose ear Peter had cut off" | οὐκ ἐγώ σε εἶδον; = "did I not see you?"

18:28 | τὸ πάσχα – could be (1) the Passover proper, or (2) the Feast of Unleavened Bread (cp. Luke 22:1). Option (1) implies that John views crucifixion as occurring on same day as the Passover. Option (2) is to be preferred, since it avoids conflict with united witness of Synoptics that crucifixion occurred the day following the Passover (cp. Matt 26:17 || Mk 14:12 || Lk 22:7). See "Excursus: The Day and Date of the Crucifixion" in Geldenhuys 649–70; Carson 455–8, 589.

18:30 | οὐκ ἄν σοι ... αὐτόν = "we would not have handed him over to you"

18:31 | ἔξεστιν τινι + inf. = "it is permitted/lawful for someone to"

18:32 | ἵνα = "[this happened] so that" (cp. 19:24) | σημαίνων ποίῳ θανάτῳ ἤμελλεν ἀποθνῄσκειν = "indicating by what kind of death he was about to die" (e.g., Roman crucifixion)

18:34 | ἀπὸ σεαυτοῦ = "of your own accord"

18:37 | οὐκοῦν βασιλεὺς εἶ σύ; = "so then, you *are* a king?" (BDAG οὐκοῦν 2; BDF §451(1)) | γεγέννημαι = "I was born," aoristic perf. (W 574) | μου τῆς φωνῆς = τῆς φωνῆς μου

18:38 | εὑρίσκω αἰτίαν = "find a basis for legal action" (BDAG αἰτία 3)

18:39 | ἔστιν συνήθεια ὑμῖν = "you have a custom," dat. of possession | βούλεσθε ἀπολύσω ὑμῖν; = "do you want me to release to you?" deliberative subj. (W 467) introduced with βούλομαι (BDF §366(3))

John 19
19:3 | ἔλεγον = "they kept on saying," iterative impf. (W 547)

19:4, 6 | εὑρίσκω αἰτίαν – see 18:38

19:5 | φορῶν = "wearing"

19:8 | μᾶλλον ἐφοβήθη = "he became even more afraid"

19:11 | εἶχες = "you would have," imperfect w/o ἄν in apodosis of an unreal condition (ZG; BDF §§358, 360(1)) | κατ᾽ ἐμοῦ = "against me" (BDAG κατά A2bγ), "over me" (ESV) | ἦν δεδομένον – plupf. periphrastic (W 649) | ὁ παραδούς μέ = "he who delivered me over"

19:12 | ἐκ τούτου = either (1) temporal, "from then on" (M 72–3), or (2) logical, "for this reason" (ZG; BDAG ἐκ 3e) (cp. 6:66)

19:14 | παρασκευή = "Friday," the day of preparation for the Sabbath (see vv. 31, 42; Mk 15:42). Thus, παρασκευὴ τοῦ πάσχα is not "the day of preparation for the Passover," but "the Friday of Passover week"

(see Geldenhuys 664; Carson 603–4, 622) | ὡς with numerals = "about" (BDAG ὡς 6) (cp. v. 39)

19:17 | βαστάζων αὐτῷ τὸν σταυρόν = "bearing his own cross," αὐτῷ = ἑαυτῷ

19:18 | ἐντεῦθεν καὶ ἐντεῦθεν = "one on either side" | μέσος = "in the middle, in between"

19:19 | ἔγραψεν δὲ καὶ τίτλον ὁ Πιλᾶτος = "Pilate *also* wrote a notice"

19:20 | τῶν Ἰουδαίων goes with πολλοί = "many of the Jews" | Interlocking word order: ἐγγύς ... τῆς πόλεως = "near the city," and ὁ τόπος ... ὅπου = "the place where" ("For the place where Jesus was crucified was near the city")

19:22 | γέγραφα (2x) – extensive perf. (W 577)

19:23 | μέρη – pl. of μέρος (neut.) | ἔλαβον τὰ ἱμάτια αὐτοῦ ... καὶ τὸν χιτῶνα = "they took his outer garments ... and his shirt/tunic" | ἐκ τῶν ἄνωθεν = "from top to bottom" | δι' ὅλου = "throughout" (BDAG ὅλος 2)

19:24 | σχίσωμεν & λάχωμεν – hortatory subjs. | τίνος ἔσται = "[to decide] whose it shall be" | ἵνα = "[this happened] so that" (cp. 18:32) | βάλλω κλῆρον ἐπί + acc. = "cast lots for something" (BDAG ἐπί 14bα; κλῆρος 1)

19:24–25 | μέν ... δέ = "Therefore [οὖν – in fulfillment of Scripture] the soldiers did these things, but standing by the cross of Jesus were his mother ..."

19:25 | ἡ τοῦ Κλωπᾶ = "the wife of Clopas" (cp. Matt 1:6)

19:27 | εἰς τὰ ἴδια = "into his home"

19:29 | ὄξους (2x) – gen. | μεστός + gen. (2x) = "full of" | "A jar full of sour wine was standing there; so they put a sponge full of the sour wine upon a branch of hyssop and brought it up to his mouth" (NASB)

19:31 | ἦν γὰρ μεγάλη ἡ ἡμέρα ἐκείνου τοῦ σαββάτου = lit. "for the day of that Sabbath was great," i.e., "for that Sabbath was a high day" (NASB, ESV), taking τοῦ σαββάτου as gen. of apposition (W 95) | Attenuated ἵνα after verb of asking = "that" (BDAG ἵνα 2aγ) | αὐτῶν τὰ σκέλη = τὰ σκέλη αὐτῶν

19:32–33 | μέν ... δέ = "So the soldiers came and broke the legs of the first (τοῦ πρώτου), and of the other (τοῦ ἄλλου) who had been crucified with him. *But* when they came to Jesus and saw that he was already dead, they did not break his legs" (ESV)

19:34 | λόγχῃ = "with a spear," instrumental dat. (W 162) | αὐτοῦ τὴν πλευράν = τὴν πλευρὰν αὐτοῦ | ἐξῆλθεν αἷμα καὶ ὕδωρ – sg. verb bec. "blood and water" viewed as whole (BDF §135(1a))

19:35 | ὁ ἑωρακώς = "he who has seen" | αὐτοῦ ... ἡ μαρτυρία = ἡ μαρτυρία αὐτοῦ | ἀληθῆ λέγει = lit., "he speaks truly," adv. acc. (W 200–1), i.e., "he is telling the truth"

19:36 | ὀστοῦν αὐτοῦ = "his bones," collective sg. (BDF §139); contracted form of ὀστέον

19:37 | ὅν = "[him] whom"

19:38 | ὢν μαθητὴς τοῦ Ἰησοῦ κεκρυμμένος δὲ διὰ τὸν φόβον τῶν Ἰουδαίων = "being a disciple of Jesus, *but a secret one* for fear of the Jews" (NASB)

19:39 | νυκτός = "at night," gen. of time (cp. 3:2) | τὸ πρῶτον = "earlier," adv. acc. | ὁ ἐλθὼν πρὸς αὐτὸν νυκτὸς τὸ πρῶτον =

"the man who earlier had come to him at night" | φέρων ... ἑκατόν
= "bringing a mixture of myrrh and aloes, about [ὡς] 75 pounds in
weight" (ESV)

19:40 | καθὼς ἔθος ἐστὶν τοῖς Ἰουδαίοις ἐνταφιάζειν = "as is
the burial custom of the Jews," ἔθος + dat. of possession + inf. as complement of noun

19:42 | ἐκεῖ goes with ἔθηκαν – "they laid Jesus there," i.e., in the tomb

John 20
20:1 | τῇ μιᾷ τῶν σαββάτων = "on the first day of the week" (BDAG
σαββάτον 2b) (cp. v. 19) | σκοτίας ἔτι οὔσης = "while it was still
dark," gen. abs.

20:4 | τάχιον + gen. of comparison = "faster than"

20:7 | χωρὶς ἐντετυλιγμένον εἰς ἕνα τόπον = "rolled up in one
place by itself," χωρίς used here as an adverb, "separately, by itself"
(BDAG χωρίς 1)

20:9 | οὐδέπω ᾔδεισαν = "as yet they did not understand" (ESV)

20:10 | πρὸς αὐτούς = "to their homes" (BDAG πρός 3aα)

20:11–12 πρός + dat. (3x) = "at" (BDAG πρός 2a)

20:11 | ὡς ἔκλαιεν = "as she was weeping" (BDAG ὡς 8b)

20:13 | ὅτι recitative

20:14 | στρέφομαι εἰς τὰ ὀπίσω = "turn around"

20:15 | δοκοῦσα ὅτι ὁ κηπουρός ἐστιν = "supposing that he was
the gardener"

20:17 | μή μου ἅπτου = "stop clinging to me!" (BDAG ἅπτω 2b; BDF §336(3)), verbs of touching take gen.

20:18 | Mixing direct and indirect discourse (BDF §470): "telling the disciples, 'I have seen the Lord,' and [that] he had said these things to her"

20:19 | οὔσης ὀψίας [gen. abs.] τῇ ἡμέρᾳ ἐκείνῃ = "on the evening of that day" (ESV) | τῇ μιᾷ σαββάτων – see v. 1 | εἰς τὸ μέσον = "in the midst" (cp. v. 26)

20:23 | ἄν τινων (2x) = "*whose soever* sins ye remit, they are remitted unto them; [and] *whose soever* [sins] ye retain, they are retained" (KJV) | ἀφέωνται & κεκράτηνται – proleptic perfects (W 581)

20:25 | τὸν τύπον τῶν ἥλων (2x) = "the mark/imprint of the nails" (BDAG τύπος 1)

20:26 | μεθ᾽ ἡμέρας ὀκτώ = "after eight days," μετά + acc. | τῶν θυρῶν κεκλεισμένων = "although the doors were shut," concessive gen. abs.

20:27 | φέρω (2x) = "put, reach" (BDAG φέρω 4)

20:29 | καί = "and yet" (BDAG καί 1bη)

20:30–31 | μέν ... δέ = "Jesus did many other signs ... But these have been written"

20:30 | ἃ οὐκ ἔστιν γεγραμμένα – neut. pl. subjects take sg. verbs

20:31 | Textual problem: πιστεύσητε (aorist subj. "that you might *come* to believe"), or πιστεύητε (present subj. "that you might *continue* to believe") (cp. same variant at 19:35) (see 10:38 for evidence that John distinguished between aorist and present subj.). See commentaries.

A Syntax Guide for Readers of the Greek New Testament

John 21

21:1 | ἐφανέρωσεν δὲ οὕτως = "he revealed himself in the following way"

21:3 | ὑπάγω ἁλιεύειν = "I'm going fishing" | ἐρχόμεθα καὶ ἡμεῖς σὺν σοί = "we too will go with you," futuristic present

21:4 | πρωΐας δὲ ἤδη γενομένης = "but when the day was now breaking" (NASB) | εἰς τὸν αἰγιαλόν = "on the beach" = ἐπὶ τὸν αἰγιαλόν (Matt 13:2, 48; Acts 21:5)

21:5 | προσφάγιον = "anything eaten with bread," e.g., a piece of fish | μή τι προσφάγιον ἔχετε; = "haven't you any fish?" (NIV), μή expects neg. answer

21:6 | εἰς τὰ δεξιὰ μέρη = "on the right side" | εὑρήσετε = "you will find [fish]" | οὐκέτι αὐτὸ ἑλκύσαι ἴσχυον = "they were no longer able to draw it in," ἰσχύω + inf. = "be able to" (BDAG ἰσχύω 2b) | ἀπό = "because of" (BDAG ἀπό 5a)

21:7 | τὸν ἐπενδύτην διεζώσατο = "he put his outer garment on" | ἦν γὰρ γυμνός = "for he was not wearing an outer garment" (BDAG γυμνός 3), parenthetical comment

21:8 | τῷ πλοιαρίῳ = "in the little boat," locative dat. (W 155) | ὡς ἀπὸ πηχῶν διακοσίων = "about 200 cubits away" (BDAG ἀπό 4) | τὸ δίκτυον τῶν ἰχύων = "the net [full] of fish," gen. of content (W 92–3)

21:9 | "So when they got out on the land, they see a bed of charcoals [ἀνθρακιὰν κειμένην] and a fish lying on it and bread"

21:10 | ἀπὸ τῶν ὀψαρίων = "some of the fish," ἀπό for partitive gen. (BDAG ἀπό 1f) | "bring some of the fish you have just (νῦν) caught" (NIV)

21:11 | τοσούτων ὄντων = "even though there were so many," concessive gen. abs.

21:14 | τοῦτο ἤδη τρίτον = "this was now the third time that"

21:15 | ἀγαπᾷς με πλέον τούτων; (gen. of comparison) = elliptical: could be (1) "do you love me more than [you love] these [other disciples]?" (2) "do you love me more than these [other disciples love me]?" or (3) "do you love me more than [you love] these [fish and fishing gear, i.e., your profesion]?"

21:19 | On "glorifying God" as a euphemism for suffering in times of persecution, including martyrdom (cp. 1 Pet 4:16)

21:21 | οὗτος δὲ τί; = "what about him?"

21:22–23 | τί πρὸς σέ; (2x) = "what is it to you?" or "how does it concern you?" (BDAG πρός 3eγ)

21:25 | ἔστιν ... ἄλλα πολλά = "there are many other things," neut. pl. subjects take sg. verbs | καθ᾽ ἕν = "one by one, in detail" (BDAG κατά 3a; BDF §305) | οἴομαι + acc. + inf. = "I suppose that" | οὐδ᾽ αὐτὸν τὸν κόσμον = "not even the world itself"

Chapter Five

The Acts of the Apostles

Acts 1

1:1 | πρῶτος here stands for πρότερος = "former" (BDAG πρῶτος 1bα; BDF §62; Z §151) | λόγος = "treatise" (BDAG λόγος 1b) | ἤρξατο ... ἄχρι may have sense, "from the beginning until" (see M 181)

1:2 | ἄχρι ἧς ἡμέρας ... ἀνελήμφθη = "until the day when he was taken up," incorporation of the antecedent in the relative clause (BDF §294(5)); should be ἄχρι [τῆς] ἡμέρας ἧς [or ἐν ᾗ] ἀνελήμφθη (cp. v. 22; Lk 1:20) | τοῖς ἀποστόλοις ... οὓς ἐξελέξατο = "to the apostles whom he had chosen"

1:3 | μετὰ τὸ παθεῖν αὐτόν = "after his suffering" (W 611), acc. αὐτόν as subject of inf. | ἐν πολλοῖς τεκμηρίοις = "by many proofs," Hebr./insrumental ἐν | τὰ περὶ τῆς βασιλείας τοῦ θεοῦ = "the things concerning the kingdom of God" (BDAG περί 1i) (cp. 19:8; 28:31)

1:4 | συναλίζω – see BDAG for interesting lexical discussion | περιμένω + acc. = "wait for something"

1:5 | ὕδατι – instrumental dat. | ἐν πνεύματι ἁγίῳ (cp. 11:16), Hebr./instrumental ἐν | οὐ μετὰ πολλὰς ταύτας ἡμέρας (μετά

249

+ acc. = "after") = "not many days from now" (BDAG οὗτος 2c; πολύς 1aα; BDF §226) (cp. Lk 15:13)

1:6 | εἰ = marker of direct question (BDAG εἰ 5a; Z §401) | ἀποκαθιστάνεις – ingressive-futuristic present

1:7 | οὐχ ὑμῶν ἐστιν γνῶναι = "it is not yours to know," taking inf. as subject and ὑμῶν (gen. of possession) as predicate, equivalent to ὑμέτερον (M 38)

1:8–10 | Note the gen. absolutes (3x)

1:8 | ἕν τε = ἐν + enclitic particle τέ (BDF §443)

1:10, 13, 14 | ἦσαν + present ptc. (3x) = impf. periphrastic (W 647–49)

1:10 | καὶ ἰδοὺ ἄνδρες δύο = "*that* there [were] two men," apodotic καί (BDAG καί 1bδ); supply ἦσαν (cp. Lk 5:18; 13:11) | αὐτοῖς – dat. in agreement with παρα- prefix in παρ-ειστήκεισαν, "standing beside them"

1:11 | ὃν τρόπον = "in the same way as"

1:12 | σαββάτου ἔχον ὁδόν = lit. "having a journey of a Sabbath," i.e., "a Sabbath day's journey"

1:13 | οὗ after noun denoting a locality = "where" (cp. 2:2; 7:29; 12:12; 16:13)

1:14 | ὁμοθυμαδόν – adv. acc.

1:15 | ἦν τε ὄχλος ὀνομάτων ἐπὶ τὸ αὐτὸ ὡς ἑκατὸν εἴκοσι = "(now the throng of persons together was about 120)," parenthesis (BDAG ὄνομα 2) | ἐπὶ τὸ αὐτό = "together, at the same place" (BDAG αὐτός 3b)

1:16 | τοῦ γενομένου ὁδηγοῦ τοῖς συλλαβοῦσιν Ἰησοῦν = "who became a guide to those who arrested Jesus" (ESV)

1:17 | ὅτι = "for" | ἐν ἡμῖν = "among us"

1:18–19 | Parenthesis – Luke's editorial comment

1:18 | ἐκ μισθοῦ τῆς ἀδικίας = "with the reward he got for his wickedness" (NIV 1984), ἐκ as periphrasis for gen. of price (BDAG ἐκ 4b); τῆς ἀδικίας – gen. of means or of production (W 125 n143) | μέσος = "in the middle"

1:21 | ἐν παντὶ χρόνῳ ᾧ = "during the whole time that" | ἐφ' ἡμᾶς = "among us" (BDAG ἐπί 1cγ; cp. 2 Thess 1:10)

1:21–22 δεῖ τῶν συνελθόντων ἡμῖν ἀνδρῶν ... μάρτυρα ... γενέσθαι ἕνα τούτων = "of the men who accompanied us ... it is necessary for one of them to become a witness with us of his resurrection"

1:24 | καρδιογνῶστα πάντων = "who knows the hearts of all," objective gen. (cp. 15:8) | ὃν ἐξελέξω ἐκ τούτων τῶν δύο ἕνα = ἕνα ἐκ τούτων τῶν δύο ὃν ἐξελέξω = "which one of these two you have chosen"

1:25 | τῆς διακονίας ταύτης καὶ ἀποστολῆς = "this apostolic ministry" (NIV, ZG), hendiadys (BDF §442(16))

1:26 | ἔδωκαν κλήρους αὐτοῖς = "they cast lots for them"

Acts 2

2:1 | ἐν τῷ συμπληροῦσθαι τὴν ἡμέραν τῆς πεντηκοστῆς = "when the day of Pentecost had come" (W 611) (cp. Lk 9:51) | ἐπὶ τὸ αὐτό – see 1:15

2:2 | ὥσπερ φερομένης πνοῆς βιαίας = "like a violent/mighty [βίαιος] rushing [BDAG φέρω 3c] wind," gen. abs. (BDAG ὥσπερ b) | οὗ = "where" (see 1:13)

2:3 | ὡσεὶ πυρός = "as of fire"

2:4 | Verbs of filling take the gen. ("they all were filled with the Holy Spirit") (W 94) | καθὼς τὸ πνεῦμα ἐδίδου ἀποφθέγγεσθαι αὐτοῖς = "as the Spirit was giving them utterance"

2:5 | "Now there were [non-native] residents in [εἰς = ἐν] Jerusalem who were Jews, devout men from every nation under heaven" (i.e., diaspora Jews whose mother tongue was that of the land in which they were originally born)

2:6 | γενομένης δὲ τῆς φωνῆς ταύτης = "when this sound occurred" (NASB), "at this sound" (ESV), gen. abs. | εἷς ἕκαστος = "each one"

2:6, 11 | ἀκούω + gen. of person + gen. ptc. (BDAG ἀκούω 1c); thus ἀκούω λαλούντων αὐτῶν (2x) = "hear them speaking" (cp. 15:12)

2:8 | ἡμεῖς ἕκαστος = "we each"

2:11 | τὰ μεγαλεῖα τοῦ θεοῦ = "the mighty deeds of God," subjective gen.

2:12 | ἄλλος πρὸς ἄλλον λέγοντες = "saying to one another" | τί θέλει τοῦτο εἶναι; = "what can this mean?" (BDAG θέλω 5)

2:13 | μεμεστωμένοι εἰσίν – perf. periphrastic (W 649) | μεστόω + gen. of thing with which filled = "fill with," γλεύκους is gen. of γλεῦκος

2:14 | τοῦτο ὑμῖν γνωστὸν ἔστω = "let this be known to you"

2:17 | ἀπό + gen. for partitive gen. ("I will pour out *of* my Spirit") | ἐνυπνίοις ἐνυπνιασθήσονται – Hebr. cognate dat. (BDF §198(6))

2:18 | καί γε = "even," enclitic particle γέ as intensifier (BDAG γέ bγ)

2:19 | δίδωμι = "produce/cause" signs (BDAG δίδωμι 4) | ἀτμίδα καπνοῦ = "vapor of smoke," "smoky vapor" like that of a volcanic eruption (BDAG ἀτμίς), attributive gen.

2:20 | Verbs of change + εἰς (2x) = "turn into" (BDAG εἰς 4b) | πρίν + inf. = "before" (W 596; BDF §395)

2:21 | πᾶς ὃς ἐάν = "everyone who"

2:22 | ἀπό = ὑπό (BDAG ἀπό 5eβ) | εἰς for dat. (BDAG εἰς 4g) | καθὼς αὐτοὶ οἴδατε = "as you yourselves know"

2:23 | "This man, delivered over (ἔκδοτον) by the predetermined plan and foreknowledge of God, you nailed to a cross by the hands of godless men and put him to death" (NASB) | χειρός – collective sg.

2:24 | οὐκ ἦν δυνατὸν κρατεῖσθαι αὐτὸν ὑπ' αὐτοῦ = "it was not possible for him to be held by it"

2:25 | διὰ παντός = "continually" | ἐκ = "at," answers question "where?" (BDAG ἐκ 2) (cp. v. 34)

2:26 | ἔτι δέ = "furthermore" (BDAG ἔτι 2b) | καὶ ἡ σάρξ μου = "my flesh also" | ἐπ' ἐλπίδι = "in hope" (BDAG ἐλπίς 1bα), "on the basis of hope" (BDF §235(2))

2:27, 31 | εἰς ᾅδην (2x) = possibly "to Hades," more likely "in Hades," εἰς for ἐν (M 68)

2:27 | δίδωμι = "let, permit" (BDAG δίδωμι 13)

2:28 | Verbs of filling take the gen. ("fill with joy") | μετὰ τοῦ προσώπου σου = "in your presence," LXX quotation (BDAG μετά A2aγℶ)

2:29 | ἐξὸν εἰπεῖν = "[it is] permissible (or possible) to speak" (BDAG ἔξεστιν 1–2); supply ἐστίν (BDF §353(5)) | μετὰ παρρησίας = "plainly, candidly, confidently" | ἐν ἡμῖν = "among us"

2:29, 33, 36 | καί ... καί (3x) = "both ... and"

2:30 | ὅρκῳ ὤμοσεν = "he swore with an oath" (BDF §198(6)) | ἐκ καρποῦ τῆς ὀσφύος αὐτοῦ = lit. "someone from the fruit of his loins," i.e., "one of his descendants," partitive ἐκ functioning as object of καθίσαι (BDAG ἐκ 4aγ; BDF §164(2); ὀσφῦς 2)

2:33 | τῇ δεξιᾷ = "to the right hand," dat. of destination (W 147) (cp. 5:31) | τὴν ἐπαγγελίαν τοῦ πνεύματος τοῦ ἁγίου = "the promise of the Holy Spirit," gen. of apposition (W 99)

2:35 | ἕως ἄν + aor. subj. = "until"

2:36 | καὶ κύριον ... καὶ Χριστόν = "both Lord and Christ" (see v. 29)

2:37 | τὴν καρδίαν – acc. of respect (W 203–4) | εἶπόν τε = "and so they said" (BDF §443(3)) | ποιήσωμεν – deliberative subj.

2:38 | ἐπὶ τῷ ὀνόματί τινος = "in the name of someone," authorizing function (BDAG βαπτίζω 2c; ἐπί 17; ὄνομα 1dγℶ) | εἰς ἄφεσιν τῶν ἁμαρτιῶν ὑμῶν = "for the forgiveness of sins" (BDAG εἰς 4f) (cp. Matt 26:28; Mk 1:4; Lk 3:3) | τὴν δωρεὰν τοῦ ἁγίου πνεύματος – gen. of apposition (W 95)

2:39 | πᾶσιν τοῖς εἰς μακράν = "for all who are far off," εἰς = ἐν (BDAG εἰς 1aδ) | ὅσους ἄν = "as many as"

2:40 | ἑτέροις λόγοις πλείοσιν = "with many other words," instrumental dat.

2:41 | μὲν οὖν = "so then," continuing narrative (BDAG μέν 2e; οὖν 2d)

2:42 | ἦσαν προσκαρτεροῦντες – impf. periphrastic

2:44 | ἐπὶ τὸ αὐτό – see v. 1; 1:15

2:45 | ἐπίπρασκον & διεμέριζον – distributive iterative impfs. (W 546) | καθότι ἄν τις χρείαν εἶχεν = "as any had need" (ESV)

2:46–47 | καθ' ἡμέραν (2x) = "day by day" (BDAG κατά B2c; ἡμέρα 2c)

2:46 | κατ' οἶκον = "from house to house" (BDAG κατά B1d) (cp. 5:42) | μεταλάμβανω τροφῆς (partitive gen.) = "partake of food" (BDF §169(1)) (cp. 27:33)

2:47 | ἔχοντες χάριν πρός = "having favor with," "enjoying the respect of" (BDAG χάρις 2b) | προστιθέναι ἐπὶ τὸ αὐτό = "to add to the total" (BDAG αὐτός 3b), contrast ἐπὶ τὸ αὐτό in vv. 1, 44; 1:15

Acts 3
3:1 | ἀνέβαινον – impf. describing an action in progress during which something else happened (ZG; Z §275) | ἐπὶ τὴν ὥραν τῆς προσευχῆς τὴν ἐνάτην = "at the hour of prayer, the ninth hour" (BDAG ἐπί 18cα)

3:2 | χωλὸς ἐκ κοιλίας μητρὸς αὐτοῦ ὑπάρχων = "who was lame from his mother's womb" | ἐβαστάζετο = "was being carried," pass. | ἐτίθουν = "whom they used to put," customary impf. | καθ' ἡμέραν – see 2:46–47 | πρός + acc. = "at" (BDAG πρός 3g) | τοῦ αἰτεῖν = "to beg," gen. of the articular inf. with final sense (BDF §400(5)) | παρά = "from" (BDAG παρά A3a)

3:3 | μέλλοντας εἰσιέναι = "about to enter," μέλλω + inf. = "be about to"

3:5 | ὁ = "he," article as pronoun | τι παρ᾽ αὐτῶν = "something from them" (on παρά, see v. 2)

3:6 | οὐχ ὑπάρχει μοι = "I do not have," dat. of possession

3:7 | Verbs of grasping take the gen. ("taking hold of him by the right hand") | ἡ βάσις (< βαίνω) = lit. "step," here "that with which one steps," i.e., foot

3:10 | ἐπεγίνωσκον αὐτὸν ὅτι = lit. they "recognized him, that," i.e., "recognized that," anticipation of the object (prolepsis; BDF §476(3)); impf. (ἐπεγίνωσκον) expressing relative time (BDF §330) | πρὸς τὴν ἐλεημοσύνην = "for the purpose of [begging for] alms" (BDAG πρός 3cα) | Verbs of filling take gen. | ἐπὶ τῷ συμβεβηκότι αὐτῷ = "at what had happened to him," ἐπί + dat. after words of emotion (BDAG ἐπί 6c) (cp. v. 12)

3:11 | κρατοῦντος αὐτοῦ τὸν Π. καὶ τὸν Ἰ. = "as he was clinging to Paul and John," gen. abs. | ἔκθαμβοι – pl., though ὁ λαός is sg. – *constructio ad sensum*

3:12 | ἡμῖν τί ἀτενίζετε; = "why do you gaze at us?" | ὡς = "as though" (BDAG ὡς 3c) | πεποιηκόσιν τοῦ περιπατεῖν αὐτόν = "we have caused him to walk" (BDAG ποιέω 2hα), τοῦ pleonastically prefixed to inf.; Septuagintism (BDF §400(7))

3:13 | παῖς = "servant" (see v. 26) | κρίναντος ἐκείνου ἀπολύειν = "even though he had decided to release him," concessive gen. abs. (BDAG κρίνω 4)

3:14 | ἄνδρα φονέα = "a murderer," adjectival use of substantive (BDF §242)

3:16 | ἐπὶ τῇ πίστει τοῦ ὀνόματος αὐτοῦ = "on the basis of faith his name" (BDAG ἐπί 6a), πίστις + objective gen. | Anacoluthon: "And on the basis of faith in His name – the name of Jesus has strengthened this man whom you see and know," τὸ ὄνομα αὐτοῦ is the subject of ἐστερέωσεν | ἡ πίστις ἡ δι᾽ αὐτοῦ = "faith, which [comes] through him"

3:17 | κατὰ ἄγνοιαν = "in ignorance" (BDAG κατά B5bβ)

3:18 | "The things which God announced beforehand by the mouth of all the prophets – i.e., that his Christ would suffer – he has thus fulfilled" | παθεῖν τὸν Χριστὸν αὐτοῦ – indirect discourse, although somewhat difficult when juxtaposed with "the things ..." (ἃ προκατήγγειλεν)

3:19 | εἰς τό + inf. indicating purpose (BDF §402(2))

3:20 | ὅπως ἄν + subj. = "so that" (BDAG ὅπως 2aβ)

3:21 | οἱ ἅγιοι ἀπ᾽ αἰῶνος αὐτοῦ προφῆται = "his holy prophets from of old" (cp. Lk 1:70)

3:24 | πάντες οἱ προφῆται ... ὅσοι ἐλάλησαν = "all the prophets ... who have spoken" | ἀπὸ Σαμουὴλ καὶ τῶν καθεξῆς = "from Samuel and his successors," οἱ καθεξῆς ("successors") | καὶ κατήγγειλαν = "also proclaimed"

3:25 | διατίθημι διαθήκην = "make a covenant," common LXX phrase

3:26 | ἐν τῷ ἀποστρέφειν ἕκαστον = (1) if transitive (BDAG ἀποστρέφω 2), ἕκαστον is direct object: "by turning each one," (2) if intransitive (BDAG ἀποστρέφω 1), ἕκαστον is subject of inf.: "as each one turns away" (see ZG; BDF §§308, 404(3))

Acts 4
4:1 | λαλούντων αὐτῶν – gen. abs.

4:2 | διὰ τὸ διδάσκειν ... καὶ καταγγέλλειν = "because they [αὐτούς] were teaching ... and proclaiming" (W 610)

4:3 | εἰς τὴν αὔριον = "until the next day" (BDAG εἰς 2a; αὔριον) (cp. v. 5)

4:5 | ἐγένετο + inf. = "it came to pass that" | ἐπὶ τὴν αὔριον = "on the next day" (BDAG αὔριον; BDF §233(3))

4:8 | Verbs of filling take gen.

4:9 | ἀνακρινόμεθα = "we are being questioned" (BDAG ἀνακρίνω 2) | ἐπὶ εὐεργεσίᾳ ἀνθρώπου ἀσθενοῦς = "because of a benefaction done to a sick man," objective gen. (W 117; BDF §163) | ἐν τινι = "by what means" (ESV) – Hebr./instrumental ἐν (BDF §219)

4:11 | ὑφ' ὑμῶν τῶν οἰκοδόμων = "by you the builders" | γινόμαι + εἰς functioning as predicate nom. (BDAG εἰς 8aα)

4:12 | ἡ σωτηρία = "salvation," article with abstract noun (W 226–7) | ἐν ἀνθρώποις = "among men" | ἐν ἄλλῳ οὐδενί = "in no one else" | ἐν ᾧ = "by which," Hebr./instrumental ἐν (M 77) | τὸ δεδομένον = "such as is given," odd use of article with ptc. (M 103) | δεῖ + inf. + acc. = "it is necessary for" (W 452)

4:13 | τὴν τοῦ Πέτρου παρρησίαν καὶ Ἰωάννου = "the boldness of Peter and John" | ἐπεγίνωσκόν τε αὐτοὺς ὅτι – prolepsis (cp. 3:10)

4:14 | "And seeing the man who had been healed standing with them, they had nothing to say in reply" (NASB)

4:15 | κελεύσαντες αὐτοὺς ἔξω τοῦ συνεδρίου ἀπελθεῖν = "when they had ordered them to depart out of the council room" (BDAG συνέδριον 3)

4:16 | τί ποιήσωμεν; – deliberative subj. | ὅτι μὲν γὰρ γνωστὸν σημεῖον γέγονεν δι' αὐτῶν πᾶσιν τοῖς κατοικοῦσιν ʼI. φανερόν = "for that a notable sign has been performed through them is evident to all the inhabitants of Jerusalem" (ESV)

4:17 | ἵνα μὴ ἐπὶ πλεῖον διανεμηθῇ εἰς τὸν λαόν = "so that it [= the apostles' message about Jesus (v. 2)] will not spread any further among the people" | μηδενὶ ἀνθρώπων = lit. "to no one of persons"

4:18 | τὸ καθόλου μὴ φθέγγεσθαι = "not to speak at all," τὸ καθόλου – adv. acc.

4:19 | ἀκούω takes gen. (ὑμῶν and τοῦ θεοῦ) | κρίνατε = "you be the judge"

4:21 | μηδὲν εὑρίσκοντες τὸ πῶς κολάσωνται αὐτούς = "finding no way to punish them," τό changes direct question into indirect (BDAG ὁ 2hα; πῶς 1bα) (see Lk 1:62)

4:22 | ὁ ἄνθρωπος ἐφ᾽ ὃν γεγόνει τὸ σημεῖον = "the man on whom the miracle had been performed" (BDAG ἐπί 14bα)

4:23 | ἀπήγγειλαν ὅσα πρὸς αὐτοὺς οἱ ἀρχ. καὶ οἱ πρ. εἶπαν = "they reported all that the chief priest and the elders had said *to them*"

4:24 | δέσποτα – voc.

4:25 | ὁ ... εἰπών = "who ... said," ὁ functioning as relative pronoun linking back to δέσποτα, σὺ ὁ ποιήσας (v. 24) | τοῦ πατρὸς ἡμῶν goes with Δαυίδ | στόματος = "[through] the mouth," sc. διά from the preceding prepositional phrase (διὰ πνεύματος ἁγίου) | "The text of this verse is in a very confused state" (Metzger – see discussion there)

4:26 | κατά + gen. (2x) = "against"

4:27 | ἐπ' ἀληθείας = "truly" | ἐπί + acc. = "against"

4:29 | τὰ νῦν = "now," adv. acc. | ἔπιδε ἐπί + acc. = "look upon," repeating the preposition (M 91)

4:30 | ἐν τῷ … ἐκτείνειν … καί … γίνεσθαι = "while you extend your hand to heal and [while] signs and wonders take place" | εἰς ἴασιν = "to heal" (BDAG εἰς 4f)

4:31 | δεηθέντων αὐτῶν = "when they had prayed," gen. abs. | ἦσαν συνηγμένοι = "they had gathered," plupf. periphrastic | Verbs of filling take gen.

4:32 | τοῦ πλήθους τῶν πιστευσάντων ἦν καρδία καὶ ψυχὴ μία = lit. "the full number of those who believed was one heart and soul" | οὐδὲ εἷς … ἔλεγεν = "no one said that" | τι τῶν ὑπαρχόντων αὐτῷ = "any of the things that belonged to him," dat. of possession | ἴδιον εἶναι = "was his own"

4:33 | ἀπεδίδουν τὸ μαρτύριον οἱ ἀπόστολοι τῆς ἀναστάσεως = "the apostles were bearing witness to the resurrection," objective gen.?

4:34 | ἐν αὐτοῖς = "among them" | ὅσοι κτήτορες χωρίων ἢ οἰκιῶν ὑπῆρχον = "all who were owners of lands or houses" | τὰς τιμὰς τῶν πιπρασκομένων = "the proceeds of what was sold" (BDAG τιμή 1)

34–35 | ἔφερον, ἐτίθουν, διεδίδετο – distributive iterative impfs.

4:36 | ἀπό = ὑπό

4:36–37 | Ἰωσήφ … ὑπάρχοντος αὐτῷ ἀγροῦ πωλήσας ἤνεγκεν τὸ χρῆμα = "Joseph [a.k.a. Barnabas] … a field belonging to him, sold [it] and brought the money," ὑπάρχοντος as gen. abs.; αὐτῷ as dat. of possession; πωλήσας as attendant circumstances ptc.; Ἰωσήφ is subject of ἤνεγκεν and ἔθηκεν

Acts 5

5:2 | ἐνοσφίσατο ἀπὸ τῆς τιμῆς = "he kept back for himself some of the proceeds" (ESV); ἀπό for partitive gen. (also v. 3); on τιμή, see 4:34 | συνειδυίης καὶ τῆς γυναικός = "with his wife's full knowledge" (NASB), gen. abs. | μέρος τι = "a part [of it]"

5:3 | Two infs. of result (BDF §391(4)): "How is it that Satan has so filled your heart *that you have lied* to the Holy Spirit and *have kept for yourself* some of the money you received for the land?" (NIV)

5:4 | οὐχὶ μένον σοὶ ἔμενεν = "While it remained [unsold], did it not remain your own?" (NASB), dat. of possession | καὶ πραθὲν ἐν τῇ σῇ ἐξουσίᾳ ὑπῆρχεν; = "and after it was sold, was it not under your control?" (NASB) | τί ὅτι; = "why [is it] that?" (BDAG ὅτι 2b) (see v. 9) | τίθημι ἐν τῇ καρδίᾳ = "contrive in one's heart" (BDAG τίθημι 1bε) (cp. 19:21)

5:7 | ὡς with numbers = "about" (cp. v. 36)

5:8 | εἰ = "whether" (BDAG εἰ 5bα) | τοσούτου (2x) = "for so much," gen. of price

5:9 | τί ὅτι; = "why is it that?" (see v. 4)

5:10 | πρός + acc. = "by, beside" (BDAG πρός 3g)

5:12 | ἐγίνετο σημεῖα καὶ τέρατα πολλά – neut pl. subjects take sg. verbs

5:13 | τῶν λοιπῶν οὐδείς = "none of the rest"

5:14 | μᾶλλον δέ = "but more than ever" | προσετίθεντο πιστεύοντες τῷ κυρίῳ = (1) "believers in the Lord were added to [their number]" (NASB; cp. 16:34; 18:8), or (2) "believers were added to the Lord" (ESV; cp. 11:24) (BDAG προστίθημι 1b; BDF §187(6)) | πλήθη = "multitudes" (pl. of πλῆθος)

5:15 | ὥστε + inf. = "with the result that," "to such an extent that" (NASB) (BDAG ὥστε 2aβ) | Subject of ἐκφέρειν and τιθέναι is an implied "they" or "people" | ἐρχομένου Πέτρου = "as Peter went by," gen. abs. | κἂν ἡ σκιά = "at least his shadow" (BDAG κἄν 3) | τινὶ αὐτῶν = "some of them"

5:16 | τὸ πλῆθος τῶν πέριξ πόλεων Ἰ. = "many from the towns around Jerusalem," αἱ πέριξ πόλεις = "the circumjacent cities" (Thayer πέριξ) | οἵτινες ἐθεραπεύοντο ἅπαντες = "and they were all being healed" (cp. οἵτινες clause in 9:35)

5:17 | ἡ οὖσα αἵρεσις τῶν Σ. = "i.e., the sect of the Sadducees" | Verbs of filling take gen. (also v. 28)

5:19 | διὰ νυκτός = "during the night," διά + gen., of the period of time within which something occurred (BDAG διά A2b)

5:21 | ὑπὸ τὸν ὄρθρον = "about daybreak" (BDAG ὑπό 3; M 66) | ἀπέστειλαν εἰς τὸ δεσμωτήριον ἀχθῆναι αὐτούς = "sent [orders] to the prison house for them to be brought" (NASB)

5:23, 25 | ὅτι recitative (2x)

5:24 | ὡς + aorist = "when" | διηπόρουν περὶ αὐτῶν τί ἂν γένοιτο τοῦτο = "they were greatly perplexed about them, wondering what this would come to" (ESV), either oblique optative (BDF §386(1)), or potential optative (ZG; Z §356) (cp. 10:17)

5:25 | εἰσίν ... ἑστῶτες = (1) "they *are* in the temple, *standing* and teaching," not periphrastic, or (2) "they *are standing* in the temple and teaching," perf. periphrastic

5:26 | ἄγω = "arrest" (BDAG ἄγω 2) | ἐφοβοῦντο τὸν λαόν, μὴ λιθασθῶσιν = "they were afraid of being stoned by the people" (ESV)

5:28 | βούλεσθε + inf. = "you are determined to" (NIV)

5:31 | τῇ δεξιᾷ αὐτοῦ – see 2:33

5:34 | ἐκέλευσεν ἔξω βραχὺ τοὺς ἀνθρώπους ποιῆσαι = "gave orders to put the men outside *for a little while*" (ESV) (BDAG βραχύς 1; ποιέω 2hγ), βραχύ – adv. acc.

5:35 | προσέχετε ἑαυτοῖς ἐπὶ τοῖς ἀνθρώποις τούτοις τί μέλλετε πράσσειν = (1) "take heed to yourselves in regard to these men, what you are about to do [with them]," prolepsis, or (2) "take care what you are about to do with these men" (BDAG προσέχω 1; ἐπί 14a)

5:36 | πρὸ τούτων τῶν ἡμερῶν = "some time ago" (cp. 21:38)

5:36–37 | πάντες ὅσοι ἐπείθοντο [impf. pass.] αὐτῷ (2x) = "all who were persuaded by him," i.e., all his followers (BDAG πείθω 3c)

5:37 | ἀπέστησεν λαὸν ὀπίσω αὐτοῦ = "he incited the people to revolt, so that they followed him" (BDAG ἀφίστημι 1) | κἀκεῖνος = καὶ ἐκεῖνος

5:38 | καὶ τὰ νῦν = "so in the present case" (ESV, NASB)

5:39 | μήποτε καὶ θεομάχοι εὑρεθῆτε = lit. "lest you be found even opposing God"

5:42 | κατ᾽ οἶκον – see 2:46 | παύομαι + supplementary ptc. = "cease doing something" (BDF §414(2)) (cp. 6:13)

Acts 6

6:1 | πληθυνόντων τῶν μαθητῶν = "while the disciples were increasing in number," gen. abs. | παρεθεωροῦντο – retention of impf. in direct speech (see extended comment at Z §347)

6:2 | διακονέω + dat. of thing (τραπέζαις) = "serve tables," "serve [food to people at] tables" (see BDAG διακονέω 5)

6:3 | ἄνδρας μαρτυρουμένους = "men of good reputation" (BDAG μαρτυρέω 2b)

6:3, 5, 8 | πλήρης + gen. (3x) = "full of"

6:6 | ἐπέθηκαν αὐτοῖς – dat. bec. of ἐπι- prefix

6:7 | ὑπήκουον τῇ πίστει – distributive iterative impf. (cp. Rom 1:5; 10:16)

6:8 | ποιέω τέρατα καὶ σημεῖα = "perform wonders and signs" (BDAG ποιέω 2b) (cp. 7:36) | ἐν τῷ λαῷ = "among the people"

6:9 | "But some men from what was called the Synagogue of the Freedmen, including both Cyrenians and Alexandrians, and some from Cilicia and Asia, rose up and argued with Stephen" (NASB)

6:11 | ὑποβάλλω = "suborn; induce someone to commit perjury" | ὅτι recitative | εἰς + acc. = "against" (BDAG εἰς 4cα)

6:13 | παύομαι + supplementary ptc. = "cease doing something" (cp. 5:42) | κατά + gen. = "against" (BDAG κατά A2bβ)

6:14 | Ἰησοῦς ὁ Ναζωραῖος οὗτος = "this Nazarene, Jesus" (NASB)

6:15 | εἶδον τὸ πρόσωπον αὐτοῦ ὡσεὶ πρόσωπον ἀγγέλου = they "saw his face, [that it was] like the face of an angel," prolepsis

Acts 7
7:1 | εἰ ταῦτα οὕτως ἔχει; = "are these things so?" (NASB, ESV), εἰ as marker of direct question (BDAG εἰ 5a; cp. 1:6) (BDAG ἔχω 10a)

7:2 | ὄντι ἐν = "while he was in" | πρὶν ἤ + inf. = "before"

7:3 | εἰς τὴν γῆν ἣν ἄν σοι δείξω = "into *whichever* land I show you"

7:4 | κἀκεῖθεν = καὶ ἐκεῖθεν | μετὰ τό + inf. = "after" | μετῴκισεν αὐτὸν εἰς τὴν γῆν ταύτην εἰς ἣν ὑμεῖς νῦν κατοικεῖτε = "made him move *to* that land *in* which you now dwell," first εἰς = "to," second εἰς = ἐν

7:4–5 | Subject of verbs must be inferred from context: "[God] made him to move ... [God] did not give him an inheritance ... [God] promised to give ..."

7:5 | οὐδὲ βῆμα ποδός = "not even a footstep," phrase from LXX Deut 2:5; different historical context but similar circumstances, i.e., not owning land but being a sojourner in it (cp. Deut 2:6 with Gen 23) | ἐπηγγείλατο δοῦναι αὐτῷ εἰς κατάσχεσιν αὐτήν = "promised to give it [αὐτήν = τὴν γῆν] to him *as* (or *for*) a possession" (BDAG εἰς 8b or 4f) | οὐκ ὄντος αὐτῷ τέκνου = "though he had no child," concessive gen. abs.

7:6 | δουλώσουσιν αὐτό [= τὸ σπέρμα] = "they [the people of that foreign land, i.e., the Egyptians] will enslave (BDAG δουλόω 1) Abraham's seed and mistreat it [= them]") | ἔτη τετρακόσια – acc. for extent of time

7:7 | τὸ ἔθνος ᾧ ἐὰν δουλεύσουσιν = "whichever nation to which they shall be enslaved" (cp. v. 3)

7:8 | Subject of ἔδωκεν is God. Subject of ἐγέννησεν and περιέτεμεν is Abraham | καὶ Ἰσαὰκ [...] τὸν Ἰακώβ, καὶ Ἰακὼβ [...] τοὺς δώδεκα πατριάρχας – ellipsis; supply ἐγέννησεν | τῇ ἡμέρᾳ τῇ ὀγδόῃ – dat. of time

7:9 | ἀπέδοντο εἰς Αἴγυπτον = they "sold him [to traders who brought him] into Egypt," pregnant construction (BDAG εἰς 10d) derived from

LXX Gen 37:28: ἀπέδοντο τὸν Ιωσηφ τοῖς Ισμαηλίταις εἴκοσι χρυσῶν, καὶ κατήγαγον τὸν Ιωσηφ εἰς Αἴγυπτον.

7:10 | χάρις = "favor" (BDAG χάρις 2b)

7:11 | ηὕρισκον = "our fathers could find no food," conative impf. (W550–2) (cp. Lk 19:48)

7:12 | ἀκούσας Ἰακὼβ ὄντα σιτία εἰς Αἴγυπτον = "when Jacob heard that there was grain in Egypt," ptc. ὄντα in indirect discourse; εἰς = ἐν

7:12–13 πρῶτον ... ἐν τῷ δευτέρῳ = "for their first visit ... on the second visit"

7:14 | ἀποστείλας μετεκαλέσατο = "sent [messengers who] summoned," Semitic graphic ptc. (Z §363) (cp. Matt 2:16; Mk 6:17; Rev 1:1) | ἐν ψυχαῖς ἑβδομήκοντα πέντε = "consisting of 75 souls" (M 79; BDF §220(2); BDAG ἐν 12) (cp. LXX Deut 10:22)

7:16 | ᾧ – attracted from ὅ to agree with the case of the antecedent (ZG) | τιμῆς ἀργυρίου = "for a sum of money," gen. of price (W 122)

7:17 | ὁ χρόνος τῆς ἐπαγγελίας ἧς ὡμολόγησεν ὁ θεὸς τῷ Ἀβραάμ = "the time for God to fulfill the promise that he made to Abraham" (first-level fulfillment; the second-level fulfillment is yet future; cp. Lk 1:72–3)

7:18 | ἄχρι οὗ (= ἄχρι χρόνου ᾧ) + aorist indic. = "until the time when" (BDAG ἄχρι 1bα)

7:19 | τὸ γένος ἡμῶν = "our race" | τοῦ ποιεῖν τὰ βρέφη ἔκθετα αὐτῶν εἰς τὸ μὴ ζῳογονεῖσθαι = "forced our fathers to expose their infants, so that they would not be kept alive" (ESV) (ἔκθετος < ἐκτίθημι, v. 21) | τοῦ ποιεῖν – either final ("to make them expose") or consecutive ("to the point of exposing") (ZG; Z §383)

7:20 | ἀστεῖος (LXX Exod 2:2) τῷ θεῷ = "beautiful/handsome in the sight of God," ethical dat. (BDF §192; W 147); possibly circumlocution for the superlative (BDAG θεός 3gβ) | μῆνας τρεῖς – acc. for extent of time (W 202) | τοῦ πατρός = "of his father," article as possessive pronoun

7:21 | ἐκτεθέντος δὲ αὐτοῦ – gen. abs. | ἑαυτῇ εἰς υἱόν = "as her own son," εἰς as predicate acc. (BDAG εἰς 8b; cp. LXX Exod 2:10)

7:23 | ὡς δὲ ἐπληροῦτο αὐτῷ τεσσαρακονταετὴς χρόνος = "but when he was approaching the age of forty" (NASB) | ἀνέβη ἐπὶ τὴν καρδίαν αὐτοῦ + inf. = "it entered his mind to" (NASB) (cp. 1 Cor 2:9)

7:24 | ποιέω ἐκδίκησιν = "see to it that justice is done," "avenge" (cp. Lk 18:7–8) | τῷ καταπονουμένῳ = "for the oppressed man," dat. of advantage

7:25 | Subject of ἐνόμιζεν is Moses: "[Moses] thought that his brethren would understand that God was granting them deliverance through his hand" | δίδωσιν = lit. "is granting," present retained in indirect discourse (W 537) | οἱ = "they," article as pronoun

7:26 | ὤφθη αὐτοῖς μαχομένοις = "he [= Moses] appeared to them as they were fighting" | συνήλλασσεν αὐτοὺς εἰς εἰρήνην = he "tried to reconcile them in peace," conative impf. (W 551)

7:28 | "Do you want to kill me as you killed the Egyptian yesterday?" (ESV) | μὴ ἀνελεῖν με σὺ θέλεις = μὴ σὺ θέλεις ἀνελεῖν με | ὃν τρόπον = lit. "in the manner in which" (adv. acc.), or simply "as"

7:29 | ἐν τῷ λόγῳ τούτῳ = "at this statement" (BDAG ἐν 9a; BDF §219(2)) | οὗ = "where" (see 1:13)

7:30 | Subject of ὤφθη is ἄγγελος | ἐν φλογὶ πυρὸς βάτου = "in the flame of the burning bush"

7:31 | προσερχομένου αὐτοῦ κατανοῆσαι = "as he approached [the burning bush] to inspect [it]," gen. abs.

7:33 | ἐφ' ᾧ = ἐπὶ ᾧ

7:34 | ἰδὼν εἶδον = "seeing I have seen," cognate ptc. rendering Hebr. inf. absolute (BDF §422) (LXX Exod 3:7) | καὶ νῦν δεῦρο ἀποστείλω σε = "and now come, let me send you," δεῦρο + hortatory subj. (BDF §364(1); W 464)

7:35 | τοῦτον τὸν Μωϋσῆν, ὃν ἠρνήσαντο εἰπόντες = "this is the Moses whom they disowned when they said" | καὶ ἄρχοντα καὶ λυτρωτήν = "as both ruler and redeemer" | σὺν χειρὶ ἀγγέλου = "with the help of the angel" (BDAG χείρ 2bδ), but other MSS have instrumental ἐν (BDF §217(2))

7:36 | ποιέω τέρατα καὶ σημεῖα = "perform wonders and signs" (see 6:8) | ἔτη τεσσαράκοντα – acc. for extent of time

7:37–38 οὗτός ἐστιν ὁ Μωϋσῆς ὁ εἴπας ... ὁ γενόμενος = "this is the Moses *who* said ... *who* was," articles functioning as relative pronouns (W 213)

7:38 | καὶ τῶν πατέρων ἡμῶν = "and [with] our fathers," goes with earlier μετά

7:39 | ᾧ οὐκ ἠθέλησαν ὑπήκοοι γενέσθαι = "to whom [= Moses] our fathers were not willing to be obedient"

7:40 | προπορεύσονται ἡμῶν – gen. bec. of προ- prefix

7:42 | ἔστρεψεν ὁ θεός = either (1) transitive: "God turned [the Israelites toward idolatry]" (BDAG στρέφω 1a), or (2) intransitive: "God turned [away from the Israelites]" (BDAG στρέφω 4) | μή ... προσηνέγκατέ μοι; = "you did not bring me ..., did you?"

7:43 | ἀναλαμβάνω = "take up in order to carry; take along" (BDAG ἀναλαμβάνω 2) | προσκυνεῖν – telic inf. | ἐπέκεινα + gen. = "beyond"

7:44 | ἦν + dat. of possession – "our fathers had the tabernacle of the testimony" | ὁ λαλῶν = "the one speaking" (= God) | αὐτήν = "it" (= ἡ σκήνη)

7:45 | "Having received the tabernacle, our fathers under Joshua brought it with them when they took the land from the nations God drove out before them. It remained in the land until the time of David" (NIV 1984)

7:46 | Textual problem: the reading τῷ οἴκῳ Ἰακώβ ("for the house of Jacob") has superior attestation; nevertheless, τῷ θεῷ Ἰακώβ ("for the God of Jacob") is instrinsically more likely (cp. LXX Ps 132:5) and is followed by Vulgate and most English versions (see discussion in Metzger)

7:48 | ἀλλ' οὐχ ... = "However, the Most High does not ..." (NASB) | ἐν χειροποιήτοις = "in [temples/houses] built by human hands"

7:49 | ποῖος; = "what kind of?"

7:51 | ἀπερίτμητοι καρδίαις καὶ τοῖς ὠσίν = "uncircumcised with respect to hearts and ears," dat. of respect (W 144; BDF §197) | ὡς οἱ πατέρες ὑμῶν καὶ ὑμεῖς = "*as* your fathers did, *so* do you" (ESV) (BDAG ὡς 2a; καί 2c) (cp. Matt 6:10; Gal 1:9; Phil 1:20)

7:52 | οὗ νῦν ὑμεῖς προδόται καὶ φονεῖς ἐγένεσθε = "whose betrayers and murderers you have now become" (NASB)

7:53 | εἰς διαταγὰς ἀγγέλων – either (1) "by directions of angels" (BDAG διαταγή), "by angelic mediation" (M 70), instrumental εἰς (BDAG εἰς 9; BDF §206(1)), or (2) "as the ordinances of angels," "as ordained by angels" (NASB), predicative εἰς (BDAG εἰς 8) | καί = "and yet" (BDAG καί 1bη)

7:54, 57 | ἐπ᾽ αὐτόν (2x) = "at him," in hostile sense (BDAG ἐπί 12b)

7:55 | πλήρης + gen. = "full of" (cp. 6:3, 5, 8)

7:56 | ἐκ δεξιῶν ἑστῶτα τοῦ θεοῦ = ἑστῶτα ἐκ δεξιῶν τοῦ θεοῦ (cp. v. 55)

7:57 | ὁμοθυμαδόν = "with one impulse" (NASB)

7:58 | ἐκβάλλω + plenoastic ἔξω

Acts 8

8:1 | ἦν συνευδοκῶν – impf. periphrastic (W 648) | ἐπί + acc. = "against" (BDAG ἐπί 12b) (cp. 7:54, 57) | κατὰ τὰς χώρας = "throughout/over the regions" (BDAG κατά B1a) | πάντες ... πλήν + gen. = "all except" (BDAG πλήν 2)

8:2 | ἐπ᾽ αὐτῷ = "for him," ἐπί after expressions of emotion (BDAG ἐπί 6c)

8:3 | κατὰ τοὺς οἴκους εἰσπορευόμενος = "entering house after house"

8:4 | οἱ = "they," article as pronoun

8:6 | τοῖς λεγομένοις ὑπό = "to the things said by" | ἐν τῷ ἀκούειν ... καὶ βλέπειν = "as they heard ... and saw" (BDF §404(1))

8:9 | προϋπῆρχεν μαγεύων = "who had previously practiced magic," verb mng. "be" + supplementary ptc. (BDF §414(1)) | λέγων εἶναί τινα ἑαυτὸν μέγαν = "claiming to be someone great" (NASB) (BDF §301(1))

8:11 | "And they paid attention to him because for a long time had amazed them with his magic" (ESV); διὰ τό + inf. (BDF §402(1)) | ἱκανῷ χρόνῳ – dat. of time (W 155) | ταῖς μαγείαις – dat. of means (W 162)

8:13 | ὁ δὲ Σίμων καὶ αὐτός = "even Simon himself" | ἦν προσκαρτερῶν τῷ Φιλίππῳ – impf. periphrastic; dat. bec. of προσ- prefix

8:16 | οὐδέπω ἦν ἐπιπεπτωκός = "[the Spirit] had not yet fallen," pluperf. periphrastic (W 583 n33; 649) | μόνον = "simply" (NASB), "only" (ESV) | βεβαπτισμένοι ὑπῆρχον = either (1) pluperf. periphrastic (on use of ὑπάρχω as finite verb in periphrastic constructions, see W 647 quoting Dana-Mantey), or (2) βεβαπτισμένοι as predicate adj. ptc. (ZG; BDF §414(1)) | εἰς τὸ ὄνομα = "in the name" (BDAG ὄνομα 1dγℷ) (cp. 19:5)

8:18 | δίδοται τὸ πνεῦμα = "the Spirit was bestowed," present retained in indirect discourse (W 537)

8:19 | κἀμοί = καὶ ἐμοί | ἵνα after a noun (ἐξουσία) (BDAG ἵνα 2cα) (cp. 27:42) | ᾧ ἐὰν ἐπιθῶ τὰς χεῖρας = "*everyone* on whom I lay my hands" | λαμβάνῃ – subj. following ἵνα

8:20 | εἴη – voluntative optative (W 481–3; Z §355): "May your money perish," or "To hell with you and your money!" (J. B. Phillips, *The New Testament in Modern English*)

8:21 | οὐκ ἔστιν σοι μερὶς οὐδὲ κλῆρος = "you have neither portion nor lot," σοι = dat. of possession

8:22 | μετανόησον ἀπό = "repent [so as to turn] from," pregnant construction (BDAG ἀπό 1e) | τῆς κακίας σου ταύτης = "this wickedness of yours" | δέομαι takes gen. (cp. v. 34) | εἰ ἄρα = "that, if possible," εἰ introducing indirect question, strengthened with ἄρα (BDF §375; BDAG εἰ 6aβ; ἄρα 3)

8:23 | εἰς = ἐν | ὁρῶ σε ὄντα = "I see that you are"

8:24 | μηδέν ... ὧν εἰρήκατε = "nothing of what you have said"

8:26 | κατὰ μεσημβρίαν = either (1) "about noon" (cp. 22:6 with περί) or (2) "toward the south" (BDAG μεσημβρία 1–2) | αὕτη ἐστὶν ἔρημος = "this is an isolated road," αὕτη refers back to τὴν ὁδόν, and ἔρημος (adj.) here means "isolated, unfrequented, empty" (BDAG ἔρημος)

8:27 | καὶ ἰδού = "and behold [there was]," ellipsis of the verb, common in Luke | ὃς ἐληλύθει προσκυνήσων = "who had come to worship," telic future ptc. (W 636 n57; M 103, 140)

8:28 | ἦν ὑποστρέφων = he was "on his way home" (NIV), impf. periphrastic

8:30 | Ἆρά γε γινώσκεις ἃ ἀναγινώσκεις; = "Do you after all understand what you are reading?" with interrogative particle ἆρα (≠ ἄρα); doubt heightened with addition of enclitic γέ (M 158)

8:31 | πῶς γὰρ ἂν δυναίμην = "[no,] for how could I [understand]?" potential optative (Z §356; BDF §385(1)), with γάρ functioning as reason for unexpressed negative response (BDF §452(1)) | ἐὰν μή τις = "unless someone" | ὁδηγήσει – future for subj. after ἐάν (Z §341)

8:32 | ἐπὶ σφαγήν = "to be slaughtered," ἐπί + acc. as marker of purpose (BDAG ἐπί 11)

8:36 | ὡς ἐπορεύοντο κατὰ τὴν ὁδόν = "as they went along the road" (NASB) | ἦλθον ἐπί τι ὕδωρ = "they came to some water" (NASB)

8:38–39 | καταβαίνω εἰς τὸ ὕδωρ ... ἀναβαίνω ἐκ τοῦ ὕδατος – does not prove baptism by immersion, bec. "going down" and "coming up" refer to walking down (or up) the riverbank to get to (or away from)

the water; "both Philip and the eunuch" went down into the water and came up out of the water (note the 3p verbs).

8:40 | εὑρέθη εἰς Ἄζωτον = "found himself at Azotus" (NASB, ESV; BDAG εὑρίσκω 1b), pass. with intransitive mng. (ZG; BDF §313); εἰς = ἐν | ἕως τοῦ ἐλθεῖν αὐτόν εἰς K. = "until he came to Caesarea," acc. αὐτόν as subject of inf.

Acts 9

9:1 | ἐμπνέω (trans.) + gen. = "breathe out, exhale" (BDF §174) | ἀπειλῆς καὶ φόνου = "murderous threats" (NIV), hendiadys

9:2 | εἰς Δ. πρὸς τὰς συναγωγάς = "to the synagogues in Damascus" | ὅπως ... δεδεμένους ἀγάγῃ = "so that he might bring them bound" | ἐάν τινας εὕρῃ τῆς ὁδοῦ ὄντας = "if he found any belonging to the Way" (BDF §416(2))

9:3 | ἐν τῷ πορεύεσθαι ἐγένετο αὐτὸν ἐγγίζειν τῇ Δ. = "as he was traveling, it happened that he was approaching Damascus" (NASB); ἐν τῷ + inf. (BDF §404(1); Z §387); Septuagintism: ἐγένετο + acc. (subject) + inf. (Z §389) (cp. vv. 32, 37, 43) | ἐξαίφνης τε = "and suddenly"

9:5 | ὁ = "he" [= Jesus], article as pronoun; sc. εἶπεν (ellipsis) (cp. v. 11)

9:6 | λαληθήσεται σοι ὅ τί σε δεῖ ποιεῖν = "it will be told you what you must do," ὅ τι introducing an indirect question (BDF §300(1)); acc. σέ subject of inf.

9:8 | ἀνεῳγμένων δὲ τῶν ὀφθαλμῶν αὐτοῦ = "although his eyes were open," concessive gen. abs. | οὐδὲν ἔβλεπεν = "he could not see anything," conative impf. (W 551) | χειραγωγοῦντες αὐτόν = "by leading him by the hand," adverbial ptc. of means (W 628–30)

9:9 | Subject of ἦν is Saul | ἡμέρας τρεῖς – acc. for extent of time | "he was three days without sight" (NASB)

9:11–12 | ζήτησον ... Σαῦλον ὀνόματι Ταρσέα = "look for a man from Tarsus named Saul" | The Lord's words to Ananias continue through end of v. 12 | Subject of προσεύχεται and εἶδεν is "Saul"

9:13 | ὅσα κακά = "how much evil" (ESV)

9:15 | σκεῦος ἐκλογῆς μοι = "my chosen instrument," attributive Hebr. gen., ἐκλογῆς = ἐκλεκτόν (W 86–8; BDF §§165; 190(1)), μοι – dat. of possession | τοῦ βαστάσαι – inf. in apposition to a noun (σκεῦος) (W 606–7) | τε ... καί ... τε = "before the Gentiles and their kings, and the sons of Israel" (BDF §444(4))

9:16 | ὅσα δεῖ αὐτὸν παθεῖν = "how much he must suffer," acc. αὐτόν as subj. of inf.

9:17 | ἐν τῇ ὁδῷ ᾗ ἤρχου = "on the road by which you were coming [here]" | Verbs of filling take gen.

9:18 | ἀπέπεσαν αὐτοῦ ἀπὸ τῶν ὀφθαλμῶν ὡς λεπίδες = "something like scales fell from his eyes" (ESV; BDAG λεπίς) | αὐτοῦ ἀπὸ τῶν ὀφθαλμῶν = ἀπὸ τῶν ὀφθαλμῶν αὐτοῦ

9:19 | γίνομαι μετά + gen. = "be with someone" (BDAG μετά A2aα) (cp. 20:18) | ἡμέρας τινάς = "for several days," acc. for extent of time | "Saul spent several days with the disciples in Damascus" (NIV)

9:20 | ἐκήρυσσεν – iterative impf.; as implied by "in the synagogues," i.e., on more than one occasion | Either (1) prolepsis with ὅτι as marker of discourse content: "he was preaching Jesus, that he is the Son of God," i.e., "he was preaching that Jesus is the Son of God," or (2) ὅτι recitative: "he was preaching Jesus, saying, 'He is the Son of God'"

9:21 | πορθέω = "attack and cause complete destruction, pillage, make havoc of, destroy, annihilate" (BDAG) (cp. Gal 1:13, 23) | First εἰς = ἐν | ἐληλύθει – extensive pluperf. (W 585–6; BDF §347(3)) | ἵνα equivalent to explanatory inf. after demonstrative (εἰς τοῦτο) (BDAG ἵνα 2e) | ἐπί + acc. = "before," marker of legal proceeding (BDAG ἐπί 10)

9:22 | συγχέω = "confound" (ESV, NASB, BDAG), "baffle" (NIV) | συμβιβάζων ὅτι οὗτός ἐστιν ὁ Χριστός = "by proving that [Jesus] is the Christ," adverbial ptc. of means (W 629)

9:23 | ὡς δὲ ἐπληροῦντο ἡμέραι ἱκαναί = "when many days had passed" (ESV)

9:24 | Subject of παρετηροῦντο is "the Jews"

9:24–25 | ἡμέρας τε καὶ νυκτός & νυκτός (= "by night") – gens. of time

9:25 | αὐτόν (= Saul) is understood as the direct object of the two ptcs.

9:26, 28 | εἰς (2x) = ἐν

9:26 | παραγίνομαι εἰς = "arrive at" (cp. 13:14; 15:4) | ἐστίν – present retained in indirect discourse

9:28 | Subject of ἦν is "Saul," not to be taken with the following ptcs. as periphrastic construction | ἦν μετ' αὐτῶν = "he was staying with them" | εἰσπορευόμενος καὶ ἐκπορευόμενος = "moving about freely" (NASB)

9:29 | οἱ = "they," article as pronoun

9:30 | ἐπιγνόντες = "when they found out"

9:31 | καθ' ὅλης τῆς Ἰουδαίας καί ... = "throughout all Judea and

Galilee and Samaria" (BDAG κατά A1c; BDF §225) (cp. v. 42; 10:37; Lk 4:14; 23:5)

9:32 | ἐγένετο + acc. (subject) + inf. = "it happened ... that" (see v. 3) | διὰ πάντων = "throughout all those regions" (NASB), "about the country" (NIV), "among them all" (ESV)

9:33 | ἐξ ἐτῶν ὀκτὼ κατακείμενον ἐπὶ κραβάττου = "who had been bedridden for eight years" (NASB) (BDAG ἐκ 5a)

9:34 | ἰᾶται – aoristic present (BDF §320; W 517–8) | στρῶσον σεαυτῷ = "make your bed"

9:35 | οἵτινες ἐπέστρεψαν ἐπὶ τὸν κύριον = "and they turned to the Lord" (cp. οἵτινες clause in 5:16)

9:36 | μαθήτρια = female μαθητής | Δορκάς = "gazelle" | πλήρης + gen.

9:38 | ἐγγὺς οὔσης Λύδδας τῇ Ἰόππῃ = "since Lydda is near Joppa," causal ptc. (W 631); for ἐγγύς + dat., see 27:8 | ἐστίν – present retained in indirect discourse | ἐν αὐτῇ = "in her," i.e., in the town of Lydda

9:39 | μετ' αὐτῶν οὖσα ἡ Δορκάς = "while Dorcas was with them"

9:42 | καθ' ὅλης τῆς Ἰόππης = "throughout all Joppa" (see v. 31)

9:43 | ἐγένετο ἡμέρας ἱκανὰς μεῖναι = "it came about that he stayed for many days" (see vv. 3, 32, 37)

Acts 10

10:2 | ποιῶν ἐλεημοσύνας πολλὰς τῷ λαῷ = lit. "doing many alms for the [Jewish] people," dat. of advantage | δεόμενος τοῦ θεοῦ = "praying to God," δέομαι takes gen. | διὰ παντός = "continually"

10:3 | ὡσεὶ περί = "about," ὡσεί (like ὡς) with numerals means "about," as does περί + acc. (BDAG περί 2b) (cp. v. 9); pleonasm | ὥραν ἐνάτην = "at the ninth hour," acc. denoting a point in time (ZG) (cp. 20:16)

10:4 | ὁ = "he," article as pronoun, subject of εἶπεν | εἰς μνημόσυνον = "as a memorial offering," predicate εἰς (BDAG εἰς 8b) (BDAG μνημόσυνον 3; cp. LXX Lev 2:2, 9, 16; 5:12)

10:6 | ᾧ ἐστιν = "who has," dat. of possession

10:7 | ὡς + aorist – "when the angel had left" | δύο τῶν οἰκετῶν = "two of his servants" | τῶν προσκαρτερούντων αὐτῷ – partitive gen., the two servants and the soldier are "from among those who attended him" (ESV)

10:9 | ὁδοιπορούντων ... ἐγγιζόντων = "as they [= the messengers from Cornelius] were on their way and approaching the city," gen. abs.

10:10 | ἤθελεν γεύσασθαι = "he was desiring to eat" (BDAG γεύομαι 1) | παρασκευαζόντων αὐτῶν = "as they were preparing [Peter's meal]," gen. abs.; indef. "they"

10:11 | σκεῦός τι ὡς ὀθόνην μεγάλην = "*something* like a large sheet" (NIV), σκεῦος (neut.) = "a material object used to meet some need in an occupation or other responsibility" (BDAG σκεῦος 1) | τέσσαρσιν ἀρχαῖς καθιέμενον = "lowered by four corners" (BDAG ἀρχή 4), καθιέμενον is neut. in agreement with σκεῦος (cp. 11:6)

10:13 | ἀναστάς – attendant circumstances ptc. with imperatival mng. | Πέτρε – voc. (cp. 11:7)

10:14 | οὐδέποτε ἔφαγον πᾶν κοινὸν καὶ ἀκάθαρτον = "I have never eaten anything common or unclean," Hebr. οὐ ... πᾶς construction (BDF §302(1); Z §446); ἤ would be expected instead of καί, as in some MSS (BDF §446) and as in v. 28; 11:8

10:15 | ἐκ δευτέρου = "a second time" (BDAG ἐκ 5bβ) (cp. 11:9)

10:16 | ἐπὶ τρίς = "three times" or "a third time" (BDAG ἐπί 13; τρίς) (cp. 11:10)

10:17 | τί ἂν εἴη τὸ ὅραμα = "what this vision might mean," either oblique optative (BDF §386(1)), or potential optative (ZG; Z §356) (cp. 5:24) (BDAG εἰμί 2cα) | διερωτήσαντες τὴν οἰκίαν τοῦ Σίμωνος = having "found out where Simon's house was" (NIV), or "having asked directions for Simon's house" (NASB)

10:18 | πυνθάνομαι εἰ + indic. = "inquire whether" (BDAG εἰ 5bα) | ξενίζεται – present retained in indirect discourse

10:19 | τοῦ Π. διενθυμουμένου – gen. abs.

10:20 | μηδὲν διακρινόμενος = "without hesitation" (ESV), "without misgivings" (NASB) (BDAG διακρίνω 6; cp. Jas 1:6) (contrast 11:12) | ὅτι = "for"

10:21 | ὅν = "[the one] whom"

10:22 | μαρτυρούμενος = "well spoken-of" (cp. 6:3) | ἐχρηματίσθη = "[divinely] directed" (BDAG χρηματίζω 1bα) (see Matt 2:12) | μεταπέμψασθαί σε εἰς τὸν οἶκον αὐτοῦ = "to send for you [to come] to his house," pregnant construction (BDAG εἰς 10d)

10:23–24 | τῇ ἐπαύριον (2x) = "the next day," dat. of time

10:24 | ἦν προσδοκῶν – impf. periphrastic | συγκαλεσάμενος = "having called together," aorist ptc. referring to an action preceding the main verb | τοὺς ἀναγκαίους φίλους = "his close friends"

10:25 | ὡς ἐγένετο τοῦ εἰσελθεῖν τὸν Πέτρον is highly unusual; either (1) "when Peter's entry took place" (M 129; cp. BDF §400(7)), or (2) "as Peter was about to enter" (Fitzmyer). Option (2) is to be preferred in light of narrative context (vv. 25–27): As Peter was about to enter, Cornelius met him (συναντήσας), presumably at the door, prostrated himself, and was raised up. Only then did Peter actually enter the house (v. 27).

10:26 | καὶ ἐγὼ αὐτός = "I too"

10:28 | ὡς = "that," marker of discourse content (BDAG ὡς 5) | ἀθέμιτόν ἐστιν τινι + inf. = "it is forbidden for someone to" | προσέρχεσθαι τινι = "to visit someone" | κἀμοί = καὶ ἐμοί – "*and yet* God has shown *me*" (BDAG καί 1bη) | μηδένα ... ἄνθρωπον = "no one" | λέγω = "call" (BDAG λέγω 4)

10:29 | τίνι λόγῳ = "for what reason" (BDAG λόγος 2d)

10:30 | Ἀπὸ τετάρτης ἡμέρας μέχρι ταύτης τῆς ὥρας = "four days ago to this hour" | ἤμην τὴν ἐνάτην προσευχόμενος = "I was praying during the ninth [hour]," impf. periphrastic | τὴν ἐνάτην – could be direct object: "I was praying the ninth-hour [prayer]" (M 34); but probably acc. for extent of time (W 202)

10:33 | σύ καλῶς ἐποίησας παραγενόμενος = "you have been kind enough to come" (NASB, ESV; BDAG καλῶς 4a) | ἀκοῦσαι – inf. of purpose (W 590)

10:34 | ἐπ' ἀληθείας = "truly"

10:35 | δεκτός + ethical dat. (W 146–7) = "welcome to Him" (NASB)

10:37 | τὸ γενόμενον ῥῆμα = "the event that took place" (BDAG ῥῆμα 2) | καθ' ὅλης τῆς Ἰουδαίας = "throughout all Judea" (see 9:31)

10:40 | ἔδωκεν αὐτὸν ἐμφανῆ γενέσθαι = "granted that he should be plainly seen" (BDAG δίδωμι 13); ἐμφανῆ γενέσθαι = "to become visible" (BDAG ἐμφανής 1)

10:41 | μάρτυσιν … ἡμῖν = apposition | τοῖς προκεχειροτονη-μένοις ὑπὸ θεοῦ = "who had been chosen beforehand by God," article as relative pronoun | μετὰ τὸ ἀναστῆναι αὐτὸν ἐκ νεκρῶν = "after he rose from the dead" (BDF §402(3)); acc. αὐτόν as subject of inf.

10:43 | μαρτυρέω + dat. of person about whom testimony is given (BDAG μαρτυρέω 1aα); τούτῳ = "about him" | Indirect discourse: "that everyone who believes in him receives forgiveness of sins through his name"

10:44 | ἔτι λαλοῦντος τοῦ Πέτρου τὰ ῥήματα ταῦτα = "while Peter was still speaking these words," gen. abs.

10:45 | οἱ ἐκ περιτομῆς πιστοί = "the believers from among the circumcision," i.e., Jewish Christians; ancestral ἐκ (cp. Rom 4:12; Col 4:11) (but see 11:2) | καὶ ἐπὶ τὰ ἔθνη = *"even* on the Gentiles" (cp. 11:1)

10:47 | "Surely no one can [justly] withhold the water with the result that these people who have received the Holy Spirit just as we [did] would not be baptized, can they?" (BDAG κωλύω 2: "keep something back, refuse, deny, withhold")

Acts 11
11:1 | ἤκουσαν … ὅτι = they "heard … that" | οἱ ἀδελφοὶ οἱ ὄντες κατὰ τὴν Ἰουδαίαν = "the brothers who were throughout Judea" | καὶ τὰ ἔθνη = *"even* the Gentiles" (cp. 10:45)

11:2 | οἱ ἐκ περιτομῆς = either (1) "those from the circumcision," ancestral ἐκ (as in 10:45), or (2) "the circumcision party" (ESV) (cp. Gal 2:12; Tit 1:10), characteristic ἐκ (these two uses of ἐκ are closely linked and discussed together under BDAG ἐκ 3b) | διακρίνω πρός τινα = "take issue with (or criticize) someone" (BDAG διακρίνω 5b)

11:3 | ὅτι could be translated "why?" (M 132, 159), but probably ὅτι recitative | ἄνδρας ἀκροβυστίαν ἔχοντας = lit. "men having foreskin," i.e., uncircumcised men

11:4 | ἀρξάμενος Π. ἐξετίθετο καθεξῆς = "Peter began and explained in order" (BDAG ἄρχω 2b)

11:5 | ἤμην προσευχόμενος – impf. periphrastic | For καταβαῖνον σκεῦός τι, etc., see 10:11; but note that here καθιεμένην is fem. in agreement with ὀθόνην

11:7 | ἀναστάς – attendant circumstances ptc. with imperatival mng. | Πέτρε – voc. (cp. 10:13)

11:9 | ἐκ δευτέρου = "a second time" (BDAG ἐκ 5bβ) (cp. 10:15)

11:10 | ἐπὶ τρίς = "three times" or "a third time" (BDAG ἐπί 13; τρίς) (cp. 10:16) | ἀνασπάω = "draw/pull up" (BDAG)

11:11 | ἐφίστημι ἐπὶ τὴν οἰκίαν = "stand at [the gate of] the house" (cp. 10:17)

11:12 | μηδὲν διακρίναντα – could be: (1) "without misgivings" (NASB; cp. 10:20); or (2) "making no distinction" (ESV; BDAG διακρίνω 2)

11:14 | ἐν οἷς = "by which," Hebr./instrumental ἐν

11:15 | ἐν τῷ ἄρξασθαί με λαλεῖν = "as I began to speak" (BDF §404(1)), acc. μέ as subject of inf.

11:16 | μιμνήσκομαι takes gen. | ἐν πνεύματι ἁγίῳ (cp. 1:5) – Hebr./instrumental ἐν

11:17 | "If then God gave the same gift to them as he gave to us when we believed in the Lord Jesus Christ, who as I that I could stand in God's way?" (ESV)

11:18 | Ἄρα καὶ τοῖς ἔθνεσιν = "So then, to the Gentiles *also*" (cp. 10:45; 11:1)

11:19 | ἀπὸ τῆς θλίψεως = "because of the persecution" (BDAG ἀπό 5a) (cp. 22:11) | ἐπί Στεφάνῳ – possibilities: "in connection with Stephen" (NASB), "over Stephen" (ESV), "against Stephen" (BDAG ἐπί 12), "at the time of [the death of] Stephen" (BDF §234(8)) | μηδενί … εἰ μὴ μόνον = "to no one except only" (BDAG μόνος 2cα) (cp. Matt 21:19; Mk 6:8)

11:22 | ἠκούσθη ὁ λόγος εἰς τὰ ὦτα … περὶ αὐτῶν = "news about them reached the ears" (NASB) (cp. εἰς τὰ ὦτα in Matt 10:27; Lk 1:44; Jas 5:4)

11:24 | πλήρης takes gen.

11:26 | ἐγένετο + aor. infs. (συναχθῆναι … διδάξαι … χρηματίσαι) = "it came to pass that [S. and B.] gathered together," etc., constative/global aorists – repeated activity viewed as a single event (BDF §332(2); W 557) | αὐτοῖς … συναχθῆναι = "gathered together with them," i.e, the believers in Antioch | καὶ ἐνιαυτὸν ὅλον = "even for an entire year," acc. for extent of time

11:28 | εἷς ἐξ αὐτῶν = αὐτῶν τις (ZG; Z §§80, 155) | μέλλειν ἔσεσθαι = "that [something] was about to be," first inf. in indirect discourse; second inf. as complementary inf.; μέλλω + future inf. denotes certainty (BDAG μέλλω 1a) (cp. 24:15; 27:10) | ἐπὶ Κλαυδίου = "during the reign of Claudius" (NIV; BDAG ἐπί 18a)

Acts 12

12:1 | κατά + acc. = "at," marker of temporal aspect (BDAG κατά B2a) | τινας τῶν ἀπὸ τῆς ἐκκλησίας = "some who belonged to the church"

12:2 | μαχαίρῃ = "with the sword," instrumental dat.

12:3 | ἐστίν – present retained in indirect discourse | προστίθημι + inf. = "proceed to," "do something again" (Septuagintism; BDAG προστίθημι 1c; BDF §435; M 177)

12:4 | παραδοὺς τέσσαρσιν τετραδίοις στρατιωτῶν φυλάσσειν αὐτόν = "delivering him over to four squads of soldiers to guard him" (ESV), φυλάσσειν = inf. of purpose | τετράδιον = "a squad of four soldiers" (4 squads = 16 soldiers)

12:5 | οὖν = "so," marker of continuation of narrative, resuming subject after interruption (BDAG οὖν 2a) | προσευχὴ ἦν γινομένη = "prayer was being made," impf. periphrastic

12:6 | μέλλω + inf. = "be about to" | τῇ νυκτὶ ἐκείνῃ – dat. of time | ἦν κοιμώμενος – impf. periphrastic | φύλακές τε ... ἐτήρουν τὴν φυλακήν = "and sentries were guarding the prison" (τέ is enclitic) | πρὸ τῆς θύρας = "before the door," local (rather than temporal) use of πρό (BDAG πρό 1; BDF §213) (cp. v. 14; 14:13)

12:7 | ἐν τάχει = "quickly," periphrasis for adv. (BDAG ἐν 11) | αὐτοῦ appears to modify ἁλύσεις ("his chains") | ἐκ for ἀπό (ZG; M 72; BDAG ἐκ 2)

12:8 | ἐποίησεν οὕτως = "he did so"

12:9 | "He did not know that what occurred [τὸ γινόμενον] through the angel was real," i.e., not imaginary (BDAG ἀληθής 3) | ἐδόκει ὅραμα βλέπειν = "he thought he was seeing a vision," inf. in indirect discourse

12:10 | "When they had passed the first and second guard, they came to the iron gate" | τὴν φέρουσαν εἰς τὴν πόλιν = "that leads into the city" (BDAG φέρω 6) | ἐξελθόντες προῆλθον ῥύμην μίαν = "they went out and proceeded a distance of one (cross-)street," i.e., one block;

ῥύμην – acc. for extent of space (W 202) (BDAG προέρχομαι 1)

12:11 | ἐν ἑαυτῷ γενόμενος = "having come to his senses" (BDAG γίνομαι 5c)

12:12 | συνιδών = "when he realized [this]" (NASB) | οὗ = "where" (see 1:13) | ἱκανοί = "many" | ἦσαν + perf. ptc. + καί + present ptc. = "had gathered and were praying" (NIV), plupf. and impf. periphrastics (W 648–9)

12:13 | κρούσαντος αὐτοῦ = "when he knocked," gen. abs. | ὑπακοῦσαι = "to answer," inf. of purpose

12:14 | ἀπὸ τῆς χαρᾶς = "because of her joy" (BDAG ἀπό 5c) | ἀπήγγειλεν ἑστάναι τὸν Πέτρον = "she announced that Peter was standing at the door" (indirect discourse: inf. + subject in the acc.)

12:15 | οἱ = "they" (2x) and ἡ = "she," article for pronoun | οὕτως ἔχειν = "that [it] was so" (indirect discourse) (BDAG ἔχω 10a)

12:17 | κατασείσας αὐτοῖς σιγᾶν = "he motioned to them to be silent and," attendant circumstance ptc. | εἶπέν τε = "and said" (cp. v. 6)

12:18 | τάραχος οὐχ ὀλίγος = "no small commotion" | τί ἄρα ὁ Πέτρος ἐγένετο = "as to what had become of Peter" (NIV; M 35; BDAG γίνομαι 4d; ἄρα 1b; BDF §299(2))

12:20 | Subject of ἦν + ptc. (impf. periphrastic) is Herod; αὐτόν = Herod | ὁ ἐπὶ τοῦ κοιτῶνος = "the one in charge of the bedchamber, chamberlain" (BDAG κοιτών; ἐπί 9a) | διὰ τὸ τρέφεσθαι αὐτῶν τὴν χώραν ἀπὸ τῆς βασιλικῆς = "because their country depended on the king's country for food" (ESV), i.e., the Tyrians and Sidonians imported grain from land personally owned by Herod.

12:21 | τακτῇ ἡμέρᾳ = "on an appointed day," dat. of time

12:23 | ἀνθ' ὧν = ἀντὶ ὧν = "because" | σκωληκόβρωτος (< σκώληξ + βιβρώσκω)

12:25 | πληρώσαντες τὴν διακονίαν = "when they had completed their service" (ESV), i.e., famine relief (cp. διακονία in 11:29) | συμπαραλαβόντες = "bringing [John Mark] with them" (ESV)

Acts 13
13:1 | ἐν Ἀ. κατὰ τὴν οὖσαν ἐκκλησίαν = κατὰ τὴν ἐκκλησίαν τὴν οὖσαν ἐν Ἀ. = "in the church that is in Antioch" (BDF §474(5c)) | Ἡρῴδου σύντροφος = "who had been brought up with Herod" (NIV, NASB; BDAG σύντροφος)

13:2 | λειτουργούντων ... νηστευόντων – gen. abs. | δή adds urgency to impv. (BDAG δή 2; BDF §451(4)) | εἰς τὸ ἔργον [sc. εἰς] ὃ προσκέκλημαι αὐτούς = "for the work [to] which I have called them"

13:5 | εἶχον δὲ καὶ Ἰωάννην ὑπηρέτην = "they also had John as their helper," ἔχω + double acc.

13:8 | "Elymas the magician (for so [οὕτως] his name is translated)" (NASB); whether "Elymas" translates "Bar-Jesus," or "magician" translates "Elymas," the linguistic connections are no longer perspicuous to us.

13:9 | ὁ καὶ Παῦλος = "who [is] also [known as] Paul"

13:10 | ῥᾳδιουργία = "fraud" (NASB), "trickery" (NIV), "chicanery" (BDAG) | υἱέ, ἐχθρέ – vocatives | παύω + ptc. = "cease/stop doing something" | οὐ παύσῃ = "will you never stop ...?" (NIV)

13:12 | BDAG ἐπί 6c

13:13 | οἱ περὶ Παῦλον = "Paul and his companions" (M 62; BDF §228) (cp. Mk 4:10; the shorter ending of Mk; Lk 22:49)

13:14 | διελθόντες ἀπὸ τῆς Π. = "they went on from Perga and" (BDAG διέρχομαι 1bβ) | παραγίνομαι εἰς = "arrive at" (cp. 9:26; 15:4) | τῇ ἡμέρᾳ τῶν σαββάτων = "on the Sabbath day," dat. of time; also, pl. for sg. (BDAG σάββατον 1bβ)

13:15 | εἴ τίς ἐστιν ἐν ὑμῖν λόγος παρακλήσεως πρὸς τὸν λαόν = "if you have any word of encouragement for the people" (ESV)

13:17 | ἐξ αὐτῆς = "out of it" (= the land [γῆ, fem.] of Egypt)

13:18 | ὡς τεσσαρακονταετῆ χρόνον = "for a period of *about* 40 years," ὡς with numerals; acc. for extent of time | ἐτροποφόρησεν – other MSS have ἐτροφοφόρησεν = "care for someone" (from LXX Deut 1:31, which has the same π/φ textual variants)

13:19 | κατεκληρονόμησεν τὴν γῆν αὐτῶν = God "caused [his people] to inherit their [= the Canaanites'] land"

13:20 | Textual problem: either (1) ὡς ἔτεσιν τετρακοσίοις καὶ πεντήκοντα. καὶ μετὰ ταῦτα ...: "All this took about 450 years. And after that ..." (ESV), or (2) καὶ μετὰ ταῦτα ὡς ἔτεσιν τετρακοσίοις καὶ πεντήκοντα ...: "and after that he gave unto them judges about the space of 450 years" (KJV) (see Metzger); in any case, temporal dat. answering question "how long?" (BDF §201) | ἔδωκεν κριτάς = "appointed judges" (BDAG δίδωμι 7)

13:21 | κἀκεῖθεν = καὶ ἐκεῖθεν = usually means "and from there," but here with a temporal mng., "and then" (BDAG κἀκεῖθεν 2)

13:22 | The subject of ἤγειρεν is God | εἰς βασιλέα = "to be king," "as king," predicate εἰς (BDAG εἰς 8b; M 70)

13:23 | τούτου ἀπὸ τοῦ σπέρματος = ἀπὸ τοῦ σπέρματος τούτου = "from this man's seed," i.e., from the seed of David (cp. Rom 1:3 which uses ἐκ)

13:24 | προκηρύξαντος Ἰωάννου = "after John had preached beforehand," gen. abs. | πρὸ προσώπου + gen. = "before" in temporal sense (M 74); allusion to LXX Mal 3:1: ἰδοὺ ἐγὼ ἐξαποστέλλω τὸν ἄγγελόν μου, καὶ ἐπιβλέψεται ὁδὸν πρὸ προσώπου μου = "behold, I will send my messenger, and he will look upon the way before me"

13:25 | ὡς + impf. = "as" | οὐκ εἰμὶ ἐγώ = "I am not [he]" | ἔρχεται = "[one] is coming" | οὗ ... τὸ ὑπόδημα τῶν ποδῶν = "the sandal of whose feet"

13:26 | οἱ ἐν ὑμῖν φοβούμενοι τὸν θεόν = "those among you who fear God"

13:27 | "For those who live in Jerusalem and their rulers, failing to acknowledge him [= Jesus] and the utterances of the prophets which are read every Sabbath, by condemning (the one) [= Jesus], they fulfilled (the other) [= the utterances of the prophets]" | κατὰ πᾶν σάββατον = "every Sabbath" (BDAG κατά B2c)

13:28 | μηδεμίαν αἰτίαν θανάτου = "no ground for [putting him to] death" (NASB) | ᾐτήσαντο Π. ἀναιρεθῆναι αὐτόν = "they asked Pilate that he be killed," indirect discourse; acc. αὐτόν as subject of inf.

13:31 | ἐπὶ ἡμέρας πλείους = "for many days" (BDAG ἐπί 18cβ)

13:32 | τὴν πρὸς τοὺς πατέρας ἐπαγγελίαν γενομένην = "the promise that came to the fathers" (cp. John 10:35 for γίνομαι πρός applied to revelation)

13:33 | ὅτι = "namely that," discourse content of εὐαγγελιζόμεθα | ταύτην refers to τὴν ἐπαγγελίαν (v. 32) | ἀναστήσας = "by raising," ptc. of means

13:34 | First ὅτι = "as for the fact that" (NASB, ESV); second ὅτι is recitative | τὰ ὅσια Δαυὶδ τὰ πιστά = "the holy and sure blessings

of David" (ESV), "the unfailing divine assurances or decrees relating to
David" (BDAG ὅσιος 3)

13:35 | ἐν ἑτέρῳ = "in another [psalm]" | δίδωμι = "grant, allow,
permit" (BDAG δίδωμι 13)

13:36 | ἰδίᾳ γενεᾷ = "in his own generation," temporal dat. (BDF
§§200(4); 286(2)) | προσετέθη πρὸς τοὺς πατέρας αὐτοῦ = "he
was gathered to his fathers," referring to the state of death (cp. LXX
Judges 2:10; 4 Kgdms 22:20; 1 Macc 2:69)

13:37 | ὃν δέ = "but [he] whom"

13:38 | δικαιόω ἀπό = "cause someone to be released from legal
claims" (BDAG δικαιόω 3) (cp. Rom 6:7)

13:41 | "Look, you scoffers, be astounded and perish" (ESV) | οὐ
μὴ πιστεύσητε = "you will never believe," emphatic negation subj.
(W 468–9) | ἐάν τις ἐκδιηγῆται ὑμῖν = "even if someone told
you" (NIV)

13:42 | ἐξιόντων αὐτῶν = "as they [Paul and Barnabas] were going
out," gen. abs. | Subject of παρεκάλουν is "they," i.e., the people
of the synagogue = "the people kept begging," iterative impf. | εἰς
τὸ μεταξὺ σάββατον = "on the next Sabbath" (BDAG εἰς 2aβ;
μεταξύ 1bβ)

13:43 | λυθείσης τῆς συναγωγῆς = "after the meeting of the syn-
agogue had broken up" (ESV), gen. abs. (BDAG λύω 3) | οἵτινες
προσλαλοῦντες αὐτοῖς ἔπειθον αὐτούς = "who [= Paul and
Barnabas], as they spoke to them, were urging them"

13:44 | ἐρχομένος = "following, next" (BDAG ἔρχομαι 4aβ)

13:45 | ζήλου – verbs of filling take gen. (cp. v. 52)

13:46 | ἄξιος + gen. = "worthy of"

13:47 | Predicate εἰς (2x) = "to be," "as" (cp. v. 22) | τοῦ εἶναί σε = "that you may be," τοῦ + inf. expressing purpose (BDF §400(5)); acc. σε as subject of inf.

13:48 | ἐπίστευσαν ὅσοι ἦσαν τεταγμένοι εἰς ζωὴν αἰώνιον = "as many as *had been appointed* to eternal life believed" (NASB), plupf. periphrastic (W 649); predestination is the cause of faith, not vice versa: *crediderunt quotquot erant praeordinati ad vitam aeternam* (Vulgate)

Acts 14

14:1 | ἐγένετο + infs. = "it came to pass that" | κατὰ τὸ αὐτό = modifies the verb εἰσελθεῖν and means either "in the same way" (i.e., "as usual," NIV), or "together" (NASB, ESV) (see BDAG αὐτός 3b) | οὕτως ὥστε = "in such a way that" (ESV), "so effectively that" (NIV)

14:2 | κακόω τὴν ψυχὴν τινος κατά = "poison someone's mind against"

14:3 | παρρησιαζόμενοι ἐπὶ τῷ κυρίῳ = "speaking boldly [with reliance] *upon* the Lord" (NASB; BDAG ἐπί 6b; BDF §235(2); M 50) | τῷ μαρτυροῦντι ... γίνεσθαι = "who was testifying to the word of his grace by granting signs and wonders to be done" (see 13:35 on δίδωμι)

14:4 | οἱ μέν ... οἱ δέ = "some ... others"

14:5 | ὁρμή + subjective gen. + inf. = "an attempt on the part of someone to" (BDF §393(6))

14:7 | κἀκεῖ = καὶ ἐκεῖ = "and there" | ἦσαν εὐαγγελιζόμενοι – impf. periphrastic

14:8 | ἀδύνατος τοῖς ποσίν = "powerless with respect to his feet," dat. of respect; "who could not use his feet" (ESV)

14:9 | πίστιν τοῦ σωθῆναι = πίστιν ὥστε σωθῆναι = "faith necessary for healing (lit. 'salvation')" (BDF §400(2))

14:11 | Λυκαονιστί = "in the Lycaonian language"

14:12 | ὁ ἡγούμενος τοῦ λόγου = "the chief speaker"

14:12–13 | Δία, Διός – acc., gen. of Ζεύς

14:13 | τοῦ Διὸς τοῦ ὄντος πρὸ τῆς πόλεως = "of the Zeus who is before the city," a local Zeus whose temple was located in front of the city gates; on πρό, see 12:6 | ὁ ἱερεύς ... ἤθελεν θύειν = "the priest ... wanted to offer sacrifice"

14:15 | τί; = "why?" | καὶ ἡμεῖς = "we too"

14:17 | οὐκ ἀμάρτυρον ἑαυτὸν (or αὐτὸν) ἀφῆκεν = "he did not leave himself without witness" | Verbs of filling take gen.

14:18 | "Even with these words, they had difficulty keeping the crowds from sacrificing to them" (NIV; BDAG μόλις 1)

14:19 | "But Jews came from Antioch and Iconium ..."

14:22 | καὶ ὅτι = "and saying," ὅτι recitative | δεῖ + acc. + inf. = "it is necessary for one to"

14:23 | κατ᾽ ἐκκλησίαν = "in every church" (BDAG κατά B1d) | μετά of accompanying phenomena (BDAG μετά A3b)

14:26 | κἀκεῖθεν = καὶ ἐκεῖθεν | "From there they sailed to Antioch, where they had [originally] been entrusted to the grace of God for the work [τὸ ἔργον, cp. 13:2] which they have [now] completed"

14:27 | ὅσα ἐποίησεν ὁ θεὸς μετ᾽ αὐτῶν (cp. 15:4, 12) – possibilities (see BDAG μετά A2aγכ): (1) supply ptc. ὤν, "all that God had done [being] *with* them," (2) "all that God had done *for* them" (Tobit 12:6; 13:7; Judith 8:26; 15:10; 1 Macc 10:27), (3) "all that God had done *through* them" (NIV), but had Luke intended this, he would have used δι᾽ αὐτῶν (as in 15:12), (4) "all that God had done *with* them" (NASB, ESV), i.e., the signs God did to accompany their message | καὶ ὅτι = "and how" | Subject of ἤνοιξεν is God

14:28 | χρόνον οὐκ ὀλίγον = "a long time," acc. for extent of time

Acts 15

15:1 | ἐὰν μή + subj. = "unless" | τῷ ἔθει τῷ Μωϋσέως = "according to the custom of Moses," unusual use of dat. (M 45); article as relative pronoun (W 214) | ὅτι recitative

15:2 | γενομένης ... – gen. abs. (cp. v. 7) | τῷ Παύλῳ καὶ τῷ Βαρναβᾷ πρὸς αὐτούς = "on the part of P. and B. with (or against) them" | Subject of ἔταξαν is "they," i.e., the believers at Antioch | BDAG περί 1e (cp. v. 6)

15:3 | διέρχομαι + acc. = "pass through some place" | ποιέω χαράν + dat. of advantage = "bring joy to someone" (BDAG ποιέω 2c)

15:4 | ἀπό = ὑπό (BDAG ἀπό 5eβ) | ὅσα ὁ θεὸς ἐποίησεν μετ᾽ αὐτῶν – see 14:27

15:5 | τινες τῶν ἀπὸ τῆς αἱρέσεως τῶν Φαρισαίων πεπιστευκότες = "some of those who had believed from the sect of the Pharisees," τινες goes with πεπιστευκότες; also, ἀπό is substitute for partitive gen. (BDAG ἀπό 1f) | δεῖ + inf. = "it is necessary to" | αὐτούς as object of περιτέμνειν does double duty as object of παραγγέλειν | παραγγέλειν τε τηρεῖν τὸν νόμον Μωϋσέως = "and to direct them to keep the law of Moses"

15:6 | ἰδεῖν περὶ τοῦ λόγου = "to look into this matter" (NASB), "to consider this matter" (ESV) (BDAG λόγος 1aε) (cp. v. 2)

15:7 | ἀφ᾽ ἡμερῶν ἀρχαίων = "in the early days" (ESV, NASB), "some time ago" (NIV) | ἐν ὑμῖν ἐξελέξατο ὁ θεός = "God made a choice among you" (NASB) (BDAG ἐν 1d) | ἀκοῦσαι τὰ ἔθνη ... καὶ πιστεῦσαι = "that the Gentiles should hear ... and believe"

15:8 | δούς – ptc. of means

15:9 | οὐθέν = οὐδέν

15:11 | καθ᾽ ὃν τρόπον κἀκεῖνοι (= καὶ ἐκεῖνοι) = "in the same way as they *also* [are saved]," brachylogy (cp. 27:25)

15:12 | ἀκούω + gen. of person + gen. ptc. = "listen to someone speaking, telling," etc. (BDAG ἀκούω 1c) (cp. 2:6, 11) | ὅσα ἐποίησεν ὁ θεὸς σημεῖα καὶ τέρατα ... δι᾽ αὐτῶν = "all the signs and wonders God had done ... through them" (cp. v. 4; 14:27)

15:13 | μετὰ τό + aorist inf. + acc. = "after x did y" (BDF §402(3)); αὐτούς (the subject of the inf.) refers to Paul and Barnabas, "after they stopped speaking" (BDAG σιγάω 1b), not the assembly, as in v. 12, where the verb means "keep silent" (BDAG σιγάω 1a)

15:14 | καθώς introducing indirect discourse = "how" (BDAG καθώς 5) | ἐπεσκέψατο λαβεῖν ἐξ ἐθνῶν λαὸν τῷ ὀνόματι αὐτοῦ = (1) God "visited the Gentiles, to take from them a people for his name" (ESV), or (2) "concerned himself about taking from among the Gentiles a people for his name" (NASB; cp. BDAG ἐπισκέπτομαι 3)

15:17 | ἐφ᾽ οὓς ἐπικέκληται τὸ ὄνομά μου ἐπ᾽ αὐτούς = "upon whom my name has been called," "who bear my name" (NIV); ἐπ᾽ αὐτούς – Semitic pleonastic personal pronoun (BDF §297)

15:17–18 | κύριος ποιῶν ταῦτα γνωστὰ ἀπ᾽ αἰῶνος – either (1) "the Lord who makes these things known from long ago" (NASB), or (2) "the Lord who does these things that have been known for ages" (NIV 1984; cp. LXX Amos 9:12)

15:19 | ἐγὼ κρίνω = "it is my judgment that" (BDAG κρίνω 3) | τοῖς ἀπὸ τῶν ἐθνῶν (= τοῖς ἐξ ἐθνῶν, v. 23), ἀπό as partitive gen. (BDAG ἀπό 1f)

15:20 | τοῦ ἀπέχεσθαι + gen. = "[telling them] to abstain from," pleonastic τοῦ (BDF §400(7)); appositional inf. (W 607) | τῶν ἀλισγημάτων τῶν εἰδώλων – could be (1) general: "the pollutions associated with idols," or more likely (2) specific: "the polluted food of idols" (= εἰδωλόθυτα, cp. v. 29; 21:25) (cp. ἀλισγέω w.r.t. food in LXX Dan 1:8; Mal 1:7, 12; Sirach 40:29)

15:21 | κατὰ πόλιν = "in every city" (BDAG κατά B1d) | ἔχει – extending-from-past present (W 519–20) | κατὰ πᾶν σάββατον = "every Sabbath" (BDAG κατά B2c)

15:22 | ἐν τοῖς ἀδελφοῖς = "among the brothers"

15:23 | γράφω διὰ χειρός τινος = "write/send a letter [to be delivered and orally explained, cp. v. 27] by another" (BDAG γράφω 2c) | κατά + acc. of place = "in" (BDAG κατά B1a) | χαίρειν = "greetings," standard formula in Hellenistic letters (cp. 23:26; James 1:1)

15:24 | λόγοις = "with words," dat. of means | ἀνασκευάζοντες τὰς ψυχὰς ὑμῶν = "unsettling your souls," ptc. of result (W 637)

15:25 | ἔδοξεν ἡμῖν + ptc. = "it seemed good to us to" | γενομένοις ὁμοθυμαδόν = "having become of one mind" (NASB), dat. pl. in agreement with ἡμῖν | ἐκλεξαμένους ἄνδρας πέμψαι πρὸς ὑμᾶς = "to select men to send to you"

15:26 | παραδεδωκόσι τὰς ψυχὰς αὐτῶν = "who have risked their lives"

15:27 | καὶ αὐτούς ... ἀπαγγέλλοντας τὰ αὐτά = "who will themselves tell you the same things" (ESV) | διὰ λόγου = "by word of mouth" (not merely "by letter") (BDAG λόγος 1aα) (cp. v. 32)

15:28 | μηδὲν πλέον βάρος = "no greater burden" | τὰ ἐπάναγκες = "the necessary things"

15:29 | ἐξ ὧν διατηροῦντες ἑαυτούς = "if you keep yourselves from these things," conditional ptc. (W 633) | εὖ πράσσειν = καλῶς ποιεῖν (BDF §414(5)) | ἔρρωσθε = "be in good health," "farewell," formulaic epistolary closing

15:30 | οἱ μὲν οὖν ἀπολυθέντες = "so when they had been sent off"

15:31 | BDAG ἐπί 6c

15:32 | καὶ αὐτοὶ προφῆται ὄντες = "being also prophets themselves" | διὰ λόγου πολλοῦ = "with a lengthy message" (NASB) (BDAG λόγος 1aβ)

15:33 | ποιέω + acc. of time = "spend time" (BDAG ποιέω 5c) (cp. 18:23; 20:3)

15:35 | μετὰ καὶ ἑτέρων πολλῶν = "with many others also"

15:36 | πῶς ἔχουσιν = "and see how they are doing" (NIV)

15:37 | "Now Barnabas wanted to take along John also, the one called Mark"

15:38 | "But Paul thought best not to take with them one who had withdrawn from them in Pamphylia and had not gone with them to the work" (ESV)

Acts 16

16:1 | Subject of κατήντησεν is Paul | πιστῆς = "a believer" (cp. v. 15)

16:2 | μαρτύρομαι ὑπό τινος = "be well spoken of by someone" (cp. 10:22)

16:3 | σὺν αὐτῷ goes with ἐξελθεῖν = "to go out [on the mission] with him"

16:4 | φυλάσσειν τὰ δόγματα = "the decrees ... for them to observe" (NASB)

16:5 | καθ᾽ ἡμέραν = "daily"

16:7 | πειράζω + inf. = "attempt to do something" (BDAG πειράζω 1)

16:9 | ἦν ἑστώς = "was standing," plupf. periphrastic with impf. force (W 586, 649) (cp. 22:20)

16:10 | ζητέω + inf. = "aim, strive for, seek to do something" (BDAG ζητέω 3) – with ἐζητήσαμεν, the "we" section of Acts begins

16:12 | πρώτης μερίδος τῆς Μακεδονίας πόλις, κολωνία = "a leading city of the district of Macedonia, a [Roman] colony" | ἦμεν διατρίβοντες = "we were staying," impf. periphrastic | ἡμέρας τινάς – acc. for extent of time

16:13, 16 | προσευχή (2x) = "place of prayer," frequently technical term for synagogue building; here, open-air meeting place. "In places with no official synagogue, Jewish people preferred to meet in a ritually pure place near water" (*IVP Bible Background Commentary: New Testament* [ed. Craig S. Keener; Downers Grove: IVP Academic, 1994], 368).

16:13 | οὗ = "where" (see 1:13) | ταῖς συνελθούσαις γυναιξίν = "to the women who had come together"

16:14 | ἧς ... τὴν καρδίαν = "whose heart"

16:16, 19 οἱ κύριοι αὐτῆς (2x) = "her masters" (she was a slave girl or παιδίσκη)

16:16 | "It came to pass, as we were going to the place of prayer, that a slave girl ... met us" (ἐγένετο + inf. with gen. abs. in between) | ἔχουσαν πνεῦμα πύθωνα = "who had a spirit of divination," adjectival use of substantive (BDF §242) | μαντευομένη = "by fortune-telling," ptc. of means

16:18 | ἐποίει – iterative impf.

16:19 | ἐπί + acc. = "before," marker of legal proceeding (BDAG ἐπί 10) (cp. 17:6; 18:12)

16:21 | "They advocate customs that are not lawful for us as Romans to accept or practice" (ESV) | Neut. pl. subjects (ἅ) take sg. verbs (ἔξεστιν) | Ῥωμαίοις οὖσιν – dat. in agreement with ἡμῖν

16:24 | ὅς refers to the δεσμοφύλαξ | παραγγελίαν τοιαύτην λαβών = "upon receiving such an order" (BDAG τοιοῦτος bⅎ) | τοὺς πόδας ... αὐτῶν = "their feet"

16:27 | μέλλω + inf. = "be about to"

16:33 | ἔλουσεν ἀπὸ τῶν πληγῶν = lit. "he washed [them] from the blows"

16:34 | πανοικεί (adverbial dat.) could modify ἠγαλλιάσατο ("he rejoiced along with his entire household") or πεπιστευκώς ("he rejoiced because he had believed in God along with his entire household") | πεπιστευκώς – ptc. of cause (W 632)

16:36 | ὅτι recitative

16:37 | ἀνθρώπους Ῥωμαίους ὑπάρχοντας = "even though we are Roman citizens" (NIV), concessive ptc. (W 634) | ἐκβάλλω = "send away, release" | οὐ γάρ, ἀλλὰ ἐλθόντες αὐτοὶ ἡμᾶς ἐξαγαγέτωσαν = "No indeed! But let them come themselves and bring us out" (NASB)

16:38 | εἰσίν – present retained in indirect discourse

16:40 | ἰδόντες παρεκάλεσαν τοὺς ἀδελφούς = "when they saw the brethren, they encourage them" (NASB)

Acts 17

17:2 | κατὰ τὸ εἰωθὸς τῷ Παύλῳ = "according to Paul's custom," dat. of possession

17:3 | δεῖ + acc. + inf. = "it is necessary for someone to" | Mixture of indirect to direct discourse (BDF §470), with switch to direct discourse introduced by ὅτι recitative: "... and [saying], '...'" | οὗτός ἐστιν ὁ Χριστὸς ὁ Ἰησοῦς = "this Jesus ... is the Christ"

17:4 | γυναῖκες αἱ πρῶται = "the prominent women" (BDAG πρῶτος 2aβ)

17:5 | τῶν ἀγοραίων ἄνδρας τινὰς πονηρούς = "some bad characters from the marketplace" (NIV) | ἐφίστημι = "attack" (BDAG ἐφίστημι 3) | ἐζήτουν αὐτοὺς προαγαγεῖν εἰς τὸν δῆμον = "seeking to bring them out to the crowd" (ESV)

17:6 | BDAG ἐπί 10 (cp. 16:19; 18:12) | ὅτι recitative | οἱ τὴν οἰκουμένην ἀναστατώσαντες οὗτοι καὶ ἐνθάδε πάρεισιν = "these men who have upset the world have come here also" (NASB)

17:9 | λαμβάνειν τὸ ἱκανόν = "to receive money as bail" = *satis accipere* (Latinism; BDF §5(3)(b))

17:10 | οἵτινες παραγενόμενοι εἰς τὴν συναγωγὴν ἀπῄεσαν = "when they arrived, they went into the synagogue"

17:11 | εὐγενέστεροι + gen. of comparison = "more noble-minded than" | καθ' ἡμέραν = "daily" | εἰ ἔχοι ταῦτα οὕτως = "[to see] whether these things were so" (BDAG εἰ 5bγ; ἔχω 10a); oblique optative used in indirect question (W 483; Z §346; BDF §386(2))

17:13 | κἀκεῖ = καὶ ἐκεῖ

17:14 | ἕως ἐπὶ τὴν θάλασσαν = "as far as the sea;" other MSS read ὡς ἐπὶ τὴν θάλασσαν = "as it were, toward the sea" (see commentaries)

17:15, 16 | Ἀθῆναι (= Athens) is always pl. (cp. 18:1)

17:15 | ὡς τάχιστα = "as quickly as possible" (BDAG ὡς 8d)

17:16 | ἐκδεχομένου αὐτοὺς τοῦ Παύλου = "while Paul was waiting for them [= Silas and Timothy]," gen. abs.

17:17 | οἱ παρατυγχάνοντες = "those who happened to be there"

17:18 | τί ἂν θέλοι ... λέγειν; = "what would this seed picker say?" potential optative (W 484) | σπερμολόγος (< σπέρμα + λέγω in sense "pick out, collect") = lit. "picking up seeds" as a bird, "scrap-monger, scavenger" (BDAG), "one who picks up and retails scraps of knowledge" (LSJ); substantival use of adj.

17:19 | Δυνάμεθα γνῶναι τίς ἡ καινὴ διδαχή; = "May we know what this new teaching is?"

17:20 | ξενίζοντα τινα εἰσφέρεις εἰς τὰς ἀκοὰς ἡμῶν = "you are bringing some strange ideas to our ears" (NIV) | βουλόμεθα γνῶναι τίνα θέλει ταῦτα εἶναι = "we want to know what these things mean" (BDAG θέλω 5; cp. 2:12)

17:21 | εἰς οὐδὲν ἕτερον ηὐκαίρουν [customary impf.] ἢ λέγειν τι ἢ ἀκούειν τι καινότερον = they "used to spend their time in nothing other than telling or hearing something new" (NASB) (ἕτερον ἤ = "other than")

17:22 | κατὰ πάντα ὡς δεισιδαιμονεστέρους ὑμᾶς θεωρῶ = "I see that in every way you are very religious" (NIV)

17:25 | προσδεόμενός τινος = "as though he needed anything" | διδούς = "since he gives," causal ptc.

17:26 | ἐπὶ παντὸς προσώπου τῆς γῆς = "on all the face of the earth," i.e., everywhere on earth

17:27 | εἰ ἄρα γε ψηλαφήσειαν αὐτὸν καὶ εὕροιεν = "if perhaps they might grope for him and find him" (NASB), "feel their way toward him" (ESV), conditional optative (W 484) | καί γε = "though" (BDAG γέ bγ)

17:28 | τινες τῶν καθ' ὑμᾶς ποιητῶν = "some of your own poets" (cp. 18:15)

17:29 | γένος [sg.] ὑπάρχοντες [pl.] τοῦ θεοῦ = "since we are God's offspring," causal ptc; *constructio ad sensum* | ὅμοιον + dat. = "like"

17:30 | τὰ νῦν = "now," adv. acc.

17:31 | ἐν ἀνδρί = "by [the] man," Hebr./instrumental ἐν | πίστιν παρασχών = "having furnished proof" (BDAG πίστις 1c) | ἀναστήσας = "by raising," ptc. of means

17:32 | οἱ μέν ... οἱ δέ = "some ... but others"

Acts 18
18:2 | διὰ τό + inf. = "because"

18:3 | σκηνοποιός = (1) maker of stage properties, or (2) tentmaker (see extensive discussion in BDAG) | τῇ τέχνῃ = "by trade"

18:4 | κατὰ πᾶν σάββατον = "every Sabbath"

18:5 | εἶναι τὸν Χριστὸν Ἰησοῦν = "that Jesus was the Christ," indirect discourse (cp. v. 28)

18:6 | ἀντιτασσομένων ... βλασφημούντων – gen. abs. | καθαρὸς ἐγώ· ἀπὸ τοῦ νῦν εἰς τὰ ἔθνη πορεύσομαι = "I am clean. From now on I will go to the Gentiles"

18:8 | ἐπίστευον καὶ ἐβαπτίζοντο – distributive iterative impfs. (W 546)

18:10 | ἐστί μοι = "I have," dat. of possession

18:11 | ἐνιαυτὸν καὶ μῆνας ἕξ = "for a year and six months," acc. for extent of time

18:12 | Γαλλίωνος ἀνθυπάτου ὄντος τῆς Ἀχαΐας = "when Gallio was proconsul of Achaia," gen. abs. | κατέπεστησεν ὁμοθυμαδόν = "made a united attack" (ESV) | BDAG ἐπί 10 (cp. 16:19; 17:6)

18:13 | ὅτι recitative | παρά + acc. = "against, contrary to" (BDAG παρά C6)

18:14 | κατὰ λόγον ἂν ἀνεσχόμην ὑμῶν = "it would be reasonable for me to put up with you" (BDAG κατά B5bβ; λόγος 2d), ἀνέχω takes gen.

18:15 | ζητήματα ἐστιν – neut. pl. subjects take sg. verbs | ζητήματα περὶ λόγου καὶ ὀνομάτων = "controversial issues involving disputes about words (or teaching) and persons" (BDAG λόγος 1aβ; ὄνομα 2) | νόμου τοῦ καθ᾽ ὑμᾶς = "your own law" (BDF §224(1)) | ὄψεσθε – imperatival future (W 569)

18:17 | οὐδὲν τούτων τῷ Γαλλίωνι ἔμελεν = lit. "none of these things were a concern to Gallio," i.e., he "was not concerned about any of these things"

18:18 | ἔτι ἡμέρας ἱκανάς = "many days longer," acc. for extent of time | εἶχεν εὐχήν = "he was under a vow" (ESV)

18:19 | κἀκείνους = καὶ ἐκείνους | αὐτοῦ (adv.) = "there"

18:20 | ἐρωτώντων αὐτῶν ... μεῖναι = "when they were asking him to stay for a longer time," gen. abs.

18:21 | τοῦ θεοῦ θέλοντος = "if God wills," conditional gen. abs. (W 632–3)

18:23 | ποιήσας χρόνον τινά = "having spent some time," ποιέω + acc. of time (BDAG ποιέω 5c) (cp. 15:33; 20:3)

18:25 | οὗτος ἦν κατηχημένος τὴν ὁδὸν τοῦ κυρίου = "this man had been instructed in the way of the Lord" | τὰ περὶ τοῦ Ἰησοῦ = "the things concerning Jesus" (M 63)

18:27 | βουλομένου αὐτοῦ + inf. = "when he wanted to," gen. abs. | προτρεψάμενοι οἱ ἀδελφοὶ ἔγραψαν τοῖς μαθηταῖς ἀποδέξασθαι αὐτόν = "the brethren encouraged him [to do it] and wrote to the disciples [in Achaia] to welcome him," προτρέπω = "promote a particular course of action" (BDAG) | ὃς παραγενόμενος = "who upon his arrival" | πολύ = "greatly," adv. acc. | διὰ τῆς χάριτος could modify συνεβάλετο but most likely modifies τοῖς πεπιστευκόσιν, "those who through grace had believed" (ESV)

18:28 | ἐπιδεικνὺς διὰ τῶν γραφῶν εἶναι τὸν Χριστὸν Ἰησοῦν = "demonstrating by the Scriptures that Jesus was the Christ" (cp. v. 5)

Acts 19

19:1 | ἐγένετο + inf. = "it came to pass ... that" | ἐν τῷ τὸν Ἀπολλῶ εἶναι ἐν Κορίνθῳ = "while Apollos was in Corinth" | τὰ ἀνωτερικὰ μέρη = "the upper regions"

19:2 | Ἀλλ' οὐδ' εἰ πνεῦμα ἅγιον ἔστιν ἠκούσαμεν = "No, we have not even heard *that* there is a Holy Spirit" (NIV, ESV) (for rendering εἰ as "that," see BDAG εἰ 2)

19:4 | τῷ λαῷ λέγων ... ἵνα πιστεύσωσιν = "telling the people to believe in the one coming after him," unusual word order (M 169)

19:5 | εἰς τὸ ὄνομα = "in the name" (BDAG ὄνομα 1dγ⅁) (cp. 8:16)

19:6 | ἐπιθέντος ... = "when Paul had laid his hands on them," gen. abs.

19:8 | πείθων περί + gen. = "persuading [them] concerning"

19:9 | ἀποστὰς ἀπ' αὐτῶν ἀφώρισεν τοὺς μαθητάς = Paul "withdrew from them and separated the disciples" (BDAG ἀφορίζω 1) | καθ' ἡμέραν = "daily"

19:10 | τοῦτο ἐγένετο ἐπὶ ἔτη δύο = "this went on for two years" (NIV) | ὥστε + inf. = "so that," expressing result

19:11 | οὐ τὰς τυχούσας = "extraordinary" (see note at 28:2)

19:12 | ἀπὸ τοῦ χρωτὸς αὐτοῦ = "from his [Paul's] skin," i.e., "that had touched his skin" (ESV)

19:13 | τινες καί τῶν περιερχομένων ἐξορκιστῶν = "*even* some traveling exorcists" | ὁρκίζω + double acc. = "I adjure you by so-and-so" (BDF §149; W 204–5); instantaneous/performative present (W 517–8)

19:16 | ἀμφότεροι when more than two = "all of them" (BDAG ἀμφότερος 2)

19:19 | κατέκαιον – distributive iterative impf. | συνεψήφισαν τὰς τιμὰς αὐτῶν καὶ εὗρον ἀργυρίου μυριάδας πέντε = "they counted up the price of them and found it 50,000 pieces of silver" (NASB)

19:20 | κατὰ κράτος = "powerfully"

19:21 | τίθημι ἐν τῷ πνεύματι = either (1) "resolve in one's spirit," or (2) "resolve in the Spirit" (BDAG τίθημι 1bε) (cp. 5:4) | ὅτι recitative | μετὰ τὸ γενέσθαι με ἐκεῖ δεῖ με καὶ Ῥώμην ἰδεῖν = "after I have been there, it is necessary for me to visit Rome as well"

19:24 | ναοὺς ἀργυροῦς Ἀρτέμιδος = "silver shrines of Artemis," replicas of the famous temple of Artemis at Ephesus, one of the seven wonders of the ancient world

19:25 | τοὺς περὶ τὰ τοιαῦτα ἐργάτας = "the workmen in similar trades" (ESV), "the workers who were occupied with such things" (BDAG περί 2c) | ἡμῖν ἐστιν = "we have," dat. of possession

19:26 | οὐ μόνον Ἐφέσου ἀλλὰ σχεδὸν πάσης τῆς Ἀσίας – either (1) genitives of place (BDF §186(1)), or (2) partitive genitives with ἱκανὸν ὄχλον (M 39) | ὁ Παῦλος οὗτος = "this Paul person" | ἱκανὸν ὄχλον = "large numbers of people" (NIV)

19:27 | τοῦτο ἡμῖν τὸ μέρος = "this line of business of ours" (BDAG μέρος 1bη) | Subject of καθαιρεῖσθαι is Artemis; takes gen. (τῆς μεγαλειότητος) bec. of κατα- prefix (BDF §180(1)) | "And that she whom all of Asia and the world worship will even be dethroned from her magnificence" (NASB)

19:28 | πλήρης + gen. = "full of"

19:29 | ἐπλήσθη ἡ πόλις τῆς συγχύσεως = "the city was filled with confusion," verbs of filling take gen. | συνεκδήμους Παύλου = "Paul's traveling companions," gen. of association (W 128–30)

19:30 | Παύλου βουλομένου + inf. = "although Paul wanted to," concessive gen. abs.

19:31 | μὴ δοῦναι ἑαυτὸν εἰς τὸ θέατρον = "not to venture into the theater" (BDAG δίδωμι 11)

19:32 | ἄλλοι ἄλλο τι ἔκραζον = "some were shouting one thing and some another" (cp. 21:34), distributive iterative impf. | τίνος ἕνεκα συνεληλύθεισαν = "why they had come together"

19:33 | ἐκ τοῦ ὄχλου = "some in the crowd" | προβαλόντων αὐτὸν τῶν Ἰουδαίων = "the Jews having pushed him to the front," gen. abs.

19:34 | ἐπιγνόντες ὅτι Ἰουδαῖός ἐστιν = "when they recognized that he was a Jew" | ὡς ἐπὶ ὥρας δύο = "for about two hours"

19:35 | τίς γάρ ἐστιν ἀνθρώπων ὃς οὐ γινώσκει; = "after all, who is there who does not know?" (ZG; BDAG γάρ 3) | νεωκόρος = "honorary temple keeper," a city responsible for the maintenance of a pagan temple and the associated emperor cult (BDAG) | τὸ διοπετές [sc. ἄγαλμα] = "her image, which fell from heaven" (NIV; lit. "from Zeus"), ellipsis of understood substantive (BDF §241(7)); possibly a meteorite

19:36 | δέον ἐστὶν ὑμᾶς κατεσταλμένους ὑπάρχειν = "you ought to be quiet"

19:37 | οὔτε ... οὔτε ... = "who are neither robbers of temples [cp. Rom 2:22] nor blasphemers of our goddess"

19:38 | εἰ ... ἔχουσι πρός τινα λόγον = "if [they] have a grievance against anybody" (NIV) | ἀγοραῖοι ἄγονται = "the courts are open" = *fora aguntur* (Latinism; BDF §5(3)(b)) | ἐγκαλείτωσαν ἀλλήλοις = "let them bring charges against one another"

19:40 | καὶ γὰρ κινδυνεύομεν ... περὶ τῆς συστροφῆς ταύτης = "For indeed we are in danger of being charged with rioting for today's events, since there is no cause with reference to which we will be able to give an account of this uproar" (leaving out [οὐ]; see Metzger)

Acts 20
20:1 | μετὰ τό + inf. = "after" (W 594–5)

20:2 | λόγῳ πολλῷ = "in much discourse," dat. of manner (ZG; W 161)

20:3 | ποιήσας μῆνας τρεῖς = "and spent three months" (see 15:33; 18:23) | αὐτῷ = "against him," dat. of disadvantage | μέλλοντι + inf. = "as he was about to," dat. in agreement with αὐτῷ (BDF §356) | ἐγένετο γνώμης + inf. = "he decided to" (M 38; BDAG γίνομαι 7); γνώμης is predicate gen. (BDF §162(7)), lit. "he was of a mind to" | Pleonastic τοῦ with inf. (BDF §400(7))

20:4 | Σώπατρος Πύρρου Βεροιαῖος = "Sopater son of Pyrrhus, from Berea" | Θεσσαλονικέων = "[both] of the Thessalonians" | Δερβαῖος = "from Derbe" | Ἀσιανοί = "Asians," i.e., from Asia Minor

20:5 | μένω + acc. = "wait for someone"

20:6 | ἄχρι ἡμερῶν πέντε = "within five days," unique usage (M 205)

20:7 | ἐν τῇ μιᾷ τῶν σαββάτων = "on the first [day] of the week" (BDAG σάββατον 2b) | συνηγμένων ἡμῶν + inf. = "when we were gathered together to," gen. abs.

20:8 | οὗ ἦμεν συνηγμένοι = "where we had gathered," plupf. periphrastic

20:9 | καταφερόμενος ὕπνῳ βαθεῖ = "sinking into a deep sleep" | διαλεγομένου τοῦ Παύλου – gen. abs. | First ἀπό = ὑπό

20:11 | ἐφ᾽ ἱκανόν ὁμιλήσας ἄχρι αὐγῆς οὕτως ἐξῆλθεν = "he talked with them a long while until daybreak, and then left" (NASB) | On οὕτως, see BDF §425(6) (cp. 27:17)

20:13 | οὕτως γὰρ διατεταγμένος ἦν μέλλων αὐτὸς πεζεύειν = "for so he had arranged it, intending himself to go by land" (NASB)

20:15 | κἀκεῖθεν = καὶ ἐκεῖθεν | τῇ ἐπιούσῃ ... τῇ δὲ ἑτέρᾳ ... τῇ δὲ ἐχομένη = "the next [day] ... and the next [day] ... and the [day] after that," datives of time (W 155)

20:16 | ὅπως μὴ γένηται ... γενέσθαι εἰς Ἱεροσόλυμα = "so that he would not have to spend time in Asia; for he was hurrying to be in Jerusalem, if possible, on the day of Pentecost" (NASB) | εἰ εἴη = "if possible," conditional optative (W 484), fourth class conditional (W 701) | τὴν ἡμέραν τῆς πεντηκοστῆς = "on the day of Pentecost," acc. denoting a point in time (ZG) (cp. 10:3); gen. of apposition (W 95) | εἰς = ἐν

20:18 | γίνομαι μετά + gen. = "be with someone" (BDAG μετά A2aα) (cp. 9:19) | τὸν πάντα χρόνον = "the whole time," acc. for extent of time (M 94)

20:19 | μετά ... πειρασμῶν τῶν συμβάντων μοι ἐν ταῖς ἐπιβουλαῖς τῶν Ἰουδαίων = "with trials that happened to me through the plots of the Jews" (ESV), Hebr./instrumental ἐν

20:20 | ὡς οὐδὲν ὑπεστειλάμην τῶν συμφερόντων τοῦ μὴ ἀναγγεῖλαι ὑμῖν = "how I did not shrink from declaring to you anything that was profitable" (ESV, NASB); the two negatives reinforce each other (cp. v. 27) | κατ᾽ οἴκους = "from house to house"

20:22 | τὰ ἐν αὐτῇ συναντήσοντά μοι μὴ εἰδώς = "not knowing what will happen to me there," lit. "in her" (= in Jerusalem)

20:23 | κατὰ πόλιν = "in every city" | με μένουσιν = "await me"

20:24 | ἀλλ' οὐδενὸς λόγου ποιοῦμαι τὴν ψυχὴν τιμίαν ἐμαυτῷ = either (1) "I don't consider my life as something of value for myself" (BDAG ποιέω 7b), or (2) "I do not consider my life worth a single word" (BDAG λόγος 1aα) | ὡς + inf. = "so that," rare construction in NT (M 138 n1; BDF §391(1); BDAG ὡς 9b) (cp. Lk 9:52); see scribal variants, e.g., changing ὡς to ὥστε, or inf. to subj. | διακονίαν ... διαμαρτύρασθαι = "ministry of testifying," epexegetical inf. (W 607)

20:25, 27 | ἐν οἷς/ᾧ = "among whom" (cp. v. 32)

20:31 | παύομαι + ptc. = "cease doing something"

20:32 | τὰ νῦν = "now," adv. acc.

20:35 | πάντα = "in everything" (NASB), "in everything I did" (NIV), acc. of respect | οὕτως κωπιῶντας = "by working hard in this way" (ESV), ptc. of means; on οὕτως, see BDF §425(6) | Sc. ἡμᾶς as subject of δεῖ ("we must") | ἀντιλαμβάνομαι takes gen. | μᾶλλον ... ἤ = "better ... than"

20:37 | ἱκανὸς κλαυθμὸς ἐγένετο πάντων = "there was much weeping on the part of all" (ESV) | κατεφίλουν – distributive iterative impf.

20:38 | BDAG ἐπί 6c

Acts 21

21:1 | Ὡς ἐγένετο ἀναχθῆναι ἡμᾶς ἀποσπασθέντας ἀπ' αὐτῶν = "After we had torn ourselves away from them, we put out to sea" (NIV; cp. BDAG ἀποσπάω 2b); note word order | τῇ ἑξῆς = "on the next day" | κἀκεῖθεν = καὶ ἐκεῖθεν

21:2 | εὑρόντες πλοῖον διαπερῶν εἰς Φοινίκην ἐπιβάντες ἀνήχθημεν = "we found a ship crossing over to Phoenicia, boarded it, and set sail"

21:3 | καταλιπόντες αὐτὴν [= τὴν Κύπρον] εὐώνυμον = "leaving it on the left" | ἦν ἀποφορτιζόμενον = "was to unload," either (1) impf. periphrastic (BDF §353(3)) with ingressive sense (W 544), or (2) impf. + futuristic present ptc. (BDF §339(2)(b))

21:4 | ἀνευρίσκω = "seek out" | αὐτοῦ (adv.) = "there" | ἡμέρας ἑπτά – acc. for extent of time (cp. vv. 7, 10)

21:5 | ὅτε ἐγένετο ἡμᾶς ἐξαρτίσαι τὰς ἡμέρας = "when our days there were ended" (NASB, ESV) | ἐπορευόμεθα = "we started on our journey," inceptive impf. | προπεμπόντων ἡμᾶς πάντων = "while they all accompanied us," gen. abs. | ἕως ἔξω τῆς πόλεως = "until we were out of the city"

21:6 | εἰς τὰ ἴδια = "home" (BDAG ἴδιος 4b)

21:8 | ὄντος ἐκ τῶν ἑπτά = "who was one of the seven" (cp. 6:5)

21:9 | τούτῳ ἦσαν = "he had," dat. of possession

21:11 | δέω τινα τοὺς πόδας καὶ τὰς χεῖρας = "bind someone hand and foot," acc. of respect (W 203; BDF §160; BDAG δέω 1b) | τάδε λέγει = "thus says," the formula τάδε λέγει κύριος (= "thus says the Lord") is extremely common in LXX; see HR ὅδε) (W 328)

21:12 | οἱ ἐντόπιοι = "the local residents" (NASB, BDAG ἐντόπιος), substantivized adj.

21:13 | τί ποιεῖτε; + present ptcs. = "what are you doing, weeping and breaking my heart?" | ἑτοίμως ἔχω + inf. = "I am ready to" (BDAG ἔχω 10b) (cp. 2 Cor 12:14; 1 Pet 4:5) | εἰς = ἐν

21:14 | μὴ πειθομένου αὐτοῦ = "since he would not be dissuaded," gen. abs.

21:16 | καὶ τῶν μαθητῶν ἀπὸ Καισαρείας = "also [some] of the disciples from Caesarea," partitive gen. as subject (BDF §164(2)); the text may be corrupt, since τινές or ἐκ would normally be present before τῶν, and τῶν would be repeated before ἀπό | ἄγοντες παρ' ᾧ ξενισθῶμεν Μνάσωνί = "taking us to Mnason ... with whom we were to lodge" (NASB) (M 130 n1; BDF §294(5))

21:17 | γενομένων ἡμῶν = "when we arrived," gen. abs.

21:18 | τῇ ἐπιούσῃ = "the following [day]"

21:19 | καθ' ἕν = "one after the other, in detail" (BDAG εἷς 5e; cp. John 21:25) | ἕκαστον ὧν ἐποίησεν ὁ θεός ("each of the things God did") is the object of ἐξηγεῖτο | NA punctuation sets off καθ' ἓν ἕκαστον as a phrase, but ἐξηγέομαι takes acc. (10:8; 15:12; Lk 24:35)

21:20 | ζηλωταὶ τοῦ νόμου = "zealots for the law," objective gen. (cp. Gal 1:14)

21:21 | τοὺς κατὰ τὰ ἔθνη πάντας Ἰουδαίους = "all the Jews throughout the nations" (BDAG κατά B1a), i.e., Diaspora Jews

21:22 | τί οὖν ἐστιν; = "What, then, is [to be done]?" (NASB)

21:23 | εὐχὴν ἔχοντες ἐφ' ἑαυτῶν = lit. "who have a vow over themselves," i.e., who are under a vow

21:24 | δαπανάω ἐπί + acc. = "pay someone's expenses" | ἵνα ξυρήσονται – one of the rare cases of ἵνα + future indic. (M 139); but note textual variant ξυρήσωνται (BDF §369(3)) | τὴν κεφαλήν – acc. of respect ("that they may be shaved with respect to the head") | ὅτι ὧν κατήχηνται περὶ σοῦ οὐδέν ἐστιν = "that there is nothing to the things which they have been told about you" (NASB) | στοιχεῖς καὶ αὐτὸς φυλάσσων τὸν νόμον = "you yourself are living in obedience to the law" (NIV) (see BDAG στοιχέω)

21:25 | ἡμεῖς ἐπεστείλαμεν κρίναντες φυλάσσεσθαι αὐτούς = "we have sent a letter with our judgment that they should abstain from" (ESV)

21:26 | διαγγέλλων τὴν ἐκπλήρωσιν … ἡ προσφορά = "to give notice of the date when the days of purification would end and the sacrifice would be made for each of them" (NIV)

21:27 | ὡς ἔμελλον αἱ ἑπτὰ ἡμέραι συντελεῖσθαι = "when the seven days were almost completed" (ESV); μέλλω + inf.; note that the augment for the impf. of μέλλω can be either ἐ- or ἠ- (cp. 12:6; 16:27) (BDF §66(3)) | συνέχεον πάντα τὸν ὄχλον = "they were stirring up the whole crowd"

21:28 | ὁ … διδάσκων = "who teaches" | κατά + gen. = "against" | ἔτι τε καὶ Ἕλληνας εἰσήγαγεν εἰς τὸ ἱερόν = "and besides he has even brought Greeks into the temple" (NASB) (BDAG ἔτι 2b)

21:29 | ἦσαν προεωρακότες = "they had previously seen," plupf. periphrastic

21:30, 33 | Verbs of grasping, seizing (e.g., ἐπιλαμβάνομαι) take gen.

21:31 | ζητούντων αὐτὸν ἀποκτεῖναι = "while they were trying to kill him" (NIV), gen. abs.; sc. αὐτῶν as subject of ζητούντων | φάσις … ὅτι = "a report that" – the verb ἀνέβη is used bec. the report "went up" to the Tower Antonia where the tribune was (BDAG φάσις)

21:32 | παύομαι + ptc. = "cease doing something"

21:33 | ἐπυνθάνετο τίς εἴη καὶ τί ἐστιν πεποιηκώς = "he was inquiring who he was and what he had done," εἴη as oblique optative (W 483; BDF §386)

21:34 | ἄλλοι ἄλλο τι ἐπεφώνουν – see 19:32 | μὴ δυναμένου αὐτοῦ γνῶναι τὸ ἀσφαλές = "since he was unable to determine the facts," causal gen. abs. | τὸ ἀσφαλές = "the facts," substantivized adj. (cp. 22:30) | διὰ τὸν θόρυβον = "because of the uproar" (of the mob), the reason the commander was unable to determine the facts | ἐκέλευσεν ἄγεσθαι αὐτόν = "ordered him [= Paul] to be led"

21:35 | ὅτε ἐγένετο ἐπὶ τοὺς ἀναβαθμούς = "when he was at the steps" (BDAG γίνομαι 6c) | συνέβη βαστάζεσθαι αὐτόν = "he had to be carried" (NIV)

21:36 | αἶρε αὐτόν = "away with him!"

21:38 | οὐκ ἄρα σὺ εἶ ὁ Αἰγύπτιος; = "Aren't you the Egyptian ...?" (NIV) | πρὸ τούτων τῶν ἡμερῶν = "some time ago" (cp. 5:36) | ὁ ἀναστατώσας καὶ ἐξαγαγών = "who incited a revolt and led," article functioning as relative pronoun and governing both ptcs. | ἄνδρας τῶν σικαρίων = "men from the *sicarii*," partitive gen.; Latin *sica* = curved dagger; hence *sicarius* = a dagger man – here in reference to Jewish nationalist extremists who would hide daggers in their garments and mingle in crowd to assassinate their enemies (Josephus, *Jewish War* 2.254–57; *Antiquities* 20.186–88)

21:40 | ἐπιτρέψαντος αὐτοῦ & πολλῆς σιγῆς γενομένης – gen. abs.

Acts 22
22:1 | ἀκούω + gen. (τῆς ἀπολογίας) (cp. v. 7) | μου τῆς πρὸς ὑμᾶς νυνὶ ἀπολογίας = "my defense [which I] now [make] to you"

22:2 | μᾶλλον παρέσχον ἡσυχίαν = "they became even more quiet"

22:3 | ζηλωτὴς τοῦ θεοῦ = "zealous for God," objective gen. (cp. Rom 10:2)

22:4 | ὅς refers back to ἐγώ (v. 3)

22:5 | ἄξων = "in order to lead away, arrest," telic future ptc. (BDF §418(4); W 635–7) | καὶ τοὺς ἐκεῖσε ὄντας = "even those who were there"

22:6 | ἐγένετο μοι + inf. = "it happened to me that …" (cp. v. 17) | φῶς ἱκανόν = "a very bright light"

22:9 | ἀκούω here could be translated "understand" (BDAG ἀκούω 7), alleviating apparent contradiction with 9:7; semantic issue; change of case not part of the solution (see W 133–4) | τὴν φωνήν … τοῦ λαλοῦντός μοι = "the voice of the one who was speaking to me"

22:10 | ποιήσω – deliberative subj. | κἀκεῖ = καὶ ἐκεῖ

22:11 | ὡς οὐκ ἐνέβλεπον = "since I could not see" (NASB) (BDF §358) | ἀπὸ τῆς δόξης τοῦ φωτός = "because of the brilliance of the light" (BDAG ἀπό 5a) (cp. 11:19) | ὑπὸ τῶν συνόντων μοι = "by those who were with me"

22:12 | μαρτυρούμενος ὑπό = "well spoken of by" (cp. 10:22; 16:2)

22:13 | "'Receive your sight!' And so I [κἀγώ = καὶ ἐγώ], at that very hour, received my sight" | ἀνέβλεψα εἰς αὐτόν = "I received my sight [and looked] at him," pregnant construction; εἰς αὐτόν demands an understood βλέπω derived from ἀναβλέπω

22:15 | ὅτι = "for" | μάρτυς αὐτῷ … ὧν ἑώρακας καὶ ἤκουσας

= "a witness for him ... [of the things] which you have seen and heard," αὐτῷ = dat. of advantage

22:16 | τί μέλλεις; = "why are you delaying?" (BDAG μέλλω 4)

22:18 | ἐν τάχει = "quickly," periphrasis for adv.

22:19 | ἤμην φυλακίζων καὶ δέρων = "I used to imprison and beat," customary periphrastic impfs. (W 548) | κατὰ τὰς συναγωγάς = "in one synagogue after another"

22:20 | αὐτὸς ἤμην ἐφεστώς = "I myself was standing by," plupf. periphrastic with impf. force (ZG; W 586, 649) (cp. 16:9)

22:24 | λέγω = "command, order" (BDAG λέγω 2c)

22:25 | εἰ – marker of direct question (BDAG εἰ 5a)

22:28 | πολλοῦ κεφαλαίου = "for a large sum of money," gen. of price (W 122)

22:29 | ἀπέστησαν ἀπ᾽ αὐτοῦ = "withdrew from him" | ἐπιγνοὺς ὅτι ... δεδεκώς = "when he realized that he had put Paul, a Roman citizen, in chains" (NIV)

22:30 | τὸ ἀσφαλὲς τὸ τί κατηγορεῖται = lit. "the truth, the reason why he is being accused" (apposition); putting the two phrases together: "exactly why Paul was being accused" (NIV); on τὸ ἀσφαλές, see 21:34; τό changes direct question into indirect (BDAG ὁ 2hα) (see Lk 1:62); present (κατηγορεῖται) retained in indirect discourse

Acts 23
23:1 | πεπολίτευμαι τῷ θεῷ = "I have lived my life before God" (ESV), ethical dat. (W 146; BDF §192)

23:2 | αὐτοῦ τὸ στόμα = τὸ στόμα αὐτοῦ

23:3 | τοῖχε κεκονιαμένε = "you whitewashed wall," voc.

23:6 | τὸ ἓν μέρος ... τὸ δὲ ἕτερον = "one party ... the other" (BDAG μέρος 1bζ) | κρίνομαι = "I am on trial" (BDAG κρίνω 5aα) (cp. 24:21)

23:7 | στάσις τῶν Φαρισαίων καὶ Σαδδουκαίων = "a dispute between the Pharisees and Sadducees," two genitives joined by καί with mng. "between" (W 135) | τοῦτο αὐτοῦ εἰπόντος = "when he said this," gen. abs.

23:8 | τὰ ἀμφότερα = "all" (cp. 19:16)

23:9 | τὸ μέρος τῶν Φαρισαίων = "the party of the Pharisees" (cp. v. 6) | εἰ δὲ πνεῦμα ἐλάλησεν αὐτῷ ἢ ἄγγελος = "what if a spirit or an angel has spoken to him?" (BDAG εἰ 6aβ); aposiopesis (BDF §482)

23:10 | πολλῆς γινομένης στάσεως = "when the dispute [cp. v. 7] became violent," gen. abs. (BDAG πολύς 3aα) | φοβέομαι μή + aor. subj. = "be afraid *that*" (BDF §370(1)) (cp. 27:17, 29)

23:11 | τῇ ἐπιούσῃ νυκτί = "the following night" | ὡς ... οὕτω = "as ... so" | τὰ περὶ ἐμοῦ = "my cause" (NASB), "the facts about me" (ESV) (cp. v. 15) | εἰς (2x) = ἐν | οὕτω σε δεῖ καὶ εἰς Ῥώμην μαρτυρῆσαι = "so you must *also* testify in Rome," δεῖ + acc. (σε as subject of inf.) + inf.

23:12 | γενομένης ἡμέρας = "when it was day," gen. abs.

23:12, 14, 21 | ἕως οὗ + subj. (3x) = "until"

23:13 | συνωμοσίαν ποιεῖσθαι = "form a conspiracy," ποιέω (mid.) + noun as periphrasis for simple verbal idea (BDAG ποιέω 7a; Z §227) (cp. 25:17; 27:18) | "There were more than forty who formed this plot" (NASB)

23:14 | ἀναθέματι ἀνεθεματίσαμεν ἑαυτούς = "we have bound ourselves by a solemn oath," cognate dat. in imitation of Heb. inf. abs. (BDF §198(6)) | γεύομαι takes the gen. (μηδενός)

23:15 | σὺν τῷ συνεδρίῳ goes with ὑμεῖς | ὡς + ptc. = "on the pretext of" (BDF §425(3); BDAG ὡς 3b) | "Now then, you and the Sanhedrin petition the commander to bring him before you on the pretext of wanting more accurate information about his case" (NIV) | πρὸ τοῦ + inf. + acc. (subject of inf.) = "before he comes near" (W 596) | ἕτοιμος + inf. = "ready to," inf. as complement to adj. (BDF §393(3)); here with pleonastic τοῦ (BDF §400(7))

23:17–19 | ἔχω τι + inf. (3x) = "have something to"

23:19 | ἐπιλαμβάνομαι takes gen. | κατ᾽ ἰδίαν = "privately"

23:20 | ὅτι recitative | ὡς μέλλον – see v. 15

23:21 | Adversative οὖν (BDAG οὖν 4) | ἐξ αὐτῶν ἄνδρες πλείους τεσσεράκνοτα = "more than 40 of them," ἐκ for partitive gen.; ἄνδρες is best left untranslated | προσδεχόμενοι τὴν ἀπὸ σοῦ ἐπαγγελίαν = "waiting for your consent"

23:22 | μέ – mixture of indirect and direct speech (BDF §470(2)) (cp. 1:4)

23:23 | ἱππεύς (pl. ἱππεῖς) = "horseman, cavalryman" (cp. v. 32), not to be confused with ἵππος (pl. ἵπποι) = "horse" | ἀπὸ τρίτης ὥρας τῆς νυκτός = "at the third hour of the night" (BDAG ἀπό 2bα)

23:24 | διασώζω πρός = "bring [someone] safely to"

23:25 | ἔχουσαν τὸν τύπον τοῦτον = either (1) "having the following content" (BDAG τύπος 5), or (2) "as follows" (NIV), "to this effect" (ESV) (BDAG τύπος 4)

23:26 | κράτιστος = "excellent, noble," superlative in form but elative ("very") in force (BDF §60; W 303) (cp. 24:3; 26:25; Lk 1:3)

23:27 | ἐστίν – present retained in indirect discourse (W 537)

23:28 | τὴν αἰτίαν δι᾽ ἣν ἐνεκάλουν αὐτῷ = "the charge for which they were accusing him" (NASB, ESV)

23:29 | ὃν εὗρον ἐγκαλούμενον = "whom I found to be accused" | ἔχω ἔγκλημα = "be charged with," "be under an accusation" (BDAG ἔχω 7aδ)

23:30 | μηνυθείσης μοι ἐπιβουλῆς εἰς τὸν ἄνδρα ἔσεσθαι = "when it was disclosed to me that there would be a plot against the man" (ESV), gen. abs. | ἔπεμψα – epistolary aorist (W 563) | παραγγείλας καὶ τοῖς κατηγόροις λέγειν πρὸς αὐτὸν ἐπὶ σοῦ = "I also ordered his accusers to present to you their case against him" (NIV)

23:31 | μὲν οὖν – resumptive, returning to narrative; no corresponding δέ (see BDF §451(1)) | κατὰ τὸ διατεταγμένον αὐτοῖς = "in accordance with their orders" (BDAG διατάσσω 2) | διὰ νυκτός = "through/during the night" (BDAG διά A2b; νύξ 1b)

23:32 | ἐάσαντες τοὺς ἱππεῖς ἀπέρχεσθαι σὺν αὐτῷ = "letting the horsemen go on with him" (ESV) (on ἱππεύς, see v. 23)

23:35 | διακούω τινος = "give someone a hearing in court," legal term (see BDAG) | οἱ κατήγοροί σου = "your accusers," not possessive gen.; cognate verb κατηγορέω takes gen. (cp. 24:8)

Acts 24

24:1 | ῥήτορος Τερτύλλου τινός = "a lawyer, a certain Tertullus" | ἐμφανίζω κατά τινος = "bring charges against someone" (BDAG ἐμφανίζω 3) (cp. 25:2)

24:2 | κληθέντος αὐτοῦ = "after Paul had been summoned," gen. abs. | πολλῆς εἰρήνης τυγχάνοντες = "we having enjoyed a long period of peace" (NIV) | διορθωμάτων γινομένων τῷ ἔθνει τούτῳ = "since reforms are being made for this nation," gen. abs.

24:3 | κράτιστος – see 23:26

24:4 | ἵνα δὲ μὴ ἐπὶ πλεῖόν σε ἐγκόπτω = "but in order not to weary you further" (NIV) | παρακαλῶ ἀκοῦσαί σε ἡμῶν = παρακαλῶ σε ἀκοῦσαι ἡμῶν = "I beg you to hear us," hyperbaton

24:6–8 | On the significant textual issue, see Metzger

24:8 | παρ᾿ οὗ δυνήσῃ + inf. (ἐπιγνῶναι) = "from whom you will be able to ascertain" | ὧν = "[the things] of which" | κατηγορέω takes gen. (cp. v. 13; 25:5)

24:9 | συνεπιτίθημι + ptc. = "join in doing something" | ταῦτα οὕτως ἔχειν = "that these things were so"

24:10 | νεύσαντος αὐτῷ τοῦ ἡγεμόνος λέγειν = "when the governor nodded for him [= Paul] to speak," gen. abs. | ἐκ πολλῶν ἐτῶν = "for many years" (BDAG ἐκ 5a)

24:11 | δυναμένου σου ἐπιγνῶναι ὅτι = "you can verify that" (ESV) | οὐ πλείους εἰσίν μοι ἡμέραι δώδεκα = "it was no more than 12 days ago" | ἀφ᾿ ἧς = "since" (cp. v. 21) | ἀνέβην προσκυνήσων = "I went up to worship," future ptc. (BDF §351; M 103) (cp. v. 17; 8:27; 22:5)

24:13 | οὐδὲ παραστῆσαι δύνανταί σοι περὶ ὧν νυνὶ κατηγοροῦσίν μου = "Nor can they prove to you [the charges] of which they now accuse me" (NASB)

24:14 | ὁμολογῶ – instantaneous present (W 517–8) | ἣν λέγουσιν αἵρεσιν = "which they call a sect" (BDAG λέγω 4)

24:15 | ἐλπίδα ἔχων ... ἀνάστασιν μέλλειν ἔσεσθαι = "having the hope ... namely, that there will be a resurrection," appositional inf. (W 606–7); μέλλω + future inf. denotes certainty (BDAG μέλλω 1a) (cp. 11:28; 27:10)

24:16 | διὰ παντός = "always"

24:17 | δι᾽ ἐτῶν πλειόνων = "after several years" (BDAG διά A2c; M 56) | ἐλεημοσύνας ποιήσων ... παρεγενόμην καὶ προσφοράς = "I came to bring alms ... and offerings," future ptc. | εἰς = "for" (BDAG εἰς 4g), equivalent to dat. (M 69)

24:18 | ἐν αἷς = "while I was doing this" (ESV)

24:19 | οὓς ἔδει ἐπὶ σοῦ παρεῖναι καὶ κατηγορεῖν = "who ought to be here before you and bring charges" (NIV) | εἴ τι ἔχοιεν πρὸς ἐμέ = "if they should have anything against me," potential optative (BDF §385(2))

24:20 | ἤ = "or else" | τί εὗρον ἀδίκημα = τί ἀδίκημα εὗρον = "what misdeed/crime they found" | BDAG ἐπί 3

24:21 | ἤ = "unless it was" (BDAG ἤ 2c) | φωνή = "statement, declaration" (BDAG φωνή 2c) | ὅτι recitative | ἐφ᾽ ὑμῶν = "before you" (cp. ἐπί in v. 20 – BDAG ἐπί 3)

24:22 | ἀκριβέστερον εἰδὼς τὰ περὶ τῆς ὁδοῦ = "having a rather accurate knowledge of the Way" (ESV) | διαγνώσομαι τὰ καθ᾽ ὑμᾶς = "I will decide your case" (BDAG κατά B6)

24:23 | τηρεῖσθαι αὐτὸν ἔχειν τε ἄνεσιν = "for Paul to be kept and yet have some freedom" (NASB) | μηδένα τῶν ἰδίων αὐτοῦ = "none of his friends" (BDAG ἴδιος 4a)

24:24 | περὶ τῆς εἰς Χριστὸν Ἰησοῦν πίστεως = "about faith in Christ Jesus"

24:25 | Τὸ νῦν ἔχον ... μετακαλέσομαί σε = "Go away for the present, and when I find time I will summon you" (NASB); τὸ νῦν ἔχον as adv. acc. (M 160; BDAG ἔχω 10a)

24:27 | ἔλαβεν διάδοχον ὁ Φῆλιξ Πόρκιον Φῆστον = "Felix was succeeded by P. F."

Acts 25
25:1 | Narrative οὖν | μετὰ τρεῖς ἡμέρας = "three days later," modifies ἀνέβη

25:2 | ἐμφανίζω κατά τινος – see 24:1 | αὐτόν = Felix

25:3 | αἰτούμενοι χάριν κατ᾽ αὐτοῦ = "requesting a favor against Paul" | ἐνέδραν ποιοῦντες = "setting an ambush" | κατὰ τὴν ὁδόν = "along (or on) the way" (BDAG κατά B1a; ὁδός 2)

25:4 | τηρεῖσθαι τὸν Παῦλον εἰς Καισάρειαν = "that Paul was being kept in custody at Caesarea" | ἐν τάχει = "shortly," periphrasis for adv. (BDAG ἐν 11; τάχος 2) | ἐκπορεύομαι = "leave"

25:5 | οἱ ἐν ὑμῖν δυνατοί = "the influential men among you" | τι ἄτοπον = "anything wrong" (cp. Lk 23:41) | συγκαταβάντες ... κατηγορείτωσαν αὐτοῦ = "let them come down and prosecute him," κατηγορέω takes gen. (cp. v. 11; 24:8)

25:6 | ἡμέρας οὐ πλείους ὀκτὼ ἢ δέκα = "no more than eight or ten days"

25:7 | πολλὰ καὶ βαρέα αἰτιώματα = "many weighty charges," the καί is unnecessary in English (BDF §442(11))

25:8 | οὔτε εἰς ... οὔτε εἰς ... οὔτε εἰς ... τι ἥμαρτον = "neither against ... nor against ... nor against ... have I committed any offense"

25:9 | ἐπ᾽ ἐμοῦ = "before me" (BDAG ἐπί 3) (cp. vv. 10, 12)

25:10 | Ἰουδαίους οὐδὲν ἠδίκησα = "I have done no wrong to the Jews," here ἀδικέω is trans. (contrast v. 11)

25:11 | εἰ ἀδικῶ καὶ ἄξιον θανάτου πέπραχά τι = "If I am a wrongdoer and have committed anything worthy of death" (NASB); here ἀδικέω is intrans.; also, perfective present (BDF §322) | οὐ παραιτοῦμαι τὸ ἀποθανεῖν = "I do not refuse to die," acc. articular inf. as object (BDF §399(1)) | ἐπικαλοῦμαι – instantaneous performative present (W 517)

25:13 | Aorist ptc. ἀσπασάμενοι to refer to action subsequent to main verb is "extraordinarily problematic" (M 100); possible solutions: (1) telic aorist ptc. (W 636–7 n58; debated), "to pay their respects" (NIV); (2) aorist ptc. of simultaneous action (Z §264; BDF §339(1)); or (3) adopt textual variant ἀσπασόμενοι (telic future ptc.)

25:14 | ὡς = "while" | ἀνέθετο τὰ κατὰ τὸν Παῦλον = "he presented Paul's case" (BDAG κατά B6) (cp. 24:22) | καταλελειμμένος δέσμιος = "left as a prisoner"

25:15 | γενομένου μου εἰς Ἱερ. = "when I was at Jerusalem," gen. abs. | ἐμφανίζω περί + gen. = "present charges concerning someone" (cp. with κατά + gen., 24:1; 25:2) | αἰτούμενοι κατ᾽ αὐτοῦ καταδίκην = "asking for a condemning verdict against him"

25:16 | πρὶν ἤ = "before" | "It is not the custom of the Romans to hand over any man before the accused meets his accusers face to face and has an opportunity to make his defense against the charges" (NASB) | ἔχοι & λάβοι – oblique optatives (BDF §386(4))

25:17 | ἀναβολὴν μηδεμίαν ποιησάμενος = "having made no delay (or postponement)," ποιέω (mid.) + noun as periphrasis for simple verbal idea (BDAG ποιέω 7a; Z §227) (cp. 23:13; 27:18) | τῇ ἑξῆς = "on the next [day]"

25:18 | περὶ οὗ ... οὐδεμίαν αἰτίαν ἔφερον ὧν ἐγὼ ὑπενόουν πονηρῶν = "they brought no charge in his case of such evils as I supposed" (ESV)

25:19 | ζητήματα τινα ... εἶχον πρὸς αὐτόν = "they [simply] had some points of disagreement with him" (NASB) | περί τινος Ἰησοῦ = "about a certain Jesus" | ὃν ἔφασκεν ὁ Παῦλος ζῆν = "whom Paul asserted to be alive" (NASB, ESV)

25:20 | ἀπορούμενος τὴν περὶ τούτων ζήτησιν = "because I was at a loss concerning the investigation of these things" (BDAG ζήτησις 1), "being at a loss how to investigate such matters" (NASB) | ἔλεγον εἰ βούλοιτο πορεύεσθαι = "I asked whether he was willing to go" (NASB), εἰ as marker of indirect question (BDAG εἰ 5bγ) + oblique optative (W 483; M 154)

25:21 | τοῦ Παύλου ἐπικαλεσαμένου ... διάγνωσιν = "when Paul appealed to be held in custody for the Emperor's decision," gen. abs. | ὁ Σεβαστός = translation of Latin title Augustus, i.e., "the Emperor" (in this case, Nero) | ἕως οὗ + aor. subj. = "until I could send him"

25:22 | Ἀγρίππας πρὸς τὸν Φῆστον = "Then Agrippa [said] to Festus"

25:23 | τῇ ἐπαύριον = "on the next day" | ἀνδράσιν τοῖς κατ' ἐξοχὴν τῆς πόλεως = "the prominent men of the city"

25:24 | τοῦτον περὶ οὗ ἅπαν τὸ πλῆθος τῶν Ἰουδαίων ἐνέτυχόν μοι = "this man about whom all the people of the Jews appealed to me" (NASB) | ἔν τε Ἱεροσολύμοις καὶ ἐνθάδε = "both in Jerusalem and here" (ἔν = ἐν with accent from the enclitic τε) | βοῶντες μὴ δεῖν αὐτὸν ζῆν μηκέτι = "shouting that he ought not to live any longer," acc. αὐτόν as subject of inf. ζῆν

25:25 | κατελαβόμην μηδὲν ἄξιον αὐτὸν θανάτου πεπραχέναι = "I found that he had committed nothing worthy of death" | αὐτοῦ τούτου ἐπικαλεσαμένου τὸν Σεβαστόν = "since he himself appealed to the Emperor," gen. abs. | ἔκρινα πέμπειν = "I decided to send [him]"

25:26 | ὅπως τῆς ἀνακρίσεως γενομένης σχῶ τί γράψω = "so that after the investigation has taken place [gen. abs.], I may have something to write"

25:27 | "For it seems to me unreasonable, in sending a prisoner, not to indicate the charges against him" (ESV)

Acts 26
26:1 | Ἐπιτρέπεταί σοι = "you are permitted"

26:2 | ἥγημαι – perf. with present force (W 579; BDF §341) | μακάριον ἐπὶ σοῦ μέλλων σήμερον ἀπολογεῖσθαι = "fortunate that it is before you I am going to make my defense today" (ESV); note emphatic position of ἐπὶ σοῦ (BDAG ἐπί 3)

26:3 | μάλιστα γνώστην ὄντα σε + objective gen. = "especially since you are an expert in," ὄντα – causal ptc.; should be gen. in agreement with σοῦ (v. 2) (ZG; BDF §137(3))

26:5 | προγινώσκοντές με ἄνωθεν = "since they have known me for a long time," extending-from-past present (W 519); causal ptc. (BDAG ἄνωθεν 3) | ἐὰν θέλωσι μαρτυρεῖν = "if they are willing to testify" | ἔζησα Φαρισαῖος = "I lived as a Pharisee"

26:6 | ἐπ ἐλπίδι τῆς εἰς τοὺς πατέρας ἡμῶν ἐπαγγελίας γενομένης ὑπὸ τοῦ θεοῦ = "because of my hope in the promise made by God to our fathers" (ESV), τῆς ἐπαγγελίας as objective gen.

26:7 | εἰς ἥν – could refer back to ἐλπίς or ἐπαγγελία (v. 6)

26:8 | τί; = "why?"

26:9 | πρός = "against" (BDAG πρός 3dα) | πολλὰ ἐναντία = "many hostile things"

26:10 | ὃ καὶ ἐποίησα = "and this is just what I did" (NASB), ὃ as loose connective (BDF §458) | τέ … τέ = "not only … but also" (BDAG τέ 2b) | ἀναιρουμένων αὐτῶν = "when they were being put to death," gen. abs.

26:11 | κατὰ πάσας τὰς συναγωγάς = "in all the synagogues" (ESV, NASB), "from one synagogue to another" (NIV) | ἠνάγκαζον = "I tried to force them" (NASB), conative impf. that is also iterative like ἐδίωκον (BDF §326; W 551) | ἕως καὶ εἰς τὰς ἔξω πόλεις = "even to foreign cities"

26:12 | ἐν οἷς = "in the course of which activity" (M 131)

26:13 | ὑπὲρ τὴν λαμπρότητα τοῦ ἡλίου = "brighter than the sun"

26:14 | πάντων καταπεσόντων ἡμῶν – gen. abs.

26:16 | μάρτυρα ὧν τε εἶδές με ὧν τε ὀφθήσομαί σοι = "a witness not only to the things in which you saw me but also to those in which I shall appear to you" (BDAG ὁράω A1b)

26:18 | ἐν = "among"

26:20 | πᾶσάν τε τὴν χώραν τῆς Ἰουδαίας = "and throughout all the region of Judea," acc. for extent of space (W 202) | dat. + ἀπήγγελλον + inf. = "I was declaring to them that [they should] repent and turn to God"

26:21 | με is direct object of both συλλαβόμενοι & διαχειρίσασθαι

26:22 | ἐπικουρίας τυχὼν τῆς ἀπὸ τοῦ θεοῦ = "having obtained help from God" (NASB) | οὐδὲν ἐκτὸς λέγων ... Μωϋσῆς = "stating nothing but what the Prophets and Moses said was going to take place" (NASB)

26:23 | εἰ (2x) = "that," marker of content (BDAG εἰ 2) | παθητός = "subject to suffering," verbal adj. from πάσχω (BDAG παθητός; BDF §65(3)) | πρῶτος ἐξ ἀναστάσεως νεκρῶν = "as the first to rise from the dead" (NIV) | φῶς (acc.) μέλλει καταγγέλλειν = "he would proclaim light"

26:25 | κράτιστε – see 23:26 | ἀληθείας καὶ σωφροσύνης ῥήματα = "true and rational words" (ESV), "words of sober truth" (NASB), attributive gen.

26:26 | πρὸς ὃν καὶ παρρησιαζόμενος λαλῶ = "to whom [= King Agrippa] I *also* speak freely/boldly," ptc. of manner (W 627) | λανθάνειν αὐτὸν τούτων οὐ πείθομαι οὐθέν [= οὐδέν] = "I am persuaded that none of these things escapes his notice"

26:28 | Ἐν ὀλίγῳ με πείθεις Χριστιανὸν ποιῆσαι – difficult; either (1) a statement: (a) "Soon you will persuade me to play the Christian" (BDF §405(1)), taking πείθω in the sense "persuade" (BDAG πείθω 1b), ποιέω as technical term for playing a part (cp. LXX 3 Kgdms 20:7), and με as both object of πείθεις and subject of inf. ποιῆσαι; (b) "In too short a time you believe you are making me into a Christian" (BDAG πείθω 3a), taking πείθω in the sense "believe," ποιέω + double acc. = "make x into y," with με not as object of πείθεις but only of ποιῆσαι; or

(2) as a question: "In such a short time would you persuade me to become a Christian?" taking πείθω in the sense "persuade," ποιῆσαι as equivalent to γενέσθαι (which is also a textual variant), and με as both object of πείθεις and subject of inf. ποιῆσαι

26:29 | Εὐξαίμην ἂν τῷ θεῷ = "I would to God" (ESV), potential optative (BDF §385(1)) | καὶ ἐν ὀλίγῳ καὶ ἐν μεγάλῳ = "whether in a short or long time" (NASB; BDAG καί 1f; ὀλίγος 2bβ) | τοιούτους [pl.] ὁποῖος [sg.] καὶ ἐγώ εἰμι = "of such a kind such as even I am"

26:31 | ὅτι recitative

26:32 | Ἀπολελύσθαι ἐδύνατο ... εἰ μὴ ἐπεκέκλητο Καίσαρα = "This man could have been set free if he had not appealed to Caesar" (NIV, ESV)

Acts 27

27:1 | Ὡς ἐκρίθη τοῦ ἀποπλεῖν ἡμᾶς εἰς τὴν Ἰταλίαν = "when it was decided that we would set sail for Italy" | σπείρης Σεβαστῆς = "who belonged to the Imperial Regiment" (NIV)

27:2 | πλοίῳ Ἀδραμυττηνῷ μέλλοντι πλεῖν εἰς τοὺς κατὰ τὴν Ἀσίαν τόπους = "a ship from Adramyttium about to sail for ports along the coast of the province of Asia" (NIV) | κατά + acc. = "along the coast of" (cp. vv. 5, 7 [2x])

27:3 | τῇ ἑτέρᾳ = "the next [day]" | χράομαι + dat. + adv. = "treat someone in a certain way" (BDAG χράομαι 3) | φιλανθρώπως ὁ Ἰούλιος ... ἐπιμελείας τυχεῖν = "Julius treated Paul kindly (or humanely) and let him go to his friends to receive care"

27:4 | κἀκεῖθεν = καὶ ἐκεῖθεν = "and from there" | διὰ τὸ τοὺς ἀνέμους εἶναι ἐναντίους = "because the winds were contrary," διὰ τό + inf. = "because" (cp. v. 9)

27:6 | κἀκεῖ = καὶ ἐκεῖ = "and there" | πλοῖον Ἀλεξανδρῖνον πλέον εἰς τὴν Ἰταλίαν = "a ship from Alexandria sailing for Italy"

27:7 | ἐν ἱκαναῖς ἡμέραις = "for many days" (BDAG ἐν 10c) | μὴ προσεῶντος ἡμᾶς τοῦ ἀνέμου = "since the wind did not allow us to go farther," gen. abs.

27:8 | παραλεγόμενοι αὐτήν = "sailing past it," i.e., Salmone | ᾧ ἐγγὺς πόλις ἦν Λασαία = "near which was the city of Lasea," for ἐγγύς + dat., see 9:38

27:9 | διὰ τὸ καὶ τὴν νηστείαν ἤδη παρεληλυθέναι = "because *even* the Fast [= the Day of Atonement] was already over" (cp. v. 4). "Luke uses a Jewish calendaric reference for a secular problem, which was what the Romans called *mare clausum*, 'the closed sea,' the time when the Mediterranean was no longer navigable, often as of mid-October, but usually from 11 November to 10 March" (Fitzmyer).

27:10 | μετὰ ὕβρεως = "with damage" | μέλλειν ἔσεσθαι τὸν πλοῦν = "the voyage will certainly be" (NASB), μέλλω + future inf. denotes certainty (BDAG μέλλω 1a) (cp. 11:28; 24:15)

27:11 | dat. + μᾶλλον ἐπείθετο ἤ + dat. = "was more persuaded by x than by y"

27:12 | ἀνεύθετος πρός + acc. = "unsuitable for" | τίθημι βουλήν = "decide" | εἴ πως δύναιντο = "if somehow they could," oblique (BDF §386) or conditional optative (W 484) | λιμένα is in apposition to Φοίνικα – "Phoenix, a harbor of Crete" | βλέποντα κατὰ λίβα καὶ κατὰ χῶρον = "facing southwest and northwest" (BDAG βλέπω 8)

27:13 | δόξαντες τῆς προθέσεως κεκρατηκέναι = "supposing that they had achieved their purpose," κρατέω + gen. | ἆσσον παρελέγοντο τὴν Κρήτην = they "sailed along Crete, close to the shore" (ESV), or "as near as possible" (BDF §244(2))

27:14 | μετ᾽ οὐ πολύ = lit. "after not much time," i.e., "not long afterward" (BDAG μετά B2c) | BDAG βάλλω 6 | κατ᾽ αὐτῆς = lit. "down from her [= Crete]" (BDAG κατά A1a)

27:15 | ἐπιδόντες ἐφερόμεθα = "we gave way to it and were driven along" (ESV) (cp. v. 17; BDAG φέρω 3a)

27:16 | ἰσχύσαμεν μόλις περικρατεῖς γενέσθαι τῆς σκάφης = "we were scarcely able to become in control of the ship's boat (in danger of being smashed against the ship's hull)" (ZG); περικρατεῖς ("in control of") is pl. in agreement with 1p verb ἰσχύσαμεν ("we"); it is predicate acc. with γενέσθαι

27:17 | βοηθείαις ἐχρῶντο ὑποζωννύντες τὸ πλοῖον = "they used supporting cables in undergirding the ship" (NASB) | φοβούμενοι μή ... ἐκπέσωσιν = "fearing *that* they might run aground" (see 23:10) (cp. v. 29) | οὕτως ἐφέροντο = "and in this way let themselves be driven along" (NASB) (see v. 15); on οὕτως, see BDF §425(6) (cp. 20:11)

27:18 | σφοδρῶς χειμαζομένων ἡμῶν = "since we were violently storm-tossed" (ESV), causal gen. abs. | τῇ ἑξῆς = "the next [day]" | ἐκβολὴν ἐποιοῦντο = "they began to jettison the cargo" (NASB); ingressive impf. (W 544); ποιέω (mid.) + noun as periphrasis for simple verbal idea (BDAG ποιέω 7a; Z §227) (cp. 25:17) | "We took such a violent battering from the storm that the next day they began to throw the cargo overboard" (NIV)

27:19 | τῇ τρίτῃ = "on the third [day]" | αὐτόχειρες (< αὐτός + χείρ) = "with their own hands" | τὴν σκευὴν τοῦ πλοίου = "the ship's tackle"

27:20 | λοιπόν = "finally," adv. acc. | περιῃρεῖτο ἐλπὶς πᾶσα τοῦ σῴζεσθαι ἡμᾶς = "all hope of our being saved was given up," with τοῦ σῴζεσθαι as objective gen., and ἡμᾶς as acc. subject of the inf. (W 234)

27:21 | πολλῆς ἀσιτίας ὑπαρχούσης = "when they had gone a long time without food" (NASB), gen. abs.; either from suspense (v. 33) or seasickness | ἔδει μέν, ὦ ἄνδρες ... τὴν ζημίαν = "Men, you should have taken my advice not to sail from Crete; then you would have spared yourselves this damage and loss" (NIV) | κερδαίνω = "gain"; with nouns of loss/injury, "spare oneself" (BDAG, Thayer)

27:22 | τὰ νῦν = "now," adv. acc. | ἀποβολὴ ψυχῆς = "loss of life"

27:23 | τοῦ θεοῦ ... ἄγγελος = "an angel of the God to whom I belong and whom I serve"

27:25 | καθ᾽ ὃν τρόπον = "just as" (cp. 15:11)

27:27 | κατὰ μέσον τῆς νυκτός = "about midnight" (BDAG μέσος 1b) | ὑπενόουν οἱ ναῦται προσάγειν τινὰ αὐτοῖς χώραν = "the sailors suspected that some land was coming near to them," inf. with verbs of perception (BDF §397)

27:29 | φοβέομαι μή + aor. subj. (see v. 17) | που κατὰ τραχεῖς τόπους = "somewhere along the rocky places" (BDAG κατά B1a) | ηὔχοντο ἡμέραν γενέσθαι = they "prayed for day to come" (ESV)

27:30 | τῶν ναυτῶν ζητούντων φυγεῖν = "as the sailors were trying to escape," gen. abs. | προφάσει ὡς + ptc. = "on the pretense of intending to lay out anchors from the bow" (NASB)

27:33 | ἄχρι οὗ ἡμέρα ἤμελλεν γίνεσθαι = "until day was about to dawn," ingressive impf. (W 544–5) (BDAG ἄχρι 1bα) | μεταλάμβανω τροφῆς = "partake of food," partitive gen. (BDF §169(1)) (cp. v. 36; 2:46) | τεσσαρεσκαιδεκάτην σήμερον ἡμέραν προσδοκῶντες ἄσιτοι διατελεῖτε = "today is the 14th day that you have continued in suspense and without food" (ESV), taking διατελεῖτε as extending-from-past present (W 519–20) | μηθέν = μηδέν

27:38 | κορέννυμι takes gen. | ἐκβαλλόμενοι = "by throwing out" (NASB), ptc. of means

27:39 | τὴν γῆν οὐκ ἐπεγίνωσκον = "they did not recognize the land" | εἰ δύναιντο = "if possible," oblique (BDF §386(2)) or conditional optative (W 484)

27:40 | τῇ πνεούσῃ = "to the wind"

27:41 | τόπον διθάλασσον = "a point of land jutting with water (sea) on both sides" (BDAG), "a reef" (ESV), "a sandbar" (NIV)

27:42 | βουλὴ ἵνα = "a plan to," ἵνα after a noun (BDAG ἵνα 2cα) (cp. 8:19) | "The soldiers' plan was to kill the prisoners, lest any should swim away and escape" (ESV)

27:43 | ἐκώλυσεν αὐτοὺς τοῦ βουλήματος = "he kept them from [carrying out] their plan" (BDAG κωλύω 1a), gen. of separation (W 107) | κέλευσεν ... ἐξιέναι = "he ordered those who could swim to jump overboard first and make for the land" (ESV)

27:44 | οὓς μέν ... οὓς δέ = "some ... others" | ἐπί τινων τῶν ἀπὸ τοῦ πλοίου = "on pieces of the ship," ἀπό as substitute for partitive gen. (BDAG ἀπό 1f)

Acts 28

28:2 | οἱ βάρβαροι παρεῖχον οὐ τὴν τυχοῦσαν φιλανθρωπίαν ἡμῖν = "the natives showed us extraordinary kindness" (NASB) (BDAG παρέχω 2a) | ὁ τυχών = "the first person one happens to meet in the way" → οὐχ ὁ τυχών = "not the ordinary one" (BDAG τυγχάνω 2d) | ἅπτω + acc. = "light, kindle"

28:3 | φρυγάνων τι πλῆθος = "a bundle of sticks" | ἀπὸ τῆς θέρμης = "because of the heat" (BDAG ἀπό 5a) | καθάπτω takes gen.

28:4 | ὃν διασωθέντα ἐκ τῆς θαλάσσης ἡ δίκη ζῆν οὐκ εἴασεν
= "whom, though escaped from the sea, Justice has not allowed to live,"
concessive ptc.

28:5–6 | ὁ μέν ... οἱ δέ = "he [= Paul] ... but they ..."

28:6 | ἐπὶ πολὺ αὐτῶν προσδοκώντων = "after they had waited a
long time" | μεταβαλόμενοι ἔλεγον = "they changed their minds
and began to say," ingressive impf.

28:7 | τὰ περί + acc. = "the regions around" | ὑπῆρχεν χωρία + dat.
of possession = "there were lands belonging to" | ὁ πρῶτος = "the
chief man"

28:8 | ἐγένετο + inf. (κατακεῖσθαι) = "it came to pass that" |
πυρετοῖς καὶ δυσεντερίῳ συνεχόμενον = "afflicted with fevers
and dysentery"

28:9 | καὶ οἱ λοιποί ... = "the rest of the people on the island ... *also*
came" | προσήρχοντο & ἐθεραπεύοντο – distributive iterative impfs.

28:10 | πολλαῖς τιμαῖς ἐτίμησαν = "they honored us with many
honors," cognate dat. (BDF §198(6); W 168) | ἀναγομένοις =
"when we were about to sail" (ESV), present ptc. with future nuance
(BDF §339(2)) | ἐπιτίθημι – either "give" (BDAG ἐπιτίθημι 1b) or
"put on board" (ESV) | τὰ πρὸς τὰς χρείας = "the things for our
needs" (BDAG πρός 3eβ), "the supplies we needed" (NIV)

28:11 | παρακεχειμακότι = "that had wintered" | παρασήμῳ
Διοσκούροις = "marked by the Dioscuri" (BDAG παράσημος 2),
"which had the Twin Brothers for its figurehead" (NASB)

28:13 | μετὰ μίαν ἡμέραν ἐπιγενομένου νότου δευτεραῖοι
ἤλθομεν εἰς Ποτιόλους = "after one day a south wind sprang
up [gen. abs.], and on the second day we came to Puteoli" (ESV) |

δευτεραῖοι – predicate adj., rendered as adv. in English (BDF §243)
(cp. ὀρθριναί, Lk 24:22)

28:14–15, 21 | ἤλθαμεν = ἤλθομεν; ἦλθαν = ἦλθον; εἶπαν = εἶπον
(BDF §§80–81)

28:14 | οὗ (adv.) = "where" | παρ᾽ αὐτοῖς modifies ἐπιμεῖναι – "we
were invited to stay with them"

28:15 | κἀκεῖθεν = καὶ ἐκεῖθεν | ἦλθαν εἰς ἀπάντησιν ἡμῖν
ἄχρι = "they came as far as [these two towns] to meet us"

28:16 | καθ᾽ ἑαυτόν = "by himself," in a private, rented dwelling
(ξενία [v. 23], μίσθωμα [v. 30]) (BDAG κατά B1c)

28:17 | Ἐγένετο ... συγκαλέσασθαι αὐτὸν τούς ... πρώτους = "it
came to pass that Paul [αὐτόν] called together the leading men of the
Jews" | δέσμιος ἐξ Ἱεροσολύμων = "as a prisoner of/from Jerusalem"

28:18 | διὰ τὸ μηδεμίαν αἰτίαν θανάτου ὑπάρχειν ἐν ἐμοί =
"because there was no reason for the death penalty in my case" (ESV)
(BDAG ἐν 8)

28:19 | οὐχ ὡς τοῦ ἔθνους μου ἔχων τι κατηγορεῖν = "not that I
had any accusation against my nation" (NASB), κατηγορέω takes gen.
(τοῦ ἔθνους)

28:20 | παρεκάλεσα ὑμᾶς ἰδεῖν καὶ προσλαλῆσαι = "I have sum-
moned you to see [you] and speak with [you]" (BDAG παρακαλέω 1a),
ὑμᾶς understood as direct object of the two infs. | τὴν ἅλυσιν ταύτην
περίκειμαι = "I am bound with this chain," acc. with pass. (BDF §159)

28:22 | ἀξιοῦμεν παρὰ σοῦ ἀκοῦσαι = "we would like to hear from
you" (BDAG ἀξιόω 2a) | ἃ φρονεῖς = "the views that you hold"
(BDAG φρονέω 1)

28:23 | πλείονες = "in large numbers" (NASB)

28:24 | οἱ μέν … οἱ δέ = "some … but others"

28:25 | ἀπελύοντο, εἰπόντος τοῦ Παύλου ῥῆμα ἕν = "they [began] leaving after Paul had spoken one [parting] word" (NASB), gen. abs. | ὅτι recitative | καλῶς = "rightly" (BDAG καλῶς 4b) (cp. Matt 15:7 ‖ Mk 7:6)

28:27 | μήποτε + subj. = "otherwise they may …" | ἰάσομαι – future continuing subj. to designate some further consequence (BDF §369(3))

28:28 | τὸ σωτήριον = "means of deliverance" (BDAG)

28:30 | ἐνέμεινεν – constative/global aorist (M 13; W 557) | διετίαν ὅλην = "for two whole years," acc. for extent of time

Chapter Six

The Epistle to the Romans

Romans 1

1 | κλητὸς ἀπόστολος = "called [to be] an apostle" | ἀφωρισμένος – cp. Acts 13:2; Gal 1:15

1:3–4 | τοῦ γενομένου ... τοῦ ὁρισθέντος = "who was ... who was"

1:3 | ἐκ σπέρματος Δαυίδ = lit. "of/from the seed of David," i.e., a descendant of David (cp. ἐκ σπέρματος Ἀβραάμ, 11:1)

1:4 | ἐν δυνάμει could modify (1) υἱοῦ θεοῦ, "Son-of-God-in-power," ἐν of concomitant circumstances (ZG), or (2) ὁρισθέντος, "powerfully marked out or declared," with ἐν as periphrasis for adv. (BDAG ἐν 11) | πνεῦμα ἁγιωσύνης = "the Spirit of holiness" = "the Holy Spirit," Hebr. attributive gen.

1:5 | ἐλάβομεν – epistolary pl. (W 394–5) | χάριν καὶ ἀποστολήν – (1) "the grace of being commissioned to be an apostle" (hendiadys), or (2) "the grace of conversion/salvation and the office of apostleship" | ὑπακοὴ πίστεως (also 16:26) – gen. of apposition (W 95) = "obedience which consists in believing [the gospel]" (cp. 10:16; 15:18; 2 Th 1:8; Acts 6:7) | ὑπὲρ τοῦ ὀνόματος αὐτοῦ = "for the sake of [i.e., to spread] his name" (BDAG ὑπέρ A1b) (cp. John 11:4)

1:5–6 | ἐν πᾶσιν τοῖς ἔθνεσιν ... ἐν οἷς ἐστε καὶ ὑμεῖς κλητοί = "among all the Gentiles ... among whom you *also* are called," ἐν does not signify merely geographical location; Paul did not receive apostleship to bring about the obedience of faith of people living among the Gentiles but of the Gentiles themselves (cp. 11:13) | κλητοὶ Ἰησοῦ Χριστοῦ – (1) "the called ones of Jesus Christ," possessive gen., or (2) "called by Jesus Christ," gen. of agency (W 126; cp. v. 7)

1:7 | ἀγαπητοῖς θεοῦ = "beloved by God," gen. of agency (cp. v. 6)

1:8 | πρῶτον μέν – adv. acc. enumerating a series (BDAG πρῶτος 1bβ), but here w/o a "second" or "third" (cp. 3:2; 1 Cor 11:18) | ἐν ὅλῳ = "throughout the whole" (NASB) (cp. Phil 1:13)

1:9 | μάρτυς μου – objective gen. | ἐν τῷ πνεύματί μου – Hebr./ instrumental ἐν | μάρτυς ... ὡς = "witness ... that," with ὡς as marker of discourse content (BDAG ὡς 5) | μνείαν ποιεῖσθαί τινος = "to mention someone," ποιέω (mid.) + noun as periphrasis for simple verbal idea (BDAG ποιέω 7a; μνεία 2) (cp. Phm 4)

1:10 | πάντοτε ἐπὶ τῶν προσευχῶν μου = "always in my prayers" (BDAG ἐπί 18a), this adverbial phrase could modify ποιοῦμαι or δεόμενος | εἴ πως ἤδη ποτέ = "if perhaps now at last" (NASB)

1:11 | τι ... χάρισμα ... πνευματικόν = "some spiritual gift" | εἰς τὸ στηριχθῆναι ὑμᾶς = "that you may be strengthened," εἰς τό + inf. (BDF §402(2))

1:12 | τοῦτο δέ ἐστιν (≠ τοῦτ' ἐστιν) = "or rather" | ἐν ὑμῖν = "when I am among you," difficult bec. it implies that the subject of συμπαρακληθῆναι is "I" rather than "we." Possible solutions include: (1) ignore (!) ἐν ὑμῖν and translate "that we may be mutually encouraged" (ESV), (2) delete ἐν (per some MSS) or change it to ἐμέ (conjectural emendation proposed in 1881 by J. H. A. Michelsen) leaving ὑμῖν to go with συν- prefix, "that I may be encouraged with you," (3)

retain ἐν ὑμῖν, "that I may be encouraged together with you while
among you" (NASB; cp. Thayer συμπαρακαλέω), assuming συν-
prefix carries with it an implied ὑμῖν (cp. the συν- verbs at 6:6; 8:17
and the implied αὐτῷ) | διὰ τῆς ἐν ἀλλήλοις πίστεως = "by each
other's faith"

1:13 | καὶ ἐκωλύθην ἄχρι τοῦ δεῦρο = "but I have been prevented
thus far," parenthetical; adversative καί (BDAG καί 1bη) | ἵνα τινὰ
καρπὸν σχῶ καὶ ἐν ὑμῖν καθὼς καὶ ἐν τοῖς λοιποῖς ἔθνεσιν
= "in order that I might have a harvest among you, just as I have had
among the other Gentiles" (NIV) (BDAG καί 2c)

1:15 | οὕτως τὸ κατ᾽ ἐμὲ πρόθυμον ... εὐαγγελίσασθαι = (1)
"so my eagerness is to preach the gospel," taking κατ᾽ ἐμέ = "my" (cp.
Acts 17:28; 18:15; Eph 1:15; BDF §224(1); BDAG κατά B7b) and
τὸ πρόθυμον as substantivized neut. adj. equivalent to abstract noun
ἡ προθυμία (Z §140); or (2) "so, as far as I am concerned, I am eager
to preach the gospel," taking τὸ κατ᾽ ἐμέ as a self-contained adverbial
phrase, and πρόθυμον as a slip for πρόθυμος (M 58), either due to attraction to the acc. ἐμέ, or in agreement with the implied acc. subject of
the inf. (cp. οὕτως φιλοτιμούμενον εὐαγγελίζεσθαι – see 15:20)

1:17 | δικαιοσύνη θεοῦ – could be (1) "God's righteousness," possessive
or subjective gen. (cp. 3:5, 25–26); (2) "a righteousness acceptable before
or approved by God," objective gen.; but more likely (3) "a righteousness
from God" (NIV 1984), gen. of source or author (cp. 3:21–22; 5:17;
10:3–4; Phil 3:9) | ἐκ πίστεως εἰς πίστιν – could be taken (1) with
ἀποκαλύπτεται: "revealed by means of faith [and] unto faith," or more
likely (2) with δικαιοσύνη θεοῦ: "a righteousness from God [received]
by means of faith [and given] to [all who have] faith" (cp. 3:22; 10:4) | ὁ
δίκαιος ἐκ πίστεως ζήσεται = "the person who is righteous by faith
shall live," taking ἐκ πίστεως as modifying ὁ δίκαιος

1:18 | ἐπί + acc. = "against" (BDAG ἐπί 12b) | ἀνθρώπων τῶν ...
κατεχόντων = "of humans who suppress," article as relative pronoun

1:19, 21 | διότι (2x) = "for" (BDAG διότι 3)

1:19 | τὸ γνωστὸν τοῦ θεοῦ = "that which is known about God," objective gen. | ἐν αὐτοῖς = "to them," ἐν for simple dat. (BDF §220(1))

1:20 | τὰ ἀόρατα αὐτοῦ ... καθορᾶται = "his invisible [attributes] are clearly perceived" | ἀπὸ κτίσεως κόσμου = "since the creation of the world," temporal (BDAG ἀπό 2b) | τοῖς ποιήμασιν νοούμενα = "being understood through what is made," instrumental dat. | εἰς τὸ εἶναι + double acc. = "with the result that x is y," same construction can express purpose ("so that x might be y") or be ambiguous (cp. 3:26; 4:11, 16; 8:29; 15:16; James 1:18); double acc. with equative verb inf. (W 195); εἰς τό + inf. (BDF §402(2)) (cp. v. 11)

1:20, 21 | ἀΐδιος, ἀσύνετος – two-termination adjectives (masc./fem., -ος; neut., -ον), here fem. Each adj. is in first attributive position (W 306); so the fem. article ἡ does not substantivize the adj., but rather goes with its respective noun: ἡ ἀΐδιος αὐτοῦ δύναμις (= "his eternal power") and ἡ ἀσύνετος αὐτῶν καρδία (= "their foolish hearts")

1:21 | γνόντες τὸν θεόν = "although they knew God," concessive ptc. (W 634)

1:23, 25 | ἀλλάσσω τι ἔν τινι (2x) = "exchange something for something [else]," idiom (BDAG ἐν 5b)

1:24 | τοῦ + inf. – purpose or result | ἐν αὐτοῖς = "among themselves" (ESV), "with one another" (NIV)

1:25 | παρά = "rather than," Hebr. comparative expressing exclusion (BDF §245a; παρά C3) (cp. Lk 18:14; Heb 1:9)

1:26 | χρῆσις = "use, intercourse" (BDAG χρῆσις 3) | παρά =

"contrary to" (BDAG παρά 8) – τὴν παρὰ φύσιν = "that [use] which is contrary to nature," brachylogy

1:27 | τὴν φυσικὴν χρῆσιν τῆς θηλείας = "the natural use of (or intercourse with) the female," objective gen. | ἄρσενες ἐν ἄρσεσιν = "men with [other] men" (BDAG ἐν 5), goes with κατεργαζόμενοι | τὴν ἀντιμισθίαν ἣν ἔδει τῆς πλάνης = "the due penalty for their error" (ESV), ἣν ἔδει = lit. "which is proper or due" | ἐν ἑαυτοῖς = "in their own persons"

1:28 | ἔχειν ἐν ἐπιγνώσει = "to acknowledge" (ESV, NASB)

1:29 | πληρόω (pass.) + dat. = "filled with" (BDF §195(2)) | μεστούς + gen. = "full of"

1:30 | ἐφευρετὰς κακῶν = "inventors of evil things," objective gen.

Romans 2

2:1 | ὦ ἄνθρωπε πᾶς ὁ κρίνων = "O man, every one of you who passes judgment," articular ptc. with personal pronoun (BDF §412(5)) (cp. v. 3 w/o πᾶς; 14:4) | ἐν ᾧ κρίνεις – could be (1) circumstantial: "in passing judgment" (ESV) (BDAG ἐν 7), (2) specific: "at whatever point you judge" (NIV), or (3) causal: "because you pass judgment" (BDAG ἐν 9; BDF §219(2))

2:4 | τὸ χρηστὸν [= ἡ χρηστότης] τοῦ θεοῦ = "the kindness of God" (BDF §263(2)) (cp. 9:22)

2:5 | κατὰ τὴν σκληρότητά σου... = "because of your hardness and impenitent heart" (BDAG κατά B5aδ) | ἐν ἡμέρᾳ ὀργῆς καὶ ἀποκαλύψεως δικαιοκρισίας τοῦ θεοῦ = "on the day of wrath when God's righteous judgment is revealed"

2:7–8 | τοῖς μὲν ζητοῦσιν ... τοῖς δὲ ἀπειθοῦσι = "to those who seek ... but to those who are disobedient" | In both verses, one must supply the verb "he will repay" (ἀποδώσει) from v. 6

2:7 | καθ' ὑπομονὴν ἔργου ἀγαθοῦ = "by perseverance in doing good" (NASB), objective gen. (BDAG κατά B5aδ)

2:8 | τοῖς ἐξ ἐριθείας καὶ ἀπειθοῦσι τῇ ἀληθείᾳ πειθομένοις δὲ τῇ ἀδικίᾳ = "to those who as a result of (or because of) selfishness are *also* disobedient to the truth *and yet* obedient to unrighteousness" (BDAG ἐκ 3e)

2:9-10 | In both verses, one must supply a verb such as "will come"

2:11 | BDAG παρά B4

2:12 | ὅσοι ἀνόμως ἥμαρτον, ἀνόμως καὶ ἀπολοῦνται = "all who have sinned apart from the law will *also* perish apart from the law" | ἐν νόμῳ = "under the law" (cp. Gal 3:11; 5:4; Phil 3:6) | κριθήσονται = "will be condemned" (cp. 2 Thess 2:12)

2:13 | οἱ ἀκροαταὶ νόμου ... οἱ ποιηταὶ νόμου = "the hearers of the law ... the doers of the law," objective gens. | δίκαιοι παρὰ τῷ θεῷ = "righteous before God," *coram Deo* (cp. Gal 3:11) (BDAG παρά B2)

2:14 | ὅταν + subj. = "whenever" | ἔθνη is anarthrous bec. Paul is not saying that *all* the Gentiles do the things of the law – "whenever [certain/some/any] Gentiles" | φύσει (adverbial dat.; W 161) could go equally with ἔχοντα or ποιῶσιν – hard to decide | νόμον μὴ ἔχοντες – concessive ptc.

2:15 | γραπτόν is neut. in agreement with τὸ ἔργον; thus it is misleading to say that "the law (masc.) is written on their hearts" | τὸ ἔργον τοῦ νόμου = "the functional equivalent of the law," i.e., conscience (see commentaries for other possibilities) | συμμαρτυρούσης αὐτῶν ... ἀπολογουμένων – gen. abs. (cp. 9:1) | ἢ καί = "or even"

2:16 | ἐν ἡμέρᾳ ὅτε + pres. = "on the day when," would expect ὅταν + subj. (BDF §382(3)); but note textual variant ἐν ᾗ ἡμέρᾳ (= ἐν τῇ ἡμέρᾳ ᾗ) | κρίνει – present (note placement of accent; contrast fut. κρινεῖ in v. 27)

2:19 | ὁδηγὸν τυφλῶν, φῶς τῶν ἐν σκότει = "a guide to the blind, a light to those who are in darkness," objective gens.

2:22 | ἱεροσυλέω = "rob temples," usually in reference to pagan temples (cp. Acts 19:37), but here possibly in reference to keeping back tithes due to the temple of Yahweh (cp. Mal 3:8–9; Neh 13:10–11)

2:23 | ὃς ἐν νόμῳ καυχᾶσαι = "you who boast in the law"

2:24 | διά + acc. = "because of"

2:26 | οὐχ or οὐχί (textual issue) = "will not ...?" | λογίζομαι εἰς = "regard something as" (cp. 4:3; 9:8) (BDAG εἰς 8aγ)

2:27 | κρινεῖ – future (contrast v. 16) | σὲ τὸν διὰ γράμματος καὶ περιτομῆς παραβάτην νόμου = "you, who with all your obser-vances of the letter and your circumcision, are a transgressor of the law" (M 57), διά + gen. as marker of attendant or prevailing circumstance (BDAG διά A3c)

Romans 3

3:1 | τὸ περισσόν = "the advantage"

3:2 | πολὺ κατὰ πάντα τρόπον = "much in every way" (BDAG κατά B5ba) | πρῶτον μέν – see 1:8 | ἐπιστεύθησαν τὰ λόγια τοῦ θεοῦ = "they were entrusted with the oracles of God," pass. + acc. of retained object (W 438; BDF §159(4))

3:3 | τί γάρ; = "what then?" (NASB)

3:4 | ὅπως ἄν + subj. + future to designate some further consequence (BDF §369(3)) | ἐν τῷ κρίνεσθαί σε – either (1) pass.: "when you are judged" (NASB, ESV, BDAG κρίνω 2b), or (2) mid.: "when you judge" (NIV), "when you go to law" (ZG); in both options, acc. σε is subject of inf.

3:5 | ὁ ἐπιφέρων τὴν ὀργήν = "who inflicts wrath" (BDAG ἐπιφέρω 3) | κατὰ ἄνθρωπον λέγω = "I speak in a human way" (BDAG ἄνθρωπος 2b)

3:6 | ἐπεί = "otherwise" (BDF §456(3)) (cp. 11:6, 22) | κρινεῖ – future (cp. 2:27)

3:7 | ἐν τῷ ἐμῷ ψεύσματι = "through my lie," Hebr./insrumental ἐν | τί ἔτι καί; = "why still?" καί after interrogative (Z §459; BDF §442(14))

3:8 | καὶ μή ... ὅτι; = "And why not say ...?" (NASB, BDF §427(4)), carrying over τι from v. 7 and supplying λέγομεν from λέγειν in the parenthetical clause; but see commentaries for other solutions | καθὼς βλασφημούμεθα καὶ καθώς φασίν τινες ἡμᾶς λέγειν (parenthetical clause) = "as we are slanderously reported and as some claim that we say" (NASB) | ὅτι recitative | ποιήσωμεν – hortatory aorist subj., "let us do"

3:9 | προεχόμεθα; = either (1) "are we Jews any better off?" or (2) "are we Gentiles any better off?" | προῃτιασάμεθα = "I have [in the preceding discourse] already charged," epistolary "we" | ὑφ' ἁμαρτίαν = ὑπὸ ἁμαρτίαν – cp. Gal 3:22

3:10 | ὅτι recitative

3:12 | ἅμα (adv.) = "together" (BDAG ἅμα 2a) | οὐκ ἔστιν ἕως ἑνός = "there is not even one" (BDAG ἕως 5)

3:14 | ὧν τὸ στόμα ἀρᾶς καὶ πικρίας γέμει = "whose mouth is full of curse and bitterness," verbs of filling take gen.

3:15 | ὀξεῖς οἱ πόδες αὐτῶν ἐκχέαι αἷμα = "their feet are swift (lit. sharp) when it comes to shedding blood" (BDAG ὀξύς 2)

3:18 | φόβος θεοῦ – objective gen. | ἀπέναντι τῶν ὀφθαλμῶν αὐτῶν = "before their eyes," i.e., "with them" (BDAG ἀπέναντι 1bβ; BDF §214(6))

3:19 | τοῖς ἐν τῷ νόμῳ = "those who are subject to the law" (BDAG ἐν 4c) (cp. 2:12)

3:20 | διότι could be translated (1) "because" (NASB), (2) "for" (ESV), or (3) "therefore" (NIV) (see BDAG) | Hebr. οὐ ... πᾶς construction (BDF §302; Z §446) (cp. 1 Cor 1:29)

3:21–22 | δικαιοσύνη θεοῦ – see 1:17

3:22 | δικαιοσύνη δὲ θεοῦ ... = "even the righteousness of God which comes through faith in Jesus Christ," explanatory and/or intensifying δέ (BDF §447(8)) (cp. 9:30) | πίστεως Ἰησοῦ Χριστοῦ – either (1) "the faith(fulness) of Jesus Christ," subjective gen., or more likely (2) "faith in Jesus Christ," objective gen. (cp. Mk 11:22; Acts 3:16; James 2:1)

3:22–23 | (οὐ γάρ ἐστιν διαστολή· πάντες γὰρ ἥμαρτον καὶ ὑστεροῦνται τῆς δόξης τοῦ θεοῦ) – best treated as a parenthesis

3:24 | δικαιούμενοι δωρεάν – picks up and interprets δικαιοσύνη θεοῦ διὰ πίστεως Ἰ. Χρ. (v. 22), suggesting that δικαιοσύνη θεοῦ is not God's own attribute or activity but the righteousness that comes from God as a gift | δωρεάν = "freely, as a gift," adv. acc.

3:25 | ἱλαστήριον = "means of propitiation" (used in LXX, Philo, and Heb 9:5 to refer to the mercy seat) | διὰ πίστεως ἐν τῷ αὐτοῦ αἵματι – could be taken together ("through faith in his blood," for πίστις ἐν, see Gal 3:26) or as two separate prepositional phrases ("through faith, by means of his blood") | διά + acc. = "because of"

3:25–26 | εἰς (or πρὸς τὴν) ἔνδειξιν + gen. = "in order to demonstrate"

3:26 | ἐν τῷ νῦν καιρῷ = "at the present time" | εἰς τὸ εἶναι – see 1:20 | τὸν ἐκ πίστεως Ἰησοῦ = "the one who has faith in Jesus" (ESV, NASB)

3:27 | διὰ ποίου νόμου; = "by what kind of law?"

3:28 | λογίζομαι = "think, hold, maintain" (BDAG λογίζομαι 3) | πίστει – dat. of means

3:29 | οὐχὶ καὶ ἐθνῶν; = "Is he not [the God] of the Gentiles too?"

3:30 | εἴπερ = "if," first class condition (W 694) | εἷς ὁ θεός = "God is one" (cp. LXX Deut 6:4) | δικαιώσει – future used in logical sense

Romans 4

4:1 | κατὰ σάρκα – could modify προπάτορα ("our forefather according to the flesh") or εὑρηκέναι ("what has Abraham found according to the flesh?") | εὑρηκέναι = either (1) active for mid. (BDF §310(1)), "found for himself, obtained" (BDAG εὑρίσκω 3); "was gained by" (ESV), or (2) active, "discovered" (NIV)

4:3, 5, 9, 22 | λογίζομαι εἰς (4x) = "reckon/credit something as something" (BDAG εἰς 8αγ)

4:6 | λέγω + acc. = "speak of"

4:7 | μακάριοι ὧν = "blessed [are those] whose"

4:8 | οὗ οὐ μὴ λογίσηται κύριος ἁμαρτίαν = "whose sin the Lord will never count," but some MSS have ᾧ instead: "to whom the Lord will never count sin" | οὐ μή + aorist subj. – emphatic negation (BDF §365) = "will never"

4:9 | ἐπί (2x) + acc. – "marker indicating the one to whom, for whom, or about whom something is done" (BDAG ἐπί 14bα); verb must be supplied, e.g., "cometh upon" (KJV), "is pronounced on" (NRSV), "is for" (ESV, NIV); most likely, "is said concerning" (Hodge; cp. Heb 7:13)

4:10–12 | ἐν περιτομῇ (2x) / ἐν ἀκροβυστίᾳ (4x) = "while un/circumcised," ἐν as marker of state or condition (BDAG ἐν 2b); note ὄντι

4:11 | σημεῖον περιτομῆς – gen. of apposition (W 95) | εἰς τό + inf. (2x), here indicating result (cp. 3:26) | δι' ἀκροβυστίας = "while uncircumcised" (διά of attendant circumstance, BDAG A3c)

4:12 | πατέρα ... τοῖς ἐκ περιτομῆς = "father ... to those [believers in Jesus] who are from the circumcised" (see Acts 10:45; Col 4:11), ancestral ἐκ (not same as "the circumcision party" in Acts 11:2; Gal 2:12; Tit 1:10) | οὐ μόνον ... ἀλλὰ καί = "not only ... but also" (also v. 16) | τοῖς before στοιχοῦσιν is called "a simple mistake" by Cranfield (but cp. v. 16) | τῆς ἐν ἀκροβυστίᾳ πίστεως = "the faith that he had while uncircumcised"

4:13 | ἡ ἐπαγγελία ... τὸ κληρονόμον αὐτὸν εἶναι κόσμου = "the promise ... that he is heir of the world," τό does not go with κληρονόμον (which is masc.) but with the inf. | τὸ εἶναι is an anaphoric substantivized inf. epexegetical to ἡ ἐπαγγελία (BDF §399(1)) | αὐτόν (= Abraham or his seed) is the acc. subj. of the inf. εἶναι | κόσμου (objective gen.) modifies κληρονόμον, i.e., "one who is to inherit the world"

4:15 | οὗ = "where," gen. of ὅς that has become adv. of place (W 676) (cp. 5:20)

4:16–17 | ὅς ἐστιν πατὴρ πάντων ἡμῶν ... κατέναντι οὗ ἐπίστευσεν θεοῦ = "who is the father of us all ... in the sight of God, in whom he believed," taking quotation of Gen 17:5 as parenthesis (cp. NASB); from a κατὰ σάρκα point of view (v. 1), Abraham is the father of the Jews only, but "in the sight of God," he is the father of all who believe, whether Jew or Gentile | κατέναντι οὗ ἐπίστευσεν θεοῦ = κατέναντι τοῦ θεοῦ ᾧ ἐπίστευσεν – incorporation of the antecedent into the relative clause, with omission of article (Z §18; BDF §294(5)) | ὅτι recitative

4:18 | παρ’ ἐλπίδα = "contrary to (all human) expectation" (BDAG ἐλπίς 1a) | ἐπ’ ἐλπίδι = "full of hope" (BDAG ἐλπίς 1bα; ἐπί 5)

4:19 | πού = "about, approximately" (BDAG πού 2)

4:21 | ὃ ἐπήγγελται δυνατός ἐστιν καὶ ποιῆσαι = "what was promised he was able *also* to perform"

4:23–24 | δι’ αὐτόν & δι’ ἡμᾶς – "for" his/our sake

4:24 | μέλλω + inf. = "be about to"

4:25 | Parallelism of διά + acc. (2x) is stylistic not semantic: "for [causal sense] our transgressions ... for [final sense] our justification" (BDAG διά B2a) (cp. 11:28) | παρεδόθη & ἠγέρθη are divine passives

Romans 5

5:1 | δικαιωθέντες = "since we have been justified," causal ptc. (W 631) | Textual issue: although ἔχωμεν (hortatory subj.) has better MS support, ἔχομεν (indic.) is recommended by context (see Metzger; W 464)

5:2 | ἐσχήκαμεν = "we have obtained" (NASB), intensive perf. (W 574–6)

5:3 | οὐ μόνον δέ = "not only so" (NIV) (cp. v. 11)

5:4 | δοκιμή = "the experience of going through a test with special reference to the result, standing a test, character ... a test that promotes and validates the character of the one undergoing it" (BDAG)

5:5 | ὅτι = "for" | ἡ ἀγάπη τοῦ θεοῦ – subjective gen. (as proved by the γάρ in v. 6 and τὴν ἑαυτοῦ ἀγάπην in v. 8)

5:6 | ἔτι ὄντων ἡμῶν ἀσθενῶν ἔτι – gen. abs.; first ἔτι placed up front for emphasis; second ἔτι added for clarity (M 166; Cranfield) | κατὰ καιρόν = "at the right time"

5:7 | ἀποθανεῖται – gnomic future (BDF §349(1); W 571) (cp. χρηματίσει, 7:3) | τάχα τις καὶ τολμᾷ ἀποθανεῖν = "possibly someone would even dare to die"

5:8 | ὅτι = ἐν τούτῳ ὅτι = "in that" (BDAG ὅτι 2b) | ἔτι ἁμαρτωλῶν ὄντων ἡμῶν = "while we are still sinners," gen. abs.

5:9, 10, 15, 17 | πολλῷ μᾶλλον (4x) = "much more surely/certainly," the phrase "does not express a higher degree of efficacy, but of evidence or certainty" (Hodge)

5:9, 10 | ἐν τῷ αἵματι αὐτοῦ (= "by his blood") & ἐν τῇ ζωῇ αὐτοῦ (= "by his [resurrection] life") – Hebr./instrumental ἐν (BDF §219)

5:11 | καυχώμενοι – use of ptc. as finite verb (M 179; BDF §468(1))

5:12 | διὰ τοῦτο is difficult – see commentaries | ὥσπερ demands οὕτως καί ("just as ... so also"), but Paul interrupts himself; it is not until vv. 18–19 that he repeats the first half of the comparison and provides the expected second half introduced by οὕτως καί (2x) | ἐφ' ᾧ is highly contested; options include "on the basis of which," "because," "inasmuch as," "with the result that" (see BDAG ἐπί 6c; BDF §235(2); M 132; commentaries)

5:13 | μὴ ὄντος νόμου – gen. abs.

5:14 | ἐβασίλευσεν – constative/global aorist (W 558) (cp. Rev 20:4) | καὶ ἐπὶ τοὺς μὴ ἁμαρτήσαντας ἐπὶ τῷ ὁμοιώματι τῆς παραβάσεως Ἀδάμ = "even over those who had not sinned in the likeness of the transgression of Adam," that is, even over those who did not sin by breaking a law-covenant the way Adam did; see usage of παράβασις and cognates in LXX (cp. Rom 2:23, 25, 27; 4:15; Gal 2:18; 3:19; Heb 2:2; 9:15)

5:15 | Ἀλλ᾽ οὐχ ὡς τὸ παράπτωμα, οὕτως καὶ τὸ χάρισμα = lit. "But it is not 'As the trespass, so also the gift,'" i.e., "But the gift is not like the trespass" | ἡ δωρεὰ ἐν χάριτι = "the free gift in grace" (BDAG ἐν 12)

5:5:16 | δι᾽ ἑνός = "the result which came through the one ..." (cp. v. 18 (2x)) | Assonance, playing on nouns ending in -μα (BDF §488(3)) | ἐξ ἑνὸς [sc. παραπτώματος] & ἐκ πολλῶν παραπτωμάτων = "following one/many trespasse(s)" (BDAG ἐκ 5b)

5:17 | οἱ ... λαμβάνοντες = "those who receive"

5:18 | εἰς ... εἰς ... (2x) – note different uses of εἰς (BDAG εἰς 4e/g); it also helps to switch the order: "*resulting in* condemnation/justification *for* all men" | δικαίωσις ζωῆς = "justification that brings life" (NIV 1984)

5:20 | οὗ = "where" (see 4:15)

Romans 6
6:1 | ἐπιμένωμεν – deliberative rhetorical subj. (W 467) (cp. v. 15)

6:2–3 | οἵτινες/ὅσοι + 1p verb = "those of us who"

6:3 | ἐβαπτίσθημεν εἰς Χρ. Ἰ. – probably means "baptized *in the name of* Christ Jesus" (cp. Matt 28:19; Acts 8:16; 19:5; 1 Cor 1:13, 15), or "in reference to" (cp. 1 Cor 10:2) (BDAG εἰς 5)

6:4 | αὐτῷ – dat. bec. of the συν- prefix in συνθάπτω

6:5 | ἀλλά in apodosis of conditional sentence = "certainly" (BDAG ἀλλά 4a)

6:6 | Sc. αὐτῷ ("with him," explicit in vv. 4, 8) with συνεσταυρώθη (cp. 8:17; 2 Tim 2:11–12) | τοῦ μηκέτι δουλεύειν ἡμᾶς = "so that we would no longer be slaves," acc. ἡμᾶς as subject of inf.

6:7 | δικαιόω ἀπό = "cause someone to be released from legal claims" (BDAG δικαιόω 3) (cp. Acts 13:38)

6:9 | κυριεύω + gen. = "be lord over someone" (cp. v. 14; 7:1)

6:10 | ὃ ἀπέθανεν ... ὃ ζῇ = either (1) "the [death] that he died ... the [life] that he lives" (BDF §154); or (2) ὅ could be acc. of respect, "whereas" (M 34, 131)

6:12 | εἰς τὸ ὑπακούειν = "with the result that [you] obey" (BDF §402(2)); non-sequential, almost epexegetical, inf. of result (W 592 n7)

6:15 | ἁμαρτήσωμεν – cp. v. 1

6:16 | δοῦλοι ἐστε ᾧ ὑπακούετε = "you are slaves [of the one] whom you obey"

6:16, 19, 22 | εἰς (6x) = "resulting in," "leading to"

6:17 | χάρις τῷ θεῷ = "thanks be to God" (BDAG χάρις 5) | ὑπηκούσατε εἰς ὃν παρεδόθητε τύπον διδαχῆς = ὑπηκούσατε τῷ τύπῳ διδαχῆς εἰς ὃν παρεδόθητε = "you became obedient to the pattern of teaching to which you were given over [by God]" (BDAG παραδίδωμι 1b end; τύπος 4)

6:19 | ἀνθρώπινον = "in a human way," adv. acc.

6:21 | τίνα οὖν καρπὸν εἴχετε = "what benefit were you then deriving?" (NASB) | ἐφ᾽ οἷς νῦν ἐπαισχύνεσθε = "of which you are now ashamed" (BDAG ἐπί 6c)

Romans 7

7:1 | γινώσκουσιν = "to those who know the law," anarthrous substantival dat. pl. ptc. (W 619) | κυριεύω takes gen. | ἐφ᾽ ὅσον χρόνον ζῇ = "as long as he lives" (BDAG ἐπί 18cβ)

7:2–3 | ἀνήρ (7x) = "husband"

7:2 | ὕπανδρος (< ὑπό + ἀνήρ) (two-termination adj.) = "under the power of or subject to a man" (BDAG; cp. LXX Num 5:20, 29) | δέδεται & κατήργηται – gnomic intensive perfs. (W 581) | νόμῳ = "by law," dat. of means (W 162)

7:3 | ζῶντος τοῦ ἀνδρός goes with the protasis – "if [ἐάν], *while her husband is alive* [gen. abs.], she is joined to another man" | χρηματίσει – gnomic future (cp. 5:7) | γίνομαι + dat. of possession = "come to belong to someone" (W 150 n31) | τοῦ μὴ εἶναι αὐτὴν [subject] μοιχαλίδα [predicate] = "so that she is not an adulteress," double acc. with equative verb inf. (W 195); inf. of result (W 592–4) (see 1:20) | γενομένην ἀνδρὶ ἑτέρῳ = "even though she has come to belong to another husband," concessive ptc. (W 634)

7:4 | ὥστε introducing independent clause = "therefore" (BDAG ὥστε 1) (cp. v. 12) | καὶ ὑμεῖς = "you too," like the woman in the analogy who was "made to die" representatively by virtue of being under (ὕπανδρος, v. 2) her husband who died | θανατόω (pass.) does not mean "die" generically but "be put to death" as punishment | εἰς τὸ γενέσθαι ὑμᾶς ἑτέρῳ = "so that you may come to belong to another [husband]"

7:5 | τὰ παθήματα τῶν ἁμαρτιῶν τὰ διὰ τοῦ νόμου ἐνηργεῖτο = "the the sinful passions, *which* were aroused by the Law" (NASB); second τά functions as relative pronoun (W 213; BDF §269(2))

7:6 | ἀποθανόντες ἐν ᾧ κατειχόμεθα = "having died [to that] in which we were held fast," κατέχω has connotations of confinement and restraint (BDAG κατέχω 4)

7:7–25 | Paul's use of the first person is not autobiographical but a rhetorical device called *prosōpopoiia* in which the "I" represents a typical character (W 392; 532 n52; BDF §281) (cp. 1 Cor 10:29–30; Gal 2:18); Stanley K. Stowers, "Romans 7.7–25 as a Speech-in-Character (προσωποποιΐα)," in *Paul in His Hellenistic Context* (ed. Troels Engberg-Pedersen; Minneapolis: Fortress, 1995), 180–202

7:7 | In τὴν τε ἐπιθυμίαν, the τέ is ascensive = "even" (BDAG τέ 3), ἐπιθυμία as well as ἁμαρτία (BDF §443(3)) | ἐπιθυμία = "coveting" (NASB), "desire for something forbidden or simply inordinate, *craving, lust*" (BDAG ἐπιθυμία 2) | ἐπιθυμήσεις – LXX imperatival future (BDF §362; W 569) (cp. 13:9)

7:8 | πᾶσαν ἐπιθυμίαν = "coveting of every kind" (NASB) (BDAG πᾶς 5)

7:9 | ἐγὼ ἔζων χωρὶς νόμου ποτέ = "I was once alive apart from the Law," proof that ἐγώ is not autobiographical | ἐλθούσης δὲ τῆς ἐντολῆς = "but when the commandment came," gen. abs. (cp. Gal 3:25)

7:10 | εὑρέθη μοι ἡ ἐντολὴ ἡ εἰς ζωὴν αὕτη εἰς θάνατον = "the commandment that was intended to bring life, that very one [αὕτη] proved in my experience [to be, sc. οὖσα] a cause of death," taking μοι (= "in my experience") with εὑρέθη as ethical dat. (W 146) (BDAG εὑρίσκω 2)

7:13 | καθ' ὑπερβολὴν ἁμαρτωλός = "sinful in the extreme" (BDAG ὑπερβολή), "sinful beyond measure" (ESV; BDAG κατά B5bβ), "utterly sinful" (NASB)

7:17, 20 | ἡ οἰκοῦσα ἐν ἐμοὶ ἁμαρτία (2x) = "sin that dwells within me"

7:19 | The two relative clauses (ὃ [οὐ] θέλω) go with ἀγαθόν/κακόν: "The good *that I want*, I do not do, but I practice the very evil *that I do not want*" (NASB)

7:21 | εὑρίσκω τὸν νόμον ... ὅτι = "I find it to be a law that" (ESV), "I find the principle that" (NASB); wordplay on Paul's usual mng. of "law" (BDAG νόμος 1a) (cp. v. 23)

7:23 | αἰχμαλωτίζοντά με ἐν + dat. = either (1) "making me a prisoner to," taking ἐν as equivalent to simple dat. (BDF §220), or (2) "making me a prisoner under," taking ἐν νόμῳ = "under the law" (cp. 2:12; 3:19)

7:25 | χάρις τῷ θεῷ – cp. 6:17

Romans 8

8:2 | On textual issue (σε vs. με), see Metzger

8:3 | τὸ ἀδύνατον τοῦ νόμου – acc. in apposition to whole sentence (M 35), "in view of the inability of the law" | ἐν ᾧ = "in that" (M 131) or "because" (BDF §219(2)) | περὶ ἁμαρτίας = either (1) "to deal with sin" (BDAG περί 1g), or (2) "to be a sin offering" (cp. LXX Lev 5:6–13)

8:7 | εἰς in hostile sense (BDAG εἰς 4cα) | οὐδὲ γὰρ δύναται = "for it is not even able [to submit]," brachylogy

8:9 | εἴπερ = "if indeed" (cp. v. 17)

8:10 | τὸ πνεῦμα = either (1) "the [human] spirit" (contrasted with τὸ σῶμα); (2) "the [Holy] Spirit" (as in vv. 9, 11); or (3) "the human spirit as indwelt by the Holy Spirit" (combined view) | ζωή = either (1) "life," or (2) "alive," adjectival noun (W 49 n43)

8:12 | ὀφειλέτης + inf. = "under obligation to" (BDAG ὀφειλέτης 2b) (cp. Gal 5:3), in this case with pleonastic τοῦ prefixed to inf. (BDF §400(7))

8:13 | ζήσεσθε – for some reason many active verbs become mid. in the future (BDF §77)

8:13–14 | πνεύματι (2x) – instrumental dat.

8:14 | ὅσοι ἄγονται = "all who are led," customary/habitual present (W 521)

8:15 | "The Spirit you received does not make you slaves, so that you live in fear again; rather, the Spirit you received brought about your adoption to sonship" (NIV 2011)

8:16 | συμμαρτυρεῖ τῷ πνεύματι ἡμῶν = either (1) "bears witness along with our spirit," dat. of association, or (2) "bears witness to our spirit" (see W 160–1)

8:17 | καὶ κληρονόμοι = "then heirs," apodotic καί (BDAG καί 1bδ) | συγκληρονόμοι Χριστοῦ = "fellow-heirs with Christ," gen. of association (W 129) | συμπάσχομεν ... συνδοξασθῶμεν [sc. αὐτῷ] – an implied "with him" goes with the two συν- verbs (cp. 6:6)

8:18 | οὐκ ἄξια πρός + acc. = "not worthy to be compared with" (BDAG πρός 3eδ) | τὴν μέλλουσαν δόξαν ἀποκαλυφθῆναι = "the glory that is about to be revealed," curious word order; one expects τὴν δόξαν τὴν μέλλουσαν, etc. (M 169–70; BDF §474(5a)) (cp. Gal 3:23; but 1 Pet 5:1 is normal)

8:20 | ματαιότης = "futility" (cp. LXX Eccl 1:2, 14; etc. [32x])

8:20–21 | Punctuation options, depending on mng. of ὅτι: (1) ὑποτάξαντα, ἐφ' ἐλπίδι ὅτι ("subjected [it] in the hope *that* ..."), or (2) ὑποτάξαντα ἐφ' ἐλπίδι, ὅτι ("subjected [it] in hope; *for* ...") | ἐφ' ἐλπίδι (< ἐλπίς) alternative spelling for the usual ἐπ' ἐλπίδι (BDF §14) (cp. 4:18; 5:2); note textual variant

8:21 | ἀπὸ τῆς δουλείας τῆς φθορᾶς = "from its enslavement to corruption," objective gen. | τὴν ἐλευθερίαν τῆς δόξης τῶν τέκνων τοῦ θεοῦ = "the glorious freedom of the children of God," taking τῆς δόξης as attributive gen. (W 87–8)

8:23 | οὐ μόνον δέ – cp. 5:3 | ἡμεῖς καὶ αὐτοί = "even we ourselves"

8:24 | ὃ βλέπει τίς ἐλπίζει; = "who hopes for what he sees?"

8:25 | δι' ὑπομονῆς = "with patience," attendant circumstances (BDAG διά A3c)

8:26 | τὸ γὰρ τί προσευξώμεθα καθὸ δεῖ οὐκ οἴδαμεν = "for we do not know the 'what shall we pray for?' as we ought," τό changes direct question into indirect (BDAG ὁ 2hα) (see Lk 1:62); προσευξώμεθα – deliberative subj. | στεναγμοῖς ἀλαλήτοις = "along with [our] inarticulate groanings," dat. of association (W 159)

8:27 | τί [sc. ἐστιν] | κατὰ θεόν = "according to [the will of] God" | Subject of ἐντυγχάνω is not "he who searches the hearts" but "the Spirit"

8:28 | πάντα συνεργεῖ εἰς ἀγαθόν – three options: (1) taking πάντα as subject (neut. pl. subjects take sg. verbs), "all things work together for good" (ESV); (2) taking "God" subject: (a) "in all things [acc. of respect] God works for the good" (NIV), or (b) "God causes all things [acc. as direct object] to work together for good" (NASB)

8:29 | οὕς ... καί = "those whom ... he also" (would expect τούτους as in v. 30) | εἰς τὸ εἶναι αὐτὸν [subject] πρωτότοκον [predicate] = "so that he might be the firstborn" (see 1:20) | ἐν = "among"

8:31 | πρός + acc. = "with reference to" (BDAG πρός 3eα)

8:31, 33 | κατά + gen. (2x) = "against" (BDAG κατά A2bγ)

8:32 | φείδομαι takes gen. (cp. 11:21)

8:36 | ὅτι recitative | ὅλην τὴν ἡμέραν = "all day long," acc. for extent of time | πρόβατα σφαγῆς = "sheep destined for slaughter," gen. of destination (W 100–1)

8:37 | ἀλλά = "no, not at all!" (BDAG ἀλλά 3)

Romans 9
9:1 | συμμαρτυρούσης μοι τῆς συνειδήσεώς μου – gen. abs. (cp. 2:15)

9:2 | λύπη μοί ἐστιν μεγάλη = "I have great sorrow," dat. of possession

9:3 | ηὐχόμην ἀνάθεμα εἶναι αὐτὸς ἐγώ = "I could almost wish myself to be accursed," desiderative impf. (W 552; M 9) | ἀπό designates separation in pregnant construction (BDAG ἀπό 1e; BDF §211), "and cut off from Christ" (ESV)

9:5 | τὸ κατὰ σάρκα – adv. acc. (M 111) | ὁ ὢν ἐπὶ πάντων θεὸς εὐλογητὸς εἰς τοὺς αἰῶνας – possible construals: (1) taking θεός with what follows: "who is over all, God blessed for ever" (NASB), or (2) taking θεός with what precedes: "who is God over all, blessed forever" (ESV)

9:6 | οὐχ οἷον δὲ ὅτι = "but it is not as though," combination of οὐχ οἷον and οὐχ ὅτι (BDAG οἷος) | οὐ πάντες οἱ ἐξ Ἰσραήλ, οὗτοι Ἰσραήλ = "not all who are descended from Israel are Israel"

9:7 | οὐδ᾽ ὅτι εἰσὶν σπέρμα Ἀβραάμ, πάντες τέκνα = "nor, [just] because (ὅτι) they are Abraham's seed, are they all children" | σοι σπέρμα = "your seed," dat. of possession

9:8 | λογίζεται εἰς – cp. 2:26

9:9 | κατὰ τὸν καιρὸν τοῦτον = "at this very season [next year]"

(LXX Gen 18:10, 14) | ἔσται τῇ Σάρρᾳ υἱός = "Sarah will have a son," dat. of possession (LXX Gen 18:14)

9:10 | οὐ μόνον δέ – cp. 5:3, 11; 8:23 | ἐξ ἑνός = "by one man" | κοίτην ἔχω = "conceive" (BDAG κοίτη 2b)

9:11 | "though [Jacob and Esau] were not yet born and had not done anything good or bad," concessive gen. abs. | ἡ κατ' ἐκλογὴν πρόθεσις τοῦ θεοῦ = "God's electing purpose," "the purpose of God which operates by selection" (BDAG ἐκλογή 1)

9:12, 17 | ὅτι recitative (2x)

9:15 | ὃν ἄν (2x) = "on whomever"

9:16 | οὐκ + gen. = "[it] does not depend on," gen. of source (W 109–10)

9:20 | μενοῦνγε σὺ τίς εἶ = "you, who in the world are you?" (BDAG μενοῦν; BDF §450(4)), prolepsis (see 14:4)

9:21 | ἐξουσία + gen. (τοῦ πηλοῦ) + inf. = "right/authority over ... to" (BDF §393(3)) | ὃ μέν ... σκεῦος ὃ δέ = "this vessel ... that [vessel]," brachylogy | εἰς τιμήν/ἀτιμίαν = "for (dis)honorable use" (BDAG εἰς 4d)

9:22–23 | Probably anacoluthon (but see BDF §467) | εἰ δέ = "what if?" (BDAG εἰ 6aβ) | τὸ δυνατόν = ἡ δύναμις (BDF §263(2)) (cp. 2:4)

9:26 | οὗ (adv.) = "where"

9:28 | "For the Lord will carry out his sentence on earth with speed and finality" (NIV)

9:30 | κατέλαβεν – neut. pl. subjects (ἔθνη) take sg. verbs | δικαιοσύνην δὲ τὴν ἐκ πίστεως = "that is, the righteousness which is by faith," explanatory and/or intensifying δέ (BDF §447(8)) (cp. 3:22)

9:32 | ὅτι οὐκ ἐκ πίστεως ἀλλ' ὡς ἐξ ἔργων = "because [they pursued righteousness] not by faith but as if [they could attain it] by works" (BDAG ὡς 3c) | προσέκοψαν – would expect sg. (Ἰσραήλ, v. 31), but it is pl. ("they") (*constructio ad sensum*)

9:32–33 | λίθος προσκόμματος (2x) = "a stone which causes stumbling," gen. of production (W 104)

Romans 10
10:1 | εἰς σωτηρίαν = "that they may be saved" (NIV) (BDAG εἰς 4f) | Ellipsis of the copula "is"

10:2 | ζῆλον θεοῦ = "zeal for God," objective gen. (cp. Acts 22:3)

10:3 | τοῦ θεοῦ δικαιοσύνην = "the righteousness that comes from God," gen. of source (W 110)

10:4 | Since τέλος is anarthrous, it is the predicate: "Christ is the end of the law" (not "the end of the law is Christ") (cp. 13:10b) | εἰς δικαιοσύνην = "so that there may be (or with the result that there is) righteousness," adverbial purpose or result clause (cp. εἰς σωτηρίαν – 1:16; 10:1) (BDAG εἰς 4e/f)

10:5 | γράφω + acc. = "write about something" (would expect περί) | ὁ ποιήσας = "whoever does," substantival gnomic aorist ptc. with generic reference (W 615 n8) (cp. Gal 3:12) | ἐν αὐτοῖς = "by them," Hebr./instrumental ἐν

10:9 | First ὅτι could be (1) marker of causality, "because" (ESV), or (2) marker of discourse content, "that" (NASB)

10:10 | Present passives, with impersonal force, "one believes ... one confesses" (M 27) | εἰς (2x) = "resulting in" (BDAG εἰς 4e)

10:12 | Two genitives joined by καί mng. "between" (W 135)

10:14–15 | πῶς + deliberative aorist subj. (4x) = "how can they ...?" (NIV), "how are they to ...?" (ESV)

10:14 | κηρύσσοντος = "someone preaching," anarthrous substantival ptc.

10:15 | ὡς ὡραῖοι οἱ πόδες = "how timely is the arrival" (BDAG ὡς 7; ὡραῖος 1)

10:18 | "But I ask: Did they not hear? Of course they did [μενοῦνγε]" (NIV)

10:19 | ἐπ᾽ οὐκ ἔθνει = "by that which is not a nation"

10:20 | ἀποτολμᾷ καὶ λέγει = "boldly says" (NIV), "is so bold as to say" (BDAG ἀποτολμάω) | [ἐν] τοῖς ἐμὲ μὴ ζητοῦσιν = "among (or by) those not seeking me" – if ἐν is read, then it would be rendered "among" (ZG); if ἐν is not read, then dat. of agent (BDF §191(3)) | τοῖς ἐμὲ μὴ ἐπερωτῶσιν = "to those not asking for me"

10:21 | ὅλην τὴν ἡμέραν = "all day long," acc. for extent of time

Romans 11
11:1 | λέγω = "I ask" (cp. v. 11) | μή expects neg. answer | καὶ γὰρ ἐγώ = "for I too" | ἐκ σπέρματος Ἀβραάμ = lit. "of/from the seed of Abraham," i.e., a descendant of Abraham (cp. ἐκ σπέρματος Δαυίδ, 1:3)

11:2 | ἐν Ἠλίᾳ = "in the passage about Elijah" (NASB) (see BDF §219(1)) | Subject of ἐντυγχάνει is Elijah | ἐντυγχάνω τινὶ κατά τινος = "appeal to someone against a third person" (BDAG ἐντυγχάνω 1a)

11:3 | κἀγώ = καὶ ἐγώ

11:4 | κατέλιπον ἐμαυτῷ = "I have kept for myself" | τῇ Βάαλ – fem. article for male deity, reflecting the Jewish custom of substituting בֹּשֶׁת (= "the shameful thing" = ἡ αἰσχύνη [e.g., LXX Jer 3:24]) for names of pagan deities (BDAG Βάαλ; BDF §53(4); M 183)

11:5 | οὕτως οὖν καὶ ἐν τῷ νῦν καιρῷ = "so also at the present time" | γέγονεν = "has come to be," "there is"

11:6 | ἐπεί = "otherwise" (BDF §456(3)) (cp. v. 22; 3:6)

11:8 | πνεῦμα κατανύξεως = "a spirit of stupor," attributive gen. (W 88)

11:8, 10 | τοῦ μή + inf. (3x) = "so that they may not ..."

11:9 | γίνομαι εἰς = "become," with εἰς functioning as predicate nom. (BDAG εἰς 8aα) | αὐτοῖς = "to them," dat. of disadvantage (W 142)

11:10 | σύγκαμψον – impv. addressed to God, "bend their backs" | διὰ παντός = "continually" (BDAG διά A2a)

11:11 | ἡ σωτηρία τοῖς ἔθνεσιν = "salvation [sc. has come] to the Gentiles" | εἰς τό + inf. = "in order to ..."

11:12, 15 | Must supply a verb: "is" (NASB), or "mean(s)" (ESV)

11:13 | ἐφ' ὅσον = "to the degree that, in so far as" (BDAG ἐπί 13) | ἐθνῶν ἀπόστολος = "an apostle to the Gentiles" (ESV), gen. of direction (W 100)

11:14 | μου τὴν σάρκα = τὴν σάρκα μου = "my fellow countrymen"

(NASB) (cp. 9:3) (BDAG σάρξ 4) | παραζηλώσω ... σώσω – subj. followed by future to indicate some further consequence (BDF §369(3))

11:16 | εἰ ... καί (2x) = "if ... so (is/are)"

11:17 | ἀγριέλαιος ὤν = "although being a wild olive tree," concessive ptc. (W 634) | ἡ ῥίζα τῆς πιότητος = "the root with its oily richness" (BDAG πιότης), "the rich root" (NASB), attributive gen. | συγκοινωνός + gen. of thing in which one shares

11:18 | κατα-καυχάομαι + gen. = "boast down upon/over/against"

11:20 | καλῶς = "Quite right! That is true!" (BDAG καλῶς 4c)

11:21 | οἱ κατὰ φύσιν κλάδοι = "the natural branches" | [μὴ πῶς] οὐδὲ σοῦ φείσεται – textual problem: either (1) retain the "typically Pauline expression" μὴ πῶς (Metzger): "he will not somehow spare you either, will he?" or (2) delete it: "neither will he spare you" | φείδομαι takes gen. (cp. 8:32)

11:22 | ἐπεί = "otherwise" (see v. 6)

11:23 | κἀκεῖνοι = καὶ ἐκεῖνοι

11:24 | εἰ σὺ ἐκ τῆς κατὰ φύσιν ἐξεκόπης ἀγριελαίου = "if you were cut off from what is by nature a wild olive tree" (NASB), makes better sense if verb ἐξεκόπης is moved before ἐκ (M 91) | παρὰ φύσιν = "contrary to nature" (cp. 1:26)

11:25 | [παρ'] ἑαυτοῖς φρόνομοι = "wise in your own estimation" (NASB) (BDAG παρά B2) (cp. 12:16; LXX Prov 3:7) | ἀπὸ μέρους = "partial" (modifies "hardening") | ἄχρις οὗ + subj. = "until"

11:26 | καὶ οὕτως = "and in this way"

11:27 | παρ' ἐμοῦ = "made/given by me" (BDAG παρά A3b), or just "my" | Supply some form of the copula, "this [is, or will be] my covenant with them"

11:28 | κατὰ μέν ... κατὰ δέ = "from the standpoint of ... but from the standpoint of" (NASB) | Parallelism of διά + acc. (2x) is stylistic not semantic: "for the sake of you [final sense] ... on account of the fathers [causal sense]" (cp. 4:25)

11:30–31 | τῇ τούτων ἀπειθείᾳ ... τῷ ὑμετέρῳ ἐλέει = "because of their disobedience ... because of the mercy shown to you" (NASB), dat. of cause (BDF §196)

Romans 12
12:1 | διά + gen. as part of an urgent request = "by" (BDAG διά A3f; BDF §223(4)) (cp. 15:30; 1 Cor 1:10) | παρακαλῶ ... παραστῆσαι – verb of urging followed by inf. in indirect discourse (W 604) | θυσίαν = "as a sacrifice," predicate acc. | θυσίαν ζῶσαν ἁγίαν εὐάρεστον τῷ θεῷ = either (1) taking ζῶσαν as predicate ptc.: "as a sacrifice – alive, holy, acceptable to God," or (2) taking ζῶσαν as attributive ptc.: "as a living sacrifice – holy [and] acceptable to God" (see discussion at W 618–9) | ἡ λογικὴ λατρεία ὑμῶν – either (1) "your rational service" (ESV alt.) or (2) "your spiritual worship" (ESV) (see BDAG λογικός) (cp. 1 Pet 2:2)

12:2 | τῇ ἀνακαινώσει τοῦ νοός = "by the renewal of the [= your] mind," dat of means; objective gen. | εἰς τό + inf. + acc. (ὑμᾶς) as subject of inf. = "so that you may be able to ..." | τί τὸ θέλημα τοῦ θεοῦ = "what the will of God [is]" | τὸ ἀγαθόν, etc. – the article either (1) signals an abstract concept, "the good," etc., or (2) functions anaphorically, "that [will] which is good," etc.

12:3 | παρ' ὃ δεῖ φρονεῖν = "than he ought to think" | ἑκάστῳ ὡς ὁ θεὸς ἐμέρισεν μέτρον πίστεως = "to each one as God has apportioned a measure of faith" (BDAG μερίζω 2b; μέτρον 2b) (cp. 2 Cor 10:13); on ἑκάστῳ ὡς, see BDAG ὡς 1bγ (cp. 1 Cor 3:5; 7:17)

12:4–5 | καθάπερ ... οὕτως = "just as ... so"

12:4 | τὰ μέλη πάντα οὐ τὴν αὐτὴν ἔχει πρᾶξιν = τὰ μέλη πάντα οὐκ ἔχει τὴν αὐτὴν πρᾶξιν = "all the members do not have the same function" (NASB), neut. pl. subjects take sg. verbs

12:5 | τὸ καθ᾽ εἷς = "individually," adv. acc.; κατά + nom. looks like bad grammar, but it was an accepted colloquial expression (BDF §§224(3), 305) (cp. Mark 14:19; John 8:9)

12:9 | ἡ ἀγάπη ἀνυπόκριτος = "[let] love [be] sincere" (sc. ἔστω)

12:9–19 | Series of ptcs./adjs./infs. used imperatively (BDF §§468(2), 389; W 650–1)

12:10–11a | Three datives of respect (W 144) (τῇ φιλαδελφίᾳ ... τῇ τιμῇ ... τῇ σπουδῇ) = "With regard to brotherly love, be devoted to one another. With regard to honor, outdo one another. With regard to zeal, do not shrink back."

12:16 | τὸ αὐτὸ φρονέω = "be in agreement," "be like-minded" (cp. 15:5; 2 Cor 13:11; Phil 2:2; 4:2); but note that we are called to agree κατὰ Χριστὸν Ἰησοῦν (15:5) | φρόνιμοι παρ᾽ ἑαυτοῖς = "wise in your own estimation" (NASB) (see 11:25)

12:18 | τὸ ἐξ ὑμῶν = "so far as it depends on you" (NASB, ESV; cp. BDAG ἐκ 3e), adv. acc. (M 34, 111, 160) or acc. of respect (BDF §160)

12:19 | Anacoluthon: shift from imperatival ptc. (ἐκδικοῦντες) to impv. (δότε) | ἐμοί – dat. of possession

12:20 | τοῦτο ποιῶν = "in so doing," ptc. of means (W 630)

12:21 | ἐν τῷ ἀγαθῷ = "by means of the good," Hebr./instrumental ἐν (BDF §219)

Romans 13

13:1 | πᾶσα ψυχή = "every person" (cp. 2:9) | "The presence of the preposition ὑπό in both clauses suggests that we should read back into the first clause a form of the verb τάσσω, which Paul uses in the second clause" (Moo 798 n29)

13:2 | ὥστε = "therefore" (cp. 7:4, 12)

13:3 | φόβος = "a cause of fear" (NASB) | "Do you wish to have no fear of the authority? [Then] do what is good," parataxis in place of conditional subordination (BDF §§471(3), 494) | ἐξ αὐτῆς = "from it (= ἡ ἐξουσία)"

13:4 | σοὶ εἰς τὸ ἀγαθόν = "for your good" (ESV) | ἔκδικος εἰς ὀργὴν τῷ τὸ κακὸν πράσσοντι = "an avenger who brings wrath on the one who practices evil" (NASB) (BDAG εἰς 4e)

13:5 | διὸ ἀνάγκη ὑποτάσσεσθαι = "Therefore [it is] necessary to be in subjection," noun + ἐστίν + inf. (BDF §393(3); BDAG ἀνάγκη 1), but here with ἐστίν omitted (BDF §127(2))

13:6 | διὰ τοῦτο γὰρ καὶ φόρους τελεῖτε = "this is also why you pay taxes" (NIV) | εἰς αὐτὸ τοῦτο προσκαρτεροῦντες = "devoting themelves to this very thing" (NASB), "who give their full time to governing" (NIV)

13:7 | τῷ τὸν φόρον τὸν φόρον = "to whom revenue [is owed, pay] revenue," etc. (brachylogy – 4x)

13:8 | πεπλήρωκεν – proleptic perf. (W 581) (cp. 14:23)

13:9 | τό used to introduce quotations (BDAG ὁ 2hα) | Future tense employed to render categorical injunctions and prohibitions in LXX (cp. 7:7)

13:10 | πλήρωμα οὖν νόμου ἡ ἀγάπη = "love is the fulfillment of the law," ἡ ἀγάπη is the subject bec. it is articular/definite (cp. 10:4)

13:11 | καὶ τοῦτο = "and [do] this" | ὥρα + inf. (BDF §393(3)) | ἐγγύτερον ... ἢ ὅτε = "nearer ... than when," comparative + ἤ (BDAG ἤ 2a) | ἡμῶν ἡ σωτηρία = ἡ σωτηρία ἡμῶν = "our salvation," objective gen.

13:13 | περιπατήσωμεν = "let us walk," hortatory subj. | περιπατέω + six datives of attendant circumstance (BDAG περιπατέω 2aβ; BDF §198(5))

13:14 | ποιοῦμαι πρόνοιαν + gen. = "make provision for something," ποιέω (mid.) + noun as periphrasis for verbal idea (BDAG ποιέω 7a) | εἰς ἐπιθυμίας = "to gratify its desires" (ESV) (BDAG εἰς 4f)

Romans 14
14:1 | μὴ εἰς διακρίσεις διαλογισμῶν = "but not for the purpose of getting into quarrels about opinions" (BDAG διάκρισις 2; εἰς 4f)

14:2 | ὃς μέν ... ὁ δὲ ἀσθενῶν = "the one ... the weak person," anacoluthon; the ὃς μέν ... ὃς δέ ("the one ... the other") construction (cp. v. 5) is not continued in the second clause (BDAG ὅς 2b; BDF §250) | πιστεύει φαγεῖν πάντα = "is convinced [that it is permissible] to eat anything" (BDF §397(2); BDAG πιστεύω 4–5)

14:4 | σὺ τίς εἶ ὁ κρίνων = "you, who are you who judges?" (= Jas 4:12), prolepsis (BDF §476) (cp. 9:20), articular ptc. with personal pronoun (BDF §412(5)) (cp. 2:1, 3) | δυνατεῖ ὁ κύριος στῆσαι αὐτόν = "the Lord is able to make him stand," στῆσαι is trans. (BDAG ἵστημι 5)

14:5 | κρίνω = "recognize" (BDAG κρίνω 1), "regard" (NASB), "consider" (NIV) | ἡμέραν παρ᾽ ἡμέραν = "one day more sacred than another" (NIV) (BDAG παρά C3) | κρίνει πᾶσαν ἡμέραν = "considers every day alike" (NIV)

14:9 | εἰς τοῦτο = "to this end" (BDAG εἰς 4f) | καί ... καί = "both ... and" (BDAG καί 1f) | κυριεύω + gen. of that over which rule is exercised

14:11 | Ζῶ ἐγώ = "as surely as I live," biblical oath formula (cp. LXX Num 14:28; Isa 49:18)

14:12 | λόγον δίδωμι = "give an account" (BDAG λόγος 2a)

14:13 | κρίνωμεν – hortatory subj. | Second κρίνω = "decide" (BDAG κρίνω 4), play on words with the first κρίνω mng. "judge"

14:14 | δι᾽ ἑαυτοῦ = "in itself" | λογίζομαι = "be of the opinion" (BDAG λογίζομαι 3) | τῷ λογιζομένῳ ... ἐκείνῳ – ethical datives (W 146) (cp. v. 20)

14:15 | λυπέω (pass.) = "be sad, distressed, grieved," but can also mean "be injured" (BDAG λυπέω 2b)

14:16 | "Do not let what is for you a good thing be spoken of as evil" (NASB)

14:19 | τά + gen. (2x) = "the things which make for ..." (BDF §266(3))

14:20 | τῷ διὰ προσκόμματος ἐσθίοντι = either (1) of the weak, "the one who eats and stumbles in the process" (BDAG πρόσκομμα 1b), or (2) of the strong, "he who eats in a way which causes stumbling" (M 58); in either case, διά of attendant circumstance (BDAG διά A3c)

14:21 | καλόν + inf. = "[it is] better to," positive for comparative (BDAG καλός 2dγ; BDF §245) | μηδὲ ἐν ᾧ = "nor [sc. to do anything] whereby" (BDF §480(1); ZG; BDAG ἐν 5b)

14:22 | ἐν ᾧ δοκιμάζει = "in [that] which he approves"

14:23 | κατακέκριται – proleptic perf. (W 581) (cp. 13:8) | ὅτι οὐκ ἐκ πίστεως = "because [his eating is] not from faith" (NASB)

Romans 15
15:2 | εἰς τὸ ἀγαθὸν πρὸς οἰκοδομήν = "for his good, to build him up" (ESV) (BDAG πρός 3c)

15:3 | καὶ γὰρ ὁ Χριστός = "for even the Christ"

15:4 | The repetition of διά means that τῶν γραφῶν only goes with τῆς παρακλήσεως – we have hope through two things: (1) through endurance, and (2) through the encouragement of the Scriptures

15:5 | ὁ θεὸς δῴη ὑμῖν = "may God grant you," voluntative optative, used in prayers (W 481–3) (cp. v. 13) | τὸ αὐτὸ φρονέω – see 12:16 | ἐν ἀλλήλοις = either (1) "with one another," or (2) "among yourselves"

15:8 | διάκονος περιτομῆς = "a servant to the circumcision," objective gen.

15:9 | τὰ δὲ ἔθνη ὑπὲρ ἐλέους δοξάσαι τὸν θεόν = "and so that the Gentiles would glorify God for his mercy" (vv. 8–9 are an anacoluthon, since subject of βεβαιῶσαι is Christ, but subject of δοξάσαι is the Gentiles, thus breaking the εἰς τό + inf. construction) | ἐν ἔθνεσιν = "among the Gentiles"

15:12 | ἄρχω (when it means "rule") takes gen. of what/who is ruled

15:13–14 | Verbs of filling take gen. | μεστός also takes gen.

15:13 | πληρῶσαι – optative (see v. 5) | ἐν τῷ πιστεύειν = "in believing/trusting," "as you believe/trust" (BDF §404(1))

15:14 | πέπεισμαι ... περὶ ὑμῶν ὅτι = "I am convinced concerning you, that ...," prolepsis (BDF §476); could be translated "I am convinced that you ..." | καὶ αὐτὸς ἐγώ = "I myself also"

15:15 | ἔγραψα – probably not epistolary aorist; refers what has been written up to this point (W 563; BDF §334) | ἀπὸ μέρους = "on some points" | ὡς + ptc. expresses purpose

15:16 | εἰς τὸ εἶναι – see 1:20 | ἡ προσφορὰ τῶν ἐθνῶν = either (1) subjective gen.: "the offering that the Gentiles bring," or (2) gen. of apposition: "the offering which consists of the Gentiles themselves" | εὐπρόσδεκτος – two-termination adj.; here fem. (προσφορά) | Hebr./instrumental ἐν

15:17 | τὰ πρὸς τὸν θεόν = "in things pertaining to God," acc. of respect (M 33) or adv. acc. (BDF §160); seems to have a cultic connotation (cp. Heb 2:17; 5:1)

15:18 | τι ... ὧν οὐ κατειργάσατο Χριστός = "anything except what Christ has accomplished" (NASB) | εἰς ὑπακοὴν ἐθνῶν = "to bring the Gentiles to obedience" (ESV) (BDAG εἰς 4f), subjective gen. (cp. "the obedience of faith," see 1:5; 16:26)

15:19 | ὥστε με + inf. = "so that I," acc. με as subject of inf.

15:20 | οὕτως δὲ φιλοτιμούμενον εὐαγγελίζεσθαι = "and thus I make it my ambition to preach the gospel" (ESV); φιλοτιμούμενον is acc. in agreement with με (v. 19); "since the subject of the infinitive generally is ... in the acc., it is natural that adjuncts and predicates going with the subject follow suit" (BDF §410) (cp. 1:15)

15:21 | οἷς = "[those] to whom"

15:22 | τὰ πολλά = "many times," adv. acc. | ἐνεκοπτόμην τοῦ ἐλθεῖν = "I have been prevented from coming," gen. of the articular inf. (BDF §400(4)); gen. of separation (W 107)

15:24 | ὡς ἄν + subj. = "whenever," "as soon as" (M 133; BDF §455(2); BDAG ὡς 8cα) | ἐλπίζω γάρ ... ἐμπλησθῶ – parenthesis | ἐὰν ὑμῶν πρῶτον ἀπὸ μέρους ἐμπλησθῶ = "after I have first enjoyed your company for a while," ἐμπίμπλημι + gen. = "enjoy something" (BDAG ἐμπί(μ)πλημι 3)

15:25 | διακονῶν = "to serve," present ptc. with future sense (BDF §339(2))

15:26 | BDAG εἰς 4g

15:27 | ὀφειλέται εἰσὶν αὐτῶν = "they owe it to them," objective gen.

15:29 | ἐρχόμενος ... ἐλεύσομαι = "when I come to you, I will come in the fullness of the blessing of Christ"

15:30 | διά (2x) – see 12:1

Romans 16
16:1 | διάκονος – common (masc./fem.) gender, here fem. (as οὖσαν proves); should not be rendered "servant" but "deacon" in the sense of office, as indicated by several factors: (1) Paul's recommendation (συνίστημι) of her, which may imply that she is also the letter carrier, (2) her office as "deacon" distinuished from her role as "sister," (3) the use of the ptc. (οὖσαν) + noun construction, showing διάκονος is something that she *is*, and (4) the added phrase τῆς ἐκκλησίας τῆς ἐν Κεγχρεαῖς

16:2 | Probably imperatival ἵνα (BDAG ἵνα 2g; BDF §387(3); but see M 145) | ἐν ᾧ ἂν ὑμῶν χρήζῃ πράγματι = "in whatever matter she may have need of you" (NASB); χρήζω takes gen. of person/thing needed

16:3 | τοὺς συνεργούς μου = "my fellow-workers," gen. of association (W 128–30)

16:5 | ἡ κατ᾽ οἶκον αὐτῶν ἐκκλησία = "the church that meets at their house" (NIV) (BDAG κατά B1a) (1 Cor 16:19) | ἀπαρχή ... εἰς Χριστόν = "the first convert to Christ" (ESV)

16:6, 12 | πολλὰ ἐκοπίασεν (2x) = "has worked hard," πολλά as adv. acc. amplifies the mng. of the verb (cp. v. 12)

16:6 | BDAG εἰς 4g

16:7 | ἐπίσημοι ἐν τοῖς ἀποστόλοις = (1) taking ἐν as equivalent to ordinary dat. (BDAG ἐν 8; BDF §220(1)): "well known to the apostles" (ESV), or (2) taking ἐν as "among" (BDAG ἐν 1d): "outstanding among the apostles" (NASB, BDAG ἐπίσημος 1) | On whether "Junia(s)" is the name of a man or a woman, see BDAG's two entries as well as recent commentaries and articles

16:10–11 | τοὺς ἐκ τῶν (2x) = "those of the household of ..."

16:16 | Hebr./instrumental ἐν

16:17 | τούς ... ποιοῦντας = "those who cause" | παρά + acc. = "contrary to" (BDAG παρά C6)

16:18 | κοιλία = "appetites" (many English versions)

16:19 | χαίρω ἐπί = "rejoice over" (BDAG ἐπί 6c) | εἰς (2x) = "with reference to" (BDAG εἰς 5)

16:20 | ἐν τάχει = "soon," periphrasis for adv. (BDAG ἐν 11)

16:22 | ὁ γράψας τὴν ἐπιστολήν = "who wrote down this letter" (NIV), deictic use of the article (W 221); Tertius was the amanuensis to whom Paul dictated the letter | ἐν κυρίῳ modifies ἀσπάζομαι

16:25–26 | σεσιγημένου ... φανερωθέντος ... γνωρισθέντος –
genitives in agreement with μυστηρίου (not gen. abs.) | χρόνοις
αἰωνίοις = "for long ages," temporal dat. (BDF §201) | διά τε = "and
through" (the enclitic τε indicates that this entire prepositional phrase
goes with γνωρισθέντος) | On ὑπακοὴ πίστεως, see 1:5

Chapter Seven

The First Epistle to the Corinthians

1 Corinthians 1

1:2 | αὐτῶν καὶ ἡμῶν = "both their Lord and ours" (ESV)

1:4 | ἐπί + dat. = "because of," "for" (BDAG ἐπί 6c)

1:5 | ὅτι = either (1) "that," or (2) "for"

1:6 | τὸ μαρτύριον τοῦ Χριστοῦ = "the testimony about Christ," objective gen. | ἐν ὑμῖν = "among you" (also vv. 10–11)

1:7 | ὥστε + acc. as subject of inf. + inf. = "with the result that you are not lacking" | ἀπεκδεχομένους = "as you await"

1:8 | ἕως τέλους = "to the end," i.e., until the parousia (BDAG τέλος 2bβ) (ἕως as preposition + gen.)

1:9 | κοινωνίαν τοῦ υἱοῦ αὐτοῦ = "fellowship *with* his Son" (NASB; BDAG κοινωνία 1)

1:10 | διά + gen. as part of an urgent request = "by" (BDAG διά A3f; BDF §223(4)) (cp. Rom 12:1) | ἡ ... σχίσματα – neut. pl. subjects take sg. verbs

1:11 | ὑπὸ τῶν Χλόης = "by Chloe's people"

1:13 | μή expects neg. answer: "Paul was not crucified for you, was he?" (NASB)

1:13, 15 | εἰς τὸ ὄνομα = "in the name of" (BDAG ὄνομα 1dγ)

1:16 | λοιπόν = "beyond that," adv. acc. | τινα ἄλλον = "any other"

1:17 | οὐκ ἐν σοφίᾳ λόγου = "not in cleverness of speech" (NASB; cp. BDAG σοφία 1a) (cp. λόγου, 2:1) | ἵνα μή + subj. = "lest"

1:18 | τοῖς μέν ... τοῖς δέ = "to those ... but to those," ethical datives (W 146)

1:21 | ἐπειδὴ γάρ = "for since" | οὐκ ἔγνω ὁ κόσμος διὰ τῆς σοφίας τὸν θεόν = "the world through *its* wisdom did not come to know God" (NASB), article as possessive pronoun (W 215)

1:22 | ἐπειδὴ καί = "for indeed"

1:24 | θεοῦ δύναμιν καὶ θεοῦ σοφίαν = δύναμιν θεοῦ καὶ σοφίαν θεοῦ

1:25 | τὸ μωρὸν τοῦ θεοῦ ... καὶ τὸ ἀσθενὲς τοῦ θεοῦ = "the foolish-ness of God ... and the weakness of God," substantivized adjectives (BDF §263(2)) | τῶν ἀνθρώπων (2x) = "than humans," gen. of comparison

1:29 | Hebr. μή ... πᾶς construction (BDF §302; Z §446) (cp. Rom 3:20)

1:30 | ἐξ αὐτοῦ = "by His doing" (NASB) | ἡμῖν – either ethical dat. ("in our eyes"), or dat. of possession ("our")

1:31 | ἐν κυρίῳ goes with καυχάσθω

1 Corinthians 2

2:1 | κἀγώ = καὶ ἐγώ (cp. 3:1) | καθ᾽ ὑπεροχὴν λόγου ἢ σοφίας = "with superiority of speech or of wisdom" (BDAG κατά B5bβ; ὑπεροχή 1) (cp. λόγου, 1:17)

2:2 | οὐ ἔκρινά τι εἰδέναι = "I decided to know nothing" (ESV) (BDAG κρίνω 4)

2:4 | Textual problem: Either (1) ἐν πειθοῖ σοφίας (omitting everything in brackets in NA) = "with the persuasiveness of wisdom" (taking πειθοῖ as dat. sg. of noun πειθώ), or (2) ἐν πειθοῖς σοφίας λόγοις = "with persuasive words of wisdom" (taking πειθοῖς as substantival dat. pl. of adj. πειθός, a word found nowhere but here) (see Metzger; BDAG πειθός; BDF §§47(4), 112)

2:6 | σοφίαν δέ = "a wisdom, however" (NASB), explanatory adversative δέ (BDAG δέ 4a; BDF §447(8))

2:7 | σοφίαν ἐν μυστηρίῳ, τὴν ἀποκεκρυμμένην = "wisdom in a mystery, the hidden [wisdom]" | εἰς δόξαν ἡμῶν = "for our [eschatological] glory" (BDAG δόξα 1cβ)

2:8 | εἰ γὰρ ἔγνωσαν, οὐκ ἄν ... ἐσταύρωσαν = "for if they had understood it, they would not have crucified the Lord of glory," unreal or contrary-to-fact conditional (BDF §360)

2:9 | ἀναβαίνω ἐπὶ καρδίαν = "enter one's mind," Septuagintism (LXX 4 Kgdms 12:5; Isa 65:16; Jer 3:16; 51:21) (BDAG ἀναβαίνω 2)

2:10 | καί = "even" (BDAG καί 2b)

2:11 | τίς ... ἀνθρώπων = "who among humans?" partitive gen.

2:11–12 | τὸ πνεῦμα ... τό (2x) = "the s/Spirit that," second article as relative pronoun

2:13 | ἐν διδακτοῖς λόγοις + gen. (2x) = "in words taught by" | πνευματικοῖς πνευματικὰ συγκρίνοντες = "expressing spiritual truths in spiritual words" (NIV 1984), but συγκρίνω can also mean "combine, compare, or interpret" (see BDAG)

2:16 | ὃς συμβιβάσει αὐτόν = "so as to instruct him" (ESV), qualitative-consecutive relative clause (BDF §379)

1 Corinthians 3

3:1–2 | Augment of δύναμαι vacillates between ἠ- and ἐ- (BDF §66(3))

3:2 | γάλα ὑμᾶς ἐπότισα = "I gave you milk to drink" | οὔπω ἐδύνασθε = "you were not yet able [to eat meat]" | ἀλλ' οὐδὲ ἔτι νῦν δύνασθε = "Indeed, even now you are not yet able" (NASB) (BDAG ἀλλά 3)

3:3 | ὅπου = "insofar as," "since" (BDAG ὅπου 3) | κατὰ ἄνθρωπον = "in a human way" (ESV)

3:10 | ἕκαστος βλεπέτω πῶς ἐποικοδομεῖ = "let each one take care how he builds on it" (ESV) (BDAG βλέπω 6)

3:11 | ἄλλον ... παρά + acc. = "another than" (BDAG παρά C3)

3:13 | ἡ ἡμέρα = "the day of judgment"

3:15 | οὕτως δὲ ὡς διὰ πυρός = lit. "yet so as through fire" (NASB), i.e., "but only as one escaping through the flames" (NIV 1984); οὕτως implies repetition of σωθήσεται (BDAG διά A1b; ὡς 1a) (cp. 1 Pet 3:20)

3:19 | παρά + dat. = "in the sight of" (BDAG παρά B2)

3:20 | Prolepsis (BDF §476)

3:21 | ὥστε = "so then"

1 Corinthians 4

4:1 | οὕτως ... ὡς = "in this manner ... as"

4:2 | ὧδε = "here, in this case" | λοιπόν = "moreover," adv. acc. | ζητεῖται ἐν τοῖς οἰκονόμοις ἵνα = "it is required in the case of managers that" (BDAG ζητέω 4; ἐν 8); substantival ἵνα clause (W 474–5)

4:3 | ἐμοὶ εἰς ἐλάχιστόν ἐστιν = "it is of little importance to me" (BDAG εἰμί 2cβ) ethical dat. (W 146); Semitic εἰς (BDF §145); superlative ἐλάχιστος for elative (W 303) | Attenuated ἵνα equivalent to inf. (BDAG ἵνα 2b) | ἀνθρωπίνη ἡμέρα = "a human court" (BDAG ἡμέρα 3ba)

4:4 | οὐδὲν ἐμαυτῷ σύνοιδα = "I am conscious of nothing against myself" (NASB), "my conscience is clear" (NIV), dat. of disadvantage (W 160 n54)

4:5 | ὥστε = "therefore" | μὴ πρὸς καιροῦ τι κρίνετε ἕως ἂν ἔλθῃ ὁ κύριος = either (1) "do not pronounce judgment before the time, before the Lord comes" (ESV), but ἕως + subj. does not mean "before," or (2) supply missing thought: "do not go on passing judgment before the time, [but wait] until the Lord comes" (NASB)

4:6 | ἐν ἡμῖν = "by considering our case" (M 77) (cp. 9:15) | τό functions as quote marks | εἷς ὑπὲρ τοῦ ἑνὸς κατὰ τοῦ ἑτέρου = "each one on behalf of one against the other" (BDF §247(4))

4:7 | εἰ δὲ καὶ ἔλαβες = "but if you did receive it" (BDAG εἰ 6c) | ὡς μὴ λαβών = "as if you had not received it" (BDAG ὡς 3b) (cp. v. 18)

4:8 | ὄφελόν γε ἐβασιλεύσατε = "indeed, I wish that you had become kings" (NASB); ὄφελον has become a fixed form functioning as a particle expressing an unattainable wish (BDAG ὄφελον; BDF §359(1))

4:11 | ἄχρι τῆς ἄρτι ὥρας = "to this very hour"

4:13 | ἕως ἄρτι = "until now," "up to the present"

4:14 | οὐκ ἐντρέπων ὑμᾶς = "not to shame you," final or telic ptc. (BDF §418(4); W 635)

4:15 | "For though you have countless guides in Christ, you do not have many fathers" (ESV)

4:18 | ὡς μὴ ἐρχομένου μου πρὸς ὑμᾶς = "as if I were not coming to you," gen. abs. (BDAG ὡς 3b)

4:19 | γνώσομαι ... δύναμιν = "I will find out not the talk of these arrogant people but their power" (ESV)

4:20 | οὐκ [ἐστιν] ἐν = "is not a matter of" (NIV; M 79)

4:21 | ἔλθω; = "shall I come?" deliberative subj. | ἐν ῥάβδῳ = "with a rod" (BDAG ἐν 5aβ) | ἐν ἀγάπῃ πνεύματί τε πραΰτητος = "in love and and with a gentle spirit" (NIV) (BDAG ἐν 11)

1 Corinthians 5

5:1 | ὅλως ἀκούεται = either (1) "it is bandied about *everywhere* [that there is]" (BDAG ὅλως 1), or (2) "it is *actually* reported [that there is]" (BDAG ὅλως 2) | τοιαύτη ... ἥτις = "of such a kind that" | Epexegetic ὥστε = "that" (M 140) | γυναῖκά τινα τοῦ πατρὸς ἔχειν = "someone has his father's wife," with acc. τινα as subject of inf.

5:2 | πεφυσιωμένοι ἐστέ – perf. periphrastic (W 649) | καὶ οὐχὶ μᾶλλον ἐπενθήσατε = "and have not mourned instead" (NASB), taking οὐχί as simple negative (BDAG οὐχί 1); the usual interrogative mng. of οὐχί (BDAG οὐχί 3) yields nonsense, "and have you not mourned instead?" (but see ESV/NIV for attempts to make it work) | ὁ ... πράξας – substantival aorist ptc.

5:3 | μέν ... δέ = "though absent ... but present" | ὡς παρών = either (1) "as if present" (BDAG ὡς 3b), or (2) "as actually present" (Fee) (BDAG ὡς 3aα)

5:4 | συναχθέντων ὑμῶν καὶ τοῦ ἐμοῦ πνεύματος = "when you and my spirit are assembled together," gen. abs. | σὺν τῇ δυνάμει τοῦ κυρίου ἡμῶν Ἰησοῦ = "and the power of our Lord Jesus is present" (NIV)

5:5 | παραδοῦναι is difficult: either (1) imperatival inf. (NIV, ESV; BDF §389), or (2) supply κέκρικα – "[I have decided] to deliver" (NASB)

5:8 | ὥστε = "therefore" | ἑορτάζωμεν – hortatory subj. | ἄζυμα = "the feast of unleavened bread," Semitic pl.

5:10 | ἐπεὶ ἄρα = "for otherwise, you see" (BDAG ἐπεί 2) (cp. 7:14)

5:11 | ἔγραψα – epistolary aorist (unlike v. 9; M 12)

5:12 | τί γάρ μοι τοὺς ἔξω κρίνειν; = "For what have I to do with judging outsiders?" (ESV, NASB), "What business is it of mine to judge those outside the church?" (NIV)

5:13 | κρινεῖ – future (note accent)

1 Corinthians 6

6:1 | τολμᾷ τις ὑμῶν; = "does any one of you dare?" partitive gen. | κρίνεσθαι ἐπί + gen. = "to go to law before some tribunal" (cp. v. 6) (BDAG κρίνω 5aβ; ἐπί 3)

6:2 | κρινοῦσιν – future | ἐν ὑμῖν = either (1) "by you," ἐν + dat. to express agent, or (2) "in your court," dat. of sphere (W 374 n50) | κρίνεται = "is to be judged" (ESV), futuristic present (W 536) | ἀνάξιοί ἐστε κριτηρίων ἐλαχίστων; = either (1) "Are you not competent to constitute the smallest law courts?" (NASB), or (2)

"Are you incompetent to try trivial cases?" (ESV) – depending on whether κριτήριον is taken to mean "lawcourt" or "lawsuit" (BDAG κριτήριον 1–2) (same options in v. 4)

6:3 | μήτιγε = μήτι γε = "not to mention, let alone" (BDAG μήτι)

6:4 | κριτήρια – two options (see v. 2) (NASB vs. ESV/NIV) | καθίζω = "appoint as judge" (BDAG καθίζω 2); καθίζετε could be imperative (NIV) or interrogative (NASB)

6:5 | οὕτως = "Do you mean to tell me that?" (BDAG οὕτως 1b) | ἀνὰ μέσον τοῦ ἀδελφοῦ αὐτοῦ = lit. "between his brother," but should be rendered "between brothers." The usual construction (common in LXX; see HR) is ἀνὰ μέσον + two genitives joined by καί (with optional repetition of ἀνὰ μέσον before second gen.; cp. LXX Ezek 18:8), or ἀνὰ μέσον + gen. pl. (cp. LXX Deut 1:16). Here the construction has been abbreviated (BDAG ἀνά 1b; μέσος 1b); written in full it would read: ἀνὰ μέσον ἀδελφοῦ καὶ (ἀνὰ μέσον) τοῦ ἀδελφοῦ αὐτοῦ (BDF §139)

6:6 | κρίνεσθαι μετά + gen. = "to go to law with (or against) someone" (BDAG κρίνω 5aβ; μετά A2cβ)

6:7 | "Actually, then, it is already a defeat for you, that you have lawsuits with one another. Why not rather be wronged? Why not rather be defrauded?" (NASB)

6:9 | ἀρσενοκοίτης < ἄρσην ("male") + κοίτη ("bed, intercourse") (cp. μετὰ ἄρσενος κοίτην γυναικός, LXX Lev 18:22; 20:13)

6:12 | ἔξεστιν + dat. (2x) = "be permitted to one," "be lawful for one" (libertine slogan quoted by Paul, then met with his own)

6:13 | καί ... καί = "both ... and" (cp. v. 14)

6:14 | καὶ τὸν κύριον ἤγειρεν καὶ ἡμᾶς ἐξεγερεῖ = God "has not only raised the Lord, but will also raise us" (NASB), καί ... καί = "not only ... but also"

6:15 | ποιήσω – deliberative subj.

6:16 | Semitic εἰς (BDF §145; BDAG εἰς 8)

6:18 | Paul may again be quoting and refuting a libertine slogan (M 196–7)

6:20 | τιμῆς – gen. of price (cp. 7:23) | δοξάσατε – constative aorist impv. (W 720–1)

1 Corinthians 7

7:1 | περὶ δὲ ὧν ἐγράψατε = "now concerning [the matters] that you wrote [about]" | γυναικός – verbs of touching take gen. | ἅπτομαι normally means "touch," here with sexual connotation (BDAG ἅπτομαι 4)

7:2 | διὰ τὰς πορνείας (pl.) = "because of the temptation to sexual immorality" (ESV), "since there is so much immorality" (NIV 1984); other MSS have διὰ τὴν πορνείαν (sg.) | ἕκαστος ... ἑκάστη = "each man ... each woman"

7:4 | ἐξουσιάζω takes gen.

7:5 | εἰ μήτι ἂν ἐκ συμφώνου = "except perhaps by agreement" (BDAG I. ἄν f); εἰ μήτι ἄν is a unit (BDAG εἰ 6j); hypothetical modification of εἰ μήτι by analogy with ὅστις ἄν (BDF §376) | ἐκ συμφώνου = "by mutual consent," adverbial (BDAG ἐκ 6c)

7:7 | ὡς καὶ ἐμαυτόν = "even as myself" (cp. v. 8) | ὁ μὲν οὕτως, ὁ δὲ οὕτως = "one in this manner, and another in that" (NASB)

7:8 | ὡς κἀγώ = ὡς καὶ ἐγώ = "even as I" (cp. v. 7)

7:9 | Comparative + ἐστίν + inf. + ἤ + inf. = "it is better to x than to y" (BDAG ἤ 2a) (cp. 9:15)

7:10 | τοῖς γεγαμηκόσιν = "to the married"

7:14 | Hebr./instrumental ἐν (2x) (BDF §219) | ἐστίν (2x) – neut. pl. subjects take sg. verbs | ἐπεὶ ἄρα = "for otherwise, you see" (see 5:10)

7:15 | χωριζέσθω "let him depart," permissive impv. (W 488–9) (cp. v. 36) | ἐν τοῖς τοιούτοις = "in such cases" | ἐν εἰρήνῃ = "to live in peace" (NIV; cp. M 79)

7:16 | τί οἶδας; (2x) = "how do you know?" | γύναι, ἄνερ – vocatives

7:17 | εἰ μή = "nevertheless" (NIV), "only" (ESV, NASB)

7:21 | μᾶλλον χρῆσαι is elliptical, since χράομαι needs a dat. object. Two main options: (1) supply τῇ δουλείᾳ or τῇ κλήσει – "but even if (ἀλλ᾽ εἰ καί) you are able to become free, rather (μᾶλλον) make use of [your bondage or your calling]" (cp. NRSV) (concessive use of εἰ καί – cp. 2 Cor 4:16; 7:8 [3x]; 12:11; see M 167; BDAG εἰ 6e; W 663 n16); or (2) supply τῇ ἐλευθερίᾳ – "but if (ἀλλ᾽ εἰ) you are also able (καὶ δύνασαι) to become free, by all means (μᾶλλον) avail yourself of [your freedom]" (most English versions) (not taking εἰ καί as a phrase; καί as adv. modifying δύνασαι)

7:23 | τιμῆς – gen. of price (cp. 6:20)

7:25 | ὡς ἠλεημένος ... εἶναι – "as one who by the Lord's mercy is trustworthy" (ESV)

7:26 | τὸ οὕτως εἶναι – articular inf. in which τό is anaphoric, linking back to τοῦτο (BDF §399(1)) = "I think then that this is good in view of the present distress, that it is good for a man to remain as he is" (NASB)

7:28 | φείδομαι takes gen. (ὑμῶν)

29 | τὸ λοιπόν = "from now on" | Imperatival ἵνα (BDAG ἵνα 2g; BDF §387(3)) + ὦσιν = "those who have wives *should be* as though they had none" (NASB)

7:34 | μεμέρισται = "his interests are divided" (ESV) | καί ... καί = "both ... and"

7:35 | οὐχ ἵνα βρόχον ὑμῖν ἐπιβάλω = "not to put a restraint on you" (NASB) | πρὸς τὸ εὔσχημον καὶ εὐπάρεδρον – substantivized adjectives (BDF §263) = "to promote good order and to secure your undivided devotion to the Lord" (ESV) (BDAG πρός 3cα)

7:36 | ἀσχημονέω ἐπί + acc. = "behave improperly toward" | ἐὰν ᾖ ὑπέρακμος = either (1) "if his passions are strong" (ESV), or (2) "if she is past marriageable age," ὑπέρακμος can be either masc. or fem. (two-termination adj.) (see BDAG ὑπέρακμος 1–2) | καὶ οὕτως ὀφείλει γίνεσθαι = "and if it must be so" (NASB) | γαμείτωσαν = "let them marry," permissive impv. (W 488–9) (cp. v. 15)

7:36–37 | παρθένος = either (1) "virgin daughter" (NASB), or (2) "virgin to whom one is engaged" (cp. NIV, ESV); correspondingly, τις would refer either to the virgin's father or the man engaged to the virgin

7:37 | ἐξουσίαν ἔχειν περί τινος = "be at liberty w.r.t. a thing" (BDAG ἐξουσία 1) | τηρεῖν τὴν παρθένον = "to keep his virgin inviolate as such" (BDAG τηρέω 2b), which fits either interpretation of παρθένος

7:38 | καί ... καί = "both ... and" | γαμίζω = can mean (1) "marry," or (2) "give in marriage" (consistent with the two mngs. of παρθένος)

7:39 | δέδεται – gnomic perf. (W 580) | ἐφ᾽ ὅσον χρόνον = "as long as" (cp. Rom 7:1) (BDAG ἐπί 18cβ) | ᾧ θέλει γαμηθῆναι = "to be married to whom she wishes" (ESV)

7:40 | ἐὰν οὕτως μείνῃ = "if she remains as she is" | κατὰ τὴν ἐμὴν γνώμην = "in my judgment" (ESV, BDAG γνώμη 2)

1 Corinthians 8

8:5 | καὶ γὰρ εἴπερ = "for even if," concessive (BDF §454(2)) | λεγόμενοι = "so-called"

8:6 | ἡμῖν = "for us," ethical dat. (W 146) | ἡμεῖς εἰς αὐτόν ... ἡμεῖς δι᾽ αὐτοῦ = "we [exist, or live spiritually] for him ... we [exist, or live spiritually] through him," the reason "live spiritually" is an option is bec. ἡμεῖς seems to mean "we the saved"

8:7 | οὐκ ἐν πᾶσιν ἡ γνῶσις = "not all possess this knowledge" (ESV), anaphoric article (W 217) | τῇ συνηθείᾳ ἕως ἄρτι τοῦ εἰδώλου = "because they are still accustomed to the idol," dat. of cause (BDF §196) | ὡς εἰδωλόθυτον = "as really offered to an idol" (ESV) (BDAG ὡς 3aα)

8:8 | οὔτε ... οὔτε = "neither ... nor" | περισσεύω = "have more [divine approval]" (BDAG), "be better off" (ESV)

8:9 | βλέπετε μή πως ἡ ἐξουσία ὑμῶν αὕτη πρόσκομμα γένηται = "take care lest this right of yours somehow becomes a stumbling block," αὕτη goes with ἡ ἐξουσία (BDAG βλέπω 5; cp. 10:12)

8:10 | σὲ τὸν ἔχοντα γνῶσιν = "you who have knowledge" | ἀσθενοῦς ὄντος = "if it is weak," conditional gen. abs. | οἰκοδομέω is used ironically – "will not his conscience be 'strengthened'?" (BDAG) | εἰς τό + inf. = "so as to," expressing result

8:11 | Hebr./instrumental ἐν (BDF §219)

8:12 | "When you sin against your brothers in this way and wound their weak conscience, you sin against Christ" (NIV 1984)

8:13 | οὐ μή + subj. + εἰς τὸν αἰῶνα = "I will never ..." (emphatic negation)

1 Corinthians 9

9:2 | ἄλλοις & ὑμῖν – ethical datives | ἀλλά γε = "at least" (BDAG ἀλλά 4a; BDF §439(2)) | μου τῆς ἀποστολῆς = τῆς ἀποστολῆς μου

9:4–6 | ἐξουσία + inf. (3x) = "the right to" (BDAG ἐξουσία 1; BDF §400(1))

9:4–5 | μὴ οὐκ ἔχομεν ἐξουσίαν = "are we without-the-right ...?" "οὐκ-ἔχομεν is a closely-coalescing phrase, while the μή is a separate particle, introducing a question expecting the answer 'No'" (M 156) (cp. 11:22)

9:6 | "Or is it only Barnabas and I who have no right to refrain from working for a living?" (ESV)

9:7 | ἰδίοις ὀψωνίοις = "at his own expense," dat. of means (W 162) | ἐσθίω ἐκ (for partitive gen.) = "get sustenance from" (BDAG ἐσθίω 1bβ; ἐκ 4aε)

9:8 | μή expects negative answer – "I am not ... am I?" | κατὰ ἄνθρωπον = "from a human standpoint" (BDAG ἄνθρωπος 2b) (cp. Rom 3:5; Gal 3:15) | ἢ καὶ ὁ νόμος ταῦτα οὐ λέγει; = "Or does not the Law *also* say these things?" (NASB)

9:9 | μέλει (used impersonally) + gen. of thing about which concern is felt + dat. of person to whom it is a concern – "God is not concerned about oxen, is he?" (NASB)

9:10 | ἢ δι' ἡμᾶς πάντως λέγει; = "Or is he speaking altogether for our sake?" (NASB) | ὅτι = "because" | ὀφείλει + two infs. (ἀροτριάν & τοῦ μετέχειν) = "ought to plow ... to partake," pleonastic τοῦ (BDF §400(7)) | ἐπ' ἐλπίδι (2x) = "in hope"

9:11 | μέγα εἰ = "is it an extraordinary thing if ...?" (BDAG μέγας 5)

9:12 | τῆς ὑμῶν ἐξουσίας = "the right over you" (NASB), taking ὑμῶν as objective gen. (BDAG ἐξουσία 1), i.e., the right to receive financial support from you | οὐ μᾶλλον ἡμεῖς; = "do not we even more?" (ESV)

9:12, 15 | χράομαι takes dat. (2x)

9:14 | οὕτως καί = "so also," or "in the same way" (NIV) | ζάω ἐκ + gen. = "obtain one's living from" (BDAG ζάω 1b)

9:15 | οὐκ ἔγραψα = "I am not writing," epistolary aorist | ἐν ἐμοί = "in my case" (BDAG ἐν 8; M 77) (cp. 4:6) | καλόν + dat. + inf. + μᾶλλον ἤ = "it would be better for one to x than" (BDAG καλός 2dγ; ἤ 2a) | Textual problem: Paul breaks off sentence after ἤ due to strong emotion (aposiopesis [BDF §482]), but scribes tried to rescue the construction by changing οὐδεὶς κενώσει to ἵνα τις κενώσῃ (see Metzger)

9:16 | οὐκ ἔστιν μοι καύχημα = "I have no ground for boasting," dat. of possession

9:17 | οἰκονομίαν πεπίστευμαι = "I have been entrusted with a stewardship" (cp. Gal 2:7), pass. + acc. of retained object (W 438; BDF §159(4))

9:18 | Epexegetical ἵνα explaining μισθός (W 476) | ἵνα + future (M 139) | εὐαγγελιζόμενος = "when I preach the gospel," "in my preaching of the gospel," temporal adverbial ptc. (W 623)

9:19 | ἐλεύθερος ὤν = "although I am free," concessive ptc. (W 634)

9:21 | ἔννομος Χριστοῦ = "under the law of Christ" (NASB, ESV), "subject to the jurisdiction of Christ" (BDAG ἔννομος)

9:24 | οἱ ... τρέχοντες = "the runners" | μέν ... δέ = "all run, but only one receives the prize"

9:25 | πάντα = "in all things," acc. of respect

9:26 | οὕτως ... ὡς (2x) = "in such a way ... as," ὡς refers back to οὕτως (BDAG οὕτως 2; ὡς 1bα) (cp. 3:15; 4:1)

1 Corinthians 10

10:2 | ἐβαπτίσθησαν εἰς – probably means "baptized in the name of" (cp. 1:13, 15), or "in reference to" (cp. Rom 6:3) (BDAG εἰς 5)

10:4 | πίνω ἐκ = "drink of/from," ἐκ for partitive gen.

10:5 | εὐδοκέω ἐν τινι = "be well pleased with someone" (BDAG εὐδοκέω 2a)

10:6 | τύποι ἡμῶν = either (1) "examples for us" (NASB, ESV) (BDAG τύπος 6b), or (2) "types prefiguring us" (BDAG τύπος 6c) (cp. τυπικῶς, v. 11) | ἐπιθυμητὰς κακῶν = "those who desire/crave evil things," objective gen. | κἀκεῖνοι = καὶ ἐκεῖνοι

10:8–9 | πορνεύωμεν, ἐκπειράζωμεν – hortatory subjunctives

10:8 | μιᾷ ἡμέρᾳ = "in a single day," dat. of time when (W 155)

10:11 | ταῦτα ... συνέβαινεν ... ἐγράφη – neut. pl. subjects take sg. verbs | πρὸς νουθεσίαν ἡμῶν = "for our intruction," objective gen. | τὰ τέλη τῶν αἰώνων = either (1) "the end of the ages" (BDAG τέλος 2a; αἰών 2b), or (2) "the culmination of the ages" (NIV 2011)

10:12 | ὥστε = "therefore" | BDAG βλέπω 5 (cp. 8:9)

10:13 | ὑπὲρ ὃ δύνασθε = "beyond what you are able [to endure]" | ποιέω τὴν ἔκβασιν = "provide a way out" (BDAG ποιέω 2c) | τοῦ δύνασθαι ὑπενεγκεῖν = "so that you will be able to endure it" (BDF §400(2))

10:16 | κοινωνία + gen. (2x) = "a participation in"

10:20 | ἀλλ᾽ = "no, but" (BDAG ἀλλά 3)

10:22 | αὐτοῦ = "than he," gen. of comparison

10:23 | πάντα (4x) – neut. pl. subjects take sg. verbs | ἔξεστιν (2x) = "is (are) permitted/lawful"

10:25 | πᾶν τὸ ἐν μακέλλῳ πωλούμενον = "everything sold in the meat market"

10:27 | τις ... τῶν ἀπίστων = "one of the unbelievers"

10:30 | ὑπὲρ οὗ = "concerning [that] for which" (NASB)

10:33 | τὸ τῶν πολλῶν = "the [benefit] of the many"

1 Corinthians 11

11:2 | πάντα = "in everything," acc. of respect | μιμνῄσκομαι + gen. of person remembered (μου)

11:4 | κατὰ κεφαλῆς ἔχων = lit. "having [something (e.g., a veil) hanging] down from his head" (BDAG κατά A1a; BDF §225)

11:5 | ἀκατακαλύπτῳ τῇ κεφαλῇ = "with her head uncovered," associative dat. (BDF §198(3)) | ἓν γάρ ἐστιν καὶ τὸ αὐτὸ τῇ ἐξυρημένῃ = "for it is one and the same as she who is shaven," neut. bec. viewed as class and in abstract (BDF §131); dat. used with adj. of identity (BDF §194)

11:6 | καὶ κειράσθω = "then let her cut [her hair] off," apodotic καί (BDAG καί 1bδ)

11:7 | τὴν κεφαλήν = "with respect to his head," acc. of respect | ὑπάρχων = "since he is," causal ptc.

11:9 | καὶ γάρ = "neither" (ESV) (BDF §452(3))

11:10 | ἐξουσία ἐπὶ τῆς κεφαλῆς is highly contested – four main options: (1) "freedom over her head to do as she wishes," (2) "as a means of exercising authority," as a sign of her new liberty in Christ to pray and prophesy; (3) taking ἐξουσία as metonym for "veil," (4) "a symbol of authority on her head" (ESV, NASB), "a covering ... to show she is under authority" (New Living Translation)

11:13 | ἐν ὑμῖν αὐτοῖς κρίνατε = "judge for yourselves"

11:14–15 | μέν ... δέ (cp. v. 21)

11:15 | ἀντὶ περιβολαίου = "as/for a covering" (BDAG ἀντί 2)

11:16 | εἰ τις δοκεῖ φιλόνεικος εἶναι = "if anyone is inclined to be contentious" (ESV) (BDAG δοκέω 1b) | τοιαύτην συνήθειαν οὐκ ἔχομεν = either (1) "we have no [*other*] practice" (NASB), referring to women wearing a veil; or (2) "we have no *such* practice" (ESV), referring to being argumentative

11:17 | τοῦτο παραγγέλλων = "in giving this instruction" (NASB)

11:18 | πρῶτον μέν – adv. acc. enumerating a series (BDAG πρῶτος 1bβ), but here w/o a "second" or "third" (cp. Rom 1:8; 3:2) | συνερχομένων ὑμῶν ἐν ἐκκλησίᾳ = "when you come together as a church," gen. abs. (cp. v. 20) | μέρος τι = "in part," adv. acc.

11:20 | συνέρχομαι ἐπὶ τὸ αὐτό = "come together" (cp. 14:23)

11:21 | ἐν τῷ φαγεῖν = "as you eat" (BDF §404(1)) | ὃς μέν ... ὃς δέ = "one ... another"

11:22 | μὴ οἰκίας οὐκ ἔχετε; = "do you not have houses?" (see 9:4–5) | κατα-φρονέω takes gen.

11:24 | τοῦτό μού ἐστιν τὸ σῶμα = τοῦτό ἐστιν τὸ σῶμά μου (Matt 26:26 || Mk 14:22 || Lk 22:19)

11:24–25 | εἰς τὴν ἐμὴν ἀνάμνησιν (2x) = "in remembrance of me"

11:25 | μετὰ τό + inf. = "after" (BDF §402(3))

11:25–26 | ὁσάκις ἐάν + subj. (2x) = "as often as" (cp. Rev 11:6)

11:26 | ἄχρις οὗ + subj. = "until"

11:27 | ὥστε = "therefore" (cp. v. 33) | ὃς ἄν + subj. = "whoever" | ἀναξίως = "in a careless manner" (BDAG) (see Fee)

11:28 | καὶ οὕτως = "and in so doing" (NASB) | ἐσθίω/πίνω ἐκ = "eat/drink of" (see 10:4)

11:29 | μὴ διακρίνων = "if one does not discern," conditional ptc. | Given the near reference to "the body and blood of the Lord" (v. 26), διακρίνων τὸ σῶμα probably refers to discerning the mng. of the sacramental elements, rather than recognizing the corporate body of believers (cp. 10:17)

11:30 | ἐν ὑμῖν = "among you" | κοιμῶνται ἱκανοί = "quite a few have fallen asleep" (BDAG ἱκανός 4)

11:31 | Second class (contrary-to-fact) condition (W 694–6) | οὐκ ἂν ἐκρινόμεθα = "we would not come under such judgment" (NIV 2011)

11:32–33 | κρινόμενοι (= "when we are judged") & συνερχόμενοι (= "when you come together") – temporal adv. ptcs.

11:34 | ὡς ἄν + subj. = "when," "as soon as" (M 133; BDF §455(2); BDAG ὡς 8cα) | τὰ λοιπά ... διατάξομαι = either (1) "I will put in order the remaining matters" (BDAG διατάσσω 1), or (2) "I will give instructions concerning the remaining matters" (BDAG διατάσσω 2)

1 Corinthians 12

12:2 | ὅτε ἔθνη ἦτε = "when you were pagans" | πρὸς τὰ εἴδωλα τὰ ἄφρωνα ὡς ἂν ἤγεσθε ἀπαγόμενοι – difficult; most likely, we are to take the ptc. as a substitute for the finite verb (BDF §468(2)), or understand ἦτε as repeated with the ptc. (impf. periphrastic): "whenever you were led ... you were being led away/astray" | ὡς ἄν = "whenever," denotes repetition (BDF §367; BDAG ἄγω 3) | For similar use of ἄγω in reference to being under the influence of superhuman spiritual forces, cp. Lk 4:1, 9; Rom 8:14; Gal 5:18; 2 Tim 3:6 | πρὸς τὰ εἴδωλα could be taken with ἤγεσθε or ἀπαγόμενοι

12:3, 9, 13 | Hebr./instrumental ἐν (5x) – "by the Spirit"

12:4–6 | Trinitarian formula: Spirit, Lord, God (cp. Eph 4:4–6)

12:6, 11 | ἐνεργέω τὰ πάντα (2x) = "produce/effect all [these gifts]"

12:7 | πρὸς τὸ συμφέρον = "for the common good"

12:11 | τὸ ἓν καὶ τὸ αὐτὸ πνεῦμα = "one and the same Spirit" | ἰδίᾳ ἑκάστῳ = "to each particular individual" (BDAG ἴδιος 5)

12:12 | Neut. pl. subjects take sg. verbs (also vv. 19, 22–24, 26) | πολλὰ ὄντα = "though many," concessive ptc.

12:15–16 | οὐ παρὰ τοῦτο οὐκ ἔστιν ἐκ τοῦ σώματος (2x) = "it

is not for this reason any the less a part of the body" (NASB); the two
negatives reinforce each other (BDAG παρά C5)

12:18 | ἓν ἕκαστον αὐτῶν = "each one of them"

12:22 | ἀλλὰ πολλῷ μᾶλλον = "on the contrary" | τὰ δοκοῦντα
μέλη τοῦ σώματος ἀσθενέστερα ὑπάρχειν = "the parts of the
body that seem to be weaker," would expect τὰ μέλη τοῦ σώματος
τὰ δοκοῦντα ἀσθενέστερα ὑπάρχειν (cp. Rom 8:18)

12:24 | τὰ δὲ εὐσχήμονα ἡμῶν οὐ χρείαν ἔχει = "whereas our
more presentable parts have no need [of it]" [= such special treatment]
(NASB) | τῷ ὑστερουμένῳ περισσοτέραν δοὺς τιμήν = "giving
greater honor to the part that lacked it" (ESV)

12:25 | ἵνα ... τὸ αὐτὸ ὑπὲρ ἀλλήλων μεριμνῶσιν τὰ μέλη = "so
that ... the members may have the same care for one another" (NASB)

12:27 | ἐκ μέρους = "individually," adv. (BDAG ἐκ 6c)

12:31 | ἔτι καθ᾽ ὑπερβολήν = "still more excellent" (NASB, ESV),
"far better" (BDAG ὑπερβολή)

1 Corinthians 13
13:2 | οὐθέν = οὐδέν

13:3 | κἄν = καὶ ἐάν | τὰ ὑπάρχοντά μου = "my possessions" |
Textual problem (see Metzger): (1) ἵνα καυχήσωμαι = "that I may
boast," or (2) ἵνα καυθήσομαι = "that I should be burned," ἵνα + future (BDF §369(2))

13:4 | περπερεύομαι = "behave as a πέρπερος, a braggart, a
windbag" (BDAG)

13:5 | τὰ ἑαυτῆς = "its own [interests]" | οὐ λογίζεται τὸ κακόν

= "love keeps no score of wrongs" (BDAG λογίζομαι 1a, quoting the Revised English Bible)

13:6 | BDAG ἐπί 6c

13:9, 12 | ἐκ μέρους (2x) = "in part," adv. (BDAG ἐκ 6c)

13:10 | τὸ ἐκ μέρους = "the partial, the imperfect"

13:11 | λογιζόμαι = "reason" | τὰ τοῦ νηπίου = "childish things/ways"

13:12 | ἐν αἰνίγματι = "indirectly" (BDAG), "only a reflection" (NIV 2011) (possible allusion to LXX Num 12:8, although αἴνιγμα used with different shade of mng.) | καθὼς καὶ ἐπεγνώσθην = "just as I *also* have been fully known" (NASB)

13:13 | μείζων = "greatest," comparative for superlative (W 299; BDAG μέγας 4b)

1 Corinthians 14
14:1 | μᾶλλον δέ = "but especially" (not "rather") (cp. v. 5)

14:1, 5, 12, 13 | Attenuated ἵνα = "that" or "to" (BDAG ἵνα 2)

14:2 | ἀκούω = "hear and understand" (BDAG ἀκούω 7)

14:5 | μᾶλλον δέ = "but even more" (cp. v. 1) | ἤ = "than" (also v. 19) | ἐκτὸς εἰ μή + subj. = "unless"

14:6 | τί ὑμᾶς ὠφελήσω = "what will I benefit you?" | ἢ ἐν ἀποκαλύψει ἤ ... "either by way of revelation or of ... or of ... or of ..." (NASB)

14:7–8 | δίδωμι φωνήν (2x) = "produce a sound" (BDAG δίδωμι 4)

14:7 | "Yet even lifeless things, either flute or harp, in producing a sound, if they do not produce a distinction in the tones, how will it be known what is played on the flute or on the harp?" (NASB)

14:8 | ἄδηλον φωνήν = "an indistinct sound"

14:9 | διὰ τῆς γλώσσης – "So also you, *with the tongue*, unless you utter intelligible speech," comparison between lifeless instruments and the human tongue (BDAG γλῶσσα 1; διά A3a/c) | πῶς γνωσθήσεται τὸ λαλούμενον; = "how will it be known what is spoken?" (NASB) | ἔσεσθε … λαλοῦντες = "you will be speaking," future periphrastic (W 648–9)

14:10 | εἰ τύχοι = "doubtless" (ESV), "probably" (BDAG τυγχάνω 2b), "perhaps" (ZG); conditional optative (W 484) qualifying τοσαῦτα (cp. 15:37)

14:10–11 | γένη φωνῶν = "kinds of phonetic sounds" | ἐὰν οὖν μὴ εἰδῶ τὴν δύναμιν τῆς φωνῆς = "If then I do not grasp the meaning of what someone is saying" (NIV) (BDAG δύναμις 6) | NASB, ESV render φωνή as "language(s)" in both verses, which also yields a good sense (BDAG φωνή 3)

14:11 | ἐν ἐμοί = "in my eyes," ἐν for simple dat. (BDF §220(1))

14:12 | ζηλωταί πνευμάτων = "zealous/eager for spiritual gifts," objective gen. | ζητεῖτε ἵνα περισσεύητε = "strive to excel" (ESV; BDAG περισσεύω 1bα)

14:15 | τί οὖν ἐστιν; = "What, then, is to be done?" (BDAG οὖν 1cβ) (also v. 26)

14:16 | ἐπεί = "otherwise" (cp. 15:29) | "The ἰδιῶται are neither similar to the ἄπιστοι, nor are they full-fledged Christians, but stand between the two groups, probably as prospects for membership" (BDAG ἰδιώτης 2)

14:17 | μέν ... ἀλλά = "to be sure ... but" (BDAG μέν 1aβ) | καλῶς = "well enough"

14:18 | πάντων ὑμῶν μᾶλλον = "more than you all," gen. of comparison

14:19 | θέλω + inf. ... ἤ = "I would rather do x ... than" (BDAG ἤ 2bα)

14:20 | ταῖς φρεσίν (2x) & τῇ κακίᾳ – datives of reference/respect (W 144–6)

14:21 | καὶ οὐδ᾽ οὕτως + future = "and even then they will not listen to me" (ESV)

14:22 | εἰς σημεῖον = "intended as a sign" (M 70)

14:23 | συνέρχομαι ἐπὶ τὸ αὐτό = "come together" (cp. 11:20)

14:25 | τὰ κρυπτά ... γίνεται – neut. pl. subjects take sg. verbs | ὅτι recititative

14:27 | κατὰ δύο ἢ τὸ πλεῖστον τρεῖς = "two or, at most, three at a time" (BDAG κατά B3a); τὸ πλεῖστον – adv. acc. (BDAG πολύς 3bβ) | ἀνὰ μέρος = "one at a time" (NIV), or "in turn" (BDAG ἀνά 2)

14:31 | καθ᾽ ἕνα = "one by one" (ESV)

14:38 | "If he ignores this, he himself will be ignored" (NIV 1984)

1 Corinthians 15

15:2 | τίνι λόγῳ εὐηγγελισάμην ὑμῖν εἰ κατέχετε – difficult. Many English versions switch word order and have something like, "if you hold fast to the word I preached to you." But this ignores τίνι, and κατέχω normally takes acc. (cp. 11:2) not dat. A better solution is to take this clause as reaching back to Γνωρίζω: "I make know to you ...

with what word (or form of words) I preached to you, provided you hold
it fast" (Fee; Barrett) | εἰκῇ here could mean (1) "in vain, to no purpose,"
or (2) "without due consideration, in a haphazard manner" (BDAG)

15:3 | ἐν πρώτοις = "among the first (= most important) things"
(BDAG πρῶτος 2aα; ἐν 1d)

15:4 | τῇ ἡμέρᾳ τῇ τρίτῃ = "on the third day," dat. of time when

15:6 | ἐπάνω + numbers = "more than" (BDAG ἐπάνω 2) (cp. Mk
14:5) | ἐξ ὧν οἱ πλείονες μένουσιν ἕως ἄρτι = "most of whom
are still alive" (ESV)

15:8 | ἔσχατον πάντων = "last of all," adv. acc. (cp. Mk 12:22) |
ἔκτρωμα = "a birth that violates the normal period of gestation (whether
induced as abortion, or natural premature birth or miscarriage ..., or birth
beyond term)" (BDAG) | κἀμοί = καὶ ἐμοί = "also to me"

15:10 | ἡ χάρις αὐτοῦ ἡ εἰς ἐμέ = "his grace which [was shown]
to me," second ἡ functions as relative pronoun (W 213–15) |
περισσότερον αὐτῶν πάντων ἐκοπίασα = "I worked harder than
all of them" (NIV), adv. acc. + gen. of comparison | ἡ χάρις τοῦ θεοῦ
ἡ σὺν ἐμοί = "God's grace, that came to my aid" (BDAG σύν 2)

15:12 | εἰ Χριστὸς κηρύσεται ὅτι = lit. "if Christ is preached that
...," i.e., "if it is preached that Christ ..." (NIV), prolepsis (BDF §476) |
ἐν ὑμῖν τινες = "some among you"

15:15 | εὑρισκόμεθα δὲ καὶ ψευδομάρτυρες τοῦ θεοῦ = "we
are even found to be misrepresenting God" (ESV), objective gen. |
μαρτυρέω κατὰ τινος ὅτι = "bear witness against someone by declaring that" (BDAG μαρτυρέω 1aα)

15:19 | ἠλπικότες ἐσμέν = "we have hoped," perf. periphrastic (W
649) | ἐλεεινότεροι πάντων ἀνθρώπων = (1) "of all people most

to be pitied" (ESV), comparative for superlative with partitive gen.; or (2) "to be pitied more than all men" (NIV 1984), genuine comparative with gen. of comparison

15:25 | ἄχρι οὗ + subj. = "until"

15:26 | "The last enemy to be destroyed is death" (ESV)

15:27 | δῆλον ὅτι ἐκτὸς τοῦ ὑποτάξαντος αὐτῷ τὰ πάντα = "it is evident that this does not include the one [i.e., God the Father] who put all things in subjection to him [i.e., Christ]"

15:29 | ἐπεί = "otherwise" (cp. 14:16) | εἰ ὅλως νεκροὶ οὐκ ἐγείρονται = "if the dead are not raised at all"

15:29–30 | τί καί; (2x) = "why at all, still?" καί after interrogative (Z §459; BDF §442(14))

15:31 | καθ᾿ ἡμέραν = "daily" (BDAG κατά B2c) | νὴ τὴν ὑμετέραν καύχησιν = "(I affirm that it is true) by my boasting in you," in extra-biblical Greek, νή + acc. of the divinity invoked, e.g., "I swear by Zeus" (LSJ νή)

15:32 | κατὰ ἄνθρωπον = "from human motives" (NASB), or "as a mere human being" (cp. 3:3) | θηριομαχέω could be literal (the Roman punishment *ad bestias*, in which one is condemned to fight with wild beasts in the arena), or metaphorical (Paul's struggle with Jewish opponents who wanted to kill him) (see discussion in BDAG, commentaries) | φάγωμεν & πίωμεν – deliberative subjunctives

15:33 | ὁμιλίαι κακαί is the subject; ἤθη χρηστά is the direct object

15:34 | δικαίως = "as you ought" (NASB, BDAG), "as is right" (ESV) | πρὸς ἐντροπὴν ὑμῖν = "to your shame"

Chapter Seven: The First Epistle to the Corinthians

15:36 | σὺ ὃ σπείρεις = "that which you sow" (switch order of first two words)

15:37 | εἰ τύχοι σίτου ἤ τινος τῶν λοιπῶν = "perhaps of wheat or of some other grain" (ESV) (on εἰ τύχοι, see 14:10)

15:40 | ἑτέρα μὲν ἡ ... ἑτέρα δὲ ἡ ... = "the glory of the heavenly bodies is one kind, that of the earthly bodies is another"

15:41 | ἄλλη δόξα ... καὶ ἄλλη ... καὶ ἄλλη = "there is one glory ... and another ... and another" | nom. + gen. + διαφέρει = "x differs from y" (gen. of comparison)

15:45 | ἐγένετο ... εἰς ψυχήν ... εἰς πνεῦμα – note Semitic use of εἰς as predicate nom. (BDAG εἰς 8aα); second εἰς presupposes implied repetition of verb ἐγένετο (brachylogy)

15:48 | οἷος ... τοιοῦτοι καί = "as ... so also"

15:52 | ἐν ἀτόμῳ = "in a moment," ἄτομος (< ἀ- + τέμνω) = "indivisible," here, of a moment of time so short as to be incapable of division

15:54 | εἰς νῖκος = "in victory" (BDAG εἰς 1aδ)

1 Corinthians 16
16:1 | τῆς εἰς τοὺς ἁγίους = "which is for the saints" (BDAG εἰς 4g)

16:2 | κατὰ μίαν σαββάτου = "on the first day of every week," taking κατά distributively (BDAG κατά B2c) | παρ᾽ ἑαυτῷ τίθημι = "put aside by himself," i.e., at home (BDAG παρά B1ba; τίθημι 2) | θησαυρίζων ὅ τι ἐὰν εὐοδῶται = "saving up whatever profit he makes" (Barrett) | ὅταν ... τότε = "when ... then"

16:3 | οὓς ἐάν ... τούτους = "whomever you have approved, these I will send" | δι᾽ ἐπιστολῶν = "with letters [of recommendation]," διά of attendant circumstances (ZG; BDAG διά 3c)

16:4 | ἐὰν ἄξιον ἦ τοῦ κἀμὲ πορεύεσθαι = "if it is fitting for me to go also," ἄξιος + gen. articular inf. = "fitting to" (BDF §400(3)); κἀμέ = καὶ ἐμέ (acc. subject of inf.)

16:6 | τυχόν = "perhaps," acc. absolute (BDF §424) | ἢ καί = "or even" | οὗ ἐὰν πορεύωμαι = "wherever I may go," οὗ (adv.)

16:7 | ἐν παρόδῳ = "in passing" | χρόνον τινά = "for some time," acc. for extent of time (see BDAG ἐπιμένω 1)

16:10 | ἀφόβως = "without cause to be afraid" (BDAG, NASB) | κἀγώ = καὶ ἐγώ

16:12 | παρακαλέω πολλά = "urge strongly," adv. acc. πολλά intensifies the verb | πάντως οὐκ ἦν θέλημα = "he was not at all willing" | ἵνα – final sense attenuated; functions as inf. (BDAG ἵνα 2)

16:14 | πάντα ὑμῶν = "all that you do"

16:15–16 | παρακαλῶ ὑμᾶς ... ἵνα = "I urge you ... to" (οἴδατε ... ἑαυτούς is a parenthetical comment)

16:17 | BDAG ἐπί 6c

16:18 | ἐπιγινώσκω = "give recognition to" (BDAG ἐπιγινώσκω 4)

16:19 | ἀσπάζομαι πολλά = "greet warmly" (cp. v. 12) | ἡ κατ᾽ οἶκον αὐτῶν ἐκκλησία = "the church that meets at their house" (NIV) (BDAG κατά B1a) (cp. Rom 16:5)

16:20 | Hebr./instrumental ἐν

16:23 | μεθ᾽ = μετά

Chapter Eight

The Second Epistle to the Corinthians

2 Corinthians 1

1:1 | τοῖς οὖσιν ἐν ὅλῃ τῇ Ἀχαΐᾳ = "who are throughout Achaia" (NASB)

1:4 | ἐπί + dat. – marker of time at or during which (BDAG ἐπί 18b) (cp. 3:14; 7:4) | εἰς τό + inf. + acc. (subject) = "so that we may be able" | τοὺς ἐν πάσῃ θλίψει = "those who are in *any* affliction" (BDF §275(3))

1:5 | καθώς ... οὕτως ... καί = "just as ... so also"

1:6 | ὑπέρ + gen. (2x) = "it is for," indicating purpose (BDAG ὑπέρ A1b; BDF §231(2)) | τῆς ἐνεργουμένης ... πάσχομεν = "which you experience when you patiently endure the same sufferings that we suffer" (ESV)

1:7 | ἡ ἐλπὶς ἡμῶν βεβαία ὑπὲρ ὑμῶν = "our hope for you is firm" | εἰδότες = "because we know," causal ptc. (W 631) | ὡς ... οὕτως καί = "as ... so also" | κοινωνοί ἐστε is to be understood as repeated in the second part of the comparison (brachylogy)

1:8 | ἀγνοεῖν ὑπέρ + gen. = "to be ignorant concerning" (BDAG ὑπέρ A3) | καθ' ὑπερβολήν = "exceedingly" | ὑπὲρ δύναμιν = "beyond [our] ability," ὑπέρ + acc. (BDAG ὑπέρ B) | ὥστε ἐξαπορηθῆναι ἡμᾶς καὶ τοῦ ζῆν = "so that we despaired even of life," gen. of the articular inf. (BDF §400(3))

1:9 | ἵνα μὴ πεποιθότες ὦμεν ... = "so that we would not trust in ourselves but in God" (cp. LXX Isa 10:20), periphrastic perf. subj. with present mng. (BDAG πείθω 2; BDF §§341, 352)

1:10 | ὅς & ὅν – relative pronouns referring back to θεός (v. 9) | ἐκ τηλικούτου θανάτου = "from so great a [peril of] death" (NASB), "from such a deadly peril" (NIV, ESV)

1:11 | συνυπουργούντων ὑμῶν ὑπὲρ ἡμῶν τῇ δεήσει = "while you join in helping us by your prayers" (BDAG συνυπουργέω), gen. abs.; dat. of means (W 162–3) | πρόσωπον = "person" (BDAG πρόσωπον 2) | τὸ εἰς ἡμᾶς χάρισμα διὰ πολλῶν = "the favor bestowed on us through [the prayers of] many" (NASB), though one would expect τό before διά (M 108) | ἵνα ἐκ πολλῶν προσώπων τὸ χάρισμα εὐχαριστηθῇ (aor. pass. subj.) ὑπὲρ ἡμῶν = lit. "so that the favor may be given thanks for by many persons on our behalf," i.e., so that many persons may give thanks on our behalf for the favor (BDF §312(2); BDAG εὐχαριστέω)

1:12 | τοῦ θεοῦ – either (1) "godly" (ESV), descriptive gen., or (2) "from God" (NIV 1984), gen. of source | περισσοτέρως πρὸς ὑμᾶς = "especially toward you" (NASB)

1:13 | ἄλλα ... ἀλλ' ἤ = "anything other than" (N.B.: ἄλλος ≠ ἀλλά) | ἕως τέλους = (1) "fully" (ESV) or (2) "until the end," i.e., until the parousia (BDAG τέλος 2bβ; NASB)

1:13–14 | ἐλπίζω ὅτι ... ἐπιγνώσεσθε ... ὅτι = "And I hope that, as you have understood us in part, you will come to understand fully that ..." (NIV); for the sake of clarity, in translation it is best to transpose the parenthetical ἀπὸ μέρους (= "in part") clause before the ἕως τέλους (= "fully") clause

1:14 | καύχημα ὑμῶν ἐσμεν καθάπερ καὶ ὑμεῖς ἡμῶν = either (1) take καύχημα as "the thing of which one is proud" or "reason for boasting" (see BDAG) and ὑ/ἡμῶν as possessive gens.: "we are your reason to be proud as you also are ours" (NASB), or (2) take καύχημα as verbal noun and ὑ/ἡμῶν as subjective gens.: "you will boast of us as we will boast of you" (ESV)

1:15 | ἵνα δευτέραν χάριν σχῆτε = "that you might benefit twice" (NIV)

1:17 | μήτι ἄρα; = "I was not ..., was I?" | τῇ ἐλαφρίᾳ χράομαι = "proceed with irresponsible frivolity or impetuousness" | παρ' ἐμοί = "with me" | τὸ Ναὶ ναὶ καὶ τὸ Οὒ οὔ = "yes, yes and no, no" where καί means "and at the same time" (for τό, see BDAG ὁ 2h; BDF §267)

1:18 | πιστὸς ὁ θεὸς ὅτι = "God is faithful [to bear witness] that," oath formula (cp. v. 23; 11:10) (BDAG ὅτι 1a)

1:21 | εἰς Χριστόν = "in Christ" (εἰς = ἐν) | ὁ βεβαιῶν ... καὶ χρίσας – the article governs both ptcs. (also in v. 22)

1:23 | ἐγώ ... ψυχήν = "I call God as witness against my soul," i.e., if I am lying, I will forfeit my soul/life (BDAG ψυχή 2d) | φειδόμενος = "to spare you," telic ptc. | οὐκέτι ἦλθον = "I did not come again"

1:24 | κυριεύω takes gen. | ὑμῶν τῆς πίστεως = τῆς πίστεως ὑμῶν = "your faith"

2 Corinthians 2

2:1 | κρίνω = "decide" (BDAG κρίνω 4) | τὸ μή ... ἐλθειν – articular inf. (BDF §399(3)) | "I made up my mind not to make another painful visit to you" (ESV)

2:2 | καὶ τίς; = "who then?" (BDAG καί 1bθ; BDF §442(8)) | ὁ
λυπούμενος [pass.] ἐξ ἐμοῦ = "the one whom I have pained" (ESV)

2:3 | τοῦτο αὐτό (adv. acc.) = "for this very reason" (BDAG αὐτός
1g; BDF §290(4)) | ὅτι ἡ ἐμὴ χαρὰ πάντων ὑμῶν ἐστιν = "that
my joy would be [the joy] of you all" (NASB), "that you would all share
my joy" (NIV)

2:4 | διά of attendant circumstances (BDAG διά A3c) | τὴν ἀγάπην
ἵνα γνῶτε ἣν ἔχω = ἵνα γνῶτε τὴν ἀγάπην ἣν ἔχω

2:5 | εἰ τις λελύπηκεν = "if anyone has caused pain" | ἀπὸ μέρους
= "to some extent" (NIV) | ἵνα μὴ ἐπιβαρῶ is parenthetical = "in
order not to say too much" (BDAG, NASB), "not to put it too severely"
(ESV)

2:6 | ἡ ὑπὸ τῶν πλειόνων = "which [was inflicted] by the majority"
(NASB)

2:7 | ὥστε ὑμᾶς + inf. = "so that you [ought] to ..." ("tendency to
ellipsis in use of ὥστε," M 144) | τοὐναντίον = τὸ ἐναντίον = "on
the other hand" (adv. acc.) | μή πως + subj. = "lest"

2:9 | ἵνα γνῶ τὴν δοκιμὴν ὑμῶν = "to see if you would stand the
test" (NIV) | εἰς πάντα ὑπήκοοι = "obedient in every respect"
(BDAG εἰς 5; ὑπήκοος)

2:10 | χαρίζομαι + dat. of person forgiven + acc. of thing forgiven |
κἀγώ = καὶ ἐγώ = "I also [forgive him]," brachylogy

2:11 | αὐτοῦ τὰ νοήματα = τὰ νοήματα αὐτοῦ

2:12 | εἰς τὸ εὐαγγέλιον τοῦ Χρ. = "for the gospel of Christ"
(BDAG εἰς 4f) | θύρας μοι ἀνεῳγμένης = "even though a door
was opened for me" (ESV), concessive gen. abs.

2:13 | οὐκ ἔσχηκα ἄνεσιν τῷ πνεύματί μου = "my spirit had no rest," dat. of possession (BDF §§189, 190(3)) | τῷ μὴ εὑρεῖν με Τίτον = "because I did not find Titus," dat. articular inf., indicating cause (BDF §401), with acc. με as subject of inf.

2:15 | ἐν (2x) = "among"

2:16 | οἷς μέν ... οἷς δέ = "to the one ... to the other"

2:17 | ἐσμέν καπηλεύοντες – pres. periphrastic | ὡς οἱ πολλοί = "like so many" (ESV) | Second and third ὡς – marker of character in which Paul is rightly to be viewed (BDAG ὡς 3aα)

2 Corinthians 3

3:1 | ἢ μὴ χρῄζομεν; = "Or do we need?" μή expects neg. answer

3:3 | φανερούμενοι ὅτι = "you show that," shift from sg. ptcs. to pl., connecting back to ὑμεῖς (v. 2) | ἐπιστολὴ Χριστοῦ = "a letter from Christ," gen. of source (W 109–10) | διακονηθεῖσα ὑφ' ἡμῶν = "delivered by us" (BDAG, ESV), "the result of our ministry" (NIV) | μέλανι & πνεύματι – instrumental datives | ἐν = "on" (BDAG ἐν 1b) | ἐν πλαξὶν καρδίαις σαρκίναις = "on tablets consisting of human hearts," awkward apposition (Metzger)

3:5 | ἱκανός + inf. (BDF §393(4)) | λογίσασθαι τι ὡς ἐξ ἑαυτῶν = "to claim anything as coming from ourselves" (mixture of ESV & NASB)

3:7 | λίθοις = "on stone," locative dat. (W 153) | διά + acc. = "because of"

3:9 | εἰ τῇ διακονίᾳ ... δόξα = "if the ministry of condemnation had glory," dat. of possession

3:10 | οὐ δεδόξασται τὸ δεδοξασμένον = "what was glorious has no glory now" (NIV) | ἐν τούτῳ τῷ μέρει = "in this case" (BDAG μέρος 1bθ) (cp. 9:3)

3:11 | διὰ δόξης = "[was/came] with glory," διά of attendant circumstance

3:12 | πολλῇ παρρησίᾳ χρώμεθα = "we are very bold"

3:13 | πρὸς τὸ μή + inf. = "so that they might not" | τὸ τέλος τοῦ καταργουμένου = (1) temporal sense: "the end of what was fading away" (NASB) (BDAG τέλος 1), or (2) teleological sense: "the outcome of what was being brought to an end" (ESV) (BDAG τέλος 3)

3:14 | ἐπὶ τῇ ἀναγνώσει τῆς παλαιᾶς διαθήκης = "when the old covenant is read" (NIV), temporal ἐπί (see 1:4) | μὴ ἀνακαλυπτόμενον ὅτι ἐν Χριστῷ καταργεῖται – (1) ὅτι as marker of discourse content: "the veil remains, it not being revealed to them *that* it is done away in Christ" (cp. the American Standard Version), but it is doubtful that ἀνακαλύπτω can mean "reveal" (it clearly does not have that meaning in v. 18), or (2) causal ὅτι: "the veil remains unlifted, *because* it is removed [only] in Christ"

3:15–16 | ἡνίκα ἄν/ἐάν (2x) = "whenever"

3:17 | οὗ (adv.) = "where"

3:18 | τὴν αὐτὴν εἰκόνα μεταμορφούμεθα = "we are being transformed into the same image," acc. with pass. (BDF §159(4)) | ἀπὸ κυρίου πνεύματος = "from the Lord, who is the Spirit" (BDAG ἀπό 5d)

2 Corinthians 4

4:2 | τὰ κρυπτὰ τῆς αἰσχύνης = "secret and shameful ways" (NIV), "disgraceful, underhanded ways" (ESV), attributive gen. | τῇ φανερώσει τῆς ἀληθείας = "by the open statement of the truth" (ESV), dat. of means; objective gen.

4:3 | εἰ καί = "even if" (cp. v. 16) | ἐν τοῖς ἀπολλυμένοις = "to those who are perishing," ἐν for simple dat. (BDF §220(1))

4:4 | ἐν οἷς = "in whose case" (NASB) (BDAG ἐν 8) | εἰς τὸ μή + inf. = "so that they might not" | "the light emanating from the gospel which proclaims the glory of Christ," concatenation of gens. with different mngs. (BDF §168(2))

4:4, 6 | φωτισμός (2x) = "light" but with different nuances: objective light (v. 4) vs. subjective illumination (v. 6) (see BDAG φωτισμός a/b)

4:5 | διὰ Ἰησοῦν = "for Jesus' sake"

4:6 | λάμψει – imperatival future (W 569) | ὅς = "[is the one] who," some scribes deleted ὅς to improve sentence flow | πρὸς φωτισμὸν τῆς γνώσεως τῆς δόξης τοῦ θεοῦ = "to give us the illumination which consists in knowing God's glory" (BDAG πρός 3cα)

4:7 | τοῦ θεοῦ – gen. of source (cp. "the righteousness of God," Rom 1:17; 10:3; cp. Phil 3:9)

4:8 | ἐν παντί = "in every way"

4:8–10 | Independent ptcs. functioning as indicatives (W 653; BDF §468; M 179) (cp. 5:6; 9:11)

4:12 | ὥστε = "so"

4:13 | καὶ ἡμεῖς = "we also"

4:14 | εἰδότες = "since we know," causal ptc.

4:15 | "All this is for your benefit, so that the grace that is reaching more and more people may cause thanksgiving to overflow to the glory of God" (NIV)

4:16 | εἰ καί = "even if," "though" (M 167; BDAG εἰ 6e) | Second ἀλλά (in apodosis) = "yet" (BDF §448(5); BDAG ἀλλά 4a) | ἡμέρᾳ καὶ ἡμέρᾳ = "day by day," temporal dat.

4:17 | τὸ παραυτίκα ἐλαφρόν = "the momentary lightness," taking τὸ ἐλαφρόν as substantivized adj. (BDF §263(2)); παραυτίκα as attributive adj. | καθ᾽ ὑπερβολὴν εἰς ὑπερβολήν = "far beyond all comparison" (NASB)

4:18 | μὴ σκοπούντων ἡμῶν = "while …," gen. abs., with reference to the preceding ἡμῖν (BDF §423(5))

2 Corinthians 5
5:1 | ἡ ἐπίγειος ἡμῶν οἰκία τοῦ σκήνους = "the earthly house which is our temporary abode," epexegetical/appositional gen. (BDF §168(1))

5:2 | τὸ οἰκητήριον … ἐπενδύσασθαι ἐπιποθοῦντες = "longing to be clothed with our dwelling from heaven," acc. with pass. (BDF §159) | ἐπενδύομαι = "put a garment on over an existing garment" (BDAG; Geerhardus Vos, *Redemptive History & Biblical Interpretation: The Shorter Writings of Geerhardus Vos* [ed. Richard B. Gaffin, Jr.; Phillipsburg: Presbyterian and Reformed, 1980], 46–47)

5:3 | εἴ γε καί = "inasmuch as," "assuming, of course" (BDAG εἰ 6b); some MSS have εἴπερ καί = "even if" | Textual problem: either (1) ἐνδυσάμενοι = "having put it on," or (2) ἐκδυσάμενοι = "having put it off" – difficult to decide: (1) has superior external support, but is banal, even tautologous; conversely, (2) has weak support but makes better sense in context ("although having put it off [i.e., having died], we shall not [at the end] be found naked," Vos, p. 47)

5:4 | ἐφ᾽ ᾧ = "because" (BDAG ἐπί 6c)

5:5 | εἰς αὐτὸ τοῦτο = "for this very purpose/reason" (BDAG εἰς 4f)

5:6 | Independent ptcs. (see 4:8–10) | ἐνδημοῦντες = "while we are at home," temporal ptc.

5:10 | τὰ διὰ τοῦ σώματος = "the things [done] in/via the body" | πρὸς ἃ ἔπραξεν = "in accordance with what he has done" (BDAG πρός 3εδ)

5:11–20 | All first person pl. verbs and pronouns ("we/us") are literary plurals refering to Paul himself (BDF §280), though he is probably setting himself forth as an example (note expanded use of "we/us" to include all believers by the end, v. 21).

5:12 | ἀφορμὴν καυχήματος ὑπὲρ ἡμῶν = "an opportunity to boast about us" | ἵνα ἔχητε πρὸς τούς = "so that you will have [an answer] for those who" (NASB)

5:14 | συνέχω = "press in and around so as to leave little room for movement" (BDAG συνέχω 3), here figuratively, "impel" or "control" (BDAG συνέχω 7–8)

5:16–17 | ὥστε (2x) = "therefore"

5:16 | ἀπὸ τοῦ νῦν = "from now on" | εἰ καί ... ἀλλά = "even though ... yet"

5:19 | ὡς ὅτι = "that" (BDF §396; BDAG ὅτι 5b) | θεὸς ἦν ἐν Χριστῷ κόσμον καταλλάσσων – either (1) "in Christ God was reconciling the world" (ESV), taking ἦν καταλλάσσων as impf. periphrastic, or (2) "God was in Christ, reconciling the world" (KJV, NASB), taking ἐν Χριστῷ with ἦν, and καταλλάσσων as a separate adverbial ptc. | Take ὡς ὅτι ... αὐτῶν as a parenthesis, highlighting parallelism of three ptcs: τοῦ καταλλάξαντος ... καὶ δόντος ... καὶ θέμενος (vv. 18–19) (Seyoon Kim, *Paul and the New Perspective: Second Thoughts on the Origin of Paul's Gospel* [Grand Rapids: Eerdmans, 2002], 220–22) | θέμενος ἐν ἡμῖν = "having committed/entrusted to us," ἐν for simple dat. (BDF §220(1)) (cp. δόντος ἡμῖν, v. 18)

5:20 | ὑπὲρ Χριστοῦ (2x) = "on Christ's behalf," i.e., in his name and as his representative | ὡς τοῦ θεοῦ παρακαλοῦντος δι' ἡμῶν = "as though God were making his appeal through us" (NIV), gen. abs.

5:21 | Subject of ἐποίησεν is "God"

2 Corinthians 6

6:1 | συνεργοῦντες = "working together [with God]" | εἰς κενόν = "in vain" (BDAG εἰς 4e; κενός 3)

6:2 | καιρῷ δεκτῷ = "in the time of my favor" (NIV), dat. of time | καιρὸς εὐπρόσδεκτος = "the time of God's favor" (NIV)

6:3 | μηδεμίαν ... προσκοπήν = "no cause for offense" | ἐν μηδενί = (1) "in anything" (NASB), (2) "to anyone," ἐν for simple dat. (BDF §220(1)), (3) "in anyone's way/path" (ESV)

6:4–10 | "An impassioned and almost lyrical passage, where precision in the interpretation of the prepositions is probably impossible" (M 196)

6:7–8 | διά of attendant circumstances (3x) (BDAG διά A3c)

6:8–10 | ὡς ... καί (7x) = "as ... and yet" (BDAG καί 1bη)

6:11 | τὸ στόμα ἡμῶν ἀνέῳγεν πρὸς ὑμᾶς = "our mouth is open toward you," i.e., I have spoken freely and openly | ἀνοίγω = "be candid" (BDAG ἀνοίγω 7)

6:12 | ἐν ἡμῖν = "by us," "on our part" | Lit. "You are not restricted by us, but you are restricted in your own hearts." More idiomatically: "We are not withholding our affection from you, but you are withholding yours from us" (NIV).

6:13 | τὴν αὐτὴν ἀντιμισθίαν = "as a fair exchange" (NIV), adv. acc., or acc. in apposition to sentence (M 34–36, 160) (BDF §154 suggests it is pregnant form of cognate acc.: τὸν αὐτὸν πλατυσμὸν ὡς ἀντιμισθίαν πλατύνθητε) | ὡς τέκνοις λέγω – parenthesis

6:14 | μὴ γίνεσθε ἑτερογυζοῦντες ἀπίστοις = "do not be unequally yoked with unbelievers" (ESV), present periphrastic (W 648); associative dat. (W 160) | τίς μετοχὴ δικαιοσύνη καὶ ἀνομία; = "what do righteousness and wickedness have in common?" (NIV) (BDAG μετοχή)

6:14–16 | τίς + noun + dat. of possession (φωτί, πιστῷ, ναῷ) + πρός/μετά + gen. (3x) = "what fellowship (etc.) does x have with y?"

6:16 | ὅτι recitative | ἐν αὐτοῖς = "among them"

6:17 | Verbs of touching take gen. | κἀγώ = καὶ ἐγώ

6:18 | Semitic εἰς with εἰμί (2x) (BDAG εἰς 8aβ)

2 Corinthians 7

7:1 | ταύτας τὰς ἐπαγγελίας = "these promises" | καθαρίσωμεν – hortatory subj.

7:2 | χωρήσατε ἡμᾶς = "make room for us in your hearts" (NASB; BDAG χωρέω 3bα)

7:3 | πρὸς κατάκρισιν οὐ λέγω = "I do not say this to condemn you" (ESV) (BDAG πρός 3cα) | εἰς τό + infs. = "in suchwise that" (ZG); "you have such a place in our hearts that we would live or die with you" (NIV)

7:4 | [ἐστίν] μοι (2x) = "I have," dat. of possession | πληρόω (pass.) + dat. = "filled with" (BDF §195(2)) | ἐπὶ πάσῃ τῇ θλίψει ἡμῶν = "in all our affliction" (ESV), temporal use of ἐπί + dat. (see 1:4)

7:5 | ἐλθόντων ἡμῶν = "when we came into Macedonia," gen. abs. | ἐν παντὶ θλιβόμενοι = "we were afflicted at every turn" (ESV), finite verb continued with ptc. (BDF §468(1))

7:7 | παρεκλήθη ... ἀναγγέλλων – Titus is the subject, "the comfort with which he was comforted in you, as he reported" (NASB) | ὥστε με μᾶλλον χαρῆναι = "so that I rejoiced still more" (BDF §244(2)), acc. με as subject of inf.

7:8 | εἰ καί (3x) = "even if," concessive (M 167; BDAG εἰ 6e) | εἰ καὶ πρὸς ὥραν = "though only for a while" (ESV)

7:9–11 | κατὰ θεόν (3x) = "according to [the will of] God" (NASB) (cp. Rom 8:27; 1 Pet 5:2)

7:10 | ἀμεταμέλητον (two-termination adj.) could modify (1) μετάνοιαν ("a repentance not to be regretted," BDAG; cp. NASB), or (2) σωτηρίαν ("salvation without regret," ESV)

7:11 | αὐτὸ τοῦτο τὸ λυπηθῆναι = "this very sorrow" | πόσην is in apposition to the articular inf., modifies σπουδήν, and is understood throughout the series of nouns that follows: "Look at this godly sorrow, what eagerness it has produced in you, what defense," etc. | ἀλλά (6x) introduces additional point in emphatic way (BDAG ἀλλά 4b; BDF §448(6)) | τῷ πράγματι = "in this matter," dat. of respect (BDF §197)

7:12 | εἰ καί = "although" (cp. v. 8) | πρὸς ὑμᾶς goes with τοῦ φανερωθῆναι – "that before God you could see for yourselves how devoted to us you are" (NIV)

7:13 | ἐπὶ τῇ παρακλήσει ἡμῶν = "in addition to our own encouragement" (BDAG ἐπί 7) | περισσοτέρως ... ἐπὶ τῇ χαρᾷ Τίτου = "we were especially delighted to see how happy Titus was" (NIV)

7:14 | ὅτι = "for" | εἴ τι αὐτῷ ὑπὲρ ὑμῶν κεκαύχημαι = "if in anything I have boasted to him about you" (NASB); "whatever boasts I made to him about you" (ESV) | ἡ καύχησις ἡμῶν ἡ ἐπὶ Τίτου = "our boast [about you] which [we made] to Titus"

7:15 | τὰ σπλάγχνα ... ἐστιν = "his affection for you is even greater," neut. pl. subjects take sg. verbs | ἀναμιμνησκομένου = "as he remembers," gen. abs. | ὡς = "how," indirect question (BDAG ὡς 1bδ)

2 Corinthians 8

8:2 | ἐν πολλῇ δοκιμῇ θλίψεως = "in a severe test of affliction" (ESV) (BDAG δοκιμή 1) | ἡ κατὰ βάθους πτωχεία αὐτῶν = "their deep/extreme poverty" (BDF §225)

8:3 | κατὰ δύναμιν ... παρὰ δύναμιν = "according to their means ... beyond their means" (ESV) | μαρτυρῶ is a slight parenthesis (BDF §465(2))

8:4 | "begging us with much urging for *the favor of participating* in this ministry for the saints," hendiadys

8:5 | καὶ οὐ καθὼς ἠλπίσαμεν = "and this, not as we had expected" (NASB, ESV)

8:6 | εἰς τὸ παρακαλέσαι ἡμᾶς Τίτον = "with the result that we urged Titus" | Subject of προενήρξατο and ἐπιτελέσῃ is Titus | καθώς ... οὕτως καί = "as ... so also"

8:7 | ἡ ἐξ ἡμῶν ἐν ὑμῖν ἀγάπη = "the love we inspired in you" (NASB) | Imperatival ἵνα, translated "see that" (BDAG ἵνα 2g)

8:8 | κατ᾽ ἐπιταγήν = "as a command" | διά ... δοκιμάζων = lit. "by means of the earnestness of others testing the sincerity of your love as well," or, "I want to test the sincerity of your love by comparing it with the earnestness of others" (NIV) (telic ptc.) | τὸ τῆς ὑμετέρας ἀγάπης γνήσιον = "the genuineness of your love" (BDF §263(2))

8:9 | πλούσιος ὤν = "though he was rich," concessive ptc.

8:10 | οἵτινες ... ἀπὸ πέρυσι = "who a year ago started not only to do this work but also to desire to do it" (ESV), προ- prefix explained by ἀπὸ πέρυσι, while νυνί in v. 11 forms contrast (BDAG προενάρχομαι)

8:11 | καθάπερ ἡ προθυμία τοῦ θέλειν, οὕτως καὶ τὸ ἐπιτελέσαι = "just as [there was] the readiness to desire it, so [there may be] also the completion of it" (NASB), ellipsis requiring verbs to be supplied | ἐκ τοῦ ἔχειν = "according to your means" (NIV)

8:12 | καθὸ ἐὰν ἔχῃ = "according to what [a person] has," taking ἐάν = ἄν and supplying τις as subject (ZG)

8:13 | ἐξ ἰσότητος = "as a matter of equality" (BDAG ἰσότης 1)

8:15 | ὁ τὸ πολύ ... ὁ τὸ ὀλίγον = "the one [who had gathered] much/ little," συλλέγω must be supplied by knowledge of OT context (LXX Exod 16:16–18)

8:17 | τὴν παράκλησιν ἐδέξατο = "he accepted our appeal" | μέν ... δέ = "not only ... but also"

8:18 | οὗ ὁ ἔπαινος ... ἐκκλησιῶν = "whose fame in connection with the gospel [i.e., 'for his preaching of the gospel' (ESV)] has gone out through all the churches" (BDAG ἔπαινος)

8:19 | χειροτονηθεὶς συνέκδημος ἡμῶν = "he [= 'the brother'] has been appointed to travel with us" | πρός ... καὶ προθυμίαν ἡμῶν = "and to show our good will" (ESV)

8:20 | "taking precaution so that no one will discredit us in our administration of this generous gift" (NASB), μή τις + subj. = "lest someone," i.e., "that no one"

8:22 | ὃν ἐδοκιμάσαμεν ... σπουδαῖον ὄντα = "whom we have tested and found to be earnest/diligent," supplementary ptc. with verbs of cognition (BDF §416(2)) | πεποιθήσει πολλῇ τῇ εἰς ὑμᾶς = "because of his confidence in you," dat. of cause (W 167)

8:23 | εἴτε ὑπέρ ... εἴτε = "whether it concerns x ... or whether [it concerns] y" (BDF §454(3); BDAG ὑπέρ A3)

8:24 | ἐνδεικνύμενοι – imperatival ptc. (BDF §468(2)) | εἰς πρόσωπον + gen. = "in the face of, before" (BDAG πρόσωπον 1bβ⊐)

2 Corinthians 9

9:2 | Μακεδόσιν = "to the Macedonians," dat. pl. | καυχάομαι ὑπέρ τινος = "boast about someone" (cp. v. 3)

9:3 | ἐν τῷ μέρει τούτῳ = "in this matter/case" (BDAG μέρος 1bθ) (cp. 3:10)

9:4 | μή πως ... καταισχυνθῶμεν ἡμεῖς, ἵνα μὴ λέγω ὑμεῖς = "lest *we* should be put to shame, to say nothing of *you*," brachylogy (ὑμεῖς is nom. in parallel with ἡμεῖς) | ἐν τῇ ὑποστάσει ταύτῃ = "for being so confident" (ESV), ἐν equivalent to dat. of cause

9:5 | ἡγέομαι ἀναγκαῖον + inf. = "think it necessary to" (cp. Phil 2:25) | παρακαλέω τινα ἵνα = "urge someone to," attenuated ἵνα as inf. (BDAG ἵνα 2aγ) | προέρχομαι καὶ προκαταρτίζω = "go on ahead and make arrangements in advance" | εὐλογία (2x) = "generous gift, bounty" (BDAG εὐλογία 3c or 4); thus, ἡ προεπηγγελμένη εὐλογία ὑμῶν = "the generous gift you had promised" (NIV), taking ὑμῶν as subjective gen. | ταύτην ἑτοίμην ... πλεονεξίαν = "so that in this way it may be ready as a willing gift, not as an exaction" (ESV mod.); acc. ταύτην as subject of inf. (ZG); consecutive/final εἶναι w/o ὥστε (M 141) + οὕτως = "that in this way" (ZG)

9:6 | Τοῦτο δέ = "The point is this" (ESV) | ἐπ’ εὐλογίαις (2x) = "bountifully"

9:7 | καθώς demands οὕτως – "As each has decided in his heart, [so must he give], not reluctantly or under compulsion" (cp. Gal 3:6; 1 Tim 1:3) | ἐκ λύπης = "reluctantly," adverbial (BDAG ἐκ 6c)

9:9 | ἐσκόρπισεν, ἔδωκεν – gnomic aorists (W 562) | ἡ δικαιοσύνη αὐτοῦ – the subject of the verbs and the pronoun αὐτοῦ could refer to (1) God (cp. v. 8), or (2), more likely, the man who fears the Lord and gives to the poor (see Harris 639–41)

9:10 | εἰς βρῶσιν = "for food" (BDAG εἰς 4d)

9:11, 13 | πλουτιζόμενοι (= "you will be enriched"), δοξάζοντες (= "they [the recipients] will glorify"), independent ptcs. (see 4:8–10)

9:13 | διὰ τῆς δοκιμῆς τῆς διακονίας ταύτης = "by testing and approving this [your] service," objective gen. (W 119) | ἡ ὑποταγὴ τῆς ὁμολογίας ... = "your confession's submission to the gospel of Christ," ὑποταγή + εἰς (functioning as dat., cp. Rom 10:3; BDAG εἰς 4g); ὁμολογία does not take εἰς but gen.

9:13, 15 | Praise/thanks to God + ἐπί + dat. (2x) = "for"

9:14 | καὶ αὐτῶν ... ἐπιποθούντων = "while they also, by prayer on your behalf, yearn for you" (NASB), gen. abs. | ἐφ’ ὑμῖν = "upon you," i.e., "given to you"

2 Corinthians 10

10:1 | κατὰ πρόσωπον μέν ... ἀπὼν δέ = "when face to face ... but when absent" | ταπεινός = "timid" (NIV), "meek" (NASB), "pliant, subservient, abject" (BDAG ταπεινός 2) | ἐν ὑμῖν = either "among you" (BDAG ἐν 1d) or "in your presence" (BDAG ἐν 1e) | εἰς ὑμᾶς = "toward you" (BDAG εἰς 4c)

10:2 | τὸ μή … θαρρῆσαι = "that I may not be bold," articular inf., equivalent to ἵνα μή clause (BDF §399(3)) | παρών = "when I am present" | λογίζομαι (2x) used with different nuances: "I ask that when I am present I may not have to be bold with the confidence that I *have in mind* (BDAG λογίζομαι 2) to undertake toward some who *regard* (BDAG λογίζομαι 1b) us as if we walk according to the flesh" | ἐπί + acc. = "toward, against," of feelings (BDAG ἐπί 15) | ὡς = "as if" (BDAG ὡς 3aγ and 3c)

10:4 | δυνατὰ τῷ θεῷ = either (1) "divinely powerful" (NASB), Hebraism (M 184); or (2) "powerful for God [to use]," dat. of advantage (BDF §§192, 188) | καθαίρεσις = "destruction," καθαιρέω = "destroy"

10:5 | εἰς τὴν ὑπακοὴν τοῦ Χριστοῦ = "to make it obedient to Christ" (NIV), τοῦ Χρ. – objective gen. (BDAG ὑπακοή 1b); εἰς – entry into a state of being (BDAG εἰς 4f)

10:6 | ἐν ἑτοίμῳ ἔχω + inf. = "be ready to"

10:7 | τὰ κατὰ πρόσωπον βλέπετε – could be indic.: "you are looking only on the surface of things" (NIV 1984), or impv.: "look at what is before your eyes" (ESV) | λογίζομαι (used here with yet a third nuance; cp. v2) = "consider" (BDAG λογίζομαι 2) (also v. 11) | λογιζέσθω ἐφ᾽ ἑαυτοῦ = "let him consider within himself" (NASB), "based on himself" (BDAG ἐπί 8)

10:8 | ἐὰν περισσότερόν … τῆς ἐξουσίας ἡμῶν = "even if I boast a little too much of our authority" (ESV)

10:9 | Options: (1) "I do not want to seem to be trying to frighten you with my letters" (NIV), implied verb of wishing + ἵνα of content (M 145), or (2) "So as not to seem to be trying to frighten you with [mere] letters … let such a person consider this," ἵνα clause put ahead of main clause (v. 11), with v. 10 as parenthesis (BDF §483) | ὡς ἄν (or ὡσάν) = (1) "so to speak" (BDF §453(3)), or (2) "as if" (BDAG I. ἄν f)

10:10 | ἡ παρουσία τοῦ σώματος = "his bodily presence" (ESV), "in person" (NIV)

10:11 | ἀπόντες ... παρόντες = "when we are absent ... when we are present" (cp. 13:10)

10:12 | ἐν ἑαυτοῖς ἑαυτοὺς μετροῦντες = "measuring (i.e., evaluating) themselves by one another" (BDAG μετρέω 1b), Hebr./instrumental ἐν

10:13, 15 | εἰς τὰ ἄμετρα (2x) = "beyond [our] limits"

10:13 | κατὰ τὸ μέτρον ... μέτρου "is difficult; οὗ is probably attracted from ὅ (referring to μέτρον) to κανόνος and then μέτρου repeated, lest οὗ be referred to κανόνος" (BDF §294(5)) | κανών = "mission assignment, which included directions about geographical area" (BDAG), "area of influence" (ESV), "field" (NIV 1984) | ἐφικέσθαι ἄχρι καὶ ὑμῶν = "a field that reaches even to you" (NIV 1984)

10:14 | οὗ goes with ὑπερεκτείνομεν | ὡς μὴ ἐφικνούμενοι εἰς ὑμᾶς = "as though we did not reach to you" (ESV), parenthetical | φθάνειν ἐν τῷ εὐαγγελίῳ = "come with the preaching of the gospel" (BDAG ἐν 5aβ)

10:15–16 | "Our hope is that, as your faith increases [gen. abs.], we may be greatly enlarged in [BDAG κατά B1a] our area of influence, so that we may preach the gospel in the regions beyond you, not so that we may boast of work already done in someone else's area of influence," in all three infs. the implicit subject is ἡμᾶς; the first inf., μεγαλυνθῆναι, is used in indirect discourse supplementing ἐλπίδα (BDF §396); last two, εὐαγγελίσασθαι and καυχήσασθαι, are infs. of purpose (BDF §390)

10:18 | ὅν = "[the one] whom"

2 Corinthians 11
11:1 | ὄφελον = "would that!" "The word ὄφελον ... has crystallized

in the NT into a particle introducing a wish, and is followed by the
Indic." (M 137) | ἀνέχομαι + gen. + acc. = "put up with someone
with regard to something" | ἀλλὰ καί = either (1) "but indeed," taking
ἀνέχεσθε as indic. (NASB), or (2) "nay, you must" (ZG), taking
ἀνέχεσθε as impv. (cp. ESV)

11:2 | θεοῦ ζήλῳ = "with a godly (NASB), or divine (ESV), jealousy,"
attributive gen.

11:3 | Hebr./instrumental ἐν | Interestingly, φθείρω can also mean
"seduce a virgin" (BDAG φθείρω 1c, 2b) | ἀπό designates separation
in pregnant construction: "be ruinously diverted from wholehearted
commitment" (BDAG ἀπό 1e) | τῆς εἰς τὸν Χριστόν = "of [your
devotion] to Christ"

11:4 | καλῶς ἀνέχεσθε = "you put up with it all right," ironic (BDAG
καλῶς 6)

11:5 | Acc. of respect + ὑστερέω + gen. of comparison = "in some way
to be inferior to someone" (μηδέν = "in no way")

11:6 | Supply εἰμί 2x in first half of verse | First ἀλλά (in apodosis)
= "yet" (BDF §448(5); BDAG ἀλλά 4a); second ἀλλά = "in fact"
(BDAG ἀλλά 4b) | ἐν παντὶ φανερώσαντες ἐν πᾶσιν εἰς ὑμᾶς
= "in every way we have made this plain to you in all things" (ESV), ptc.
instead of finite verb (M 179–80; BDF §468)

11:7 | ταπεινῶν – ptc. of means (W 628–30) | ὅτι = "because"

11:8 | λαβών – ptc. of means (cp. v. 7) | πρὸς τὴν ὑμῶν διακονίαν
= "in order to serve you" (ESV) (BDAG πρός 3cα); taking ὑμῶν as
objective gen.

11:9 | καταναρκάω takes gen. bec. of κατα- prefix (cp. 12:13) | ἐλθόντες
= "who came" or "when they came" | ἐν παντὶ ἀβαρῆ ἐμαυτὸν ὑμῖν

ἐτήρησα καὶ τηρήσω = "I have kept myself from being a burden to you in any way, and will continue to do so" (NIV), τηρέω + double acc. = "keep x as y"

11:10 | ἔστιν ἀλήθεια Χριστοῦ ἐν ἐμοὶ ὅτι – oath formula; ὅτι = "[when I say] that" (BDF §397(3)) (cp. 1:18) | εἰς ἐμέ = "with reference to me" (BDAG εἰς 5)

11:11 | διὰ τί; = "why?" | ὁ θεὸς οἶδεν = "God knows [I do]"

11:12 | ὃ δὲ ποιῶ καὶ ποιήσω = "what I am doing I will *also* continue to do," adverbial καί (BDAG καί 2) | Second ἵνα supplements ἀφορμήν like an inf. (BDAG ἵνα 2ca) – "an opportunity to be regarded just as we are in the matter about which [ἐν ᾧ – BDAG ἐν 7] they are boasting" (NASB) (NA confusingly puts a comma after ἀφορμήν)

11:13–15 | μετασχηματίζομαι εἰ (or ὡς) = "transform onself into" (BDAG εἰς 4b) or "masquerade as" (BDAG ὡς 3aα)

11:15 | μέγα = "surprising" (BDAG μέγα 5)

11:16 | μή τίς με δόξῃ ἄφρονα εἶναι = "let no one think that I am foolish," subj. of prohibition (BDF §364(3)) | εἰ δὲ μήγε = "but if you do" | κἄν = "even if only" (BDAG κἄν 3)

11:16, 18, 21, 22 | κἀγώ (6x) = καὶ ἐγώ = "I also"

11:17 | κατὰ κύριον = "as the Lord would" (NASB), "with the Lord's authority" (ESV) | ἡ ὑπόστασις τῆς καυχήσεως = (1) "this boastful frame of mind," epexegetical gen., or (2) "this boasting project of mine" (see BDAG ὑπόστασις 2 or 3)

11:19 | φρόνιμοι ὄντες = "since you are so wise" (NIV), causal ptc.

11:20 | ἀνέχεσθε εἴ τις = "you put up with [it] if anyone ..." |

λαμβάνω = "take advantage of" (BDAG λαμβάνω 3) (cp. 12:16)

11:21 | κατὰ ἀτιμίαν = "to my shame" | ὡς ὅτι = "that" (cp. 5:19) | ἡμεῖς ἠσθενήκαμεν = "we were too weak for that!" (ESV), ironic | ἐν ᾧ δ' ἄν τις τολμᾷ = "whatever anyone else dares to boast of" (ESV) | ἐν ἀφροσύνῃ λέγω = "I am speaking as a fool" (ESV), parenthesis; ἐν as periphrasis for adv. (BDAG ἐν 11)

11:23 | παραφρονῶν λαλῶ = "I am talking like a madman" (ESV), concessive ptc. (W 635) | ὑπὲρ ἐγώ = "I even more," rare adverbial use (BDAG ὑπέρ C)

11:24 | παρὰ μίαν = "less one" (BDF §236(4); BDAG παρά C7)

11:25 | ποιέω + acc. of time (νυχθήμερον) = "spend" (BDAG ποιέω 5c)

11:26 | ἐν ψευδαδέλφοις = "among false brethren" (NASB) (BDAG ἐν 1d)

11:28 | χωρὶς τῶν παρεκτός = either (1) "besides everything else" (NIV), or (2) "apart from such external things" (NASB) | ἡ ἐπίστασίς μοι ἡ καθ' ἡμέραν = "my daily burden"

11:30 | τὰ τῆς ἀσθενείας μου = "the things that show my weakness" (ESV), "the occasions of my weakness" (ZG), gen. of reference (W 127–8)

11:32 | Ἀρέτα is gen. = "the ethnarch *under* King Aretas"

2 Corinthians 12
12:1 | οὐ συμφέρον [sc. ἐστίν] = "there is nothing to be gained by it" (BDAG; BDF §353(5)) | μέν … δέ = "although … yet" | ἔρχομαι εἰς = "come to," of a writer dealing with a new subject (BDAG ἔρχομαι 5) | ἀποκαλύψεις κυρίου = (1) "revelations from the Lord" (NIV), gen. of source, or (2) "revelations of the Lord" (NASB, ESV), objective gen.

12:2 | πρὸ ἐτῶν δεκατεσσάρων = "fourteen years ago" (M 74)

12:2–3, 5 | ὁ τοιοῦτος (3x) = "such a man"

12:4 | ἄρρητα ῥήματα – ἄρρητος can mean "cannot be expressed" or "must not be expressed" (BDAG ἄρρητος 1–2), and ῥήματα can mean "words" or "things" (BDAG ῥῆμα 1–2), resulting in four options: (1a) "words that cannot be expressed," (1b) "words that must not be expressed," (2a) "things that cannot be told" (ESV), (2b) "things that must not be told" | ἃ οὐκ ἐξόν – neut. pl. subjects take sg. verbs

12:6 | ἐὰν θελήσω = "even if I should choose" (NIV), aor. subj. with futuristic nuance (BDF §363) | φείδομαι δέ ... ἐξ ἐμοῦ = "but I refrain from this, so that no one will credit me with more than he sees in me or hears from me" (NASB) | λογίζομαι εἰς τινα = "credit someone" (BDAG λογίζομαι 1a) | ὑπέρ + acc. = "more than" (cp. v. 13)

12:7 | καὶ τῇ ὑπερβολῇ τῶν ἀποκαλύψεων διό – punctuation problem: Does διό go with what precedes or with what follows? Options: (1) "... even considering the exceptional character of the revelations. Therefore, to keep me from being too elated ..." (NRSV, following NA punctuation); or (2) "Because of the surpassing greatness of the revelations, for this reason, to keep me from exalting myself, there was given me ..." (NASB) | What was Paul's thorn? See variety of proposals at BDAG κολαφίζω | ἄγγελος Σατανᾶ = "a messenger from Satan," probably an evil spirit (BDAG ἄγγελος 2c)

12:9, 15 | ἥδιστα (2x) = either (1) "very gladly," superlative as elative (BDF §246), or (2) "most gladly" (ZG, NASB), true superlative. With μᾶλλον = "all the more gladly" (NIV, ESV; BDAG ἡδέως)

12:10 | ὅταν + subj. ... τότε = "when ... then"

12:11 | ἐγὼ ὤφειλον ὑφ' ὑμῶν συνίστασθαι = "I ought to have been commended by you" (ESV) | acc. + ὑστερέω + gen. (cp. 11:5)

| ὑφ᾽ ὑμῶν = ὑπὸ ὑμῶν | εἰ καὶ οὐδέν εἰμι = "even though I am nothing" (BDAG εἰ 6e)

12:12 | ἐν ὑμῖν = "among you" | ἐν πάσῃ ὑπομονῇ = "with utmost patience" (ESV) (BDAG ἐν 11)

12:13 | τί γάρ ἐστιν ὃ ἡσσώθητε ὑπὲρ τὰς λοιπὰς ἐκκλησίας; = "for what is there in regard to which you were treated as inferior to the rest of the churches?" taking ὅ as acc. of respect (M 131) | καταναρκάω takes gen. (cp. 11:9)

12:14 | τρίτον τοῦτο = "for the third time" (ESV), adv. acc. (cp. 13:1) | ἑτοίμως ἔχω + inf. = "I am ready to" (BDAG ἔχω 10b) (cp. Acts 21:13; 1 Pet 4:5) | τὰ ὑμῶν = "what is yours" (ESV, NASB), "your possessions" (NIV)

12:15 | ἧσσον ἀγαπῶμαι; = "am I to be loved less?" (NASB, ESV)

12:16 | ἔστω δέ = "be that as it may" (NASB), permissive impv. (W 488–9) | ὑπάρχων πανοῦργος = "crafty fellow that I am" (NASB), causal ptc. | δόλῳ τινα λαμβάνω = "catch someone by a trick" (BDAG λαμβάνω 3) (cp. 11:20)

12:17 | "Certainly I have not taken advantage of you through any of those whom I have sent to you, have I?" (NASB)

12:18 | παρεκάλεσα Τίτον = "I urged Titus [to go]" | μήτι expects negative answer: "Titus did not take advantage of you, did he?" (NASB) | οὐ τῷ αὐτῷ πνεύματι ... ἴχνεσιν; = "Did we not act in the same spirit and follow the same course?" (NIV)

12:19 | πάλαι δοκεῖτε – could be (1) indic.: "you imagine all along" (BDAG), or (2) interrogative: "Have you been thinking all along ...?" (ESV). One might think that this whole time (in the course of the epistle until now – πάλαι) Paul has been defending himself against his critics, but in reality everything he has said (τὰ πάντα) was intended for their edification | ἀπολογούμεθα = "I have been defending myself," extending-from-past present (BDF §322; W 519–20; M 8)

12:20 | οὐχ οἵους θέλω εὕρω ὑμᾶς = εὕρω ὑμᾶς οὐχ οἵους θέλω = "that I will find you not such as I want [to find you]"

20–21 | φοβοῦμαι governs μή πως (2x; BDAG πώς 2b) and μή (v. 21): "I am afraid *that* I will find ... *that* [there will be] quarreling, etc. ... *that* my God will humble me and I will grieve"

12:21 | πάλιν ἐλθόντος μου = "when I come again," gen. abs. | πρὸς ὑμᾶς = "before you" (BDAG πρός 3g)

2 Corinthians 13

13:1 | τρίτον τοῦτο ἔρχομαι πρὸς ὑμᾶς = "this is the third time I am coming to you," futuristic present (M 7) | ἐπί + gen. = "on the basis of" (BDAG ἐπί 8) | ῥῆμα = "fact" (NASB), "charge" (ESV)

13:2 | προείρηκα καὶ προλέγω ... = "I have previously said when present the second time, and though now absent I say in advance" (NASB) | ὡς παρών ... καὶ ἀπών νῦν = "as when present ... *so* now while absent" (BDAG ὡς 2a) | εἰς τὸ πάλιν = πάλιν

13:3 | ἐπεὶ δοκιμὴν ζητεῖτε τοῦ ἐν ἐμοὶ λαλοῦντος Χριστοῦ = "since you seek proof that Christ is speaking in me" (ESV), "... through me" (NIV) | ὅς refers to "Christ"

13:4 | ἐξ ἀσθενείας = "as a result of his weakness/frailty/vulnerability" as a human being (BDAG ἀσθένεια 2b; ἐκ 3e) | εἰς ὑμᾶς = "to serve you" (NIV 1984), "in dealing with you" (ESV)

13:5 | εἰ = "[to see] whether" (BDAG εἰ 5bα) | εἰ μήτι ἀδόκιμοί ἐστε = "unless indeed you fail the test" (BDAG εἰ 6j)

13:6 | γνώσεσθε (fut.) = "you will realize"

13:7 | εὐχόμεθα … μὴ ποιῆσαι ὑμᾶς κακὸν μηδέν = "we pray that you do nothing wrong," indirect discourse with acc. ὑμᾶς as subj. of inf. ποιῆσαι | ἡμεῖς δὲ ὡς ἀδόκιμοι ὦμεν = "even though we may seem to have failed" (NIV); ὦμεν is subj. after ἵνα

13:8 | Supply ποιεῖν – "We can do nothing against the truth" (BDAG δύναμαι c) | κατά + gen. = "against"

13:10 | ἀπών … παρών = "while absent … when present" (cp. v. 2) | ἵνα … μὴ ἀποτόμως χρήσωμαι κατὰ τὴν ἐξουσίαν = "that … I may not have to be severe in my use of the authority" (ESV), χράομαι + adv. = "act in a certain way" (BDAG χράομαι 2)

13:11 | λοιπόν = "finally," adv. acc. (BDAG λοιπός 3b) | καταρτίζεσθε = "mend your ways" (BDAG) | παρακαλεῖσθε = "listen to my appeal" (NIV 1984, ESV alt.) | μεθ᾽ ὑμῶν = μετὰ ὑμῶν

13:12 | Hebr./instrumental ἐν

Chapter Nine

The Epistle to the Galatians

Galatians 1

1:1 | οὐκ ἀπ' ἀνθρώπων = "not [sent] from men" (NASB), ἀπό links back to ἀπόστολος (< ἀπο-στέλλω) and carries forward an implied "sent"

1:6 | οὕτως ταχέως = "so quickly" | μετατίθημι ἀπό = "turn away from, desert" | Textual issue: either (1) ἐν χάριτι = "graciously" (BDAG ἐν 11), or (2) ἐν χάριτι Χριστοῦ = "by the grace of Christ," Hebr./instrumental ἐν

1:7 | Epidiorthosis (BDF §495(3)), i.e., self-correction followed by improved restatement. Paraphrase: "In reality, of course, there is no other gospel. But there are some who are troubling you and trying to pervert the gospel of Christ," εἰ μή = "but" (BDAG εἰ 6iβ; BDF §448(8))

1:8 | καὶ ἐὰν ἡμεῖς = "even if we"

1:8–9 | παρ' ὅ (2x) = "contrary to that which" (BDAG παρά C6)

1:9 | ὡς ... καί = "as ... so" (BDAG καί 2c; ὡς 2a) (cp. Matt 6:10; Acts 7:51; Phil 1:20)

1:9–10 | ἄρτι (2x) = "now, at the present time" (BDAG ἄρτι 3)

1:10 | πείθω = "win over, strive to please" (BDAG πείθω 1c) | εἰ ἔτι ἤρεσκον = "if I were still trying to please," conative impf.

1:12 | ἀποκάλυψις Ἰησοῦ Χριστοῦ – could be (1) "a revelation given by Jesus Christ," subjective gen. (i.e., Jesus Christ revealed the gospel to Paul), or (2) "a revelation whose content was Jesus Christ," objective gen. (i.e., God revealed Jesus Christ to Paul – cp. v. 16)

1:13 | καθ᾽ ὑπερβολήν = "beyond measure" | ἐπόρθουν = "I tried to destroy it," conative impf. (also v. 23)

1:14 | ἐν τῷ γένει μου = "among my people" (BDAG ἐν 1d) | ζηλωτής + objective gen. = "zealous for something"

1:15 | ὁ ἀφορίσας … καὶ καλέσας – article governs both ptcs.

1:16 | ἐν ἐμοί = "to me," ἐν for ordinary dative (BDF §220(1)) | ἐν τοῖς ἔθνεσιν = "among the Gentiles" (BDAG ἐν 1d) (cp. 2:2)

1:17 | οἱ πρὸ ἐμοῦ ἀπόστολοι = "those who were apostles before I was," i.e., the original apostles; temporal use of πρό (BDAG πρό 2)

1:18 | μετά + acc. = "after" in temporal sense | ἱστορέω = "visit for the purpose of coming to know someone" | ἐπιμένω πρός τινα = "stay with someone" (BDAG ἐπιμένω 1; πρός 3g) | ἡμέρας δεκαπέντε = "for 15 days," acc. for extent of time

1:20 | ἐνώπιον τοῦ θεοῦ ὅτι = "before God [I swear] that," ὅτι after implicit verb of swearing (BDAG ὅτι 1a)

1:22 | ἤμην ἀγνοούμενος = "I was unknown," impf. periphrastic | τῷ προσώπῳ = "in person" (ESV), "personally" (NIV; BDAG πρόσωπον 1bα), dat. of respect (BDF §197)

1:23 | ἀκούοντες ἦσαν = "they were hearing," impf. periphrastic | ὅτι recitative

1:24 | ἐν ἐμοί = "in my case" (BDAG ἐν 8), or "because of me" (BDAG ἐν 9)

Galatians 2

2:1 | διά + interval of time = "after" (BDAG διά A2c) | συμπαραλαβὼν καὶ Τίτον = "taking Titus along as well"

2:2 | κατὰ ἀποκάλυψιν = "in response to" (NIV) or "because of a revelation" (BDAG κατά B5aδ) | κατ' ἰδίαν = "privately" | οἱ δοκοῦντες = "the reputed ones" (cp. vv. 6, 9 – with εἶναι) | μὴ πώς = "[fearing] that perhaps" (BDAG πώς 2c) (cp. 4:11) | εἰς κενόν = "in vain" (BDAG εἰς 4e; κενός 3) (cp. Phil 2:16; 1 Thess 3:5)

2:3 | οὐδέ = "not even" (cp. v. 5) | ὁ σὺν ἐμοί = "who was with me," article as relative pronoun (W 213) | Ἕλλην ὤν = "even though he was a Greek," concessive ptc. (W 634)

2:4–5 | Principal options: (1) follow scribal omission of οἷς, or even οἷς οὐδέ (!) (see Metzger), and take διά + acc. as forward looking, providing the reason for v. 5; (2) accept the anacoluthon (BDF §467) and take vv. 4–5 as a single, awkward sentence (ESV); (3) take διά + acc. as backward looking, with general reference to the preceding, "This matter arose because" (NIV); (4) take vv. 3–5 as one sentence, with διά + acc. as backward looking, providing the reason why Paul refused to let Titus be circumcised (v. 3)

2:5 | οὐδὲ πρὸ ὥραν = "not even for a moment" (BDAG ὥρα 2b) | εἴκω τῇ ὑποταγῇ = "yield in submission," dat. of manner (W 161)

2:6 | Anacoluthon caused by self-interruption | οἱ δοκοῦντες εἶναί τι = "those reputed to be something special" (BDF §301(1)) | πρόσωπον λαμβάνω = "show favoritism" (Septuagintism)

2:7 | τοὐναντίον = τὸ ἐναντίον = "on the contrary" | πεπίστευμαι
τὸ εὐαγγέλιον = "I have been entrusted with the gospel" (cp. 1 Cor
9:17), pass. + acc. of retained object (W 197, 438; BDF §159(4)) |
τὸ εὐαγγέλιον τῆς ἀκροβυστίας/περιτομῆς = "the gospel to/for
the (un)circumcised," gen. of destination (W 101)

2:8 | εἰς (2x) = "for," equivalent to dat. of advantage (BDAG εἰς 4g)

2:9 | ἵνα ... εἰς = "that we should [go] to the Gentiles"

2:10 | μόνον ... ἵνα = "[they] only [asked] us to" (NASB), "all they
asked was that" (NIV), imperatival ἵνα (BDAG ἵνα 2g) | μνημονεύω
takes gen.

2:11 | κατὰ πρόσωπον = "to his face"

2:12 | πρὸ τοῦ ἐλθεῖν = "prior to the coming of" | συνήσθιεν = "he
used to eat," customary impf. | οἱ ἐκ περιτομῆς = "the circumcision
party" (see Acts 11:2; Tit 1:10), characteristic ἐκ (BDAG ἐκ 3b); the
phrase here should not be interpreted as referring merely to circumcised
believers of Jewish ancestry (as in Acts 10:45; Rom 4:12; Col 4:11)

2:13 | καὶ Βαρναβᾶς = "even Barnabas" | αὐτῶν τῇ ὑποκρίσει =
"their hypocrisy"

2:14 | πρός = "in accordance with" (BDAG πρός 3εδ) | Ἰουδαῖος
ὑπάρχων = "though being a Jew," concessive ptc. | πῶς = "how is it
that? with what right?" (BDAG πῶς 1αγ)

2:16 | ἐὰν μή = "but" (cp. 1:7); the usual mng. ("unless") does not fit
here | πίστις ['Ἰησοῦ] Χριστοῦ (2x; cp. 3:22) = "faith in [Jesus]
Christ" (although some scholars take as subjective gen., it is probably
objective)

2:17 | καὶ αὐτοί = "even we ourselves"

2:20 | ὃ δέ νῦν ζῶ = "the life that I now live" (BDF §154) (cp. Rom 6:10)

Galatians 3

3:1 | οἷς κατ᾽ ὀφθαλμούς = "before whose eyes"

3:2 | μανθάνειν τι ἀπὸ τινος = "learn something from someone" (BDAG ἀπό 3d)

3:2, 5 | ἐξ ἀκοῆς πίστεως (2x) = "by a hearing characterized by faith," "by hearing with faith," attributive gen. (W 86)

3:4 | πάσχω here probably means "experience" (BDAG πάσχω 1) | εἴ γε καὶ εἰκῇ = "if it really was in vain" (BDAG γέ ba), εἴ γε = "if indeed"

3:5 | "Does he who supplies the Spirit to you and works miracles among you [do these things] by the works of the law, or by hearing with faith?" | ὁ ἐπιχορηγῶν ... καὶ ἐνεργῶν – article governs both ptcs.

3:6 | καθώς demands οὕτως: "Just as Abraham believed and it was credited to him for righteousness, [so have you]" (cp. 2 Cor 9:7; 1 Tim 1:3)

3:8 | Second ὅτι is recitative (cp. vv. 10–11)

3:9 | ὥστε = "therefore" | σὺν τῷ πιστῷ Ἀβραάμ = "along with Abraham, the man of faith" (ESV)

3:10 | τοῦ ποιῆσαι αὐτά = "to do them," pleonastic τοῦ (BDF §400(7))

3:11 | First ὅτι = "that"; second ὅτι = "for" | δικαιόω ἐν νόμῳ (cp. 5:4) – either (1) "justification by the law," Hebr./instrumental ἐν, or (2) "justification under the law" (cp. Rom 2:12; Phil 2:6)

3:12 | ὁ ποιήσας = "whoever does" (NRSV), substantival gnomic aorist ptc. with generic reference (W 615 n8) (cp. Rom 10:5) | ἐν αὐτοῖς = "by means of [doing] them," Hebr./instrumental ἐν (BDF §219)

3:13 | γενόμενος = "by becoming," ptc. of means (W 628)

3:15 | κατὰ ἄνθρωπον λέγω = "to give a human example" (ESV) | ὅμως here could mean (1) "even though" (NASB) or (2) "likewise" (BDAG; BDF §450(2)) | ἀνθρώπου διαθήκην = "a human covenant or testament," gen. of description | κεκυρωμένην = "once it has been ratified" (ESV), "that has been duly established" (NIV)

3:16 | λέγει ... ὡς ἐπί + gen. (2x) = "he speaks not as one would of a plurality, but as of a single thing" (BDAG ὡς 1ba; ἐπί 8) | ὅς – should be neut. ὅ in agreement with τῷ σπέρματι, but changed to masc. in agreement with predicate Χριστός – gender attraction (W 338; BDF §134)

3:17 | ὁ ... νόμος | εἰς τό + inf. = "so as to ..."

3:19 | τῶν παραβάσεων χάριν (this preposition comes after the word it governs) – could be (1) retrospective, "because of the presence of transgressions" (BDAG χάριν b), or more likely (2) prospective, "to bring about transgressions" (BDAG χάριν a) | ἄχρις οὗ + subj. = "until" | ᾧ ἐπήγγελται = "to whom the promise had been made" (NASB) | ἐν χειρὶ μεσίτου – cp. ἐν χειρὶ Μωυσῆ (LXX Lev 26:46)

3:20 | ὁ δὲ μεσίτης ἑνὸς οὐκ ἔστιν = "now a mediator is not for one party only" (NASB)

3:21 | κατά + gen. = "against, contrary to" (cp. 5:17) | ἂν ἦν = "would have been"

3:22 | ὑπὸ ἁμαρτίαν – cp. Rom 3:9 | πίστις Ἰησοῦ Χριστοῦ – see 2:16

3:23 | πρὸ τοῦ ἐλθεῖν = "prior to the coming of" (cp. 2:12) | τὴν μέλλουσαν πίστιν ἀποκαλυφθῆναι = τὴν πίστιν τὴν μέλλουσαν ἀποκαλυφθῆναι = "the faith which was later be revealed" (NASB) (see Rom 8:18; cp. 1 Cor 12:22)

3:24 | εἰς Χριστόν = either (1) "until the coming of the Messiah" (BDAG εἰς 2aα) (cp. ESV), or (2) "[to lead us] to Christ" (NASB), pregnant construction with παιδαγωγός (< παῖς + ἄγω) (BDAG εἰς 10d)

3:25 | ἐλθούσης δὲ τῆς πίστεως = "but now that faith has come," gen. abs. (cp. Rom 7:9); metonymy for the object of faith, Christ

3:28 | ἔνι (3x) = ἔνεστιν = "there is"

Galatians 4
4:1 | ἐφ᾽ ὅσον χρόνον = "as long as" (BDAG ἐπί 18cβ) | οὐδὲν διαφέρει δούλου = "he is no different from a slave" (ESV), acc. of respect; gen. of comparison | κύριος πάντων ὤν = "even though he is master/owner of everything," concessive ptc.

4:2 | ἡ προθεσμία τοῦ πατρός = "the time set by the father," subjective gen.

4:3 | ἤμεθα δεδουλωμένοι = "we were enslaved," either plupf. periphrastic or perf. ptc. as predicate adjective (W 649 n90)

4:6 | ὅτι ἐστε υἱοί, ἐξαπέστειλεν ὁ θεός = "proof that you are sons is the fact that God sent" (M 147)

4:7 | εἰ ... καί = "if ... then," apodotic καί (BDAG καί 1bδ) | διὰ θεοῦ = either (1) "through the [triune] God" (see activity of each person of the Trinity in vv. 4–6), or (2) "by the will of God" (ZG)

4:9 | νῦν δὲ γνόντες τὸν θεόν = "but now that you have come to know God," inceptive aor. (W 558) | πάλιν ἄνωθεν = lit. "again again," "all over again"

4:11 | φοβοῦμαι ὑμᾶς μὴ πώς = "I am afraid for you that perhaps" (BDAG πώς 2b), prolepsis of object (ὑμᾶς) (BDF §476(3)) | εἰς – see 2:8

4:12 | κἀγώ = καὶ ἐγώ | γίνομαι in perfect or aorist is to be understood: "Become as I am, for I also [sc. have become] as you are," brachylogy (cp. Phil 2:5) | δέομαι + gen. of person begged | ἀδικέω + double acc. = "you have done me no wrong" (BDAG ἀδικέω 1c)

4:13 | δι᾽ ἀσθένειαν τῆς σαρκός = "because of a physical/bodily ailment" (BDAG διά B2a; ἀσθένεια 1), attributive gen. (W 86) | τὸ πρότερον = lit. "the first time" (NASB, ZG), implying there was a second time; but it may just mean "at first" (ESV), "originally" (M 98), adv. acc. (see BDAG πρότερος 1bβ)

4:14 | τὸν πειρασμὸν ὑμῶν ἐν τῇ σαρκί μου – difficult. If we follow NA, there are two main options: (1a) "That which was a trial to you in my bodily condition you did not despise or loathe" (NASB) (taking τὸν πειρασμὸν ὑμῶν as direct object); (1b) "During your time of trial in connection with my physical disability, you showed no disdain" (BDAG ἐξουθενέω) (taking τὸν πειρασμὸν ὑμῶν as acc. for extent of time). But if we follow one of the variant readings, the sentence makes more sense: (2a) τὸν πειρασμόν μου ἐν τῇ σαρκί μου ("my trial in my flesh"), (2b) τὸν πειρασμόν μου τὸν ἐν τῇ σαρκί μου ("my trial which was in my flesh"), or (2c) τὸν πειρασμόν τὸν ἐν τῇ σαρκί μου ("the trial which was in my flesh"), in all cases taking the phrase as the direct object of "you did not despise or loathe" (see Metzger) | ἐκπτύω = lit. "spit as a sign of contempt"

4:15 | ποῦ οὖν ὁ μακαρισμὸς ὑμῶν; = "What then has become of the blessing you felt?" (ESV) | εἰ δυνατόν ... ἐδώκατε = "if possible ... you would have given," second class (contrary-to-fact) condition (W

694–5 n26); addition of ἄν to the apodosis expected but not obligatory (BDF §360(1))

4:16 | ὥστε = "so now" | ἀληθεύων ὑμῖν = "by telling you the truth," ptc. of means (W 628)

4:17–18 | ζηλόω (3x) = "be deeply interested in someone, court someone's favor" (BDAG ζηλόω 1b; on active/passive voice, see M 25–26) | οὐ καλῶς ... ἐν καλῷ = "for no good purpose ... for a good purpose" (ESV)

4:18 | καλόν + inf. = "it is good to ..." (BDAG καλός 2dγ) | πάντοτε modifies ζηλοῦσθαι (NASB) not καλόν (ESV) | ἐν τῷ + inf. = "when" | Acc. μέ as subject of inf.

4:19 | οὓς ὠδίνω = "with whom I am in labor" (NASB), "whom I bring forth in birth-pains" (BDAG ὠδίνω b), the acc. direct object concretizes the verb as the act of giving birth itself | μέχρις οὗ + subj. = "until"

4:20 | ἤθελον + inf. = "how I wish I could be with you now!" (NIV), impf. used to express unattainable wish (BDF §359(2)) | ἀλλάξαι τὴν φωνήν μου = "to change my tone" (BDAG ἀλλάσσω 1; φωνή 2b) | ἐν ὑμῖν = "about you" or "because of you" (BDAG ἐν 9b; ἀπορέω)

4:22–23, 30–31 | ἡ ἐλευθέρα (4x) = "the free woman," substantivized adj. with article (BDF §263)

4:23 | ὁ μέν ... ὁ δέ = "the one [son] ... the other [son]"

4:24 | ἅτινά ἐστιν ἀλληγορούμενα = "these things are spoken allegorically," neut. pl. subjects take sg. verbs | εἰς δουλείαν γεννῶσα = "bearing children for slavery" (ESV), "... who are to be slaves" (NASB), εἰς indicating vocation (BDAG εἰς 4d)

4:27 | πολλά ... μᾶλλον ἤ + gen. of comparison = "more numerous ... than" (NASB)

4:28 | κατὰ Ἰσαάκ = "just as Isaac" (BDAG κατά B5bα)

4:29 | ὁ κατὰ σάρκα γεννηθείς ... ὁ κατὰ πνεῦμα [γεννηθείς] = "he who was born according to the flesh ... he who [was born] according to the Spirit"

Galatians 5

5:1 | τῇ ἐλευθερίᾳ ... ἠλευθέρωσεν – could be (1) cognate dat. (M 178; W 168); (2) dat. of purpose (?): "for this freedom" (ἐπί is needed; cp. v. 13); (3) dat. of destination (W 147): "to this freedom," (4) dat. of sphere (W 153): "in this freedom," or (5) instrumental dat. (W 162): "by [bestowing] this freedom Christ has set us/you free" (Burton) | The article τῇ is anaphoric, "this freedom," referring back to the freedom from the law that Paul has been discussing in chs. 2–4 | For survey of the numerous textual issues, see Burton 270–1

5:3 | ὀφειλέτης + inf. = "under obligation to" (BDAG ὀφειλέτης 2b) (cp. Rom 8:12) | ὅλον τὸν νόμον is direct object of ποιῆσαι

5:4 | κατηργήθητε & ἐξεπέσατε – futuristic or proleptic aorists dramatically representing the consequences as historical fact (BDF §333(2); Z §257) | οἵτινες ἐν νόμῳ δικαιοῦσθε = "you who are trying to be justified by the law" (NIV), conative present (BDF §319; M 8) | δικαιόω ἐν νόμῳ – see 3:11 | ἐκπίπτω + gen. of separation (W 107–8; BDF §180) = "fall away from"

5:5 | ἐλπίδα δικαιοσύνης ἀπεκδεχόμεθα – Option (1) "we wait eagerly for the hope of righteousness," taking ἐλπίς as the act of hoping (BDAG ἐλπίς 1bβ), implying that we are hoping for an eschatological verdict of righteousness (on this view, δικαιοσύνης could be objective gen., or gen. of apposition); but this interpretation "would not be in keeping with the Pauline doctrine, according to which righteousness, as the privilege and state of the believer, is already present, cf. 2 Tim 4:8; Gal 2:17; Rom 5:1" (Cremer 254); therefore, option (2) "we wait eagerly for the hope [namely, glorification] which righteousness secures," taking ἐλπίς as that for which one hopes (BDAG ἐλπίς 3) (cp. Rom 8:24; Col 1:5; Tit 2:13); on this view, δικαιοσύνης could be gen. of source, gen. of production (W 104), or possessive gen. | ἀπεκδέχομαι = "wait eagerly," in Paul it always has an eschatological object (cp. Rom 8:19, 23, 25; 1 Cor 1:7; Phil 3:20)

5:6 | τι ἰσχύει = "counts for anything," "has any validity," with legal connotation (BDAG ἰσχύω 4) (cp. Heb 9:17) | πίστις δι᾽ ἀγάπης ἐνεργουμένη – it is not that faith is "energized, made effective, or formed" by means of love (Roman Catholic theology), but that faith itself is "at work, actively expressing itself (mid.)" through love (BDAG ἐνεργέω 1b)

5:7 | τίς ὑμᾶς ἐνέκοψεν τῇ ἀληθείᾳ μὴ πείθεσθαι; = "who hindered you from obeying the truth?" πείθω (mid./pass.) + dat. of person or thing to be obeyed (BDAG πείθω 3b)

5:8 | ἡ πεισμονή = "that kind of persuasion" (NIV) (cp. BDAG), or "that sort of obedience/acquiescence" (BDF §488(1)(b)), anaphoric def. article

5:10 | πείθω εἰς ὑμᾶς = "I have confidence in you" (BDAG εἰς 4cβ) | οὐδὲν ἄλλο φρονήσετε = "you will take no other view" (NIV) | ὅστις ἐὰν ᾖ = "whoever he may be" (NIV)

5:12 | ὄφελον + fut. indic. = "would that they would ..." (BDF §384)

5:13 | ἐπ᾽ ἐλευθερίᾳ = "for freedom" (BDAG ἐπί 16) | μόνον μὴ τὴν ἐλευθερίαν εἰς ἀφορμὴν τῇ σαρκί – an impv. must be supplied, depending on which mng. of εἰς is understood: "only do not [turn] your freedom *into* (BDAG εἰς 4b) an opportunity for the flesh" (NASB), or "only do not [use] your freedom *as* (BDAG εἰς 8b) an opportunity for the flesh" (ESV)

5:14 | On τῷ before quotation, see BDAG ὁ 2hα | ἀγαπήσεις – imperatival future (W 569–70; Z §280)

5:15 | βλέπετε μή + subj. = "watch out lest" (BDAG βλέπω 5)

5:16 | τελέω = "carry out"

5:17 | κατά + gen. – see 3:21 | ἵνα μὴ ἃ ἐὰν θέλητε ταῦτα ποιῆτε = "with the result that you do not do *anything and everything* [ἃ ἐάν] that your flesh desires," ἵνα goes with ποιῆτε and has ecbatic mng. (BDAG ἵνα 3; W 473; M 142)

5:19 | φανερά ἐστιν & ἅτινά ἐστιν – neut. pl. subjects take sg. verbs

5:21 | τὰ ὅμοια τούτοις = "things like these" | ἃ προλέγω ὑμῖν καθὼς προεῖπον = "of which I tell you in advance, as I said previously" – Since προ- is a relative time-indicator, the mng. of προλέγω is tense-dependent: present indic. = "tell in advance," whereas aorist/impf. indic.= "said/was saying previously"

5:25 | εἰ ζῶμεν ... καὶ στοιχῶμεν = "if we are alive by the Spirit, by the Spirit let us *also* walk" – στοιχῶμεν is hortatory subj.; bec. "we live" in Eng. is ambiguous, ζῶμεν should be translated "we are alive" or "we have life" (in Gk. ζάω rarely denotes one's way of life or conduct)

Galatians 6

6:1 | σκοπῶν σεαυτὸν μὴ καὶ σὺ πειρασθῇς = "watching yourself lest *you too* be tempted," note shift from pl. (ὑμεῖς) to sg. (σύ)

6:2 | καὶ οὕτως = "and so" or "and in this way"

6:3 | εἰ δοκεῖ τις εἶναί τι = "if anyone thinks he is something" | μηδὲν ὤν = "when he is nothing"

6:4 | ἔχω καύχημα εἰς = "have reason for boasting in," where καύχημα means "a thing of which one is proud; reason for boasting" (BDAG καύχημα 1), rather than "an expression of pride; boasting" (BDAG καύχημα 2) (cp. twofold mng. of ἐλπίς – see 5:5) | "And then his reason to boast will be in himself alone and not in his neighbor" (ESV), i.e., "without comparing himself to somebody else" (NIV 1984)

6:5 | ἕκαστος τὸ ἴδιον φορτίον βαστάσει – either (1) "each one should carry their own load" (NIV 2011), imperatival fut. (which is in tension with v. 2); or (2) "each one will bear their own load," genuine fut., referring to standing alone before God at final judgment

6:6 | ὁ κατηχούμενος τὸν λόγον = "the one who is taught the word," pass. + acc. of retained object – see 2:7 | τῷ κατηχοῦντι = "with the one who teaches"

6:7 | ὃ ἐάν = "whatever" | τοῦτο καὶ θερίσει = "that will he also reap"

6:9 | τὸ καλὸν ποιοῦντες μὴ ἐγκακῶμεν = "let us not grow tired of doing what is good," supplementary ptc.; hortatory subj. | καιρῷ ἰδίῳ = "in due time" | μὴ ἐκλυόμενοι = "if we do not give up," conditional ptc.

6:10 | καιρὸν ἔχω = "have opportunity" (BDAG καιρός 1b) | ἐργαζώμεθα – hortatory subj.

6:11 | ἔγραψα – epistolary aorist (W 563)

6:12 | ἀναγκάζουσιν – conative present (BDF §319) | μόνον ἵνα = "solely in order that" (BDAG μόνος 2d) | τῷ σταυρῷ τοῦ Χρ. = "for the cross of Christ," dat. of cause (BDF §196; M 45)

6:14 | δι' οὗ – either (1) "through whom [= Christ]", or (2) "through which [= the cross]" | ἐμοὶ & κόσμῳ – datives of respect (W 144) | κἀγώ = καὶ ἐγώ

6:16 | καὶ ἐπὶ τὸν Ἰσραὴλ τοῦ θεοῦ – debated: either (1) connective marker of addition, or (2) epexegetical καί (= "even" [NIV 1984] or "that is") (BDF §442(9); Z §455ζ)

6:17 | τοῦ λοιποῦ [sc. χρόνου] = "from now on, henceforth" (BDAG λοιπός 3aβ), gen. of time (BDF §186(2); M 39, 161) (cp. Eph 6:10)

6:18 | Sc. ἔστω

Chapter Ten

The Epistle to the Ephesians

Ephesians 1

1:1 | Textual issue – since ἐν Ἐφέσῳ is lacking in some important MSS, it has been hypothesized that Eph was a circular letter sent to multiple churches (Metzger)

1:4 | καθώς = "since" (BDAG καθώς 3; BDF §453(2)) | εἶναι ἡμᾶς = "that we would be," inf. of purpose (BDF §390); acc. ἡμᾶς as subject of inf. (cp. v. 12)

1:5 | εἰς αὐτόν = "to himself"

1:6 | Relative pronoun ἧς should be ᾗ ("by/with which") but was changed from dat. to gen. by attraction to τῆς χάριτος (ZG; BDF §294(2)) (cp. 4:1) | ἐχαρίτωσεν means more than "freely bestowed" (NASB, NRSV) and has a rich positive sense; it has "a certain inclination towards the conception embraced in δεκτός" (Cremer 576): "accepted" (KJV), "blessed" (ESV), "highly favored" (BDAG χαριτόω) (cp. Lk 1:28); Semitic cognate: "his grace/favor, with which he graced/favored us in the Beloved"

1:12 | εἰς τὸ εἶναι ἡμᾶς = "so that we would be" (cp. v. 4)

1:13 | ἀκούσαντες ... πιστεύσαντες ἐσφραγίσθητε – "*when* you heard ... and believed, you were sealed," contemporaneous attendant circumstances ptcs. (W 640); not "*after* you heard ... and believed" (W 625 n33) | Second ἐν ᾧ could go with πιστεύσαντες ("and believed in him," ESV), but more likely it goes with ἐσφραγίσθητε ("you were sealed in Him," NASB)

1:14 | Textual issue – ὅ (neut. in agreement with πνεῦμα) or ὅς (masc. by gender attraction to ἀρραβών) (see W 338 n59) | εἰς ἀπολύτρωσιν τῆς περιποιήσεως – probably future (bodily) redemption in view (Rom 8:23; Eph 4:30); but περιποίησις is ambiguous – could refer to God's possession of us (1 Pet 2:9), or our possession of the inheritance (1 Thess 5:9; 2 Thess 2:14); thus: (1) "with a view to the redemption of [those who are] God's own possession" (NASB/NIV), or (2) "until we acquire possession of it" (= our inheritance) (ESV)

1:15 | κἀγώ = καὶ ἐγώ | ἡ καθ' ὑμᾶς πίστις = "your faith" (BDAG κατά B7b; Z §130)

1:16 | παύομαι + ptc. = "stop doing something" | μνείαν ποιεῖσθαι = "to mention," ποιέω (mid.) + noun as periphrasis for simple verbal idea (BDAG ποιέω 7a; μνεία 2), gen. object must be supplied (cp. Rom 1:9; 1 Thess 1:2; Phm 4)

1:17 | ἵνα of content (M 145)

1:18 | πεφωτισμένους τοὺς ὀφθαλμοὺς τῆς καρδίας ὑμῶν – awkward syntax; possibilities: (1) acc. in apposition to whole sentence (M 25; BDF §480(6)), (2) dependent on ὑμῖν (v. 17) but changed to acc. in anticipation of ὑμᾶς (v. 18), or (3) second direct object of δώῃ (v. 17) ("that he would grant you ... enlightened hearts") | εἰς τὸ εἰδέναι ὑμᾶς = "that you may know," εἰς + articular inf. as purpose clause (BDF §402(2)); acc. ὑμᾶς as subject of inf.

1:20 | ἐγείρας – ptc. of means (W 630)

1:22 | In view of 1 Cor 15:25, ὑπέταξεν could be a proleptic aorist (W 563–4) | αὐτὸν ἔδωκεν κεφαλήν = "appointed him [as] head," δίδωμι + double acc. (BDAG δίδωμι 7) (cp. 4:11) | τῇ ἐκκλησίᾳ = "for the church" (NIV), dat. of advantage

1:23 | τὸ πλήρωμα τοῦ τὰ πάντα ἐν πᾶσιν πληρουμένου = "the fulness of him who fills all in all," mid. in form, active in mng. (M 25; BDF §316(1)) | τὸ πλήρωμα – probably best taken in apposition, not to the church, but to Christ (M 25) (cp. 3:19; 4:10, 13; Col 1:19; 2:9) (see comments in ZG)

Ephesians 2

2:1 | Anacoluthon: the acc. demands a verb and its subject, but these do not appear until vv. 4–5 (ὁ θεός ... συνεζωοποίησεν), where the participial phrase of v. 1 is repeated.

2:2–3 | οἱ υἱοὶ τῆς ἀπειθείας ... τέκνα φύσει ὀργῆς = "those who are disobedient ... by nature objects of wrath" (NIV 1984), Hebr. "son of" idiom (BDAG υἱός 2cβ; τέκνον 6)

2:3 | ἐν οἷς = "among whom" (W 336)

2:5, 8 | ἐστε σεσῳσμένοι (2x) – intensive (resultative) perf. periphrastic (W 574–5, 649; M 18–19)

2:7 | χρηστότης ἐφ᾽ ἡμᾶς = "kindness toward us" (BDAG ἐπί 15)

2:8 | καὶ τοῦτο – could refer to (1) the whole preceding idea (cp. Rom 13:11; 1 Cor 6:6, 8; Eph 6:1; 1 Pet 2:19–21 [τοῦτο 3x]), or (2) πίστις (in spite of gender mismatch, BDF §132; cp. 1 Cor 6:11 [ταῦτα]; Eph 5:5 [ὅ]; 6:17 [ὅ]; Phil 1:28 [τοῦτο]; 1 Pet 3:4 [ὅ]; 1 John 2:8 [ὅ])

2:10 | ἐπὶ ἔργοις ἀγαθοῖς = "for good works" (BDAG ἐπί 16)

2:11 | λεγόμενος (2x) = "so-called"

2:12 | τῆς πολιτείας – gen. of separation (W 107–8)

2:13 | ἐν τῷ αἵματι τοῦ Χρ. = "by the blood of Christ," Hebr./instrumental ἐν (BDF §219)

2:14 | τὸ μεσότοιχον [< μέσος + τοῖχος] τοῦ φραγμοῦ = "the barrier formed by the diving wall" (BDAG μεσότοιχον)

2:15 | ἐν δόγμασιν = "consisting of decrees" (M 79) | καταργήσας – ptc. of means (W 630) | Direct object of καταργήσας could be (1) τὴν ἔχθραν with τὸν νόμον in apposition ("by abolishing in his flesh the enmity, which is the law of commandments contained in ordinances," NASB), or (2) τὸν νόμον, taking τὴν ἔχθραν in apposition with τὸ μεσότοιχον ("the dividing wall of hostility, by abolishing in his flesh the law with its commandments and regulations," NIV 1984) | κτίζω εἰς = "make something into something else" (BDAG εἰς 4b) | ποιῶν εἰρήνην = "thus making peace," ptc. of result (W 637–9)

2:16 | ἐν αὐτῷ = "by it [= the cross]," Hebr./instrumental ἐν (cp. v. 13)

2:19 | συμπολῖται τῶν ἁγίων = "fellow-citizens with the saints," gen. of association (W 129) (cp. 5:7)

2:20 | ὄντος ἀκρογωνιαίου – gen. abs.

Ephesians 3
3:1 | τούτου χάριν = "for this reason," χάριν as preposition takes gen. (cp. v. 14) | Paul breaks off sentence and never completes it

3:3 | ὅτι = "namely that" (ZG) | καθὼς προέγραψα ἐν ὀλίγῳ = "as I have already written briefly" (NIV)

3:4 | πρὸς ὅ = "in accordance with which" (BDAG πρός 3εδ), "in the light of which" (ZG) | ἀναγινώσκοντες = "in reading," "when you read," temporal ptc. (W 623) or ptc. of means (W 628)

3:5 | ἑτέραις γενεαῖς = "in other generations," temporal dat. (M 43)

3:6 | εἶναι – epexegetical inf. (BDF §394) explicating the content of "the mystery of Christ" (v. 4)

3:8 | πάντων ἁγίων – gen. of comparison

3:8–9 | εὐαγγελίσασθαι, φωτίσαι – more epexegetical infs.

3:10 | ἵνα connects back to vv. 8–9 as a whole, rather than to κτίσαντι (*pace* Robert L. Reymond, *A New Systematic Theology of the Christian Faith* [Nashville: Thomas Nelson, 1998], 487, 490–92)

3:11 | ἐποίησεν = "accomplished" (NIV), "carried out" (NASB)

3:12 | διὰ τῆς πίστεως αὐτοῦ = "through faith in him," objective gen.

3:13 | αἰτοῦμαι μή + inf. = "I ask [you] not to"

3:15 | ὀνομάζω ἔκ τινος = "receive one's name from one" | πᾶσα πατριά = either (1) "every family," including angels (BDAG πατριά 3), or (2) "the whole family" (M 94–5) | ἐρριζωμένοι καὶ τεθεμελιωμένοι – hanging nominatives (M 105; BDF §468(2))

3:19 | τὴν ὑπερβάλλουσαν τῆς γνώσεως ἀγάπην τοῦ Χρ. = "the love of Christ that surpasses knowledge," ὑπερβάλλω + gen. of comparison | ἵνα πληρωθῆτε εἰς πᾶν τὸ πλήρωμα τοῦ θεοῦ = "that you may be filled *up to* [not 'with'] all the fullness of God" (NASB)

3:20 | τῷ δὲ δυναμένῳ ... νοοῦμεν = "Now to Him who is able to do far more abundantly *beyond all* that we ask or think" (NASB, moving ὑπὲρ πάντα after ὑπερεκπερισσοῦ) | ὑπερεκπερισσοῦ ὧν (= τούτων ἅ) = "infinitely more than" (BDAG), gen. of comparison

Ephesians 4

4:1 | ὁ δέσμιος ἐν κυρίῳ = "the prisoner in/for the Lord" (cp. Phil 1:13) | ἀξίως + gen. = "in a manner worth of" | ἥ becomes ἧς by attraction (see 1:6)

4:2–3 | ἀνεχόμενοι and σπουδάζοντες – either (1) imperatival ptcs. (BDF §468(2)), or (2) ptcs. of means (W 652)

4:4–6 | Trinitarian formula: Spirit, Lord, God (cp. 1 Cor 12:4–6)

4:7 | ἑνὶ ἑκάστῳ ἡμῶν = "to each one of us"

4:9 | τὸ Ἀνέβη – article used to quote a single word (BDAG ὁ 2hβ) | τί ἐστιν; = "what does it mean?" (BDAG εἰμί 2cα)

4:10 | ὁ καταβὰς αὐτός ἐστιν καὶ ὁ ἀναβάς = "he who descended is the same one who also ascended" (BDAG αὐτός 3)

4:12 | Punctuation options: (1) two parallel prepositional phrases, with first εἰς supplementing καταρτισμός ("equipping for the work of ministry") (many English versions; BDAG καταρτισμός), or (2) three parallel prepositional phrases set off by commas (πρός ... εἰς ... εἰς) (KJV; T. David Gordon, "'Equipping' Ministry in Ephesians 4?" *JETS* 37.1 [1994]: 69–78, critiquing "every member ministry" view)

4:14 | πρὸς τὴν μεθοδείαν τῆς πλάνης = "in deceitful scheming" (BDAG, NASB), "in accordance with the wiles of error" (M 53–4)

4:15 | αὐξήσωμεν – could be hortatory subj. ("let us grow"), but probably a second subj. dependent on ἵνα (v. 14) (note chiastic structure of vv. 14–15; Lincoln) | τὰ πάντα = "in all things," acc. of respect

4:16 | διὰ πάσης ἀφῆς τῆς ἐπιχορηγίας = "by every supporting ligament" (NIV, cp. BDAG) | κατ' ἐνέργειαν ἐν μέτρῳ ἑνός ἑκάστου μέρους = "according to the proper working (or functioning capacity [BDAG μέτρον]) of each individual part" (NASB) | τὴν αὔξησιν ποιεῖται = "grows," ποιέω (mid.) + noun as periphrasis for simple verbal idea (BDAG ποιέω 7a) | τοῦ σώματος is pleonastic (see πᾶν τὸ σῶμα earlier); added for clarity

4:17 | μηκέτι ὑμᾶς περιπατεῖν = "that you no longer walk," indirect discourse; acc. ὑμᾶς as subject of inf.; inf. seems to have added imperatival force (BDF §389) | τὰ ἔθνη περιπατεῖ – neut. pl. subjects take sg. verbs

4:18 | τῇ διανοίᾳ – dat. of respect (cp. Col 1:21) | τῆς ζωῆς – gen. of separation (cp. 2:12)

4:22–24 | ἀποθέσθαι … ἀνανεοῦσθαι … ἐνδύσασθαι – three infs. complementing ἐδιδάχθητε, could be taken as (1) indirect discourse ("you were taught that you *have* put off ..."), or (2) imperatival infs. ("you were taught that you *should* put off ...") (see W 605)

4:22 | κατὰ τὰς ἐπιθυμίας τῆς ἀπάτης = "in accordance with deceitful desires," attributive gen.

4:23 | τῷ πνεύματι – dat. of respect

4:24 | κατὰ θεὸν κτισθέντα = "created after the likeness of God" (ESV) (BDAG κατά B5ba)

4:25 | τὸ ψεῦδος = "falsehood"

4:26 | ὀργίζεσθε – impv. used to express a concession (BDF §387(1)) | ἐπὶ τῷ παροργισμῷ ὑμῶν = "while you are still angry" (NIV), temporal use of ἐπί (BDAG ἐπί 18b)

4:28 | ἐργαζόμενος – ptc. of means (W 630) | ἵνα ἔχῃ μεταδιδόναι = "so that he might have [something] to share"

4:29 | πᾶς λόγος σαπρός ... μή = "no unwholesome word," Hebr. (Z §446) (cp. 5:5) | ἀλλὰ εἴ τις ἀγαθὸς πρὸς οἰκοδομήν = "but only such [a word] as is good for edification" (NASB) | τῆς χρείας is difficult – "according to the need of the moment" (NASB), "where it is necessary" (BDAG χρεία 3), "needed, in case of need" (ZG), "as fits the occasion" (ESV)

4:30 | ἐν ᾧ = "by whom," Hebr./instrumental ἐν

Ephesians 5

5:2 | εἰς ὀσμὴν εὐωδίας = "as a fragrant aroma" (LXX Gen 8:21; Exod 29:18; Lev 1:9, etc.), Semitic predicate εἰς (BDAG εἰς 8b)

5:4 | ἃ οὐκ ἀνῆκεν – neut. pl. subjects take sg. verbs

5:5 | τοῦτο ἴστε [impv. of οἶδα] γινώσκοντες = "of this you can be sure" (NIV), finite verb + Hebr. cognate ptc. (BDF §422; Z §61) | πᾶς πόρνος ... οὐκ ἔχει = "no immoral person ... has" (cp. 4:29) | ὅ (neut.) does not agree with either the antecedent or the predicate; ὅ ἐστιν is a stereotyped expression, "that is" (cp. 6:17; Col 3:14)

5:6 | ἔρχεται – futuristic present (W 537)

5:7 | συμμέτοχοι αὐτῶν = "fellow-sharers with them," gen. of association (W 129) (cp. 2:19)

5:9 | Must supply a verb, e.g., "consists" (NIV, NASB), "is found" (ESV)

5:12 | αἰσχρόν ἐστιν καὶ λέγειν = "it is shameful *even* to mention" (NIV)

5:12–13 | Neut. pl. subjects take sg. verbs

5:13–14 | φανερόω (pass.) (2x) = "become visible" (BDAG φανερόω 1b)

5:15 | βλέπετε ἀκριβῶς = "be very careful" (βλέπετε already means "be careful")

5:16, 19–21 | Imperatival ptcs. (BDF §468(2))

5:22 | αἱ γυναῖκες – nom. for voc. (W 58)

5:23 | ἀνήρ is the subject (and κεφαλή the predicate), since ἀνήρ is the known entity, previously mentioned in v. 22 (W 42, 44 n23)

5:24 | ἀλλά – options: (1) rhetorically ascensive, "indeed," (2) used with an impv. (implied via brachylogy) to strengthen command, "now then," (3) to introduce an inference, "so, therefore, accordingly" (see BDAG ἀλλά 4b/5)

5:31 | ἀντὶ τούτου = "for this reason" | ἔσονται εἰς – Semitic predicate εἰς, or εἰς with verbs of changing, or perhaps both (BDAG εἰς 8aβ, 4b)

5:32 | λέγω εἰς = "speak with reference to" (BDAG εἰς 5)

5:33 | πλήν = "in any case" (BDAG πλήν c) | ὑμεῖς οἱ καθ᾽ ἕνα ἕκαστος = "each of you individually" | οὕτως ... ὡς = "so ... as" | Imperatival ἵνα (BDAG ἵνα 2g)

Ephesians 6
6:2 | ἐντολὴ πρώτη ἐν ἐπαγγελίᾳ = "the first commandment with a promise" (NASB), ἐν of accompaniment (M 78; BDAG ἐν 5a)

6:4 | κυρίου – either (1) subjective gen. (the Lord's own discipline [cp. LXX Prov 3:11] mediated through the parents), or (2) gen. of quality (in the sphere of the Lord, i.e., Christian)

6:6–7 | ποιοῦντες ... δουλεύοντες – imperatival ptcs.

6:7 | μετ' εὐνοίας = "with good will" (NASB), "with a good attitude, willingness" (BDAG εὔνοια), "with enthusiasm" (NRSV)

6:8 | ἕκαστος, ἐάν τι ποιήσῃ ἀγαθόν = "whatever good thing each one does" (NASB) (cp. use of κομίζω in Col 3:25)

6:9 | καὶ αὐτῶν καὶ ὑμῶν ὁ κύριος = "both their Master and yours," καί ... καί (BDAG καί 1f)

6:10 | τοῦ λοιποῦ [sc. χρόνου] = "finally" (BDAG λοιπός 3aβ), gen. of time (BDF §186(2); M 39, 161) (cp. Gal 6:17)

6:11 | πρὸς τὸ δύνασθαι ὑμᾶς στῆναι = "so that you will be able to stand" (BDF §402(5); W 592)

6:11–12 | πρός (6x) = "against" (BDAG πρός 3da)

6:12 | οὐκ ἔστιν ἡμῖν ἡ πάλη = "our struggle is not" (BDF §190) | τὰ πνευματικὰ τῆς πονηρίας = "the spiritual [forces] of wickedness" (NASB)

6:13 | καὶ ἅπαντα κατεργασάμενοι στῆναι = "and having done everything, to stand firm" (NASB), ἅπαντα as direct object of κατεργασάμενοι

6:14–15 | τὴν ὀσφύν, τοὺς πόδας – accusatives of respect

6:16 | ἐν πᾶσιν = "in all circumstances, above all" (M 78) | ἐν ᾧ = "with which" (M 77)

6:17 | ὅ – should be fem. ἥ in agreement with τὴν μάχαιραν but changed to neut. in agreement with predicate ῥῆμα – gender attraction (W 338; BDF §134)

6:18 | προσευχόμενοι, ἀγρυπνοῦντες – imperatival ptcs. | καὶ εἰς αὐτό = "and with this in view" (NASB)

6:19 | λόγος = "words, utterance"

6:20 | ὑπὲρ οὗ & ἐν αὐτῷ both refer back to τὸ εὐαγγέλιον

6:21 | τὰ κατ' ἐμέ, τί πράσσω = "how I am and what I am doing" (NIV) (cp. Phil 1:12; Col 4:7)

6:22 | ἔπεμψα – epistolary aorist (M 12; BDF §334)

6:24 | Options: (1) ἀφθαρσία may mean (a) "incorruption, sincerity" or (b) "immortality" (perhaps both, M 197); (2) ἐν ἀφθαρσίᾳ may modify (a) τῶν ἀγαπώντων ("those who love our Lord Jesus with a sincere [or undying] love"), (b) χάρις ("grace with immortality," the twofold blessing that Paul wishes upon his readers), or (c) Ἰησοῦν Χριστόν who is now in the state of immortality

Chapter Eleven

The Epistle to the Philippians

Philippians 1

1:3 | ἐπὶ πάσῃ τῇ μνείᾳ ὑμῶν = "every time I remember you" (NIV), temporal use of ἐπί (BDAG ἐπί 18b)

1:4 | τὴν δέησιν ποιούμενος = "praying," ποιέω (mid.) + noun as periphrasis for simple verbal idea (BDAG ποιέω 7a)

1:5 | ἐπὶ τῇ κοινωνίᾳ ὑμῶν εἰς τὸ εὐαγγέλιον = "because of your partnership in the gospel," providing the reason for Paul's thanksgiving and joyful prayers (vv. 3–4) (BDAG ἐπί 6c)

1:7 | καθώς = "since" (BDAG καθώς 3; BDF §453(2)), connecting to vv. 3–6 | ὑπέρ + gen. = "about" (BDAG ὑπέρ A3) | διὰ τὸ ἔχειν με ἐν τῇ καρδίᾳ ὑμᾶς = "because I have you in my heart" (NASB); in theory, could be "because *you* have *me* in your heart," but the acc. closest to the inf. is normally the subject (Jeffrey T. Reed, "The Infinitive with Two Substantival Accusatives: An Ambiguous Construction?" *NovT* 33 [1991]: 1–27) | ἔν τε τοῖς δεσμοῖς ... ὑμᾶς ὄντας = "since both in my imprisonment and in the defense and confirmation of the gospel, you are all partakers of grace with me" (NASB)

1:9 | τοῦτο προσεύχομαι, ἵνα = "this I pray, that," taking ἵνα as substitute for explanatory inf. after demonstrative (BDAG ἵνα 2e; BDF §394)

1:10 | εἰς τὸ δοκιμάζειν ὑμᾶς = "so that you may discern/approve," acc. ὑμᾶς as subject of inf. (cp. v. 7) | Second εἰς could be translated "for" (ESV), "until" (NASB), or "on" (NRSV; cp. 2:16)

1:11 | καρπόν ... τὸν διὰ Ἰ. Χρ. = "the fruit ... which [comes] through Jesus Christ"

1:12 | τὰ κατ᾽ ἐμέ = "my circumstances" (NASB) (cp. Eph 6:21; Col 4:7); neut. pl. subjects take sg. verbs (ἐλήλυθεν) | μᾶλλον ... ἐλήλυθεν = "have led rather to the progress of the gospel" (ZG) (BDAG ἔρχομαι 5)

1:13 | ὥστε ... γενέσθαι = "as a result it has become clear that I am a prisoner because I am a Christian" (Hawthorne) | ἐν ὅλῳ τῷ πραιτωρίῳ = "throughout the whole praetorian guard," assuming Paul is imprisoned in Rome; but could refer to a governor's palace guard (see BDAG πραιτώριον); ἐν ὅλῳ = "throughout the whole," cp. Rom 1:8 (NASB)

1:14 | ἐν κυρίῳ – could modify the noun ("the brothers in the Lord," NIV 1984) or the ptc. ("confident in the Lord," ESV) | τοῖς δεσμοῖς μου = "because of my imprisonment," dat. of cause (BDF §196) | τολμᾶν – this is the second inf. (after γενέσθαι) continuing the ὥστε result clause that began in v. 13 | λαλεῖν is complementary to τολμᾶν ("emboldened to speak")

1:15 | τινὲς μέν ... τινὲς δέ = "some ... others" | διά + acc. = "because of"

1:16–17 | οἱ μέν ... οἱ δέ = "the latter ... the former"

1:16 | κεῖμαι εἰς = "I am put here for" (ESV)

1:17 | ἐγείρω = "bring into being, cause" (BDAG ἐγείρω 5) | τοῖς δεσμοῖς μου = lit. "for my chains," pregnant for "for me in my imprisonment"

1:18 | τί γάρ; = "What difference does it make?" (BDF §299(3)) | πλὴν ὅτι = "in any case" (BDF §449(2); BDAG πλήν 1c) | εἴτε ... εἴτε = "whether ... or" (cp. vv. 21, 27) | ἀλλὰ καί = "[not only this] but also" (BDF §448(6); BDAG ἀλλά 3)

1:19 | ἐπιχορηγία τοῦ πνεύματος – could be (1) subjective gen. ("the help given by the Spirit," NIV 1984), (2) objective gen. ("the provision of the Spirit," NASB; cp. Z §184), implying that God or Jesus provided the Spirit, or (3) epexegetical gen. ("the provision which consists of the Spirit")

1:20 | ὡς πάντοτε καὶ νῦν = "as always *so* now" (BDAG καί 2c; ὡς 2a) (cp. Matt 6:10; Acts 7:51; Gal 1:9)

1:21 | ἐμοί = "to me, as far as I am concerned," ethical dat. (W 146–7) | τὸ ζῆν is the subject and Χριστός is the predicate (see insightful comments at Z §173)

1:22 | εἰ δὲ τὸ ζῆν ἐν σαρκί τοῦτό μοι καρπὸς ἔργου = "But if I am to live on in the flesh, this will mean fruitful labor for me" (NASB), taking ἔργου as attributed gen. (W 89–90)

1:25 | τοῦτο refers back to the thought expressed in v. 24 | τῆς πίστεως = "in the faith"

1:26 | τὸ καύχημα ... ἐν ἐμοι = "your proud confidence in me" (NASB)

1:27 | ἀξίως + gen. = "in a manner worthy of"

1:28 | ἥτις ... σωτερίας is difficult – either (1) "although your loyalty to the faith is proof to them that you will perish, it is in fact proof that you will be saved" (Hawthorne), or (2) "this is a sign to them that they will be destroyed, but that you will be saved" (NIV) | καὶ τοῦτο ἀπὸ θεοῦ (cp. Eph 2:8) – could refer to entire preceding thought, which fits best with option (1), or to σωτηρία which works with either option

1:29 | τὸ ὑπὲρ Χριστοῦ – adv. acc. (BDF §160) | τὸ πιστεύειν, τὸ πάσχειν – articular infs., "the privilege of believing/suffering"

1:29–30 | ὑμῖν continued by nom. ἔχοντες – solecism (M 30–31)

1:30 | εἴδετε ἐν ἐμοὶ καὶ νῦν ἀκούετε ἐν ἐμοί = "you saw I had, and now hear that I still have" (NIV, ESV) (BDAG ἐν 8)

Philippians 2

2:1 | εἴ τις/τι (4x) = "if [there is] any," indef. pronoun (not the interrogative τίς) (cp. 4:8) | παραμύθιον ἀγάπης = "comfort from love" (ESV), gen. of source | κοινωνία πνεύματος = "participation in" or "fellowship with the Spirit" (cp. 1 Cor 1:9; 2 Cor 13:13), just as κοινωνέω takes gen. | εἴ τις σπλάγχνα καὶ οἰκτιρμοί – unusual lack of concord in number and gender: (1) some MSS have εἴ τι (indeclinable stereotyped τι), others have the grammatically correct εἴ τινα; (2) it could be an instance of indeclinable τις (see discussion in Z §9; BDF §137(2)); (3) σπλάγχνα καὶ οἰκτιρμοί could be viewed as hendiadys and therefore as a single concept; (4) ultimately, the reason for τις is probably rhetorical: it sounds more powerful to have a series beginning with τις, or an alternation between τις and τι (depending on one's decision with the other textual variant before παραμύθιον), than to have the series end with a grammatically correct but rhetorically dull τινα

2:2 | μου τὴν χαράν = τὴν χαράν μου | ἵνα τὸ αὐτὸ φρονῆτε = "by being of the same mind" (NASB, ESV), ἵνα could be imperatival or explanatory (M 145 n3)

2:2–4 | Four imperatival ptcs.

2:3 | μηδέν ... κενοδοξίαν – must supply a ptc., e.g., ποιοῦντες | ἑαυτῶν – gen. of comparison

2:5 | τοῦτο φρονεῖτε ἐν ὑμῖν ὃ καὶ ἐν Χριστῷ Ἰησοῦ – debated; two main options: (1) take ἐν ὑμῖν as "among yourselves" (BDAG ἐν 1d), take ἐν Χρ. in the "union with Christ" sense, and supply ἐστίν ὑμῶν: "Have this mind among yourselves, which is yours in Christ Jesus" (ESV) (this interpretation must downplay the καί, which implies a comparison between the two ἐν clauses), or (2) supply τὸ φρόνημα after τοῦτο and ἐφρονεῖτο in second half of comparison (brachylogy, cp. Gal 4:12; Eph 5:24), and take the two ἐν-clauses as parallel: "Have this attitude in yourselves which was *also* in Christ Jesus" (NASB)

2:6 | ἐν μορφῇ θεοῦ ὑπάρχων – could be (1) causal ptc.: "because he existed in the form of God," or (2) concessive ptc.: "although he existed in the form of God" (see discussion at W 634–5) | ἁρπαγμός (*hapax*) – see BDAG, commentaries | ἡγέομαι + double acc. = "consider x to be y," object-complement construction – anarthrous ἁρπαγμόν is complement and articular inf. τὸ εἶναι ἴσα θεῷ (= "equality with God") is direct object (W 186, 220, 602)

2:7 | μορφὴν δούλου λαβών = "by taking the form of a servant," ptc. of means (W 630)

2:8 | θανάτου δὲ σταυροῦ = "even death on a cross," explanatory and/or intensifying δέ (BDF §447(8))

2:10 | ἐν τῷ ὀνόματι Ἰησοῦ = "at the name," i.e., when the name of Jesus is spoken (M 78); ἐν as marker of cause or occasion (BDAG ἐν 9a) (cp. Acts 7:29)

2:12 | ὥστε = "therefore" | μὴ μόνον ... ἀλλά = "not only ... but"

2:13 | καί ... καί = "both ... and" | ὑπὲρ τῆς εὐδοκίας = "for [God's] good will/pleasure"

2:15 | μέσον + gen. = "in the midst of," neut. of μέσος functioning as improper preposition (BDAG μέσος 1c; BDF §215(3)) | ἐν οἷς = "among whom," referring back to γενεᾶς (sg.), *constructio ad sensum*

2:16 | ἐπέχοντες = (1) "holding fast," or (2) "holding forth," imperatival ptc. | εἰς καύχημα ... ὅτι = "in order that I may boast on the day of Christ that" | εἰς κενόν (2x) = "in vain" (BDAG εἰς 4e; κενός 3) (cp. Gal 2:2; 1 Thess 3:5)

2:17 | ἀλλὰ εἰ καί = "but even if" | τῆς πίστεως ὑμῶν = "coming from your faith" (NIV), gen. of source

2:18 | τὸ δὲ αὐτό = "in the same way," adv. acc. (M 34; BDF §154)

2:19 | κἀγώ = καὶ ἐγώ (cp. v. 28) | γνούς + acc. = "when I learn of" | τὰ περὶ ὑμῶν (cp. vv. 20, 23) = "your circumstances, situation, condition, affairs" (BDAG περί 1i; M 62–3)

2:20 | ὅστις = "such that," qualitative-consecutive relative clause (BDF §379)

2:22 | ὡς πατρὶ τέκνον = "like a child [serving with] his father," brachylogy

2:23 | τοῦτον μὲν οὖν = "this one, therefore," resumptive/transitional (M 162–3) | ὡς ἂν ἀφίδω τὰ περὶ ἐμὲ ἐξαυτῆς = "as soon as I see how things go with me" (NASB); ὡς ἂν + subj. = "when," "as soon as" (M 133; BDF §455(2); BDAG ὡς 8cα)

2:24 | καὶ αὐτός + 1s verb = "I myself"

2:25 | ἡγέομαι ἀναγκαῖον + inf. = "think it necessary to" (cp. 2 Cor 9:5)

2:26 | ἐπιποθῶν ἦν πάντας ὑμᾶς = "he was longing for you all," impf. periphrastic (W 648)

2:26–27 | ἠσθένησεν (2x) = "he fell ill"

2:27 | καὶ γάρ = "for indeed" | παραπλήσιον + dat. = "near to," improper preposition (M 86) | ἵνα μὴ λύπην ἐπὶ λύπην σχῶ = "to spare me sorrow upon sorrow" (NIV)

2:28 | ἔπεμψα – epistolary aorist (W 563) | ἵνα + two subjunctives (χαρῆτε & ὦ) | ἰδόντες αὐτὸν πάλιν = "when you see him again" (but πάλιν could go with χαρῆτε)

2:29 | τοὺς τοιούτους ἐντίμους ἔχετε = "hold men like him in high regard" (NASB)

2:30 | τὸ ὑμῶν ὑστέρημα τῆς πρός με λειτουργίας = "what was lacking in your service to me"

Philippians 3
3:1 | τὸ λοιπόν = "finally," adv. acc. (cp. 4:8)

3:2–3 | κατατομή – play on words with περιτομή – paronomasia (BDF §488(1b))

3:4 | ἔχων πεποίθησιν ἐν & πεποιθέναι ἐν = "have [reason for] confidence in" | καὶ ἐν σαρκί = "in the flesh also" (ESV), "even in the flesh" (NASB) | εἴ τις ἄλλος = "if anyone else"

3:5 | περιτομῇ ὀκταήμερος = lit. "a person-of-eight-days relative to circumcision" (BDAG ὀκταήμερος), dat. of respect (BDF §197)

3:6 | ἐν νόμῳ = "under the law" (ESV), "based on the law" (NIV 2011); possibly Hebr./instrumental ἐν, "by the law"

3:7 | ἅτινα (< ὅστις) – neut. pl. subjects take sg. verbs

3:8 | ἀλλὰ μενοῦνγε καί – strengthened form of ἀλλὰ καί (cp. 1:18) = "more than that" (NASB, BDAG μενοῦν), "what is more" (NIV)

3:9 | εὑρίσκω has eschatological connotation, "be found [at the last day]" (cp. Matt 24:46; Mk 13:36; Lk 18:8; 1 Cor 4:2; 2 Cor 5:3; 2 Tim 1:18; 1 Pet 1:7; 2 Pet 3:10, 14; Rev 14:5; 16:20; 18:14, 21, 22, 24; 20:11, 15) | Second τήν carries with it an implied repetition of δικαιοσύνην, "that [righteousness] which" | πίστεως Χριστοῦ – many recent scholars argue for "the faith(fulness) of Christ" (subjective gen.); but more likely, "faith in Christ" (objective gen.) | ἐπὶ τῇ πίστει = "that depends on faith" (ESV) (cp. Acts 3:16)

3:10 | τοῦ γνῶναι αὐτόν = "so as to know him," gen. articular inf. – could be final, consecutive, or epexegetical (M 128–9)

3:12 | εἰ καταλάβω = "[to see] if I can lay hold," εἰ + subj. to express expectation (BDAG εἰ 5bβ; BDF §§368, 375) | καταλάβω ἐφ᾽ ᾧ – either (1) taking καταλαμβάνω absolutely (i.e., w/o a direct object; cp. 1 Cor 9:24) and ἐφ᾽ ᾧ as "because" (see ESV), or (2) taking ἐφ᾽ ᾧ as direct object of καταλαμβάνω, "so that I may lay hold of that for which also I was laid hold of" (NASB)

3:13 | ἓν δέ – must supply a verb, e.g., "but one thing [I do]"

3:14 | κατὰ σκοπὸν διώκω = "I press on toward the goal"

3:15 | φρονῶμεν – hortatory subj. | τι = "in anything," acc. of respect (W 203)

3:16 | στοιχεῖν – imperatival inf. (M 126; BDF §389)

3:17 | οὕτω … καθώς | ἔχετε τύπον ἡμᾶς = "you have us as/for an example," τύπον as predicate acc. (BDF §157(1))

3:21 | τοῦ δύνασθαι – articular inf., epexegetical of ἐνέργειαν (M 129) | καὶ ὑποτάξαι = "even to subject," complement of δύνασθαι | "by the power that enables him even [καί] to subject all things to himself" (ESV)

Philippians 4

4:1 | Ὥστε = "therefore, so" | οὕτως = "in the manner [just described]"

4:3 | γνήσιε σύζυγε – voc.

4:5 | τὸ ἐπιεικές – substantived adj. (BDF §263)

4:6 | μηδὲν μεριμνᾶτε = "be anxious for nothing," acc. of respect (M 34)

4:7 | ἡ ὑπερέχουσα πάντα νοῦν = "which surpasses all understanding," article as relative pronoun; use of concrete noun for abstract

4:8 | τὸ λοιπόν = "finally" (cp. 3:1) | ὅσα – neut. pl. subjects take sg. verbs | εἴ τις (2x) = "if [there is] any" (cp. 2:1) | λογίζομαι = "ponder, dwell on" (BDAG λογίζομαι 2)

4:9 | μεθ᾽ ὑμῶν = μετὰ ὑμῶν

4:10 | ἤδη ποτέ = "now at last" | τὸ ὑπὲρ ἐμοῦ φρονεῖν = "your concern for me," articular inf. | ἐφ᾽ ᾧ καὶ ἐφρονεῖτε = "with regard to which you were indeed concerned," referring back to τὸ ὑπὲρ ἐμοῦ φρονεῖν (M 132) | ἠκαιρεῖσθε δέ = "but you lacked the opportunity" (until now)

4:11 | καθ᾽ ὑστέρησιν = "out of need" | ἐν οἷς εἰμι = "in whatever circumstances I am"

4:12 | καί … καί (3x) = "both … and" | ἐν παντὶ καὶ ἐν πᾶσιν =

"in any and every circumstance" (ESV) | μυέω + inf. = "learn the secret of doing/being x," technical term for being initiated into a mystery religion

4:13 | πάντα ἰσχύω = "I am able to endure all circumstances," i.e., whether need or abundance (v. 12) | Could be Hebr./instrumental ἐν (BDF §219), or "union with Christ" ἐν

4:14 | συγκοινωνήσαντές μου τῇ θλίψει = "to share [with me] in *my* affliction" (NASB); since συγκοινωνέω takes dat., μου goes with τῇ θλίψει

4:15 | ἐν ἀρχῇ τοῦ εὐαγγελίου – see commentaries | εἰς λόγον δόσεως καὶ λήμψεως = "in the settlement of a mutual account" (BDAG λόγος 2b; cp. v. 17), or "in the matter of giving and receiving" (NASB)

4:17 | εἰς λόγον ὑμῶν = "to your account"

4:19 | πληρώσει – future indic. ("God will fill/supply"); other MSS have πληρώσαι – voluntative optative ("May God fill/supply")

Chapter Twelve

The Epistle to the Colossians

Colossians 1

1:4 | ἀκούσαντες = either "because we have heard" (NIV), or "since we heard" (NASB, ESV)

1:5 | διὰ τὴν ἐλπίδα = "the faith and love that spring from the hope" (NIV), διά + acc. expressing cause or reason

1:6 | τοῦ παρόντος εἰς ὑμᾶς = "which has come to you" | καθὼς καί ... καθὼς καί = "just as ... so also" | ἀφ᾽ ἧς ἡμέρας = "from the day that" (cp. v. 9)

1:7 | μανθάνειν τι ἀπὸ τινος = "learn something from someone" (BDAG ἀπό 3d)

1:9 | παύομαι + ptc. = "cease doing something" | ἵνα – final sense attenuated, "asking that" (BDAG ἵνα 2aγ)

1:10 | περιπατῆσαι – inf. of purpose | ἀξίως + gen. = "in a manner worthy of" | εἰς πᾶσαν ἀρεσκείαν = "to please Him [= the Lord] in all respects" (NASB, BDAG ἀρεσκεία)

1:13 | τοῦ υἱοῦ τῆς ἀγάπης αὐτοῦ = τοῦ ἀγαπητοῦ υἱοῦ αὐτοῦ – adjectival gen. (M 175)

1:15 | πρωτότοκος πάσης κτίσεως – could be (1) "firstborn out of all creation," partitive gen. (W 84) (with an implied ἐκ, as in v. 18), (2) "firstborn with reference to all creation," gen. of reference (W 128), or (3) "firstborn over all creation," gen. of subordination (W 104); options (2) and (3) are more consistent with the ὅτι clause which follows (v. 16)

1:16 | ἐν αὐτῷ = "by him," Hebr./instrumental ἐν designating personal agent (BDF §219(1); BDAG ἐν 5–6) | On εἰς αὐτόν, see Z §109 | Note shift from aorist ἐκτίσθη ("were created") to extensive perf. ἔκτισται ("are created") (see Z §287)

1:18 | τοῦ σώματος τοῦ ἐκκλησίας = "of the body, the church," gen. of simple apposition (W 99) | ἵνα γένηται ἐν πᾶσιν αὐτὸς πρωτεύων = "so that he might come to have first place in everything" (BDAG πρωτεύω), taking the present ptc. as predicate adj.

1:19 | ἐν αὐτῷ εὐδόκησεν πᾶν τὸ πλήρωμα κατοικῆσαι – either (1) supply θεός as subject of εὐδόκησεν and take πᾶν τὸ πλήρωμα as subject of κατοικῆσαι: "For God was pleased to have all his fulness dwell in him" (NIV), or (2) take πᾶν τὸ πλήρωμα as subject of both verbs: "For in him all the fullness of God was pleased to dwell" (ESV) (cp. 2:9)

1:20 | εἰς αὐτόν = "to himself"

1:21 | τῇ διανοίᾳ – dat. of respect (cp. Eph 4:18) | ἐν τοῖς ἔργοις τοῖς πονηροῖς = either (1) "because of your evil behavior" (NIV) (BDAG ἐν 9), or (2) "as shown by your evil behavior" (NIV alt.) (BDAG ἐν 8)

1:22 | ἐν τῷ σώματι τῆς σαρκός = "by his fleshly body," Hebr./instrumental ἐν; attributive gen. (W 88) or gen. of material (W 91)

1:23 | εἴ γε = "if indeed" | ἐν πάσῃ κτίσει = either (1) "in all creation" (NASB, ESV), or (2) "to every creature" (NIV, BDAG κτίσις 2a), ἐν for simple dat. (BDF §220); on the duality of πᾶς, see M 93–95

1:25 | κατὰ τὴν οἰκονομίαν τοῦ θεοῦ = "according to the stewardship from God" (NASB, ESV), gen. of source | εἰς ὑμᾶς = "for you," equivalent to dat. of advantage (BDAG εἰς 4g)

1:26 | Note transition from ptc. to finite verb (M 180; BDF §468(3))

1:29 | εἰς ὃ καὶ κοπιῶ = "for this purpose also I labor" (NASB; BDAG εἰς 4f) | ἐν δυνάμει = "powerfully" (BDAG ἐν 11)

Colossians 2
2:2 | Note variety of mngs. of συμβιβάζω (BDAG) | εἰς ἐπίγνωσιν = "resulting in the true knowledge" (NASB) (BDAG εἰς 4e)

2:5 | εἰ καί ... ἀλλά = "although ... yet" (BDAG εἰ 6e; ἀλλά 4a) | ὑμῶν τὴν τάξιν = τὴν τάξιν ὑμῶν | τὸ στερέωμα τῆς εἰς Χριστὸν πίστεως ὑμῶν = "the firmness of your faith in Christ" (for πίστις εἰς, cp. Acts 20:21; 24:24; 26:18)

2:7 | τῇ πίστει – dat. of respect | περισσεύοντες ἐν εὐχαριστίᾳ – imperatival ptc.

2:8 | βλέπετε μή τις + future instead of subj. (BDF §369(2)) = "see to it that no one" | ὑμᾶς is the direct object of ὁ συλαγωγῶν

2:10 | ἐστὲ πεπληρωμένοι = "you have been brought to fullness" (NIV 2011), "you have been made complete" (NASB), perf. periphrastic (W 649)

2:11 | ἡ περιτομὴ τοῦ Χριστοῦ – could be (1) adjectival gen. ("Christian circumcision"), (2) subjective gen. ("the circumcision that Christ performs"), or (3) objective gen. ("the circumcision that Christ himself received," i.e., his being cut off in death)

2:12 | ἡ πίστις τῆς ἐνεργείας τοῦ θεοῦ – could be (1) objective gen. ("faith in the working of God"), or (2) gen. of production (W 104–6) ("faith which is produced by the working of God")

2:14 | καθ' ἡμῶν ... ὃ ἦν ὑπεναντίον ἡμῖν = "which stood against us and condemned us" (NIV 2011), redundant for sake of emphasis | τοῖς δόγμασιν – a "problematic and unparalleled" use of the dat. (M 45 n2); possibly "with its legal demands" (ESV) or "consisting of decrees" (NASB) (cp. ἐν δόγμασιν, Eph 2:15) | αἴρω ἐκ τοῦ μέσου = "take [something] out of the way" (cp. NASB)

2:15 | ἀπεκδύομαι – could be (1) true mid., "strip oneself" of clothes, here metaphorically, as if the powers had encircled Christ like a garment, or (2) deponent (mid. with active mng., BDF §316(1)), "disarm," i.e., strip one's foe of his armor/weapons | δειγματίζω ἐν παρρησίᾳ = "make a public spectacle of" (cp. BDAG παρρησία 2) | θριαμβεύω – see discussion in BDAG | ἐν αὐτῷ [= τῷ σταυρῷ] (Hebr./instrumental ἐν)

2:16 | ἐν = "in connection with" (BDAG ἐν 8) | ἐν μέρει + gen. = "in the matter of, with regard to" (BDAG μέρος 1c)

2:17 | ἅ ἐστιν – neut. pl. subjects take sg. verbs (cp. vv. 22–23) | τοῦ Χριστοῦ (sc. ἐστιν) = "belongs to Christ"

2:18 | θέλων ἐν = "delighting in" (NASB, cp. BDAG) (possible Septuagintism [1 Chron 28:4; Pss 1:2; 111:1; 146:10], M 183; but BDF §148(2)) | ἃ ἑόρακεν ἐμβατεύων – see discussion at BDAG ἐμβατεύω – main options: (1) "going into great detail about what he has seen" (NIV 1984); (2) "taking his stand on visions he has seen" (NASB); (3) "which he has seen upon entering" (technical term used when initiates enter sanctuary – see commentaries) | εἰκῇ φυσιούμενος = "puffed up without cause" | ὑπὸ τοῦ νοὸς τῆς σαρκὸς αὐτοῦ = "by his fleshly mind" (NASB), attributive gen.

2:19 | αὔξει τὴν αὔξησιν – cognate acc., serves purpose only when qualifying word or phrase is added (τοῦ θεοῦ) (BDF §153)

2:20 | Paul normally uses the dat. with ἀποθνήσκω ("die to," e.g., Rom 6:2, 10), but here he uses ἀπό in a pregnant construction; by death one is freed from the control of the στοιχεῖα (BDAG ἀπό 1e) | τί δογματίζεσθε; = "why do you permit yourselves to be put under rules and regulations?" (BDAG) | ὡς = "as if"

2:22 | ἅ ἐστιν πάντα εἰς φθορὰν τῇ ἀποχρήσει – parenthesis: "(referring to things that all perish as they are used)" (ESV)

2:23 | ἅτινά ἐστιν ... οὐκ ἐν τιμῇ τινι πρός = "which are of no value against" (BDAG τιμή 1; πρός 3da) | λόγον μὲν ἔχοντα σοφίας = "although having an appearance of wisdom" (BDAG λόγος 1aβ or 2f)

Colossians 3

3:1 | εἰ οὖν = "since then" | τῷ Χριστῷ – dat. bec. of the συν- prefix in συνεγείρω | ἐν δεξιᾷ = "at the right hand" | Punctuation options: (1) "where Christ is seated at the right hand of God" (NIV 1984), taking ἐστιν καθήμενος as perf. periphrastic, or (2) "where Christ is, seated at the right hand of God" (NIV 2011)

3:4 | ὅταν + aorist subj. ... τότε + fut. = "when ... then" | καὶ ὑμεῖς = "you also"

3:6 | δι' ἅ = "because of which things" (διά + acc.)

3:7 | ἐζῆτε = "you used to walk," customary impf. (W 648)

3:9-10 | ἀπεκ- & ἐν-δυσάμενοι = "since you have put off/on," causal ptcs.

3:11 | ἔνι = ἔνεστιν = "there is"

3:12 | σπλάγχνα οἰκτιρμοῦ = "compassionate hearts," attributive gen. (W 86)

3:13 | ἀνεχόμενοι, χαριζόμενοι – imperatival ptcs. (cp. vv. 16–17) (W 652) | ἐάν τις πρός τινα ἔχῃ μομφήν = "if one has a complaint against another" (ESV)

3:14 | ἐπὶ πᾶσιν τούτοις τὴν ἀγάπην = "in addition to all these things [put on] love" (BDAG ἐπί 7) | ὅ (neut.) does not agree with either the antecedent or the predicate; ὅ ἐστιν is a stereotyped expression, "that is" (cp. Eph 5:5; 6:17)

3:16 | ἐν χάριτι ... ἐν ταῖς καρδίαις ὑμῶν τῷ θεῷ = "with thankfulness in your hearts to God" (ESV, NASB) (BDAG χάρις 5)

3:17 | πᾶν ὅ τι ἐὰν ποιῆτε = "everything whatsoever that you do"

3:18-22; 4:1 | αἱ γυναῖκες, οἱ ἄνδρες, τὰ τέκνα, οἱ πατέρες, οἱ δοῦλοι, οἱ κύριοι – nom. for voc. (W 56-8)

3:20, 22 | κατὰ πάντα (2x) = "in all respects" (BDAG κατά B6)

3:23 | ὅ ἐὰν ποιῆτε = "whatever you do"

3:24 | τὴν ἀνταπόδοσιν τῆς κληρονομίας = "the reward which is the inheritance" or "the inheritance as your reward" (ESV), gen. of apposition

3:25 | ὁ ἀδικῶν κομίσεται ὃ ἠδίκησεν = lit. "the wrongdoer will receive back the wrong that he committed," i.e., "the wrongdoer will be paid back for the wrong he has done" (ESV) (cp. use of κομίζω in Eph 6:8)

Colossians 4
4:2–5 | γρηγοροῦντες, προσευχόμενοι, ἐξαγοραζόμενοι – imperatival ptcs.

4:3 | ἅμα καί = "at the same time" | θύραν τοῦ λόγου = "a door for the word," what kind of gen.? | δι᾽ ὅ = "because of which" (cp. 3:6) | λαλῆσαι = "so that we may proclaim" (NIV)

4:4 | ὡς δεῖ με λαλῆσαι = "as I ought to speak," acc. με as subject of inf. (cp. v. 6)

4:7 | τὰ κατ᾽ ἐμὲ πάντα = "all the news about me" (NIV)

4:8 | ἔπεμψα – epistolary aorist (W 562–3; BDF §334) | εἰς αὐτὸ τοῦτο, ἵνα = "for this very purpose, that" (ESV)

4:9 | πάντα τὰ ὧδε = "everything that is happening here" (NIV)

4:10 | ὁ συναιχμάλωτός μου = "fellow-prisoner with me," gen. of association (W 129) (cp. Phm 24)

4:11 | οἱ ὄντες ἐκ περιτομῆς = "who are from the circumcised" (see Acts 10:45; Rom 4:12), i.e., Jewish Christians; ancestral ἐκ (BDAG ἐκ 3b)

4:12 | Ἐπαφρᾶς ὁ ἐξ ὑμῶν = "Epaphras, who is one of your number" (NASB)

4:13 | ἔχει πολὺν πόνον = "he is working hard" (NIV)

4:15 | ἡ κατ᾽ οἶκον αὐτῆς ἐκκλησία = "the church that meets in her house" (BDAG κατά B1c)

4:16 | παρ᾽ ὑμῖν = "among you" (ESV) (BDAG παρά B1bβ) | ποιέω + ἵνα functioning as inf. = "cause or bring it about that" (BDAG ποιέω 2hα)

4:18 | μνημονεύω takes gen. | μου τῶν δεσμῶν = τῶν δεσμῶν μου

Chapter Thirteen

The First Epistle to the Thessalonians

1 Thessalonians 1

1:2 | μνείαν ποιεῖσθαι = "to make mention," ποιέω (mid.) + noun as periphrasis for simple verbal idea (BDAG ποιέω 7a; μνεία 2), gen. obj. must be supplied (cp. Rom 1:9; Eph 1:16; Phm 4) | ἐπὶ τῶν προσευχῶν ἡμῶν = "in our prayers" (BDAG ἐπί 18a)

1:3 | ὑμῶν goes with the following head nouns ("your work of faith," etc.) | Genitives in need of interpretation – perhaps: "the work that manifests the reality of your faith" (subjective gen.; cp. Gal 5:6); "your labor motivated by love" (gen. of source); and "your patience produced by hope" (gen. of production; W 104–6) | μνημονεύω takes gen. | ἔμπροσθεν (adv., "in the presence of") could modify μνημονεύοντες (ESV, NIV) or the verbal idea contained in ἐλπίδος (NASB)

1:5 | γίνομαι εἰς = "come to," "reach" (BDAG γίνομαι 6a) | οἷοι ἐγενήθημεν ἐν ὑμῖν δι' ὑμᾶς = "what kind of men we proved to be among you for your sake" (NASB, ESV)

1:6 | μιμηταί + objective gen. (cp. 2:14) | ἐν of attendant circumstances (ZG; M 78)

1:7 | ὑμᾶς is the subject of γενέσθαι

1:8 | ὥστε μὴ χρείαν ἔχειν ἡμᾶς λαλεῖν τι = "so that we have no need to say anything [about your faith]" (acc. ἡμᾶς as subject of inf. ἔχειν)

1:9 | αὐτοί = "they themselves" (the believers in Macedonia and Achaia) | περὶ ἡμῶν ("concerning us") – an alternative (albeit inferior) reading has περὶ ὑμῶν ("concerning you"), which makes more sense | εἴσοδος = "reception" (NASB), "welcome" (BDAG εἴσοδος) (cp. 2:1)

1 Thessalonians 2

2:1 | Lit. "you yourselves know our coming to you, that it was not in vain," prolepsis (BDF §476), i.e., "you yourselves know that our coming to you was not in vain"

2:2 | προπαθόντες καὶ ὑβρισθέντες ... ἐν Φιλίπποις = "after we had previously suffered and been outrageously mistreated in Philippi" | ἐν πολλῷ ἀγῶνι = "amid much opposition" (NASB)

2:4 | πιστευθῆναι + acc. = "be entrusted with something"

2:5 | ἐν of attendant circumstances (M 78) | οὔτε ποτε ἐν λόγῳ κολακείας ἐγενήθημεν = "we never came with words of flattery" (ESV) | οὔτε ἐν προφάσει πλεονεξίας = "nor with a pretext for greed" (ESV)

2:5–6a | οὔτε ... οὔτε ... οὔτε = "neither ... nor ... nor"

2:6b | οὔτε ... οὔτε = "either ... or"

2:7 | δυνάμενοι (concessive ptc.) ... ἀπόστολοι = "even though as apostles of Christ we could have been burdensome" (cp. NASB; M 78) – referring to the right to receive financial support (cp. use of lexemes from the βαρ- group in v. 9; 2 Thess 3:8; 2 Cor 11:9; 12:16) | Textual problem: νήπιοι (= "infants") vs. ἤπιοι (= "gentle," which fits context better) (see Metzger)

2:7–8 | ὡς ἐάν ... οὕτως = "as when ... so"

2:8 | ὁμείρομαι takes gen.

2:9 | νυκτὸς καὶ ἡμέρας (gen. of time) (cp. 3:10) | πρὸς τὸ μή + inf. = "in order not to" | τινα ὑμῶν = "to any of you"

2:11–12 | οἴδατε ὡς ... παρακαλοῦντες ... = "you know that ... we exhorted," etc. (BDAG ὡς 5) | ἕνα ἕκαστον ὑμῶν = "each one of you" | Continuation of a finite verb with ptcs. (BDF §468(1))

2:12 | εἰς τό + inf. = "so that" | ἀξίως + gen. = "in a manner worthy of"

2:13 | λόγον ἀκοῆς παρ' ἡμῶν τοῦ θεοῦ = "the word of God which you heard from us" (ESV), or "the word of divine proclamation that goes out from us" (BDAG ἀκοή 4b)

2:14 | ὑπὸ τῶν ἰδίων συμφυλετῶν = "from your own countrymen"

2:15 | τῶν = "who," article as relative pronoun (W 213–15)

2:16 | κωλυόντων ἡμᾶς λαλῆσαι = "hindering us from speaking" | εἰς τό + inf. = "with the result that" | αὐτῶν τὰς ἁμαρτίας = τὰς ἁμαρτίας αὐτῶν | εἰς τέλος = (1) "to the limit" (NIV 1984), or (2) "at last" (NIV 2011), "in the end" (BDAG τέλος 2bγ)

2:17 | πρὸς καιρὸν ὥρας = "for a short time," a combination of πρὸς καιρόν and πρὸς ὥραν (BDAG καιρός 1a) | ἐν πολλῇ ἐπιθυμίᾳ = "with great desire," ἐν of attendant circumstances (M 78)

2:18 | καὶ ἅπαξ καὶ δίς = "both once and twice," καί ... καί (BDAG καί 1f) | Third καί = "and yet" (NASB) or "but" (ESV) (BDAG καί 1bη)

2:19 | ἢ οὐχὶ καὶ ὑμεῖς; = "is it not you?"

1 Thessalonians 3

3:1 | μηκέτι στέγοντες = "when we could endure [it] no longer,"
temporal ptc. (W 623) (cp. v. 5) | Ἀθῆναι (= Athens) is always pl.

3:2 | συνεργὸν τοῦ θεοῦ = "fellow-worker with God," gen. of association (W 128) | παρακαλέσαι ὑπὲρ τῆς πίστεως ὑμῶν = "to encourage you in your faith" (NIV) (BDAG παρακαλέω 4; ὑπέρ A1b)

3:3 | τὸ μηδένα σαίνεσθαι = "that no one be disturbed," equivalent of ἵνα μή clause (BDF §399(3)) | ἐν ταῖς θλίψεσιν ταύταις = "because of these afflictions," causal ἐν with verbs of emotion (BDAG ἐν 9b)

3:4 | καὶ γάρ = "for indeed" | ὅτε πρὸς ὑμᾶς ἦμεν = "when we were with you" (BDAG πρός 3g) | προελέγομεν = "we kept telling you beforehand," iterative impf. (W 546) | ὅτι μέλλομεν θλίβεσθαι = "that we are [were] going to suffer affliction/persecution," present retained in indirect discourse (W 537) | καί ... καί = "both ... and"

3:5 | κἀγώ = καὶ ἐγώ | εἰς τὸ γνῶναι τὴν πίστιν ὑμῶν = "to find out about your faith" (NASB) | εἰς κενόν = "in vain" (BDAG εἰς 4e; κενός 3) (cp. Gal 2:2; Phil 2:16)

3:6 | Ἄρτι δὲ ἐλθόντος Τιμοθέου ... καὶ εὐαγγελισαμένου = "But now that Timothy has come and brought the good news," gen. abs. | ἔχω μνείαν ἀγαθήν τινος = "remember someone kindly" (cp. 2 Tim 1:3) | ἐπιποθοῦντες ἡμᾶς ἰδεῖν καθάπερ καὶ ἡμεῖς ὑμᾶς = "that you long to see us, just as we [long to see] you," brachylogy

3:7 | παρεκλήθημεν ἐφ᾽ ὑμῖν = "we were comforted over you" (KJV), ἐπί after verbs of emotion (BDAG ἐπί 6c) | ἐπὶ πάσῃ ... = "in the midst of all our distress and affliction," temporal ἐπί (BDAG ἐπί 18b) (cp. 2 Thess 1:4) | διὰ τῆς ὑμῶν πίστεως modifies παρεκλήθημεν

3:8 | ἐάν + present indic. = "*since* you are standing firm in the Lord" (NIV) (BDAG ἐάν 1bβ; BDF §372(1)(a))

3:10 | νυκτὸς καὶ ἡμέρας – gen. of time | ὑμῶν τὸ πρόσωπον = τὸ πρόσωπον ὑμῶν

3:11 | Compound subject ("our God and Father himself and our Lord Jesus") with sg. verb κατευθύναι is perhaps suggestive of the deity of Christ (see W 482)

3:11–12 | κατευθύναι, πλεονάσαι, περισσεύσαι – voluntative optatives (W 481–2)

3:13 | ὑμῶν τὰς καρδίας = τὰς καρδίας ὑμῶν

1 Thessalonians 4

4:1 | λοιπόν = "finally," adv. acc. | τὸ πῶς δεῖ ὑμᾶς περιπατεῖν καὶ ἀρέσκειν θεῷ = "how you ought to walk and to please God," τό changes direct question into indirect (BDAG ὁ 2hα) (see Lk 1:62) and causes the indirect question to function as a noun (BDAG πῶς 1bα) | περιπατεῖν καὶ ἀρέσκειν θεῷ = "to walk in a way that pleases God," hendiadys | ἵνα (2x) = "that," final mng. attenuated

4:3–6 | ἀπέχεσθαι ... εἰδέναι ... τὸ μὴ ὑπερβαίνει – series of epexegetical infs. in apposition to ἁγιασμός

4:4 | εἰδέναι + inf. = "to know [how] to" | κτᾶσθαι τὸ ἑαυτοῦ σκεῦος = either (1) "to acquire his own wife" (rabbinic background), or (2) "to gain control over his own body [or sex organ]" (see BDAG κτάομαι 1; σκεῦος 3)

4:6 | τὸ μή + two infs. – equivalent to ἵνα μή clause (BDF §399(3)), but here with an imperatival nuance

4:7 | ἐπὶ ἀκαθαρσίᾳ = "for impurity" (BDAG ἐπί 16) | ἐν ἁγιασμῷ – perhaps "for sanctification," rare use of ἐν for εἰς (M 205 note to p. 76; BDF §218)

4:8 | ὁ ἀθετῶν = "the one who rejects [this instruction]"

4:9 | οὐ χρείαν ἔχετε γράφειν ὑμῖν = "you have no need [for anyone] to write to you" (cp. 5:1 but in pass. voice)

4:10 | καὶ γάρ = "for indeed"

4:11 | πράσσειν τὰ ἴδια = "to mind your own business" (BDAG ἴδιος 4b)

4:13 | οἱ λοιποί = "the others," i.e., unbelievers (cp. 5:6)

4:14 | διὰ τοῦ Ἰησοῦ – options: (1) διά of attendant circumstances with τοὺς κοιμηθέντας: "God will bring with Him those who have fallen asleep *in Jesus*" (NASB), "... *in contact with Jesus*" (M 57); or (2) instrumental διά with ἄξει: "*through Jesus*, God will bring with him those who have fallen asleep" (ESV)

4:15 | ἐν λόγῳ κυρίου = "by a word from the Lord" (ESV), Hebr./ instrumental ἐν (cp. v. 18); gen. of source | εἰς = "until" (BDAG εἰς 2aα)

4:16 | ἐν κελεύσματι, etc. = "with a cry of command" (ESV), ἐν (3x) of attendant circumstances (M 78)

4:17 | εἰς ἀπάντησιν τοῦ κυρίου = "to meet the Lord," objective gen. | εἰς ἀέρα = "in the air," εἰς = ἐν

1 Thessalonians 5
5:1 | οὐ χρείαν ἔχετε ὑμῖν γράφεσθαι = "you have no need [of anything] to be written to you" (cp. 4:9 but in active voice)

5:2 | οὕτως – either (1) pleonastic, or (2) prolepsis: "that the day of the Lord – as a thief [comes] in the night, *so* shall [it] come"

5:3 | ὅταν λέγωσιν = "when people are saying," indef. subject | ὅταν ... τότε = "when ... then" | αἰφνίδιος ὄλεθρος = "sudden destruction" | ἐν γαστρὶ ἔχω = "be pregnant" | ὥσπερ clause is ellipsis; sc. ἐφίσταται – "as the birthpang [comes upon] the pregnant woman" | οὐ μή + aorist subj. for emphatic negation

5:4 | ἡ ἡμέρα = "that day," anaphoric use of article | Ecbatic ἵνα (BDAG ἵνα 3; W 473; M 142)

5:5 | υἱοὶ φωτός & υἱοὶ ἡμέρας – Hebr. "son of" idiom (BDF §162(6); BDAG υἱός 2cβ; M 174–5), immediately restated w/o using the idiom: οὐκ ἐσμὲν νυκτὸς οὐδὲ σκότους (cp. ἡμέρας, v. 8)

5:6 | καθεύδωμεν, γρηγορῶμεν, νήφωμεν (also v. 8) – hortatory subjunctives | οἱ λοιποί – see 4:13

5:7 | νυκτός (2x) = "at night," gen. of time

5:8 | ἡμεῖς ἡμέρας ὄντες = "since we belong to the day" (ESV), causal ptc. | ἐνδυσάμενοι – aorist ptc. after hortatory subj. takes on imperatival nuance | καὶ περικεφαλαίαν ἐλπίδα σωτηρίας = "and for a helmet the hope of salvation"

5:9 | εἰς περιποίησιν σωτηρίας = "to obtain salvation"

5:11 | εἰς τὸν ἕνα = "one another"

5:12 | εἰδέναι = "to respect, honor" (BDAG οἶδα 6) | προΐστημι takes gen. (ὑμῶν)

5:13 | διὰ τὸ ἔργον αὐτῶν = "on account of the work they do," subjective gen.

5:14 | ἀντέχεσθε τῶν ἀσθενῶν – ἀντέχομαι takes gen.

5:22 | εἶδος can mean "kind" (NIV, BDAG), "form" (NASB, ESV), or "appearance" (KJV)

5:23 | "May your spirit and soul and body be kept whole" | ὁλόκληρος = "whole, complete, intact" (BDAG) (-ον = neut. nom.) | ὑμῶν goes with πνεῦμα, ψυχή, σῶμα | ἀγιάσαι & τηρηθείη – voluntative optatives (W 481–3; BDF §384; M 136) (cp. 3:11–12)

5:28 | μεθ' ὑμῶν = μετὰ ὑμῶν

Chapter Fourteen

The Second Epistle to the Thessalonians

2 Thessalonians 1

1:3 | εὐχαριστεῖν ὀφείλομεν τῷ θεῷ = ὀφείλομεν εὐχαριστεῖν τῷ θεῷ (cp. 2:13), ὀφείλω + complementary inf. | καθὼς ἄξιόν ἐστιν = "as is fitting" (BDAG ἄξιος 1c) | ἑνὸς ἑκάστου πάντων ὑμῶν = "of each and every one of you"

1:4 | ὥστε = "therefore" | αὐτοὺς ἡμᾶς = "we ourselves," acc. as subject of inf. | ἐγκαυχάομαι ἔν τινι = "boast about someone" | ἐν πᾶσιν τοῖς διωγμοῖς ὑμῶν καὶ ταῖς θλίψεσιν = "in the midst of all your persecutions and afflictions" (NASB), temporal ἐν (BDAG ἐν 10c) | ἀνέχομαι usually takes gen. or acc., but here dat. due to attraction (BDAG ἀνέχω 2)

1:5 | ἔνδειγμα τῆς δικαίας κρίσεως τοῦ θεοῦ = "[This is] evidence of the righteous judgment of God" | εἰς τὸ καταξιωθῆναι ὑμᾶς + gen. = "so that you will be considered worthy of"

1:6 | παρὰ τῷ θεῷ = "in the sight of God" (BDAG παρά B2)

1:7 | ἐν τῇ ἀποκαλύψει τοῦ κυρίου Ἰησοῦ = "when the Lord Jesus is revealed," temporal ἐν (BDAG ἐν 10b); objective gen. | μεθ' ἡμῶν = μετὰ ἡμῶν | μετ' ἀγγέλων = μετὰ ἀγγέλων

1:9 | τίνω δίκην + acc. (ὄλεθρον) = "pay the penalty of" | ἀπὸ προσώπου ... τῆς ἰσχύος αὐτοῦ (cp. LXX Isa 2:10, 19, 21) – either (1) "They will pay the penalty of eternal destruction, excluded from the presence of the Lord and from the glory of his might" (cp. NIV), pregnant construction (BDAG ἀπό 1e/4; πρόσωπον 1bβℵ), or (2) "They will pay the penalty of eternal destruction which comes from the presence of the Lord and from the glory of his might" (cp. ESV alt.), ἀπό of source (BDAG ἀπό 3)

1:10 | ἐν τοῖς ἁγίοις αὐτοῦ = "among his holy ones" (could be saints or angels) | ἐν + dat. pl. (2x) = "among" (BDAG ἐν 1d) | ἐφ᾽ ὑμᾶς = either "among you" (BDAG ἐπί 1cγ) (cp. Acts 1:21), or "to you" (NASB)

1:11 | εἰς ὅ = "with this end in view" | ἀξιόω + acc. + gen. = "consider someone worthy of something" (cp. v. 5) | πᾶσαν εὐδοκίαν ἀγαθωσύνης = "every desire for goodness," objective gen.

1:12 | καὶ ὑμεῖς ἐν αὐτῷ = "and you in him," brachylogy

2 Thessalonians 2

2:1 | ὑπέρ = "concerning, with reference to" (BDAG ὑπέρ 3) | ἐπ᾽ αὐτόν = "to him" (NASB; BDAG ἐπί 4)

2:1–2 | ἐρωτῶμεν ὑμᾶς ... εἰς τὸ μὴ ταχέως σαλευθῆναι = "we urge you not to be quickly shaken," final sense of εἰς τό + inf. is attenuated, similar to attenuated ἵνα (BDAG ἵνα 2)

2:2 | ὡς δι᾽ ἡμῶν = "as if from us" (NASB), "seeming to be from us" (ESV) (BDAG ὡς 3c; διά A4b) | ὡς ὅτι = ὅτι (BDF §396; BDAG ὅτι 5b) = "to the effect that" (NASB, ESV)

2:3 | μή τις ὑμᾶς ἐξαπατήσῃ κατὰ μηδένα τρόπον = "let no one decive you in *any* way," double negatives reinforce | ὅτι ἐὰν μή – apodosis must be supplied: "for [that day will not come] unless" | τῆς ἀνομίας, τῆς ἀπωλείας – adjectival genitives (M 174–5)

2:4 | ἐπὶ πάντα λεγόμενον θεόν = "above every so-called god" (NASB) (BDAG ἐπί 9c) | ἀποδεικνύντα ἑαυτὸν ὅτι ἐστιν θεός = "proclaiming himself to be God" (ESV), prolepsis (BDF §476)

2:5 | ἔτι ὢν πρὸς ὑμᾶς = "when I was still with you" (BDAG πρός 3g) (cp. 3:10) | ταῦτα ἔλεγον ὑμῖν = "I kept telling you these things," iterative impf. (W 546)

2:6 | The εἰς τό + inf. clause goes with τὸ κατέχον – he is presently being held back, *so that* he may be revealed at the proper time

2:7 | τὸ μυστήριον ... τῆς ἀνομίας | ὁ κατέχων ἄρτι = "he who now restrains [will continue to do so]" | ἕως ἐκ μέσου γένηται = "until he [= the restrainer] is taken out of the way" (NASB) (BDAG γίνομαι 6b), or possibly "until he [= the man of lawlessness] arises out of the midst"

2:9 | οὗ ἐστιν ἡ παρουσία = "whose [= the lawless one's] coming is" | ψεύδους – gen. sg., "false signs and wonders," adjectival gen.

2:10 | ἀνθ' ὧν – they perish "because" | τὴν ἀγάπην τῆς ἀληθείας οὐκ ἐδέξαντο = "they refused to love the truth" (NIV), objective gen.

2:11 | ἐνέργειαν πλάνης = "a deluding influence" (BDAG), adjectival gen.

2:13 | εἵλατο ... εἰς σωτηρίαν – textual problem: (1) "God chose you as the firsfruits [ἀπαρχήν] to be saved" (ESV, following NA text), or (2) "God chose you from the beginning [ἀπ' ἀρχῆς] to be saved" (cp. NASB); see Metzger

2:14 | εἰς περιποίησιν δόξης = "to obtain the glory"

2:15 | εἴτε ... εἴτε = "whether ... or" | διὰ λόγου = "by word [of mouth]"

2:16 | ἐν χάριτι = "graciously" (BDAG ἐν 11)

2:17 | παρακαλέσαι, στηρίξαι – voluntative optatives (cp. 3:5, 16; 1 Thess 3:11–12; 5:23)

2 Thessalonians 3
3:1 | τὸ λοιπόν = "finally," adv. acc. | καθὼς καὶ πρὸς ὑμᾶς = "just as [the word sped on and was honored] with reference to you also" (BDAG πρός 3eα)

3:2 | οὐ πάντων ἡ πίστις = "not all have faith"

3:3 | ἀπὸ τοῦ πονηροῦ = either "from evil" (neut.) or "from the evil one" (masc.) (same ambiguity in Matt 6:13)

3:4 | ἐφ᾿ ὑμᾶς = "concerning you," marker of feelings directed toward someone (BDAG ἐπί 15); Paul's confidence is not in them, but in the Lord concerning them | ἃ παραγγέλλομεν καὶ ποιεῖτε [present] καὶ ποιήσετε [future] = "you are doing and will continue to do the things we command" (NIV)

3:5 | ὑμῶν τὰς καρδίας = τὰς καρδίας ὑμῶν | τὴν ἀγάπην τοῦ θεοῦ – could be objective, subjective, or plenary gen. (W 121) | τὴν ὑπομονὴν τοῦ Χριστοῦ – could be (1) "patient waiting for Christ" (objective gen.), (2) "the fortitude that comes from Christ" (gen. of source), or (3) "the fortitude that Christ himself had" (subjective gen.) (see BDAG ὑπομονή 1–2)

3:8 | νυκτὸς καὶ ἡμέρας – genitives of time | πρὸς τὸ μὴ ἐπιβαρῆσαί τινα ὑμῶν = "so as not to be a [financial] burden to any of you"

3:9 | ἵνα ἑαυτούς ... ἡμᾶς = "in order to offer ourselves as a model for you to imitate" (NIV 2011)

3:10 | καὶ γὰρ ὅτε = "for even when" | BDAG πρός 3g (cp. 2:5)

3:12 | Attenuated ἵνα equivalent to inf.

3:13 | μὴ ἐγκακήσητε καλοποιοῦντες = "do not grow weary of doing good" (NASB), complementary ptc. (W 646)

3:14 | τοῦτον σημειοῦσθε μὴ συναναμίγνυσθαι αὐτῷ = "take note of this person, so as not to associate with him"

3:15 | καί = "yet" (BDAG καί 1bη)

3:16 | διὰ παντὸς ἐν παντὶ τρόπῳ = "at all times and in every way" (NIV)

3:17 | σημεῖον = "mark of genuineness" (BDAG σημεῖον 1)

Chapter Fifteen

The First Epistle to Timothy

1 Timothy 1

1:3 | Clause accompanying καθώς must be supplied from context: "Just as I have urged you to stay on in Ephesus [do so] ... so that you may command" (BDAG καθώς 1) | πορευόμενος = "when I was on my way," conative present ptc., nom. in agreement with the subject of παρεκάλεσα | Attenuated ἵνα equivalent to inf.

1:4 | μᾶλλον ἤ = "rather than" | τὴν ἐν πίστει = "which is (realized) in faith" (ZG), "which is by faith" (ESV)

1:5 | τὸ τέλος τῆς παραγγελίας = "the goal of this instruction" (BDAG τέλος 3)

1:6 | ὧν = "from which," gen. of separation (M 41)

1:7 | μὴ νοοῦντες μήτε ... μήτε = "without understanding either ... or" (ESV), double negatives reinforce

1:8 | χράομαι takes dat.

1:9–10 | κεῖμαι takes dat. (15x); one would expect τι ἕτερον to be dat. as well (anacoluthon)

481

1:10 | ἀρσενοκοίτης – see 1 Cor 6:9 | ἀντίκειμαι takes dat.

1:11 | πιστεύω (pass.) + acc. = "be entrusted with something," acc. of the thing retained with pass. (BDF §159), thus ὅ = "with which"

1:12 | χάριν ἔχω = "I give thanks" | ἡγέομαι + double acc. = "consider x to be y" | θέμενος εἰς διακονίαν = "appointing me to his service" (ESV) – would expect, "having considered me trustworthy, he appointed me," but inversion of ptc. & verb not uncommon (ZG; Z §263)

1:13 | τὸ πρότερον = "formerly," adv. acc. | ὄντα = "although I was," concessive ptc. (W 634), with an implied με | ἀγνοῶν ἐποίησα = "I acted ignorantly," ptc. of manner (W 627)

1:16 | ἐν ἐμοί = "in my case" (BDAG ἐν 8; M 77) | ἅπας, intensive form of πᾶς = "entire" (M 94), "perfect" (NASB, ESV), "immense" (NIV 2011) | πρὸς ὑποτύπωσιν = "as a model or prototype" (BDAG) | τῶν μελλόντων πιστεύειν = "for those who would believe" (NIV, NASB)

1:17 | τῶν αἰώνων = either (1) "[who rules] over the ages," gen. of subordination (W 103–4), or (2) "eternal," Hebr. attributive gen. (W 88)

1:18 | κατὰ τὰς προαγούσας ἐπὶ σὲ προφητείας = "in accordance with the prophecies previously made concerning you" (NASB) | ἐν αὐταῖς = "by them," Hebr./instrumental ἐν (BDF §219)

1 Timothy 2
2:1 | πρῶτον πάντων = "first of all"

2:3 | Antecedent of τοῦτο is vv. 1–2a (praying for all people, for kings, and for all who are in high positions) rather than v. 2b (leading a peaceful and quiet life)

2:5 | μεσίτης θεοῦ καὶ ἀνθρώπων = "mediator between God and humans," two genitives joined by καί with mng. "between" (W 135)

2:6 | τὸ μαρτύριον καιροῖς ἰδίοις = "the testimony [given by God] at the proper time" (NASB), taking phrase in apposition to all of vv. 5–6a; temporal dat., idiomatic pl. referring to one time, viz., the present time of God's testimony through the preaching of the gospel

2:7 | εἰς ὅ = "for this purpose" (NIV) (BDAG εἰς 4f); antecedent of ὅ is μαρτύριον

2:9–10 | κοσμεῖν ἑαυτάς … δι᾽ ἔργων ἀγαθῶν = "to adorn themselves … with good deeds"

2:12 | ἐπιτρέπω + dat. + inf. = "permit someone to do something" | Mng. of αὐθεντέω (*hapax* in NT and rare elsewhere) is contested: could be (1) neutral, "have/exercise authority over" (NIV 1984), or (2) negative, "assume authority over" (NIV 2011), "assume a stance of independent authority, give orders to, dictate to" (BDAG); see Leland E. Wilshire, "The TLG Computer and Further Reference to αυθεντεω in 1 Timothy 2.12," *NTS* 34 (1988): 120–34; H. Scott Baldwin's word study in *Women in the Church: A Fresh Analysis of 1 Timothy 2:9–15* (ed. Andreas J. Köstenberger, Thomas R. Schreiner, and H. Scott Baldwin; Grand Rapids: Baker, 1995), 65–80, 269–305 | ἀνδρός could be the object of both αὐθεντεῖν and διδάσκειν (case being determined by nearest verb), or more likely, of αὐθεντεῖν only (note distance between διδάσκειν and ἀνδρός)

2:15 | σωθήσεται διὰ τεκνογονίας – main options: (1) "she will be brought safely through the dangers of childbirth" (BDAG διά A1b or A3c); (2) "she will be saved by *the* childbirth," i.e., the birth of Jesus; (3) "she will work out her salvation by accepting her God-given role, of which childbearing is the main function" (synecdoche)

1 Timothy 3

3:4 | τέκνα ἔχοντα ἐν ὑποταγῇ μετὰ πάσης σεμνότητος – either (1) taking μετὰ πάσης σεμνότητος as modifying ἐν ὑποταγῇ (and thus the children): "keeping his children submissive and respectful in every way" (NRSV), or (2) taking μετὰ πάσης σεμνότητος as modifying ἔχοντα (and thus the father): "keeping his children under control with all dignity" (NASB).

3:6–7 | ἐμπίπτω εἰς (2x) = "fall into" | Gen. τοῦ διαβόλου used in different ways: κρίμα τοῦ διαβόλου (v. 6) = "the condemnation incurred by the devil" (NASB), objective gen.; but παγίδα τοῦ διαβόλου (v. 7) = "the devil's trap" (NIV 1984), subjective or possessive gen.

3:7 | μαρτυρίαν καλὴν ἔχειν ἀπὸ τῶν ἔξωθεν = "have a good attestation [of character] from outsiders" (BDAG μαρτυρία 3; ἀπό 5d)

3:8 | δεῖ ... εἶναι must be supplied from v. 2

3:10 | ἀνέγκλητοι ὄντες = "if they are beyond reproach," conditional ptc.

3:11 | γυναῖκας is contested – either (1) "their wives," or (2) "women [deacons]" | διάβολος (adj.) = "slanderous" (cp. 2 Tim 3:3; Tit 2:3)

3:14 | ἐν τάχει = "quickly," periphrasis for adv. (BDAG ἐν 11)

3:15 | "But if I am delayed [I am writing these things] so that you may know ...," supplying ταῦτα γράφω from v. 14 | ἥτις – should be masc. ὅστις in agreement with οἶκος, but changed to fem. in agreement with predicate ἐκκλησία – gender attraction (W 338; BDF §134)

3:16 | ὁμολογουμένως = "by common confession" (NASB) | Textual issue: ὅς, ὅ, or θεός. According to NA, ὅς is most likely reading (see Metzger); what then is the antecedent? (1) Some suggest it is τὸ τῆς εὐσεβείας μυστήριον, which is interpreted as Christ; but more likely, (2) this is a case of omission of the antecedent, with relative pronoun being used to introduce an early Christian hymn or confession (see W 339–42) | ὤφθη ἀγγέλοις – either (1) "he appeared to messengers/angels," indirect object, or (2) "he was seen by messengers/angels," dat. of agent (see W 165)

1 Timothy 4
4:1 | ἀφίστημι takes gen. (τῆς πίστεως)

4:2 | ἐν ὑποκρίσει ψευδολόγων = "by means of the hypocrisy of liars" (NASB), "through the insincerity of liars" (ESV), "such teachings come through hypocritical liars" (NIV) | κεκαυστηριασμένων τὴν ἰδίαν συνείδησιν = "who have been seared with respect to their own conscience," acc. of respect

4:3 | [κελευόντων] ἀπέχεσθαι = "[commanding] to abstain from" (BDF §479(2)), zeugma

4:4 | μετὰ εὐχαριστίας λαμβανόμενον = "if it is received with thanksgiving," conditional ptc.

4:8 | πρὸς ὀλίγον ὠφέλιμος = "profitable for a little," i.e., has some value (BDAG ὀλίγος 3) | ζωῆς τῆς νῦν καὶ τῆς μελλούσης = "for the present life and for the [life] to come"

4:12 | σου τῆς νεότητος = τῆς νεότητός σου = "your youthfulness" | καταφρονέω takes gen. | τύπος τῶν πιστῶν = "an example for the believers"

4:14 | ἀμελέω takes gen.

4:15 | ἐν τούτοις ἴσθι = "immerse yourself [ESV] in these things" | σου ἡ προκοπή = ἡ προκοπή σου

4:16 | καὶ σεαυτόν ... καὶ τοὺς ἀκούοντάς σου = "both yourself and your hearers," καί ... καί (BDAG καί 1f)

1 Timothy 5
5:4 | εὐσεβέω τινα = "act piously or reverently toward someone" (LSJ, Thayer)

5:5 | ἤλπικεν ἐπὶ θεόν = "puts her hope in God" (NIV) (BDF §344), gnomic perf. | νυκτὸς καὶ ἡμέρας – genitives of time

5:6 | ἡ δὲ σπαταλῶσα ζῶσα τέθνηκεν = "but she who is self-indulgent is dead even while she lives" (ESV), taking ζῶσα as concessive ptc.

5:8 | προνοέω takes gen. | χείρων + gen. of comparison (ἀπίστου)

5:9 | Χήρα καταλεγέσθω μὴ ἔλαττον ἐτῶν ἑξήκοντα γεγονυῖα = "A widow is to be put on the list only if she is not less than sixty years old" (NASB), taking γεγονυῖα as conditional ptc.

5:11 | ὅταν καταστρηνιάσωσιν τοῦ Χριστοῦ = "when their passions draw them away from Christ" (ESV), gen. bec. of κατα- prefix (BDF §181)

5:12 | ἔχω κρίμα ὅτι = "be subject to condemnation because" | τὴν πρώτην πίστιν = "their previous pledge" (NASB), "a solemn promise to be faithful and loyal" (BDAG πίστις 1b), referring either to (1) a pledge of faithfulness to first husband (unlikely in light of v. 14), or (2) a pledge of celibacy upon entrance into order of widows

5:13 | ἄμα δὲ καί = "Besides, they also ..." | μανθάνουσιν [εἶναι] ἀργαί = "they learn [to be] idle" (BDF §416(2)) | περιερχόμεναι τὰς οἰκίας = "going about from house to house" | λαλοῦσαι τὰ μὴ δέοντα = "saying things they ought not to" (NIV), or "... what is not proper" (BDAG δεῖ 2a)

5:14 | ἀφορμήν ... λοιδορίας χάριν = "opportunity for slander" (NIV), χάριν + gen., this preposition follows noun it governs (cp. Tit 1:5, 11)

5:16 | τις πιστή = "any female believer" | ἔχω χήρας = "have [relatives who are] widows" | Subject of ἐπαρκείτω is "any female believer," while the subject of ἐπαρκέσῃ is "the church"

5:19 | κατά + gen. = "against" | ἐκτὸς εἰ μή = "except"

5:23 | ὑδροποτέω = "prefer water for drinking," "drink only water as an abstemious way of life," cp. ὑδροπότης = "party-pooper" (see BDAG)

5:24 | Subject of ἐπακολουθοῦσιν is αἱ ἁμαρτίαι

5:25 | τὰ ἄλλως ἔχοντα = "those [deeds] which are otherwise," ἔχω + adv. = "be in a condition or situation" (BDAG ἔχω 10a)

1 Timothy 6
6:1 | ἡγέομαι + double acc. = "regard x as y"

6:2 | οἱ πιστοὺς ἔχοντες δεσπότας = "those who have believing masters" | ἀλλὰ μᾶλλον δουλευέτωσαν = "rather they must serve them all the better" (ESV) (BDAG μᾶλλον 2a) | οἱ τῆς εὐεργεσίας ἀντιλαμβανόμενοι – depending on whether εὐεργεσία is performed by the slaves or the masters, and on mng. of ἀντιλαμβάνω, either (1) "those who benefit from their [= the slaves'] service" (NIV 1984) (BDAG ἀντιλαμβάνω 4), or (2) "are devoted to the welfare of their slaves" (NIV 2011), "those who devote themselves to kindness" (BDAG ἀντιλαμβάνω 2)

6:3 | προσέρχεται is difficult – some MSS have προσέχεται (προσέχω = "cling to, devote oneself to"); but it is possible that we have a rare usage of προσέρχομαι = "come over to, assent to" (Thayer), hence "agree with" (ESV)

6:4 | ὑπόνοιαι πονηραί = "evil suspicions"

6:5 | διαπαρατριβαὶ διεφθαρμένων ἀνθρώπων τὸν νοῦν = "constant friction among people who are depraved in mind" (ESV), acc. of respect | τῆς ἀληθείας – gen. of separation after verb with ἀπο- prefix

6:6 | ἔστιν πορισμὸς μέγας ἡ εὐσέβεια – the article indicates that ἡ εὐσέβεια is the subject and πορισμὸς μέγας the predicate (cp. v. 10)

6:7 | ὅτι is difficult – scribes inserted "[it is true (or evident)] that" or tried other fixes; but the text as printed has strong support (Metzger), thus encouraging us to consider a rare mng. for ὅτι, perhaps "so that" (BDAG ὅτι 5c)

6:10 | ῥίζα πάντων τῶν κακῶν = "a root of all kinds of evils" (BDAG πᾶς 5) | ἡ φιλαργυρία is the subject, ῥίζα the predicate (cp. v. 6)

6:12 | ἐπιλαμβάνομαι takes gen. (also v. 19) | εἰς ἣν ἐκλήθης καὶ ὡμολόγησας – grammatically rough; possible translation: "to which you were called *and about which* you made the good confession" (ESV), implicit repetition of εἰς ἥν but with different mng. (BDAG εἰς 5)

6:13 | BDAG ἐπί 3

6:14 | Acc. σε as subject of inf. τηρῆσαί

6:15 | ἥν refers back to ἡ ἐπιφανεία | καιροῖς ἰδίοις = "at the proper time" (BDF §200(4)), temporal dat.

6:16 | φῶς οἰκῶν ἀπρόσιτον = "dwelling in unapproachable light," οἰκέω + acc. (φῶς) = "dwell in"

6:17 | ἐπὶ πλούτου ἀδηλότητι = "in the uncertainty of wealth" (ἐπί + dat.) | εἰς ἀπόλαυσιν = "for enjoyment," "to enjoy" (BDAG εἰς 4f)

6:18 | Infs. (ἀγαθοεργεῖν, πλουτεῖν & εἶναι) dependent on παράγγελε (v. 17): "Instruct [them] to do good," etc.

6:19 | εἰς τὸ μέλλον = "for the future"

6:21 | ἥν refers back to ἡ γνῶσις | περὶ τὴν πίστιν ἠστόχησαν = "have missed the mark (or deviated) with regard to the faith" (BDAG), "swerved" (ESV) (cp. 2 Tim 2:18) | μεθ' ὑμῶν = μετὰ ὑμῶν

Chapter Sixteen

The Second Epistle to Timothy

2 Timothy 1

1:3 | χάριν ἔχω = "give thanks" | ἀπὸ προγόνων = "from/since [the time of] my ancestors," which can only mean "as my ancestors did" (BDAG πρόγονος) | ὡς ἀδιάλειπτον ... τὴν μνείαν = "as I make constant mention of you" | ἔχω μνείαν = "remember" or "make mention" (cp. 1 Thess 3:6) | νυκτὸς καὶ ἡμέρας – genitives of time

1:4 | μεμνημένος σου τῶν δακρύων – when translating, move this clause to the front, thereby more clearly linking the ἵνα clause to ἰδεῖν: "Recalling your tears, I long to see you, so that I may be filled with joy" (NIV) | σου τῶν δακρύων = τῶν δακρύων σου

1:5 | ὑπόμνησιν λαμβάνειν τινός = lit. "to receive a remembrance of something," i.e., "to be reminded of something" | πέπεισμαι δὲ ὅτι καὶ ἐν σοί = "I am persuaded that [it dwells] in you as well," brachylogy

1:7 | "For the Spirit God gave us does not make us timid, but gives us power, love and self-discipline" (NIV 2011), genitives of product (W 106)

1:8 | συν- prefix in συγκακοπάθησον requires "with [me]" (cp. 2:3) | τῷ εὐαγγελίῳ = "for the gospel," dat. of advantage | κατὰ δύναμιν θεοῦ = "by God's power"

1:9–10 | τοῦ σώσαντος ... καλέσαντος ... καταργήσαντος ... φωτίσαντος = "who saved ... called ... abolished ... brought to light," article functioning as relative pronoun; aorist ptcs. are gen. in agreement with θεοῦ

1:12 | δι' ἣν αἰτίαν καὶ ταῦτα πάσχω = "That is why I am suffering as I am" (NIV) | ᾧ = "whom" | τὴν παραθήκην μου – could be (1) "what I have entrusted to him" (NASB), subjective gen., or (2) "what has been entrusted to me" (ESV), objective gen.

1:13 | ὑποτύπωσιν ἔχε (pres. impv.) = "hold fast the standard" (BDAG)

1:15 | Οἶδας τοῦτο, ὅτι = "You know that"

1:16, 18 | δῴη ὁ κύριος (2x) = "may the Lord grant," voluntative optative (W 481)

1:18 | ὅσα ... σὺ γινώσκεις = "you know very well what services he rendered at Ephesus" (NASB)

2 Timothy 2

2:2 | διὰ πολλῶν μαρτύρων = "in the presence of many witnesses," διά of attendant circumstances (M 57) | ἱκανός + inf. = "able, competent, qualified to"

2:3 | συγκακοπάθησον – see 1:8

2:4 | ὁ στρατολογήσας = "the one who enlisted him as a soldier," i.e., "his commanding officer" (NIV)

2:6 | μεταλαμβάνω takes gen. | πρῶτος = "be the first to" (NASB)

2:8 | κατὰ τὸ εὐαγγέλιόν μου = "as my gospel declares" (cp. Rom 2:16)

2:9 | ἐν ᾧ (referring back to τὸ εὐαγγέλιον) = "for which," marker of cause or reason (BDAG ἐν 9) | μέχρι δεσμῶν ὡς κακοῦργος = "even to the point of being chained like a criminal" (NIV)

2:10 | διὰ τοὺς ἐκλεκτούς = "for the sake of the elect," final use of διά + acc. (cp. Rom 4:25; 11:28) | τυγχάνω (= "obtain") takes gen. object (σωτηρίας)

2:11–12 | συναπεθάνομεν, συζήσομεν & συμβασιλεύσομεν – sc. αὐτῷ ("with him"), implied by συν- prefix (cp. Rom 6:6; 8:17)

2:12 | κἀκεῖνος = καὶ ἐκεῖνος

2:14 | First ἐπί is part of construction – χρήσιμος ἐπί + dat. = "useful/beneficial for" | Second ἐπί + dat. = "leading to," marker of purpose/result (BDAG ἐπί 16; BDF §235(4)) (cp. v. 16)

2:15 | ὀρθοτομοῦντα τὸν λόγον τῆς ἀληθείας = "accurately handling the word of truth" (NASB), or "guiding the word of truth along a straight path" (BDAG ὀρθοτομέω, citing LXX Prov 3:6; 11:5)

2:16 | ἐπὶ πλεῖον προκόψουσιν ἀσεβείας = "it will lead to further ungodliness" (NASB) (cp. v. 14)

2:17 | νομὴν ἔχω = "spread," medical simile, used of ulcers, gangrene, etc.

2:18 | οἵτινες περὶ τὴν ἀλήθειαν ἠστόχησαν = "who have swerved from the truth" (ESV) (cp. 1 Tim 6:21) | ἤδη γεγονέναι = "has aldredy taken place" (NASB), extensive perf. (W 577)

2:20 | οὐ μόνον ... ἀλλὰ καί = "not only ... but also" (cp. 4:8) | ἔστιν ... σκεύη – neut. pl. subjects take sg. verbs ("there are") | ἃ μέν ... ἃ δέ = "some ... others"

2:23 | ἀπαιδεύτους ζητήσεις = "uninformed speculations" (BDAG ἀπαίδευτος)

2:25 | μήποτε + subj. = "if perhaps" (NASB) (BDF §370(3); BDAG μήποτε 3)

2:26 | εἰς τὸ ἐκείνου θέλημα = "to [do] his will"

2 Timothy 3

3:3 | διάβολος (adj.) = "slanderous" (cp. 1 Tim 3:11; Tit 2:3)

3:4 | μᾶλλον ἤ = "rather than"

3:6 | ἐκ τούτων = "among them," partitive ἐκ | σεσωρευμένα ἁμαρτίαις = "weighed down with sins," dat. of material or content (W 169–71) | ἀγόμενα ἐπιθυμίαις ποικίλαις = "led by a variety of desires," dat. of means (W 162)

3:7 | μανθάνοντα ... δυνάμενα – neut. pl. ptcs. describing the γυναικάρια of v. 6

3:8 | ὃν τρόπον ... οὕτως καί = "just as ... so also" | κατεφθαρμένοι τὸν νοῦν = "corrupted in mind" (ESV), acc. of respect

3:9 | οὐ προκόψουσιν ἐπὶ πλεῖον = "they will not get very far" (ESV) | ὡς καὶ ἡ [sc. ἄνοια] ἐκείνων ἐγένετο = "just as theirs [= Jannes' and Jambres' folly] was also [clearly evident]," brachylogy

3:10 | μου modifies the following nouns, e.g., τῇ διδασκαλίᾳ μου, etc.

3:11 | τοῖς διωγμοῖς, τοῖς παθήμασιν, οἷά μοι ἐγένετο = "persecutions, [and] sufferings, such as happened to me" (NASB), οἷα refers back only to "persecutions and sufferings," not back to the other items listed in v. 10; neut. pl. subjects (οἷα) take sg. verbs (ἐγένετο)

3:13 | γόης = "swindler, cheat" (BDAG), used to describe self-proclaimed philosophers deemed to be charlatans

3:14 | σὺ δὲ μένε ἐν οἷς [= τούτοις ἃ] ἔμαθες καὶ ἐπιστώθης = "but you must stand by what you have learned and become convinced of" (BDAG πιστόω)

3:15 | βρέφους – gen. sg.

3:16 | πᾶσα γραφὴ θεόπνευστος – either (1) "every inspired scripture," or (2) "every scripture is inspired" (see W 313–4)

2 Timothy 4

4:1 | διαμαρτύρομαι + acc. = "I solemnly charge you ... by"

4:2 | κήρυξον – constative aorist impv. (W 720–1) | εὐκαίρως ἀκαίρως = "when it is convenient and when it is inconvenient," i.e., whether or not the preaching comes at a convenient time for the hearers (BDAG ἀκαίρως); asyndeton (BDF §460(1))

4:3–4 | ἀκοή (2x) = "ear" (BDAG ἀκοή 3)

4:3 | ἀνέχομαι takes gen. | κνηθόμενοι τὴν ἀκοήν = "feeling an itching in their ears," taking τὴν ἀκοήν as acc. of respect

4:4 | Here τὴν ἀκοήν is the direct object of ἀποστρέψουσιν – they "will turn away their ears from the truth"

4:6 | ἤδη σπένδομαι = "I am already being poured out," ingressive-futuristic present (W 537)

4:7 | Extensive perfects (W 577)

4:8 | λοιπόν = "from now on," "in the future" (BDAG λοιπός 3a), "henceforth" (ESV), adv. acc. | ἀποδίδωμι = "requite, recompense," in a good sense or a bad sense (cp. v. 14) (Thayer), "award" (NASB) | οὐ μόνον ... ἀλλὰ καί = "not only ... but also" (cp. 2:20)

4:14 | πολλὰ κακά = "many evil things," "much harm" | ἐνδείκνυμι = "show, display conduct," hence, "do"

4:15 | ὃν καὶ σὺ φυλάσσου (present mid. impv.) = "you too should be on your guard against him" (NIV)

4:16 | λογισθείη – voluntative optative (W 481)

4:22 | μεθ' ὑμῶν = μετὰ ὑμῶν

Chapter Seventeen

The Epistle to Titus

Titus 1

1:2 | ἐπ᾿ ἐλπίδι = "with a view to the hope," "for the sake of the hope" (BDAG ἐπί 16), modifying ἀπόστολος

1:3 | πιστεύω (pass.) + acc. of retained object (W 197) = "be entrusted with something"

1:5 | τούτου χάριν – see 1 Tim 5:14 | κατὰ πόλιν = "from city to city," "in every city" (BDAG κατά B1d)

1:6 | μὴ ἐν κατηγορίᾳ ἀσωτίας = "not open to the charge of debauchery" (ESV), prep. phrase modifies τέκνα; κατηγορία + gen. of the content of the charge | ἢ ἀνυπότακτα = "or rebellious," acc. adj. modifies τέκνα (*pace* NASB which takes ἀνυπότακτα as second gen. of the content of the charge: "not accused of dissipation or rebellion")

1:9 | ἀντεχόμαι takes gen. | δυνατὸς καὶ παρακαλεῖν ... καὶ ἐλέγχειν = "able both to exhort ... and to refute," δυνατός + inf. (BDF §393(4)); καί ... καί (BDAG καί 1f)

1:10 | οἱ ἐκ τῆς περιτομῆς = either (1) "those from the circumcised" (cp. Acts 10:45; Rom 4:12; Col 4:11), ancestral ἐκ, or more likely (2)

"those of the circumcision party" (ESV) (cp. Acts 11:2; Gal 2:12), characteristic ἐκ (these two uses of ἐκ are closely linked – see BDAG ἐκ 3b)

1:11 | ἃ μὴ δεῖ = "what ought not [to be taught]," would expect οὐ (see BDF §428(4); Z §440 n1) | αἰσχροῦ κέρδους χάριν = "for the sake of dishonest gain," on the prep. χάριν, see 1 Tim 5:14

1:12 | ἴδιος αὐτῶν προφήτης = "a prophet of their own"

1:13 | δι' ἣν αἰτίαν = "for this reason"

1:15 | αὐτῶν καὶ ὁ νοῦς καὶ ἡ συνείδησις = "both their mind and their conscience," καί ... καί (BDAG καί 1f)

1:16 | τοῖς ἔργοις = "by their deeds," dat. of means | πᾶν = "any"

Titus 2
2:1 | λάλει – impv. (cp. v. 15) | ἃ πρέπει τῇ ὑγιαινούσῃ διδασκαλίᾳ = "the things which are fitting for sound doctrine" (NASB)

2:2 | εἶναι – either (1) imperatival inf. (BDF §389; M 126), or (2) inf. complementary to λάλει (v. 1) understood loosely as "teach/exhort/remind" (cp v. 15) (cp. similar construction at v. 6 and 3:1–2) | ὑγιαίνοντας τῇ πίστει, etc. = "sound in faith, in love, in perseverance," datives of reference/ respect (W 144)

2:3 | διάβολος (adj.) = "slanderous" (cp. 1 Tim 3:11; 2 Tim 3:3)

2:7 | περὶ πάντα = "in all respects" (M 62) | σεαυτόν = "yourself," addressing Titus | παρέχω (mid.) ἑαυτόν τι = "show oneself to be something" (BDAG παρέχω 2b) | ἐν τῇ διδασκαλίᾳ ἀφθορίαν = "in your teaching show integrity" (ESV), continuing παρέχω but w/o the ἑαυτόν construction

2:8 | λόγον ὑγιῆ ἀκατάγνωστον = "sound speech that cannot be

condemned" (ESV) | ὁ ἐξ ἐναντίας = "the opponent" (BDAG
ἐκ 2) | μηδὲν ἔχων λέγειν περὶ ἡμῶν φαῦλον = ἔχων μηδὲν
φαῦλον λέγειν περὶ ἡμῶν – note that μηδέν goes with φαῦλον;
adj. (φαῦλον) + inf. (λέγειν) construction (BDF §393(4))

2:9 | ὑποτάσσεσθαι & εἶναι – see note on εἶναι (v. 2)

2:10 | πᾶσαν πίστιν ἐνδεικνυμένους ἀγαθήν – could be (1)
"showing all faith [to be] good," double acc. construction with ἀγαθήν
as complement to πίστιν (see W 188–9, 312–3), or (2) "showing all
good faith" (NASB, ESV), "to show that they can be fully trusted"
(NIV), taking ἀγαθήν as attributive adj. | τὴν διδασκαλίαν τὴν
τοῦ σωτῆρος ἡμῶν θεοῦ – could be (1) "the doctrine of God our
Savior" (NASB, ESV), gen. of source or possessive gen., (2) "the
teaching of God our Savior," subjective gen., or (3) "the teaching about
God our Savior" (NIV), objective gen. or gen. of reference (W 127)

2:12 | παιδεύουσα ἡμᾶς ἵνα ... ζήσωμεν = "training/leading us to
live," attenuated ἵνα functioning as inf. (BDAG ἵνα 2)

2:13 | τοῦ μεγάλου θεοῦ καὶ σωτῆρος ἡμῶν Ἰ. Χρ. – the (contested) Granville Sharp Rule may apply here, possibly identifying
Christ as θεός (see W 272–76, 290) (cp. 2 Pet 1:1)

2:14 | ζηλωτὴν καλῶν ἔργων = "eager to do good deeds," objective
gen. (cp. 1 Pet 3:13); ζηλωτήν is sg. in apposition to λαόν

Titus 3
3:1 | ἀρχαῖς ἐξουσίαις = "to rulers [and] authorities" | ἕτοιμος
πρός + acc. = "ready for" (BDAG ἕτοιμος b; πρός 3cβ) (cp. 1 Pet
3:15)

3:2 | πᾶσαν πραΰτητα = "perfect courtesy" (ESV)

3:3 | καὶ ἡμεῖς = "we too"

3:5 | οὐκ ἐξ ἔργων τῶν ἐν δικαιοσύνῃ ἃ ἐποιήσαμεν ἡμεῖς = "not because of works done by us in righteousness" (ESV), ἃ – non-attraction of the relative (should be ὧν in agreement with ἔργων), due to separation from antecedent (BDF §294(1))

3:8 | Acc. σε as subject of inf. | προΐστημι + gen. (καλῶν ἔργων) = "busy oneself with, engage in" (BDAG προΐστημι 2) (cp. v. 14) | ταῦτά ἐστιν – neut. pl. subjects take sg. verbs

3:10 | μετά + acc. = "after"

3:12 | κρίνω + inf. = "decide to" (BDAG κρίνω 4)

3:13 | Ζηνᾶν ... πρόπεμψον = "Diligently help Zenas the lawyer and Apollos on their way" (NASB) | ἵνα μηδὲν αὐτοῖς λείπῃ = lit. "so that nothing is lacking to them," i.e., "so that they lack nothing"

3:14 | οἱ ἡμέτεροι = "our people" | εἰς τὰς ἀναγκαίας χρείας = "to meet pressing needs" (NASB)

3:15 | τοὺς φιλοῦντας ἡμᾶς ἐν πίστει = "those who love us in the faith"

Chapter Eighteen

The Epistle to Philemon

Philemon

2 | ἡ κατ᾽ οἶκόν σου ἐκκλησία = "the church that meets in your house"

4 | μνείαν ποιεῖσθαί τινος = "to mention someone," ποιέω (mid.) + noun as periphrasis for simple verbal idea (BDAG ποιέω 7a; μνεία 2) (cp. Rom 1:9; Eph 1:16; 1 Thess 1:2) | ἐπὶ τῶν προσευχῶν μου = "in my prayers" (BDAG ἐπί 18a)

5 | σου τὴν ἀγάπην καὶ τὴν πίστιν = "your love and faith" | Chiasm: "your ᵃlove and ᵇfaith, which you have ᵇtoward the Lord Jesus and ᵃfor all the saints"

6 | ἡ κοινωνία τῆς πίστεώς σου – main options: (1) "the sharing of your faith," objective gen., (2) "your (financial) sharing done out of faith," subjective gen. | παντὸς ἀγαθοῦ τοῦ ἐν ἡμῖν εἰς Χριστόν – could be (1) "of every good thing we have in Christ" (NIV 1984), εἰς = ἐν (BDAG εἰς 1aδ), or (2) "... in honor of Christ" (BDAG εἰς 4g), "... for the sake of Christ" (NIV 2011), εἰς equivalent to dat. of advantage

7 | BDAG ἐπί 6c | τὰ σπλάγχνα ... ἀναπέπαυται – neut. pl. subjects take sg. verbs

8 | ἔχων – concessive ptc. | ἐπιτάσσειν σοι τὸ ἀνῆκον = "to command you [to do] what is appropriate"

9 | τοιοῦτος ὢν ὡς Παῦλος πρεσβύτης = "since I am such a one as Paul the old man" (for more on this phrase, see M 113)

12 | ἀνέπεμψα – epistolary aorist (BDF §334; M 12) (also ἔγραψα in vv. 19, 21)

14 | τὸ ἀγαθόν σου = lit. "your good thing," i.e., "any favor you do" (NIV), subjective gen.

15 | πρὸς ὥραν = "for a little while"

16 | ὑπὲρ δοῦλον = "more than a slave" (BDAG ὑπέρ B) | καὶ ἐν σαρκὶ καὶ ἐν κυρίῳ = "both in the flesh and in the Lord," καί ... καί (BDAG καί 1f)

17 | ἔχω + double acc. = "regard/consider someone to be something" (BDAG ἔχω 6)

19 | ἵνα μὴ λέγω σοι ὅτι = "(not to mention to you that ...)"

20 | ἐγώ σου ὀναίμην = "let me have some benefit from you," voluntative optative; ὀνίνημι + gen. of person/thing that is source of benefit | μου τὰ σπλάγχνα = τὰ σπλάγχνά μου

21 | καὶ ὑπὲρ ἃ λέγω = "even more than what I say" (BDAG ὑπέρ B)

24 | ὁ συναιχμάλωτός μου = "fellow-prisoner with me," gen. of association (W 128–30) (cp. Col 4:10)

Chapter Nineteen

The Epistle to the Hebrews

Hebrews 1

1:1 | ἐν τοῖς προφήταις = "by means of the prophets," Hebr./instrumental ἐν

1:2 | ἐπ’ ἐσχάτου τῶν ἡμερῶν τούτων = lit. "in [the] last of these days," i.e., "in these last days" (BDAG ἐπί 18a); Hebr. phrase (BDF §264(5); LXX Num 24:14; Jer 23:20; 25:19; cp. 2 Pet 3:3; Jude 18) | ἐν υἱῷ = "in one who is Son" (M 114), anarthrous qualitative substantive: "God, in his final revelation, has spoken to us in one who has the characteristics of a son" (W 245), as opposed to a mere prophet

1:1–2 | Although there is a grammatical parallel between ἐν τοῖς προφήταις (v. 1) and ἐν υἱῷ (v. 2), there is also a contrast and a progression ("in the past" vs. "in these last days"), so that ἐν υἱῷ is not to be taken in the same instrumental sense as ἐν τοῖς προφήταις – God's climactic revelation has come in the very person of his incarnate Son. For other examples of parallel prepositional phrases used with different mngs., see Rom 4:25; 11:28.

1:3 | ἐν δεξιᾷ = "at the right hand" (BDAG ἐν 1c) | τῷ ῥήματι τῆς δυνάμεως αὐτοῦ = "by his powerful word" (NIV), dat. of means; attributive gen. (W 188) | καθαρισμὸν τῶν ἁμαρτιῶν ποιησάμενος

= "after making purification for sins," antecedent aorist temporal ptc. (W 624–7)

1:4 | τοσούτῳ ... ὅσῳ = "as much ... as" | κρείττων + gen. of comparison (τῶν ἀγγέλων) = "better than" | διαφορώτερον ὄνομα = "a superior name" | παρ' αὐτούς = "than they," παρά + acc. as marker of comparison (BDAG παρά C3) (common in Hebrews – see 2:7, 9; 3:3; 9:23; 11:4; 12:24) | "having become as much better than the angels, as He has inherited a more excellent name than they" (NASB) | On the elegent word order frequently found in Hebrews, see BDF §473(2)

1:5 | τίνι τῶν ἀγγέλων = "to which of the angels?" (cp. v. 13) | Semitic εἰς (2x) as predicate with forms of εἰμί (BDAG εἰς 8aβ)

1:7–8 | πρὸς μέν ... πρὸς δέ = "with reference to angels he says ... but with reference to the Son [he says]" (BDAG πρός 3ea), brachylogy

1:8 | ὁ θρόνος σου ὁ θεός – options (see discussion at W 59): (1) "God is your throne," (2) "your throne is God," (3) "your throne, O God," nom. for voc. (BDF §147) (common in LXX) | ἡ ῥάβδος τῆς εὐθύτητος = "the righteous scepter" (NASB), attributive gen.

1:9 | ἔχρισέν σε ἔλαιον = "anointed you with oil," double acc. (M 33) | παρά = "rather than," Hebr. comparative expressing exclusion (BDF §245a; παρά C3) (cp. Lk 18:14; Rom 1:25)

1:10 | κατ' ἀρχάς = "in the beginning" (BDAG κατά B2a) | ἔργα τῶν χειρῶν σού εἰσιν οἱ οὐρανοί = "the heavens are the works of your hands," οἱ οὐρανοί (articular) is subject; ἔργα (anarthrous) is predicate

1:12 | ὁ αὐτός = "the same"

1:13 | ἐκ δεξιῶν μου = "at my right [hand]" (BDAG ἐκ 2) | ἕως ἄν + subj. = "until"

1:14 | οὐχί εἰσιν = "are they not?" expecting affirmative answer | διὰ τοὺς μέλλοντας κληρονομεῖν σωτηρίαν = "for the sake of those who are destined to inherit salvation" (BDAG μέλλω 2a; διά B2a)

Hebrews 2

2:1 | δεῖ προσέχειν ἡμᾶς = "it is necessary for us to pay close attention," acc. ἡμᾶς as subject of inf. | τοῖς ἀκουσθεῖσιν (aorist pass. ptc.) = "to the things that have been heard [by us]"

2:2 | ὁ goes with λόγος | λαληθείς (aorist pass. ptc.) = "spoken"

2:3 | πῶς ἡμεῖς ἐκφευξόμεθα = "how shall we escape?" rhetorical question, implying impossibility (BDAG πῶς 1aδ); deliberative future (W 570) | ἀμελέω takes gen. (τηλικαύτης σωτηρίας = "such a great salvation"); ἀμελήσαντες = "if we neglect," conditional ptc. | ἀρχὴν λαμβάνειν λαλεῖσθαι = "to be proclaimed at first" (BDAG ἀρχή 1a) | ὑπὸ τῶν ἀκουσάντων (aorist active ptc.) modifies ἐβεβαιώθη

2:4 | συνεπιμαρτυροῦντος τοῦ θεοῦ = "while God bears witness," gen. abs.

2:6 | πού τις = "someone somewhere" | μιμνῄσκομαι takes gen.

2:7 | βραχύ τι – could be either spatial ("a little lower") or temporal ("for a little while"); Hebrews interprets Ps 8:5 temporally in terms of Jesus's suffering and death (v. 9)

2:7, 9 | παρ' ἀγγέλους (2x) = "than the angels," παρά + acc. as marker of comparison (see 1:4)

2:8 | ἐν ᾧ + inf. = "in subjecting" (BDAG ἐν 7; BDF §404) | αὐτῷ (2x) is indirect object of ἀνυπότακτον & ὑποτεταγμένα

2:9 | τόν ... Ἰησοῦν = "Jesus, who was made lower than the angels for a little while" (NIV 2011) | γεύομαι takes gen. (θανάτου)

2:9–10 | διά + acc. = "because of the suffering of death," vs. διά + gen. = "through sufferings"

2:10 | ἔπρεπεν αὐτῷ ... τελειῶσαι = "it was fitting for him [= God] to make perfect" | The principal action is expressed by the ptc. (ἀγαγόντα); could be rendered: "it was fitting that he should bring many sons to glory by making the pioneer of their salvation perfect through suffering" (see Z §263) | ἀρχηγός (cp. 12:2) = "pioneer" (NIV 2011), "captain" (KJV) – Christ is the first to experience the eschatological state of perfection, and since he does so as our representative and covenant head, he establishes and guarantees our eschatological perfection as well; cp. πρόδρομος (6:20) and ἀπαρχή (1 Cor 15:20)

2:11 | ὁ τε γὰρ ἁγιάζων καὶ οἱ ἁγιαζόμενοι ἐξ ἑνὸς πάντες = "for a consecrating priest and those whom he consecrates are all of one stock" (New English Bible), gnomic present (W 523) (cp. 3:4; 5:4; 6:16; 7:7, 12; 8:3) | δι' ἣν αἰτίαν = "for which reason" | ἀδελφοὺς αὐτοὺς καλεῖν – double acc., "to call someone something"

2:13 | ἔσομαι πεποιθώς = "I will put my trust," future perf. periphrastic (W 647–9; BDF §352) (cp. Matt 16:19; 18:18; Lk 12:52)

2:14 | κοινωνέω and μετέχω both take gen. | τῶν αὐτῶν = "the same," referring to "flesh and blood"

2:15 | τούτους, ὅσοι = "those who" | φόβῳ θανάτου = "by/through fear of death," instrumental dat. | διὰ παντὸς τοῦ ζῆν (gen. articular inf.) = "through the whole of life" (M 56; cp. BDF §398), "all their lives" (NASB), "throughout the lifetime" (BDAG διά A2a) | ἔνοχος + gen. = "subject to, held in" (BDAG ἔνοχος 1)

2:16 | δήπου = "of course, surely" | ἐπιλαμβάνομαι (2x) takes gen.

2:17 | ὤφειλεν (impf.) + inf. = "he had to be ..." | κατὰ πάντα =

"in every way" | τὰ πρὸς τὸν θεόν = "in things pertaining to God," acc. of respect (M 33); seem to have a cultic connotation (cp. 5:1; Rom 15:17) | εἰς τό + inf. = "in order to"

2:18 | ἐν ᾧ = "because" (BDAG ἐν 9a; BDF §219(2)) | πειρασθείς – though subordinate grammatically, the ptc. actually expresses the principal action (cp. v. 10): "Since He Himself was tempted (πειρασθείς) in that which He has suffered, He is able to come to the aid of those who are tempted (τοῖς πειραζομένοις)" (NASB)

Hebrews 3

3:2 | ὁ ποιήσας αὐτόν = "the one who appointed him" (BDAG ποιέω 1b)

3:3 | πλείονος δόξης ἠξίωται = "he has been considered worthy of greater honor" | παρὰ Μωϋσῆν = "than Moses," παρά + acc. as marker of comparison (see 1:4) | καθ᾽ ὅσον = "inasmuch as" (BDAG κατά B5aδ) | τοῦ οἴκου – gen. of comparison

3:4 | κατασκευάζεται – gnomic present (cp. 2:11)

3:5–6 | Μωϋσῆς μέν ... Χριστὸς δέ = "now Moses ... but Christ"

3:5 | εἰς μαρτύριον τῶν λαληθησομένων = "for a testimony of those things which were to be spoken later," only instance of future pass. ptc. in NT (BDF §351)

3:6 | οὗ = "whose"

3:8 | κατὰ τὴν ἡμέραν = "in the day" (BDAG κατά B2a)

3:9 | οὗ (adv.) = "where" | εἶδον is pl.

3:10 | τεσσαράκοντα ἔτη – modifies εἶδον; acc. for extent of time (cp. v. 17)

3:11 | ὡς ὤμοσα = "so I swore" (NIV 1984) (BDAG ὡς 4) (cp. 4:3)
| εἰ εἰσελεύσονται = "they shall certainly not enter," Hebr. oath formula; emphatic denial expressed by aposiopesis (BDF §454(5); BDAG εἰ 4; M 179) (cp. 4:3, 5)

3:12 | μήποτε + fut. indic. for aor. subj. (BDF §§369(2); 370(2)) (cp. Mk 14:2) | καρδία πονηρὰ ἀπιστίας ἐν τῷ ἀποστῆναι ἀπὸ θεοῦ ζῶντος = "an evil, unbelieving heart that falls away from the living God" (NASB) | ἀπιστίας = "unbelieving," attributive gen.

3:13 | καθ' ἑκάστην ἡμέραν = "daily" | ἄχρις οὗ = "as long as" (BDAG ἄχρι 1bα) | τις ἐξ ὑμῶν = "any of you," partitive ἐκ (cp. 4:1)

3:15 | ἐν τῷ λέγεσθαι = "while it is said" (NASB) (BDAG ἐν 10c)

3:16 | Accent trouble: (1) If τινές (= "some"), then next sentence is a statement and ἀλλά is interepreted normally (BDF §448(4)): "For some heard and rebelled, but not all who came out of Egypt through Moses," but (2) if τίνες; (= "who?"), then next sentence is a question and ἀλλά = "indeed" (BDAG ἀλλά 3): "For who heard and rebelled? Indeed, was it not all who came out of Egypt through Moses?"

3:17–18 | τίσιν; (2x) = "with/to whom?"

3:19 | καί = "and so" (BDAG καί 1bζ)

Hebrews 4
4:1 | Φοβηθῶμεν μήποτε ... δοκῇ τις ἐξ ὑμῶν = "Let us fear lest any of you should seem" | καταλειπομένης ἐπαγγελίας ... αὐτοῦ = "while the promise of entering his rest remains," gen. abs. | Inf. εἰσελθεῖν is complementary to ἐπαγγελία | τις ἐξ ὑμῶν – see 3:13 | δοκέω + inf. (ὑστερηκέναι) serves to moderate the statement (BDAG δοκέω 2aα)

4:2 | καὶ γάρ = "for indeed" | ἐσμεν εὐηγγελισμένοι = "we had the good news preached to us," perf. periphrastic (W 649) | κἀκεῖνοι = καὶ ἐκεῖνοι | ὁ λόγος τῆς ἀκοῆς = "the message they heard" (ESV)

4:3 | ὡς ὤμοσα – see 3:11 | τῶν ἔργων ... γενηθέντων – concessive gen. abs.

4:3, 5 | εἰ εἰσελεύσονται (2x) – see 3:11

4:5 | ἐν τούτῳ = "in this [passage]"

4:6 | ἀπολείπεται τινὰς εἰσελθεῖν εἰς αὐτήν = "it remains for some to enter it," ἀπολείπεται is used 3x in Heb (4:6, 9; 10:26) (BDAG ἀπολείπω 2)

4:7–8 | μετά + acc. (2x) = "after"

4:8 | Second class (contrary-to-fact) conditional (W 694–6) | Ἰησοῦς = "Joshua" | οὐκ ἄν ... ἐλάλει = "he would not have spoken" (BDF §360(4)) | περὶ ἄλλης ... ἡμέρας = "concerning another day"

4:10 | καὶ αὐτός = "himself also" (cp. 5:2)

4:11 | ἵνα μή ... τις ... πέσῃ = "so that no one will fall"

4:12 | Two genitives joined by καί mng. "between" (2x) (W 135) (cp. 5:14)

4:13 | πρὸς ὃν ἡμῖν ὁ λόγος = "to whom we must give account" (ESV), "with whom we have to do, i.e., to reckon, in his capacity as judge" (BDAG λόγος 2e) (for similar use of λόγος, cp. 13:17)

4:15 | κατὰ πάντα καθ᾽ ὁμοιότητα = lit. "in every respect according to likeness [to us]," i.e., "in every way just as we are"

4:16 | προσερχώμεθα – hortatory subj.

Hebrews 5

5:1 | Partitive ἐκ | τὰ πρὸς τὸν θεόν – see 2:17

5:2 | περίκειται ἀσθένειαν = "beset with weakness" (NASB, ESV) (cp. 7:28)

5:2–3 | αὐτός ... περὶ αὐτοῦ – "he himself ... for himself"

5:4 | οὐχ ... τις = "one does not," i.e., "no one" | λαμβάνει – gnomic present (see 2:11) | καλούμενος is awkward – either (1) "[is] called," supplying ἐστίν, resulting in a present periphrastic (although it would then be translated, "is being called"), or (2) "[receives it] when he is called" (NASB; ZG), understanding a second λαμβάνει and taking καλούμενος as temporal ptc.

5:5 | οὕτως καί – looks back to vv. 1–4 as the implied protasis | Ellipsis: "but the one who said to him ... [made him a high priest]"

5:6 | ἐν ἑτέρῳ = "in another [passage]"

5:7 | δεήσεις τε καὶ ἱκετηρίας – direct object of προσενέγκας | ἀπό = "because of" (BDAG ἀπό 5a)

5:8 | καίπερ ὤν = "although he was/is," concessive ptc. (M 102; W 634–5) | τὴν ὑπακοήν is direct object of ἔμαθεν | ἔμαθεν ... ἔπαθεν – *parēchēsis*, i.e., similar sounding words used in close succession (BDF §488(2)) | ἀφ' ὧν = ἀπὸ τούτων ἅ – the relative pronoun, which includes the demonstrative, has been assimilated to the case of the omitted demonstrative (BDF §294(4))

5:11 | "Concerning him [or 'about this,' ESV] we have much to say, and it is hard to explain, since you have become dull of hearing" (NASB) (BDF §393(6))

5:12 | ὀφείλοντες εἶναι διδάσκαλοι = "though you ought to be teachers," concessive ptc. | διὰ τὸν χρόνον = lit. "because of the time," or "by this time" (BDAG διά B2a) | χρεία + gen. articular inf. + ὑμᾶς (object of inf.) + τινά (acc. as subject of inf.) = "need for someone to teach you" | τὰ στοιχεῖα τῆς ἀρχῆς τῶν λογίων τοῦ θεοῦ = "the elementary principles of the oracles of God" (NASB), taking τῆς ἀρχῆς as attributive gen. (BDAG ἀρχή 5) (cp. 6:1)

5:13 | μετέχω takes gen. | ἄπειρος λόγου δικαιοσύνης = "unacquainted with the teaching about uprightness" (BDAG I. ἄπειρος), gen. of reference (W 127–8), adj. + gen. construction (BDF §182)

5:14 | τελείων ἐστιν = "is for the mature," with ἡ στερεὰ τροφή as subject, as indicated by the article | τῶν ... ἐχόντων = "those who have their faculties trained," article functioning as relative pronoun | διὰ τὴν ἕξιν = "because of practice" (NASB), but would expect διά + gen. here (M 204 note on p. 58) | πρὸς διάκρισις καλοῦ τε καὶ κακοῦ = "to distinguish between good and evil," two genitives joined by καί mng. "between" (see 4:12)

Hebrews 6

6:1 | ὁ τῆς ἀρχῆς τοῦ Χριστοῦ λόγος = "the elementary teaching about the Christ" (NASB) (BDAG ἀρχή 5) (cp. 5:12) | φερώμεθα ἐπί + acc. = lit. "let us be moved along to," i.e., "let us move on to" (BDAG φέρω 3d; ἐπί 4bε), hortatory subj. | πίστις ἐπὶ θεόν = "faith in God" (BDAG ἐπί 15)

6:2 | διδαχή + genitives = "instruction about ..."

6:4 | ἀδύνατον + object acc. (τοὺς φωτισθέντας, etc.) + inf. (ἀνακαινίζειν, v. 6) = "it is impossible ... to renew those who have once been enlightened" | μέτοχος + gen. = "partaker of, participator/sharer in"

6:4–5 | γεύομαι (2x) normally takes gen. (v. 4; cp. 2:9), but occasionally acc. (ῥῆμα & δυνάμεις, v. 5) (BDF §169(3); M 36) (cp. John 2:9)

6:6 | ἀνασταυροῦντας & παραδειγματίζοντας = "since they are crucifying," etc., causal ptcs. | ἑαυτοῖς = "to their own harm" (ESV), "to their loss" (NIV)

6:7 | τόν ... ὑετόν = "the rain that often falls on it" | εὔθετος takes dat. (ἐκείνοις) – "useful to those for whom also it is cultivated" | μεταλαμβάνω takes gen.

6:8 | ἐκφέρουσα δέ = "but if it produces," conditional ptc. | ἐγγύς + gen. of verbal noun (κατάρας) = "close to being cursed" (cp. 8:13)

6:9 | τὰ ἐχόμενα σωτηρίας = "things that belong to salvation" (BDAG ἔχω 11a) | εἰ καί = "even if" (M 167)

6:10 | εἰς τὸ ὄνομα αὐτοῦ = "in his name" (BDAG ὄνομα 1dγ) | διακονήσαντες = "by serving," ptc. of means

6:12 | τῶν ... κληρονομούντων = "of those who are inheriting," ingressive-futuristic present (W 537) (cp. 1:14)

6:13 | ὀμνύω κατά + gen. (2x) = "swear by someone/thing" (cp. v. 16) (M 60)

6:14 | εἰ μήν = "surely, certainly" (BDF §24) (not same as oath formula in 3:11; 4:3, 5; the underlying Hebrew is different) | On Semitism of cognate ptc. + verb, see M 177–8.

6:15 | τυγχάνω takes gen.

6:16 | ὀμνύουσιν – gnomic present (cp. 2:11) | πάσης ... ὁ ὅρκος = "for them [= ἄνθρωποι/humans] an oath is an end of every dispute, resulting in confirmation," note postposition of πέρας (BDF §474(4)); ὁ ὅρκος – generic use of article (W 227)

6:17 | ἐν ᾧ = "because" (cp. 2:18) ("Because God wanted...," NIV) | ὅρκῳ = "with an oath," dat. of means

6:18 | ψεύδομαι ἐν = "lie about something," περί would be expected; but see LXX Lev 5:21 where both prepositions are used | ἵνα ... ἔχωμεν | κρατέω takes gen.

6:19 | Antecedent of ἥν could be παράκλησις but is probably ἐλπίς understood objectively | τὸ ἐσώτερον τοῦ καταπετάσματος = "the inner sanctuary behind the curtain" (NIV)

6:20 | γενόμενος = "having become"

Hebrews 7
7:1 | The second ὁ functions as a relative pronoun and governs both συναντήσας and εὐλογήσας: "who met ... and blessed" | Ἀβραάμ ὑποστρέφοντι = "Abraham as he was returning," taking ὑποστρέφοντι is a dat. sg. attributive adjectival ptc. modifying Ἀβραάμ, which is dat. bec. συναντάω takes dat. (cp. v. 10) | ἡ κοπή τῶν βασιλέων = "the slaughter of the kings," objective gen.

7:2 | ἀπό – substitute for partitive gen. (BDAG ἀπό 1f) | πρῶτον μέν ... ἔπειτα δέ = "first of all ... then," an enumeration of items for consideration | δικαιοσύνης & εἰρήνης – attributive genitives (W 86–8)

7:1–3 | Οὗτος ὁ Μελχισέδεκ ... μένει ἱερεὺς εἰς τὸ διηνεκές = "This Melchizedek ... remains a priest forever" – all of the material prior to the verb μένει is simply an adjunct to the subject, οὗτος ὁ Μελχισέδεκ

7:4 | θεωρεῖτε πηλίκος οὗτος = "observe how great this man was" (NASB) | Ἀβραὰμ ὁ πατριάρχης | Partitive ἐκ

7:5–6 | οἱ μέν ... ὁ δέ = "they ... but this man" (W 213)

7:5 | ἐντολή + inf. = "a commandment to"

7:6 | ἐξ αὐτῶν goes with ὁ μὴ γενεαλογούμενος = "he whose descent is not traced from them," i.e., from the sons of Levi

7:7 | εὐλογεῖται – gnomic present (cp. 2:11)

7:8 | ὧδε μέν ... ἐκεῖ δέ = "in the one case ... but in the other case" | μαρτυρέω (pass.) + ὅτι = "it is testified that" (cp. v. 17)

7:9 | ὡς ἔπος εἰπεῖν = "so to speak, one might almost say" (BDAG ἔπος; ὡς 9b)

7:11 | Second class (contrary-to-fact) conditional (see 4:8) | ὁ λαὸς γὰρ ἐπ᾽ αὐτῆς νενομοθέτηται = "(for on the basis of it [= the Levitical priesthood] the people received the law)," parenthetical comment; νομοθετέω (pass.) means to be furnished with a code of laws by a νομοθέτης or lawgiver like Solon or Moses (BDAG ἐπί 8) | λέγεσθαι = "to be designated, named" (BDAG λέγω 4)

7:12 | μετατιθεμένης τῆς ἱερωσύνης – gen. abs. | καὶ νόμου μετάθεσις = "a change of law as well," objective gen. | γίνεται – gnomic present (cp. 2:11)

7:13 | ἐφ᾽ ὅν = "[the one] about whom" (BDAG ἐπί 14bα) | λέγεται (pass.) ταῦτα = "these things are said," neut. pl. subjects take sg. verbs | μετέχω takes gen.

7:17 | μαρτυρεῖται = "it is witnessed of him" | ὅτι recitative

7:18–19 | μὲν γάρ ... δέ = "for, on the one hand ... and on the other hand"

7:18 | τὸ ἀσθενὲς καὶ ἀνωφελές = "the weakness and uselessness," substantivized adjectives (BDF §263)

7:20–22 | καὶ καθ' ὅσον ... κατὰ τοσοῦτο καί = "and inasmuch as ... so much the more also" (NASB); vv. 20b–21 (οἱ μέν ... ὁ δέ ...) is a parenthesis

7:20, 23 | εἰσὶν ἱερεῖς γεγονότες (2x) = "they became priests," perf. periphrastic

7:20–21 | ὁρκωμοσία (3x) = "the swearing of an oath" (< ὅρκος + ὀμνύω – cp. Lk 1:73) | οἱ μέν ... ὁ δέ ... = "they [= the Levitical priests] ... but he [= the priest according to the order of Melchizedek]" (cp. vv. 23–24)

7:21 | Brachylogy: "but he [sc. became a priest] with the swearing of an oath" | μετά + gen. = "with" of accompanying activity (BDAG μετά A3b) | διὰ τοῦ λέγοντος πρὸς αὐτόν = "by the One who says to him"

7:22 | κρείττονος διαθήκης ἔγγυος = "the guarantor of a better covenant" (NIV 2011), "surety" (KJV), *sponsor* (Vulg.) (cp. 8:6)

7:23 | διὰ τὸ θανάτῳ κωλύεσθαι παραμένειν = "because they were prevented by death from continuing in office" (ESV); διά + articular inf. (cp. v. 24); τό goes with κωλύεσθαι; θανάτῳ is dat. of means modifying κωλύεσθαι; κωλύεσθαι + complementary inf. (παραμένειν)

7:24 | ὁ δέ = "but he" (W 211–12)

7:25 | δύναται + inf. (σῴζειν) = "he is able to save" | εἰς τὸ παντελές = "to the uttermost" (ESV), "completely" (NIV), or "forever" (NASB)

7:26 | τοιοῦτος ἀρχιερεύς = "such a high priest" (cp. 8:1), τοιοῦτος could be retrospective or prospective | ἔπρεπεν takes dat. (ἡμῖν) (cp. 2:10) – either (1) "Such a high priest was fitting for us," omitting καί per Majority text, or (2) if the καί is read, it must be taken adverbially:

"Such a high priest was *precisely* appropriate for us" (Lane citing A. T. Robertson) | τῶν οὐρανῶν – gen. of comparison

7:27 | καθ᾽ ἡμέραν = "daily"

7:28 | ἀνθρώπους καθίστησιν ἀρχιερεῖς ἔχοντας ἀσθένειαν = "appoints as high priests men who are weak" (NIV 1984), double acc. construction; taking ἔχοντας with ἀνθρώπους | τῆς μετὰ τὸν νόμον = "which came after the law," τῆς functioning as relative pronoun referring back to ὁρκωμοσίας; μετά + acc. = "after" | Sc. καθίστησιν in second half of comparison (brachylogy)

Hebrews 8

8:1 | κεφάλαιον δὲ ἐπὶ τοῖς λεγομένοις = "Now the main point in what has been said [is this]" (NASB, BDAG κεφάλαιον 1)

8:2 | τὰ ἅγια = "the sanctuary, the holy place" (BDAG ἅγιος 2b), Hebr. pl. (BDF §141(8)) (cp. 9:2ff; 10:19; 13:11) | τῶν ἁγίων λειτουργὸς καὶ τῆς σκηνῆς = "a minister in the holy places and in the true tabernacle," genitives of place within which (W 124)

8:3 | εἰς τό + inf. expresses purpose, completing καθίσταται ("is appointed to offer") | καθίσταται – gnomic present (see 2:11) | ὅθεν ... προσενέγκῃ = "so it was necessary for this one also to have something to offer" (NIV), ἔχειν τι ὃ προσενέγκῃ = lit. "to have something such that he may offer," qualitative-consecutive relative clause (BDF §379)

8:4 | Second class (contrary-to-fact) conditional, use of present tense in (BDF §360(4)) | ὄντων τῶν προσφερόντων = "since there [already] are [priests] who ...," causal gen. abs.

8:5 | λατρεύω takes dat. | μέλλων ἐπιτελεῖν τὴν σκηνήν = "as he was about to build the tabernacle"

8:6 | τυγχάνω + gen. of thing obtained (cp. 11:35) | λειτουργίας – gen. of comparison | ὅσῳ καὶ κρείττονός ἐστιν διαθήκης μεσίτης = "by as much as He is also the mediator of a better covenant" (NASB), "to the degree that" (BDAG ὅσος 3) (cp. 7:22; 9:15; 12:24) | νομοθετέω = "enact on the basis of a legal sanction, ordain, found by law" (BDAG), different nuance than in 7:11 | ἐπὶ κρείττοσιν ἐπαγγελίαις = "on the basis of better promises" (BDAG ἐπί 6a) (cp. 9:17; 10:28)

8:7 | Second class (contrary-to-fact) conditional | ἡ πρώτη ἐκείνη = ἡ πρώτη διαθήκη (cp. v. 13; 9:1, 18) | τόπος + gen. (δευτέρας [sc. διαθήκης]) = "occasion for a second [covenant]" (BDAG τόπος 1f) | ἐζητεῖτο is pass.; subject is τόπος – "occasion would not have been sought"

8:8 | αὐτούς – i.e., the Israelites | First καί = "when," Hebr. (BDAG καί 1bγ) | συντελέω διαθήκην ἐπί + acc. – "consummate (i.e., establish) a covenant with" (cp. v. 10)

8:9 | ἐν ἡμέρᾳ ἐπιλαβομένου μου τῆς χειρός αὐτῶν = "in the day of my taking them by their hand," ἐπιλαμβάνομαι takes gen. | ὅτι = "because," explaining why God is making a new covenant unlike the old one | κἀγώ = καὶ ἐγώ | ἀμελέω takes gen. of person rejected

8:10 | διατίθημι διαθήκην + dat. = "make a covenant with" (LXX) | διδούς = "I will put," futuristic present ptc. | διδούς ... ἐπιγράψω – transition from ptc. to finite verb (M 180) (cp. 10:16) | ἔσομαι εἰς (2x) – see 1:5

8:11–12 | οὐ μή + aorist subj. (2x) – emphatic negation, "will certainly never" (BDF §365)

8:12 | μιμνῄσκομαι + gen. of thing remembered | οὐ μὴ ἔτι = "never again" (BDAG ἔτι 1bβ) (cp. 10:17)

8:13 | ἐν τῷ λέγειν = "in/by saying," non-temporal use (BDF §404(3)) | ἡ πρώτη [sc. διαθήκη] (cp. v. 7; 9:1, 18) | ἐγγύς + gen. of verbal noun (ἀφανισμοῦ) = "close to disappearing" (cp. 6:8)

Hebrews 9

9:1 | "Now the first covenant had regulations for worship and also an earthly sanctuary" (NIV) | ἡ πρώτη [sc. διαθήκη] (cp. 8:7, 13; v. 18)

9:2 | σκηνὴ ἡ πρώτη = "the first or outer sanctuary," in contrast with the holy of holies (vv. 3, 6–7) | ἐν ᾗ ἡ λυχνία = "in which [was] the lampstand," the article ἡ becomes ᾗ, receiving acute accent from enclitic particle τε | ἥτις refers back to σκηνή

9:2–3, 8, 12, 24–25 | On pl. (τὰ) ἅγια (7x), see 8:2

9:3 | μετὰ τὸ δεύτερον καταπέτασμα = "behind the second curtain [was] ..." (BDAG μετά B1)

9:4 | χρυσοῦν ἔχουσα θυμιατήριον = ἔχουσα χρυσοῦν θυμιατήριον = "having the golden incense-altar," ἔχουσα is fem. in agreement with σκηνή (v. 3)

9:5 | κατασκιάζοντα is neut. pl. in agreement with Χερουβίν | περὶ ὧν ... μέρος = "Of these things we cannot now speak in detail" (ESV) (BDAG μέρος 1c)

9:6 | τούτων δὲ οὕτως κατεσκευασμένων = "once these things are arranged in this way," gen. abs. | διὰ παντός = "continually, regularly"

9:7 | ἅπαξ τοῦ ἐνιαυτοῦ = "once a year," gen. of time when

9:8 | τοῦτο δηλοῦντος τοῦ πνεύματος τοῦ ἁγίου – gen. abs. | τὴν τῶν ἁγίων ὁδόν = "the way into the sanctuary," gen. of direction (BDF §166; W 100–1) | ἔτι τῆς πρώτης σκηνῆς ἐχούσης στάσιν – gen. abs. | The outer and inner sanctuaries are viewed as symbols of the earthly and heavenly sanctuary respectively

9:9 | ἥτις παραβολή = "which [is] a symbol," ἥτις refers to all that is described in vv. 6–8, and is fem. by attraction to παραβολή (ZG) | εἰς τὸν καιρὸν τὸν ἐνεστηκότα – either (1) "for the age then present" (ESV alt), i.e., the old covenant age, or (2) "for (or pointing to [ZG]) the age now present," i.e., the new covenant age | καθ᾽ ἥν = "in accordance with which" (M 59), antecedent of ἥν could be παραβολή or πρώτη σκηνή (other MSS read καθ᾽ ὅν = "during which," taking καιρόν as antecedent) | κατὰ συνείδησιν = "in respect to the conscience" (BDAG κατά B6)

9:10 | ἐπί + dat. – either (1) "on the basis of" (BDAG ἐπί 6a; BDF §235(2)), or (2) "relate to" (NASB), "deal with" (ESV) (BDAG ἐπί 14a)

9:12 | διά of attendant circumstances = "with" (M 57) | αἰωνίαν λύτρωσιν εὑράμενος = "having obtained eternal redemption" (NASB) (BDAG εὑρίσκω 3; BDF §310)

9:13 | σποδὸς δαμάλεως – LXX Num 19:9–10 | τὴν τῆς σαρκὸς καθαρότητα = "the purification of the flesh," objective gen.

9:14 | καθαριεῖ – future (note circumflex) | εἰς τό + inf. expresses purpose

9:15 | ὅπως ... λάβωσιν | θανάτου γενομένου – gen. abs. | τῶν ἐπὶ τῇ πρώτῃ διαθήκῃ παραβάσεων = "the transgressions [that were committed] under the first covenant," temporal ἐπί (BDAG ἐπί 18b) | τὴν ἐπαγγελίαν ... τῆς αἰωνίου κληρονομίας = "the promise of the eternal inheritance"

9:16 | θάνατον ἀνάγκη φέρεσθαι τοῦ διαθεμένου = "the death of the one who made the will must be established" (BDAG φέρω 8), ἀνάγκη [ἐστίν] + inf. – impersonal construction (BDF §127(2)) (cp. v. 23)

9:17 | ἐπὶ νεκροῖς – either (1) "at death" (ESV), "when somebody has died" (NIV), temporal (BDAG ἐπί 18b), or (2) "on the basis of dead bodies," legal (BDAG ἐπί 6a) | βέβαιος = "valid, in force" (BDAG βέβαιος 3)

9:18 | ἡ πρώτη [sc. διαθήκη] – see v. 1

9:19 | λαληθείσης πάσης ἐντολῆς – gen. abs.

9:19–20 | Moses is the subject of λαβών, ἐράντισεν (2x), and λέγων

9:22 | σχεδὸν πάντα = "nearly everything" (NIV) | ἐν αἵματι = "with blood," Hebr./instrumental ἐν | αἱματεκχυσία = "the pouring out of blood" at the base of the altar – key ritual of the sin offering, resulting in forgiveness (see LXX Lev 4:7, 18–20, 25–26, 30–31, 34–35 – τὸ αἷμα ἐκχεεῖ ... καὶ ἀφεθήσεται αὐτῷ/αὐτοῖς)

9:23 | ἀνάγκη + inf. – see v. 16 | τούτοις (= "with these [sc. sacrifices]") does not go with τοῖς οὐρανοῖς but modifies καθαρίζεσθαι adverbially (instrumental dat.) | αὐτὰ τὰ ἐπουράνια = "the heavenly things themselves" | παρὰ ταύτας = "than these [sc. Levitical sacrifices]," παρά + acc. as marker of comparison (see 1:4)

9:24 | χειροποίητα ἅγια = "a man-made sanctuary" (NIV 1984) | εἰς αὐτὸν τὸν οὐρανόν = "into heaven itself"

9:25 | οὐδ' ἵνα = "nor [did he enter heaven] to," οὐδέ introduces second contrast between Christ and the Levitical priests: the first contrast is that he entered the heavenly sanctuary, not the earthly copy (v. 24); the second contrast is that he offered one sacrifice for sins for all time, not repeated sacrifices year after year (vv. 25–6) | κατ' ἐνιαυτόν = "year after year" (cp. 10:1, 3) | ἐν of attendant circumstances = "with" (M 57, 78)

9:26 | ἐπεί = "otherwise" (cp. 10:2) | ἔδει αὐτὸν πολλάκις παθεῖν = "he would have had to suffer repeatedly" (ESV) (on omission of ἄν, see M 149; BDF §358) | Temporal ἐπί (BDAG ἐπί 18b) | εἰς ἀθέτησιν [τῆς] ἁμαρτίας = "for the putting away of sin," "to put away sin," objective gen. (BDAG εἰς 4f) | διὰ τῆς θυσίας αὐτοῦ = "by the sacrifice of himself," modifying the verbal idea in ἀθέτησις; objective gen.; αὐτοῦ = ἑαυτοῦ (cp. v. 25)

9:26, 28 | ἁμαρτία (2x) – metonymy for sin's guilt and/or punishment (the κρίσις of v. 27) (Thayer ἀναφέρω 3) (also 10:2–4, 11–12)

9:27–28 | καθ᾽ ὅσον ... οὕτως καί = "just as ... so also" (BDAG κατά B5bα)

9:27 | ἀπόκειταί τινι + inf. = "it is one's destiny to" (ZG) | μετά + acc. = "after" | τοῦτο refers back to the ἀποθανεῖν

9:28 | εἰς τὸ πολλῶν ἀνενεγκεῖν ἁμαρτίας (position of πολλῶν is confusing; it can be moved to end: εἰς τὸ ἀνενεγκεῖν ἁμαρτίας πολλῶν) = "to take upon himself the sins of many," i.e., to take up the guilt of their sins as a burden in order to undergo punishment in their place (cp. LXX Isa 53:12) (see Thayer ἀναφέρω 3; BDAG ἀναφέρω 4) | ἐκ δευτέρου = "a second time" | χωρὶς ἁμαρτίας = "without reference to sin" (NASB), i.e., not for the purpose of atoning for sin (BDAG χωρίς 2bδ) | χωρὶς ἁμαρτίας ... τοῖς αὐτὸν ἀπεκδεχομένοις εἰς σωτηρίαν = "not to deal with sin but to save those who are eagerly waiting for him" (ESV)

Hebrews 10
10:1 | κατ᾽ ἐνιαυτόν – see 9:25 | εἰς τὸ διηνεκές = "continually" (cp. v. 12)

10:2 | ἐπεί = "otherwise" (cp. 9:26) | Conditional sentence: implied protasis; unreal (contrary-to-fact) indic. with ἄν in apodosis (BDF §360(2)): "would not [the offerings] have ceased to be offered [if

the law could have perfected its adherents]?" (M 151) | παύομαι +
supplementary present pass. ptc. (προσφερόμεναι) (BDF §414(2))
| διὰ τό + inf. indicates cause (W 610) | συνείδησις ἁμαρτιῶν
= "consciousness of guilt" | ἅπαξ κεκαθαρισμένους = "since they
would have been cleansed once for all," causal ptc.

10:3 | ἐν αὐταῖς = "in these [sc. sacrifices]"

10:4 | ἀδυνατον + inf. = "it is impossible for"

10:6 | περὶ ἁμαρτίας = "sin offering(s)," technical LXX term (LXX
Lev 4:3, 14, 28, 32; 5:6–10, etc.)

10:7 | ἥκω ... τοῦ ποιῆσαι ... = "I have come ... to do your will" (cp. v. 9
which omits the parenthetical comment, "in the scroll of the book it is
written of me"), inf. prefixed with pleonastic τοῦ (BDF §400(7)) (also
v. 9) | ὁ θεός = "O God," nom. for voc. (BDF §147)

10:8–9 | ἀνώτερον λέγων ὅτι ... τότε εἴρηκεν = "after saying
above ... then he said" (NASB) (M 101), ἀνώτερον – adv. acc.; ὅτι
recitative

10:10 | Hebr./instrumental ἐν (BDF §219) | ἡγιασμένοι ἐσμέν –
perf. periphrastic

10:11 | καθ᾽ ἡμέραν = "daily" | τὰς αὐτάς ... θυσίας = "the same
sacrifices"

10:11–12 | πᾶς μὲν ἱερεύς ... οὗτος δέ = "every priest ... but this
[priest]" | μίαν ... θυσίαν = "a single sacrifice" (word order places
emphasis on μίαν)

10:12 | εἰς τὸ διηνεκές = "for all time" (cp. v. 14)

10:13 | τὸ λοιπόν = "from that time onward" (NASB) (BDAG λοιπός 3aα), adv. acc. | ἕως + aorist subj. = "until" | τίθημι + double acc. = "make x y"

10:14 | μιᾷ προσφορᾷ = "by one offering," dat. of means

10:15 | μετὰ τό + inf. (εἰρηκέναι) = "after saying" (W 611) (cp. v. 26)

10:16 | διδούς ... ἐπιγράψω – see 8:10

10:17 | Supply "he then says" to complete "after saying" of v. 15 | οὐ μή + future + ἔτι = "I will no longer ..." (BDF §365) (see 8:12)

10:19 | εἰς τὴν εἴσοδον τῶν ἁγίων = "for access *into* the sanctuary," gen. of direction (BDF §166), or objective gen. (BDF §163); on pl. τὰ ἅγια, see 8:2 | Hebr./instrumental ἐν

10:20 | ἐγκαινίζω = "bring about the beginning of something, with implication that it is newly established; to ratify, inaugurate, dedicate with solemn rites" (BDAG) (LXX word used with reference to dedicating houses, temples, altars, etc.) | ὁδόν is in apposition to ἥν (εἴσοδον → ἥν → ὁδόν) | Note that τῆς σαρκός and καταπετάσματος are matching in case; thus the veil is interpreted as a type prefiguring the flesh of Jesus (see N. H. Young, "τουτ᾽ εστιν της σαρκος αυτου: (Heb. x. 20): Apposition, Dependent or Explicative?" *NTS* 20 [1973]: 100–104; commentaries)

10:22 | ῥεραντισμένοι τὰς καρδίας ... λελουσμένοι τὸ σῶμα = lit. "sprinkled with respect to our hearts ... washed with respect to our body," accs. of respect

10:22–24 | προσερχώμεθα, κατέχωμεν, κατανοῶμεν – hortatory subjunctives

10:24 | εἰς παροξυσμὸν ἀγάπης = lit. "for stirring up of love," i.e., to stir one another up to love

10:25 | ἑαυτῶν functions here as 1p reflexive pronoun, "of ourselves" (BDF §283(3)) | καθὼς ἔθος τισίν = "as is the habit of some," dat. of possession (cp. v. 30) | τοσούτῳ μᾶλλον ὅσῳ = "all the more as"

10:26 | ἑκουσίως ἁμαρτανόντων ἡμῶν = "if we sin deliberately," referring to the sin of apostasy (vv. 28–9), conditional gen. abs. | μετὰ τό + inf. (λαβεῖν) = "after receiving" (cp. v. 15) | ἀπολείπεται – see 4:6, 9

10:27 | πυρὸς ζῆλος ἐσθίειν μέλλοντος τοὺς ὑπεναντίους = "the zeal of a fire that will consume the adversaries" (cp. LXX Ps 79:5; Zeph 1:18; 3:8; Isa 26:11); ζῆλος is nom.; μέλλοντος is gen. in agreement with πυρός; μέλλω + inf. as equivalent to future

10:28 | ἀθετήσας τις νόμον = "anyone who rejected the law" | ἐπί + dat. = "on the basis of [the testimony of]" (BDAG ἐπί 6a)

10:29 | πόσῳ = lit. "by how much" (author probably began with a πόσῳ μᾶλλον construction in mind; translate as gen. in agreement with χείρονος τιμωρίας) | ἀξιόω (pass.) + gen. = "be considered worthy of something" | δοκεῖτε is parenthetical (BDF §465(2); BDAG δοκέω 1e) | Article governs all three ptcs.: ὁ καταπατήσας … ἡγησάμενος … ἐνυβρίσας | "Of how much worse punishment, do you think, the one who trampled on, etc., will be considered worthy?" | ἡγέομαι + double acc. = "consider x to be y"

10:30 | ἐμοὶ ἐκδίκησις = "vengeance [is] mine," dat. of possession | κρινεῖ – future (note circumflex)

10:32 | αἱ πρότερον ἡμέραι = "the former days" (BDF §62; BDAG πρότερος 1bβ) (cp. 1 Pet 1:14) | πολλὴν ἄθλησιν παθημάτων – could be (1) "a hard struggle with sufferings" (ESV; cp. BDAG ἄθλησις), objective gen., or (2) "a great conflict full of suffering" (NIV 2011), gen. of content (W 92)

10:33 | τοῦτο μέν … τοῦτο δέ = "sometimes … at other times" (NIV), adv. acc. | κοινωνοὶ τῶν οὕτως ἀναστρεφομένων γενηθέντες = "becoming partners with those living in such a way [amid reproach and affliction]"

10:34 | τῶν ὑπαρχόντων ὑμῶν = "of your possessions," objective gen. | μένουσαν = "lasting, abiding" (cp. 13:14)

10:36 | ὑπομονῆς ἔχετε χρείαν = ἔχετε χρείαν ὑπομονῆς

10:37 | ἔτι μικρὸν ὅσον ὅσον = "in a very little while" (BDAG ὅσος 1b; ἔτι 1c)

10:39 | "We are not of those who shrink back and are destroyed, but of those who have faith and preserve their souls" (ESV)

Hebrews 11
11:1 | πίστις is the subject (and ὑπόστασις & ἔλεγχος the predicates), since πίστις is the known entity, previously mentioned in 10:38–9 (W 42, 44 n23) | πραγμάτων ἔλεγχος οὐ βλεπομένων = ἔλεγχος πραγμάτων οὐ βλεπομένων

11:2 | ἐν ταύτῃ = "by it [= faith]," Hebr./instrumental ἐν

11:3ff | πίστει (18x) = "by faith," instrumental dat. (cp. Rom 3:28)

11:3 | ῥήματι θεοῦ = "by the word of God," instrumental dat. (cp. 1:3) | μὴ ἐκ φαινομένων = ἐκ μὴ φαινομένων (M 168; BDF §433(3); see commentaries) | εἰς τό + inf. (γεγονέναι), here expressing result (consecutive) rather than purpose (final)

11:4 | πλείονα θυσίαν παρά = "a better sacrifice than," παρά + acc. as marker of comparison (see 1:4) | ἐμαρτυρήθη εἶναι δίκαιος = "he was commended as righteous" | μαρτυροῦντος ἐπὶ τοῖς δώροις αὐτοῦ τοῦ θεοῦ = "God bearing witness 'upon his gifts,'" gen. abs. (cp. 2:4); normally the construction would be μαρτυρέω + dat. ("bear witness to") (cp. John 5:33; 18:37; Acts 10:43; 22:5), but the phrase ἐπὶ τοῖς δώροις αὐτοῦ is quoted from LXX Gen 4:4 ("God looked upon Abel and *upon his gifts*") | δι' αὐτῆς = "through it [= faith]" | ἀποθανών = "though he is dead," concessive ptc.

11:5 | τοῦ μὴ ἰδεῖν – gen. of articular inf. with μή in either final or consecutive sense (BDF §400) | πρό + gen. = "prior to" | μεμαρτύρηται εὐαρεστηκέναι τῷ θεῷ = "he was commended as one who pleased God" (NIV)

11:6 | δεῖ + inf. + acc. (τὸν προσερχόμενον) = "it is necessary for one to"

11:7 | εὐλαβηθεὶς κατεσκεύασεν κιβωτόν = "in reverent fear built an ark," ptc. of manner/attitude (W 627) | τῆς κατὰ πίστιν δικαιοσύνης κληρονόμος = κληρονόμος τῆς δικαιοσύνης [τῆς] κατὰ πίστιν = "heir of the righteousness that comes by faith" (BDAG κατά B7c), cp. the Pauline phrase, "the righteousness of faith" (Rom 4:11, 13; 9:30; 10:6; Phil 3:9)

11:8 | καλούμενος = "when he was called" | ὑπήκουσεν ἐξελθεῖν = "obeyed so as to go out," non-sequential, almost epexegetical, inf. of result (W 592 n7) | μέλλω + inf. = "be about to" | εἰς = "for" or "as" (BDAG εἰς 4d; 8b) | ἔρχεται – present retained in indirect discourse (W 537) (cp. v. 13)

11:9 | εἰς γῆν ... ὡς ἀλλοτρίαν = "in a land as if it were foreign" (BDAG ἀλλότριος 1a), εἰς = ἐν | τῆς ἐπαγγελίας τῆς αὐτῆς = "of the same promise"

11:11 | καὶ αὐτὴ Σάρρα στεῖρα – bec. καταβολὴ σπέρματος normally refers to the male role in conception ("sowing of seed," BDAG καταβολή 2) this verse is a famous *crux interpretum* – options: (1) Westcott & Hort read dat. αὐτῇ Σάρρα, interpreted either as "together with Sarah," associative dat. (see BDF §194(1)), or as "for Sarah," dat. of advantage (W 144); (2) Black (83–9) suggests supplying οὖσα (found in a few MSS) and taking the phrase as a Hebr. circumstantial clause, "even though Sarah was barren" (followed by Metzger; NIV 1984); (3) NASB, ESV, and NIV 2011 omit στεῖρα (per some MSS) and take καταβολὴ σπέρματος as referring to the female role in conception: "By faith Sarah herself received power to conceive" | δύναμιν ἔλαβεν = "(s)he received the ability" | καὶ παρὰ καιρὸν ἡλικίας = "even though (s)he was past the age" (BDAG παρά C3) | ἡγέομαι + double acc. = "consider x to be y" (cp. v. 26)

11:12 | καὶ ταῦτα is an expression mng. "and at that, although" (BDAG οὗτος 1bγ; BDF §§290(5), 425(1)) | νενεκρωμένου – gen. abs. | Hebr. ὡς + substantive, taking place of substantive (BDAG ὡς 2cα‎ℵ) | ἡ ἄμμος ἡ ... ἡ ... = "the sand which is ... which is ..."

11:13 | κατὰ πίστιν = "in faith" (NASB, ESV), "living by faith" (NIV) | εἰσιν – present retained in indirect discourse (cp. v. 8)

11:14 | οἱ τοιαῦτα λέγοντες = "people who say such things"

11:15 | Second class (contrary-to-fact) conditional | ἐκείνης ... ἀφ' ἧς ἐξέβησαν = "that [sc. country] from which they went out," looking back to πατρίς (v. 14) | μνημονεύω takes gen. (ἐκείνης) | εἶχον ἄν = "they would have had" | καιρός + inf. = "opportunity to" (BADG καιρός 1b)

11:16 | ὀρέγω takes gen. | κρείττονος ... τοῦτ' ἔστιν ἐπουρανίου = "a better [sc. country], that is, a heavenly [one]," looking back to πατρίς (vv. 14–15) | θεὸς ἐπικαλεῖσθαι αὐτῶν = "to be called their God"

11:17 | πειραζόμενος = "when he was tested" | προσέφερεν = "was about to offer," conative impf. (W 550–1)

11:19 | ἐν παραβολῇ = "as a type" (BDAG, NASB), "parabolically" (M 78)

11:20 | καὶ περὶ μελλόντων = "even concerning things to come"

11:21 | ἀποθνῄσκων = "as he was dying" | προσεκύνησεν ἐπί ... = "he bowed in worship (or prayed) over the head of his staff" (BDAG)

11:22 | τελευτῶν = "as he was dying" | μνημονεύω περί + gen. = "make mention concerning"

11:23 | γεννηθείς = "when he was born" | τρίμηνον = "for three months," acc. for extent of time

11:24 | ἠρνήσατο λέγεσθαι = "refused to be called" (BDAG ἀρνέομαι 1; λέγω 4)

11:25 | ἤ = "than" | πρόσκαιρον ἔχειν ἁμαρτίας ἀπόλαυσιν = "to enjoy the short-lived pleasures of sin" (BDAG ἀπόλαυσις)

11:26 | ἡγέομαι + double acc. (see v. 11) | τῶν Αἰγύπτου θησαυρῶν = "than the treasures of Egypt," gen. of comparison

11:27 | τὸν ἀόρατον ὡς ὁρῶν ἐκαρτέρησεν = ἐκαρτέρησεν ὡς ὁρῶν τὸν ἀόρατον = "he persevered because he saw him who is invisible" (NIV), ὡς + ptc. = "as one who, because" (BDAG ὡς 3aβ)

11:28 | πεποίηκεν = "he kept [the Passover]" (BDAG ποιέω 2f), perf. bec. this first Passover became a permanent institution (BDF §342(4)) | Verbs of touching take gen.

11:29 | ὡς διὰ ξηρᾶς γῆς – not "as if on dry land," bec. they really did cross on dry land, but "as (one travels) over dry land" (see BDAG ὡς 1bα) | λαμβάνω πεῖραν + gen. = "make an attempt of something" (contrast mng. in v. 36) | Antecedent of ἧς is τὴν Ἐρυθρὰν Θάλασσαν

11:30 | ἐπὶ ἑπτὰ ἡμέρας = "for seven days" (BDAG ἐπί 18cβ)

11:31 | δεξαμένη = "because she welcomed," causal ptc.; fem. in agreement with Ῥαὰβ ἡ πόρνη | μετ᾽ εἰρήνης = "in peace"

11:32 | καὶ τί ἔτι λέγω; = "And what more shall I say?" | ἐπιλείψει με διηγούμενον ὁ χρόνος = "time would fail me to tell" (ESV)

11:33 | ἐπιτυγχάνω + gen. of thing obtained (cp. v. 35)

11:34 | ἐδυναμώθησαν ἀπὸ ἀσθενείας = "were made strong out of weakness" (ESV), ἀπό = ἐκ, "out of the former state of" (ZG)

11:35 | "Others were tortured, not accepting release," allusion to 2 Macc 6:18–7:42 | τυγχάνω + gen. of thing obtained (cp. v. 33; 8:6)

11:36 | ἕτεροι = ἄλλοι (as in v. 35) (ZG; Z §153) | ἔτι δέ = "and even" | λαμβάνω πεῖραν + gen. (ἐμπαιγμῶν, μαστίγων, δεσμῶν, φυλακῆς) = "experience something" (contrast mng. in v. 29)

11:37 | "They were sawn in two," categorical pl. referring to Isaiah the prophet (W 404–5) (*Martyrdom of Isaiah* 1:9; 5:1–2, 14) | ἐν φόνῳ μαχαίρης = lit. "by murder of the sword," i.e., by being murdered with the sword; Hebr./instrumental ἐν; gen. of means | μηλωτή – mantle worn by Elijah (LXX 3 Kgdms 19:13, 19; 4 Kgdms 2:8, 13–14)

11:38 | ἄξιος + gen. = "worthy of" | ἐπί + dat. = "in" (BDAG ἐπί 1bα)

11:39 | μαρτυρηθέντες = "having gained approval" (NASB), "commended" (ESV)

11:40 | τοῦ θεοῦ … προβλεψαμένου – gen. abs. | κρεῖττόν τι = "something better"

Hebrews 12

12:1 | καὶ ἡμεῖς τοσοῦτον … μαρτύρων = "since we also have so great a host of witnesses surrounding us" (BDAG νέφος), ἔχοντες is a causal ptc. | τοσοῦτον = τοσοῦτο when preceding a vowel; emphatic position (BDF §473(2)); modifies νέφος (neut.) | τρέχωμεν – hortatory subj.; ptc. ἀποθέμενοι takes on the hortatory/imperatival "mood" of the main verb: "let us lay aside … and run" (W 644)

12:2 | ἀφοράω εἴς τινα = "fix one's eyes on" (BDAG ἀφοράω 1; cp. NASB) | ἀντί + gen. is ambiguous: "Does this mean that Jesus chose a cross instead of the joy that he might have had (cf. Phil. 2:6), or that he chose a cross for the sake of winning the joy which lay beyond and through it?" (M 204; cp. W 367–8) | καταφρονέω takes gen. (αἰσχύνης)

12:3 | τὸν ὑπομεμενηκότα = "he [= Jesus] who endured" | τοιαύτην ὑπὸ τῶν ἁμαρτωλῶν εἰς ἑαυτὸν ἀντιλογίαν = "such hostility by sinners against himself" | ταῖς ψυχαῖς ὑμῶν = "in your souls," dat. of sphere (W 153–5) | ἐκλυόμενοι – ptc. of result (W 637–9)

12:4 | μέχρις αἵματος = "to the point of [shedding] blood" | πρὸς τὴν ἁμαρτίαν ἀνταγωνιζόμενοι = "in your struggle against sin," adds clarity if this phrase is moved to the front of the sentence

12:5 | ἐκλανθάνομαι takes gen. | υἱέ – voc. | ὀλιγωρέω takes gen. | ὑπ᾽ αὐτοῦ ἐλεγχόμενος = "when you are corrected by him"

12:6 | First ὅν = "[the one] whom," but second ὅν = "whom"

12:7 | εἰς παιδείαν ὑπομένετε = "it is for discipline that you endure" (NASB) | προσφέρω τινι = "treat someone in a certain way" (BDAG προσφέρω 3)

12:8 | "If you are not disciplined (and everyone undergoes discipline), then you are illegitimate children and not true sons" (NIV 1984), treating ἧς μέτοχοι γεγόνασιν πάντες as a parenthesis; μέτοχος + gen. = "sharing in a thing"

12:9 | εἶτα usually means "then" or "next" in a chronological sense, but here it enumerates the next argument: "moreover" (BDAG εἶτα 2) | ἔχω + double acc. = "have x as y" | καὶ ἐνετρεπόμεθα = "and we respected [them]" | οὐ πολὺ μᾶλλον + fut. = "shall we not much more ...?"

12:10 | οἱ μέν ... ὁ δέ = "they [= our human fathers] ..., but he [= the Father of spirits]" | πρὸς ὀλίγας ἡμέρας = "for a few days" | κατὰ τὸ δοκοῦν αὐτοῖς = "as seemed best to them" | ἐπὶ τὸ συμφέρον = "for our good" | εἰς τὸ μεταλαβεῖν τῆς ἁγιότητος αὐτοῦ = "so that [we] may share in his holiness," μεταλαμβάνω + partitive gen. (see W 132–3)

12:11 | πρὸς τὸ παρόν = "for the moment" | χαρᾶς, λύπης = "joyful, painful," adjectival genitives | ὕστερον δέ = "but later," adv. acc. | δι᾿ αὐτῆς = "by it [= παιδεία]" | καρπὸν εἰρηνικὸν δικαιοσύνης – either (1) "the peaceful fruit which is righteousness," gen. of apposition (W 95), or (2) "the peaceful fruit which comes from righteousness," gen. of source (W 109)

12:14 | οὗ χωρίς = "without which" (M 87)

12:15–16 | ἐπισκοποῦντες μή τις (3x) = "taking care that no person/root," etc.

12:17 | μετανοίας τόπον οὐχ εὗρεν – either (1) "he found no opportunity for repentance" (on his own part), or (2) "he found no chance to change his father's mind" (NRSV alt.) | Antecedent of αὐτήν could be or ἡ εὐλογία or μετανοία

12:18 | ψηλαφωμένῳ = "to what may be touched" (ESV) – pass. ptc. may serve as a substitute for the verbal adj. ending in -τός, which is the usual way of expressing "may be" (BDF §65(3)) (cp. σαλευόμενα, v. 27); the rendering "to a *mountain* that can be touched" (NASB) captures the sense, but the word ὄρει itself is probably a scribal gloss derived from v. 22 (Metzger)

12:19 | σάλπιγγος ἤχῳ = ἤχῳ σάλπιγγος = "to the sound of a trumpet" | ἧς οἱ ἀκούσαντες παρῃτήσαντο μὴ προστεθῆναι αὐτοῖς λόγον = "which [sound was such that] those who heard begged that no further word be spoken to them" (NASB)

12:20 | οὐκ ἔφερον τὸ διαστελλόμενον = "they could not bear what was commanded" (NIV), impf. to express "could" (BDF §358) | κἄν = "if even"

12:21 | οὕτω φοβερόν ... εἶπεν = "so terrifying was the sight that Moses said" (ESV)

12:22 | πανηγύρει could go with (1) μυριάσιν ἀγγέλων, "to innumerable angels in festal gathering" (ESV), or (2) καὶ ἐκκλησίᾳ πρωτοτόκων (v. 23), "to the general assembly and church of the firstborn" (NASB)

12:24 | αἵματι ῥαντισμοῦ – either (1) "to the sprinkled blood," Hebr. attributive gen., or (2) "to the blood for sprinkling," modeled on ὕδωρ ῥαντισμοῦ = "the water for sprinkling" (LXX Num 19:9, 13, 20, 21) | παρὰ τὸν Ἄβελ = "than [sc. the blood of] Abel," παρά + acc. as marker of comparison (see 1:4)

12:25 | βλέπετε μή + inf. = "see to it that you do not" | ἐπὶ γῆς goes with τὸν χρηματίζοντα = "him who warned them on earth" (i.e., Moses) | παραιτησάμενοι = "when they refused" | εἰ ... πολὺ μᾶλλον = "if ... then much more surely" (BDAG μᾶλλον 2b), supplying "we will not escape" in apodosis (brachylogy) | τὸν ἀπ᾽ οὐρανῶν = "him [sc. who warned them] from heaven" (i.e., God) (brachylogy)

12:26–27 | ἔτι ἅπαξ (2x) = "yet once more"

12:26 | οὐ μόνον ... ἀλλὰ καί = "not only ... but also"

12:27 | τό functions as quote marks (BDAG ὁ 2hβ) | σαλευομέν -ων, -α – pres. pass. ptcs.; πεποιημένων – perf. pass. ptc.; all three are neut. pl. | σαλευόμενα = "things that *can* be shaken" (see v. 18) | ὡς πεποιημένων = "that is, created things" (BDAG ὡς 3aα)

12:28 | παραλαμβάνοντες = "since we are receiving," causal ingressive-futuristic pres. ptc. (W 537, 631) | ἔχωμεν χάριν = "let us have gratitude" (see BDAG χάρις 5), hortatory subj. | δι' ἧς λατρεύωμεν = "through which let us worship," with ἧς referring back to χάρις, and λατρεύωμεν functioning as hortatory subj. in relative clause (BDF §377(3))

12:29 | καὶ γάρ = "for indeed" | LXX Deut 4:24; 9:3

Hebrews 13

13:2 | ἐπιλανθάνομαι takes gen. (cp. v. 16) | διὰ ταύτης = "through it [= φιλοξενία]" | λανθάνω + ptc. = "do something unawares"

13:3 | μιμνῄσκομαι takes gen. | ὡς ... ὡς ... = "as if you were their fellow prisoners ... as if you yourselves were suffering" (NIV), taking ὄντες ἐν σῶμα negatively, in the sense "subject to mortal ills" (BDAG σῶμα 1b)

13:4 | κρινεῖ – fut. (note circumflex)

13:4–5 | Continuing 3s impv. of v. 1 (μενέτω), supply ἔστω (3x) = "let x be y"

13:5 | ἀφιλάργυρος ὁ τρόπος = "[Let] your life [be] free from the love of money" | οὐ μή + aorist subj. (2x) = "I will never," emphatic negation subj. (BDF §365(3); W 468)

13:6 | ὥστε θαρροῦντας ἡμᾶς λέγειν = "so we [sc. δύνασθαι/can] confidently say" (ESV), ὥστε has tendency to ellipsis (see M 144)

13:7 | μνημονεύω takes gen. | ὧν ἀναθεωροῦντες τὴν ἔκβασιν τῆς ἀναστροφῆς = "considering the outcome of their manner of life," object of ἀναθεωροῦντες is τὴν ἔκβασιν; ὧν is possessive pronoun going with τῆς ἀναστροφῆς | τὴν πίστιν = "their faith"

13:9 | καλὸν χάριτι βεβαιοῦσθαι τὴν καρδίαν = "it is good for the heart to be strengthened by grace," καλὸν [ἐστίν] + acc. + inf. (BDF §409(3))

13:10 | ἔχω ἐξουσίαν + inf. (φαγεῖν) = "have a right to"

13:11 | ὧν ... τούτων ... = "for [those] animals *whose* blood is brought into the holy place by the high priest as an offering for sin, *of these* the bodies are burned up outside the camp" | On pl. τὰ ἅγια, see 8:2

13:13, 15 | ἐξερχώμεθα, ἀναφέρωμεν – hortatory subjunctives

13:14 | μένουσαν ... μέλλουσαν – assonance

13:15 | διὰ παντός = "continually"

13:17 | ὡς λόγον ἀποδώσοντες = "as those who will give an account" (BDAG λόγος 2a; ὡς 3aβ), note the future ptc. (BDF §425(3))

13:18 | ἐν πᾶσιν καλῶς θέλοντες ἀναστρέφεσθαι = "desiring to act honorably in all things" (ESV), or "commendably" (BDAG καλῶς 2)

13:19 | "And I urge you all the more to do this [= to pray for us, v. 18], so that I may be restored to you the sooner" (NASB)

13:21 | καταρτίσαι – voluntative optative; only optative in Hebrews (BDF §384) | εἰς τὸ ποιῆσαι τὸ θέλημα αὐτοῦ = "that [you] may do his will" | τὸ εὐάρεστον = "that which is pleasing," substantivized adj. (BDF §263)

13:22 | διὰ βραχέων = "briefly" (M 57) | καὶ γάρ = "for indeed"

13:23 | "You should know that our brother Timothy has been released, with whom I shall see you if he comes soon" (ESV)

13:24 | οἱ ἀπὸ τῆς Ἰταλίας = "those from Italy"

Chapter Twenty

The Epistle of James

James 1

1:1 | χαίρειν = "greetings," standard formula in Hellenistic letters (cp. Acts 15:23; 23:26)

1:2 | ἡγέομαι + acc. + ὅταν = "consider [it] x when ..." | πᾶσαν χαράν = "pure joy" (BDF §275(3); NIV)

1:3 | γινώσκοντες = "because you know," causal ptc. | τὸ δοκίμιον here = "testing" (BDAG δοκίμιον 1), contrast usage in 1 Pet 1:7 | ὑμῶν τῆς πίστεως = τῆς πίστεως ὑμῶν

1:4 | ἐν μηδενὶ λειπόμενοι = "lacking in nothing" (BDAG ἐν 12)

1:5 | τις ὑμῶν = "any of you," partitive gen. | λείπω takes gen. (BDF §180(4)) (cp. 2:15) | τοῦ διδόντος θεοῦ πᾶσιν ἁπλῶς = "the God who gives generously to all"

1:6 | μηδέν = "in nothing," acc. of respect | ἔοικα takes dat. (cp. v. 23)

1:8 | ἐστίν is to be understood

1:10 | καυχάσθω is to be understood from v. 9 (brachylogy)

1:11 | Four gnomic aorists (BDF §333(1); W 562) | ἡ εὐπρέπεια τοῦ προσώπου αὐτοῦ = "the beauty of its appearance" (NASB), or simply "its beauty" (ESV)

1:13 | πειραζόμενος = "when he is tempted" | ὅτι recitative | ἀπό = ὑπό (as in v. 14) | ἀπείραστος κακῶν – options: (1) "inexperienced with reference to evil" (cp. Heb 5:13), gen. of reference (W 127–8), (2) "ought not to be tested by evil persons" (Peter H. Davids, "The Meaning of Ἀπείραστος in James 1.13," *NTS* 24 [1977–78]: 386–92), or more likely (3) "cannot be tempted by evil" (NASB), κακῶν as gen. of means (W 125); ἀπείραστος as pass. verbal adj. with ἀ- privative (BDF §117(1); BDAG ἀπείραστος); adj. + gen. construction (BDF §182(3))

1:16 | συλλαβοῦσα = "when it has conceived" | ἀποτελεσθεῖσα = "when it is fully grown"

1:17 | ἐστίν could go with ἄνωθεν ("every perfect gift is from above, coming down") (M 17), or with καταβαῖνον ("every perfect gift from above is coming down") (periphrastic) (W 648 n86) | καταβαῖνον – neut. nom. present active ptc. | παρ' ᾧ οὐκ ἔνι = "with whom there is no" | τροπῆς ἀποσκίασμα = "darkening caused by turning" (BDAG τροπή), e.g., solstices or eclipses caused by turning of heavenly bodies

1:18 | βουληθείς = "according to his will" (BDAG βούλομαι), "in the exercise of his will" (NASB) | λόγῳ – dat. of means | τινα softens the metaphor – "so to say, a kind of" (BDF §301(1))

1:19 | ἴστε = "know [this]"

1:20 | δικαιοσύνη θεοῦ = "the righteousness that God approves or desires"

1:22–23 | λόγου (2x) – objective gen.

1:23 | τὸ πρόσωπον τῆς γενέσεως αὐτοῦ = lit. "the face of his birth," i.e., "his natural face" (BDAG γένεσις 2a)

1:24 | Two gnomic aorists (cp. v. 11), and one gnomic perf. (BDF §344; W 580–1) | ὁποῖος ἦν = lit. "what kind of person he was," i.e., "what he looks like" (NIV)

1:25 | ὁ παρακύψας ... καὶ παραμείνας = "the one who looks into ... and perseveres," two ptcs. governed by one article (W 275) | ἀκροατὴς [nom.] ἐπιλησμονῆς [gen.] = "a forgetful hearer," adjectival gen. | ποιητὴς ἔργου = "a doer who acts" (ESV; BDAG ἔργον 1a), "an effectual doer" (NASB)

1:26 | μὴ χαλιναγωγῶν = "yet does not bridle," concessive ptc. | τούτου μάταιος ἡ θρησκεία = "that person's religion is worthless" (ESV)

1:27 | ἄσπιλος ἀπό = "unstained from" (ESV) (BDF §182(3))

James 2

2:1 | ἐν προσωπολημψίαις = "while showing partiality" (BDAG προσωπολημψία), sociative use of ἐν (BDF §198(2); Z §116); abstract pl. (BDF §142) | ἡ πίστις τοῦ κυρίου ἡμῶν Ἰ. Χρ. = "the faith in our Lord Jesus Christ," objective gen. (W 116) | τοῦ κυρίου ἡμῶν ... τῆς δόξης = (1) "our Lord Jesus Christ, the Lord of glory" (ESV), or (2) "our glorious Lord Jesus Christ" (NASB), taking τῆς δόξης as attributive gen.

2:2–4 | Vv. 2–3 is the protasis (ἐάν + five subjunctives); v. 4 is the apodosis

2:3 | κάθου ὧδε καλῶς = "be seated here in a good place" (BDAG καλῶς)

2:4 | ἐν ἑαυτοῖς = "among yourselves" | κριταὶ διαλογισμῶν πονηρῶν – either (1) "judges who make evil decisions" (BDF §165), or (2) "judges with evil motives" (NASB) (see BDAG διαλογισμός 2)

2:5 | τοὺς πτωχοὺς τῷ κόσμῳ = "the poor with respect to the world," dat. of respect | Supply εἶναι to connect the object acc. with the predicate acc. (BDAG ἐκλέγομαι 2cγ) – "has not God chosen the poor ... [to be] rich?"

2:6 | καταδυναστεύω takes gen. (ὑμῶν) bec. of κατα- prefix (cp. v. 13)

2:7 | Passive of ἐπικαλέω used with ὄνομα to designate ark/temple/people as belonging to God (see LXX 2 Kgdms 6:2; 3 Kgdms 8:43; 2 Chron 7:14; Jer 7:30; 14:9; Amos 9:12) (BDAG ἐπικαλέω 2)

2:10 | γέγονεν – either proleptic or gnomic perf. (W 580–1)

2:12 | ὡς ... μέλλοντες κρίνεσθαι = "as [those] who will be judged"

2:13 | ποιέω ἔλεος = "show mercy" (Septuagintism) | κατακαυχάομαι takes gen. (κρίσεως) bec. of κατα- prefix (cp. v. 6)

2:14, 16 | τί τὸ ὄφελος; (2x) = "what good is it?"

2:14 | ἐὰν πίστιν λέγῃ τις ἔχειν = "if someone says he has faith," inf. in indirect discourse (W 604) | ἡ πίστις = "such faith," anaphoric definite article (W 219; M 111)

2:15 | λείπω takes gen. (see 1:5)

2:16 | τις ἐξ ὑμῶν = "one of you," partitive ἐκ | τὰ ἐπιτήδεια τοῦ σώματος = "the things necessary for the body"

2:17 | ἡ πίστις ... καθ' ἑαυτήν = "faith by itself" (ESV)

2:18 | The ally hypothesis: v. 18 is an argument that a person who is sympathetic with James' viewpoint might bring against the person who claims to have faith without works | κἀγώ (2x) = καὶ ἐγώ

2:21 | Ἀβραάμ ... οὐκ ἐξ ἔργων ἐδικαιώθη; = "Was not Abraham justified by works?" – note that οὐκ modifies the verb (cp. v. 25)

2:23 | λογίζομαι εἰς = "reckon/credit something as something" (BDAG εἰς 8aγ)

2:24 | οὐκ ἐκ πίστεως μόνον = "not by faith viewed in isolation" (BDAG μόνος 2cβ), adv. acc.

2:25 | ὑποδεξαμένη ... ἐκβαλοῦσα = "when she welcomed them ... and sent them off" (BDAG ἐκβάλλω 2) | ἄγγελος = "a human messenger serving as an envoy" (BDAG ἄγγελος 1)

2:26 | ὥσπερ ... οὕτως καί = "just as ... so also"

James 3
3:2 | πολλά = "in many ways," adv. acc. | δυνατός + inf. = "able to" | καὶ ὅλον τὸ σῶμα = "the whole body as well" (same phrase in v. 3)

3:3 | If the reading εἰ δέ is correct (some MSS have ἴδε), apodosis is καὶ ὅλον ... μετάγομεν – "If we put bits into the mouths of horses, we guide their whole body as well") | τῶν ἵππων modifies either (1) τοὺς χαλινούς, "horses' bridles," or (2) τὰ στόματα, "horses' mouths" | εἰς τὸ πείθεσθαι αὐτοὺς ἡμῖν = "to make them obey us" (NIV)

3:4 | ὄντα ... ἐλαυνόμενα = "although they are so large and are driven by strong winds," concessive ptcs. | ὅπου ἡ ὁρμὴ τοῦ εὐθύνοντος βούλεται = "wherever the impulse of the steersman leads him" (BDAG ὁρμή)

3:5 | ἡλίκος can mean both "how great" and "how small," play on words (BDAG ἡλίκος): "How *great* a forest is set ablaze by such a *small* fire!" (ESV)

3:6 | Supply ἐστίν | ὁ κόσμος is predicate | ἡ γλῶσσα καθίσταται

... ἡ σπιλοῦσα = "the tongue is set among our members as that which defiles" (NASB), anaphoric use of article | τὸν τροχὸν τῆς γενέσεως = lit. "the wheel (or cycle) of existence," i.e., "the whole course of life" (see BDAG τροχός; γένεσις 2b)

3:7 | δαμάζεται καὶ δεδάμασται = "can be tamed and has been tamed" (ESV; ZG), customary present (W 521) | τῇ φύσει τῇ ἀνθρωπίνῃ = "by humankind" (BDAG φύσις 4; ἀνθρώπινος b), dat. of agent (BDF §191; Z §59; W 165), extremely rare

3:8 | οὐδεὶς ἀνθρώπων = lit. "no one of humans" (partitive gen.), i.e., "no human being" | μεστός + gen. (cp. v. 17)

3:9 | ἐν αὐτῇ (2x) = "with it," Hebr./instrumental ἐν | καθ' ὁμοίωσιν θεοῦ = "in the likeness of God" | τοὺς γεγονότας = "who have been made"

3:10 | χρή + inf. = "it ought to," impersonal

3:12 | ποιέω (2x) = "produce"

3:13 | ἐν ὑμῖν = "among you"

3:14 | μὴ κατακαυχᾶσθε καὶ ψεύδεσθε κατὰ τῆς ἀληθείας = "do not be arrogant and [so] lie against the truth" (NASB), κατά + gen. = "against" (BDAG κατά A2bβ)

3:16 | ὅπου ... ἐκεῖ = "where ... there"

3:18 | καρπὸς δικαιοσύνης = "fruit (i.e., harvest) which consists of righteousness," gen. of apposition

James 4
4:1 | πόθεν; (2x) = "from what source [sc. do they come]?" | ἐν ὑμῖν = "among you" | ἐντεῦθεν = "from this, namely"

4:2 | διὰ τὸ μὴ αἰτεῖσθαι ὑμᾶς = "because you do not ask," acc. articular inf., with acc. ὑμᾶς as subject of inf. (W 611)

4:3 | δαπανάω ἐν + dat. = "spend on"

4:4 | ὃς ἐάν + subj. = "whoever"

4:5 | Textual problem (see Metzger) and translation options (as listed in BDAG ἐπιποθέω): (1) Reading an iota, κατῴκισεν (causitive): (a) "The spirit that God has caused to dwell in us yearns jealously," or (b) "God yearns jealously over the spirit that he has put in us." (2) Reading an ēta, κατῴκησεν (intrans.): "The spirit that has taken up abode in us yearns jealously" | πρὸς φθόνον = φθονερῶς = "jealously" (BDAG πρός 3f)

4:9 | εἰς with verbs of changing (2x) (BDAG εἰς 4b)

4:11 | καταλαλέω (3x) takes gen. bec. of κατα- prefix

4:12 | σὺ δὲ τίς εἶ ὁ κρίνων; = "but you, who are you who judges?" (= Rom 14:4), prolepsis (BDF §476), articular ptc. with personal pronoun (BDF §412(5))

4:13 | οἱ λέγοντες = "you who say" (BDF §412(5)) (cp. 5:1) | ποιήσομεν ἐκεῖ ἐνιαυτόν = "we will spend a year there," ποιέω + acc. of time (BDAG ποιέω 5c)

4:14 | οἵτινες = lit. "who" (οἱ λέγοντες), but translate "you" | οἵτινες οὐκ ... ἡ ζωὴ ὑμῶν – punctuation options and textual problem: (1) omitting τό: "Yet you do not know what your life will be like tomorrow" (NASB), (2) reading τό: "Yet you do not know what tomorrow will bring. What is your life?" (ESV; NIV), taking τὸ τῆς αὔριον as a substantivized adv. (BDF §266(3)) | πρὸς ὀλίγον = "for a little while"

4:15 | ἀντὶ τοῦ λέγειν ὑμᾶς = "instead, you ought to say" (NASB) | ἐάν ... καί = "if ... then," Hebr./LXX influence (BDAG καί 1bδ; BDF §442(7))

4:17 | εἰδότι ... αὐτῷ = "to the one who knows ... to him," καλόν
as anarthrous substantivized adj. (BDF §264(2)); αὐτῷ as Hebr. pleonastic personal pronoun (BDF §297)

James 5
5:1 | οἱ πλούσιοι = "you rich people" (see 4:13) | ἐπί + dat. after
verbs expressing emotion = "over" (BDAG ἐπί 6c) | ἐπὶ ταῖς
ταλαιπωρίαις ὑμῶν ταῖς ἐπερχομέναις = lit. "over your miseries
that are coming upon [sc. you]" (BDAG ἐπέρχομαι 2bα)

5:3 | εἰς μαρτύριον ὑμῖν ἔσται = "will be a witness against you"
(NASB), Semitic predicate εἰς with εἶναι (BDAG εἰς 8αβ; BDF
§145(1)); ὑμῖν as dat. of disadvantage (W 143–4)

5:4 | ἀφ᾽ ὑμῶν = "by you" (ἀπό = ὑπό) | αἱ βοαὶ τῶν θερισάντων
εἰς τὰ ὦτα κυρίου Σαβαὼθ εἰσεληλύθασιν = "the cries of the har-
vesters have reached the ears of the Lord of hosts" (ESV) (cp. εἰς τὰ
ὦτα – Matt 10:27; Lk 1:44; Acts 11:22)

5:7 | μακροθυμῶν ἐπ᾽ αὐτῷ = "being patient about it" (NASB, ESV)
| [sc. ὑετὸν] πρόϊμον καὶ ὄψιμον – "rain" (cp. v. 18) is to be under-
stood; is in fact included in many MSS

5:9 | πρὸ τῆς θύρας = "at the door," local use of πρό (BDAG πρό 1)

5:10 | λαμβάνω + double acc. = "take x as y" ("as an example of suf-
fering and patience, take the prophets")

5:11 | τὸ τέλος κυρίου = "the outcome of the Lord's dealings"
(NASB); "what the Lord finally brought about" (NIV) (BDAG
τέλος 3)

5:12 | πρὸ πάντων = "above all" (BDAG πρό 3) (cp. 1 Pet 4:8) |
ὀμνύω + acc. of person or thing by which one swears (BDF §149) |
τό – BDAG ὁ 2h

5:13–14 | ἐν ὑμῖν (2x) = "among you"

5:15 | κἂν ᾖ πεποιηκώς = "and if he has committed," perf. subj. periphrastic | ἀφεθήσεται αὐτῷ = "it will be forgiven him," impersonal

5:16 | πολὺ ἰσχύει δέησις δικαίου ἐνεργουμένη – options: (1) taking ἐνεργουμένη to modify δέησις as adjectival ptc.: "The effective prayer of a righteous person has great power" (ESV alt.), or (2) taking ἐνεργουμένη as adverbial ptc.: (a) "The prayer of a righteous person has great power as it is working" (ESV), (b) "The prayer of a righteous person is powerful and effective" (NIV 2011)

5:17 | προσευχῇ προσηύξατο = "he prayed earnestly," Hebr. cognate dat. (M 178; BDF §198(6)) | τοῦ μὴ βρέξαι = "so that it would not rain" (BDF §400(4)) | ἐνιαυτοὺς ... ἕξ – acc. for extent of time

5:19–20 | ἐπιστρέφω (2x) = "turn someone," here used transitively (BDAG ἐπιστρέφω 3)

Chapter Twenty-One

The First Epistle of Peter

1 Peter 1

1:1 | ἐκλεκτοῖς παρεπιδήμοις διασπορᾶς + gen. of place = "to the chosen sojourners of the dispersion in," διασπορᾶς could be taken as partitive gen. ("among the dispersion in") or attributive gen. ("scattered throughout")

1:2 | κατὰ πρόγνωσιν θεοῦ πατρός = "destined by God the Father" (NRSV; BDAG πρόγνωσις 2; cp. cognate verb, v. 20); modifies ἐκλεκτοῖς παρεπιδήμοις | ἐν ἁγιασμῷ πνεύματος = "by the Spirit's sanctification," Hebr./instrumental ἐν; subjective gen. | εἰς ... ῥαντισμὸν αἵματος = "to be sprinkled with the blood," gen. of means | πληθυνθείη – voluntative optative (BDF §384; W 483)

1:3 | ὁ θεός ... ὁ ... ἀναγεννήσας ἡμᾶς = "God, who has begotten us again," substantival aorist ptc. with article functioning as pronoun

1:4 | εἰς ὑμᾶς = "for you," equivalent to dat. of advantage (BDAG εἰς 4g)

1:5 | ἐν δυνάμει θεοῦ = "by the power of God," Hebr./instrumental ἐν | ἕτοιμος + pass. inf. = "ready to be" (BDF §393(4))

1:6 | ἐν ᾧ = "in which" (referring to the eschatological hope of v. 5) | ὀλίγον
ἄρτι εἰ δέον [ἐστὶν] λυπηθέντας = "though now for a little while, if
necessary, you have been grieved" (ESV); other MSS read λυπηθέντες

1:7 | τὸ δοκίμιον here = "genuineness" (BDAG δοκίμιον 2), contrast
usage in Jas 1:3 | ὑμῶν τῆς πίστεως = τῆς πίστεως ὑμῶν | χρυσίου
... δοκιμαζομένου – gens. of comparison: "more precious than gold
that perishes though it is tested by fire" (ESV), taking δοκιμαζομένου
as concessive ptc. | ἐν ἀποκαλύψει Ἰ. Χρ. = "at [the time of] the rev-
elation of Jesus Christ," temporal ἐν (BDAG ἐν 10b) (cp. v. 13; 4:13)

1:8 | πιστεύω εἰς (M 69) – "though you do not see [him] now,
yet as you believe in him [εἰς ὅν] you rejoice" | ἄρτι ("now")
probably modifies entire phrase μὴ ὁρῶντες πιστεύοντες δέ
("not-seeing-but-believing")

1:9 | σωτηρίαν is in apposition to τὸ τέλος

1:10 | οἱ περὶ τῆς εἰς ὑμᾶς χάριτος προφητεύσαντες = "who
prophesied of the grace meant for you" (BDAG εἰς 4d)

1:11 | τίνα ἢ ποῖον καιρόν – either (1) taking καιρόν with both
τίνα and ποῖον: "what [time] or what sort of time," i.e., "the time and
circumstances" (NIV), or more likely (2) taking καιρόν only with
ποῖον: "what person or time" (NASB, ESV) | δηλόω εἰς = "indicate,
refer to" (BDAG) | τὰ εἰς Χριστὸν παθήματα = "the sufferings
destined for Christ" (NRSV) (see discussion, BDAG εἰς 4cβ)

1:12 | οὐκ ἑαυτοῖς ὑμῖν δὲ διηκόνουν – either (1) "they were not
acting as agents in their own behalf but for yours" (BDAG διακονέω
1), or (2) "they were serving not themselves but you" | αὐτά, ἅ = "in
the things which," acc. of respect

1:13–14 | ἀναζωσάμενοι, νήφοντες, συσχηματιζόμενοι – im-
peratival ptcs.

1:13 | τελείως ἐλπίσατε ἐπί = "fix your hope completely on" (NASB) | φερομένην ὑμῖν = "being brought to you," ingressive-futuristic present ptc. (W 537) | ἐν ἀποκαλύψει – see v. 7

1:14 | ὡς τέκνα ὑπακοῆς = "as obedient children," adjectival gen. | αἱ πρότερον ἐπιθυμίαι = "your former passions" (BDF §62; BDAG πρότερος 1bβ) (cp. Heb 10:32) | ἐν τῇ ἀγνοίᾳ ὑμῶν – either "because of your ignorance" (BDAG ἐν 9) or "when you lived in ignorance" (NIV)

1:15 | κατὰ τὸν καλέσαντα ὑμᾶς ἅγιον = "in conformity with the Holy One who called you" (BDAG κατά B5aα), i.e., "just as he who called you is holy" | καὶ αὐτοί = "yourselves also"

1:17 | εἰ πατέρα ἐπικαλεῖσθε = "if you call on him as Father" (ESV) | ὁ κρίνων κατὰ τὸ ἑκάστου ἔργον = "the One who judges according to each person's work" | ἐν φόβῳ τὸν τῆς παροικίας ὑμῶν χρόνον ἀναστράφητε = "live out your time as foreigners here in reverent fear" (NIV 2011)

1:18 | φθαρτοῖς = "with perishable things," anarthrous substantived adj. (BDF §264), dat. of means

1:19 | ὡς ἀμνοῦ = "as of a lamb" | τιμίῳ αἵματι ὡς ἀμνοῦ ἀμώμου καὶ ἀσπίλου Χριστοῦ = τιμίῳ αἵματι Χριστοῦ ὡς ἀμνοῦ ἀμώμου καὶ ἀσπίλου = "with the precious blood of Christ, as of a lamb without blemish or spot" (BDAG ὡς 3aα)

1:20 | προεγνωσμένου μέν ... φανερωθέντος δέ = "chosen ... but then manifested" (BDAG προγινώσκω 2; cp. cognate noun, v. 2), μέν ... δέ marking a contrast between eternity and time, between "before the foundation of the world" and "in these last times"

1:21 | τοὺς δι' αὐτοῦ πιστοὺς εἰς θεόν = "who through him are believers in God" (ESV) | πίστος (or πίστις) εἰς = "believer (or faith) in"

1:22 | τὰς ψυχὰς ὑμῶν ἡγνικότες = "now that you have purified yourselves" (NIV) | ἐν τῇ ὑπακοῇ τῆς ἀληθείας = "by obeying the truth" (NIV), Hebr./instrumental ἐν; objective gen.

1:23 | ἀναγεγεννημένοι = "since you have been born again," causal ptc. | ζῶντος, μένοντος – present ptcs. of ζάω, μένω, gen. in agreement with λόγου – "through the living and enduring/abiding word of God"

1 Peter 2

2:1 | ἀποθέμενοι – imperatival ptc. (cp. 1:13–14)

2:2 | τὸ λογικὸν ἄδολον γάλα – either (1) "the pure milk of the word" (NASB; cp. KJV), or (2) "pure spiritual [as opposed to literal] milk" (ESV; BDAG λογικός) (cp. Rom 12:1) | ἐν αὐτῷ = "by it," Hebr./ instrumental ἐν | εἰς σωτηρίαν – either (1) "in respect to salvation" (NASB) (BDAG εἰς 5); or (2) "so as to receive salvation" (BDAG εἰς 4e)

2:4 | μέν ... δέ marks contrast between the estimate of Christ "by humans" and "in the sight of God" | ἐκλεκτὸν ἔντιμον = "chosen [and] precious" (cp. v. 6)

2:5 | καὶ αὐτοί = "and you yourselves" | οἰκοδομεῖσθε + nom. – either (1) "build yourselves up as" (mid. impv.) (BDAG οἰκοδομέω 2), or (2) "you yourselves are being built up as" (pass. indic.) | εἰς ἱεράτευμα = "so as to become a holy priesthood" (BDAG εἰς 4e) | ἀνενέγκαι – inf. of purpose

2:6 | περιέχει ἐν γραφῇ = "it is contained in Scripture"

2:7 | ὑμῖν οὖν ἡ τιμὴ τοῖς πιστεύουσιν – how translate τιμή? Options: (1) "This *precious value*, then, is for you who believe" (NASB); (2) "So the *honor* is for you who believe" (ESV; cp. BDAG τιμή 2b); (3) "Now to you who believe, this stone is *precious*" (NIV), nom. noun used adjectivally; other examples: χάρις (vv. 19–20); ζωή (Rom 8:10); θέλημα (1 Cor 16:12); δόξα (2 Cor 3:9 when taken together with the textual variant διακονία in nom.) | ἀπιστοῦσιν – anarthrous substantived dat. pl. ptc. (BDF §264(4)) | Predicate nom. replaced by Semitic εἰς with γίνομαι (BDAG εἰς 8aα)

2:8 | τῷ λόγῳ ἀπειθοῦντες = "because they are disobedient to the word" (NASB), causal ptc. | εἰς ὃ καὶ ἐτέθησαν = "to which [sc. stumbling] they were also consigned" (BDAG τίθημι 5aα), "which is also what they were destined for" (NIV)

2:9 | λαὸς εἰς περιποίησιν = "a people for [God's] own possession" (NASB)

2:10 | οἱ (2x) = "you," articular ptc. used with personal pronoun (BDF §412(5)); οἱ [sc. ὄντες] (v. 10a) is parallel to οἱ ἠλεημένοι (v. 10b)

2:11 | παρακαλῶ [sc. ὑμᾶς] ... ἀπέχεσθαι = "I exhort [sc. you] ... to abstain" (BDF §407) | ἀπέχω takes gen. of separation bec. of ἀπο- prefix | κατά + gen. = "against"

2:12 | τὴν ἀναστροφὴν ὑμῶν ... ἔχοντες καλήν = "keep your conduct honorable" (ESV), imperatival ptc. | ἐν τοῖς ἔθνεσιν = "among the Gentiles" | ἵνα ... ἐκ τῶν καλῶν ἔργων ἐποπτεύοντες δοξάσωσιν τὸν θεόν = "so that ... they may because of your good deeds, as they observe [them], glorify God" (NASB), the ἐκ clause is adverbial, modifying δοξάσωσιν (BDAG ἐκ 3e) | ἐν ᾧ could be translated "when" (ESV), "in the thing in which" (NASB), "whereas" (BDAG ἐν 7), "though" (NIV) (ἵνα ἐν ᾧ occurs again in 3:16) | καταλαλέω takes gen. (ὑμῶν) bec. of κατα- prefix | ἡμέρα ἐπισκοπῆς (cp. LXX Isa 10:3, but with articles)

2:12, 14 | κακοποιῶν (2x), ἀγαθοποιῶν – gen. pl. nouns (not ptcs. as in vv. 15, 20 and 3:17)

2:13 | πᾶσα ἀνθρωπίνη κτίσις = "every human authority system" (BDAG κτίσις 3) | ὡς ὑπερέχοντι = "as the supreme authority" (NIV)

2:13, 17 | [ὁ] βασιλεύς (2x) = "the emperor"

2:14 | ὡς δι' αὐτοῦ πεμπομένοις = "as sent by him," i.e. by the Lord

2:15 | οὕτως (mng. "this" [BDF §434(1)] and referring to what follows) + inf. (φιμοῦν) of obligation (BDF §407) = "for [ὅτι] this is the will of God, that by doing good you should put to silence ..." (ESV) | ἀγαθοποιοῦντας – ptc. of means

2:16 | καὶ μή = "and yet not" | ἐπικάλυμμα ἔχοντες τῆς κακίας τὴν ἐλευθερίαν = ἔχοντες τὴν ἐλευθερίαν ἐπικάλυμμα τῆς κακίας = "using your liberty as a cover for wickedness," article τήν as possessive pronoun

2:18 | οἱ οἰκέται – nom. for voc. (W 56–8) (cp. 3:1, 7) | ὑποτασσόμενοι – imperatival ptc. (cp. vv. 1, 12; 3:1) | ἐν παντὶ φόβῳ = "with all respect" (BDAG φόβος 2bβ) (cp. 3:2) | οὐ μόνον ... ἀλλὰ καί = "not only ... but also"

2:19–20 | χάρις (2x) = "that which brings someone favor" (BDAG χάρις 2b), here used adjectivally (cp. v. 7), "commendable" (NIV)

2:19 | εἰ ὑποφέρει τις = "if a person endures," εἰ with indic. of reality (BDF §372) | διὰ συνείδησιν θεοῦ = "because he is conscious of God" (NIV), objective gen.

2:20 | Parallel constructions with different usages of καί: εἰ ἁμαρτάνοντες καὶ κολαφιζόμενοι = "if you do wrong and receive a beating for it" (BDAG καί 1bζ); but εἰ ἀγαθοποιοῦντες καὶ πάσχοντες = "if you do good and suffer in spite of it" (BDAG καί 1bη)

2:21 | εἰς τοῦτο = "to this" (M 70), referring back to the patient endurance of unjust suffering (vv. 19–20) | ὅτι = "because" | ὑμῖν ὑπολιμπάνων ὑπογραμμόν = "leaving you an example," could be ptc. of result (W 637) or telic ptc. (W 635)

2:23 | παρεδίδου = "continued entrusting himself" (ESV), customary impf. (W 548)

2:24 | οὗ τῷ μώλωπι = "by whose welt," instrumental dat. (M 44); οὗ is a relative pronoun; its expected dat. case has been attracted to gen. in order to do double duty as personal pronoun (cp. LXX Isa 53:5 – τῷ μώλωπι αὐτοῦ ἰάθημεν) (BDF §§294, 297) | ταῖς ἁμαρτίαις = "to sins," dat. of advantage (M 46; BDF §188(2))

1 Peter 3

3:1 | αἱ γυναῖκες – see 2:18 | ὑποτασσόμενοι – see 2:18 | καὶ εἰ = "even if" | ἄνευ λόγου = "without a word" (cp. 4:9) (M 82)

3:2 | ἐποπτεύσαντες τὴν ἐν φόβῳ ἁγνὴν ἀναστροφὴν ὑμῶν = "when they see your respectful and pure conduct" (ESV), "your chaste and respectful behavior" (NASB), see 2:18 for same use of φόβος

3:3 | ὧν ἔστω οὐχ ὁ ἔξωθεν κόσμος + descriptive gen. (W 79) = "let not your external adornment be characterized by," ὧν looks back to ὑμῶν; note that ὁ belongs with κόσμος (nine intervening words!)

3:4 | ἀλλ᾽ ὁ κρυπτὸς ἄνθρωπος = "but [let your adornment be] the hidden person," brachylogy | ἐν τῷ ἀφθάρτῳ + gen. = "consisting of the imperishable quality of a gentle and quiet spirit," substantivized adj. (BDF §263); on ἐν, see M 79

3:5 | οὕτως could be retrospective (looking back to v. 4, interpreting "adorn" literally) or prospective (interpreting "adorn" as a metaphor for ὑποτασσόμεναι) | ἐκόσμουν ἑαυτάς = "used to adorn themselves," customary impf. (W 548) | ὑποτασσόμεναι – either (1) "being in submission to," with retrospective οὕτως, or (2) "by submitting to" (ESV), ptc. of means; with prospective οὕτως

3:6 | καλέω + double acc. = "call x y" | ἀγαθοποιοῦσαι καὶ μὴ φοβούμεναι = "if you do good and do not fear," conditional ptcs.

3:7 | οἱ ἄνδρες – see v. 1; 2:18 | κατὰ γνῶσιν = "in an understanding way" (NASB, ESV) | ἀπονέμοντες τιμήν = "showing [sc. her] honor" | εἰς τὸ μή + inf. = "so that ... will not"

3:7–9 | συνοικοῦντες, ἀπονέμοντες, ἀποδιδόντες, εὐλογοῦντες – imperatival ptcs. (as well as the implied ὄντες in v. 8) (BDF §468(2))

3:8 | τὸ δὲ τέλος = "finally," adv. acc. (M 34)

3:9 | τοὐναντίον = τὸ ἐναντίον = "but on the contrary" (ESV), adv. acc. | εἰς τοῦτο is forward looking and picked up by ἵνα functioning as explanatory inf. (BDAG ἵνα 2e)

3:9, 12 | ὅτι (2x) = "for"

3:10 | τοῦ μὴ λαλῆσαι = "from speaking"

3:12 | ἐπί + acc. occurs 2x, first favorably ("toward"), then inimically ("against") (M 49; BDAG ἐπί 12, 15) (LXX Ps 34:15–16) | Supply the copula 3x

3:13 | τίς ὁ κακώσων ὑμᾶς = "who is there to harm you?" individual-indefinite article (BDF §252); on future ptc., see BDF §351 | ἀγαθοῦ ζηλωταί = "eager to do good" (NIV), objective gen. (cp. Tit 2:14)

3:14 | εἰ καὶ πάσχοιτε = "even if you should suffer," conditional optative in fourth class conditional (W 484, 699–700; BDF §385; Z §323) (cp. v. 17) | τὸν φόβον αὐτῶν μὴ φοβηθῆτε (prohibitive sub.; W 469) – options: (1) "Do not fear what they fear" (NIV 1984), taking αὐτῶν as subjective gen. (supported by LXX Isa 8:12 in context), (2) "Do not be afraid with fear of them" (M 32, 40), taking αὐτῶν as objective gen., (3) "Do not be intimidated by their intimidation" (BDAG φόβος 1a), or "their threats" (NIV 2011)

3:15 | κύριον ... ἁγιάσατε (cp. LXX Isa 8:13) | ἕτοιμος πρός + acc.

= "ready to" (BDAG ἕτοιμος b; πρός 3cβ) (cp. Tit 3:1) | λόγος = "account" (BDAG λόγος 2a)

3:16 | ἵνα ἐν ᾧ – see 2:12 | ὑμῶν τὴν ἀναστροφήν = τὴν ἀναστροφήν ὑμῶν

3:17 | κρεῖττον ἀγαθοποιοῦντας ... πάσχειν ἢ κακοποιοῦντας = "it is better to suffer for doing good ... than for doing evil" (ESV) (BDAG ἤ 2) | εἰ θέλοι τὸ θέλημα τοῦ θεοῦ = "if the will of God should so will it," conditional optative in fourth class conditional (cp. v. 14)

3:19 | ἐν ᾧ – options: (1) "in which" (taking antecedent as πνεύματι), (2) "for which reason" (causal), or (3) "on which occasion" (temporal) (see discussions in W 343 and M 131)

3:20 | κατασκευαζομένης κιβωτοῦ = "while the ark was being built" (NIV), gen. abs. | εἰς ἥν = "in which," εἰς = ἐν (BDF §205; M 68); antecedent of ἥν is κιβωτός (fem.) | διεσώθησαν δι᾽ ὕδατος – either (1) "were brought safely through water" (ESV; M 56; BDAG διά A1b), or (2) "were saved via water" (BDAG ἀντίτυπος 1; διά A3a)

3:21 | Antecedent of ὅ is ὕδωρ | ὅ ... ἀντίτυπον ... βάπτισμα = "which [water], in its corresponding symbolic form – namely, baptism – now saves you also" | συνειδήσεως ἀγαθῆς ἐπερώτημα εἰς θεόν – either (1) "an *appeal* to God for a good conscience," objective gen., or (2) "a *pledge* to God proceeding from a good conscience," gen. of source (see BDAG ἐπερώτημα)

1 Peter 4

4:1 | Χριστοῦ παθόντος – causal gen. abs. | ὁπλίζομαι (mid.) + acc. = "arm oneself with" | παύομαι (mid.) + gen. = "cease from, be done with," gen. of separation

4:2 | εἰς τὸ μηκέτι βιῶσαι = "so as to no longer live" | τὸν ἐπίλοιπον χρόνον = "the remaining time"

4:3 | ἀρκετός + inf. = "[is] sufficient to," ὁ χρόνος is subject; ἀρκετός is predicate | τὸ βούλημα τῶν ἐθνῶν = "what pagans choose to do" (NIV), "what the Gentiles want to do" (ESV), subjective gen. | πεπορευμένους = "having pursued a course of" (NASB), the ptc. is acc. in agreement with implied acc. ὑμᾶς as subject of inf. κατειργάσθαι

4:4 | ἐν ᾧ ξενίζονται μὴ συντρεχόντων ὑμῶν = "and so they are surprised when you do not run with them" (M 132), gen. abs. | βλασφημοῦντες – could be directed to the believers ("hurling insults") or to God ("blaspheming"), ptc. of manner (W 627)

4:5 | ὁ ἑτοίμως ἔχων + inf. = "the One who is ready to" (BDAG ἔχω 10b) (cp. Acts 21:13; 2 Cor 12:14)

4:6 | κατὰ ἀνθρώπους ... κατὰ θεόν – (1) "the way people are ... the way God does" (ESV), (2) "as men ... according to the will of God" (NASB), (3) "according to human standards ... according to God" (NIV 2011)

4:7 | εἰς προσευχάς = "so that you may pray" (NIV 2011) (BDAG εἰς 4f)

4:8–9 | ἔχοντες, ὄντες (to be supplied in v. 9 as in 3:8) – imperatival ptcs.

4:8 | πρὸ πάντων = "above all" (BDAG πρό 3) (cp. Jas 5:12) | τὴν ἀγάπην ἐκτενῆ ἔχοντες = "keeping your affection constant" (BDAG ἐκτενής)

4:9 | ἄνευ γογγυσμοῦ = "without grumbling" (cp. 3:1) (M 82)

4:10 | εἰς ἑαυτοὺς αὐτὸ διακονοῦντας = "serving one another with it" (BDAG διακονέω 2a), "use it to serve to one another" (ESV), εἰς for dat. (M 204 note on p. 69; BDAG εἰς 4g)

4:11 | Supply impv. (2x): "whoever speaks/serves, [is to do so] as ..." (NASB)

4:12 | γινομένη goes with τῇ πυρώσει | πρὸς πειρασμόν = "for your testing" (BDAG πρός 3cβ) | ὡς ξένου ὑμῖν συμβαίνοντος = "as though some strange thing were happening to you," gen. abs.

4:13 | ἐν τῇ ἀποκαλύψει τῆς δόξης αὐτοῦ = "when his glory is revealed," objective gen.; on ἐν, see 1:7 | ἵνα ... χαρῆτε ἀγαλλιώμενοι = "that ye may be glad ... with exceeding joy" (KJV), ptc. of manner (W 627)

4:14 | ἐν = "for, because of" (BDAG ἐν 9; ὄνομα 3) | καὶ τὸ τοῦ θεοῦ = "even the Spirit of God," on repetition of article τό, see BDF §§269(6); 442(16) (cp. LXX Isa 11:2)

4:15 | τις ὑμῶν = "any of you," with negative means "none of you" | ἀλλοτριεπίσκοπος – see various proposals in BDAG; also, "The writer seems to refer to those who, with holy but intemperate zeal, meddle with the affairs of the Gentiles – whether public or private, civil or sacred – in order to make them conform to the Christian standard" (Thayer)

4:16 | εἰ δὲ ὡς Χριστιανός = "but if [sc. anyone suffers] as a Christian" | δοξαζέτω δὲ τὸν θεὸν ἐν τῷ ὀνόματι τούτῳ (NA27) = "but let him glorify God in that name," i.e., let him suffer under the name "Christian." The Pliny/Trajan correspondence (ca. 112) indicates that Christians could be punished for *nomen Christianum*, that is, simply for being Christians apart from any other crimes. To "glorify God" may be a euphemism for martyrdom (cp. John 21:19). NA28 now follows variant μέρει instead of ὀνόματι ("let him glorify God in that matter or regard") (BDAG μέρος 1bθ or 1c)

4:17 | ὁ καιρὸς τοῦ ἄρξασθαι τὸ κρίμα = "it is time for judgment to begin" | ἄρχομαι + ἀπό (2x) indicating starting point = "begin with" (BDAG ἄρχω 2c; ἀπό 2c; cp. Luke 24:27)

4:18 | ποῦ φανεῖται; = "what will become of?" (BDAG φαίνω 2a)

4:19 | ὥστε = "therefore"

1 Peter 5
5:1 | πρεσβυτέρους τοὺς ἐν ὑμῖν παρακαλῶ = παρακαλῶ [τοὺς] πρεσβυτέρους τοὺς ἐν ὑμῖν = "I exhort the elders that are among you" | ὁ (2x) = "I who am," article functions as relative pronoun modifying implied ἐγώ | ὁ … κοινωνός | τῆς μελλούσης ἀποκαλύπτεσθαι δόξης = "of the glory that is about to be revealed," this is the normal word order in contrast with Rom 8:18 | The second καί signifies that Peter is not only a witness of the sufferings but "also" a partaker of the glory

5:2 | κατὰ θεόν = "according to the will of God" (NASB)

5:3 | κατακυριεύω take gen. bec. of κατα- prefix | τύποι τοῦ ποιμνίου = "examples to the flock," objective gen.

5:4 | φανερωθέντος τοῦ ἀρχιποίμενος = "when the chief Shepherd appears," gen. abs. | τὸν ἀμαράντινον τῆς δόξης στέφανον = τὸν ἀμαράντινον στέφανον τῆς δόξης

5:5 | "The ἐγκόμβωμα was the white scarf or apron of slaves, which was fastened to the girdle of the vest, and distinguished slaves from freemen; hence … gird yourselves with humility as your servile garb, i.e. by putting on humility show your subjection to one another" (Thayer ἐγκομβόομαι) | ὑπερηφάνοις, ταπεινοῖς = "the proud," "the humble," anarthrous substantived adjectives (BDF §264)

5:5, 7 | ὅτι (2x) = "for"

5:6 | Subject of ὑψώσῃ is God

5:7 | ἐπιρίψαντες – either (1) ptc. of means dependent on the ταπεινώθητε of v. 6 ("humble yourselves ... by casting all your anxiety on him"), or (2) independent imperatival ptc. ("Cast all your anxiety on him") (see W 340, 630) | αὐτῷ μέλει περὶ ὑμῶν = lit. "it is of concern to him concerning you," impersonal construction

5:9 | τὰ αὐτὰ τῶν παθημάτων = "the same [kinds] of sufferings" | τῇ ἐν κόσμῳ ὑμῶν ἀδελφότητι – should mean "the brotherhood in your world" (displaced pronoun; M 168); intended mng. is "your brotherhood in/throughout the (whole) world" (BDAG κόσμος 5a) | Acc. as subject of inf. + ἐπιτελεῖσθαι + dat. – either (1) "the same kinds of sufferings are being perpetrated upon your brotherhood" (ZG), or (2) "the same kinds of sufferings are being fulfilled/accomplished in the case of your brotherhood" (BDAG ἐπιτελέω 3)

5:10 | ὀλίγον παθόντας = "after you have suffered for a little while," ὀλίγον – acc. for extent of time; aorist ptc. is acc. in agreement with ὑμᾶς | αὐτός = "[God] himself" | Sc. ὑμᾶς as object of the future verbs (καταρτίσει, στηρίξει, σθενώσει, θεμελιώσει)

12 | Διὰ Σιλουανοῦ ὑμῖν goes with ἔγραψα = "I have written to you through Silvanus" as the carrier of the letter who will also provide additional explanation in person; hence his identification as a "faithful brother" | ὡς λογίζομαι = "for so I regard him" (NASB) | δι' ὀλίγων = "briefly" | εἰς = ἐν (BDF §205) (cp. 3:20)

5:14 | ἐν φιλήματι ἀγάπης = "with the kiss of love," Hebr./instrumental ἐν

Chapter Twenty-Two

The Second Epistle of Peter

2 Peter 1

1:1 | λαγχάνω = "obtain something as a portion, *receive, obtain* (by lot, or by divine will)" (BDAG λαγχάνω) | ἰσότιμον ἡμῖν πίστιν = "a faith of the same kind/value as ours" (BDAG ἰσότιμος, adding that "the recipients are not less advantaged than the apostles"), "a faith of equal standing with ours" (ESV) | ἐν δικαιοσύνῃ τοῦ θεοῦ ἡμῶν καὶ σωτῆρος Ἰ. Χρ. = "by the righteousness of our God and Savior Jesus Christ," Hebr./ insrumental ἐν; the (contested) Granville Sharp Rule may apply here, possibly identifying Chirst as θεός (see W 270–77, 290) (cp. Titus 2:13)

1:20 | πληθυνθείη – voluntative optative (W 481–3; BDF §384)

1:3 | ὡς + gen. abs. = "since his divine power has bestowed (δεδωρημένης)" (BDAG ὡς 3aβ) | πάντα τὰ πρός + acc. = "everything necessary for" (BDAG πρός 3eβ) | ἰδίᾳ δόξῃ καὶ ἀρετῇ – either (1) "to his own glory and excellence" (ESV), dat. of destination (W 147), or (2) "by his own glory and excellence" (NASB), dat. of means (W 162)

1:4 | θείας κοινωνοὶ φύσεως = κοινωνοὶ φύσεως θείας

1:5 | καὶ αὐτὸ τοῦτο = "for this very reason also," adv. acc. (BDF §290(4)), resuming ὡς (v. 3)

1:8 | ὑπάρχοντα, πλεονάζοντα – conditional ptcs. (cp. ποιοῦντες, v. 10) | καθίστησιν = "they render [sc. you]," neut. pl. subjects take sg. verbs; supply ὑμᾶς | εἰς = "with reference to" (BDAG εἰς 5)

1:9 | ᾧ μὴ πάρεστιν ταῦτα = "whoever lacks these qualities" (ESV), dat. of possession | λαμβάνω λήθην = "forget"

1:10 | οὐ μή + aorist subj. (BDF §365) | ποιεῖσθαι + double acc. = "to make x y" (BDAG ποιέω 7b)

1:11 | ἐπιχορηγέω = "grant," different mng. than in v. 5 (see BDAG)

1:12 | μελλήσω + inf. = "I intend to" (ESV; BDAG μέλλω 1cγ)

1:13 | δίκαιον ἡγοῦμαι + inf. = "I think it right to" | ἐφ' ὅσον = "as long as" (BDAG ἐπί 18cβ) | διεγείρειν ὑμᾶς ἐν ὑπομνήσει = "to stir you up by way of reminder" (NASB, ESV), "to refresh your memory" (NIV) (cp. 3:1)

1:15 | "And I will make every effort so that after my departure you may be able at any time to recall these things" (ESV); ἔχω + inf. = "be able to" (BDAG ἔχω 5); μνήμην ποιεῖσθαι = "to recall to mind," ποιέω (mid.) + noun as periphrasis of simple verbal idea (BDAG μνήμη 1; ποιέω 7a)

1:16 | Does παρουσία refer to Christ's first or second coming, or both?

1:17–18 | φέρω (2x) = "utter" a word/sound, etc. (BDAG φέρω 7) (also in v. 21a and 2:11) (aorist of φέρω is ἠνέχθη[ν])

1:17 | φωνῆς ἐνεχθείσης αὐτῷ τοιᾶσδε = "when such a voice/ sound as this was uttered to him," gen. abs. | εἰς ὃν ἐγὼ εὐδόκησα (cp. Matt 12:18; 17:5) = "with whom I am well pleased," see note at Matt 3:17 for other options

1:18 | σὺν αὐτῷ ὄντες = "when we were with him"

1:19 | καὶ ἔχομεν βεβαιότερον τὸν προφητικὸν λόγον – options: (1) "so we have the prophetic word made more sure" (NASB), (2) "we also have the prophetic message as something completely reliable" (NIV 2011), taking βεβαιότερον as a heightened positive (BDF §244(2)), (3) "and we have something more sure, the prophetic word" (ESV) | ἕως οὗ + subj. = "until"

1:20 | πᾶσα προφητεία γραφῆς ἰδίας ἐπιλύσεως οὐ γίνεται – either (1) "no prophecy of Scripture is a matter of one's own private interpretation" (BDAG ἴδιος 6; γίνομαι 9d), or (2) "no prophecy of Scripture came about from the prophet's own interpretation of things" (NIV 2011 mod.), taking ἰδίας ἐπιλύσεως as gen. of source (W 109); also note the Hebr. πᾶς ... οὐ construction (BDF §302(1))

1:21 | ἐλάλησαν ἀπὸ θεοῦ ἄνθρωποι = "men spoke what was derived from God" (M 73)

2 Peter 2

2:1 | αἱρέσεις ἀπωλείας = "destructive heresies," adjectival gen. | τὸν ἀγοράσαντα αὐτοὺς δεσπότην ἀρνούμενοι = "denying the Master who bought them"

2:2 | αὐτῶν ταῖς ἀσελγείαις = ταῖς ἀσελγείαις αὐτῶν | δι' οὕς = "because of whom"

2:3 | ἐν πλεονεξίᾳ πλαστοῖς λόγοις ὑμᾶς ἐμπορεύσονται = "in [their] greed they will exploit you with false words" (NASB, ESV) | οἷς = "whose," dat. of possession

2:4–10a | One sentence, with vv. 4–7 as the protasis, v. 8 as a parenthesis expanding on v. 7, and vv. 9–10a as the apodosis

2:4–5 | φείδω (2x) takes gen.

2:4 | σειραῖς ζόφου ταρταρώσας παρέδωκεν εἰς κρίσιν

τηρουμένους – presents a tangle of syntactical questions: (1)
Textual issue (see Metzger; BDF §23): σιροῖς (= "to/in pits")
vs. σειραῖς (= "with/to chains") (cp. δεσμοῖς, Jd 6). (2) Does
σιροῖς/σειραῖς modify ταρταρώσας ("to pits" or "with chains"),
παρέδωκεν ("to pits" or "to chains"), or τηρουμένους ("in pits"
or "with chains")? (3) Does εἰς κρίσιν complete παρέδωκεν
("handed them over to judgment") or τηρουμένους ("kept them
for/until judgment") or both? (4) εἰς κρίσιν – either "until [the
day of] judgment" (BDAG εἰς 2aα) (cp. v. 9; 3:7), or "for judgment" (BDAG εἰς 4f).

2:5 | ὄγδοον Νῶε = lit. "Noah as the eighth," i.e., "Noah with seven
others" (BDF §248(5); BDAG ὄγδοος) | δικαιοσύνης κήρυξ =
"a preacher/herald of righteousness," objective gen. | κατακλυσμὸν
κόσμῳ ἀσεβῶν ἐπάξας = "when he [= God] brought a flood upon
the world of the ungodly" (NASB)

2:6 | καταστροφῇ κατέκρινεν = "he condemned [them] to ex-
tinction/destruction" (BDF §195(2)) | ὑπόδειγμα μελλόντων
ἀσεβέ[σ]ιν τεθεικώς (NA27; BDAG τίθημι 1bθ) – textual problem
(see Metzger): (1) ἀσεβέσιν (dat. pl.): "making [them] an example of
the things about to come upon the ungodly," or (2) ἀσεβεῖν (present
inf. of ἀσεβέω) (NA28): "making [them] an example of those who
were to be ungodly in the future"

2:7 | τῆς τῶν ἀθέσμων ἐν ἀσελγείᾳ ἀναστροφῆς = "the sensual
conduct of lawless men" (ἀσελγεία = "sensuality, licentiousness")

2:8 | Lit. "For by what he saw and by what he heard, that righteous man,
by living among them day after day, was tormenting his righteous soul
with their lawless deeds"

2:9 | οἶδεν + inf. = "he knows [how] to" | κολαζομένους τηρεῖν =
"to keep under punishment" (NASB, ESV) | εἰς ἡμέραν κρίσεως =
"until the day of judgment" (BDAG εἰς 2aα) (cp. v. 4)

2:10 | μάλιστα δὲ τούς + two ptcs. = "especially those who ... and who" | τοὺς ὀπίσω σαρκὸς ἐν ἐπιθυμίᾳ μιασμοῦ πορευομένους = "those who go after the flesh in defiling passion," taking μιασμοῦ as adjectival gen. | καταφρονέω takes gen. bec. of κατα- prefix | δόξαι = "majestic beings" (BDAG δόξα 4), "the glorious ones" (ESV), i.e., angels (cp. Jd 8) | τρέμω + supplementary ptc. = "be afraid to" (BDF §415)

2:11 | ὅπου = "whereas" | ἰσχύϊ καὶ δυνάμει μείζονες ὄντες = "though greater in might and power," concessive ptc. | κατά + gen. = "against" | παρὰ κυρίῳ = "before the Lord"

2:12 | ὡς ἄλογα ζῷα = "like animals incapable of reason" | γεγεννημένα φυσικά εἰς ἅλωσιν καὶ φθοράν = "born as creatures of instinct to be captured and killed" (NASB) | ἐν οἷς ἀγνοοῦσιν βλασφημοῦντες = "blaspheming in matters of which they are ignorant" (BDF §152(1)) | ἐν τῇ φθορᾷ αὐτῶν καὶ φθαρήσονται = "will in the destruction of those creatures *also* be destroyed" (NASB), αὐτῶν refers back to ἄλογα ζῷα

2:13 | ἀδικούμενοι μισθὸν ἀδικίας – unusual construction; most likely: "suffering wrong as the wage for their wrongdoing" (ESV); for other options see BDAG ἀδικέω and commentaries. Some scribes sought to improve the syntax by changing ἀδικούμενοι to κομιούμενοι (future ptc. of κομίζω; Z §282) (see Metzger) | ἡδονὴν ἡγούμενοι τὴν ἐν ἡμέρᾳ τρυφήν = "they count it pleasure to revel in the daytime" (ESV), ἡγέομαι + double acc. (cp. 3:15) | Instead of ἐν ταῖς ἀπάταις αὐτῶν (= "in their deceptions" [ESV], or "in their lusts" [BDAG ἀπάτη 2]), some MSS read ἐν ταῖς ἀγάπαις αὐτῶν (= "in their love feasts"), but this is probably a scribal assimilation to Jd 12 (Metzger) | συνευωχούμενοι ὑμῖν = "while they feast with you" (cp. Jd 12)

2:14 | ὀφθαλμοὺς μεστοὺς μοιχαλίδος = lit. "eyes full of an adulteress," i.e., always looking for a woman with whom to commit adultery (BDAG μοιχαλίς a; μεστός 2b) | ἀκαταπαύστους ἁμαρτίας = "not ceasing with sin," adj. + gen. of separation (BDF §182(3); M 41) |

καρδίαν γεγυμνασμένην πλεονεξίας = "a heart trained in greed" (NASB), Moule calls this gen. "very curious and hard to define" (M 41 n2) | κατάρας τέκνα = lit. "children of a curse," Semitic "son of" construction (Z §43)

2:16 | ἔλεγξιν ἔσχεν ἰδίας παρανομίας = "he [Balaam] received a rebuke for his own transgression" (NASB) | ὑποζύγιον ἄφωνον = "a donkey incapable of speech," neut. nom.; subject of ἐκώλυσεν | ἐν ἀνθρώπου φωνῇ φθεγξάμενον = "having spoken with a human voice"

2:17 | ὑπὸ λαίλαπος ἐλαυνόμεναι = ἐλαυνόμεναι ὑπὸ λαίλαπος = "driven by a storm"

2:18 | ὑπέρογκα ματαιότητος φθεγγόμενοι = "by spewing empty, bombastic rhetoric" | ἐν ἐπιθυμίαις σαρκὸς ἀσελγείαις = "by fleshly desires, by sensuality" (NASB) | τοὺς ὄντως ... ἀναστρεφομένους = "those who are really escaping from those who live in error," note textual issue: ὄντως ("really," NA28) vs. ὀλίγως ("barely," NA27)

2:19 | ᾧ γάρ τις ἥττηται, τούτῳ δεδούλωται = "for by what a man is overcome, by this he is enslaved" (NASB), gnomic perf. (W 580)

2:20 | τούτοις = "by/in these," referring back to τὰ μιάσματα τοῦ κόσμου | πάλιν ἐμπλακέντες ἡττῶνται = "are again entangled and overcome," attendant circumstances ptc. | τὰ ἔσχατα = "the last state" | χείρονα τῶν πρώτων = "worse than the first state," gen. of comparison

2:21 | κρεῖττον ἦν αὐτοῖς + inf. = "it would have been better for them not to have known," impf. w/o ἄν in "would/should/could have" expressions (BDF §358(1)) | ἤ = "than" | ἐπιγνοῦσιν – aorist ptc., dat. pl. in agreement with αὐτοῖς

2:22 | τὸ τῆς ἀληθοῦς παροιμίας = "what the true proverb says"

(BDAG ὁ 2g) | ὗς λουσαμένη εἰς κυλισμὸν βορβόρου = "A sow that has bathed herself, only to roll in the mud again" (BDAG ὗς; εἰς 4f)

2 Peter 3

3:1 | ταύτην ... δευτέραν ἐπιστολήν = "this is the second epistle" | ἐν αἷς – pl. bec. both first and second epistle are in view, *constructio ad sensum* (BDF §296) | ὑμῶν displaced; goes with τὴν εἰλικρινῆ διάνοιαν (M 168; ZG) | διεγείρω ἐν ὑπομνήσει – see 1:13

3:2 | μιμνήσκομαι takes gen. of thing remembered (ῥημάτων and ἐντολῆς) | τῆς τῶν ἀποστόλων ... καὶ σωτῆρος = "the command given by our Lord and Savior through your apostles" (NIV), subjective gen. and gen. of agency

3:3 | ἐλεύσονται ... ἐν ἐμπαιγμονῇ ἐμπαῖκται = "scoffers will come with scoffing," possible Semitism (M 178) | ἐπ' ἐσχάτων τῶν ἡμερῶν = "in the last days" (BDAG ἐπί 18a); Hebr. phrase (BDF §264(5); see Heb 1:2; Jude 18)

3:4 | ἀφ' ἧς = "ever since"

3:5 | λανθάνει αὐτοὺς τοῦτο θέλοντας ὅτι = "in maintaining this it escapes their notice that" (BDAG θέλω 4) | ἦσαν ἔκπαλαι = "existed long ago" | On "out of water and through water," see M 55 | συνεστῶσα – we are probably to assume repetition of ἦσαν to form plupf. periphrastic

3:5, 7 | τῷ λόγῳ (2x) = "by the word," instrumental dat. (W 162)

3:6 | Textual problem: either (1) δι' ὅν (NA28) = "because of which [sc. word of God]," or (2) δι' ὧν (NA27) = "through which [sc. waters]" (in either case, the prepositional phrase modifies ἀπώλετο, expressing either the reason bec. of which or the means by which "the world" perished) | ὁ τότε κόσμος = "the world that then was" (KJV), with a focus on the world of humanity (cp. v. 7; 2:5) | ὕδατι κατακλυσθείς

= "being flooded with water" (NASB), ὕδατι may seem redundant in light of δι' ὧν, but it modifies κατακλυσθείς as dat. of content (W 170), expressing that which the world was flooded with

3:7 | τεθησαυρισμένοι εἰσὶν πυρί = "are stored up for fire," perf. periphrastic | τηρούμενοι εἰς ἡμέραν κρίσεως = "being kept until the day of judgment and [the day] of the destruction of the ungodly people" (see 2:4, 9)

3:8 | ἓν τοῦτο μὴ λανθανέτω ὑμᾶς = "do not let this one fact escape your notice" (NASB)

3:9 | βραδύνω + gen. = "hold back from doing something" (BDF §180(4)); thus οὐ βραδύνει ὁ κύριος τῆς ἐπαγγελίας = "the Lord is not slow to fulfill his promise" (ESV)

3:10 | ῥοιζηδόν = "with a roar," adv. acc. | λυθήσεται (also vv. 11–12) = "will be broken up into its component parts" (BDAG λύω 3; cp. Acts 27:41), "dissolved" (ESV), "destroyed" (NASB) | οὐχ εὑρεθήσεται – textual issue: NA28 has the negative οὐχ, which makes obvious sense: "the earth and the works that are in it will *not* be found" (cp. Rev 16:20; 18:14, 21, 22); however, NA27 has the more difficult reading, εὑρεθήσεται w/o the negative: lit. "will be found." If this latter reading is correct, it could be understood as an idiom pertaining to eschatological judgment, mng. "laid bare" (NIV) or "exposed" (ESV) (cp. v. 14; Matt 24:46; Mk 13:36; Lk 18:8; 1 Cor 4:2; 2 Cor 5:3; Phil 3:9; 2 Tim 1:18; 1 Pet 1:7; Rev 14:5; 18:24; 20:11, 15); see Metzger

3:11 | τούτων οὕτως πάντων λυομένων = "since all these things are to be destroyed in this way," causal gen. abs.; present with future sense

3:12 | δι' ἥν = "because of which," referring back to ἡμέρας

3:14 | αὐτῷ = "in his eyes," "before him," ethical dat. (BDF §§190(3); 192)

3:15 | ἡγέομαι + double acc. = "consider x to be y" (cp. 2:13)

3:16 | ἐν αἷς ἐστιν δυσνόητά τινα = "in which [Paul's epistles] are some things hard to understand," neut. pl. subjects take sg. verbs

3:17 | προγινώσκοντες = "knowing [sc. this] beforehand" | φυλάσσεσθε = "be on your guard" (NASB) | τῇ τῶν ἀθέσμων πλήνῃ = "with/by the error of the lawless," dat. bec. of συν- prefix of συναπάγω

3:18 | καὶ νῦν καὶ εἰς ἡμέραν αἰῶνος = "both now and to the day of eternity" (NASB, ESV) (BDAG καί 1f)

Chapter Twenty-Three

The First Epistle of John

1 John 1

1:1 | ὃ ἦν ἀπ' ἀρχῆς = "that which was from the beginning" (ἀπ' ἀρχῆς occurs 10x in the Johannine epistles: 1 John 1:1; 2:7, 13, 14, 24 [2x]; 3:8, 11; 2 John 5, 6) | τοῖς ὀφθαλμοῖς ἡμῶν = "with our eyes," instrumental dat. | ψηλαφάω – possible allusion to touching the risen Lord (Lk 24:39)

1:2 | φανερόω occurs 9x in 1 John (1:2 [2x]; 2:19, 28; 3:2 [2x], 5, 8; 4:9)

1:3 | καὶ ὑμῖν ... καὶ ὑμεῖς = "to you too ... you too" | μεθ' ἡμῶν = μετὰ ἡμῶν

1:4 | ᾖ πεπληρωμένη – subj. perf. periphrastic (W 649)

1:5 | σκοτία ἐν αὐτῷ οὐκ ἔστιν οὐδεμία = "in him there is no darkness at all," double negatives reinforce

1:7 | μετ' ἀλλήλων = "with one another" – either (1) among believers or (2) between believers and the Father/Son

1:9 | Attenuated ἵνα after adj. or ἵνα of result (BDAG ἵνα 2c; 3) | ἡμῖν – dat. of indirect object (cp. 2:12)

1 John 2

2:1 | καί = "but" (BDAG καί 1bη) (cp. v. 9)

2:2 | οὐ μόνον ... ἀλλὰ καί = "not only ... but also"

2:3 | ἐν τούτῳ = "by this," forward looking

2:3–4 | ἐγνώκα(μεν) αὐτόν (2x) = "I/we have come to know him"

2:4 | ὅτι recitative | ὁ governs both ptcs. (λέγων & τηρῶν)

2:5 | ὃς δ’ ἄν + subj. = "but whoever" (cp. 3:17) | αὐτοῦ τὸν λόγον = τὸν λόγον αὐτοῦ | First ἐν τούτῳ = "in him"; second ἐν τούτῳ = "by this," both are backward looking | τετελείωται – proleptic perf. (W 581)

2:6 | ὁ λέγων + inf. = "whoever claims that," indirect discourse (cp. v. 9) | μένω occurs 27x in Johannine epistles | ὀφείλει + inf. | καὶ αὐτός = "himself also"

2:9 | ὁ λέγων + inf. – see v. 9 | καί = "and yet" (NASB) – see v. 1 | ἕως ἄρτι = "until now," "still"

2:12 | ὑμῖν – see 1:9

2:13–14 | τὸν ἀπ’ ἀρχῆς (2x) = "him who is from the beginning" (cp. 1:1)

2:14 | ἔγραψα (3x) – epistolary aorist (cp. vv. 21, 26)

2:16 | πᾶν τὸ ἐν τῷ κόσμῳ = "all that is in the world"

2:18 | ἔρχεται = "is coming," present retained in indirect discourse (W 539) with ingressive futuristic nuance (cp. 4:3) | ὅθεν = "from which fact" (BDAG ὅθεν)

2:19 | μεμενήκεισαν ἂν μεθ᾽ ἡμῶν = "they would have remained with us," unreal, contrary-to-fact indic. with ἄν (BDF §360(3)) | ἀλλ᾽ ἵνα ... = "But [they went out], so that it would be shown that they all are not of us" (NASB), elliptical (BDF §448(7))

2:20 | Who is ὁ ἅγιος? God? The Holy Spirit? Christ? Since we have the χρῖσμα (i.e., the Holy Spirit) from him, ὁ ἅγιος is probably ὁ Χριστός | οἴδατε πάντες = "you all have knowledge" (ESV)

2:21 | οὐκ ἔγραψα = "I am not writing" – see v. 14, 26 | ὅτι (3x) = "because" | αὐτήν = "it [= the truth]" | πᾶν ψεῦδος ... οὐκ ἔστιν = "no lie is of the truth," Semitic πᾶς ... οὐ instead of οὐδείς (M 182)

2:22 | ὁ ἀρνούμενος ὅτι ᾽Ι. οὐκ ἔστιν ὁ Χρ. – redundant οὐκ with verb denoting negative idea (BDF §429; M 157 n1)

2:23 | Note contrast between οὐδέ ("not even") and καί ("also")

2:24 | καὶ ὑμεῖς = "then you too" (ESV)

2:26 | ταῦτα ἔγραψα = "I am writing these things" – see vv. 14, 21

2:27 | καὶ ὑμεῖς = "and as for you" (NASB), redundant pronoun (M 176) | χρεία ἵνα = "need for/that," attenuated ἵνα modifying a noun (BDAG ἵνα 2cα)

2:28 | ἐὰν φανερωθῇ = "when he appears," subordinate clause | μὴ αἰσχυνθῶμεν ἀπ᾽ αὐτοῦ – either (1) "may not be put to shame by him," ἀπό = ὑπό (BDAG ἀπό 5eβ), or (2) "may not shrink from him in shame" (ESV), pregnant ἀπό with Hebr. mng., "from someone's face/presence" (BDAG ἀπό 1e & 4) | Temporal ἐν = "at"

2:29 | Adverbial καί is in an unusual position – options: (1) omit καί following some scribes who saw the difficulty, or leave untranslated; (2) take καί as modifying γινώσκετε (but out of position): "If you know that he is righteous, you *also* know that everyone who does righteousness has been born of him," (3) take καί as modifying πᾶς (in position): "If you know that he is righteous (δίκαιος), you know that everyone *also* who [like him] does righteousness (δικαιοσύνη) has been born of him" | γεγέννηται ἐκ – cp. 3:9

1 John 3

3:1 | καὶ ἐσμέν = "and so we are" (ESV) | ἵνα denoting content (M 145–6); common in Johannine writings (cp. vv. 11, 23; 4:21; 5:3, 16; 2 John 5–6; 3 John 4; John 6:29, 50; 15:8, 13; 17:3) (cp. BDAG ἵνα 2e; BDF §394)

3:2 | First ὅτι is marker of discourse content; second ὅτι is causal

3:3 | ἐλπίδα ἐπ᾽ αὐτῷ = "hope in him" (i.e., in Jesus) (BDAG ἐπί 6b)

3:4 | καὶ τὴν ἀνομίαν ποιεῖ = "also practices lawlessness," adverbial καί

3:6–9 | On the problem of the apparent perfectionism advocated here, take the present tense verbs and ptcs. either (1) as proleptic of the believer's eschatological state (W 524–25), or (2) as expressing characteristic or habitual action (S. M. Baugh, *A First John Reader* [Phillipsburg: P&R, 1999], 50–52), e.g., "keeps on sinning," "makes a practice of sinning" (cp. ESV, NIV)

3:8 | ἁμαρτάνει = "has been sinning," extending-from-past present (W 519–20)

3:10 | ἐν τούτῳ – forward looking | φανερά ἐστιν τὰ τέκνα – neut. pl. subjects take sg. verbs (cp. v. 12)

3:11 | ἵνα – see v. 1 | ἀγαπῶμεν – bec. ἀγαπάω is a contract verb, the present subj. (here and vv. 18, 23) and present indic. (v. 14) are identical in form

3:12 | χάριν (as prep.) + gen. = "because of," thus χάριν τίνος; = "why?" | τὰ δὲ [sc. ἔργα] τοῦ ἀδελφοῦ αὐτοῦ δίκαια [sc. ἦν] = "but his brother's deeds were righteous," brachylogy

3:13 | θαυμάζω εἰ = "be surprised that" (BDAG εἰ 2) (cp. Mark 15:44)

3:15 | πᾶς οὐκ = "no one" | μένουσαν – fem. acc. in agreement with ζωήν

3:16 | ἐν τούτῳ – forward looking

3:17 | ὃς ἄν = "whoever" | κλείω τὰ σπλάγχνα ἀπό τινος = "close one's heart against someone" (BDAG κλείω 2)

3:18 | ἀγαπῶμεν – hortatory subj.

3:19 | ἐν τούτῳ – backward looking

3:19–20 | Options: (1) "we will assure our heart before Him in whatever (ὅ τι ἐάν) our heart condemns us; for (ὅτι) God is greater than our heart" (NASB); (2) "...; for whenever (ὅτι ἐάν) our heart condemns us, God is greater than our heart" (ESV, omitting second ὅτι following a few MSS)

3:20 | μείζων + gen. of comparison (τῆς καρδίας ἡμῶν) = "greater than"

3:22 | ὃ ἐάν = "whatever"

3:23 | ἵνα – see v. 1

3:24 | καὶ αὐτὸς ἐν αὐτῷ = "and he himself [sc. μένει/remains] in him [= in the one who keeps his commandments]," brachylogy | ἐν τούτῳ – forward looking | γινώσκω ἐκ = "know [something] by/from" (cp. 4:6) (BDAG ἐκ 3gβ)

1 John 4
4:1 | τὰ πνεύματα ... ἐστιν – neut. pl. subjects take sg. verbs | εἰ = "to see whether"

4:2 | ἐν τούτῳ – forward looking (cp. vv. 9–10, 13, 17)

4:3 | τὸ τοῦ ἀντιχρίστου = "the [spirit] of the antichrist" | ὃ ἀκηκόατε ὅτι ἔρχεται = lit. "which you have heard that it is coming," prolepsis (BDF §476); present retained in indirect discourse with ingressive futuristic nuance (cp. 2:18)

4:4 | ἤ = "than"

4:5–6 | ἀκούω (3x) takes gen. (αὐτῶν, ἡμῶν [2x])

4:6 | ὁ + ptc. ... ὅς + verb = "whoever

4:7 | ἀγαπῶμεν – hortatory subj.

4:8 | ἔγνω = either (1) "knows," gnomic aorist, or (2) "has come to know," ingressive aorist | ὁ θεὸς ἀγάπη ἐστίν – take ἀγάπη as qualitative predicate nom. (see W 264)

4:9 | ἐν ἡμῖν = "in our case," "for us," ἐν for simple dat. (BDAG ἐν 8; BDF §220(1)) (cp. v. 16)

4:10 | ἱλασμόν = "[to be] the propitiation," predicate acc. (cp. σωτῆρα, v. 14)

4:11 | καὶ ἡμεῖς = "we also" | ὀφείλω + inf. (ἀγαπᾶν)

4:13 | First ὅτι = "that," second ὅτι = "namely, because," linking back to τούτῳ | δίδωμι ἐκ = "give some of a thing" (BDAG δίδωμι 17b), partitive ἐκ

4:15 | καὶ αὐτὸς ἐν τῷ θεῷ = "and he himself [sc. μένει/remains] in God," brachylogy

4:16 | ἐν ἡμῖν – see v. 9

4:17 | μεθ᾽ ἡμῶν = "among us" (NIV) | καθώς ... καί = "as ... so also"

4:18 | ἔξω βάλλω = "drive out, expel" (BDAG βάλλω) | ἔχει = "includes in itself, brings about" (BDAG ἔχω 8), "involves" (NASB), "has to do with" (ESV)

4:21 | ἵνα – see 3:1 | ἀγαπᾷ καὶ τὸν ἀδελφὸν αὐτοῦ = "must also love his brother" (ESV), note the imperatival nuance generated by ἐντολὴν ἵνα + subj.

1 John 5

5:1 | τὸν γεννήσαντα (aorist active) = "the one who begat" vs. τὸν γεγεννημένον (perf. pass.) = "the one who is begotten" (cp. vv. 4, 18)

5:2 | ἐν τούτῳ – forward looking

5:3 | ἵνα – see 3:1

5:5 | τίς; = "who?"

5:6 | δία + gen. – could be (1) "through," in spatial sense, or (2) "with," of attendant circumstances (see BDAG δία A1a; 3c) | ἐν (3x) = "with" (BDAG ἐν 5aβ; M 57)

5:8 | εἰς τὸ ἕν εἰσιν = "are in agreement" (NIV), Semitic εἰς functioning as predicate nom. with εἰμι (BDAG εἰς 8aβ)

5:9 | First ὅτι = "for," second ὅτι = "that"

5:13 | ἔγραψα – epistolary aorist | ὑμῖν ... τοῖς πιστεύουσιν = "you ... who believe"

5:14–15 | ἀκούω (2x) takes gen. (ἡμῶν)

5:15 | ἐάν (= εἰ) + indic. – rare (BDF §372(1a)) | ὃ ἐὰν αἰτώμεθα = "in whatever we ask," acc. of respect

5:16 | αἰτήσει – subject is τις | δώσει – subject is God | αὐτῷ (dat. sg.) ... τοῖς ἁμαρτάνουσιν (dat. pl. present ptc.) = "to him, [that is,] to those whose sinning is not unto death," substantived pl. ptc. in apposition to sg. pronoun (anacoluthon) | ἵνα – see 3:1

5:18 | ὁ γεγεννημένος (perf. pass. ptc.) = "the one who is begotten" | ὁ γεννηθείς (aorist pass. ptc.) = "the begotten one" – could refer to the Son, or to the believer, depending on whether one reads αὐτόν (NA27) or ἑαυτόν (NA28); see Metzger | Verbs of touching take gen.

Chapter Twenty-Four

The Second Epistle of John

2 John

1 | Nom. (self-identification of letter author/sender) + dat. (letter recipient) | ἐκλεκτῇ κυρίᾳ = either (1) an individual Christian lady, or more likely (2) a personification for a particular church, with "her children" being the members of the church (cp. v. 13 and 1 Pet 5:13)

2 | διὰ τὴν ἀλήθειαν – modifies ἀγαπῶ (v. 1); the elder loves them "because of the truth that remains" among them | Ptc. (μένουσαν) + καί + finite verb (ἔσται) (M 180; Z §375)

4 | ἐκ τῶν τέκνων σου = "some of your children," partitive ἐκ functioning as object (BDAG ἐκ 4aγ; BDF §164(2))

5 | κυρία – voc. | γράφων – present ptc., nom. sg. in agreement with implied subject (ἐγώ) | ἥν refers back to ἐντολήν – "not as though I were writing to you a new commandment, but the one which we have had from the beginning" (NASB)

5–6 | ἵνα (3x) – see 1 John 3:1

6 | ἐν αὐτῇ = "in it," the antecedent could be ἡ ἀγάπη (v. 6a) (NIV), but more likely the antecedent is ἡ ἐντολή (v. 6b) (NASB, ESV)

7 | ὅτι = "for," introducing the reason for the elder's exhortation in vv. 4–6 | οἱ μὴ ὁμολογοῦντες Ἰ. Χρ. ἐρχόμενον ἐν σαρκί = "who do not confess the coming of Jesus Christ in the flesh" (ESV), taking ἐρχόμενον as equivalent to perf. ἐληλυθότα (cp. 1 John 4:2) (M 101) | ὁμολογέω + double acc. (BDF §416(3))

8 | Textual problem: (1) εἰργάσασθε ("that you do not lose what *you* have accomplished") (cp. NIV 1984), or (2) εἰργασάμεθα ("that you do not destroy what *we* [the presbyter] have accomplished" (cp. NIV 2011); see Metzger

9 | ἡ διδαχὴ τοῦ Χρ. – either (1) "Christ's teaching," subjective gen., or (2) "the teaching about Christ," objective gen. | καὶ τὸν πατέρα καὶ τὸν υἱόν = "both the Father and the Son," καί ... καί (BDAG καί 1f)

10–11 | χαίρειν τινὶ λέγω (2x) = "greet someone" (BDAG χαίρω 2a)

12 | πολλὰ ἔχων ὑμῖν γράφειν = "though I have many things to write to you," concessive ptc. | οὐκ ἐβουλήθην (epistolary aorist) + inf. = "I do not want [to write]," γράφειν implicitly repeated (brachylogy) | στόμα πρὸς στόμα = lit. "mouth to mouth" (LXX Jer 39:4; cp. Num 12:8 with κατά) | ᾖ πεπληρωμένη – see 1 John 1:4

13 | "The children of your elect sister greet you" (ESV)

Chapter Twenty-Five

The Third Epistle of John

3 John

1 | Nom. (self-identication of letter author/sender) + dat. (letter recipient)

2 | ἀγαπητέ – voc. (cp. vv. 5, 11) | εὔχομαι + acc. (as subject of inf.) + inf. = "I pray that you may" | σου ἡ ψυχή = ἡ ψυχή σου

3 | ἐχάρην λίαν ἐρχομένων ἀδελφῶν καὶ μαρτυρούντων = "I was very glad when brethren came and testified," gen. abs.; present ptcs. used in reference to something that happened previously (BDF §339(3)) | σου τῇ ἀληθείᾳ = τῇ ἀληθείᾳ σου = "your faithfulness to the truth" (NIV); μαρτυρέω takes dat. | καθώς = "namely how" (BDAG καθώς 5), introducing indirect discourse

4 | μειζότεραν χαράν = "greater joy," double comparative; the comparative of μέγας is μείζων, to which the comparative ending -ότερος has been added to strengthen the comparative mng. (BDF §61(2)) | τούτων ... ἵνα = "than this, namely, that," gen. of comparison (pl. for sg.) + ἵνα of content (see 1 John 3:1)

5 | πιστὸν ποιέω = "act faithfully or loyally" | ὃ ἐὰν ἐργάσῃ = "in whatever you do," acc. of respect | καὶ τοῦτο ξένους = "even though they are strangers to you" (NIV)

6 | οἵ = "who" | σου τῇ ἀγάπῃ = τῇ ἀγάπῃ σου – bec. μαρτυρέω takes dat. (cp. v. 3) | οὓς καλῶς ποιήσεις προπέμψας ἀξίως τοῦ θεοῦ = "whom you will do well to send on their way in a manner worthy of God," καλῶς ποιέω + supplementary ptc. (BDF §414(5))

7 | μηδὲν λαμβάνοντες = "accepting nothing"

8 | τοὺς τοιούτους = "such people" | τῇ ἀληθείᾳ – dat. bec. of the συν- prefix in συνεργοί – "fellow workers with the truth" (NASB)

9 | ὁ φιλοπρωτεύων αὐτῶν Διοτρέφης = "he who loves to have first rank [or preeminence – KJV] over them, namely, Diotrephes," apposition; taking αὐτῶν as gen. of subordination (W 103) | ἐπιδέχομαι here could mean (1) "acknowledge someone's authority" (cp. ESV), but BDAG says it is not lexically defensible; or (2) "receive into one's presence in a friendly manner," "welcome" (NIV 2011) (as in v. 10)

10 | ὑπομιμνῄσκω = "call attention to" (NASB), "bring up" (ESV) | αὐτοῦ τὰ ἔργα = τὰ ἔργα αὐτοῦ | οὔτε = "neither" | καὶ τοὺς βουλομένους κωλύει = "and he forbids those who desire [to receive the brethren]," brachylogy

12 | Dat. + μεμαρτύρηται = lit. "to him [a good testimony] is testified" | ὑπὸ αὐτῆς τῆς ἀληθείας = "by the truth itself" | καὶ ἡμεῖς δέ = "and we also," the presence of δέ means the καί is adverbial

15 | κατ᾽ ὄνομα = "by name"

Chapter Twenty-Six

The Epistle of Jude

Jude

1 | τοῖς ... κλητοῖς = "to those who are called, beloved by [Hebr./instrumental ἐν] God the Father," article τοῖς goes with κλητοῖς; the ptcs. ἠγαπημένοις and τετηρημένοις are attributive rather than substantival (cp. v. 3) | Ἰησοῦ Χριστῷ τετηρημένοις = either (1) "kept by Jesus Christ" or (2) "kept for Jesus Christ," unusual use of dat. (M 47)

2 | πληθυνθείη – voluntative optative (W 481–3; BDF §384)

3 | πᾶσαν σπουδὴν ποιούμενος + inf. = "being very eager to," ποιέω (mid.) + noun as periphrasis for simple verbal idea (BDAG ποιέω 7a) | ἀνάγκην ἔσχον + inf. = "I felt it necessary to" (BDAG ἔχω 7aβ) | παρακαλῶν – present ptc. followed by indirect discourse: inf. (ἐπαγωνίζεσθαι) + implied acc. ὑμᾶς as subject of inf. | Article τῇ goes with πίστει, and the ptc. παραδοθείσῃ is attributive rather than substantival (cp. vv. 1, 22)

4 | οἱ = "who," article both functions as pronoun and substantivizes the ptc. | μετατίθημι + x + εἰς + y = "turn x into y" | The two ptcs. μετατιθέντες and ἀρνούμενοι are in apposition to ἀσεβεῖς, defining what makes them so "ungodly" – also note that the direct objects precede their respective ptcs. | τὸν μόνον δεσπότην καὶ κύριον ἡμῶν – one article governing two nouns per Granville Sharp rule (W 274–5) with Ἰ. Χρ. in apposition

5 | εἰδότας ὑμᾶς πάντα = "though you already know all this" (NIV), concessive ptc. | Depending on its position (see textual variants), ἅπαξ modifies either (1) εἰδότας, which makes little sense, or (2) σώσας, in which case ἅπαξ is picked up by τὸ δεύτερον: "the Lord *at one time* delivered his people out of Egypt, *but later* destroyed those who did not believe" (NIV 2011) | Best attested reading is Ἰησοῦς (NA28, ESV); however, intrinsic improbability of Ἰησοῦς leads many to adopt ὁ κύριος (NA27, NIV, NASB) (see discussion in Metzger) | τὸ δεύτερον = lit. "the second time," but here "subsequently," adv. acc.

6 | ἀρχή = "the sphere of one's official activity, domain" (BDAG ἀρχή 7) | τούς functions as pronoun and substantivizes both ptcs. (τηρήσαντες and ἀπολιπόντας) | Subject of τετήρηκεν is still Ἰησοῦς or ὁ κύριος (v. 5); direct object is ἀγγέλους

7 | αἱ περὶ αὐτὰς πόλεις = "the cities around them" | τὸν ὅμοιον τρόπον τούτοις = "in the same way as these," adv. acc.; ὅμοιος + dat. of person/thing compared; τούτοις refers back to the angels of v. 6 | ἐκπορνεύω = "indulge in illicit sexual relations" (BDAG) | πρόκεινται δεῖγμα = "are exhibited as an example" (NASB), predicate acc. | πυρὸς αἰωνίου δίκην ὑπέχουσαι = "suffering the punishment of eternal fire"

8 | ἐνυπνιαζόμενοι = "by dreaming" (NASB), "relying on their dreams" (ESV), "on the strength of their dreams" (NIV 2011), adv. ptc. of manner indicating emotion or attitude (W 627) | δόξαι = "majestic beings" (BDAG δόξα 4), "the glorious ones" (ESV), i.e., angels (cp. 2 Pet 2:10)

9 | ὅτε ... διελέγετο = "when he was arguing" | διακρίνω τινι = "dispute with someone" (BDAG διακρίνω 5a) | κρίσιν βλασφημίας = either (1) "a charge [accusing the devil] of slander" (cp. NIV 2011; BDAG βλασφημία bβ), or (2) "a reviling charge or judgment,"

attributive gen. (BDAG κρίσις 1bβ) | οὐκ ἐτόλμησεν κρίσιν
ἐπενεγκεῖν βλασφημίας = οὐκ ἐτόλμησεν ἐπενεγκεῖν κρίσιν
βλασφημίας [sc. κατ᾽ αὐτοῦ] = "did not dare to bring a slanderous
accusation against him" (NIV 1984), τολμάω + complementary inf. =
"dare to" | ἐπιτιμῆσαι – voluntative optative (cp. v. 2)

10 | ὅσα μὲν οὐκ οἴδασιν ... ὅσα δὲ ἐπίστανται = "the things
they *don't* understand they revile ... but the things they *do* understand
...," μέν ... δέ contrast | Second ὅσα is picked up by ἐν τούτοις =
"and the things they do understand ... by these very things they are de-
stroyed," Hebr./instrumental ἐν

11 | τῇ ὁδῷ – associative dat. with verbs of walking (BDF §198(5)) |
ἐπορεύθησαν – mid./pass. in form, but translate as active | τῇ πλάνῃ
= "to the error" | μισθοῦ = "for pay/profit," gen. of price (W 122); func-
tions as adverb modifying ἐξεχύθησαν (M 39) (cp. LXX Deut 23:5;
2 Esdras 23:2 = Neh 13:2) | τῇ ἀντιλογίᾳ = "in the rebellion" (Num
16), locative or temporal dat. (cp. LXX Num 20:13; 27:14; Deut 32:51)

12 | ἀγάπαι = "love feasts, fellowship meals" | ἀφόβως = "without the
slightest qualm" (NIV) | ἑαυτοῖς ποιμαίνοντες = "shepherds who feed
only themselves" (NIV), or "caring only for themselves" (cp. Ezek 34:2) |
δὶς ἀποθανόντα = "twice dead," because (1) fruitless and (2) uprooted

13 | ἀστέρες πλανῆται = lit. "stars, wanderers," i.e., "wandering stars,"
adjectival use of substantive (BDF §242); metaphor for transgressing
the divinely ordained laws of nature (cp. *1 Enoch* 2:1; 18:15; 80:6–7) |
τετήρηται – subject is ζόφος

14 | προεφήτευσεν = ἐπροφήτευσεν – MSS are divided on proper
location of the augment (before or after προ-) for this word (BDF
§69(4)) | προφητεύω + dat. (τούτοις) – odd use of dat., but context
demands "prophesy with reference to (or about) these men" (M 47)
| καὶ τούτοις – displacement of καί, which more naturally belongs
with Ἐνώχ (M 167): "Enoch *also* prophesied about these men" (but

see NASB, ESV) | ἦλθεν = "is coming" (NIV), proleptic (futuristic) aorist (W 563–4) | ἐν = "along with" (BDAG ἐν 5aα)

15 | ποιῆσαι κρίσιν = "to execute judgment" | κατά + gen. (2x) = "against" | Antecedent of ὧν is ἔργων, thus: "all their ungodly deeds that they have committed," attributive gen. ἀσεβείας and verb ἀσεβέω meld into a single thought | οἱ σκληροί = "the harsh things/words," substantivized adj. | ἁμαρτωλοὶ ἀσεβεῖς = "ungodly sinners," subject of ἐλάλησαν

16 | γογγυσταὶ μεμψίμοιροι = "fate-blaming grumblers," μεμψίμοιρος < μέμφομαι ("blame") + μοῖρα ("lot in life, fate") (BDAG γογγυστής, μεμψίμοιρος) | κατὰ τὰς ἑαυτῶν ἐπιθυμίας πορευόμενοι = "following after their own lusts" (NASB) | θαυμάζω πρόσωπα – either (1) "flatter people" (NASB), or (2) "show favoritism" (ESV, BDAG; cp. LXX Lev 19:15; Deut 10:17) | ὠφελείας χάριν = "for their own advantage" (NIV), χάριν (prep.) + gen., χάριν following its object

17 | μιμνήσκομαι takes the gen. | τῶν ῥημάτων τῶν προειρημένων – either (1) "the things/events [BDAG ῥῆμα 2] that were predicted," i.e., "the predictions" (ESV), or (2) "the words that were spoken beforehand" (NASB); second article τῶν functioning as relative pronoun

18 | ὅτι ἔλεγον ὑμῖν – either (1) "the words [v. 17] ... *that* they were repeatedly speaking to you," ὅτι substituted for relative pronoun, or (2) "*for* they were repeatedly saying to you" – in either case, taking ἔλεγον as iterative or customary impf. (W 546–48) | Second ὅτι (but note NA27 vs. NA28) would be recitative | ἐπ᾿ ἐσχάτου [τοῦ] χρόνου = "in the last time" (BDAG ἐπί 18a), unusual placement of article (but note NA27 vs. NA28) due to Hebr. influence (BDF §264(5); see Heb 1:2; 2 Pet 3:3) | κατὰ τὰς ἑαυτῶν ἐπιθυμίας πορευόμενοι τῶν ἀσεβειῶν = "following their own ungodly desires," taking τῶν ἀσεβειῶν as attributive gen. & Hebr. pl.

20–21 | ἐποικοδομοῦντες, προσευχόμενοι, προσδεχόμενοι – these ptcs. of means all have an imperatival nuance modifying τηρήσατε (v. 21)

20 | τῇ ἁγιωτάτῃ ὑμῶν πίστει = "in your most holy faith," taking ἁγιωτάτος as superlative of ἅγιος (but see textual variants)

21 | εἰς ζωὴν αἰώνιον = "that leads to eternal life" (ESV), or "to bring you to eternal life" (NIV)

22–23 | οὓς μέν ... οὓς δέ ... οὓς δέ = "some ... others ... others," but some manuscripts distinguish between only two classes of people; see discussion in Metzger

22 | οὓς διακρινομένους = "those who are doubting," note different mng. of verb in v. 9 (see BDAG διακρίνω 5–6)

23 | ἐλεᾶτε ἐν φόβῳ = "show mercy, mixed with fear" (NIV), i.e., with fear of defiling oneself (BDAG φόβος 2aα) | μισοῦντες καὶ τὸν χιτῶνα = "hating even the garment" | ἐσπιλωμένον is attributive rather than substantival (cp. vv. 1, 3) | ἀπό = ὑπό

24 | φυλάξαι ὑμᾶς ἀπταίστους = "to keep you stumble-free," predicate acc. | ὑμᾶς is assumed after στῆσαι

Chapter Twenty-Seven

The Revelation of John

Note: "Revelation exhibits a quantity of striking solecisms which are based especially on inattention to agreement" (BDF §136) (for partial list, see Charles 1.clii–cliv). Ungrammatical expressions are identified below by indicating the correct form. It is sometimes possible to explain lack of agreement as instances of *constructio ad sensum* (BDF §134).

Revelation 1

1:1 | Ἀποκάλυψις – nom. abs. (W 49–50) | Ἰησοῦ Χριστοῦ – could be objective gen., subjective gen., or gen. of source | ἅ is direct object of δεῖξαι | Subject of ἐσήμανεν appears to be Ἰ. Χρ.; note chain of revelation: God → Jesus Christ → his angel → John → seven churches | ἐσήμανεν ἀποστείλας διά + gen. = "he made it known by sending his angel" (NIV), Semitic graphic ptc. (Z §363) (cp. Matt 2:16; Mk 6:17; Acts 7:14)

1:2 | ὅσα εἶδεν – "[viz.] to all that he saw"

1:4 | ἀπὸ ὁ ὤν, etc. – prepositions never take nom.; commonly cited as a solecism; however, "our author knows perfectly the case that should follow ἀπό [see very next prepositional phrase], but he refuses to inflect the divine name" (Charles 1.clii) | ὁ ἦν (cp. v. 8; 4:8; 11:17; 16:5) – another alleged solecism; but formed intentionally on analogy with ὁ ὤν (LXX Exod 3:14) | ἅ – rough; some scribes changed it to τῶν; others added ἐστίν (already implied)

1:5 | ὁ μάρτυς ὁ πιστός, ὁ πρωτότοκος ... ὁ ἄρχων – should be gen. after ἀπό (but cp. v. 4) | λύσαντι – aorist ptc. of λύω ("loose, free"); some MSS have λούσαντι (< λούω = "wash") | Hebr./instrumental ἐν

1:6 | ἐποίησεν – would expect dat. ptc. (ποιήσαντι), continuing ἀγαπῶντι, etc.; possible solecism, but this type of anacoluthon is common (BDF §468(3)) | τῷ θεῷ ... = "to serve his God and Father," dat. as direct object of verbal idea implied by ἱερεῖς (W 171–2) (cp. 5:10)

1:10–11 | σάλπιγγος λεγούσης – should be acc. in agreement with φωνὴν μεγάλην

1:11 | First εἰς = ἐν

1:13 | ὅμοιον υἱὸν ἀνθρώπου = "one like a son of man" – ὅμοιος should be followed by dat. (as it does in all other occurrences in Rev, except here and 14:14) (BDF §182(4)) | ποδήρης = lit. "reaching to the feet," high priest's garment (cp. LXX Exod 28:4, 27; etc.) | πρὸς τοῖς μαστοῖς = lit. "toward the pecs," the ζώνη is a very wide waistband/belt, the top of which reaches the pectoral area

1:15 | Supply copula | χαλκολίβανον – this word is found nowhere outside of Rev (here and 2:18), so its exact definition is elusive (see BDAG; commentaries) | πεπυρωμένης lacks syntactical concord with anything in sentence (scribes tried to fix; see Metzger); comparison with 3:18 suggests that it be taken as modifying χαλκολίβανῳ ("his feet were like burnished bronze, refined in a furnace," ESV)

1:16 | ἔχων = "he held," ptc. in place of finite verb (BDF §468(2))

1:19 | ἅ εἰσίν – Rev does not consistently follow the rule that pl. neut. subjects take sg. verbs (cp. 4:5) (but ἀκολουθεῖ, 14:13)

Revelation 2

2:1 | On τάδε λέγει (7x in chs. 2–3), note that the formula τάδε λέγει κύριος (= "thus says the Lord") is extremely common in LXX; see HR ὅδε) (W 328)

2:2 | τοὺς λέγοντας ἑαυτοὺς ἀποστόλους = "those who call themselves apostles" | εὑρίσκω τινά + adj. = "find someone [to be] something"

2:7 | δίδωμι regularly means "grant, allow, permit, authorize" in Rev (BDAG δίδωμι 13)

2:8 | ἔζησεν = "he came to life," ingressive aorist (W 558–9) (cp. 13:14; 20:4–5)

2:9 | σου τὴν θλῖψιν = τὴν θλῖψιν σου | ἐκ τῶν λεγόντων Ἰουδαίους εἶναι ἑαυτούς = "by those who say they are Jews" (NASB)

2:10 | μηδὲν φοβοῦ ἃ μέλλεις πάσχειν = "in no way be afraid of the things you are about to suffer," μηδέν – acc. of respect | ἐξ ὑμῶν = "some of you," partitive ἐκ functioning as object (BDAG ἐκ 4aγ; BDF §164(2)); common in Rev | ἡμερῶν δέκα = "for 10 days," gen. of time (BDF §186(2))

2:11 | οὐ μή + aorist subj. – emphatic negation (BDF §365)

2:13 | οὐκ ἠρνήσω τὴν πίστιν μου – either (1) "you did not deny my faith" (ESV) possessive gen., or (2) "you did not renounce your faith in me" (NIV), objective gen. (W 116) | καὶ ἐν ταῖς ἡμέραις = "even in the days" | Ἀντιπᾶς is gen.; thus ὁ μάρτυς, etc. should be gen. (but could be nom. of appellation, W 61) | παρ' ὑμῖν = "in your city" (NIV) (BDAG παρά B1bβ)

2:17 | ψῆφον λευκήν – possibly the white voting-pebble of acquittal (see BDAG ψῆφος)

2:19 | σου τὰ ἔργα = τὰ ἔργα σου | τῶν πρώτων – gen. of comparison

2:20 | ἡ λέγουσα should be acc.

2:21 | χρόνον ἵνα μετανοήσῃ = "time to repent," attenuated ἵνα equivalent to inf. after nouns of time (BDAG ἵνα 2d) | μετανοέω ἔκ τινος = "repent of something" (cp. v. 22; 9:20–21; 16:11)

2:24 | ὡς λέγουσιν = "as they call them" (NASB) | βάλλω = "place" | ἄλλο = "[any] other"

2:25 | ἄχρις οὗ ἄν + subj. = "until" (BDF §383(2))

2:27 | ἐν = "with"

2:28 | ὡς ... καί = "as ... so also" (BDAG καί 2c) | κἀγώ = καὶ ἐγώ

Revelation 3

3:2 | γίνου γρηγορῶν = "wake up!" (periphrastic)

3:3 | πῶς here practically means "that" (BDAG πῶς 1bα)

3:8 | δέδωκα ἐνώπιόν σου = "I have set before you" (ESV) | αὐτήν (= "door") – Semitic pleonastic pronoun in relative clause (BDF §297)

3:9 | Verse 9a is an incomplete sentence; thought resumed in v. 9b | Partitive use of ἐκ as subject or object (cp. 2:10), "those who are of the synagogue of Satan" | ποιήσω αὐτοὺς ἵνα = "I will cause them to," ἵνα as inf. (BDAG ποιέω 2hα); prolepsis (BDF §476(1)) | ἵνα + future indic. (BDF §369(2)) (cp. 6:4)

3:10 | ὅτι ... κἀγώ = "because ... I also" | Note play on words involving τηρέω, used in two different senses, "obey" and "preserve," yet forming a positive *lex talionis*) | τὸν λόγον τῆς ὑπομονῆς μου – options:

(1) "my command to endure" (Aune), or (2) "the word about my endurance" (Beale) | τηρέω ἐκ – on pre-tribulation rapture debate, see commentaries (cp. John 17:15)

3:12 | ἔξω οὐ μὴ ἐξέλθῃ ἔτι = "he will not go out from it anymore" (NASB) | ἡ καταβαίνουσα should be gen. in agreement with τῆς καινῆς Ἰερ.

3:15 | οὔτε ... οὔτε = "neither ... nor" (and v. 16) | ὄφελον = "would that" (BDAG; M 137)

3:16 | οὕτως ὅτι = "So, because"

3:19 | ἐγώ probably goes with ἐλέγχω καὶ παιδεύω (interesting word order)

3:20 | [καί] introduces apodosis (BDAG καί 1bδ) (cp. 10:7)

Revelation 4

4:1 | ὡς σάλπιγγος λαλούσης should be either nom. in agreement with ἡ φωνή or acc. in agreement with ἥν, and λέγων should be fem.

4:2 | καθήμενος = "someone sitting"

4:3 | ὅμοιος ὁράσει + dat. (2x) = "similar in appearance to" (BDAG ὅμοιος a) | ἶρις (fem.) ... ὅμοιος – either another instance of lack of agreement in gender, or ὅμοιος could be viewed here as a two-termination adj., in which -ος covers both masc. and fem. (BDF §59(2))

4:5–8 | ἐκπορεύονται ... καιόμεναι ... γέμοντα ... ἔχων ... ἔχων – finite verb continued with ptcs. (BDF §468)

4:6 | ὡς = "[there was something] like"

4:6, 8 | Verbs of filling (γέμω) take gen. (cp. 5:8)

4:7, 8 | ἔχων (2x) and λέγοντες should be neut.

4:8 | ἓν καθ᾽ ἓν αὐτῶν = "each one of them" | ἀνάπαυσιν οὐκ ἔχουσιν + ptc. = "they do not cease to" (cp. 14:11) | ἡμέρας καὶ νυκτός – gen. of time

4:9 | ὅταν + future indic. = "whensoever ... shall give," so unusual that some scribes changed verb to present subj. (BDF §382(4); M 133)

4:10 | προσκυνέω can take dat. (W 172–3)

Revelation 5

5:1 | ἔσωθεν καὶ ὄπισθεν = "recto and verso" (BDAG) | ἑπτά – indeclinable

5:4 | ἔκλαιον – ingressive impf. (W 544) | πολύ = "greatly," adv. acc.

5:5 | εἷς ἐκ = "one of," partitive (cp. 6:1; 7:13; 13:3; 15:7; 17:1; 21:9) | ἀνοῖξαι = "so as to open," inf. of result (BDF §391(4))

5:6 | ἔχων should be neut. in agreement with ἀρνίον, and ἀπεσταλμένοι should be neut. in agreement with πνεύματα

5:9 | Hebr./instrumental ἐν | Partitive use of ἐκ as object, "some from" (cp. 2:10)

5:10 | τῷ θεῷ ἡμῶν = "to serve our God" (NIV) (cp. 1:6; but 20:6 has gen.)

5:13 | λέγοντας should be neut.

Revelation 6

6:1 | εἶδον ὅτε = "I watched as" (NIV) (cp. v. 12) | φωνή should be gen.

6:2 | ἔχων – cp. 1:16 (also v. 5) | νικῶν καὶ ἵνα νικήσῃ = "conquering and [seeking] to conquer," or "as a conqueror bent on conquest" (NIV)

6:3 | Subject of ἤνοιξεν is "the Lamb" (and so in vv. 5, 7, 9, 12; 8:1)

6:4 | ἐδόθη αὐτῷ ... ἵνα ἀλλήλους σφάξουσιν = "he was given authority [cp. v. 8] ... so that people would kill one another" (see note on δίδωμι at 2:7), ἵνα + future indic. (see 3:9)

6:6 | δηναρίου (2x) = "for a denarius," gen. of price

6:8 | ὑπό after active verb (solecism)

6:10 | Ἕως πότε ... οὐ κρίνεις = "how long will you refrain from judging and avenging?" (NASB) (cp. LXX Ps 13:1) | ἐκδικέω = "avenge" with person on whom vengeance is taken designated by ἐκ (similar to 19:2) (LXX Num 31:2; 1 Kgdms 24:13)

6:11 | ἵνα + future indic. (cp. v. 4); ἵνα of content (M 145–6) | ἔτι χρόνον μικρόν = "for a little while longer," acc. for extent of time

6:13 | βάλλω = "let fall," of a tree dropping its fruit (BDAG βάλλω 1c) | ὑπό ... σειομένη = "when shaken by a great wind"

6:14 | ἀπεχωρίσθη = "was split apart" (NASB): "The division of heaven is pictured as a scroll that has been split and each of the two halves then rolled up" (Beale)

6:15 | εἰς = ἐν

Revelation 7
7:1 | ἵνα μὴ πνέῃ ἄνεμος = "so that no wind would blow" (NASB)

7:2 | οἷς ἐδόθη αὐτοῖς = "to whom it was granted" (cp. 2:7; 6:4), pleonastic pronoun (BDF §297)

7:3 | λέγων should be acc.

7:4, 5, 8 | ἐσφραγισμένων … -μένοι – disagreement in case

7:9 | Switch from gen. sg. παντός ἔθνους to gen. plurals φυλῶν, etc., dependent on παντός, and switch from sg. ὄχλος to pl. ἑστῶτες, are best regarded as *constructiones ad sensum* | περιβεβλημένους (acc.) should be nom., and φοίνικες (nom.) should be acc. and needs ἔχοντες

7:10 | τῷ θεῷ ἡμῶν = "belongs to our God," dat. of possession

7:11 | εἱστήκεισαν = "were standing" | προσκυνέω takes dat. (cp. 4:10)

7:14 | εἴρηκα – perf. for aorist (BDF §343(1); cp. 19:3)

7:15 | σκηνώσει ἐπ' αὐτούς = "will spread his tent over them" (NIV)

7:16 | οὐ … ἔτι = "no longer"

7:17 | ἐπὶ ζωῆς πηγὰς ὑδάτων = ἐπὶ πηγὰς ὑδάτων ζωῆς = "to springs of the waters of life" (cp. 21:6)

Revelation 8
8:1 | ὅταν (cp. ὅτε in 6:1, 3, etc.) + aorist indic. = "when," normally ὅταν is followed by subj. (BDF §382(4)) | ὡς ἡμίωριον (< ἡμι- + ὥρα) = "for about half an hour," acc. for extent of time; ὡς with numerals means "about" (BDAG ὡς 6)

8:3 | ἵνα δώσει ταῖς προσευχαῖς = "that he might offer it [sc. θυμιάματα] with the prayers" (BDAG δίδωμι 3), ἵνα + future indicative (cp. 3:9)

8:5 | γεμίζω τὶ ἔκ τινος = "fill something with something" (BDAG ἐκ 4aζ)

8:8 | ὡς ὄρος μέγα = "something like a great mountian"

8:9 | τὰ ἔχοντα should be gen.

8:11 | γίνομαι εἰς = "become," with Semitic εἰς as predicate marker (BDAG εἰς 8aα) | ἐκ = "because of" (BDAG ἐκ 3e) (cp. v. 13)

8:12 | ἵνα of result (BDAG ἵνα 3) | τὸ τρίτον αὐτῆς = "for a third of it," acc. for extent of time

8:13 | ἐκ τῶν λοιπῶν φωνῶν τῆς σάλπιγγος = "because of the remaining trumpet blasts"

Revelation 9
9:2 | Second ἐκ = "because of" (BDAG ἐκ 3e) (cp. v. 18)

9:3 | ἐξουσία ὡς ... τῆς γῆς = "power like that of scorpions of the earth" (NIV)

9:4 | ἵνα + future indic. (see 3:9)

9:5 | ἐδόθη αὐτοῖς ἵνα (see 6:4)

9:7 | ὡς στέφανοι ὅμοιοι χρυσῷ = "something like crowns of gold" (NIV)

9:8 | οἱ ὀδόντες αὐτῶν ὡς λεόντων ἦσαν = "their teeth were like [the teeth] of lions"

9:11 | ἐν τῇ Ἑλληνικῇ (sc. γλώσσῃ) = "in the Greek language" | Ἀπολλύων – nom. of appellation (W 61; BDF §143)

9:12 | ἔρχεται should be pl.

9:14 | λέγοντα should be fem., and ὁ ἔχων should be dat.

9:15 | οἱ ἡτοιμασμένοι εἰς τήν ... = "who had been kept ready for this very hour," etc. (NIV)

9:16 | δισμυριάδες μυριάδων = "double myriads times myriads" (a myriad = 10,000; so a double myriad = 20,000; and since δισμυριάδες is pl., total number is an unspecified multiple of 200 million)

9:17 | οὕτως – forward looking: "The horses and riders I saw in my vision looked like this" (NIV)

9:18 | ἀπό = ὑπό

9:19 | καὶ ἐν αὐταῖς ἀδικοῦσιν = "and by means of them they inflict harm," Hebr./instrumental ἐν

Revelation 10
10:2 | ἔχων should be acc.

10:4 | ἤμελλον (impf.) γράφειν = "I was about to write"

10:6 | ὀμνύω ἐν = "swear by," Hebraism (M 183) | ὅτι = "that" | χρόνος οὐκέτι ἔσται = "there will be no more delay" (BDAG χρόνος 3)

10:7 | καί = "then," introduces apodosis (BDAG καί 1bδ) (cp. 3:20) | ἐτελέσθη – proleptic (futuristic) aorist (W 563–4; cp. Rom 8:30)

10:8 | πάλιν goes with λαλοῦσαν (which, with λέγουσαν, should be nom.) = "spoke to me again," ptc. in place of finite verb

10:9 | Inf. (δοῦναι) in indirect discourse | σου τὴν κοιλίαν = τὴν κοιλίαν σου

10:10 | καὶ ὅτε = "but when" (ESV)

10:11 | ἐπί + dat. – could be "concerning" (NASB; BDAG ἐπί 14a), or "against" (BDAG ἐπί 12a)

Revelation 11
11:1 | λέγων = "and was told" (NIV), quite unusual | ἐν αὐτῷ = "in it" (= the temple)

11:3 | δίδωμι + dat. = "grant authority to" (cp. 2:7; 6:4)

11:4 | ἑστῶτες should be fem.

11:5 | θελήσει – aorist subj.; εἰ + subj. is unusual but not unattested (BDAG εἰ 1b; BDF §372(3)) | οὕτως looks backward: "in this way," i.e., by being consumed with fire

11:6 | ἵνα μὴ ὑετὸς βρέχῃ = lit. "that no rain may rain" (BDF §309(2)) | τὰς ἡμέρας = "during the days of," acc. for extent of time | εἰς = "into," with verbs of change (BDAG εἰς 4b) | ὁσάκις ἐὰν θελήσωσιν = "as often as they want" (cp. 1 Cor 11:25–26)

11:8 | Supply future form of some verb (e.g., κεῖμαι/will lie) before ἐπί

11:9 | ἐκ = "those from" (cp. 2:10)

11:10 | ὅτι = "because"

11:13 | ὀνόματα ἀνθρώπων = "people" (cp. 3:4)

11:15 | λέγοντες should be fem.

11:18 | Three aorist infs., but not grammatically parallel: subject of κριθῆναι (pass.) is "the dead" (itself peculiar, BDF §393(3)), whereas implied subject of δοῦναι and διαφθεῖραι (both active) is "you" (= God) (anacoluthon) | τούς ... μεγάλους should be dat.

Revelation 12

12:4 | ἵνα ... καταφάγῃ = "so that, the moment she gives birth [ὅταν + aor. subj.] to her child, he may devour it"

12:5 | ἄρσεν (neut.) should be masc. (as in v. 13)

12:6 | ἀπό = ὑπό

12:7 | Articular inf. (τοῦ πολεμῆσαι) in apposition to noun (πόλεμος) (M 129) | Noms. ὁ Μιχαὴλ καὶ οἱ ἄγγελοι αὐτοῦ as subject of inf. – highly anomalous; possible Septuagintism (Charles 1.322, citing LXX Hos 9:13; Ps 25:14; 1 Chron 9:25; Eccl 3:15)

12:8 | οὐκ ἴσχυσεν = "he was not strong enough" (some MSS have pl. verb) | αὐτῶν = "for them"

12:9 | ὁ δράκων ... ὁ ὄφις – cp. 20:2; LXX Gen 3:1ff; Isa 27:1

12:10 | ἡμέρας καὶ νυκτός – gens. of time

12:15 | βάλλω = "spew" (and v. 16) | ἵνα αὐτὴν ποταμοφόρητον ποιήσῃ = "that he might cause her to be swept away by the stream," ποιέω + object acc. + adj. as predicate acc. (BDAG ποιέω 2hβ)

Revelation 13

13:2 | οἱ πόδες αὐτοῦ ὡς ἄρκου = "his feet [were] like [the feet] of a bear"

13:3 | ἡ πληγὴ τοῦ θανάτου αὐτοῦ = "his fatal wound," adjectival gen. (cp. v. 12) | θαυμάζω ὀπίσω = "be amazed [and follow] after," pregnant construction (BDF §196)

13:5 | μεγάλα καὶ βλασφημίας = "haughty and blasphemous words" (ESV), taking βλασφημίας as attributive gen. | ποιῆσαι = "to be active" (BDAG ποιέω 6)

13:8 | οὖ ... αὐτοῦ should be ὧν ... αὐτῶν (cp. 17:8); note also the Hebr. pleonastic pronoun; translate together as "whose" | ἀπὸ καταβολῆς κόσμου could modify ἐσφαγμένου, but comparison with 17:8 suggests that it modifies γέγραπται

13:10 | εἴ τις ἐν μαχαίρῃ ... ἀποκτανθῆναι – difficult, and there are a dozen textual variants (see NA apparatus and Metzger); NA reading should be translated: "If anyone is to be slain with the sword, he is to be slain with the sword," taking αὐτόν as a corruption for αὐτός (Charles 1.355–7)

13:12 | τὴν ἐξουσίαν ... πᾶσαν ποιεῖ = "he exercises all the authority of the first beast" | ἐνώπιον αὐτοῦ = "on its behalf" (NIV) (BDAG ἐνώπιον 4b) (cp. v. 14; 19:20) | ποιέω ἵνα = "make/cause someone to do something" (cp. vv. 15–17); attenuated ἵνα as inf.; ἵνα + future indic. (see 3:9) | οὖ ἡ πληγή = "whose wound"

13:13 | ἵνα of result

13:14 | λέγων and ὅς should be neut. | τῷ θηρίῳ = "in honor of the beast" (NIV), dat. of advantage | ὅς ἔχει τὴν πληγὴν τῆς μαχαίρης = "who had been wounded by the sword" (BDAG ἔχω 7aα), gen. of means | ἔζησαν – see 2:8

13:15 | πνεῦμα = "breath" | Subject of ποιήσῃ is "the image of the beast" | ὅσοι ἐάν = "whoever," "all who"

13:16 | Subject of ποιεῖ is the second beast | δῶσιν – 3p aorist active subj., with impersonal, undefined subject "they" (agents of the beast?), thus forming anacoluthon after ποιεῖ πάντας, partly patched up by addition of αὐτοῖς (referring back to πάντας, etc.); best to translate: "he causes all ... to receive a mark"

Revelation 14
14:2 | ἡ φωνή ... ὡς κιθαρῳδῶν = "the sound ... [was] like [the sound] of harpists"

14:3 | οἱ ἠγορασμένοι should be fem., like ἔχουσαι (v. 1)

14:4 | ὅπου ἄν = "wherever" | ἀπό + gen. = "from among," partitive (BDAG ἀπό 1f) | ἀπαρχή = "as firstfruits"

14:7 | λέγων should be acc.

14:10 | καὶ αὐτός = "then he himself," καί introduces apodosis; *lex talionis* (cp. v. 8)

14:11 | οὐκ ἔχουσιν ἀνάπαυσιν ... (cp. 4:8) | εἴ τις = "whoever" (NASB, ESV; BDAG εἰ 7)

14:12 | οἱ τηροῦντες should be gen.

14:13 | ἀπ᾽ ἄρτι = "from now on" | Causal ἵνα = ὅτι ("because") (BDAG ἵνα 3; BDF §369(2)) | ἀκολουθεῖ – neut. pl. subjects take sg. verbs (but cp. 1:19)

14:14 | ὅμοιον υἱὸν ἀνθρώπου – see note at 1:13 | ἔχων should be acc.

14:19 | τὸν μέγαν should be fem.

14:20 | ἀπό = "for a distance of" (BDAG ἀπό 4)

Revelation 15
15:2 | τοὺς νικῶντας ἐκ – peculiar; perhaps: "those who overcame [by keeping themselves] from the beast and from his image," etc.; pregnant construction (BDF §212); present ptc. with past reference (BDF §339(3))

15:4 | τίς οὐ μὴ φοβηθῇ; – the οὐ μή + aorist subj. construction normally expresses emphatic negation (W 468), but here as question expresses emphatic affirmation (BDF §365(4)): "Who will not fear you?" (cp. Lk 18:7; John 18:11)

15:7–8 | Verbs of filling take gen.

15:8 | ἐκ = "from" (BDAG ἐκ 3g)

Revelation 16

16:2 | καὶ ἐγένετο = "and there arose," but note that in vv. 3–4 the same phrase means "and it/they became" | ἕλκος κακὸν καὶ πονηρόν = "a loathsome and malignant sore" (NASB)

16:3 | αἷμα ὡς νεκροῦ = "blood like [that of] a dead man" | πᾶσα ψυχὴ ζωῆς = "every living thing," many reliable MSS have ζῶσα (cp. LXX Gen 1:21, 24, 30); although τά should technically be fem. sg. in agreement with ψυχή, it is *constructio ad sensum* (sea creatures)

16:4 | ἐγένετο should be pl.

16:5 | ὅτι ταῦτα ἔκρινας = "because you have so judged" (NIV 1984)

16:6 | αἷμα αὐτοῖς δέδωκας πιεῖν = "you have given them blood to drink," *lex talionis* | ἄξιοί εἰσιν = "they deserve it"

16:9 | καῦμα μέγα = "with great heat," cognate acc. (BDF §153(1)) | δοῦναι = "so as to give," inf. of result (BDF §391(4))

16:10–11 | ἐκ (3x) = "because of" (BDAG ἐκ 3e) (also v. 21) | μετανοέω ἐκ – cp. 2:21

16:14 | ἃ ἐκπορεύεται ἐπί = "who go abroad to," neut. pl. subjects take sg. verbs – yet Rev is inconsistent (cp. εἰσίν πνεύματα)

16:17 | Γέγονεν = "It is done"

16:18 | οἷος οὐκ ἐγένετο ... οὕτω μέγας = "such as there had never been since [ἀφ' οὗ] man was on the earth, so great was that earthquake" (ESV)

16:19 | ἐγένετο εἰς = "it was [split] into"

Revelation 17
17:2 | μεθ' ἧς = μέτα ἧς

17:3 | Textual issue: γέμον (neut.), which agrees with θηρίον (neut.), is grammatically more correct than γέμοντα (masc.) | ὀνόματα should be gen. since it follows verb of filling (cp. v. 4) | ἔχων should be neut.

17:4 | τὰ ἀκάθαρτα should be gen., but note gen. βδελυγμάτων

17:8 | ὧν τὸ ὄνομα = "whose name" (cp. 13:8) | θαυμασθήσονται ... βλεπόντων τὸ θηρίον = "[they] will be astonished when they see the beast" (NIV), βλεπόντων should be nom. | ὅτι = "because"

17:10 | ὀλίγον αὐτὸν δεῖ μεῖναι = "he must remain a little while," acc. αὐτόν is subject of inf.; ὀλίγον is acc. for extent of time

17:12 | βασιλεία = "royal power" (ESV; BDAG βασιλεία 1a) (also in vv. 17–18)

17:17 | "For God has put it in their hearts to carry out his purpose by being of one mind and handing over their royal power to the beast, until the words of God are fulfilled" (ESV)

Revelation 18
18:2 | ἐγένετο = "she has become" | φυλακή = "a haunt" | μεμισημένος = "detestable"

18:3 | ἐκ τῆς δυνάμεως τοῦ στρήνους αὐτῆς = "from her excessive wealth" (BDAG δύναμις 4)

18:4 | ἐκ τῶν πληγῶν αὐτῆς ἵνα μὴ λάβητε = ἵνα μὴ λάβητε ἐκ τῶν πληγῶν αὐτῆς (BDF §475(1))

18:5 | αὐτῆς αἱ ἁμαρτίαι = αἱ ἁμαρτίαι αὐτῆς = "her sins" | ἐκολλήθησαν ἄχρι τοῦ οὐρανοῦ = "have touched the heaven, or reached the sky" (BDAG κολλάω 2aβ)

18:7 | ὅσα ... τοσοῦτον = "to the degree that ... to the same degree" (NASB)

18:12–13 | πᾶν ξύλον ... πρόβατα – should be gen. | ἐκ ξύλου τιμιωτάτου ... μαρμάρου = "made from very costly wood and bronze and iron and marble," ἐκ governs all five gens.

18:13 | σωμάτων, καὶ ψυχὰς ἀνθρώπων – difficult on two counts: (1) both terms mean "slaves" (see LXX Gen 34:29; Tobit 10:11; 2 Macc 8:11; Ezek 27:13), but could be epexegetical καί (= "even"); (2) shift from gen. to acc.

18:14 | ἡ ὀπώρα σου τῆς ἐπιθυμίας τῆς ψυχῆς (subjective gen.) = "the fruit for which your soul longed" (ESV) | ἀπώλετο ἀπὸ σοῦ = "are lost to you" (ESV), "have passed away from you" (NASB) | Subject of εὑρήσουσιν is impersonal "they" or "people"

18:17 | ὁ ἐπὶ τόπον πλέων = "one who sails to a place" (NASB alt.) – unusual expression, prompted several scribal emendations (see NA apparatus) | ὅσοι τὴν θάλασσαν ἐργάζονται = "all who earn their living from the sea"

18:18 | Τίς ὁμοία τῇ πόλει τῇ μεγάλῃ; = "what [city is/was] like the great city?"

18:20 | οὐρανέ – voc. | ἔκρινεν ὁ θεὸς τὸ κρίμα ὑμῶν ἐξ αὐτῆς – possibilities: (1) "God has pronounced judgment for you against her" (NASB), taking ὑμῶν as gen. of advantage; (2) "God has pronounced on her the judgment she passed on you," taking ὑμῶν as objective gen.; (3) "God has pronounced your judgment on her," taking ὑμῶν as possessive/subjective gen. (see Beale for additional options and discussion)

18:21 | εἷς = "a(n)" (cp. 19:17) | ὁρμήματι = "with violence" | βάλλω = "throw down to destruction" (BDAG βάλλω 1c)

18:21–23 | ἔτι (6x) = "any longer"

Revelation 19
19:1 | ὡς = "what sounded like" | λεγόντων should be acc. fem. sg., but could be *constructio ad sensum* (cp. v. 6) | τοῦ θεοῦ ἡμῶν = "belong to our God," supply copula

19:2 | ἐκδικέω αἷμα ἐκ – similar to 6:10, but here mixed with another construction, ἐκζητέω αἷμα ἐκ χειρός = "require someone's blood at another's hand" (LXX Gen 9:5; 2 Kgdms 4:11; Ezek 3:18, 20)

19:3 | δεύτερον = "a second time," adv. acc. | εἴρηκαν – perf. for aorist (BDF §343(1)) (cp. 7:14)

19:6 | ἐβασίλευσεν (cp. 20:4) could be constative/global or ingressive aorist (cp. LXX Ps 47:8; 93:1; 96:10; 97:1; 99:1) (W 557–59)

19:7 | χαίρωμεν, ἀγαλλιῶμεν, δώσωμεν – hortatory subjunctives, "let us"

19:8 | ἐδόθη αὐτῇ ἵνα = "she was authorized to"

19:9 | οἱ κεκλημένοι = "those who are invited"

19:10 | Ὅρα μή = "Don't do that!" (NIV 2011) | σύνδουλός σου = "a fellow-servant with you," gen. of association (W 129) | Ἰησοῦ could be objective or subjective gen. (see discussion in Beale)

19:11–13 | καλούμενος, ἔχων, περιβεβλημένος – ptcs. for finite verbs (cp. 1:16; 6:2, 5)

19:14 | ἠκολούθει – neut. pl. subjects take sg. verbs | ἐνδεδυμένοι should be neut., but could be *constructio ad sensum*

19:15 | Hebr./instrumental ἐν (2x) (and in vv. 20–21)

19:20 | ἐνώπιον αὐτοῦ – see note at 13:12 | ἐν οἷς = "with which," referring to τὰ σημεῖα | ζῶντες = "alive" | τῆς καιομένης should be acc.

19:21 | ἐκ = "with"

Revelation 20

20:2 | κρατέω = "sieze, take into custody" | ὁ ὄφις ... ὁ Σατανᾶς should be acc.

20:3 | ἔτι = "any longer"

20:4 | εἶδον + two direct objects (θρόνους and τὰς ψυχάς) with intervening parenthetical material | Subject of ἐκάθισαν is indef. "they," but beginning with τὰς ψυχάς we learn who "they" are | τὰς ψυχὰς τῶν πεπελεκισμένων ... καὶ οἵτινες οὐ προσεκύνησαν – shift from ptc. to finite verb (cp. 1:5–6; BDF §468(3)); since this is a further description of the martyrs, not a separate class, καί could be translated "even" | ἔζησαν (cp. v. 5) – see note at 2:8 | ἐβασίλευσεν – constative/global aorist (W 558) (cp. 19:6; Rom 5:14)

20:5 | οἱ λοιποί ... τὰ χίλια ἔτη is a parenthesis (see NIV), and αὕτη refers back to v. 4

20:8 | ὧν ὁ ἀριθμὸς αὐτῶν = "whose number," pleonastic pronoun (BDF §297)

20:9 | ἐπὶ τὸ πλάτος τῆς γῆς = "across the breadth of the earth" (NIV) | παρεμβολή – could refer to an army's fortified camp, or to the army itself (e.g., Heb 11:34); frequently used in LXX with reference to the camp of the Israelites in the wilderness

20:10 | ὁ πλανῶν – present ptc. with past reference (cp. 15:2; BDF §339(3))

20:11 | οὗ ἀπὸ τοῦ προσώπου = "from whose presence" | ἔφυγεν should be pl.

20:12 | ὅ ἐστιν τῆς ζωῆς = "which is [the book] of life"

20:15 | εὑρέθη γεγραμμένος = "found written"

Revelation 21
21:1 | ἀπῆλθαν should be pl.

21:3 | [αὐτῶν θεός] = "as their God"

21:4 | ἀπῆλθαν – neut. pl. subjects take sg. verbs

21:6 | Γέγοναν – cp. 16:17 | δίδωμι ἐκ = "give [to drink] from"

21:8 | Normal word for "liar" is ψεύστης, but ψευδής ("false," cp. 2:2) as a substantivized adj. can also mean "liar"

21:9 | εἷς ἐκ = "one of"

21:11 | ὁ φωστὴρ αὐτῆς – supply copula

21:12 | First ἔχουσα – ptc. for finite verb (cp. 1:16) | Second ἔχουσα should be neut.

21:13 | Supply copula ("there are")

21:14 | ἔχων should be acc.

21:16 | ὅσον = "[is] as great as" | ἐπὶ σταδίων δώδεκα χιλιάδων = "at 12,000 stadia"

21:17 | ἔκατον ... πηχῶν – "the measure arrived at is expressed by the gen. of quality" (BDAG μετρέω 1a) (BDF §165); similar to ἐπί + gen. (v. 16) | μέτρον ἀνθρώπου = "by human measurement" (ESV), perhaps pendent acc. (W 198), or acc. of respect; ἀνθρώπου and ἀγγέλου are adjectival gens.

21:19 | παντὶ λίθῳ τιμίῳ = "with every [kind of] precious stone"

21:21 | ἀνὰ εἷς ἕκαστος + gen. = "each one of"

21:23 | ἐφώτισεν = either (1) "gives it light" (ESV), taking as constative/global aorist, or (2) "has illumined it" (NASB), aorist for perf.

21:25 | ἡμέρας = "by day," "during the day," gen. of time (M 39; W 124)

21:26 | Subject of οἴσουσιν is indef. "they"

21:27 | εἰ μή = "but only"

Revelation 22
22:2 | Punctuation problem w.r.t. ἐν μέσῳ τῆς πλατείας αὐτῆς – the clause could belong (1) with v. 1, describing location of the river, or (2) with v. 2, describing location of the tree of life | τοῦ ποταμοῦ ἐντεῦθεν καὶ ἐκεῖθεν = "on each side of the river" | ποιοῦν καρποὺς δώδεκα = "bearing twelve [kinds of] fruit" (NASB) (cp. BDAG ποιέω 2g)

22:8 | κἀγώ = καὶ ἐγώ | "I, John, am the one who heard and saw these things," present ptc. with past reference (BDF §339(3)) (cp. 15:2; 20:10)

22:11 | All four verbs are aorist impvs.; however, ἀδικησάτω (= "let him do wrong") and ποιησάτω are active, whereas ῥυπανθήτω and ἁγιασθήτω are pass.

22:14 | ἵνα ἔσται ... εἰσέλθωσιν = "so that they may have the right to the tree of life, and may enter by the gates into the city" (NASB), ἵνα + future + subj. (see 3:9)

22:19 | τῶν γεγραμμένων ἐν τῷ βιβλίῳ τούτῳ – "which are described in this book" (ESV), "which" refers to the tree of life and the holy city; article functioning as relative pronoun

Index of Subjects

Entries marked with an asterisk are too numerous to be usefully indexed exhaustively. In these cases, only the first occurrence noted in the Guide in each of the following sections of the New Testament is cited: Matthew, Mark, Luke, John, Acts, Epistles of Paul, Hebrews, James, Epistles of Peter, Epistles of John, Jude, and Revelation.

ACCUSATIVE

Accusative absolute .... 1 Cor 16:6
Accusative as subject of infinitive* .Matt 6:8; Mk 8:27, 29; Lk 2:26; John 3:7, 14; Acts 1:3; Rom 1:15; Heb 2:1; Jas 4:2; 1 Pet 4:3; 3 John 2; Jude 3
Accusative closest to the infinitive is normally the subject .... Phil 1:7
Accusative for extent of space .... Matt 14:24; Mk 1:19; Lk 5:3; 22:41; 24:13; John 6:19; Acts 12:10; 26:20
Accusative for extent of time* .... Matt 4:2; Mk 1:13; Lk 1:24; John 2:20; Acts 7:6; Rom 8:36; Heb 3:10; Jas 5:17; 1 Pet 5:10; Rev 6:11
Accusative for time at which .... John 4:52; Acts 10:3; 20:16
Accusative of oath.. Mk 5:7
Accusative of respect............ Matt 27:57; Lk 21:6; John 6:10; 11:44; Acts 2:37; 20:35; 21:11, 24; Rom 6:10; 8:28; 12:18; 15:17; 1 Cor 9:25; 11:2, 7; 2 Cor 11:5; 12:13; Gal 4:1; Eph 4:15; 6:14–15; Phil 3:15; 4:6; 1 Tim 4:2; 6:5; 2 Tim 3:8; 4:3; Heb 2:17; 10:22; Jas 1:6; 1 Pet 1:12; 1 John 5:15; 3 John 5; Rev 2:10; 21:17
Accusative of retained object with passive .... Matt 16:26; Lk 7:29; 12:47–48; Acts 28:20; Rom 3:2; 1 Cor 9:17; 2 Cor 3:18; 5:2; Gal 2:7; 6:6; 1 Tim 1:11; Tit 1:3

Index of Subjects

Adverbial accusative* ....Matt 4:2; Mk 1:45; Lk 5:33; John 6:62; Acts 1:14;
                Rom 1:8; Heb 10:8–9; Jas 2:24; 1 Pet 3:8; Jude 5; Rev 5:4
Cognate accusative ....Lk 2:8–9; John 7:24; 2 Cor 6:13; Col 2:19; Rev 16:9
Double accusative* .... Matt 21:13; Mk 7:17; Lk 18:19; John 2:16; Acts 13:5;
                Rom 1:20; Heb 1:9; Jas 5:10; 1 Pet 3:6; 2 John 7
Pendent accusative ....Rev 21:17

ADJECTIVE

Attributive adjective ....2 Cor 4:17; Tit 2:10; Heb 7:1
Predicate adjective..Matt 28:14;
                Lk 1:35; 24:22; 28:13; John 4:18; Acts 28:13; Col 1:18
Substantivized adjective................. Matt 10:42; 13:48; Lk 1:35; Acts 21:12, 34;
                28:7; Rom 1:15; 1 Cor 1:25; 7:35; 2 Cor 4:17; Gal 4:22–23, 30–31;
                Heb 7:18; 13:21; Jas 4:17; 1 Pet 3:4; Jude 15
Two-termination adjective .... Matt 25:10; Rom 1:20, 21; 7:2; 15:16;
                1 Cor 7:36; 2 Cor 7:10; Rev 4:3

ADVERB OR ADVERBIAL PHRASE

Matt 5:43; Mk 15:16; Lk 1:3; 9:27; 19:28, 30; John 4:18; 20:7; Rom 1:10, 15;
                10:4; 1 Cor 7:5; 2 Cor 9:7; 11:23; 1 Pet 2:12; Jude 11

AGREEMENT

Constructio ad sensum .... Matt 21:8; Mk 1:5; 8:1;
                9:20; 13:14; Lk 2:13; 8:14–15; 21:24; John 6:2; 8:44; 11:42; Acts 3:11;
                17:29; Rom 9:32; Phil 2:15; 2 Pet 3:1; Rev 7:9; 16:3; 19:1, 14
Case attraction...............Matt 8:23; 17:25; 21:42; 24:50; Lk 19:37; John 7:31; 17:9;
                Acts 7:16; Rom 1:15; 2 Cor 10:13; Eph 1:6; 4:1; 2 Thess 1:4; 1 Pet 2:24
Gender attraction ...... Mk 15:16; Gal 3:16; Eph 1:14; 6:17; 1 Tim 3:15; Heb 9:9
Inverse attraction ....Matt 21:42
Non-attraction of the relative ....Tit 3:5
Lack of agreement .... Mk 12:28; Acts 26:3;
                Eph 5:5; Col 3:14; for Rev, see "Atypical Constructions: Solecisms"
Relative pronoun assimilated to case of omitted demonstrative ....Lk 9:36;
                John 7:31; 17:19; Heb 5:8

ANARTHROUS

Anarthrous definite noun...Mk 2:1; Lk 21:25

Index of Subjects

Anarthrous substantival adjective or participle .... Matt 2:6; 3:3; 21:16;
    Mk 1:3; Lk 3:4; 11:22; 14:8; John 11:1; Rom 7:1; 10:14; Jas 4:17;
    1 Pet 1:18; 2:7, 12, 14; 5:5
Anarthrous qualitative noun..John 1:1; 4:24; Heb 1:2
Colwell's rule.. Matt 14:33; 27:42, 54

AORIST

Consummative aorist.. Matt 27:46; Mk 15:34; John 2:20
Constative/global aorist ....Matt 3:17;
    Mk 1:11; 12:44; Lk 10:18; John 2:20; 15:4; Acts 11:26; 28:30;
    Rom 5:14; 1 Cor 6:20; 2 Tim 4:2; Rev 19:6; 20:4; 21:23
Effective aorist...John 7:26
Epistolary aorist ..... Acts 23:30; Rom 15:15; 1 Cor 5:11; 9:15; Gal 6:11; Eph 6:22;
    Phil 2:28; Col 4:8; Phm 12; 1 John 2:14, 21, 26; 5:13; 2 John 12
Gnomic aorist................ Matt 23:2; Lk 7:35; 2 Cor 9:9; Jas 1:11, 24; 1 John 4:8
Immediate past aorist ....Matt 3:17; Lk 16:4
Ingressive aorist.............Lk 15:32; John 4:52; 1 John 4:8; Rev 2:8; 19:6; 20:4, 5
Proleptic aorist.. Gal 5:4; Eph 1:22; Jude 14; Rev 10:7
Substantival gnomic aorist participle with generic reference........Matt 10:22, 39;
    23:20–22; 24:13; 26:52; Mk 13:13; 16:16; Lk 8:12, 14; 12:9; John 3:33;
    6:45; 16:2; Rom 10:5; Gal 3:12

ARTICLE

Anaphoric use of article ....Matt 15:20; 27:31;
    Rom 4:13; 12:2; 1 Cor 7:26; 8:7; Gal 5:1, 8; 1 Thess 5:4; Jas 2:14; 3:6
Article as possessive pronoun .... Lk 9:58, 62; 22:39;
    John 8:38; Acts 7:20; 1 Cor 1:21
Article as relative pronoun .....Lk 22:20; Acts 4:25; 7:37–38; 10:41; 15:1; 21:38;
    Rom 1:18; 7:5; 1 Cor 2:11–12; 15:10; Gal 2:3; Phil 4:7; 1 Thess 2:15; 2
    Tim 1:9–10; Heb 5:14; 7:28; 1 Pet 1:3; 5:1; Jude 4, 6, 17; Rev 22:19
Article as subject pronoun ....Matt 2:9, 14; 4:20, 22; 14:8; 20:31; 22:5; 26:57;
    28:9, 15, 17; Mk 1:45; 7:6; 10:3, 20, 22; 12:16; Lk 4:40; 5:33; 6:10; 8:56;
    23:21–23; John 2:8; Acts 3:5; 7:25; 8:4; 9:5, 29; 10:4; 12:15
Articular participle with personal pronoun "you"................................Matt 7:23;
    Rom 2:1, 3; 14:4; Jas 4:12; 1 Pet 2:10
Deictic use of article...Rom 16:22
Generic article...Matt 5:39; Heb 6:16
Granville Sharp Rule............... Mk 16:16; John 6:33; Tit 2:13; 1 Pet 1:1; Jude 4

Individual-indefinite article .... 1 Pet 3:13

Neuter singular article (τό) changing direct question into indirect ...... Lk 1:62; 9:46; 19:48; 22:2, 4, 23, 24; Acts 4:21; 22:30; Rom 8:26; 1 Thess 4:1

Neuter singular article (τό) functioning as quote marks .... Matt 19:18; Mk 9:23; 12:33; Lk 22:37; John 16:18; Rom 13:9; 1 Cor 4:6; 2 Cor 1:17; Eph 4:9; Heb 12:27

ATYPICAL CONSTRUCTIONS

Anacoluthon .... Matt 4:16; 5:40; 7:9–10; 12:36; 13:19; 17:25; Mk 11:32; Lk 12:48b; John 6:39; Acts 3:16; Rom 9:22–23; 12:19; 14:2; 15:9; Gal 2:4–5, 6; Eph 2:1; 1 Tim 1:9–10; 1 John 5:16; Rev 1:6; 11:18; 13:16

Difficult constructions .... Matt 5:13; 26:50, 64; Mk 14:72; Lk 12:49; John 9:6; Acts 3:18; 25:13; 26:28; Rom 1:12; 5:12; 1 Cor 5:5; 12:2; 15:2; 2 Cor 10:13; Gal 4:14; Eph 4:29; Phil 1:28; 1 Tim 6:3, 7; 1 John 2:29; Rev 13:10; 18:13

Mixing of constructions .... Mark 9:42, 43, 45, 47

Mixing direct and indirect discourse .... Mk 6:8–9; 8:23; Lk 5:14; John 20:18; Acts 17:3; 23:22

Pregnant constructions .... Matt 5:22; 10:9; 20:1; 24:17; Mk 3:3; 6:8; 7:4; Lk 14:35; Acts 7:9; 8:22; 10:22; 22:13; Rom 9:3; 2 Cor 11:3; Gal 3:24; Col 2:20; 2 Thess 1:9; Rev 13:3; 15:2

Rare constructions .... Matt 6:5; 12:34; 15:32; Mk 2:16; 4:39; 8:2; 9:11; 11:25; Lk 9:28, 52; 23:15; John 4:11; 7:4; 11:47; Acts 20:24; 21:24; 2 Cor 11:23; 1 Thess 4:7; 1 Tim 6:3, 7; Jas 3:7; 1 John 5:15

Solecisms .... Rom 4:12; Phil 1:29–30; Rev 1:4, 5, 6, 10–11, 13, 15; 2:13, 20; 3:12; 4:1, 3, 7, 8; 5:6, 13; 6:1, 8; 7:3, 4, 5, 8, 9; 8:9; 9:12, 14; 10:2, 8; 11:4, 15, 18; 12:5; 13:8, 14; 14:3, 7, 12, 14, 19; 16:3, 4; 17:3, 4, 8; 18:12–13; 19:1, 14, 20; 20:2, 11; 21:1, 12, 14

Unusual, peculiar, or anomalous constructions .... Matt 1:18; 8:23; 12:20; 20:20; 23:9; 25:29; 26:15; Mk 4:31; 9:21; 15:15; Lk 1:17; 24:20, 21; John 4:52; 7:4; 8:25; 9:6; Acts 4:12; 10:25; 15:1; 19:4; Rom 8:18; Phil 2:1; Col 2:14; 2 Pet 2:13; 1 John 2:29; Jude 1, 14, 18; Rev 4:9; 11:1, 5, 18; 12:7; 15:2; 18:17

AUGMENT

Absence of augment .... John 2:20

Double augment .... Matt 12:13; Mk 3:5; 8:25; Lk 6:10

Index of Subjects

Location of augment..Jude 14
Vacillation between ἐ- and ἠ-..Acts 21:27; 1 Cor 3:1–2

COMPARATIVES AND SUPERLATIVES

Comparative for superlative ......Matt 18:1, 4; 23:11; Mk 9:34; 1 Cor 13:13; 15:19
Positive for superlative.. Matt 18:8–9; 22:36
Superlative with elative force ....Matt 21:8;
        Mk 4:1; Lk 1:3; Acts 23:26; 1 Cor 4:3; 2 Cor 12:9, 15

CONDITIONALS

First class conditional...Lk 14:26; Rom 3:30
Second class conditional..............................Matt 23:30; 24:43; John 4:10; 8:19
Fourth class conditional.................................. Acts 20:16; 1 Pet 3:14, 17

DATIVE

Adverbial dative ....Matt 1:19; Mk 12:40; Lk 23:18; Acts 16:34; Rom 2:14
Cognate dative...Matt 8:8; 13:14; 15:4;
        Lk 7:7; John 3:29; Acts 2:17; 23:14; 28:10; Gal 5:1; Jas 5:17
Dative absolute.. Matt 14:6
Dative of advantage.........Matt 6:25; Lk 12:22; 14:12; Acts 7:24; 10:2; 15:3; 22:15;
        2 Cor 10:4; Eph 1:22; 2 Tim 1:8; Heb 11:11; 1 Pet 2:24; Rev 13:14
Dative of agent ....Lk 23:15; Rom 10:20; 1 Tim 3:16; Jas 3:7
Dative of association ....Rom 8:16, 26; 1 Cor 11:5; 2 Cor 6:14; Heb 11:11; Jude 11
Dative of cause...Lk 15:17;
        Rom 11:30–31; 1 Cor 8:7; 2 Cor 8:22; 9:4; Gal 6:12; Phil 1:14
Dative of destination... Matt 21:5;
        Lk 7:12; 10:30; 15:25; Acts 2:33; Gal 5:1; 2 Pet 1:3
Dative of disadvantage...Lk 10:11; 18:31;
        Acts 20:3; Rom 11:9; 1 Cor 4:4; Jas 5:3
Dative of indirect object ....1 John 1:9
Dative of manner .... John 7:6; Acts 20:2; Gal 2:5
Dative of material or content..................................Mk 6:13; 2 Tim 3:6; 2 Pet 3:6
Dative of means...Mk 4:33; Lk 11:36, 46; 22:48;
        Acts 8:11; 15:24; Rom 3:28; 7:2; 1 Cor 9:7; 2 Cor 1:11; 4:2; 2 Tim 3:6;
        Tit 1:16; Heb 1:3; 6:17; 7:23; 10:14; Jas 1:18; 1 Pet 1:18; 2 Pet 1:3
Dative of possession*.. Matt 13:54, 56; Mk 6:2;
        Lk 1:7; John 15:8; Acts 3:6; Rom 7:3; Heb 10:25; 2 Pet 1:9; Rev 7:10

Index of Subjects

Dative of respect/reference.............................. Matt 12:45; 13:14, 52; Lk 1:51; 18:31;
    19:3; 24:25; John 11:33; Acts 7:51; 14:8; Rom 12:10-11a; 1 Cor 14:20; 2
    Cor 7:11; Gal 1:22; 6:14; Eph 4:18, 23; Phil 3:5; Col 1:21; 2:7; Jas 2:5
Dative of sphere...1 Cor 6:2; Gal 5:1; Heb 12:3
Dative of time ....Matt 14:25; 24:20, 43; 28:1; Mk 1:21; 6:21;
    12:2; Lk 1:75; 2:38; 8:27, 29; 13:14-15; 18:33; 20:10; Acts 7:8; 8:11;
    10:23-24; 12:6, 21; 13:14, 20, 36; Rom 16:25-26; 1 Cor 10:8; 15:4;
    2 Cor 4:16; 6:2; Eph 3:5; 1 Tim 2:6; 6:15; Jude 11
Ethical dative ....Acts 7:20; 10:35; 23:1;
    Rom 7:10; 1 Cor 1:18, 30; 4:3; 8:6; 9:2; Phil 1:21; 2 Pet 3:14
Instrumental dative ....John 11:2; 19:34;
    Acts 1:5; 2:40; 12:2; Rom 1:20; 8:13-14; 2 Cor 3:3; Gal 5:1; Heb 2:15;
    9:23; 11:3ff; 1 Pet 2:24; 2 Pet 3:5, 7; 1 John 1:1
Locative dative...John 21:8; 2 Cor 3:7; Jude 11

DISCOURSE STRUCTURE

Asyndeton .... Matt 5:24; 8:4; 2 Tim 4:2
Coordination (parataxis) for subordination........John 7:4; 12:16; 13:26; Rom 13:3
Parenthesis*... Mk 7:19; Lk 2:23;
    John 1:24; Acts 1:15; Rom 1:13; Heb 7:11; 2 Pet 2:4-10a (v. 8); Rev 20:4
Period ....Lk 1:1-4

FIGURES

Aposiopesis ....Matt 26:50;
    Mk 8:12; Lk 19:42; John 6:62; Acts 23:9; 1 Cor 9:15; Heb 3:11
Assonance.. Rom 5:16; Heb 13:14
Brachylogy* .... Matt 14:19; John 1:22;
    Acts 15:11; Rom 1:26; Heb 1:7-8; Jas 1:10; 1 Pet 3:4; 1 John 3:12
Chiasm..John 9:22-23; Eph 4:15; Phm 5
Ellipsis* .... Matt 6:3;
    Mk 2:22; Lk 8:14-15; John 2:10; Acts 7:8; Rom 10:1; Heb 5:5
Epidiorthosis ....Gal 1:7
Hendiadys ....Matt 6:19; Mk 5:19; Lk 2:47; 6:48;
    John 12:16; Acts 1:25; 9:1; Rom 1:5; 2 Cor 8:4; Phil 2:1; 1 Thess 4:1
Hyperbaton... Acts 24:4
Irony...Mk 7:9; 1 Cor 8:10; 2 Cor 11:4, 21
Metonymy .... Gal 3:25; Heb 9:26, 28
Parēchēsis ....Heb 5:8

Index of Subjects

Paronomasia or play on words..Matt 21:41;
            John 15:2–3; Rom 7:21; 14:13; Phil 3:2–3; Jas 3:5; Rev 3:10
Prolepsis*.. Matt 6:26; Mk 1:24;
            Lk 4:34; John 1:19; Acts 3:10; Rom 9:20; Jas 4:12; 1 John 4:3; Rev 3:9
Prosōpopoiia .... Rom 7:7–25
Synecdoche .... 1 Tim 2:15
Zeugma .... 1 Tim 4:3

FUTURE

Deliberative future ....Matt 17:17; Lk 22:49; Heb 2:3
Imperatival future...... Matt 5:21; 6:5; Mk 12:30–31; Lk 4:8, 12; 10:27; 18:20;
                Acts 18:15; Rom 7:7; 13:9; 2 Cor 4:6; Gal 5:14
Future continuing subjunctive to designate some further consequence........... Matt
                13:15; John 12:40; Acts 28:27; Rom 3:4; 11:14
Future for subjunctive ....Lk 7:4; Acts 8:31; Col 2:8
Future infinitive ....Acts 11:28; 24:15; 27:10
Future participle... Matt 27:49; John 6:64;
        Acts 8:27; 22:5; 24:11, 17; 25:13; Heb 3:5; 13:17; 1 Pet 3:13; 2 Pet 2:13
Gnomic future..Matt 6:24; Rom 5:7; 7:3
Logical future .... Rom 3:30
Verbs that become middle in the future .... Rom 8:13

GENITIVE

Adjectival genitive ....Lk 21:22; Col 1:13; 2:11; 2 Thess 2:3, 9, 11;
            Heb 12:11; Jas 1:25; 1 Pet 1:14; 2 Pet 2:1, 10; Rev 13:3; 21:17
Attributed genitive ....Phil 1:22
Attributive genitive*... Matt 19:28; Lk 8:23; John 17:12;
            Acts 2:19; Rom 1:4; Heb 1:3; Jas 2:1; 1 Pet 1:1; Jude 9; Rev 13:5
Descriptive genitive... Matt 22:11–12;
            Lk 1:78; 2:14; John 6:29; 2 Cor 2:12; 1 Pet 3:3
Epexegetical genitive.. 2 Cor 5:1; 11:17; Phil 1:8
Genitive of agency ....Joh 6:45; 18:15–16; Rom 1:5–6, 7; 2 Pet 3:2
Genitive of apposition...John 2:21;
            8:44; 11:13; 19:31; Acts 2:33, 38; 20:16; Rom 1:5; 4:11; 15:16;
            2 Cor 5:1; Gal 5:5; Col 3:24; Heb 12:11; Jas 3:18
Genitive of association ....Matt 18:29; 23:30; Acts 19:29; Rom 8:17;
            16:3; Eph 2:19; 5:7; Col 4:10; 1 Thess 3:2; Phm 24; Rev 19:10
Genitive of cause..Lk 21:25; Acts 21:34

Index of Subjects

Genitive of comparison*...........Matt 5:20; Mk 1:7; Lk 3:16; John 1:15; Acts 17:11; 1 Cor 1:25; Heb 1:4; 1 Pet 1:7; 2 Pet 2:20; 1 John 3:20; Rev 2:19

Genitive of content...Matt 26:7; Mk 14:3, 13; Lk 1:15, 41, 67, 53; John 2:7; 6:13; 21:8; Heb 10:32

Genitive of destination or direction........Rom 8:36; 11:13; Gal 2:7; Heb 9:8; 10:19

Genitive of material............................. Matt 9:16; Mk 2:21; John 12:3; Col 1:22

Genitive of means .... Acts 1:18; Heb 11:37; Jas 1:13; 1 Pet 1:2; Rev 13:14

Genitive of place ....Lk 16:24; 19:4; Acts 19:26; Heb 8:2; 1 Pet 1:1

Genitive of price.......Matt 10:29; 20:2, 13; 26:9; Mk 6:37; 14:5; Lk 12:6; John 6:7; 12:5; Acts 1:18; 5:8; 7:16; 22:28; 1 Cor 6:20; 7:23; Jude 11; Rev 6:6

Genitive of product.........................Matt 24:15; Mk 13:14; Lk 13:11; 2 Tim 1:7

Genitive of production .... Acts 1:18; Rom 9:32–33; Gal 5:5; Col 2:12; 1 Thess 1:3

Genitive of purpose...Matt 22:19; John 10:7

Genitive of reference... Mat 21:21; 2 Cor 11:30; Col 1:15; Tit 2:10; Heb 5:13; Jas 1:13

Genitive of separation..Lk 2:37; Acts 27:43; Rom 15:22; Gal 5:4; Eph 2:12; 4:18; 1 Tim 1:6; 6:5; 1 Pet 2:11; 4:1; 2 Pet 2:14

Genitive of source ....Lk 2:35; 7:12; John 12:43; Rom 1:17; 9:16; 10:3; 2 Cor 1:12; 3:3; 4:7; 12:1; Gal 5:5; Phil 2:1, 17; Col 1:25; 1 Thess 1:3; 4:15; 2 Thess 3:5; Tit 2:10; Heb 12:11; 1 Pet 3:21; 2 Pet 1:20; Rev 1:1

Genitive of subordination ....Col 1:15; 1 Tim 1:17; 3 John 9

Genitive of time.................Matt 2:14; 24:20; 25:6; 26:42, 44; 28:13; Mk 5:5; 13:18; Lk 11:5; 17:4; 18:7, 12; 24:1; John 3:2; 8:2; 11:9, 49, 51; 19:39; Acts 9:24–25; Gal 6:17; Eph 6:10; 1 Thess 2:9; 3:10; 5:7; 2 Thess 3:8; 1 Tim 5:5; 2 Tim 1:3; Heb 9:7; Rev 2:10; 4:8; 12:10; 21:25

Objective genitive*......................Matt 12:27; Mk 1:1; Lk 2:32; John 5:42; Acts 1:24; Rom 1:9; Heb 7:1; Jas 1:22–23; 1 Pet 1:22; 2 Pet 2:5; 2 John 9; Rev 1:1

Partitive genitive .... Matt 16:28; 23:11; Lk 7:42; 14:24; 15:12; John 12:3; Acts 2:46; 10:7; 19:26; 21:16, 38; 27:33; 1 Cor 2:11; 6:1; 15:19; Col 1:15; Heb 12:10; Jas 1:5; 3:8; 1 Pet 1:1

Pendent genitive...Matt 25:29

Plenary genitive.. 2 Thess 3:5

Possessive genitive...Mk 1:41; Rom 1:5–6, 17; 2 Cor 1:14; Gal 5:5; 1 Tim 3:6–7; Tit 2:10; Heb 13:7; Rev 2:13; 18:20

Predicate genitive.. Acts 20:3

Subjective genitive*...Mk 1:1; Lk 1:41; John 5:42; Acts 2:11; Rom 1:17; 1 Pet 1:2; 2 Pet 3:2; 2 John 9; Rev 1:1

A Syntax Guide for Readers of the Greek New Testament

Index of Subjects

Two genitives joined by καί meaning "between"..........................Acts 23:7;
        Rom 10:12; 1 Cor 6:5; 1 Tim 2:5; Heb 4:12; 5:14

GRAMMATICAL WORDS

εἰ

As marker of direct question.. Acts 1:6; 7:1; 22:25
As marker of indirect question, "whether".....Mk 3:2; 8:23; 10:2; Lk 6:7;
        23:6; Acts 5:8; 10:18; 17:11; 25:20; 2 Cor 13:5; 1 John 4:1
Expressing expectation, "to see if"...Phil 3:12
In oath formula..Mk 8:12; Heb 3:11; 4:3, 5
Meaning "that" .... Mk 15:44; Acts 19:2; 26:23; 1 John 3:13
With indefinite pronoun...............................Matt 16:24; 18:28; Rev 14:11

ἤ

As interrogative particle..Matt 26:53
As relative comparative ("than") ....Matt 10:15;
        18:8–9; 19:24; Mk 9:42, 43, 45, 47; 10:25; Lk 15:7; 16:17;
        Rom 13:11; 1 Cor 7:9; 14:5, 19; Heb 11:25
ἤ ... ἤ = "either ... or" .... Matt 6:24; 12:33; Lk 16:13

ἵνα

Attenuated, denoting content................ John 17:15, 24; 19:31; 1 John 3:1
Attenuated, explanatory after demonstratives.................................Lk 1:43;
        John 6:29; Acts 9:21; Phil 1:9; 1 Pet 3:9
Attenuated, equivalent to infinitive..Matt 5:29–30;
        7:12; 28:10; Mk 10:35, 37; Lk 4:3; 6:31; 8:31–32; 18:39;
        John 5:7; 8:56; 13:2; 17:4; 1 Cor 4:3; 16:12; 2 Cor 9:5;
        2 Thess 3:12; 1 Tim 1:3; Tit 2:12; Rev 13:12
Attenuated, meaning "that" .... Matt 4:3;
        14:36; 16:20; 20:21, 31; Mk 3:9; 6:8, 12; 11:16; 14:35; Lk 17:2;
        John 6:7; 9:22; 1 Cor 14:1, 5, 12, 13; Col 1:9; 1 Thess 4:1
Attenuated, supplementary to nouns or adjectives.........Matt 8:8; Lk 7:6;
        John 4:34; 12:23; 13:1; 16:2; Acts 8:19; 27:42; 2 Cor 11:12; 1
                                John 1:9; 2:27; Rev 2:21
Causal ....Rev 14:13
Ecbatic or consecutive...........John 9:2; Gal 5:17; 1 Thess 5:4; Rev 8:12; 14:13
Epexegetical ....1 Cor 9:18

Index of Subjects

Imperatival ....Mk 5:23; 12:19; 14:49;
    Lk 20:28; John 9:3; 12:7; 13:34; Rom 16:2; 1 Cor 7:29;
    2 Cor 8:7; Gal 2:10; Eph 5:33; 1 John 4:21
With future indicative ....Lk 14:10; John 7:3; Acts 21:24;
    1 Cor 9:18; 13:3; Rev 3:9; 6:4, 11; 8:3; 9:4; 13:12; 22:14

καί

Adverbial.. Mk 1:38; 2 Cor 11:12; 1 John 2:29; 3:4
Adversative, "and yet" .... Matt 6:26; Mk 4:32; 7:24; 12:12;
    Lk 8:29; 20:19; John 5:40; 6:70; 7:19, 28; 9:30; 10:39; 16:32;
    20:29; Acts 7:53; 10:28; Rom 1:13; 2 Cor 6:8–10; 1 Thess 2:18;
    2 Thess 3:15; 1 Pet 2:20; 1 John 2:1, 9
"And it came to pass ... that"......... Matt 9:10; Mk 2:15; Lk 5:1; 9:51; 17:11
Epexegetical or intensive, "even" ....John 1:16;
    1 Cor 2:10; Gal 6:16; Rev 18:13
Introducing a question, "how/who/why then?"...........................Mk 4:13;
    9:12; 10:26; 12:37; Lk 1:43; 10:29; 18:26; 19:23; 20:44; John 9:36;
    12:27; 14:22; 2 Cor 2:2
Introducting an apodosis ....Lk 2:21; 7:12; 11:34; 13:25; Acts 1:10;
    Rom 8:17; 1 Cor 11:6; Gal 4:7; Jas 4:15; Rev 3:20; 10:7
Introducing second part of a comparison, "just as ... so also" .... Matt 6:10;
    John 6:57; 13:15; 15:9; Acts 7:51; Rom 1:13; Gal 1:9; Phil 1:20;
    Rev 2:28
καί ... καί = "not only ... but also" or "both ... and" ....Mk 9:13, 22;
    John 7:28; 9:37; 12:28; Acts 26:29; Rom 14:9; Eph 6:9;
    1 Thess 2:18; 1 Tim 4:16; Tit 1:9, 15; Phm 16; 2 Pet 3:18; 2 John 9
Meaning "and then/so".............. Mk 8:34; John 4:35; Heb 3:19; 1 Pet 2:20
Meaning "when" .... Mk 15:25; Lk 19:43; 23:44; Heb 8:8

ὅτι

Causal ....Lk 15:27
In ellipsis ....Mk 8:16–17; Acts 5:4; Rom 5:8
In oath formula.. 2 Cor 1:18; Gal 1:20
Inferential ....Lk 7:47; John 5:38
Meaning "so that" .... 1 Tim 6:7
Recitative*.........................Matt 7:23; Mk 1:15, 37, 40; Lk 1:25; John 1:20;
    Acts 5:23, 25; Rom 3:8; Heb 7:17; Jas 1:13; 1 John 2:4; Jude 18
ὡς ὅτι = "that"... 2 Cor 5:19; 11:21; 2 Thess 2:2

Index of Subjects

IMPERATIVE

Constative aorist imperative ....John 15:4; 1 Cor 6:20; 2 Tim 4:2
Imperative expressing a concession ....Eph 4:26
Imperative of ἀφίημι reinforces hortatory subjunctive to form
     single idiomatic phrase ....Matt 7:4; 28:49; Mk 15:36; Lk 6:42
Perfect imperative..Mk 4:39
Permissive imperative .... 1 Cor 7:15, 36; 2 Cor 12:16

IMPERFECT

Aoristic imperfect..Lk 5:36
Conative imperfect... Matt 3:14; 23:13; 26:59; 27:40;
    Mk 9:38; 14:55; 15:23; Lk 4:42; 9:49; 19:1; John 6:21; Acts 7:11, 26;
        9:8; 26:11; Gal 1:10, 13; Heb 11:17; 12:20
Customary imperfect .....Matt 26:55; Mk 4:33; 14:12; 15:6, 8; Lk 2:41; John 12:6;
    Acts 3:2; 17:21; 22:19; Gal 2:12; Col 3:7; 1 Pet 2:23; 3:5; Jude 18
Imperfect expressing relative time ....John 9:18; Acts 3:10
Imperfect expressing unattainable wish or desiderative imperfect..... Rom 9:3;
    Gal 4:20
Imperfect in "would/should/could have" expressions ....Mk 14:5;
    John 19:11; Acts 22:11; Heb 9:26; 12:20; 2 Pet 2:21
Inceptive or ingressive imperfect ....Matt 18:28; 20:11; 26:16; Mk 1:35; 3:6;
    Lk 23:23, 54; John 4:30; Acts 21:5; 27:18, 33; 28:6; Rev 5:4
Iterative imperfect* .... Matt 3:5–6;
    Mk 1:5; Lk 4:40; 8:29; John 3:22; Acts 2:45; 26:11; 1 Thess 3:4; Jude 18
Pluperfective imperfect.. Mk 5:8; 6:18; Lk 8:29; 23:8
Progressive imperfect..Mk 1:35; Lk 7:6; 8:42; Acts 3:1
Retention of imperfect in direct speech .... Acts 6:1
Retention of imperfect in indirect speech .... Mk 11:32
Voluntative imperfect ....Lk 1:59

INFINITIVE

Appositional infinitive ....Acts 9:15; 15:20; 24:15; Rev 12:7
Complementary or supplementary infinitive ....Matt 1:19;
    2:12; 19:14; 25:10; Mk 5:43; Lk 5:7; 8:38; Acts 11:28; Eph 4:22–24;
        Phil 1:14; 2 Thess 1:3; Tit 2:2; Heb 4:1; 7:23; Jude 9
Dative articular infinitive indicating cause...2 Cor 2:13

Index of Subjects

Epexegetical infinitive... Lk 2:1; Acts 20:24;
        Rom 4:13; 6:12; Eph 3:6, 8–9; Phil 3:21; 1 Thess 4:3–6; Heb 11:8
Genitive articular (τοῦ) infinitive expressingpurpose or result.........Matt 2:13;
        3:13; 11:1; 13:3; 21:32; Lk 1:9, 73, 77, 79; 2:21; 8:5; 12:42; 21:22;
        22:6, 31; John 1:48; Acts 3:2; 7:19; 13:47; Rom 1:24; 7:3; 15:22;
        1 Cor 16:4; 2 Cor 1:8; Phil 3:10; Heb 2:15; 5:12
Imperatival infinitive.............Lk 9:3; 1 Cor 5:5; Eph 4:17, 22–24; Phil 3:16; Tit 2:2
Infinitive as complement of adjective .... Acts 23:15; Tit 2:8; 1 Pet 4:3
Infinitive as complement of substantive ...... Lk 1:57; 2:6, 21; 12:5; John 19:40;
        Rom 9:21; 13:5; Phil 3:21; Heb 4:1; 5:12; 13:10; Rev 12:7
Infinitive equivalent to substantive...Matt 14:16; 25:35;
        Mk 5:43; 6:37; Lk 8:55; 9:13; John 4:7, 9, 10, 33
Infinitive in indirect discourse..Lk 2:26;
        John 16:2; Acts 11:28; 12:9; Rom 12:1; Jas 2:14
Infinitive of purpose....................................... Mk 7:4; Lk 6:42; 22:47; Acts 10:33;
        12:4, 13; Rom 1:24; 2 Cor 10:15–16; Eph 1:4; Col 1:10; 1 Pet 2:5
Infinitive of result ....Mk 1:27;
        Lk 1:54; Acts 5:3; Rom 1:24; 6:12; 7:3; Heb 11:8; Rev 5:4
Pleonastic τοῦ prefixed to infinitive.......................................Lk 4:10; 5:7; 10:19; 17:1;
        Acts 3:12; 15:20; 20:3; 23:15; Rom 8:12; 1 Cor 9:10; Gal 3:10; Heb 10:7

NEGATIVES

μή or μητί expecting negative answer................................Matt 12:23; 26:22, 25;
        Mk 14:19; Lk 6:39; John 4:29; 6:67; 7:41; 8:22; 21:5; Rom 11:1;
        1 Cor 1:13; 9:8; 2 Cor 3:1; 12:18
οὐχί equivalent to οὐκ...1 Cor 5:2
οὐχί expecting affirmative answer...Matt 5:46–47;
        Lk 15:8; 17:8; Rom 2:26; Heb 1:14
Redundant οὐκ .... 1 John 2:22
Reinforcing negatives.. Mk 6:5; 9:8; 11:2; 12:34;
        Lk 4:2; 10:19; 23:53; John 3:27; 5:22; 11:49; 15:5, 23; Acts 20:20; 1
        Cor 12:15–16; 2 Thess 2:3; 1 Tim 1:7; 1 John 1:5; 2:22

NOMINATIVE

Nominative absolute ....Matt 1:1; Mk 1:1; Rev 1:1
Nominative of appellation...John 13:13; Rev 2:13; 9:11
Nominative as subject of infinitive ....John 7:4; Rev 12:7
Nominative for extent of time .... Matt 15:32; Mk 8:2; Lk 9:28

A Syntax Guide for Readers of the Greek New Testament

Index of Subjects

Nominative for vocative ...... Mk 5:41; Lk 8:54; 10:21; Eph 5:22; Col 3:18–22;
4:1; Heb 1:8; 10:7; 1 Pet 2:18
Nominative after preposition........................Mk 14:19; John 8:9; Rom 12:5; Rev 1:4
Parenthetical nominative...Lk 13:16
Pendent or hanging nominative ....Matt 17:25; Mk 7:19; Lk 21:6; Eph 3:15
Qualitative predicate nominative ....John 1:1; 4:24; 1 John 4:8

NOUNS

Adjectival or qualitative noun .... Lk 24:19; John 1:1; 4:24;
Acts 3:14; Rom 8:10; Heb 1:2; 1 Pet 2:7, 19-20; 1 John 4:8; Jude 13
Collective singular noun...Matt 21:8; Mk 8:1; Lk 2:13; 21:24;
John 2:15; 6:2; 8:44; 11:42; 19:36; Acts 2:23; 3:11; Rom 9:32; Phil 2:15

OPTATIVE

Conditional optative..........Acts 17:27; 20:16; 27:12, 39; 1 Cor 14:10; 1 Pet 3:14
Oblique optative...Lk 1:29, 62; 6:11;
18:36; 22:23; Acts 5:24; 10:17; 17:11; 21:33; 25:16, 20; 27:12, 39
Potential optative...Lk 1:29, 62; 6:11; 15:36;
18:36; 22:23; John 13:24; Acts 5:24; 8:31; 10:17; 17:18; 24:19; 26:29
Voluntative optative ....Mk 11:14; Acts 8:20;
Rom 15:5, 13; Phil 4:19; 1 Thess 3:11–12; 5:23; 2 Thess 2:17;
2 Tim 1:16, 18; 4:16; Phm 20; Heb 13:21; 1 Pet 1:2; 2 Pet 1:2; Jude 2, 9

OTHER LANGUAGES

Aramaic...Matt 21:9, 15; Mk 4:8
Hebrew............................... Matt 5:13; 9:10; 21:5, 42; Lk 4:10; 22:15; Rom 11:4
Latinisms ....Matt 12:14; 22:15;
27:1; 28:12; Mk 15:1, 15, 19; Lk 7:4; 12:58; Acts 17:9; 19:38
Semitisms ....Lk 12:8; 19:2; Heb 6:14; 2 Pet 3:3

PARTICIPLES

Adjectival participle...Matt 27:37;
Mk 1:38; Lk 5:18; Acts 8:16; Gal 4:3; Col 1:18; Jas 5:16
Adverbial or circumstantial participle......................Lk 3:23; Cor 5:19; Jas 5:16
Attendant circumstances participle*..Matt 4:10;
Mk 1:7; Lk 4:40; Acts 4:36–37; Eph 1:13; 2 Pet 2:20

Index of Subjects

Attendant circumstances participle with imperative meaning .... Acts 10:13; 11:7

Causal genitive absolute .... John 6:18; Acts 21:34; 27:18; Heb 8:4; 2 Pet 3:11

Causal participle .... Lk 10:29; 23:45; Acts 9:38; 17:25, 29; 26:3, 5; Rom 5:1;
1 Cor 11:7; 2 Cor 1:7; 4:14; 11:19; 12:16; Phil 2:6; Col 3:9–10;
1 Thess 5:8; Heb 6:6; 10:2; 11:31; 12:1, 28; Jas 1:3; 1 Pet 1:23; 2:8

Cognate participle .... Acts 7:34; Eph 5:5; Heb 6:14

Complementary or supplementary participle .... Matt 1:18; 17:25;
Lk 5:4; Acts 5:42; 6:13; 8:9; 2 Cor 8:22; Gal 6:9; 2 Thess 3:13;
Heb 10:2; 2 Pet 2:10; 3 John 6

Concessive participle* Matt 13:13; Mk 4:31; Lk 11:13; John 12:37; Acts 16:37;
Rom 1:21; Heb 5:8; Jas 1:26; 1 Pet 1:7; 2 Pet 2:11; 2 John 12; Jude 5

Conditional genitive absolute .... Acts 18:21; 1 Cor 8:10; Heb 10:26

Conditional participle .... Matt 21:22;
Lk 9:25; 10:25; 18:18; John 5:44; Acts 15:29; 18:21; 1 Cor 11:29;
Gal 6:9; 1 Tim 3:10; 4:4; 5:9; Heb 2:3; 6:8; 1 Pet 3:6; 2 Pet 1:8

Genitive absolute* .... Matt 1:18; Mk 4:17; Lk 2:2;
John 2:3; Acts 2:2; Rom 2:15; Heb 2:4; 1 Pet 3:20; 2 Pet 1:3; 3 John 3

Graphic participle .... Matt 2:16; Mk 6:17; Lk 15:25; Acts 7:14; Rev 1:1

Imperatival participle .... Rom 12:9–19; 2 Cor 8:24;
Eph 4:2–3; 5:16, 19–21; 6:6–7, 18; Phil 2:2–4, 16; Col 2:7; 3:13;
4:4–5; 1 Pet 1:13–14; 2:1, 12, 18; 3:7–9; 4:8–9; 5:7; Jude 20–21

Inversion of participle and verb .... 1 Tim 1:12; Heb 2:10, 18

Participle continued by finite verb .... Matt 13:22–23;
Lk 5:18; John 1:32; Col 1:26; Heb 8:10; 2 John 2; Rev 20:4

Participle for finite verb .... Rom 5:11;
1 Cor 12:2; 2 Cor 4:8–10; 5:6; 9:11, 13; 11:6; Rev 1:16; 19:11–13

Participle of emotion or attitude .... Matt 19:22; Lk 19:37; Heb 11:7; Jude 8

Participle of manner .... Lk 2:16, 48; 7:38; 8:47;
Acts 26:26; 1 Tim 1:13; 1 Pet 4:4, 13

Participle of means .... Matt 27:35;
Lk 7:29; 11:45; 15:13; Acts 9:8, 22; 13:33; 15:8; 16:16; 17:31; 20:35;
27:38; Rom 12:20; 2 Cor 11:7, 8; Gal 3:13; 4:16; Eph 1:20; 2:15; 3:4;
4:28; Phil 2:7; Heb 6:10; 1 Pet 2:15; 3:5; 5:7

Participle of result .... Mk 7:13, 19; Acts 15:24; Eph 2:15; Heb 12:3; 1 Pet 2:21

Pendent nominative participle .... Mk 7:19; 12:40

Telic future participle .... Acts 8:27; 22:5; 25:13

Telic participle ... Matt 16:1; 19:3; 22:35; Mk 10:2; Lk 4:2; 10:25; 11:16; 13:7;
John 6:6; 8:6; Acts 24:11, 17; 1 Cor 4:14; 2 Cor 1:23; 8:8; 1 Pet 2:21

Index of Subjects

Temporal participle..Lk 5:11; 6:40b; John 3:4;
        1 Cor 9:18; 11:32–33; 2 Cor 5:6; Eph 3:4; 1 Thess 3:1; Heb 1:3; 5:4

PERFECT

Aoristic perfect.. Matt 13:46; John 18:37
Extensive perfect..........................John 19:22; Col 1:16; 2 Tim 2:18; 4:7
Gnomic perfect...John 3:18; 5:24;
        Rom 7:2; 1 Cor 7:39; 1 Tim 5:5; Jas 1:24; 2:10; 2 Pet 2:19
Intensive or resultative perfect............Lk 5:20; 13:12; Rom 5:2; 7:2; Eph 2:5, 8
Perfect with present force .... Acts 26:2
Proleptic perfect ....John 20:23; Rom 13:8; 14:23; Jas 2:10; 1 John 2:5

PERIPHRASTIC

Future periphrastic...Matt 10:18;
        Mk 13:13, 25; Lk 1:20; 5:10; 21:17; 22:69; 1 Cor 14:9
Future perfect periphrastic............................... Matt 16:19; Lk 12:52; Heb 2:13
Imperfect periphrastic*.. Matt 7:29;
        Mk 1:22; Lk 2:33; John 3:23; Acts 1:10, 13, 14; Gal 1:22
Perfect periphrastic...Lk 1:7; 14:8;
        John 6:31, 45; Acts 2:13; 5:25; 1 Cor 5:2; 15:19; Eph 2:5, 8;
        Col 2:10; 3:1; Heb 4:2; 7:20, 23; 10:10; 2 Pet 3:7; 1 John 1:4
Pluperfect periphrastic...Lk 5:17; 8:2; 9:32,
        45; 15:24; 23:51, 55; John 1:24; 3:24; 12:16; 19:11; Acts 4:31; 8:16;
        12:12; 13:48; 16:9; 20:8; 21:29; 22:20; Gal 4:3; 2 Pet 3:5
Present periphrastic ....2 Cor 2:17; 6:14; Heb 5:4

PLEONASM

General pleonasm..... Matt 6:26; Mk 5:30; 13:19; 14:47; Lk 1:23; 19:4; 22:50;
        John 9:34–35; 11:49; 12:31; Acts 7:58; 10:3; Eph 4:16; 1 Thess 5:2
Pleonastic ἄνθρωπος .... Matt 11:19; 13:28, 45, 52; 18:23; 20:1
Pleonastic pronoun .... Matt 4:16; 5:40; 25:29; Mk 1:7; 7:25; Lk 3:16; 12:48b;
        John 1:27, 33; 13:26; Acts 15:17; Jas 4:17; Rev 3:8; 7:2; 13:8; 20:8

PLUPERFECT

Extensive pluperfect..John 1:24
Intensive pluperfect...John 6:17
Pluperfect in protasis of second class condition...................Matt 24:43

Index of Subjects

Pluperfect with past or imperfect force..Matt 27:15;
Mk 1:34; Acts 16:9; 22:20

PLURALS

Abstract plural..Jas 2:1
Categorical plural .... Matt 2:20; Mk 16:17–18; Heb 11:37
Epistolary plural .... Rom 1:5; 3:9
Implied indefinite third person plural subject.....Matt 5:15; 9:2, 17, 32; 13:48;
Mk 5:35; 10:13; Lk 23:31; Acts 5:15; Rom 9:32;
Rev 13:16; 18:14; 20:4; 21:26
Neuter plural subjects take singular verbs*...Matt 10:2;
Mk 4:4; Lk 3:5; John 3:20, 21; Acts 5:12; Rom 8:28; Heb 7:13;
2 Pet 1:8; 1 John 3:10; Rev 14:13
Plural for singular...1 Tim 2:6; 3 John 4
Plural for the four directions ....Lk 12:54
Semitic plural with singular meaning ....Matt 12:1; 22:2; 26:17;
Mk 1:21; Lk 13:10; Acts 13:14; 1 Cor 5:8; Heb 8:2; 13:11

PREPOSITIONS

ἀπό (only takes genitive)
    As substitute for partitive genitive .... Mat 15:27; 27:21;
Mk 6:43; 7:28; 12:2; 16:21; John 21:10; Acts 15:5, 19; 27:44;
Heb 7:2; Rev 14:4
    Equivalent to ὑπό ....Matt 7:16, 20; 11:19; 27:9;
Lk 6:18; 7:35; 8:43; 9:22; Acts 2:22; 4:36; 15:4; 20:9; Jas 1:13, 14;
5:4; 1 John 2:28; Jude 23; Rev 9:18; 12:6
    Indicating cause, "because of" ....Matt 18:7;
Lk 19:3; 21:26; John 21:6; Acts 11:19; 22:11; 28:3; Heb 5:7
    Indicating motive or reason, "for, from" ....Matt 13:44;
Lk 21:26; 22:45; 24:41; Acts 12:14
    Spatial, indicating distance "from" ....Mk 7:17;
John 11:18; 21:8; Rev 14:20
    Temporal, indicating time "from"..Matt 13:35;
Lk 8:43; 13:7; 24:21; Acts 23:23; Rom 1:20
    With verbs of perception or learning, "from, by" .... Matt 7:16, 20;
Gal 3:2; Col 1:7

A Syntax Guide for Readers of the Greek New Testament

Index of Subjects

διά

    With accusative, causal ("because of") or final ("for the sake of") ... Matt
        13:58; 14:9; Mk 2:27; 6:6; Lk 5:19; John 6:57; 11:15, 42;
        Rom 2:24; 3:25; 4:25; 11:28; 2 Cor 3:7; Gal 2:4–5; 4:13;
        Phil 1:15; Col 1:5; 3:6; 2 Tim 2:10; Heb 1:14; 2:9–10; 5:12
    With genitive, as part of an urgent request .... Rom 12:1; 15:30; 1 Cor 1:10
    With genitive, of attendant circumstances ..... Rom 2:27; 4:11; 8:25; 14:20; 1
        Cor 16:3; 2 Cor 2:4; 6:7-8; 1 Thess 4:14; 2 Tim 2:2; Heb 9:12
    With genitive, marker of extension "through" space .... 1 Cor 3:15;
        1 Tim 2:15; 1 Pet 3:20
    With genitive, marker of extension "through" time .... Matt 26:61; Mk 2:1;
        14:58; Acts 5:19; 23:31; 24:17; Rom 11:10; Gal 2:1; Heb 2:15

εἰς (only takes accusative)

    Equivalent to dative of advantage .... Matt 20:1; Mk 8:19–20;
        Lk 9:13; 14:35; John 6:9; Acts 2:22; 24:17; Rom 5:18; 15:26; 16:6;
        1 Cor 16:1; 2 Cor 9:13; Gal 2:8; Col 1:25; Phm 6; 1 Pet 1:4; 4:10
    Equivalent to ἐν .... Matt 2:1, 23; Mk 1:9; 10:10; Lk 1:20; 4:23,
        44; 7:1; 9:61; 11:7; 13:21; 21:37; John 1:18; 9:7; Acts 2:5, 39;
        7:4, 12; 8:23, 40; 9:21; 20:16; 21:13; 1 Cor 15:54; 2 Cor 1:21; 1
        Thess 4:17; Phm 6; Heb 11:9; 1 Pet 3:20; 5:12; Rev 1:11; 6:15
    Indicating change from one state "into" another .... Acts 2:20;
        2 Cor 11:13–15; Gal 5:13; Eph 2:15; Jas 4:9; Rev 11:6
    Indicating extension in time .... Acts 4:3;
        13:42; Gal 3:24; 1 Thess 4:15; 2 Pet 2:4, 9
    Indicating purpose or result .... Matt 8:4; 26:13; Lk 5:4, 14;
        21:13; 22:19; John 1:7; 9:39; Acts 2:38; 4:30; Rom 5:18; 10:1,
        4, 10; 13:4, 14; 14:1; 15:18; Phil 2:16; Col 2:2; 1 Pet 2:2, 5
    Indicating vocation or use .... Matt 27:10;
        Lk 2:32; Rom 9:21; 2 Cor 9:10; Gal 4:24; Heb 11:8; 1 Pet 1:10
    Meaning "against" .... Lk 12:10; Acts 6:11; Rom 8:7
    Meaning "among" .... Matt 13:22; Mk 4:7, 18; Lk 21:4
    Meaning "with reference to" .... Lk 16:8; Rom 6:3; 16:19; 1 Cor 10:2; 2 Cor
        2:9; 11:10; Eph 5:32; 1 Tim 6:12; 1 Pet 2:2; 2 Pet 1:8
    Semitic predicate εἰς .... Matt 19:5; 21:42; Mk 10:8; Lk 13:19; John 1:7;
        Acts 4:11; 10:4; 13:22, 47; Rom 11:9; 1 Cor 15:45; 2 Cor 6:18;
        Eph 5:2, 31; Heb 1:5; Jas 5:3; 1 Pet 2:7; 1 John 5:8; Rev 8:11

ἐκ (only takes genitive)

    Adverbial.. 1 Cor 7:5; 12:27; 13:9, 12; 2 Cor 9:7

Index of Subjects

As periphrasis for genitive of price .... Matt 20:2; Acts 1:18
Causal ....John 6:66; 19:12;
      Rom 2:8; 12:18; 2 Cor 13:4; 1 Pet 2:12; Rev 8:11; 9:2; 16:10–11
Characteristic or ancestral............ Acts 11:2; Gal 2:12; Col 4:11; Tit 1:10
Meaning "at, on," of location ......Matt 20:21; 22:44; 27:38; Mk 10:37; 12:36;
      14:62; 15:27; 16:19; Lk 20:42; 22:69; 23:33; Acts 2:25; Heb 1:13
Partitive ....Matt 25:8; Mk 9:17; Lk 11:5; 1 Cor 9:7
Partitive ἐκ as subject or object...................................Matt 23:34; Lk 11:49;
      21:16; John 7:40; 9:40; 16:17; Acts 2:30; 2 John 4; Rev 2:10
Temporal...Matt 26:42, 44;
      Lk 23:8; John 9:1, 24, 32; Acts 9:33; 10:15; 11:9; 24:10; Rom 5:16

ἐν (only takes dative)
    As marker of cause or occasion... Matt 6:7;
      Acts 7:29; Rom 2:1; Gal 1:24; 4:20; Phil 2:10; Col 1:21;
      1 Thess 3:3; 2 Tim 2:9; Heb 2:18; 1 Pet 1:14; 4:14
    As marker of state or condition.................Lk 16:23; 23:12; Rom 4:10–12
    As periphrasis for adverb ....Lk 4:18, 32, 36; 18:8;
      Acts 12:7; 25:4; Rom 1:4; 16:20; 1 Cor 4:21; 2 Cor 11:21;
      12:12; Gal 1:6; Col 1:29; 2 Thess 2:16; 1 Tim 3:14
    As substitute for dative ....Mk 14:6; Lk 2:14; Rom 1:19; 16:7;
      1 Cor 14:11; 2 Cor 4:3; 5:19; 6:3; Col 1:23; 1 John 4:9
    Circumstantial......... Lk 1:21; Rom 2:1; 2 Cor 11:12; Heb 2:8; 1 Pet 2:12
    Equivalent to εἰς ....Lk 1:17; 4:1; John 3:35
    Hebraic/instrumental, "by, with"*..Matt 3:11;
      Mk 9:29; Lk 1:51; John 1:26, 31, 33; Acts 1:5; Rom 1:9;
      Heb 1:1; Jas 3:9; 1 Pet 1:2; Jude 1; Rev 1:5
    Hebraic/instrumental, marker of agency.....................................Matt 9:34;
      Lk 4:1; Acts 17:31; Col 1:16
    "In a particular case" .... Acts 28:18; 1 Cor 4:2; 9:15;
      2 Cor 4:4; Gal 1:24; Phil 1:30; 1 Tim 1:16; 1 John 4:9
    Meaning "along with"...Lk 14:31;
      1 Cor 4:21; 2 Cor 10:14; Eph 6:2; 1 John 5:6; Jude 14
    Meaning "among" ....John 13:35; Acts 15:7; 26:18; Rom 8:29; 16:7;
      1 Cor 15:3; 2 Cor 10:1; 11:26; Gal 1:14, 16; Phil 2:5; 2 Thess 1:10
    Meaning "at," of location...Matt 24:41; Heb 1:3
    Meaning "at," of time.. 1 John 2:28
    Meaning "consisting of " .... Acts 7:14; Rom 5:15; Jas 1:4
    Meaning "in the presence of "...2 Cor 10:1

Index of Subjects

Meaning "on" .... 2 Cor 3:3
Phrase "in (= under) the law" .... Rom 2:12; 3:19; Gal 3:11; Phil 3:6
Temporal .... John 2:19–20;
    4:31, 45; Acts 27:7; 2 Thess 1:4, 7; Heb 3:15; 1 Pet 1:7, 14

ἐπί

With accusative, answering question "where?" .... Lk 5:25, 27; Heb 11:38
With accusative, indicating movement toward .... Matt 12:49;
    21:19; Lk 15:4; 2 Thess 2:1
With accusative, indicating number or measure .... Matt 25:40, 45;
    Acts 10:16; 11:10; Rom 11:13
With accusative, meaning "among" ..... Matt 13:7; Acts 1:21; 2 Thess 1:10
With accusative, marker of feelings directed toward someone .. 2 Cor 10:2;
    Eph 2:7; 2 Thess 3:4; Heb 6:1
With accusative or dative, in hostile sense, "against" .... Matt 12:26;
    26:55; Lk 12:52–53; John 13:18; Acts 7:54, 57; 8:1; 11:19;
    Rom 1:18; 1 Pet 3:12; Rev 10:11
With accusative or dative, indicating purpose .... Matt 3:7; 26:50;
    Acts 8:32; Gal 5:13; Eph 2:10; 1 Thess 4:7; 2 Tim 2:14; Tit 1:2
With accusative or dative, indicating one to/for/about whom something
    is done .... Mk 9:12–13; Lk 3:2; John 12:16;
    Acts 4:22; 5:35; Rom 4:9; Heb 7:13; 9:10; Rev 10:11
With accusative or genitive, marker of proceeding "before" an official ... Matt
    10:18; Lk 12:11, 58; 23:1; Acts 9:21; 16:19; 17:6; 18:12; 24:20, 21;
    25:9; 26:2; 1 Tim 6:13
With accusative, dative, or genitive, marker of power/authority over .... Matt
    25:21, 23; Lk 12:44; Acts 12:20; 2 Thess 2:4
With accusative, dative, or genitive, various temporal usages* .... Matt 1:11;
    Mk 2:26; Lk 3:2; John 8:3–4; Acts 3:1; Rom 1:10; Heb 1:2;
    2 Pet 1:13; Jude 18
With dative, after verbs of emotion* .... Matt 7:28;
    Mk 1:22; Lk 1:14; Acts 3:10; Rom 6:21; Jas 5:1
With dative, as basis of action .... Matt 4:4; 19:9;
    Lk 4:4; Acts 3:16; Heb 8:6; 9:10, 17; 10:28
With dative, "in the name of," indicating authorization .... Mk 9:37;
    13:6; Acts 2:38
With dative, meaning "in addition to" .... 2 Cor 7:13; Col 3:14

With dative or genitive, indicating immediate proximity ....Matt 21:19;
        24:33; Mk 2:26; 11:4; 12:26; Lk 20:37
With genitive, for object acted on or spoken of.............John 6:2; Gal 3:16
With genitive, marker of perspective .... Mk 12:14;
        Lk 4:25; 20:21; 2 Cor 10:7; 13:1; Heb 7:11

κατά

With accusative, as periphrasis for adverb ....Mk 1:27;
        Acts 3:17; 18:14; Rom 7:13; 1 Cor 2:1
With accusative, expressing similarity .... Rom 3:2; Gal 4:28; Eph 4:24
With accusative, indicating purpose ....John 2:6
With accusative, meaning "because of" ....Matt 19:3;
        Rom 2:5, 7; Gal 2:2; Heb 3:3
With accusative, meaning "in conformity with"...........................1 Pet 1:15
With accusative, of extension in space ....Lk 8:39; 15:14; Acts 8:1;
        15:23; 21:21; 25:3; 27:29; Rom 16:5; 1 Cor 16:19; 2 Cor 10:15
With accusative, spatially distributive .... Matt 24:7;
        Mk 13:8; Lk 8:1; Acts 2:46; 14:23; 15:21; Tit 1:5
With accusative, temporally distributive ....Matt 26:55;
        Lk 9:23; Acts 2:46–47; 13:27; 15:21; 1 Cor 15:31; 16:2
With accusative numerals, meaning "at a time" .... 1 Cor 14:27
With genitive, in hostile sense, "against"............. Matt 5:11; 12:25; 26:59;
        Mk 14:55; John 19:11; Acts 6:13; Rom 8:31, 33; Jas 3:14
With genitive, meaning "down"...Matt 8:32;
        Mk 5:13; Lk 8:33; Acts 27:14

μετά

With accusative, spatial "behind" ....Heb 9:3
With accusative, temporal "after" ....Matt 17:1; Lk 15:13;
        John 20:26; Acts 1:5; Gal 1:18; Tit 3:10; Heb 4:7–8; 7:28; 9:27
With genitive, attendant circumstances ....Matt 27:66;
        Lk 17:15, 20; Acts 14:23; Heb 7:21
With genitive, "with, to" another person ....Mk 6:50;
        Lk 1:58; John 4:27; Acts 2:28; 9:19; 14:27; 20:18; 1 Cor 6:6

παρά

With accusative, "against, contrary to"...Acts 18:13;
        Rom 16:17; Gal 1:8–9
With accusative, "because of" ....1 Cor 12:15–16

       A Syntax Guide for Readers of the Greek New Testament

Index of Subjects

With accusative, "less" .... 2 Cor 11:24

With accusative, marker of position "at" ....Lk 7:38; 8:35

With accusative, expressing comparison, "than" .... Lk 3:13; 13:2, 4;
    Rom 14:5; 1 Cor 3:11; Heb 1:4; 2:7, 9; 3:3; 9:23; 11:4; 12:24

With accusative, expressing exclusion, "rather than" ....Lk 18:14;
    Rom 1:25; Heb 1:9

With dative, of spatial nearness .... Matt 22:25; 28:15;
    John 17:5; 1 Cor 16:2; Col 4:16; Rev 2:13

With dative, "in the sight of" ....Rom 2:13; 11:25; 1 Cor 3:19; 2 Thess 1:6

With genitive, "from" ....Matt 2:16;
    18:19; 21:42; Lk 10:7; Acts 3:2; Rom 11:27

περί

With accusative, of approximate times .... Matt 20:3, 5, 6, 9;
    27:46; Acts 10:3

With genitive, "about, concerning" .... Acts 1:3; Phil 2:19

πρό (only takes genitive)

"Above all" .... Jas 5:12; 1 Pet 4:8

Local ....Acts 12:6, 14; 14:13; Jas 5:9

Temporal..John 1:48; Gal 1:17; Heb 11:5

πρός

With accusative, adverbial .... Jas 4:5

With accusative, "against" .... Acts 26:9; Eph 6:11–12; Col 2:23

With accusative, "before".. 2 Cor 12:21

With accusative, "in accordance with"..Lk 12:47;
    2 Cor 5:10; Gal 2:14; Eph 3:4

With accusative, "in comparison with"... Rom 8:18

With accusative, "neart, at, beside" .... Mk 11:1, 4; Lk 16:20;
    Acts 3:2; 5:10

With accusative, "toward, for" a certain goal, purpose, or result ....John 11:4;
    Acts 3:10; 27:12; Rom 15:2; 1 Cor 7:35; 2 Cor 4:6; 7:3; 11:8;
    Tit 3:1; 1 Pet 3:15; 4:12

With accusative, "toward, for" a certain time .... Lk 24:29; John 5:35

With accusative, "with, among"...Matt 13:56;
    Lk 9:41; Gal 1:18; 1 Thess 3:4; 2 Thess 2:5; 3:10

Index of Subjects

With accusative, "with reference to"..Matt 19:8; 27:4;
Mk 10:5; 12:12; Lk 14:32; 18:1; 20:19; 28:10; John 13:28;
21:22–23; Rom 8:31; 2 Thess 3:1; Heb 1:7–8; 2 Pet 1:3
With dative, "near, at"..................................Mk 5:11; John 18:16; 20:11–12

PRESENT

Conative present...John 10:32; Gal 5:4; 6:12; 1 Tim 1:3
Customary present..Jas 3:7
Extending-from-past present..Lk 13:7; 15:29;
John 5:6; Acts 15:21; 26:5; 27:33; 2 Cor 12:19; 1 John 3:8
Futuristic present...Matt 24:43; 26:2, 18; 27:63;
Mk 9:31; 11:3, 23; Lk 3:9, 16; 13:32; 19:8; John 4:25, 35; 7:33, 41–42;
11:11; 13:11; 14:3; 15:27; 21:3; 1 Cor 6:2; 2 Cor 13:1; Eph 5:6
Futuristic present participle..Lk 1:35;
John 6:14; Acts 21:3; 28:10; Rom 15:25; Heb 8:10
Gnomic present..............................Lk 3:9; Heb 2:11; 3:4; 5:4; 6:16; 7:7, 12; 8:3
Historical present..................Matt 26:40; Mk 1:21, 40–41; 2:4; 14:51; Lk 8:49
Ingressive-futuristic present...................................Matt 26:45; Mk 10:33; 14:41;
Lk 22:21, 22, 37; John 4:23; 13:27; Acts 1:6; 2 Tim 4:6; Heb 6:12
Ingressive-futuristic present participle...Matt 26:25;
John 18:2, 5; Heb 12:28; 1 Pet 1:13
Instantaneous performative or aoristic present...Lk 19:8;
Acts 9:34; 19:13; 25:11
Ongoing/continual present..John 3:15, 16
Perfective present...........................Matt 26:50; Lk 1:34; John 15:27; Acts 25:11
Present of characteristic or habitual action..1 John 3:6–9
Present participle for conative imperfect..............Matt 23:13; 27:40; Lk 11:52
Present participle with past reference.............John 9:25; Rev 15:2; 20:10; 22:8
Present retained in indirect discourse*....................................Matt 2:4; Mk 6:49;
Lk 18:37; John 4:51; Acts 7:25; 1 Thess 3:4; Heb 11:8; 1 John 2:18
Progressive present...Matt 25:8; Mk 1:37
Voluntative present participle..Mk 15:29

RELATIVE CLAUSES

Incorporation of antecedent into relative clause........................Lk 1:20; 3:19; 12:40;
John 6:14; 9:14; 11:6; Acts 1:2; Rom 4:16–17
Qualitative-consecutive relative clause.........Lk 7:4; 1 Cor 2:16; Phil 2:20; Heb 8:3
Relative clause functioning as subject...................................Matt 11:27; Lk 10:22

A Syntax Guide for Readers of the Greek New Testament

Index of Subjects

SEPTUAGINTISMS

Matt 1:1, 2, 18, 23; 5:21, 43; 7:28; 9:10; 13:4; 16:22; 19:28; 27:24; Mk 3:10; Lk 1:8, 18, 37, 50, 58, 59; 7:50; 10:37; 11:50–51; 13:19; 19:11; 20:21; 21:23; 22:15, 29, 30; John 7:2; 8:58; Acts 3:12, 25; 7:5, 21; 9:3; 12:3; 13:36; 21:11; Rom 7:2; 8:3; 11:4; 1 Cor 2:9; 6:5, 9; Gal 2:6; 3:19; Eph 5:2; Col 2:18; Heb 1:2; 9:13, 22; 10:6, 20; 12:24; Jas 2:7, 13; 4:15; 1 Pet 2:12; 2 John 12; Jude 16; Rev 2:1; 6:10; 12:7; 19:2, 6

SUBJUNCTIVE

Aorist subjunctive with future nuance..2 Cor 12:6

Deliberative subjunctive ....Matt 11:3; 26:17; 27:17, 21, 22; Mk 6:37; 12:14; Lk 3:10, 12, 14; 7:19; 9:54; 16:3; 18:41; John 12:27; 18:39; Acts 2:37; 4:16; 22:10; Rom 6:1; 1 Cor 4:21; 6:15

Deliberative subjunctive in dubitative or rhetorical question..........Matt 23:33; 26:54; Lk 23:31; Rom 10:13–14

Deliberative subjunctive in indirect question.....................................Matt 15:32; Mk 8:1–2; 11:18; Rom 8:26

Emphatic negation subjunctive................................ Matt 24:35; Mk 9:1; 10:15; 13:2, 30, 31; Lk 18:7, 17; 21:33; John 18:11; Acts 13:41; Rom 4:8; 1 Cor 8:13; 1 Thess 5:3; Heb 8:11–12; 13:5; Rev 2:11; 15:4

Hortatory subjunctive*...Matt 7:4; Mk 1:38; Lk 2:15; John 11:7, 15, 16; Acts 7:34; Rom 3:8; Heb 4:16; 1 John 3:18; Rev 19:7

Hypothetical or parabolic subjunctive...Lk 11:5, 7

Prohibitive subjunctive .... 2 Cor 11:16; 1 Pet 3:14

Subjunctive in final relative clause...Lk 22:11

Subjunctive in indefinite relative clause .... Matt 5:19; 10:33; 12:50

TEXT CRITICAL ISSUES

Lk 7:11; 23:12; John 9:4; 13:32; 14:7; 20:31; Acts 4:25; 7:46; 13:18, 20; 19:40; 24:6–8; Rom 5:1; 8:2; 11:21; 1 Cor 2:4; 9:15; 13:3; 2 Cor 5:3; Gal 2:4–5; 4:14; 5:1; 1 Thess 2:7; 2 Thess 2:13; 1 Tim 3:16; Jas 4:5, 14; 2 Pet 2:4, 6, 13; 3:6, 10; 1 John 5:18; 2 John 8; Rev 1:15